The
Filth

Rₓ ☤ ⊕

Special thanks to Steve Bunche,
Gary Erskine, David Drage and my
wife, Karen, for all their support
during the making of this book.
— Chris Weston

For Cheesy and Toby.
— Grant Morrison

Karen Berger Editor – Original Series   Steve Bunche Zachary Rau Assistant Editors – Original Series   Jamie S. Rich Group Editor – Vertigo Comics   Jeb Woodard Group Editor – Collected Editions
Scott Nybakken Editor – Collected Edition   Steve Cook Design Director – Books   Louis Prandi Publication Design

Diane Nelson President   Dan DiDio Publisher   Jim Lee Publisher   Geoff Johns   President & Chief Creative Officer   Amit Desai Executive VP – Business & Marketing Strategy, Direct to Consumer & Global Franchise
Management   Sam Ades Senior VP – Direct to Consumer   Bobbie Chase VP – Talent Development   Mark Chiarello Senior VP – Art, Design & Collected Editions   John Cunningham Senior VP – Sales & Trade
Marketing   Anne DePies Senior VP – Business Strategy, Finance & Administration   Don Falletti VP – Manufacturing Operations   Lawrence Ganem VP – Editorial Administration & Talent Relations   Alison Gill Senior
VP – Manufacturing & Operations   Hank Kanalz   Senior VP – Editorial Strategy & Administration   Jay Kogan VP – Legal Affairs   Thomas Loftus VP – Business Affairs   Jack Mahan VP – Business Affairs   Nick J.
Napolitano VP – Manufacturing Administration   Eddie Scannell VP – Consumer Marketing   Courtney Simmons Senior VP – Publicity & Communications   Jim (Ski) Sokolowski VP – Comic Book Specialty Sales &
Trade Marketing   Nancy Spears VP – Mass, Book, Digital Sales & Trade Marketing

FSC
www.fsc.org
MIX
Paper from
responsible sources
FSC® C132124

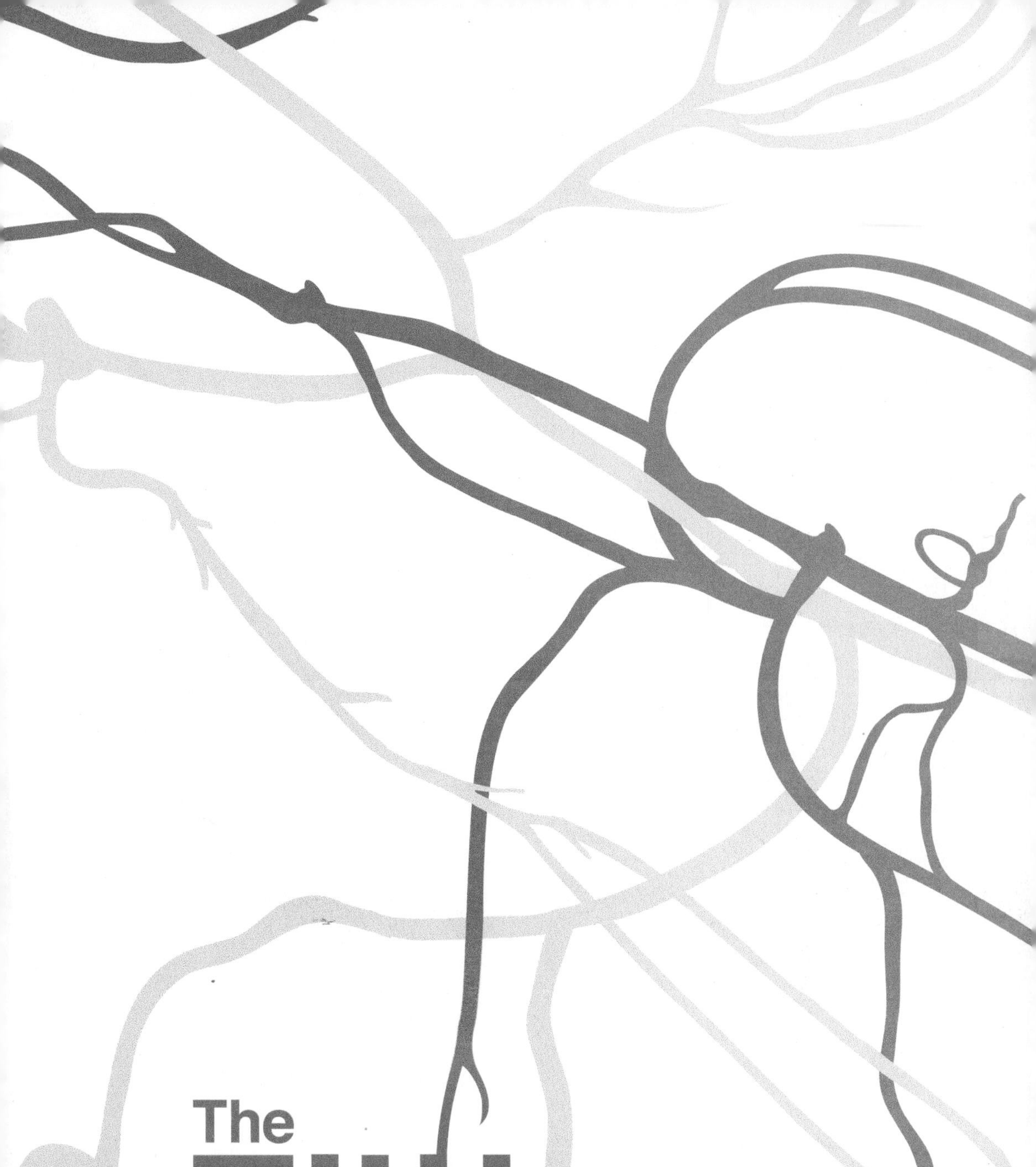

The Filth

Grant Morrison Writer   Chris Weston Penciller   Gary Erskine Inker
Matt Hollingsworth (#01-03) HI-FI (#04-13) Colorists   Clem Robins Letterer
Segura Inc. Cover Art and Original Series Covers
THE FILTH created by Grant Morrison and Chris Weston

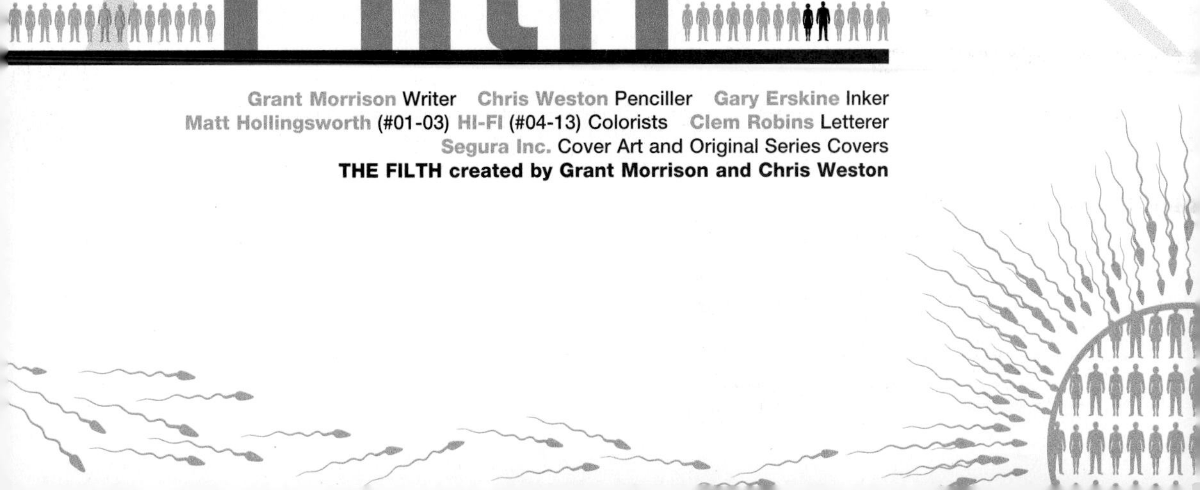

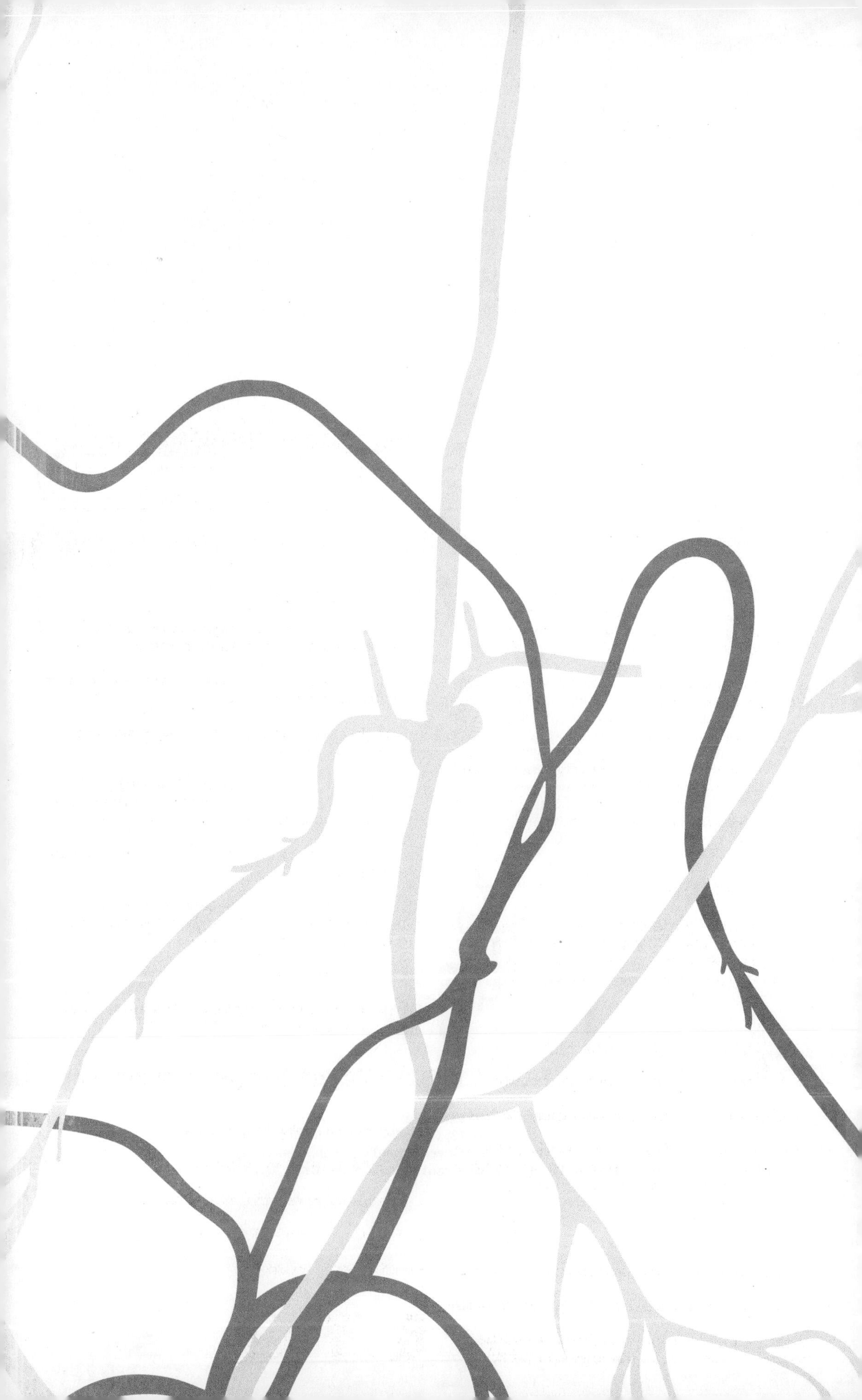

PATIENT PRODUCT INFORMATION

The
Filth ™

COMIC BOOK ISSUES 01-13

Please read this introduction carefully before you start to use THE FILTH.
If you have any questions or are not sure about anything, ask your doctor, pharmacist or comic book dealer.

WHAT IS THE FILTH?

The Filth contains the active ingredient metaphor.

- The rectangular, multi-colored comic books marked "The Filth" contain 500mg of active visual and thematic metaphor per issue. Comic books also contain the inactive ingredients paper and ink.

Metaphor is one of a group of problem-solving medicines known as figures-of-speech which are normally used to treat literal thinking and other diseases. Metaphor combines two or more seemingly unrelated concepts in a way which stimulates lateral thought processes and creativity. Patients using The Filth are required to participate in the generation of significant content by "interpreting" text and images which have been deliberately loaded with multiple, overlapping meanings and scales.

The comic book issues come in collected editions of 13 and are to be consumed optically.

WHAT IS THE FILTH USED FOR?

This comic book is used to treat all manner of disorders including internet pornography addiction, insomnia, grief, "mid-life" crisis, schizophrenia, the ignorance of samsara and the 21st century blues, especially in patients whose millennial anxiety and general paranoia has not yet responded to normal treatments.

WHEN MUST THE FILTH NOT BE USED?

- If your doctor has advised you to avoid the use of metaphor.

- If you refuse to acknowledge the mocking laughter of the Abyss.

- If you cannot face the fact that your entire immediate environment is a seething battlefield of microscopic predators, prey and excreta and, simultaneously, a rich and complex metaphor.

- If, without understanding how it happened, you have found yourself in a dark room breastfeeding two elderly men you hardly know.

- If you are taking certain "dumb" antibiotics present in most media.

- If you are allergic to comic books or any of the ingredients they contain.

- If you take high-dose vitamin A supplements or have high levels of cholesterol or triglycerides (a fat-like substance) in your blood.

WHEN SHOULD YOU BE EXTRA-CAREFUL IN USING THE FILTH?

Make sure your doctor knows if:

- You or members of your family have a history of brutality and stupidity dating back to the pre-Cambrian oceans.

- You or members of your family really think anyone is listening when you talk the shite you talk.

- You regularly use drugs to desensitize yourself against the violent entertainment you consume.

- You have a history of vague depression, all-pervading guilt and a denial of personal mortality despite living in the pampered luxury of a privileged capitalist democracy.

If you experience severe diarrhea, stop reading The Filth and contact your doctor immediately.

Your night vision may be affected by this medicine and ultraviolet light may become visible to you, so avoid sun-beds and "Insecocutor" bug-killing lamps, as the glare may lead to blindness.

Special note for blood donors:

You should not donate blood in smug imitation of Christ either during or for at least one month after reading The Filth.

MAY THE FILTH BE USED DURING PREGNANCY OR WHILE BREASTFEEDING?

The Filth must NOT be taken during pregnancy.

The Filth MUST be taken during pregnancy.

The Filth must NOT be taken during breastfeeding.

The Filth MUST be taken during breastfeeding.

Scientific opinion remains undecided.

The
Filth

WHAT ARE THE POSSIBLE UNWANTED EFFECTS OF THE FILTH?

- **Eye irritation**

Your eyes may feel abused and slightly inflamed after exposure to The Filth. This may especially be a problem if you wear contact lenses or big horse blinkers. Ask your comic dealer to suggest some less visually demanding entertainment immediately.

- **Aches and pains**

Some people have muscle aches and pains and occasionally soreness of the tendons when they are reading this comic book. This may be more likely if you remain motionless in bizarre and awkward positions while reading.

- **Hair changes**

You may notice some changes to your hair (it will have grown very slightly) after reading The Filth for a while. This is usually only temporary and your hair should return to its normal length following a brief visit to your hairdresser or barber.

- **Mood changes**

Some people have experienced mood changes (depression or other symptoms of mental disorder followed by an elated, orgasmic release phase) while reading The Filth, and in rare cases suicide and attempts of suicide have been thwarted and made to look ridiculous by use of this medicine.

IMPORTANT

The Filth will damage an unborn baby only if inserted into the body. Female readers must strictly follow these instructions.

- You must not become pregnant while reading The Filth.

- If you are a woman of childbearing age you should have been using an effective method of contraception for at least one month prior to starting The Filth.

HOW SHOULD THE FILTH BE READ?

- Always read the comic books as your doctor tells you to. Your doctor will tell you when and how much to read and what to think.

- The comic books can be read either one at a time or all at once. Take them with a meal or with a glass of milk and some recreational drugs.

- Occasionally feelings of isolation and alienation may become worse during the first phase of treatment. Your symptoms should improve with further treatment.

- A course of treatment is generally dictated by reading and interpreting speed, after which you are likely to remain free of symptoms for a long time.

- Repeated courses of therapy are not normally needed, but if your symptoms re-occur significantly, then you or your doctor may decide on repeat doses of The Filth.

- If you read too many issues at once or someone else accidentally reads your copies of The Filth, contact your doctor, comic book dealer or nearest hospital straight away.

HOW SHOULD THE FILTH BE STORED?

- Keep this medicine out of the reach and sight of all but the wisest of children.

- REMEMBER this medicine is for you. Only a right c**t would tell you anything else.

- Do not store your medicine above 451° Fahrenheit.

FURTHER INFORMATION

You can get more information about The Filth from your doctor, pharmacist or comic book dealer or from the website at www.crackcomicks.com.

DATE OF PREPARATION

March 2004

The
Filth

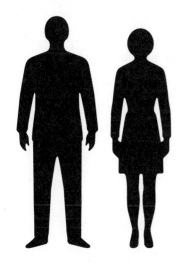 VS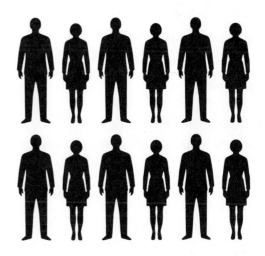

Contains
23 Pages

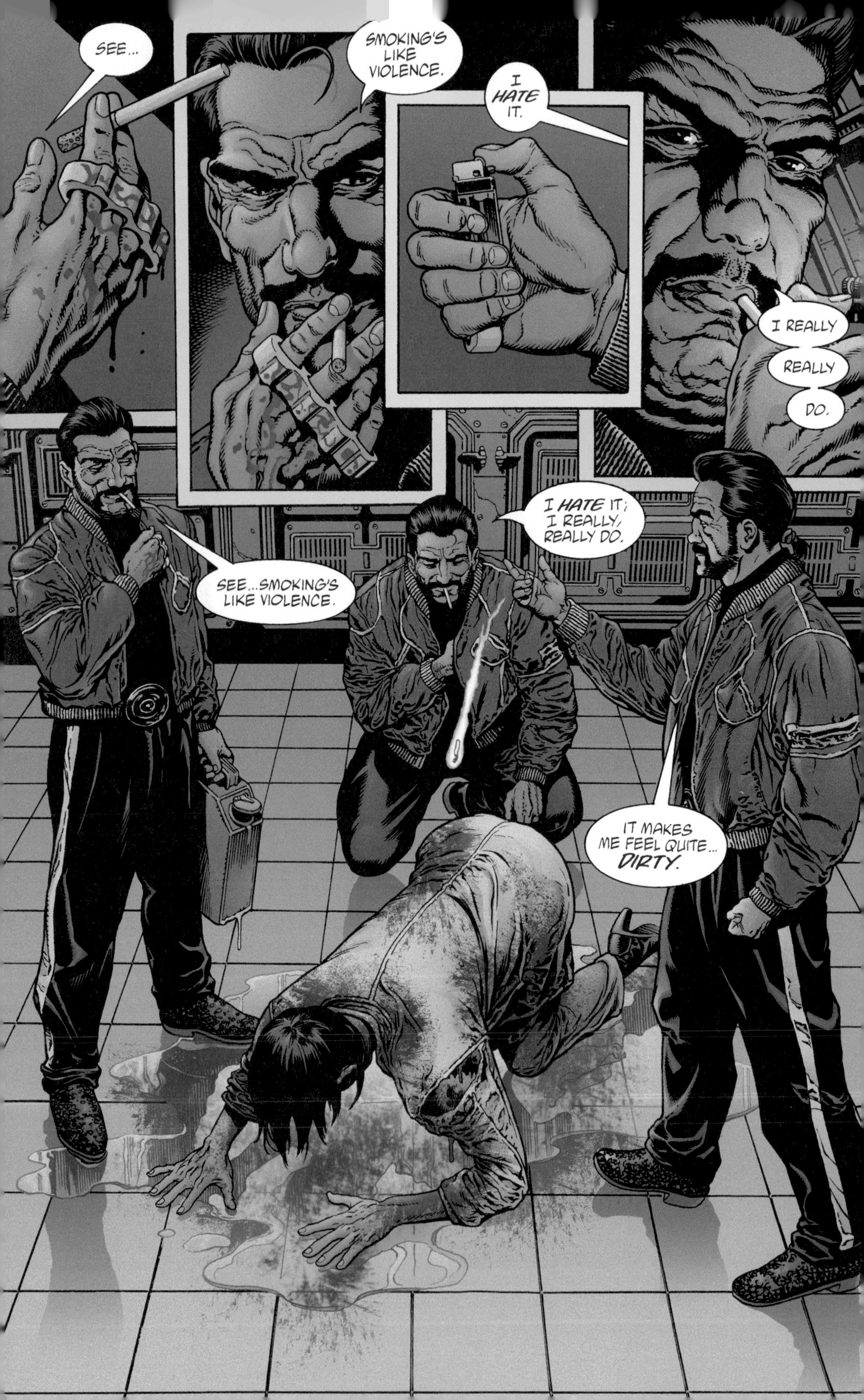
SEE...
SMOKING'S LIKE VIOLENCE.
I HATE IT.
I REALLY
REALLY
DO.
SEE...SMOKING'S LIKE VIOLENCE.
I HATE IT; I REALLY, REALLY DO.
IT MAKES ME FEEL QUITE... DIRTY.

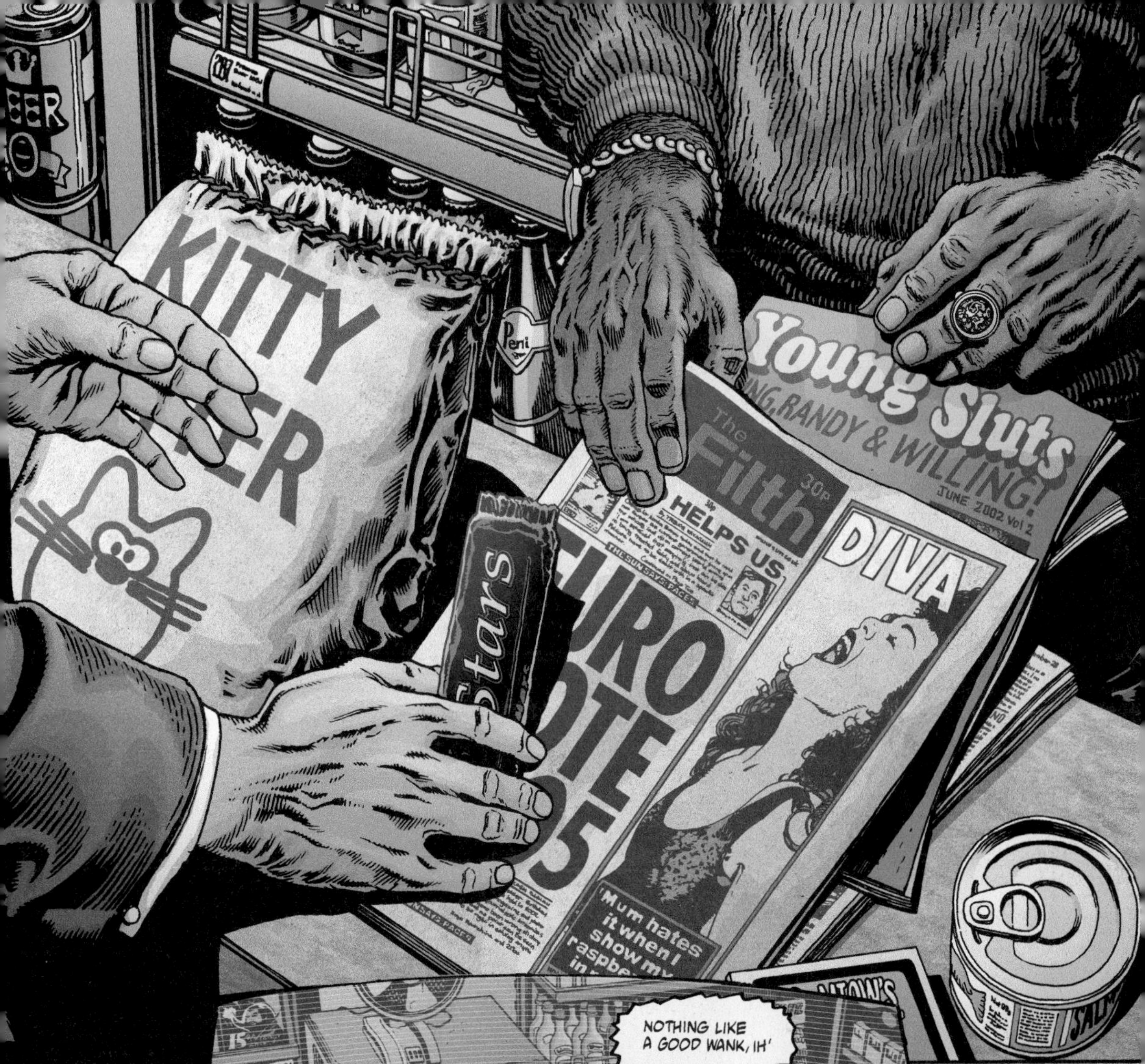
KITTY
Young Sluts
JUNE 2002 Vol 2
The Filth 30p
HELPS US
DIVA
'Mum hates it when I show my

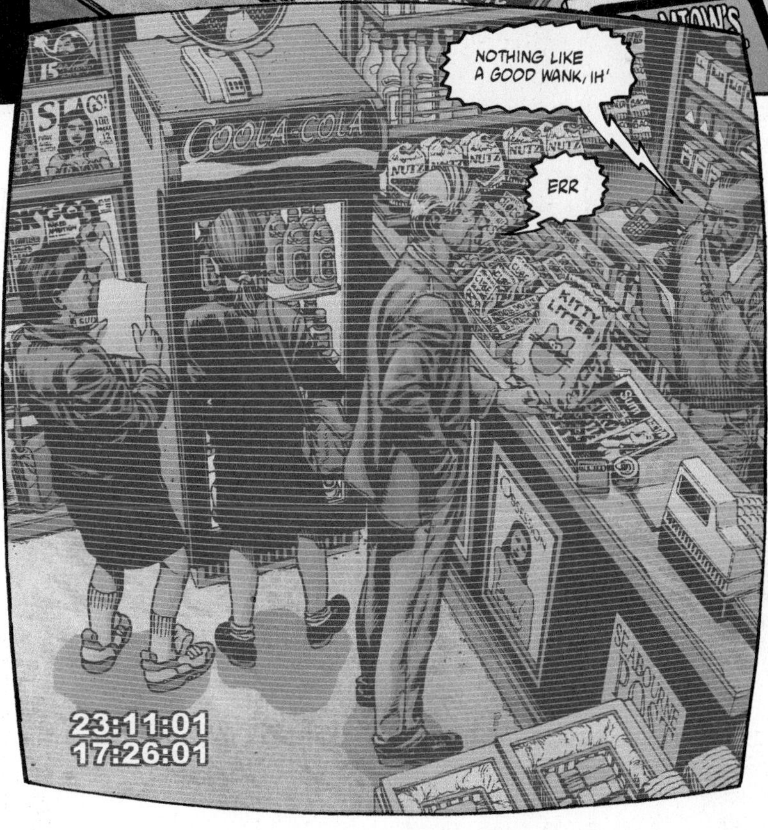
COOLA-COLA
NOTHING LIKE A GOOD WANK, IH'
ERR
KITTY LITTER
23:11:01
17:26:01

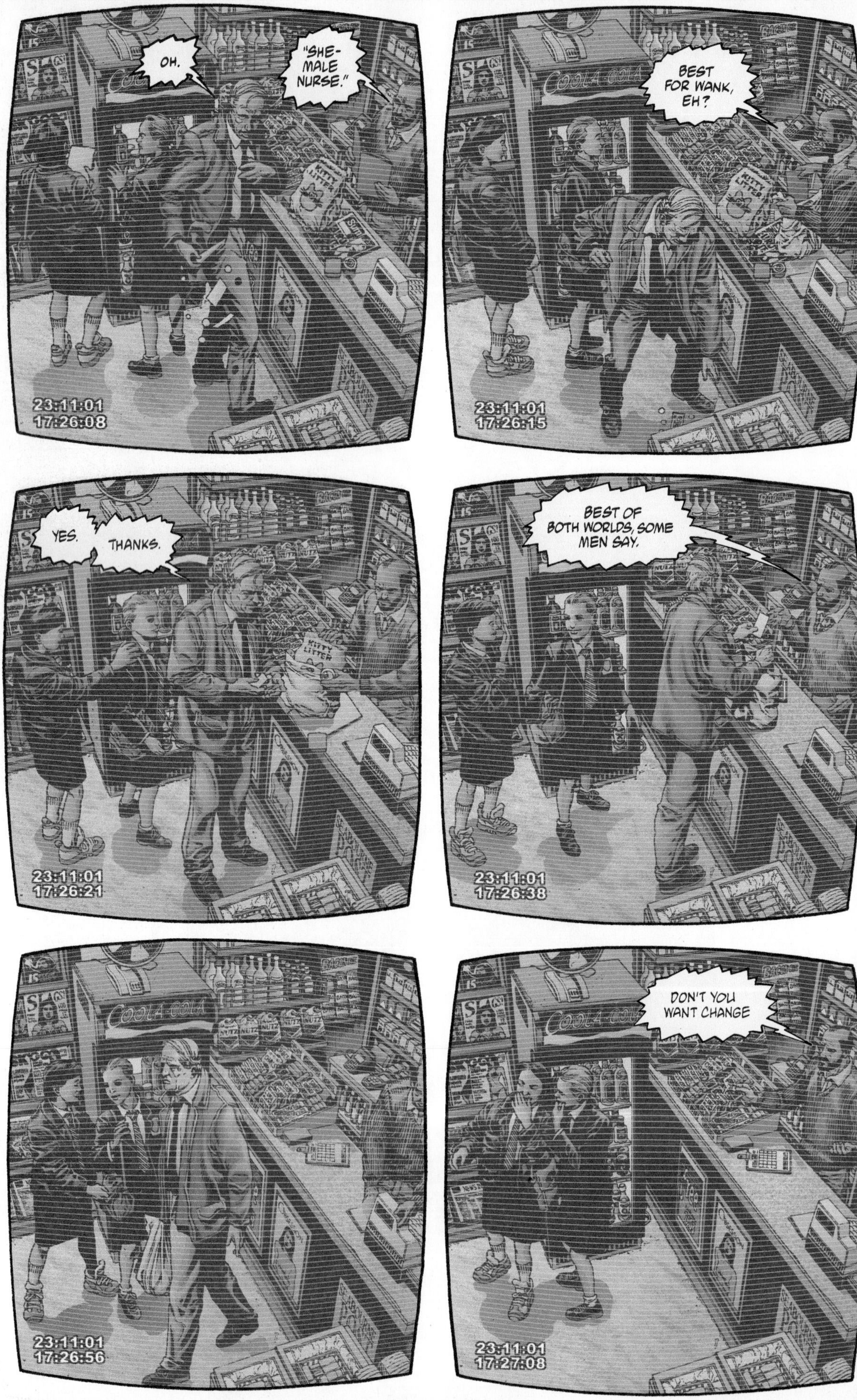
OH.
"SHE-MALE NURSE."
23:11:01
17:26:08
BEST FOR WANK, EH?
23:11:01
17:26:15
YES.
THANKS.
23:11:01
17:26:21
BEST OF BOTH WORLDS, SOME MEN SAY.
23:11:01
17:26:38
23:11:01
17:26:56
DON'T YOU WANT CHANGE
23:11:01
17:27:08

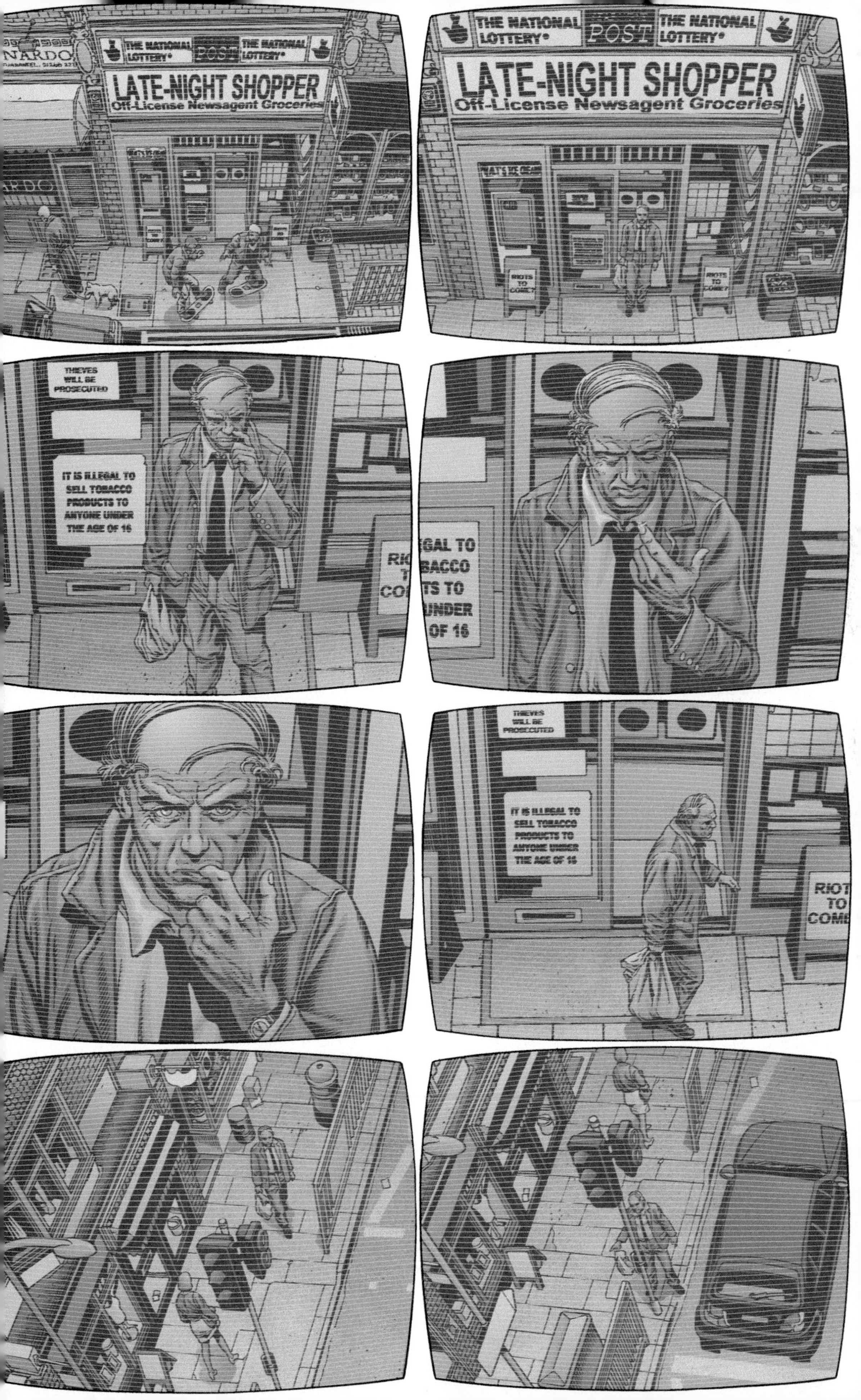
THE NATIONAL LOTTERY®
POST
THE NATIONAL LOTTERY®
LATE-NIGHT SHOPPER
Off-License Newsagent Groceries
THE NATIONAL LOTTERY®
POST
THE NATIONAL LOTTERY®
LATE-NIGHT SHOPPER
Off-License Newsagent Groceries
RIOTS TO COME?
RIOTS TO COME?
THIEVES WILL BE PROSECUTED
IT IS ILLEGAL TO SELL TOBACCO PRODUCTS TO ANYONE UNDER THE AGE OF 16
THIEVES WILL BE PROSECUTED
IT IS ILLEGAL TO SELL TOBACCO PRODUCTS TO ANYONE UNDER THE AGE OF 16

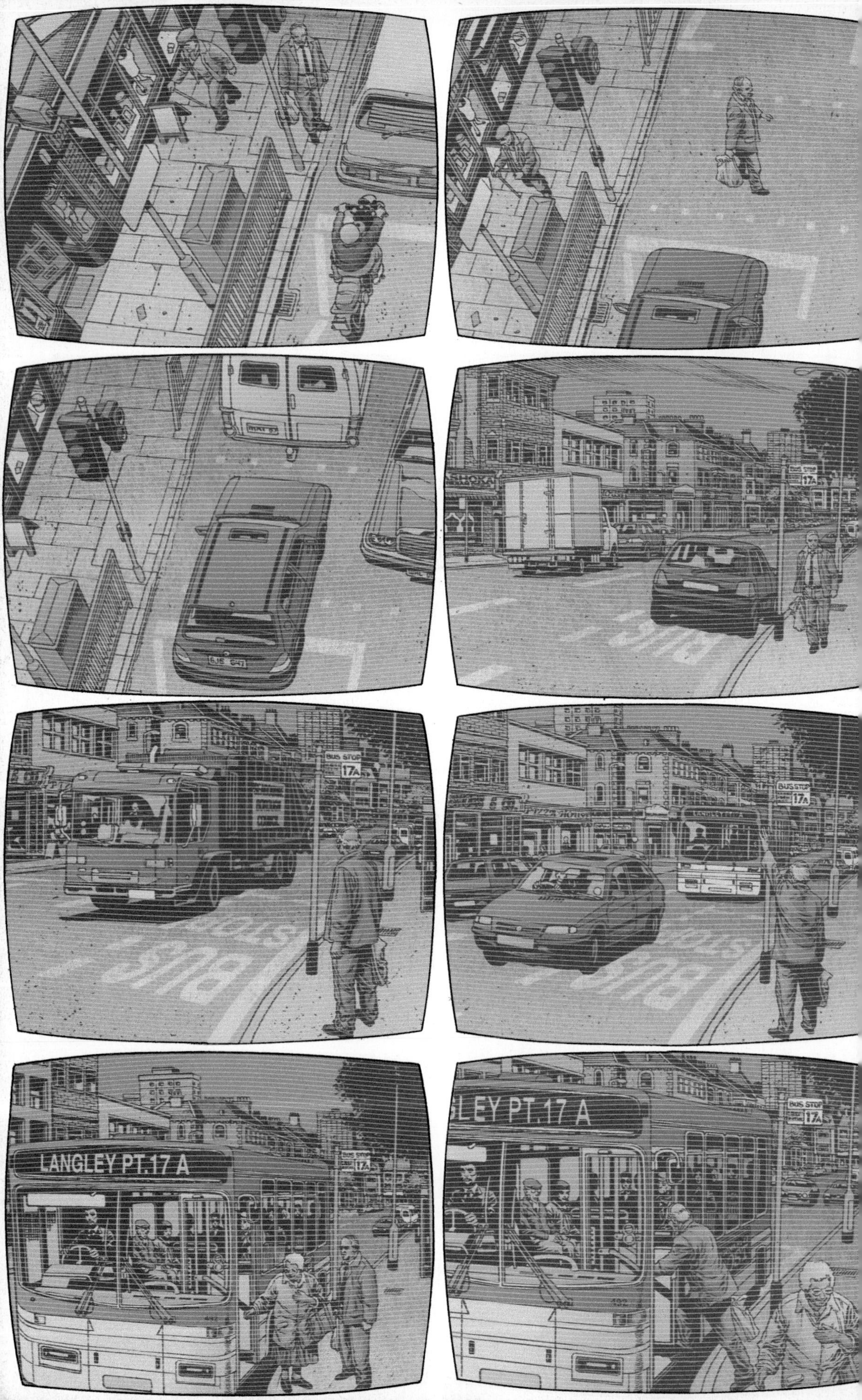
ASHOKA
BUS STOP
17A
BUS STOP
LANGLEY PT.17 A
GLEY PT.17 A

SO WHAT'S SO GOOD ABOUT JAMES BOND?

SO I'M LIKE THAT AND SHE'S LIKE THAT "IT'S LIKE THAT" THE TWO OF US ARE LIKE THAT.

HE SAYS, "WALTER, YOU'RE AHEAD OF YOUR TIME ALL RIGHT AND I ONLY HOPE THERE'S A JOB FOR YOU IN THE YEAR 2025 'CAUSE THERE'S FUCK ALL IN THIS FUCKING TIME ZONE. YOU'RE FIRED."

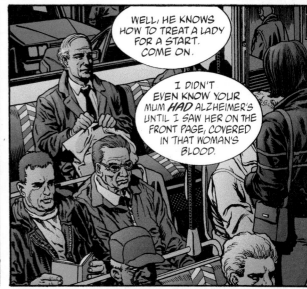

WELL, HE KNOWS HOW TO TREAT A LADY FOR A START. COME ON.

I DIDN'T EVEN KNOW YOUR MUM HAD ALZHEIMER'S UNTIL I SAW HER ON THE FRONT PAGE, COVERED IN THAT WOMAN'S BLOOD.

GAMBLING ALL NIGHT, KNOCKING HER ABOUT LIKE A RAG DOLL, USING HER AS A HUMAN SHIELD...VERY ROMANTIC!

"AT LEAST I'LL SEE THE YEAR 2025," I SAYS.

YOU'LL LIVE TO 105, WALTER. WHY WORK?

SLADE.

DON'T FUCK WITH THE FILTH.

IT'S THIS NEW THING THEY'VE GOT: IT'S WAY BEYOND ALZHEIMER'S.

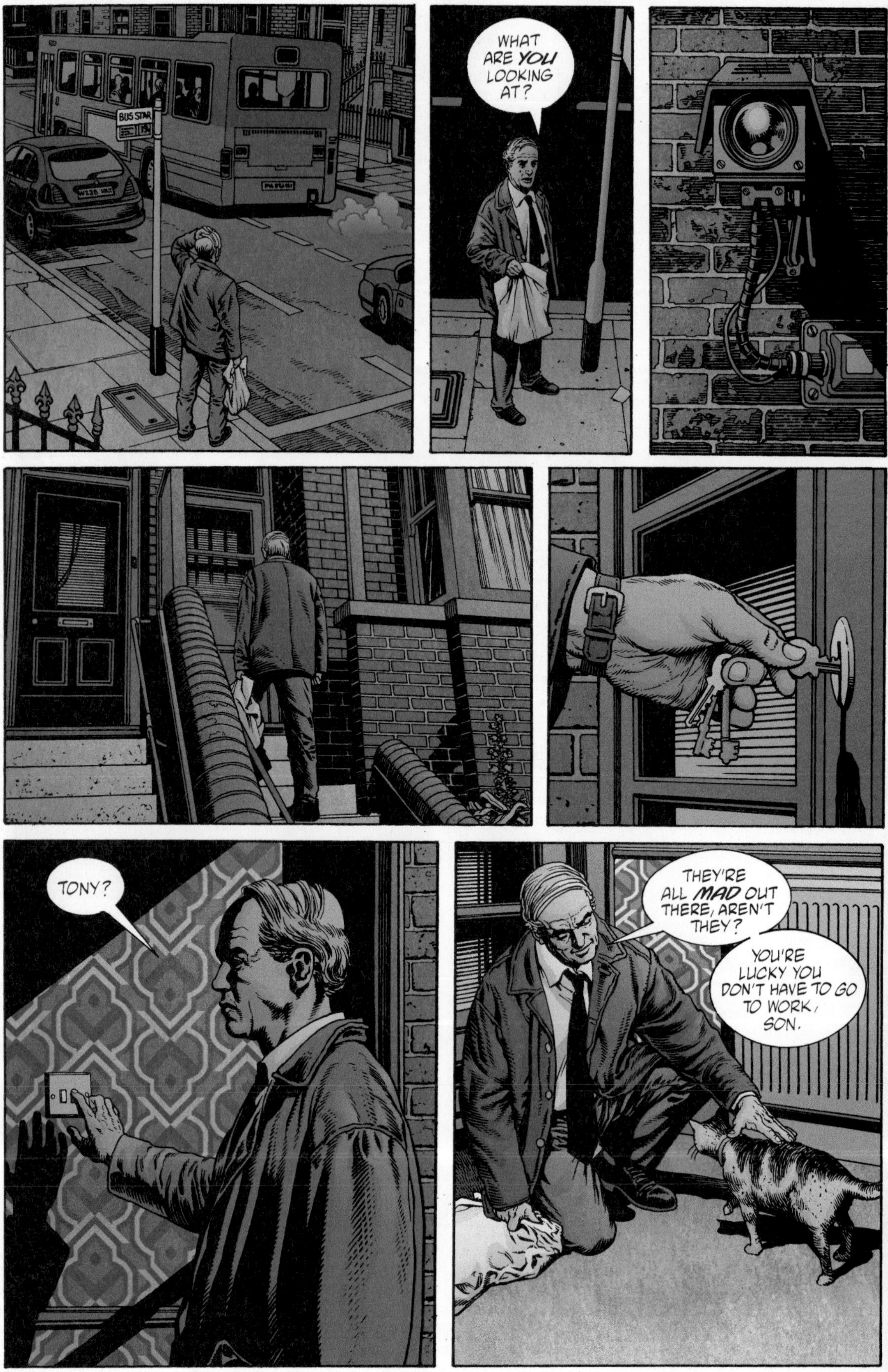
BUS STAR
WHAT ARE YOU LOOKING AT?
TONY?
THEY'RE ALL MAD OUT THERE, AREN'T THEY?
YOU'RE LUCKY YOU DON'T HAVE TO GO TO WORK, SON.

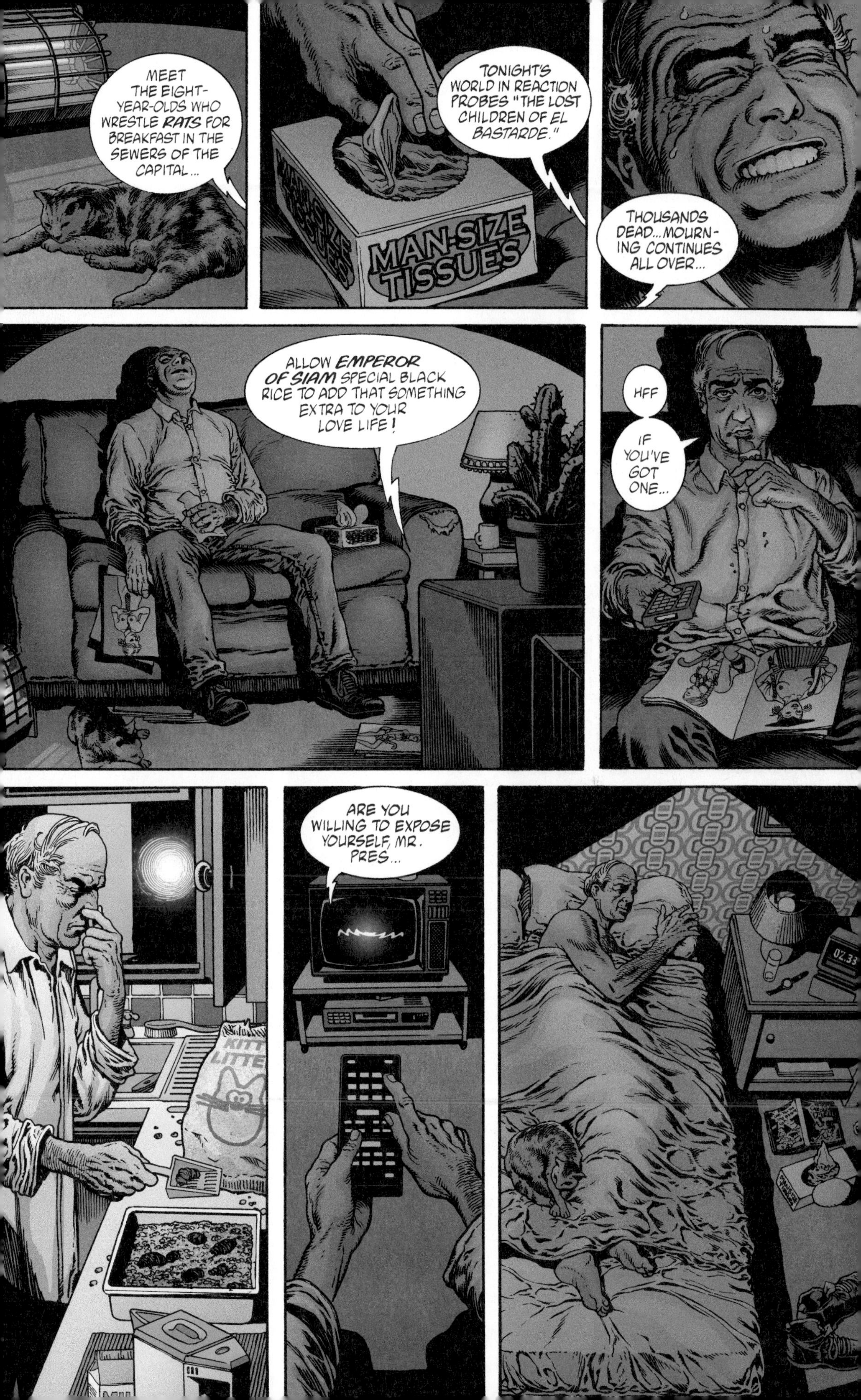
MEET THE EIGHT-YEAR-OLDS WHO WRESTLE RATS FOR BREAKFAST IN THE SEWERS OF THE CAPITAL...
MAN-SIZE TISSUES
TONIGHT'S WORLD IN REACTION PROBES "THE LOST CHILDREN OF EL BASTARDE."
THOUSANDS DEAD... MOURNING CONTINUES ALL OVER...
ALLOW EMPEROR OF SIAM SPECIAL BLACK RICE TO ADD THAT SOMETHING EXTRA TO YOUR LOVE LIFE!
HFF
IF YOU'VE GOT ONE...
KITT LITTE
ARE YOU WILLING TO EXPOSE YOURSELF, MR. PRES...
02.33

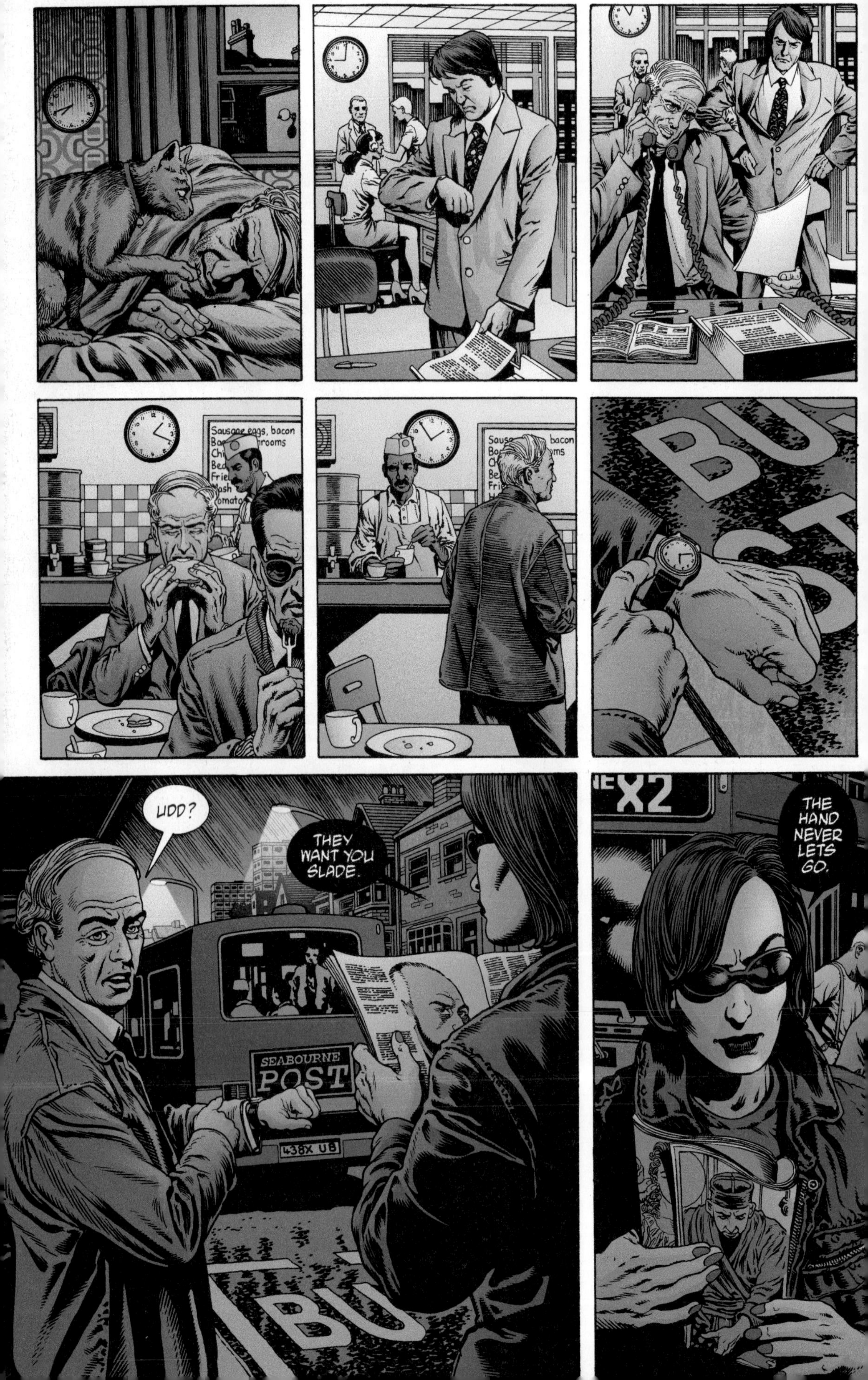
UDD?
THEY WANT YOU SLADE.
THE HAND NEVER LETS GO.

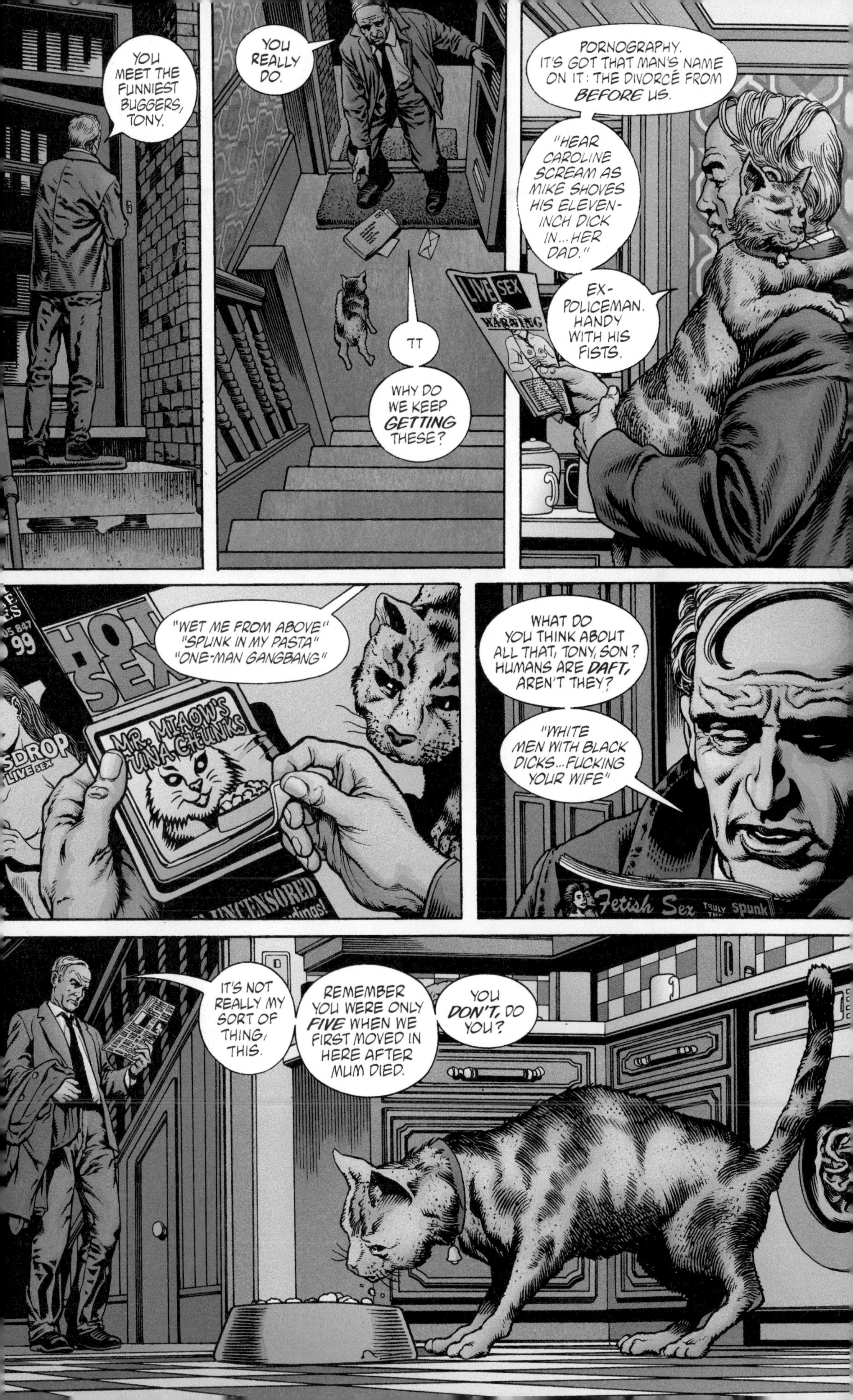
YOU MEET THE FUNNIEST BUGGERS, TONY.
YOU REALLY DO.
TT
WHY DO WE KEEP GETTING THESE?
PORNOGRAPHY. IT'S GOT THAT MAN'S NAME ON IT: THE DIVORCÉ FROM BEFORE US.
"HEAR CAROLINE SCREAM AS MIKE SHOVES HIS ELEVEN-INCH DICK IN... HER DAD."
EX-POLICEMAN. HANDY WITH HIS FISTS.
LIVE SEX
"WET ME FROM ABOVE" "SPUNK IN MY PASTA" "ONE-MAN GANGBANG"
HOT SEX
MR. MIAOW'S TUNA CHUNKS
UNCENSORED
WHAT DO YOU THINK ABOUT ALL THAT, TONY, SON? HUMANS ARE DAFT, AREN'T THEY?
"WHITE MEN WITH BLACK DICKS... FUCKING YOUR WIFE"
Fetish Sex
IT'S NOT REALLY MY SORT OF THING, THIS.
REMEMBER YOU WERE ONLY FIVE WHEN WE FIRST MOVED IN HERE AFTER MUM DIED.
YOU DON'T, DO YOU?

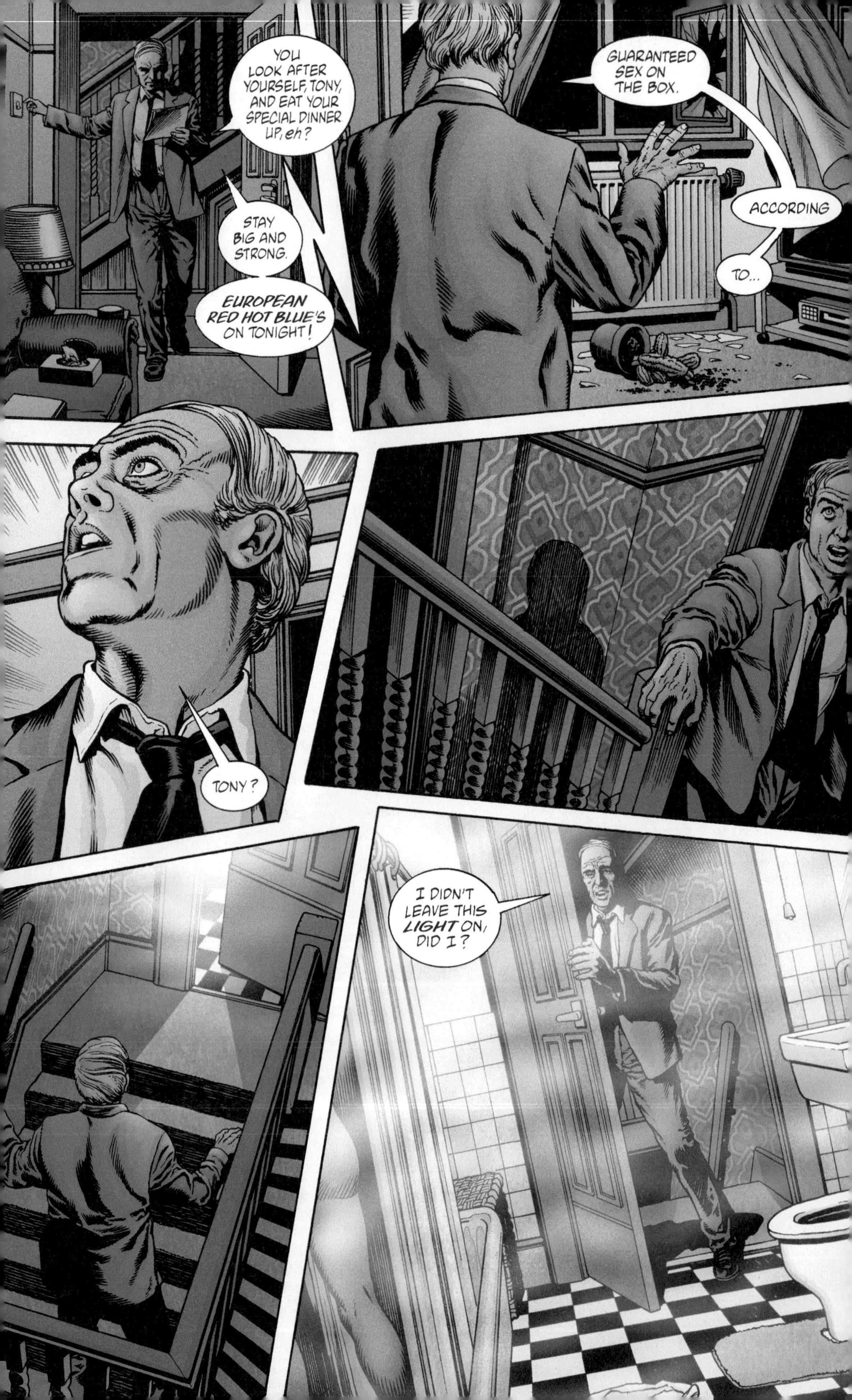
YOU LOOK AFTER YOURSELF, TONY, AND EAT YOUR SPECIAL DINNER UP, eh?
STAY BIG AND STRONG.
EUROPEAN RED HOT BLUE'S ON TONIGHT!
GUARANTEED SEX ON THE BOX.
ACCORDING
TO...
TONY?
I DIDN'T LEAVE THIS LIGHT ON, DID I?

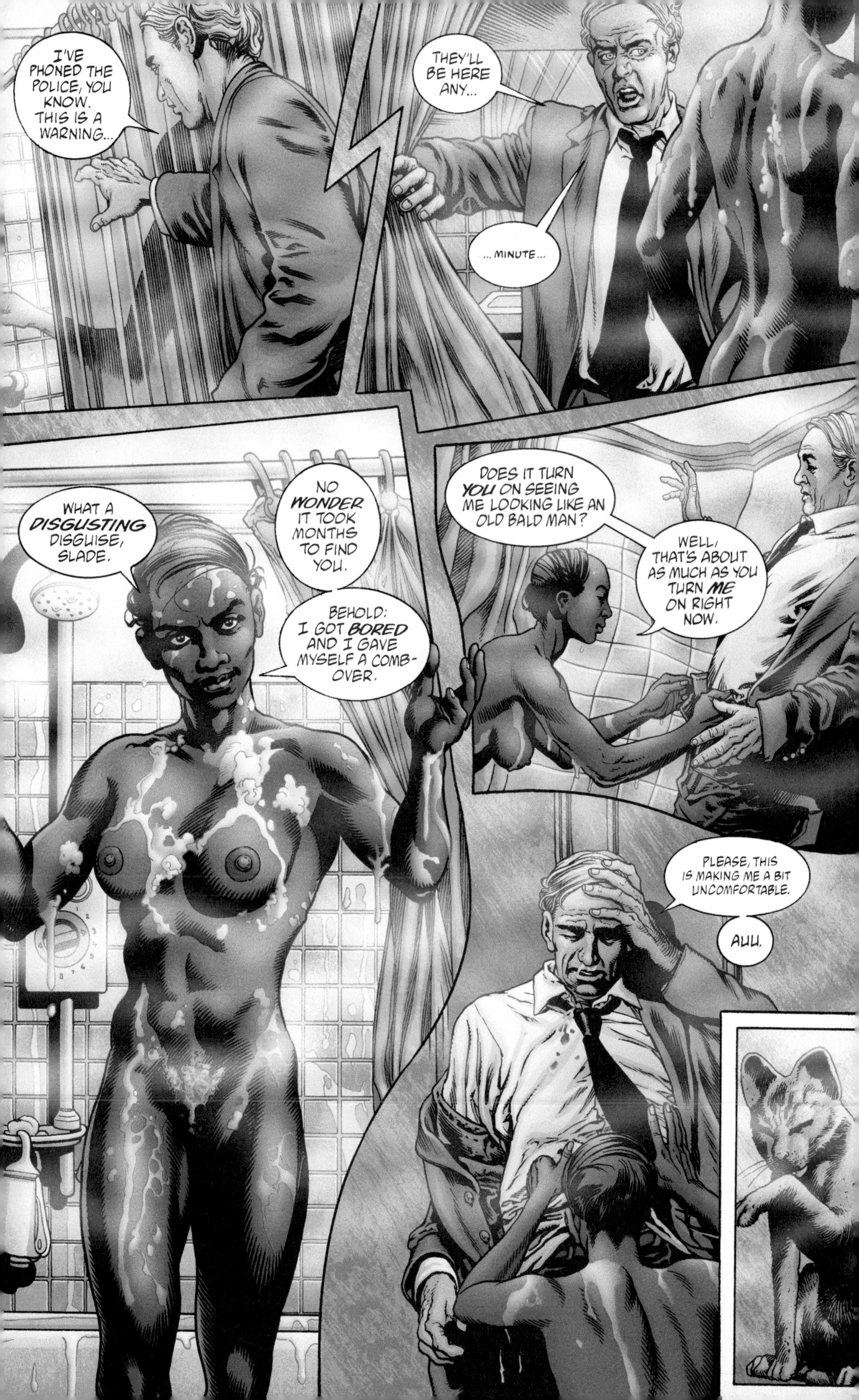
I'VE PHONED THE POLICE, YOU KNOW. THIS IS A WARNING...
THEY'LL BE HERE ANY...
...MINUTE...
WHAT A *DISGUSTING* DISGUISE, SLADE.
NO *WONDER* IT TOOK MONTHS TO FIND YOU.
BEHOLD: I GOT *BORED* AND I GAVE MYSELF A COMB-OVER.
DOES IT TURN *YOU* ON SEEING ME LOOKING LIKE AN OLD BALD MAN?
WELL, THAT'S ABOUT AS MUCH AS YOU TURN *ME* ON RIGHT NOW.
PLEASE, THIS IS MAKING ME A BIT UNCOMFORTABLE.
AUU.

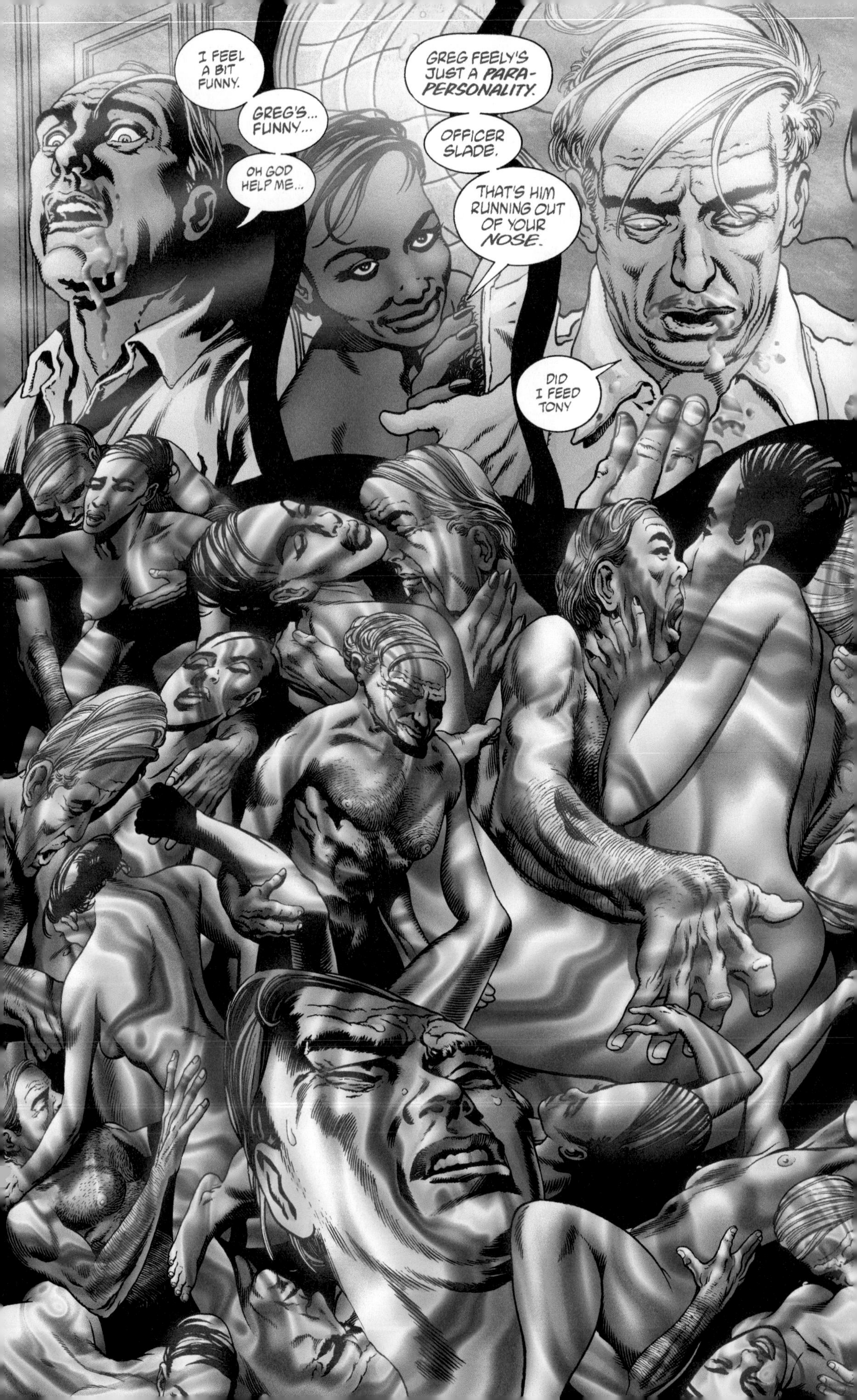
I FEEL A BIT FUNNY.
GREG'S... FUNNY...
OH GOD HELP ME...
GREG FEELY'S JUST A PARA-PERSONALITY.
OFFICER SLADE.
THAT'S HIM RUNNING OUT OF YOUR NOSE.
DID I FEED TONY

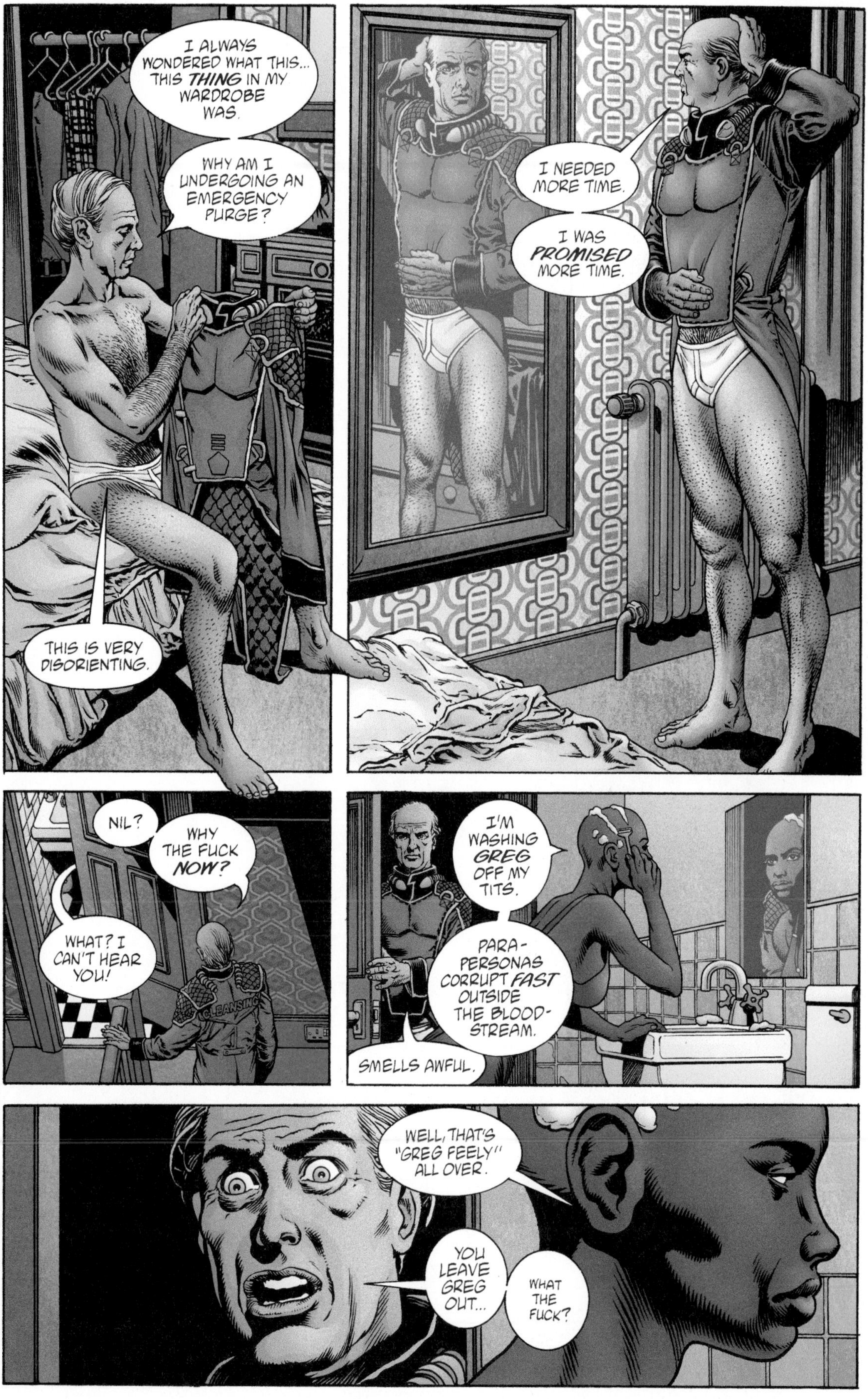
I ALWAYS WONDERED WHAT THIS... THIS THING IN MY WARDROBE WAS.
WHY AM I UNDERGOING AN EMERGENCY PURGE?
THIS IS VERY DISORIENTING.
I NEEDED MORE TIME.
I WAS PROMISED MORE TIME.
NIL?
WHY THE FUCK NOW?
WHAT? I CAN'T HEAR YOU!
CLEANSING
I'M WASHING GREG OFF MY TITS.
PARA-PERSONAS CORRUPT FAST OUTSIDE THE BLOOD-STREAM.
SMELLS AWFUL.
WELL, THAT'S "GREG FEELY" ALL OVER.
YOU LEAVE GREG OUT...
WHAT THE FUCK?

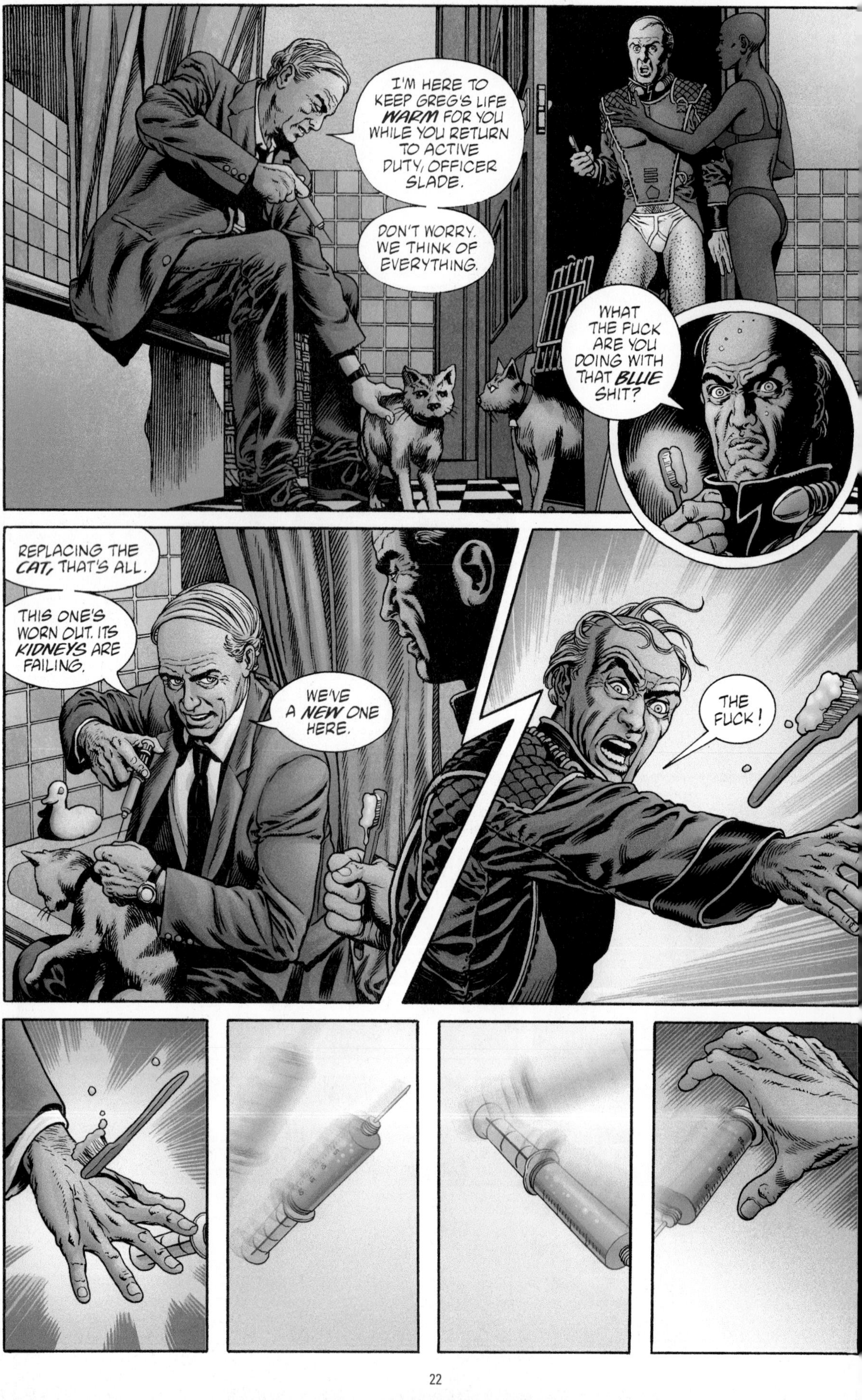
I'M HERE TO KEEP GREG'S LIFE WARM FOR YOU WHILE YOU RETURN TO ACTIVE DUTY, OFFICER SLADE.
DON'T WORRY. WE THINK OF EVERYTHING.
WHAT THE FUCK ARE YOU DOING WITH THAT BLUE SHIT?
REPLACING THE CAT, THAT'S ALL.
THIS ONE'S WORN OUT. ITS KIDNEYS ARE FAILING.
WE'VE A NEW ONE HERE.
THE FUCK!

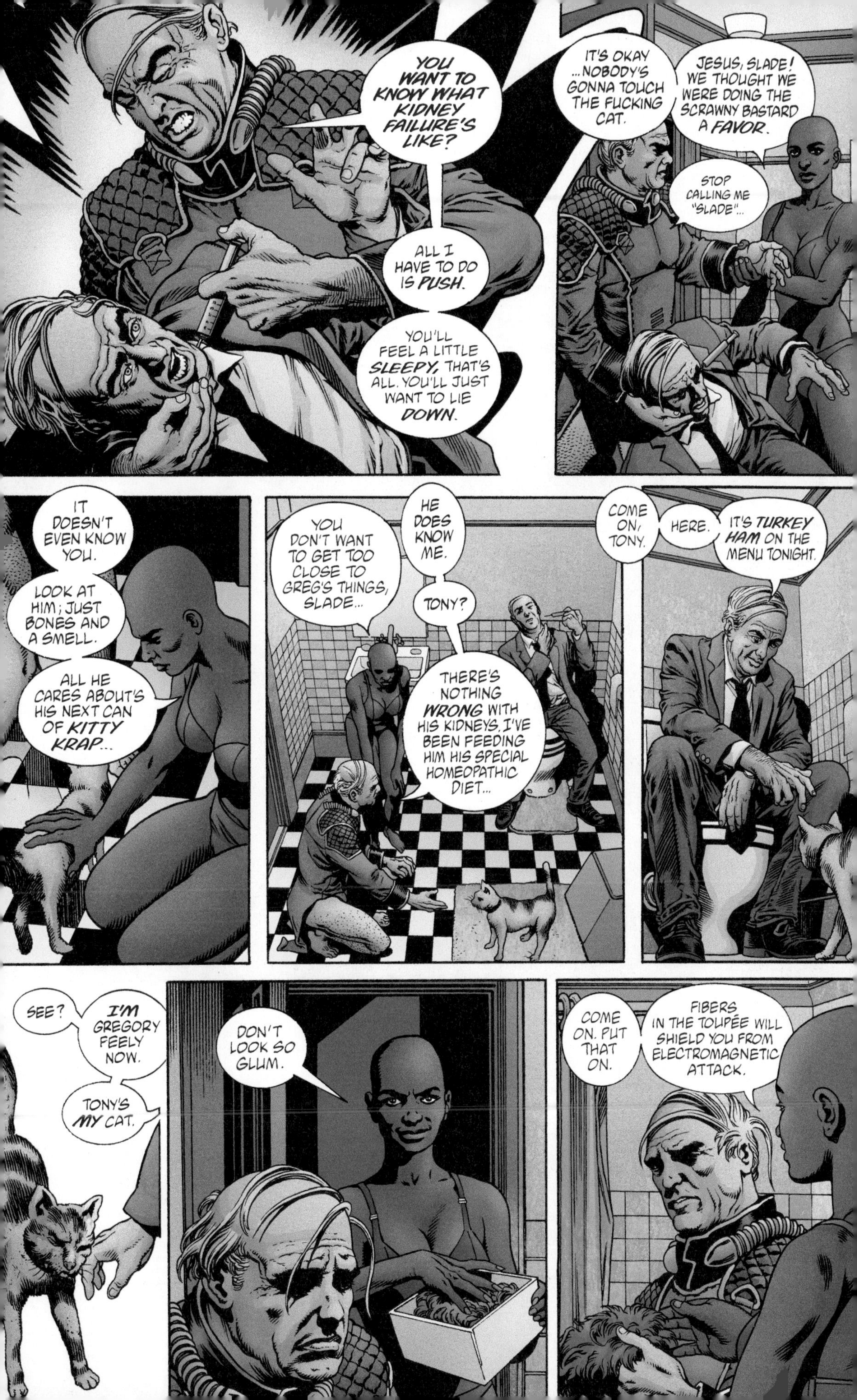
YOU WANT TO KNOW WHAT KIDNEY FAILURE'S LIKE?
ALL I HAVE TO DO IS PUSH.
YOU'LL FEEL A LITTLE SLEEPY, THAT'S ALL. YOU'LL JUST WANT TO LIE DOWN.
IT'S OKAY ...NOBODY'S GONNA TOUCH THE FUCKING CAT.
JESUS, SLADE! WE THOUGHT WE WERE DOING THE SCRAWNY BASTARD A FAVOR.
STOP CALLING ME "SLADE"...
IT DOESN'T EVEN KNOW YOU.
LOOK AT HIM; JUST BONES AND A SMELL.
ALL HE CARES ABOUT'S HIS NEXT CAN OF KITTY KRAP...
YOU DON'T WANT TO GET TOO CLOSE TO GREG'S THINGS, SLADE...
HE DOES KNOW ME.
TONY?
THERE'S NOTHING WRONG WITH HIS KIDNEYS. I'VE BEEN FEEDING HIM HIS SPECIAL HOMEOPATHIC DIET...
COME ON, TONY.
HERE.
IT'S TURKEY HAM ON THE MENU TONIGHT.
SEE?
I'M GREGORY FEELY NOW.
TONY'S MY CAT.
DON'T LOOK SO GLUM.
COME ON. PUT THAT ON.
FIBERS IN THE TOUPÉE WILL SHIELD YOU FROM ELECTROMAGNETIC ATTACK.

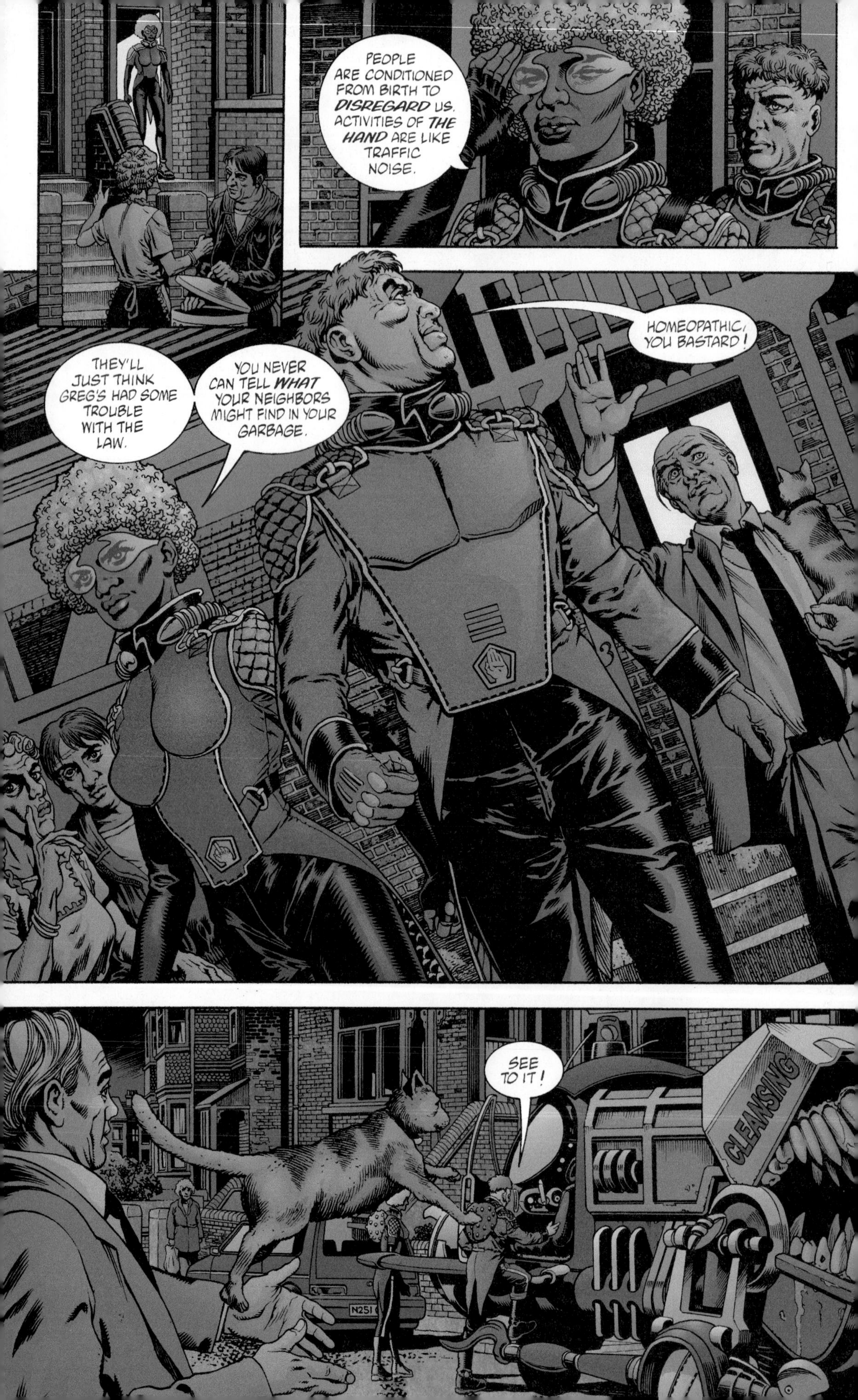
PEOPLE ARE CONDITIONED FROM BIRTH TO DISREGARD US. ACTIVITIES OF THE HAND ARE LIKE TRAFFIC NOISE.
HOMEOPATHIC, YOU BASTARD!
THEY'LL JUST THINK GREG'S HAD SOME TROUBLE WITH THE LAW.
YOU NEVER CAN TELL WHAT YOUR NEIGHBORS MIGHT FIND IN YOUR GARBAGE.
SEE TO IT!
CLEANSING

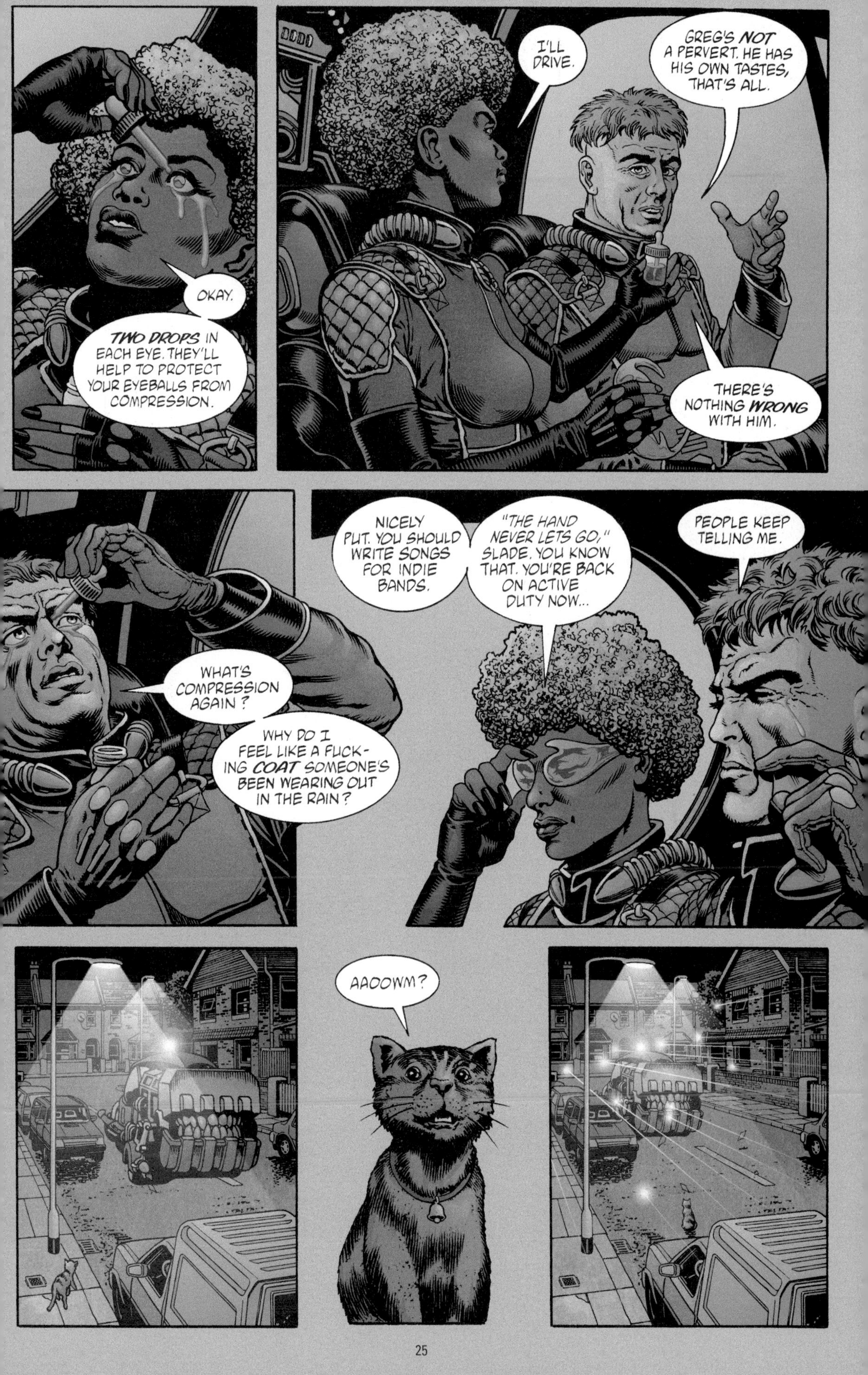
OKAY.
TWO DROPS IN EACH EYE. THEY'LL HELP TO PROTECT YOUR EYEBALLS FROM COMPRESSION.
I'LL DRIVE.
GREG'S NOT A PERVERT. HE HAS HIS OWN TASTES, THAT'S ALL.
THERE'S NOTHING WRONG WITH HIM.
WHAT'S COMPRESSION AGAIN?
WHY DO I FEEL LIKE A FUCK-ING COAT SOMEONE'S BEEN WEARING OUT IN THE RAIN?
NICELY PUT. YOU SHOULD WRITE SONGS FOR INDIE BANDS.
"THE HAND NEVER LETS GO," SLADE. YOU KNOW THAT. YOU'RE BACK ON ACTIVE DUTY NOW...
PEOPLE KEEP TELLING ME.
AAOOWM?

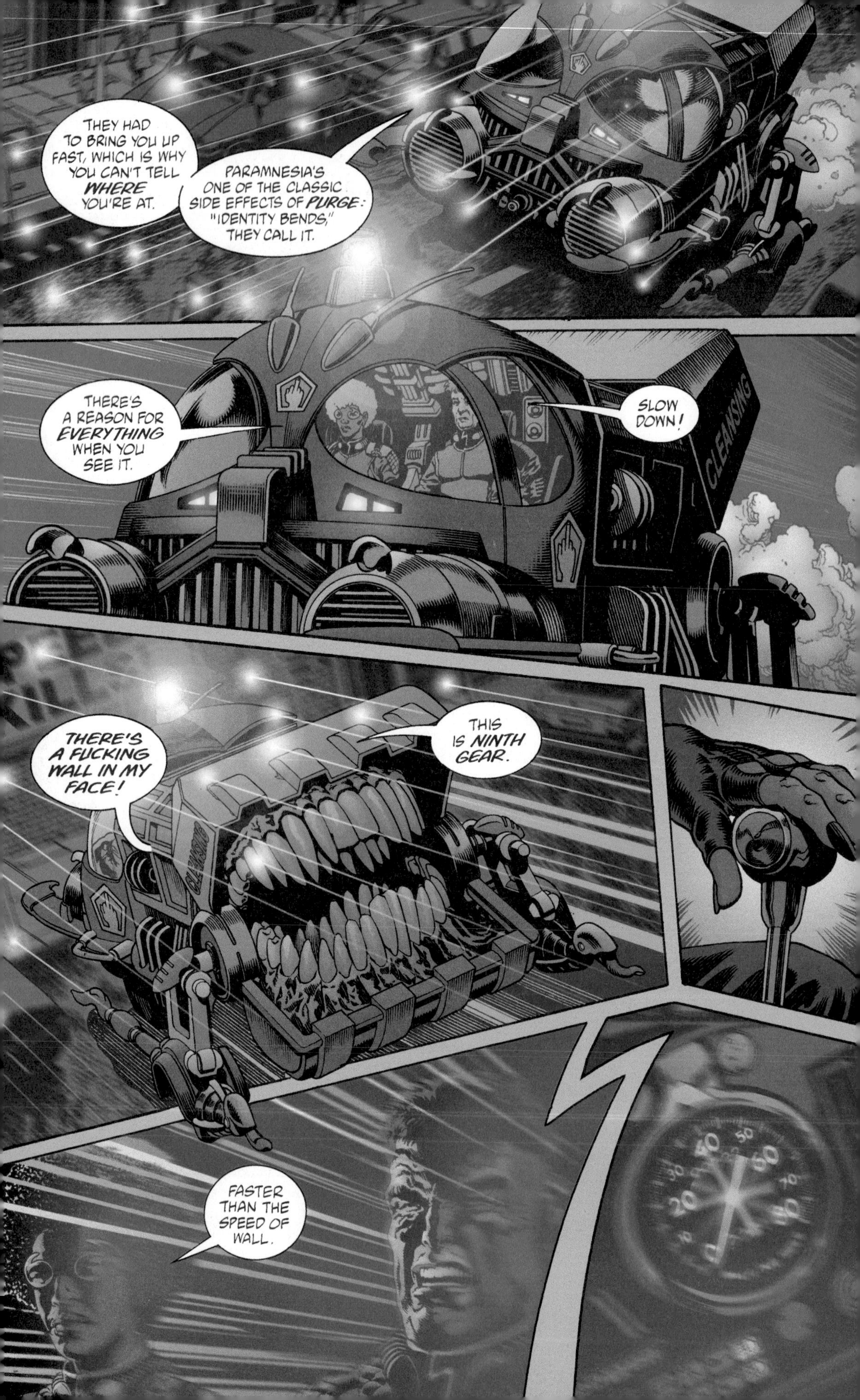
THEY HAD TO BRING YOU UP FAST, WHICH IS WHY YOU CAN'T TELL WHERE YOU'RE AT.
PARAMNESIA'S ONE OF THE CLASSIC SIDE EFFECTS OF PURGE: "IDENTITY BENDS," THEY CALL IT.
THERE'S A REASON FOR EVERYTHING WHEN YOU SEE IT.
SLOW DOWN!
CLEANSING
THERE'S A FUCKING WALL IN MY FACE!
THIS IS NINTH GEAR.
CLEANSING
FASTER THAN THE SPEED OF WALL.

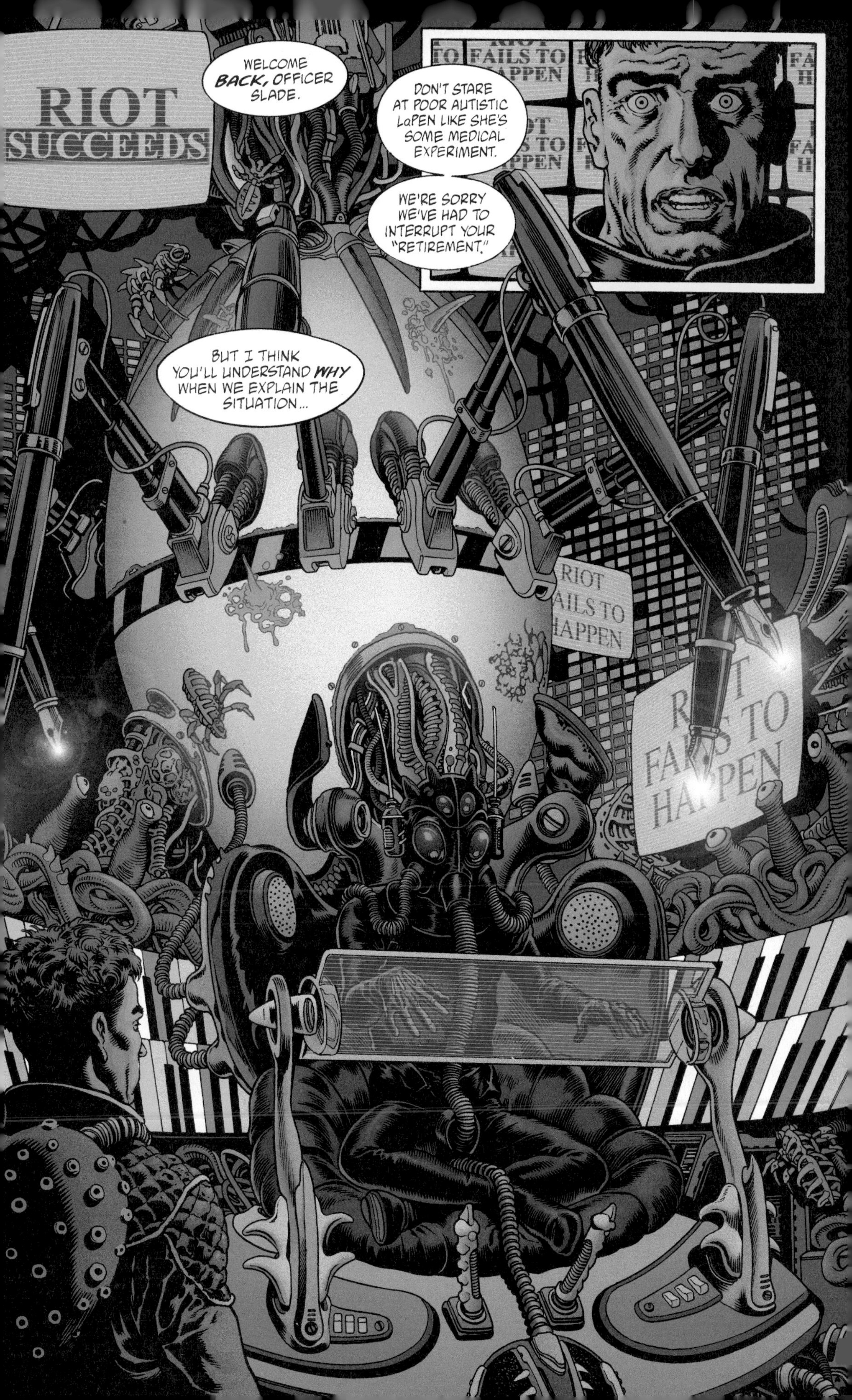
RIOT SUCCEEDS
WELCOME BACK, OFFICER SLADE.
RIOT FAILS TO HAPPEN
DON'T STARE AT POOR AUTISTIC LaPEN LIKE SHE'S SOME MEDICAL EXPERIMENT.
WE'RE SORRY WE'VE HAD TO INTERRUPT YOUR "RETIREMENT."
BUT I THINK YOU'LL UNDERSTAND WHY WHEN WE EXPLAIN THE SITUATION...
RIOT FAILS TO HAPPEN
RIOT FAILS TO HAPPEN

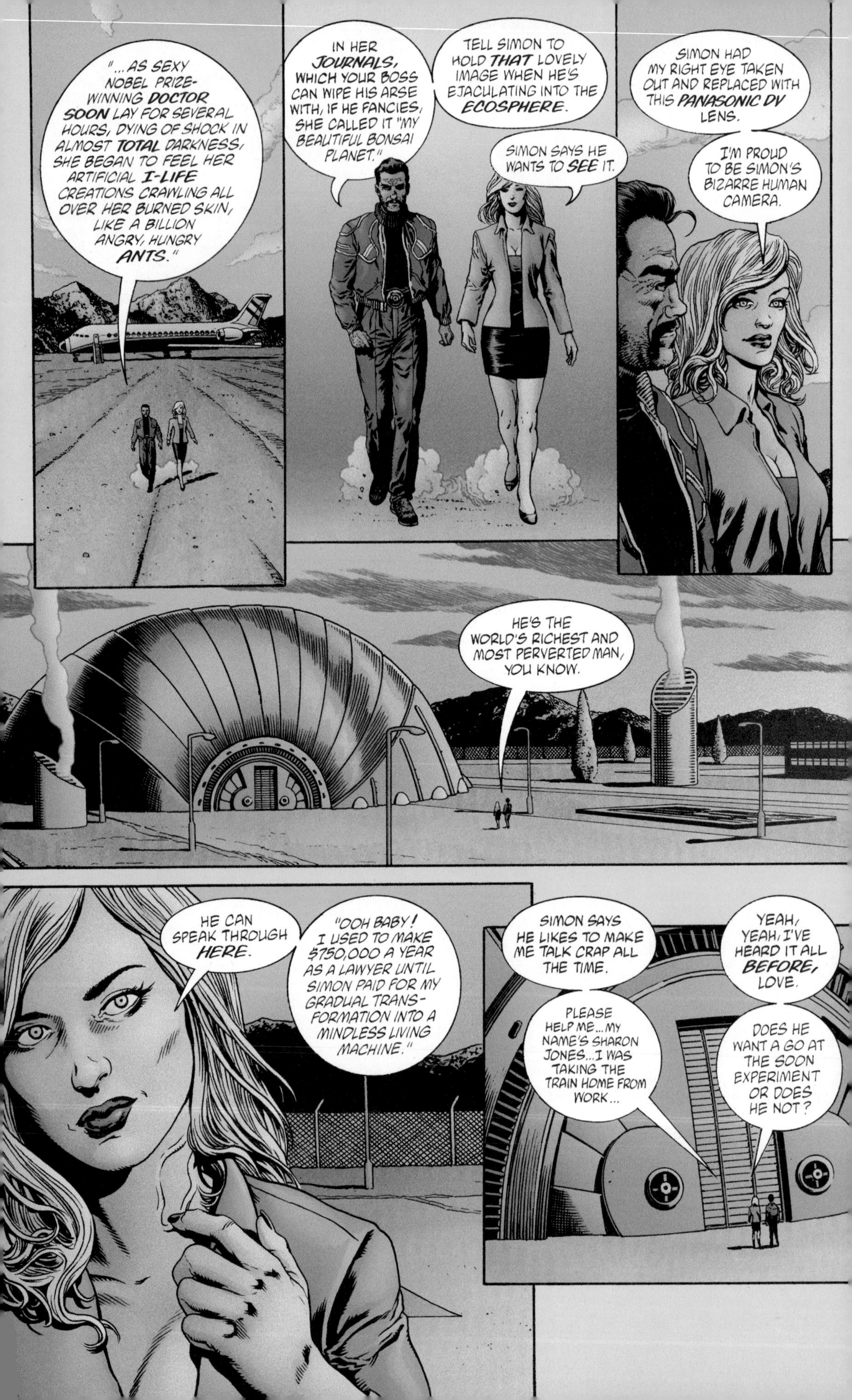
"...AS SEXY NOBEL PRIZE-WINNING DOCTOR SOON LAY FOR SEVERAL HOURS, DYING OF SHOCK IN ALMOST TOTAL DARKNESS, SHE BEGAN TO FEEL HER ARTIFICIAL I-LIFE CREATIONS CRAWLING ALL OVER HER BURNED SKIN, LIKE A BILLION ANGRY, HUNGRY ANTS."
IN HER JOURNALS, WHICH YOUR BOSS CAN WIPE HIS ARSE WITH, IF HE FANCIES, SHE CALLED IT "MY BEAUTIFUL BONSAI PLANET."
TELL SIMON TO HOLD THAT LOVELY IMAGE WHEN HE'S EJACULATING INTO THE ECOSPHERE.
SIMON SAYS HE WANTS TO SEE IT.
SIMON HAD MY RIGHT EYE TAKEN OUT AND REPLACED WITH THIS PANASONIC DV LENS.
I'M PROUD TO BE SIMON'S BIZARRE HUMAN CAMERA.
HE'S THE WORLD'S RICHEST AND MOST PERVERTED MAN, YOU KNOW.
HE CAN SPEAK THROUGH HERE.
"OOH BABY! I USED TO MAKE $750,000 A YEAR AS A LAWYER UNTIL SIMON PAID FOR MY GRADUAL TRANS-FORMATION INTO A MINDLESS LIVING MACHINE."
SIMON SAYS HE LIKES TO MAKE ME TALK CRAP ALL THE TIME.
YEAH, YEAH, I'VE HEARD IT ALL BEFORE, LOVE.
PLEASE HELP ME...MY NAME'S SHARON JONES...I WAS TAKING THE TRAIN HOME FROM WORK...
DOES HE WANT A GO AT THE SOON EXPERIMENT OR DOES HE NOT?

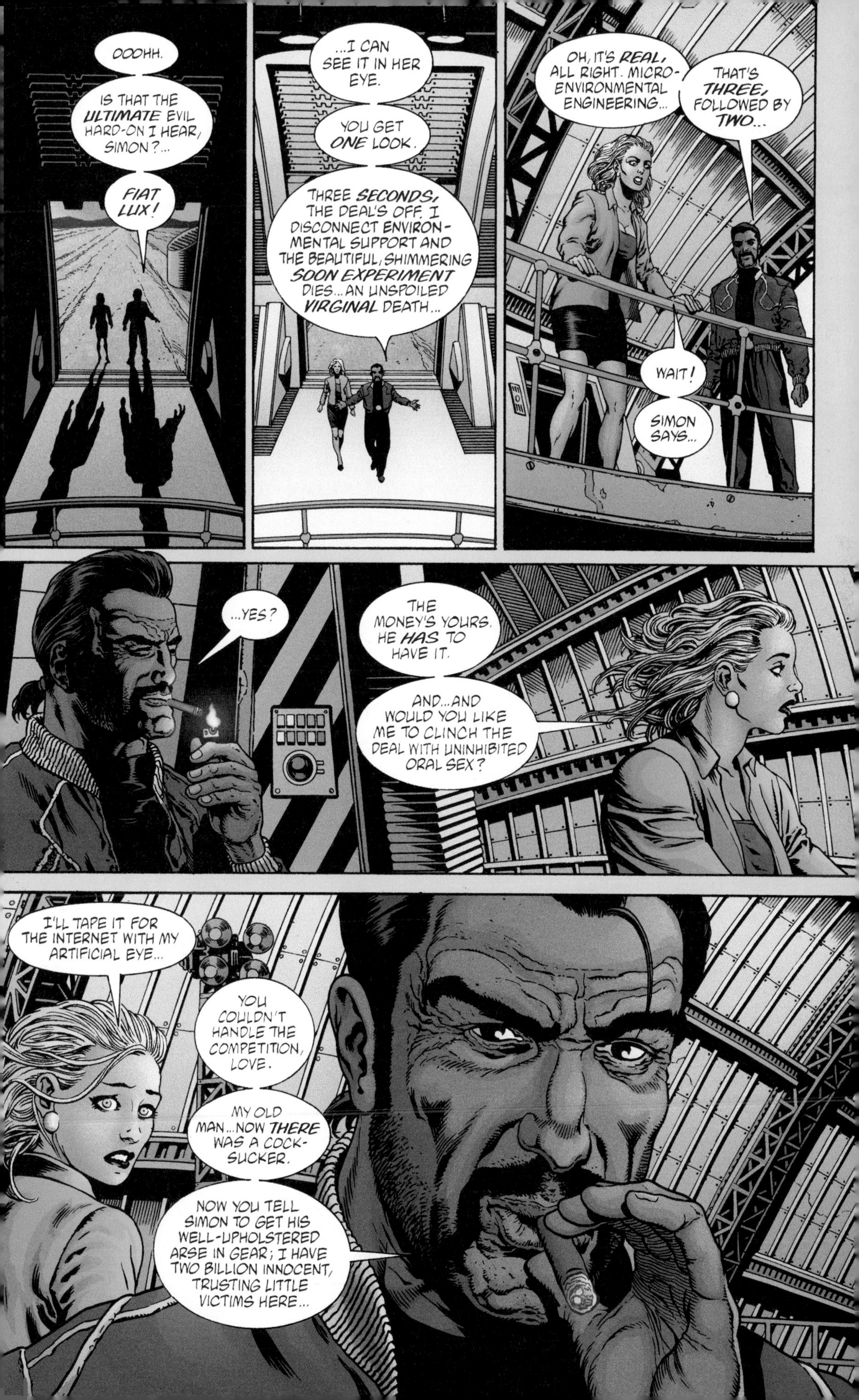
OOOHH.
IS THAT THE ULTIMATE EVIL HARD-ON I HEAR, SIMON?...
FIAT LUX!
...I CAN SEE IT IN HER EYE.
YOU GET ONE LOOK.
THREE SECONDS, THE DEAL'S OFF. I DISCONNECT ENVIRON-MENTAL SUPPORT AND THE BEAUTIFUL, SHIMMERING SOON EXPERIMENT DIES...AN UNSPOILED VIRGINAL DEATH...
OH, IT'S REAL, ALL RIGHT. MICRO-ENVIRONMENTAL ENGINEERING...
THAT'S THREE, FOLLOWED BY TWO...
WAIT!
SIMON SAYS...
...YES?
THE MONEY'S YOURS. HE HAS TO HAVE IT.
AND...AND WOULD YOU LIKE ME TO CLINCH THE DEAL WITH UNINHIBITED ORAL SEX?
I'LL TAPE IT FOR THE INTERNET WITH MY ARTIFICIAL EYE...
YOU COULDN'T HANDLE THE COMPETITION, LOVE.
MY OLD MAN...NOW THERE WAS A COCK-SUCKER.
NOW YOU TELL SIMON TO GET HIS WELL-UPHOLSTERED ARSE IN GEAR; I HAVE TWO BILLION INNOCENT, TRUSTING LITTLE VICTIMS HERE...

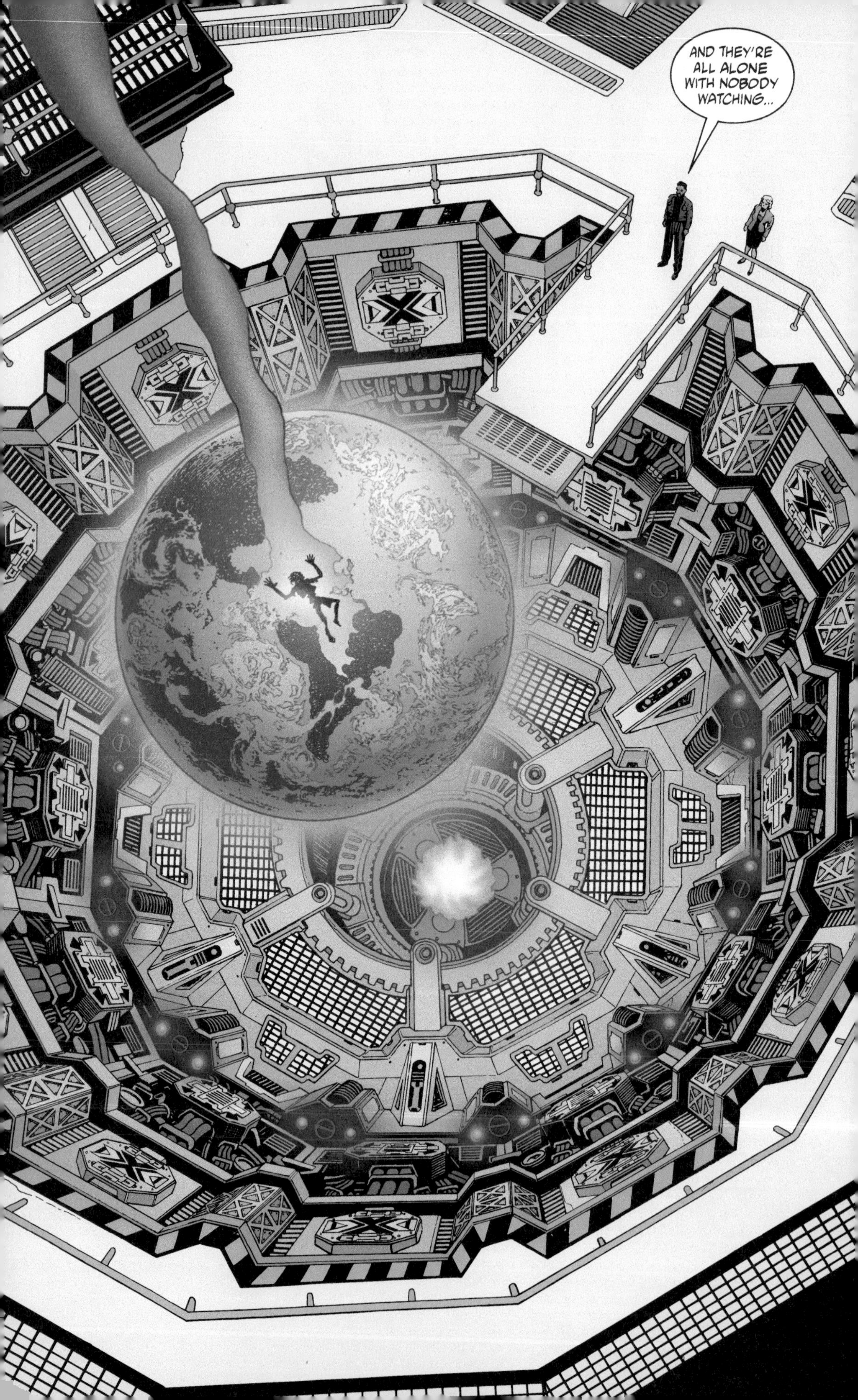
AND THEY'RE ALL ALONE WITH NOBODY WATCHING...

02. perfect victim

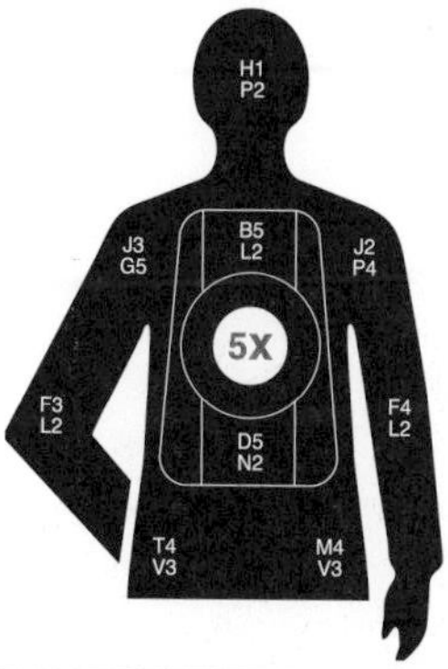
H1
P2
B5
L2
J3
G5
J2
P4
5X
F3
L2
F4
L2
D5
N2
T4
V3
M4
V3

The Filth

22
PAGES

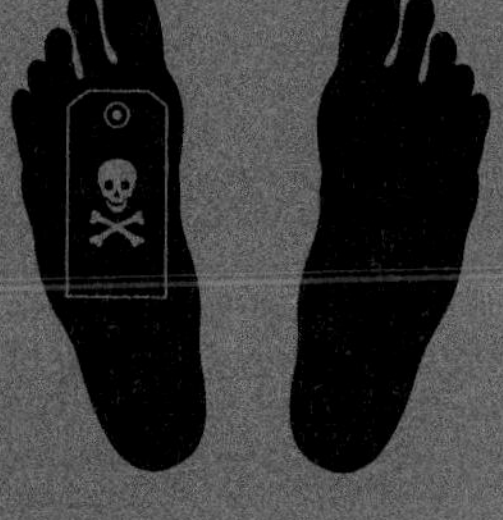

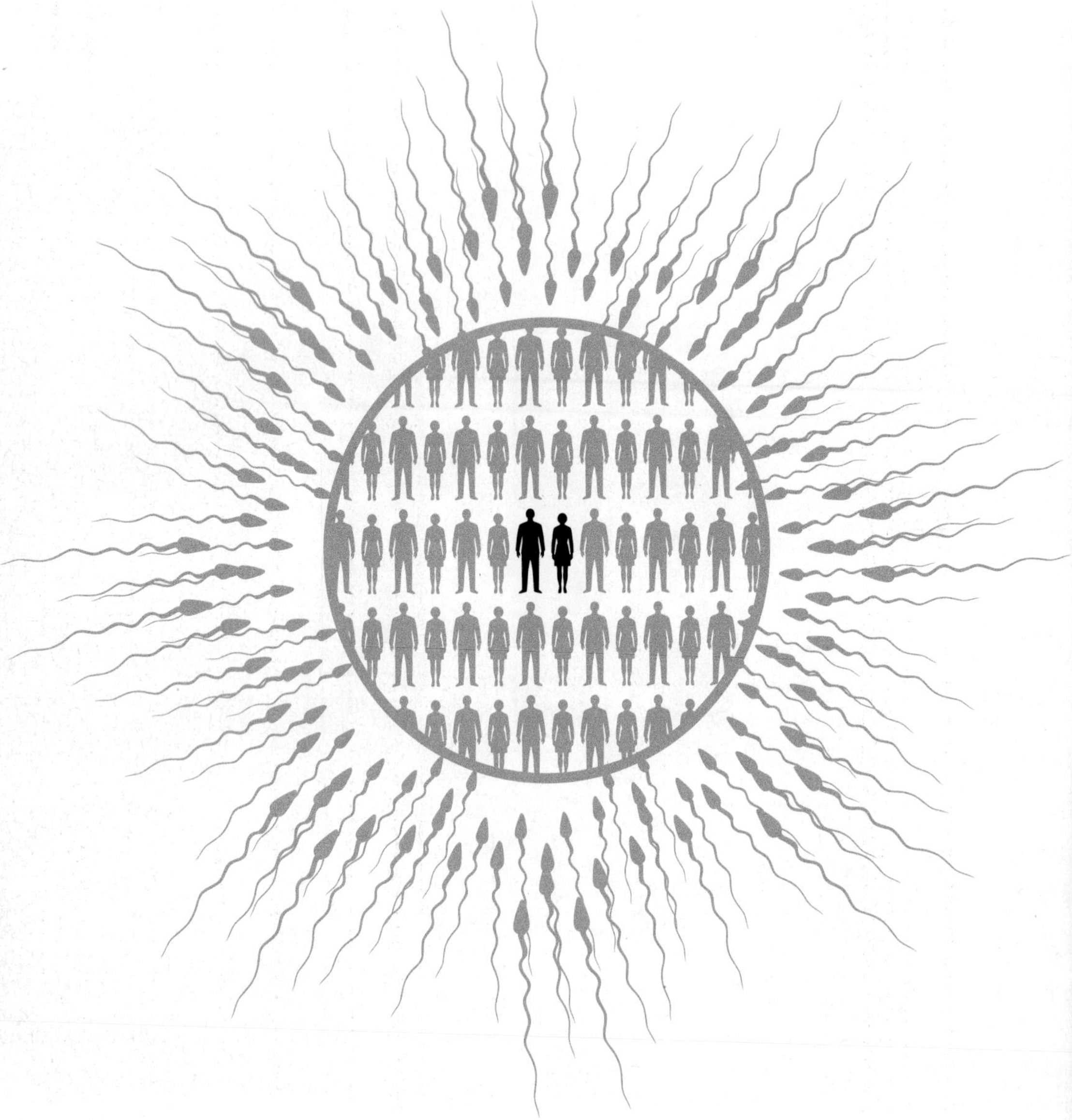

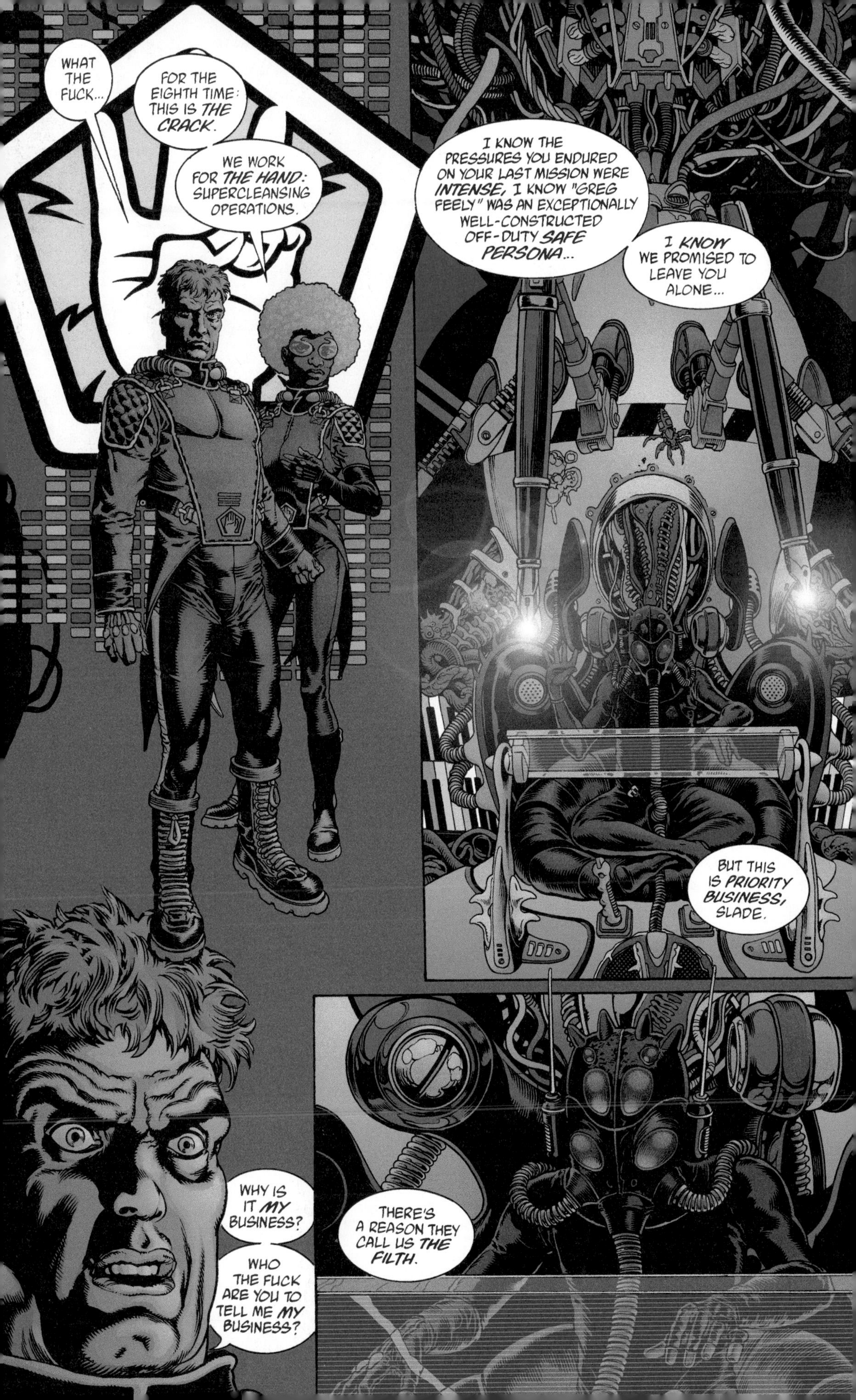
WHAT THE FUCK...
FOR THE EIGHTH TIME: THIS IS THE CRACK.
WE WORK FOR THE HAND: SUPERCLEANSING OPERATIONS.
I KNOW THE PRESSURES YOU ENDURED ON YOUR LAST MISSION WERE INTENSE, I KNOW "GREG FEELY" WAS AN EXCEPTIONALLY WELL-CONSTRUCTED OFF-DUTY SAFE PERSONA...
I KNOW WE PROMISED TO LEAVE YOU ALONE...
BUT THIS IS PRIORITY BUSINESS, SLADE.
WHY IS IT MY BUSINESS?
WHO THE FUCK ARE YOU TO TELL ME MY BUSINESS?
THERE'S A REASON THEY CALL US THE FILTH.

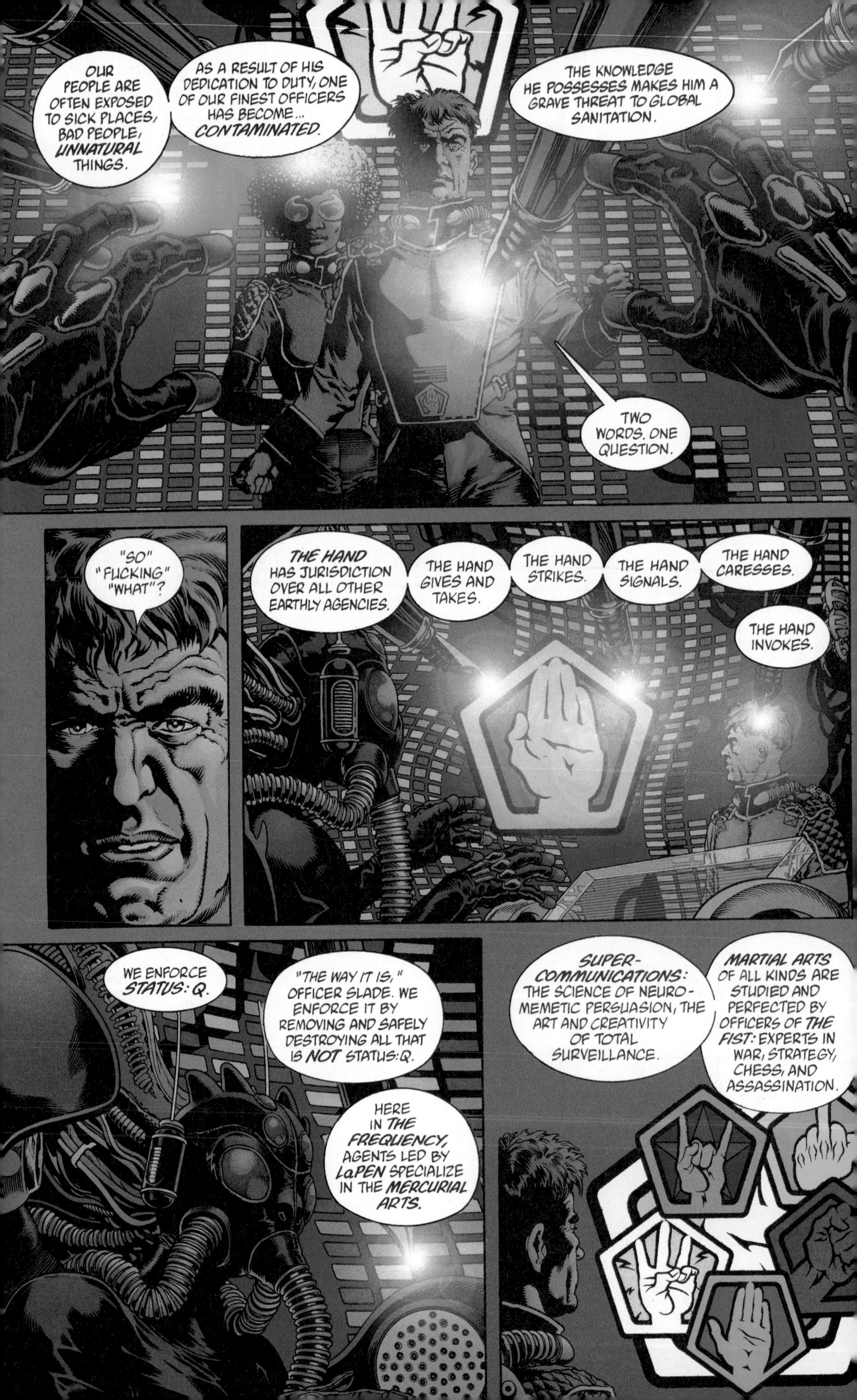
OUR PEOPLE ARE OFTEN EXPOSED TO SICK PLACES, BAD PEOPLE, UNNATURAL THINGS.
AS A RESULT OF HIS DEDICATION TO DUTY, ONE OF OUR FINEST OFFICERS HAS BECOME... CONTAMINATED.
THE KNOWLEDGE HE POSSESSES MAKES HIM A GRAVE THREAT TO GLOBAL SANITATION.
TWO WORDS. ONE QUESTION.
"SO" "FUCKING" "WHAT"?
THE HAND HAS JURISDICTION OVER ALL OTHER EARTHLY AGENCIES.
THE HAND GIVES AND TAKES.
THE HAND STRIKES.
THE HAND SIGNALS.
THE HAND CARESSES.
THE HAND INVOKES.
WE ENFORCE STATUS: Q.
"THE WAY IT IS," OFFICER SLADE. WE ENFORCE IT BY REMOVING AND SAFELY DESTROYING ALL THAT IS NOT STATUS:Q.
HERE IN THE FREQUENCY, AGENTS LED BY LaPEN SPECIALIZE IN THE MERCURIAL ARTS.
SUPER-COMMUNICATIONS: THE SCIENCE OF NEURO-MEMETIC PERSUASION, THE ART AND CREATIVITY OF TOTAL SURVEILLANCE.
MARTIAL ARTS OF ALL KINDS ARE STUDIED AND PERFECTED BY OFFICERS OF THE FIST: EXPERTS IN WAR, STRATEGY, CHESS, AND ASSASSINATION.

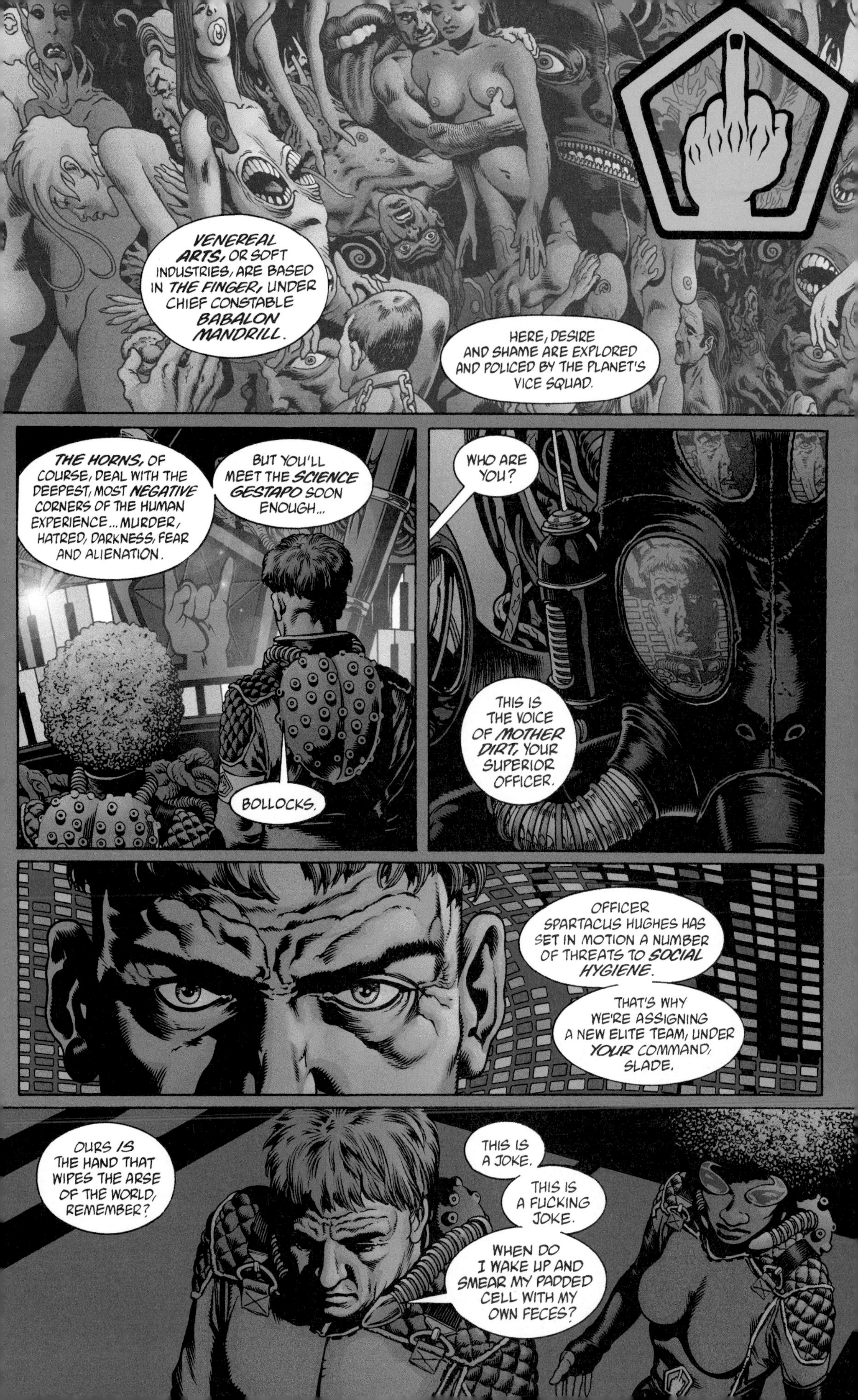
VENEREAL ARTS, OR SOFT INDUSTRIES, ARE BASED IN THE FINGER, UNDER CHIEF CONSTABLE BABALON MANDRILL.
HERE, DESIRE AND SHAME ARE EXPLORED AND POLICED BY THE PLANET'S VICE SQUAD.
THE HORNS, OF COURSE, DEAL WITH THE DEEPEST, MOST NEGATIVE CORNERS OF THE HUMAN EXPERIENCE... MURDER, HATRED, DARKNESS, FEAR AND ALIENATION.
BUT YOU'LL MEET THE SCIENCE GESTAPO SOON ENOUGH...
BOLLOCKS.
WHO ARE YOU?
THIS IS THE VOICE OF MOTHER DIRT, YOUR SUPERIOR OFFICER.
OFFICER SPARTACUS HUGHES HAS SET IN MOTION A NUMBER OF THREATS TO SOCIAL HYGIENE.
THAT'S WHY WE'RE ASSIGNING A NEW ELITE TEAM, UNDER YOUR COMMAND, SLADE.
OURS IS THE HAND THAT WIPES THE ARSE OF THE WORLD, REMEMBER?
THIS IS A JOKE.
THIS IS A FUCKING JOKE.
WHEN DO I WAKE UP AND SMEAR MY PADDED CELL WITH MY OWN FECES?

I WISH YOU'D STOP BEING SO GODDAMN *WEIRD.*

IT'S BAD FOR *MORALE,* SOME OF THESE PEOPLE WE'RE WORKING WITH CAN BE VERY HIGHLY STRUNG.

ALERT!

OFFICERS SLADE AND SPECTOR!

SLADE AND SPECTOR REPORT TO MAN GREEN/MAN YELLOW.

MAKING SURE THEY'RE ASLEEP WHILE WE OPERATE...

"SLADE"? ISN'T THAT SUPPOSED TO BE ME?

IGNORE IT.

TIME MEANS NOTHING TO MAN GREEN/MAN YELLOW AND YOU HAVEN'T EVEN *MET* CAMERON SPECTOR YET SO I WOULDN'T WORRY TOO MUCH.

FINGER ALERT: ROGUE BIO-ENGINEERED ANTI-PERSON TARGETED.

LOOK, YOU DON'T SEEM LIKE A BAD PERSON. YOU SEEM VERY... *DEDICATED,* OFFICER NIL.

BUT I WOKE UP AS SOMEONE *DIFFERENT* THIS MORNING...

FOR THE MILLIONTH TIME, SINCE WE *STARTED,* YOUR NAME IS EDWARD SLADE, SPECIAL OFFICER 999 OF *THE HAND.* I DON'T CARE *WHO* YOU GOT OUT OF BED AS.

AND MY NAME IS *MIAMI,* OKAY?

WE'RE *GARBAGEMEN,* NED.

WE STOP THE WORLD'S BACK YARD FROM *STINKING.*

HOW HARD IS THAT TO UNDER-STAND?

I'M BEGINNING TO *DESPISE* YOU.

CLEANING UP THE SHIT BEFORE THEY STEP IN IT

YOU KNOW WHAT?

YOU *ALWAYS* SAY THAT BEFORE WE FUCK LIKE TWO SPHINXES IN ESTRUS.

...I ALWAYS *DO*, DON'T I?

SO WHY DON'T I FEEL *REMOTELY* ATTRACTED TO YOU?

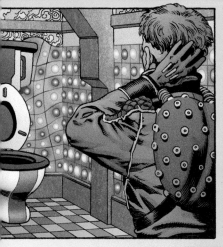

EVEN IF I *AM* "NED SLADE"... LET'S JUST SAY THAT GREG *WAS* ONLY A DISGUISE THAT'S STUCK A LITTLE...

NO ONE CAN *SERIOUSLY* EXPECT ME TO TRACK DOWN SOME FUCKING SUPER AGENT WHEN I CAN BARELY REMEMBER HOW TO FLUSH THE GENTS *TOILET* IN THIS MADHOUSE.

SPARTACUS HUGHES, EDUCATED AT ETON, MAGDALEN COLLEGE, OXFORD HONORS GRADUATE, SUPERB MARKSMAN, MARTIAL ARTS EXPERT, SEX GOD.

HE WAS BETTER THAN YOU AT *EVERYTHING* THERE IS, SLADE.

BUT YOU WERE ALWAYS *FUNNIER*, THAT'S WHAT WE ALL MISS.

HERE, YOU'LL NEED THESE *CONTACTS* TO PROTECT YOU FROM THE INK FLARE TOMORROW.

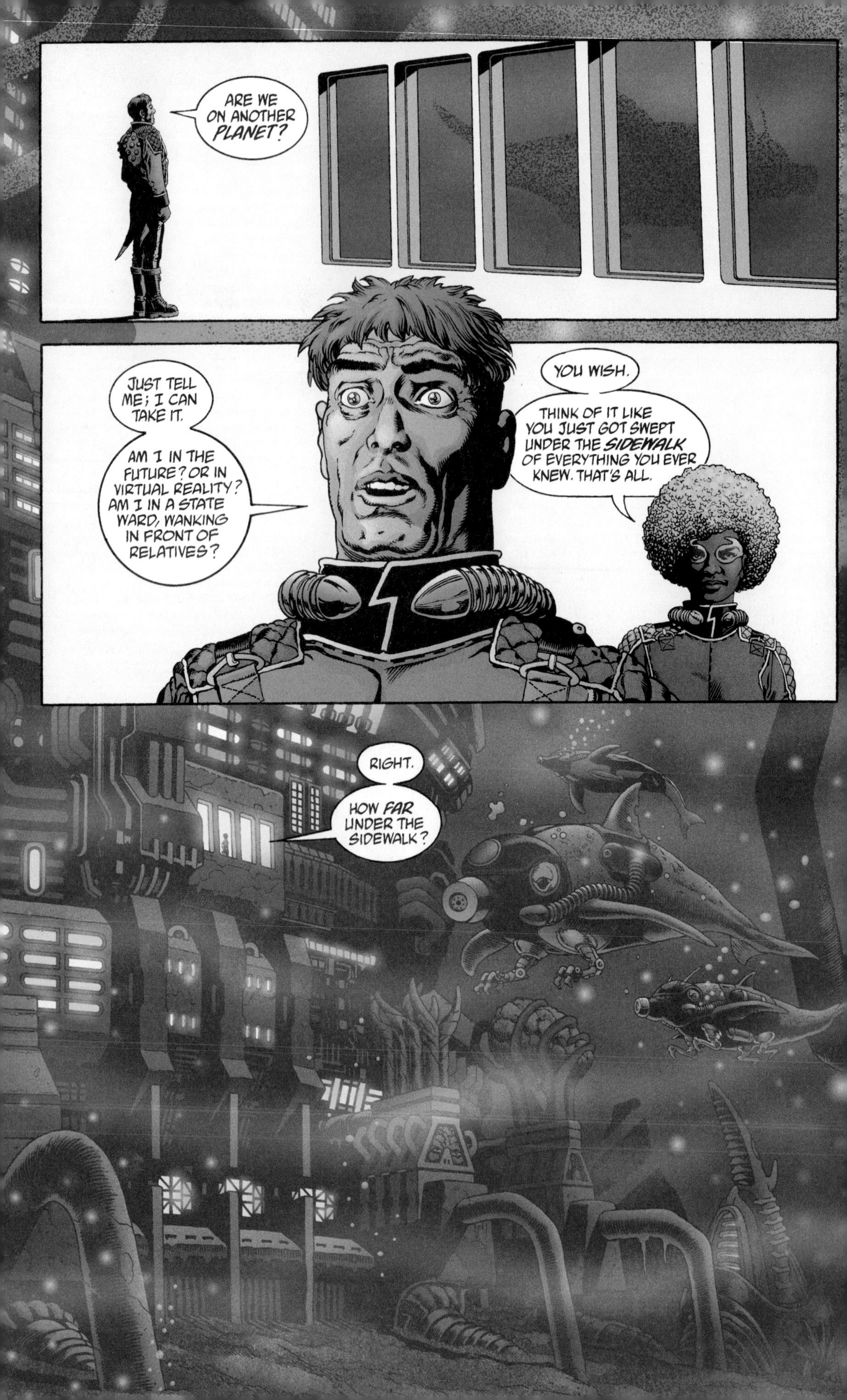
ARE WE ON ANOTHER *PLANET*?
JUST TELL ME; I CAN TAKE IT.
AM I IN THE FUTURE? OR IN VIRTUAL REALITY? AM I IN A STATE WARD, WANKING IN FRONT OF RELATIVES?
YOU WISH.
THINK OF IT LIKE YOU JUST GOT SWEPT UNDER THE *SIDEWALK* OF EVERYTHING YOU EVER KNEW. THAT'S ALL.
RIGHT.
HOW *FAR* UNDER THE SIDEWALK?

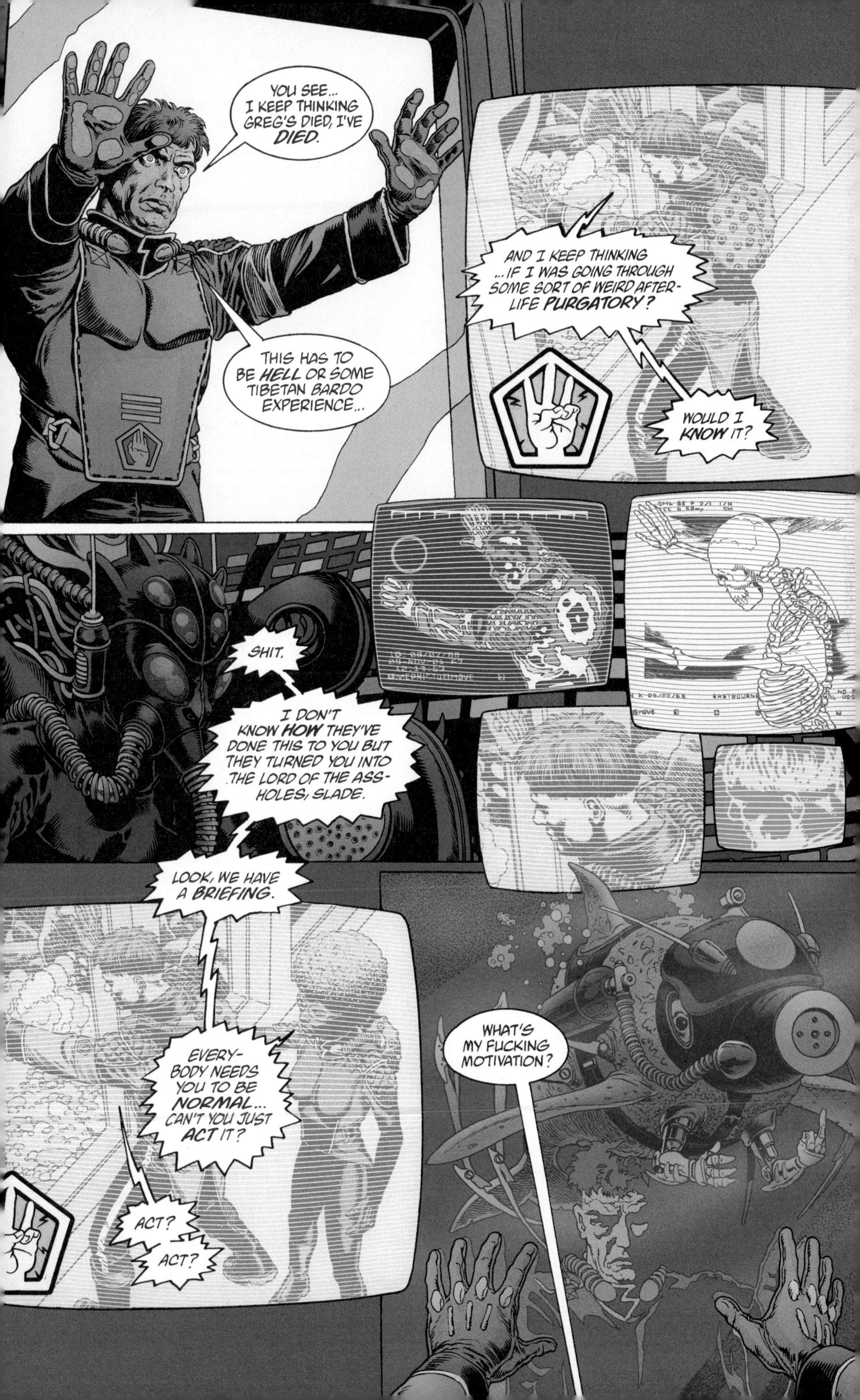
YOU SEE... I KEEP THINKING GREG'S DIED, I'VE DIED.
THIS HAS TO BE HELL OR SOME TIBETAN BARDO EXPERIENCE...
AND I KEEP THINKING ...IF I WAS GOING THROUGH SOME SORT OF WEIRD AFTER-LIFE PURGATORY?
WOULD I KNOW IT?
SHIT.
I DON'T KNOW HOW THEY'VE DONE THIS TO YOU BUT THEY TURNED YOU INTO THE LORD OF THE ASS-HOLES, SLADE.
LOOK, WE HAVE A BRIEFING.
EVERY-BODY NEEDS YOU TO BE NORMAL... CAN'T YOU JUST ACT IT?
ACT?
ACT?
WHAT'S MY FUCKING MOTIVATION?

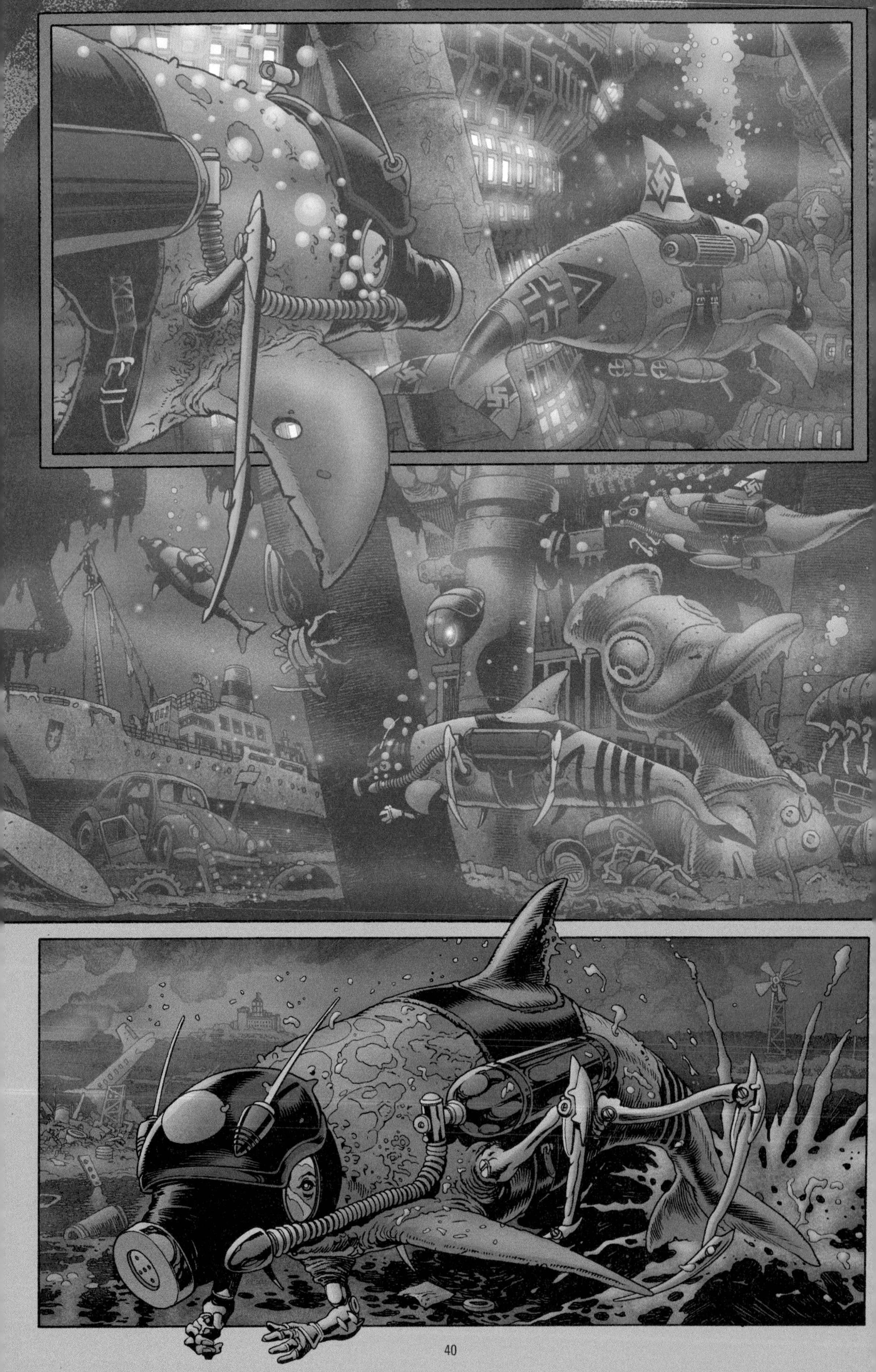

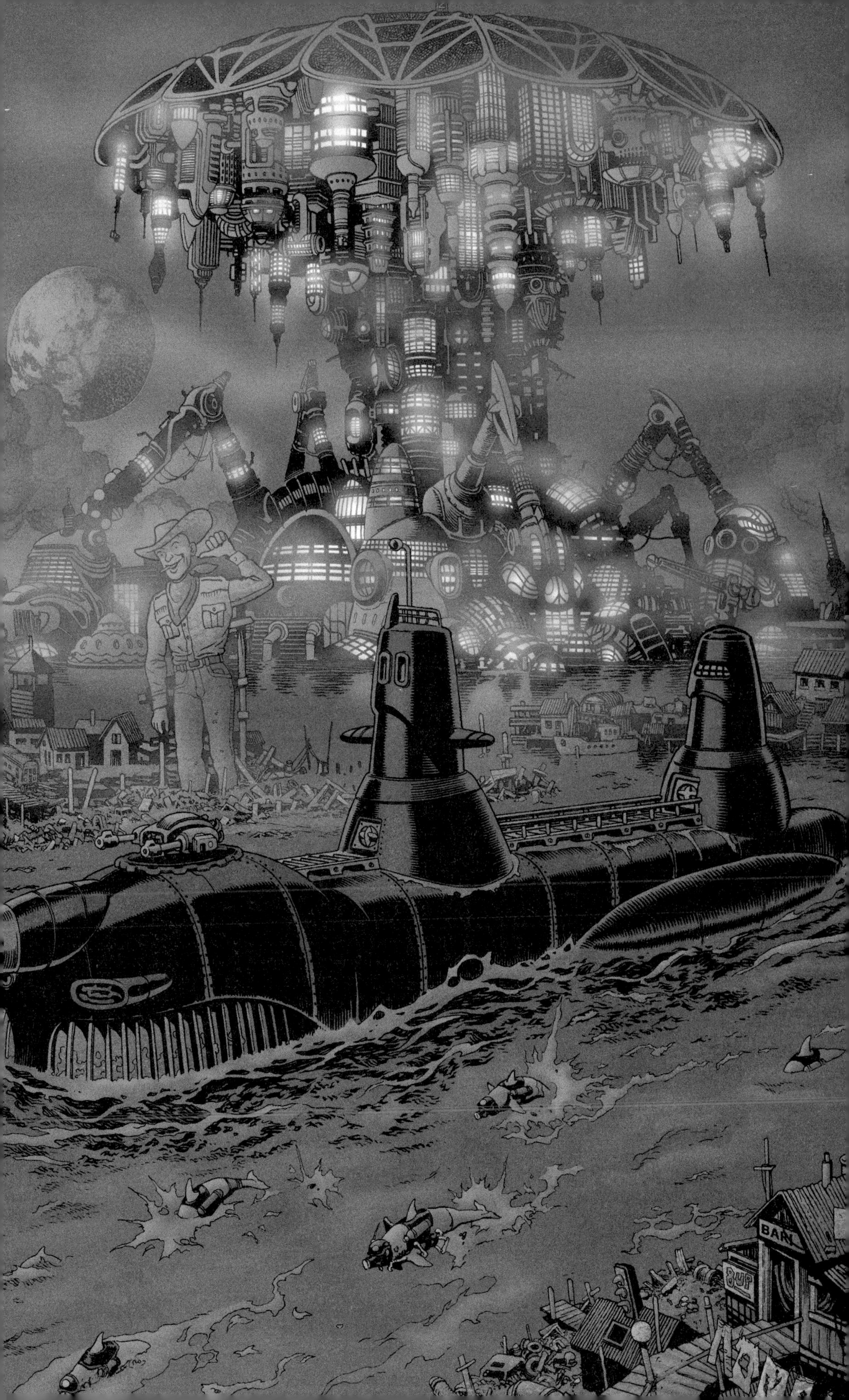
BARN
8UP

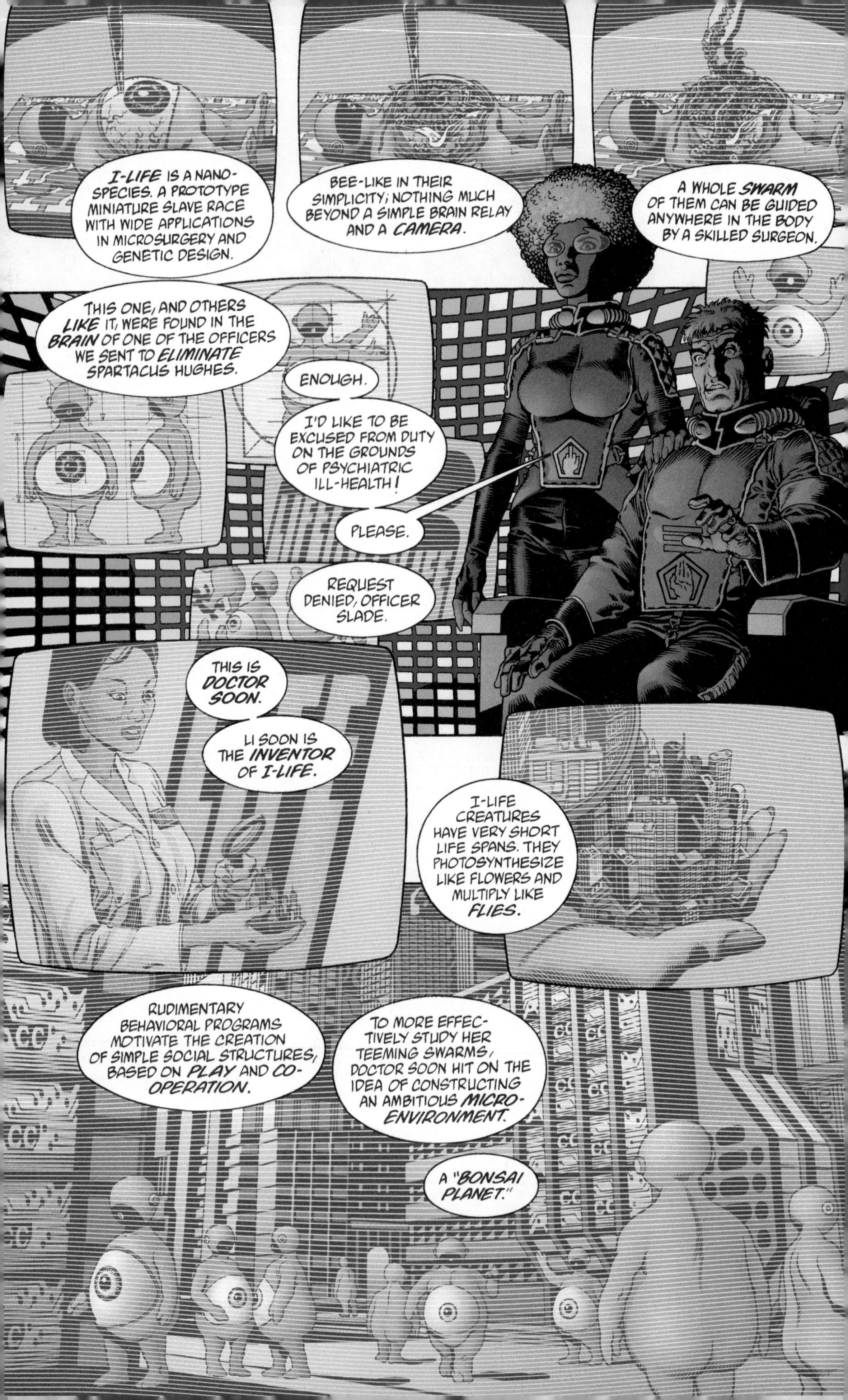
I-LIFE IS A NANO-SPECIES. A PROTOTYPE MINIATURE SLAVE RACE WITH WIDE APPLICATIONS IN MICROSURGERY AND GENETIC DESIGN.
BEE-LIKE IN THEIR SIMPLICITY; NOTHING MUCH BEYOND A SIMPLE BRAIN RELAY AND A CAMERA.
A WHOLE SWARM OF THEM CAN BE GUIDED ANYWHERE IN THE BODY BY A SKILLED SURGEON.
THIS ONE, AND OTHERS LIKE IT, WERE FOUND IN THE BRAIN OF ONE OF THE OFFICERS WE SENT TO ELIMINATE SPARTACUS HUGHES.
ENOUGH.
I'D LIKE TO BE EXCUSED FROM DUTY ON THE GROUNDS OF PSYCHIATRIC ILL-HEALTH!
PLEASE.
REQUEST DENIED, OFFICER SLADE.
THIS IS DOCTOR SOON.
LI SOON IS THE INVENTOR OF I-LIFE.
I-LIFE CREATURES HAVE VERY SHORT LIFE SPANS. THEY PHOTOSYNTHESIZE LIKE FLOWERS AND MULTIPLY LIKE FLIES.
RUDIMENTARY BEHAVIORAL PROGRAMS MOTIVATE THE CREATION OF SIMPLE SOCIAL STRUCTURES, BASED ON PLAY AND CO-OPERATION.
TO MORE EFFECTIVELY STUDY HER TEEMING SWARMS, DOCTOR SOON HIT ON THE IDEA OF CONSTRUCTING AN AMBITIOUS MICRO-ENVIRONMENT.
A "BONSAI PLANET."

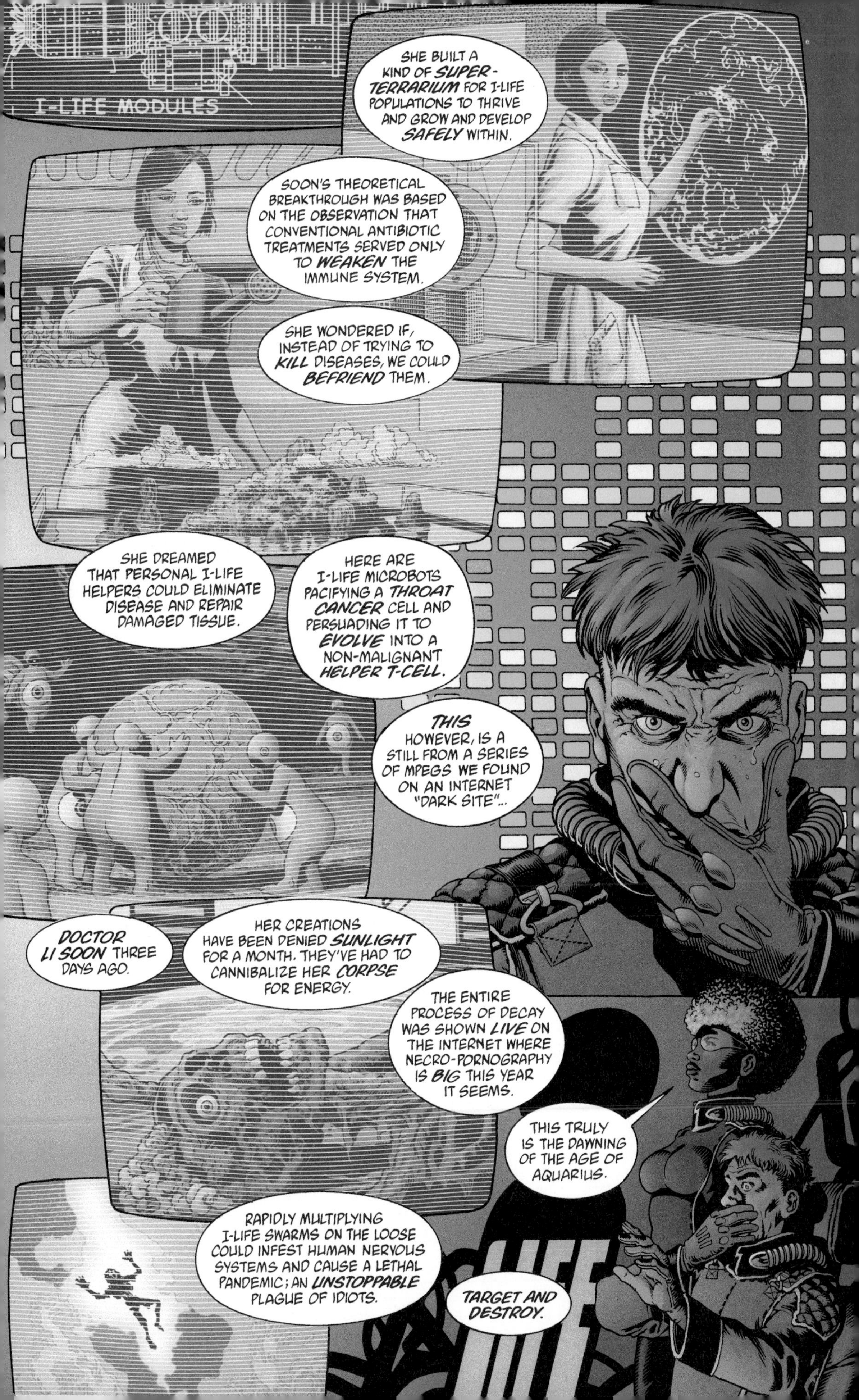
I-LIFE MODULES
SHE BUILT A KIND OF SUPER-TERRARIUM FOR I-LIFE POPULATIONS TO THRIVE AND GROW AND DEVELOP SAFELY WITHIN.
SOON'S THEORETICAL BREAKTHROUGH WAS BASED ON THE OBSERVATION THAT CONVENTIONAL ANTIBIOTIC TREATMENTS SERVED ONLY TO WEAKEN THE IMMUNE SYSTEM.
SHE WONDERED IF, INSTEAD OF TRYING TO KILL DISEASES, WE COULD BEFRIEND THEM.
SHE DREAMED THAT PERSONAL I-LIFE HELPERS COULD ELIMINATE DISEASE AND REPAIR DAMAGED TISSUE.
HERE ARE I-LIFE MICROBOTS PACIFYING A THROAT CANCER CELL AND PERSUADING IT TO EVOLVE INTO A NON-MALIGNANT HELPER T-CELL.
THIS HOWEVER, IS A STILL FROM A SERIES OF MPEGS WE FOUND ON AN INTERNET "DARK SITE"...
DOCTOR LI SOON THREE DAYS AGO.
HER CREATIONS HAVE BEEN DENIED SUNLIGHT FOR A MONTH. THEY'VE HAD TO CANNIBALIZE HER CORPSE FOR ENERGY.
THE ENTIRE PROCESS OF DECAY WAS SHOWN LIVE ON THE INTERNET WHERE NECRO-PORNOGRAPHY IS BIG THIS YEAR IT SEEMS.
THIS TRULY IS THE DAWNING OF THE AGE OF AQUARIUS.
RAPIDLY MULTIPLYING I-LIFE SWARMS ON THE LOOSE COULD INFEST HUMAN NERVOUS SYSTEMS AND CAUSE A LETHAL PANDEMIC; AN UNSTOPPABLE PLAGUE OF IDIOTS.
TARGET AND DESTROY.

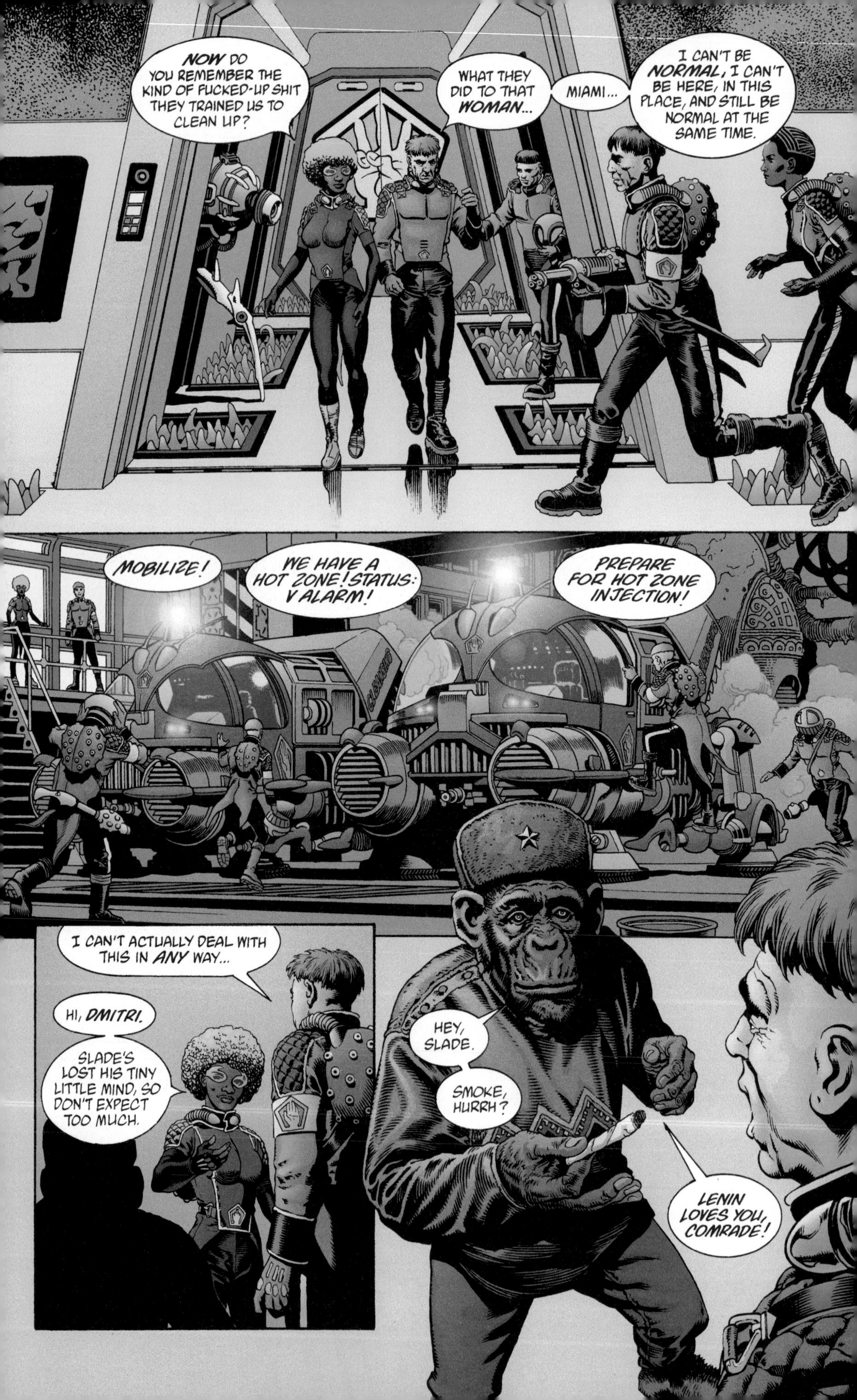
NOW DO YOU REMEMBER THE KIND OF FUCKED-UP SHIT THEY TRAINED US TO CLEAN UP?
WHAT THEY DID TO THAT WOMAN...
MIAMI...
I CAN'T BE NORMAL, I CAN'T BE HERE, IN THIS PLACE, AND STILL BE NORMAL AT THE SAME TIME.
MOBILIZE!
WE HAVE A HOT ZONE! STATUS: V ALARM!
PREPARE FOR HOT ZONE INJECTION!
I CAN'T ACTUALLY DEAL WITH THIS IN ANY WAY...
HI, DMITRI.
SLADE'S LOST HIS TINY LITTLE MIND, SO DON'T EXPECT TOO MUCH.
HEY, SLADE.
SMOKE, HURRH?
LENIN LOVES YOU, COMRADE!

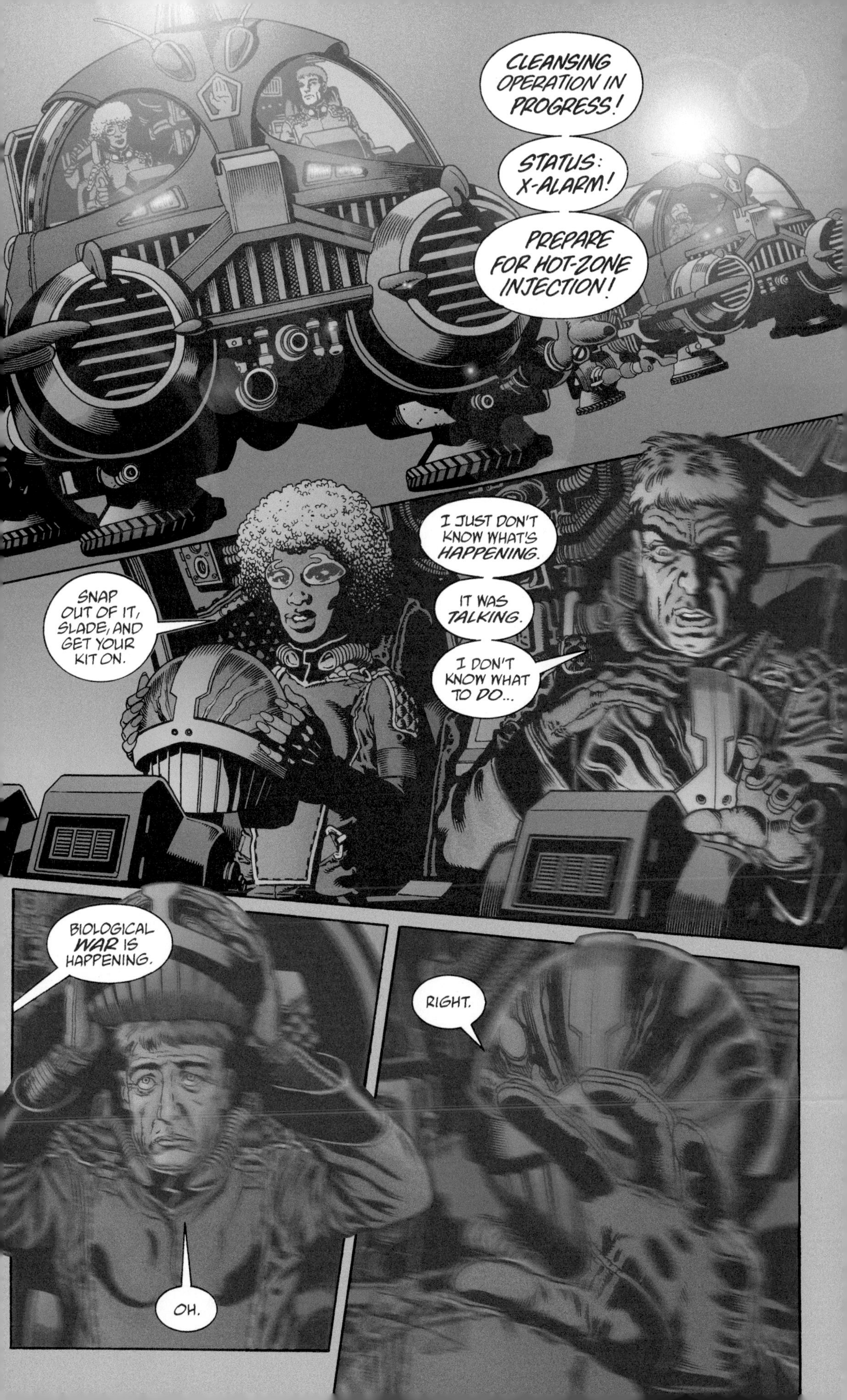
CLEANSING OPERATION IN PROGRESS!
STATUS: X-ALARM!
PREPARE FOR HOT-ZONE INJECTION!
SNAP OUT OF IT, SLADE, AND GET YOUR KIT ON.
I JUST DON'T KNOW WHAT'S HAPPENING.
IT WAS TALKING.
I DON'T KNOW WHAT TO DO...
BIOLOGICAL WAR IS HAPPENING.
OH.
RIGHT.

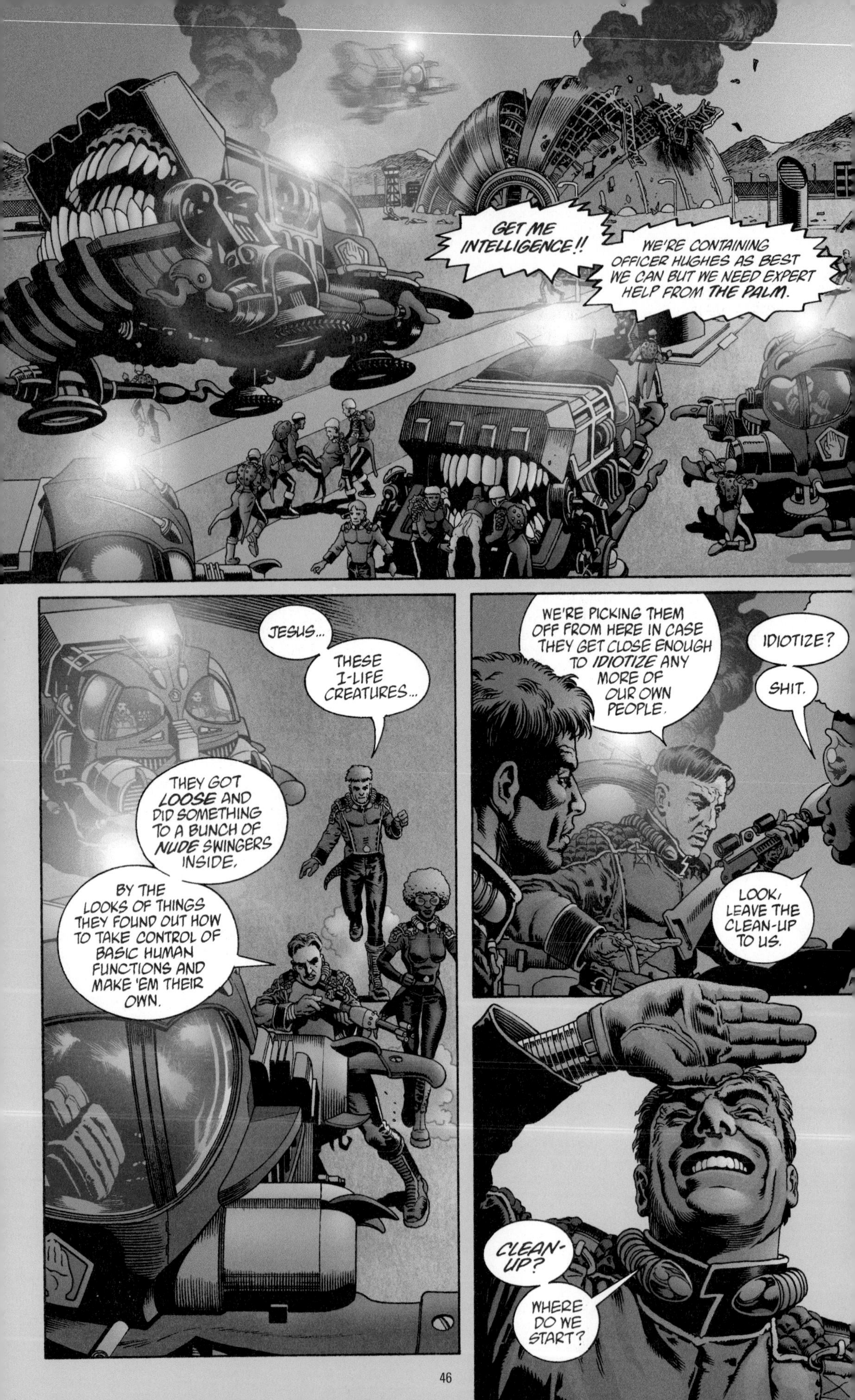
GET ME INTELLIGENCE!!
WE'RE CONTAINING OFFICER HUGHES AS BEST WE CAN BUT WE NEED EXPERT HELP FROM THE PALM.
JESUS...
THESE I-LIFE CREATURES...
THEY GOT LOOSE AND DID SOMETHING TO A BUNCH OF NUDE SWINGERS INSIDE.
BY THE LOOKS OF THINGS THEY FOUND OUT HOW TO TAKE CONTROL OF BASIC HUMAN FUNCTIONS AND MAKE 'EM THEIR OWN.
WE'RE PICKING THEM OFF FROM HERE IN CASE THEY GET CLOSE ENOUGH TO IDIOTIZE ANY MORE OF OUR OWN PEOPLE.
IDIOTIZE?
SHIT.
LOOK, LEAVE THE CLEAN-UP TO US.
CLEAN-UP?
WHERE DO WE START?

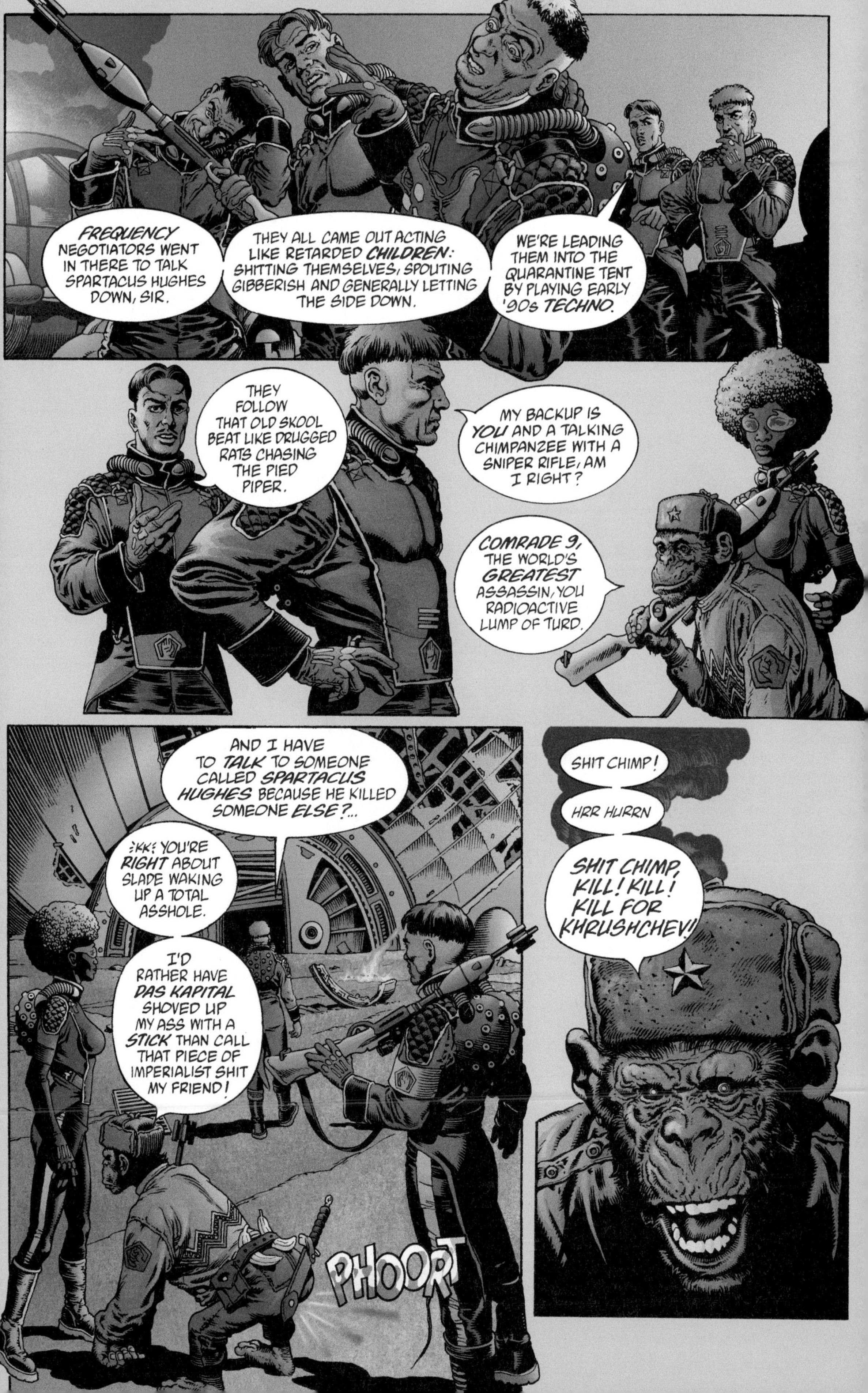

FREQUENCY NEGOTIATORS WENT IN THERE TO TALK SPARTACUS HUGHES DOWN, SIR.
THEY ALL CAME OUT ACTING LIKE RETARDED CHILDREN: SHITTING THEMSELVES, SPOUTING GIBBERISH AND GENERALLY LETTING THE SIDE DOWN.
WE'RE LEADING THEM INTO THE QUARANTINE TENT BY PLAYING EARLY '90s TECHNO.
THEY FOLLOW THAT OLD SKOOL BEAT LIKE DRUGGED RATS CHASING THE PIED PIPER.
MY BACKUP IS YOU AND A TALKING CHIMPANZEE WITH A SNIPER RIFLE, AM I RIGHT?
COMRADE 9, THE WORLD'S GREATEST ASSASSIN, YOU RADIOACTIVE LUMP OF TURD.
AND I HAVE TO TALK TO SOMEONE CALLED SPARTACUS HUGHES BECAUSE HE KILLED SOMEONE ELSE?...
KK YOU'RE RIGHT ABOUT SLADE WAKING UP A TOTAL ASSHOLE.
I'D RATHER HAVE DAS KAPITAL SHOVED UP MY ASS WITH A STICK THAN CALL THAT PIECE OF IMPERIALIST SHIT MY FRIEND!
PHOORT
SHIT CHIMP!
HRR HURRN
SHIT CHIMP, KILL! KILL! KILL FOR KHRUSHCHEV!

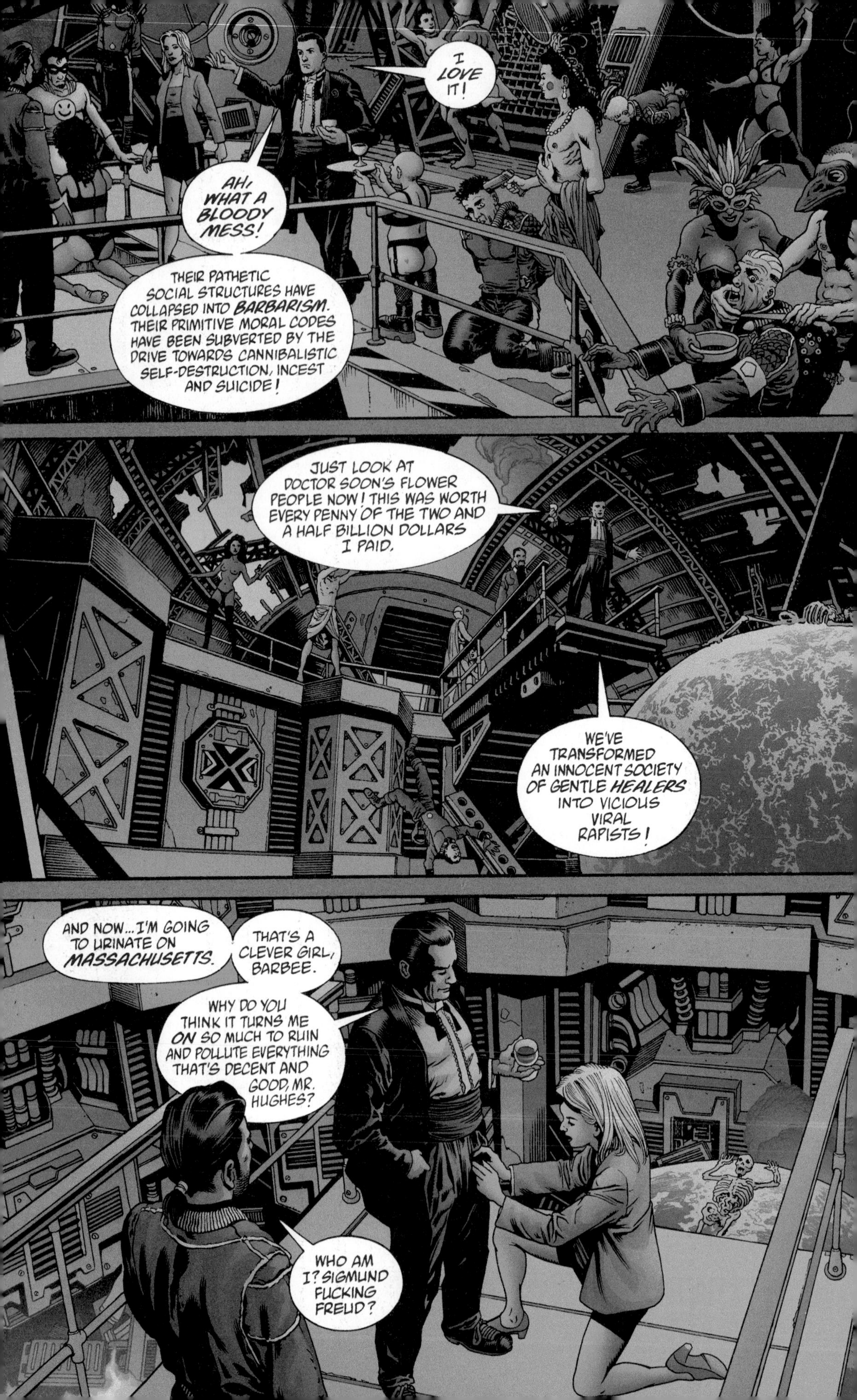
I LOVE IT!
AH, WHAT A BLOODY MESS!
THEIR PATHETIC SOCIAL STRUCTURES HAVE COLLAPSED INTO BARBARISM. THEIR PRIMITIVE MORAL CODES HAVE BEEN SUBVERTED BY THE DRIVE TOWARDS CANNIBALISTIC SELF-DESTRUCTION, INCEST AND SUICIDE!
JUST LOOK AT DOCTOR SOON'S FLOWER PEOPLE NOW! THIS WAS WORTH EVERY PENNY OF THE TWO AND A HALF BILLION DOLLARS I PAID.
WE'VE TRANSFORMED AN INNOCENT SOCIETY OF GENTLE HEALERS INTO VICIOUS VIRAL RAPISTS!
AND NOW... I'M GOING TO URINATE ON MASSACHUSETTS.
THAT'S A CLEVER GIRL, BARBEE.
WHY DO YOU THINK IT TURNS ME ON SO MUCH TO RUIN AND POLLUTE EVERYTHING THAT'S DECENT AND GOOD, MR. HUGHES?
WHO AM I? SIGMUND FUCKING FREUD?

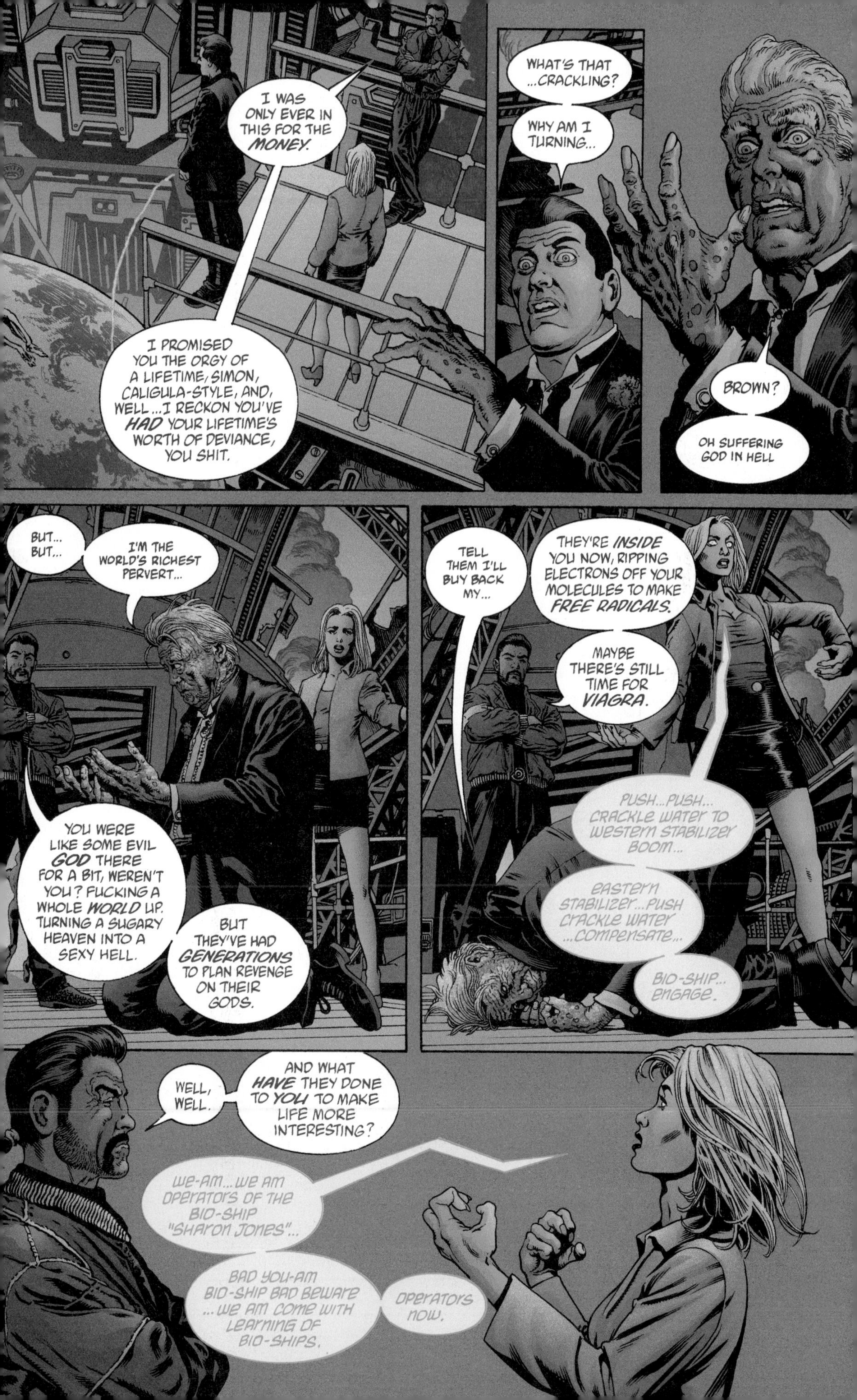
I WAS ONLY EVER IN THIS FOR THE MONEY.
I PROMISED YOU THE ORGY OF A LIFETIME, SIMON, CALIGULA-STYLE, AND, WELL...I RECKON YOU'VE HAD YOUR LIFETIME'S WORTH OF DEVIANCE, YOU SHIT.
WHAT'S THAT ...CRACKLING?
WHY AM I TURNING...
BROWN?
OH SUFFERING GOD IN HELL
BUT... BUT...
I'M THE WORLD'S RICHEST PERVERT...
YOU WERE LIKE SOME EVIL GOD THERE FOR A BIT, WEREN'T YOU? FUCKING A WHOLE WORLD UP. TURNING A SUGARY HEAVEN INTO A SEXY HELL.
BUT THEY'VE HAD GENERATIONS TO PLAN REVENGE ON THEIR GODS.
TELL THEM I'LL BUY BACK MY...
THEY'RE INSIDE YOU NOW, RIPPING ELECTRONS OFF YOUR MOLECULES TO MAKE FREE RADICALS.
MAYBE THERE'S STILL TIME FOR VIAGRA.
PUSH...PUSH... CRACKLE WATER TO WESTERN STABILIZER BOOM...
EASTERN STABILIZER...PUSH CRACKLE WATER ...COMPENSATE...
BIO-SHIP... ENGAGE.
WELL, WELL.
AND WHAT HAVE THEY DONE TO YOU TO MAKE LIFE MORE INTERESTING?
WE-AM...WE AM OPERATORS OF THE BIO-SHIP "SHARON JONES"...
BAD YOU-AM BIO-SHIP BAD BEWARE ...WE AM COME WITH LEARNING OF BIO-SHIPS.
OPERATORS NOW.

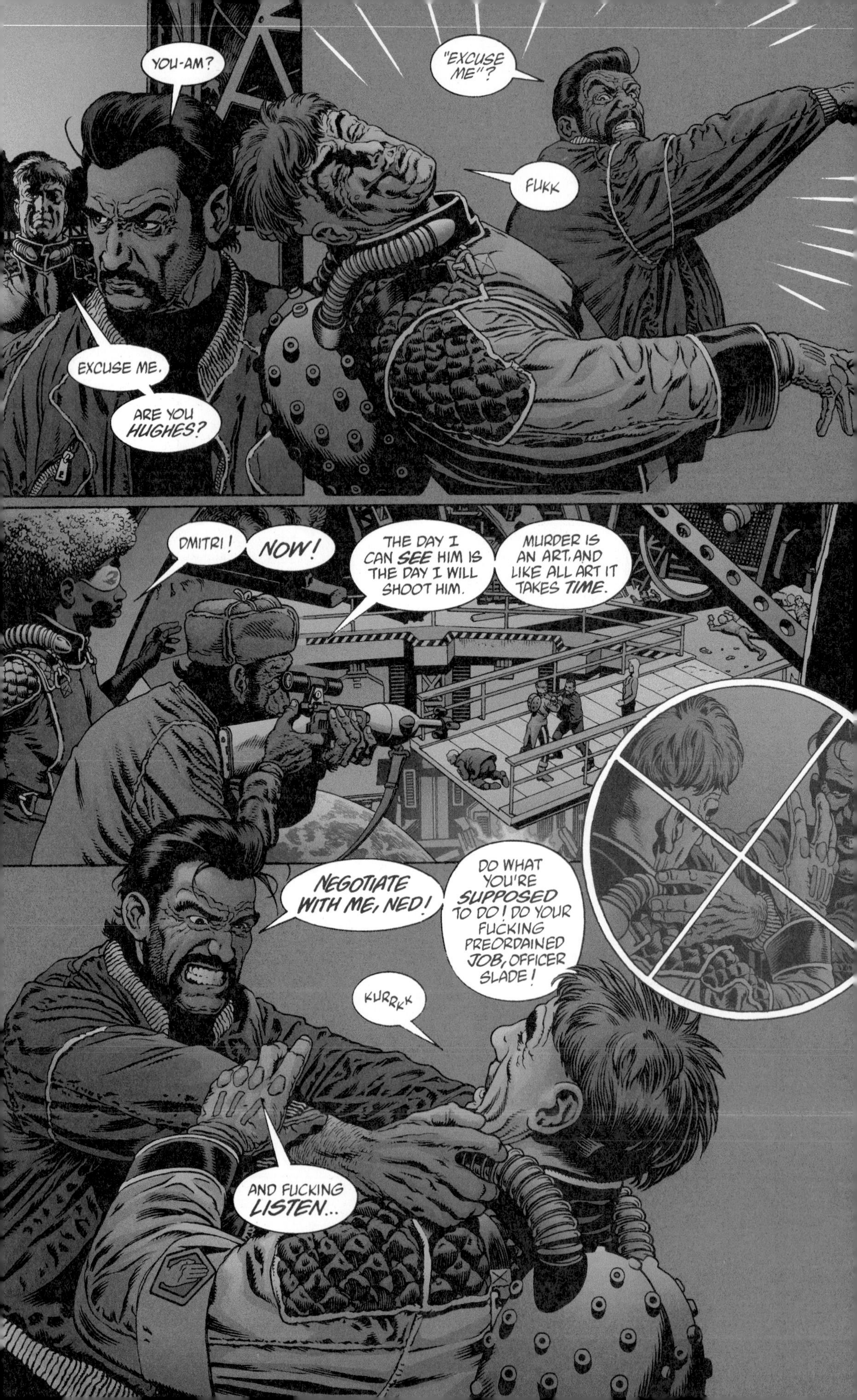
YOU-AM?
"EXCUSE ME"?
FUKK
EXCUSE ME.
ARE YOU HUGHES?
DMITRI!
NOW!
THE DAY I CAN SEE HIM IS THE DAY I WILL SHOOT HIM.
MURDER IS AN ART, AND LIKE ALL ART IT TAKES TIME.
NEGOTIATE WITH ME, NED!
DO WHAT YOU'RE SUPPOSED TO DO! DO YOUR FUCKING PREORDAINED JOB, OFFICER SLADE!
KURRKK
AND FUCKING LISTEN...

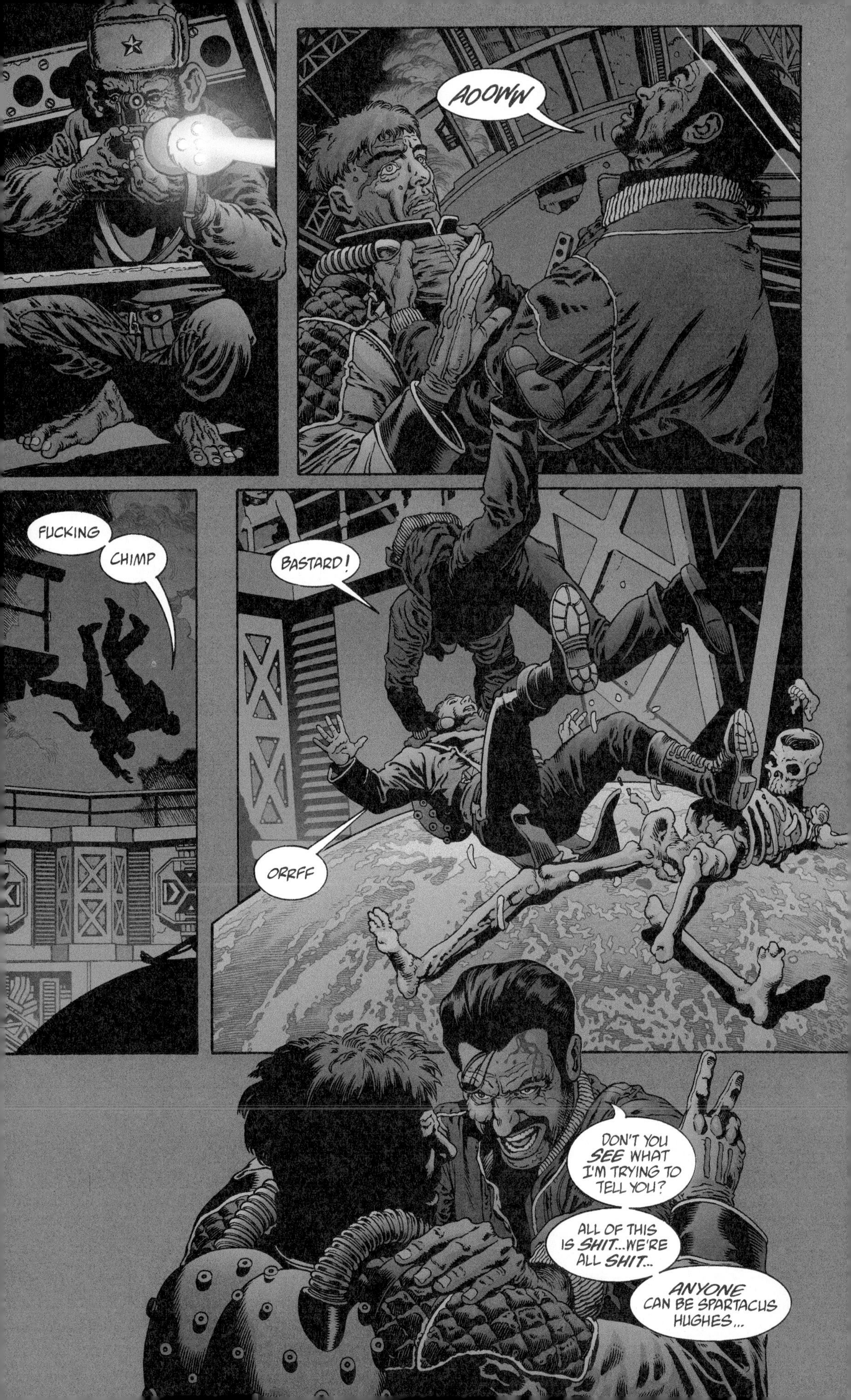
AOOWW
FUCKING
CHIMP
BASTARD!
ORRFF
DON'T YOU SEE WHAT I'M TRYING TO TELL YOU?
ALL OF THIS IS SHIT...WE'RE ALL SHIT...
ANYONE CAN BE SPARTACUS HUGHES...

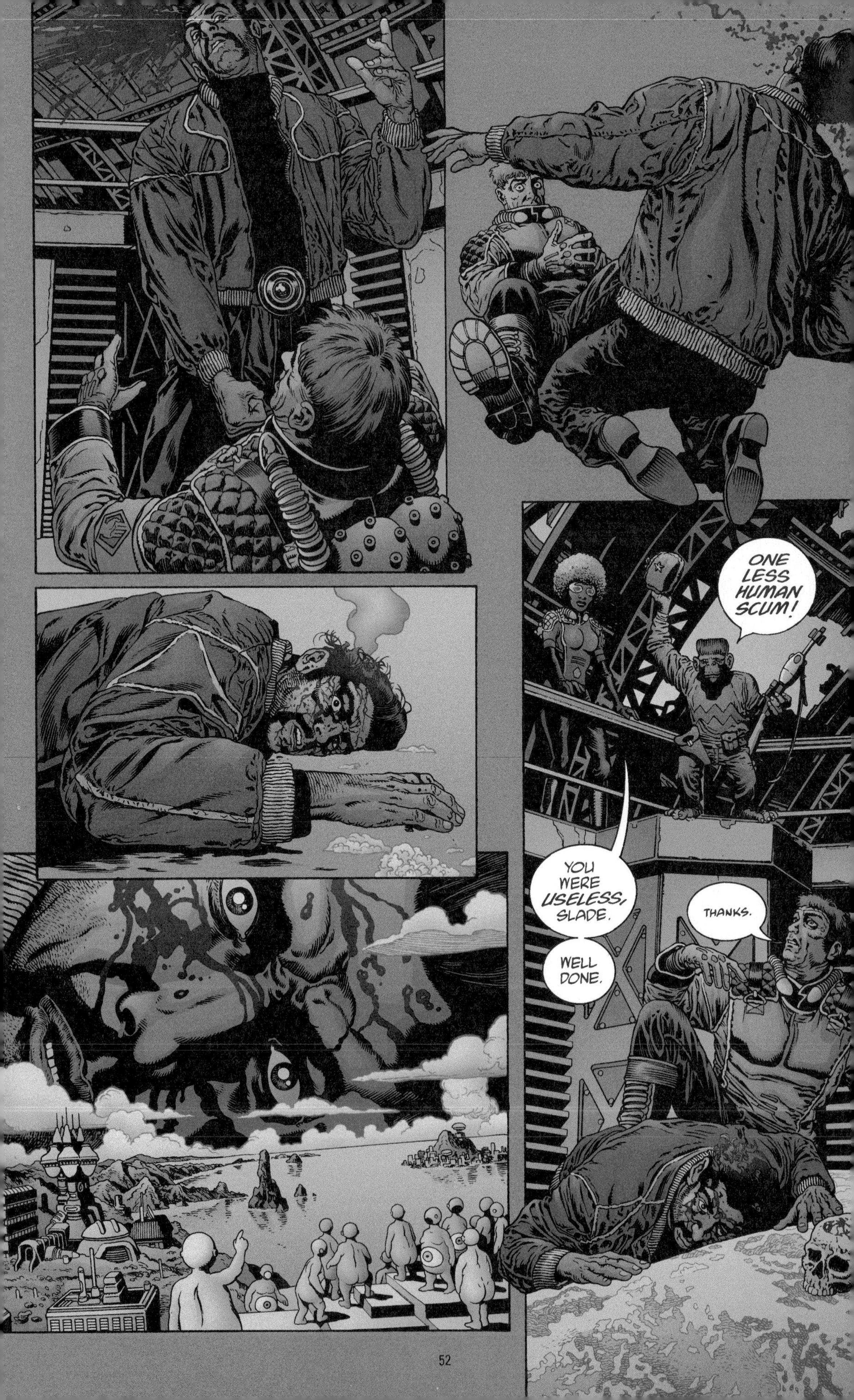
ONE LESS HUMAN SCUM!
YOU WERE USELESS, SLADE.
WELL DONE.
THANKS.

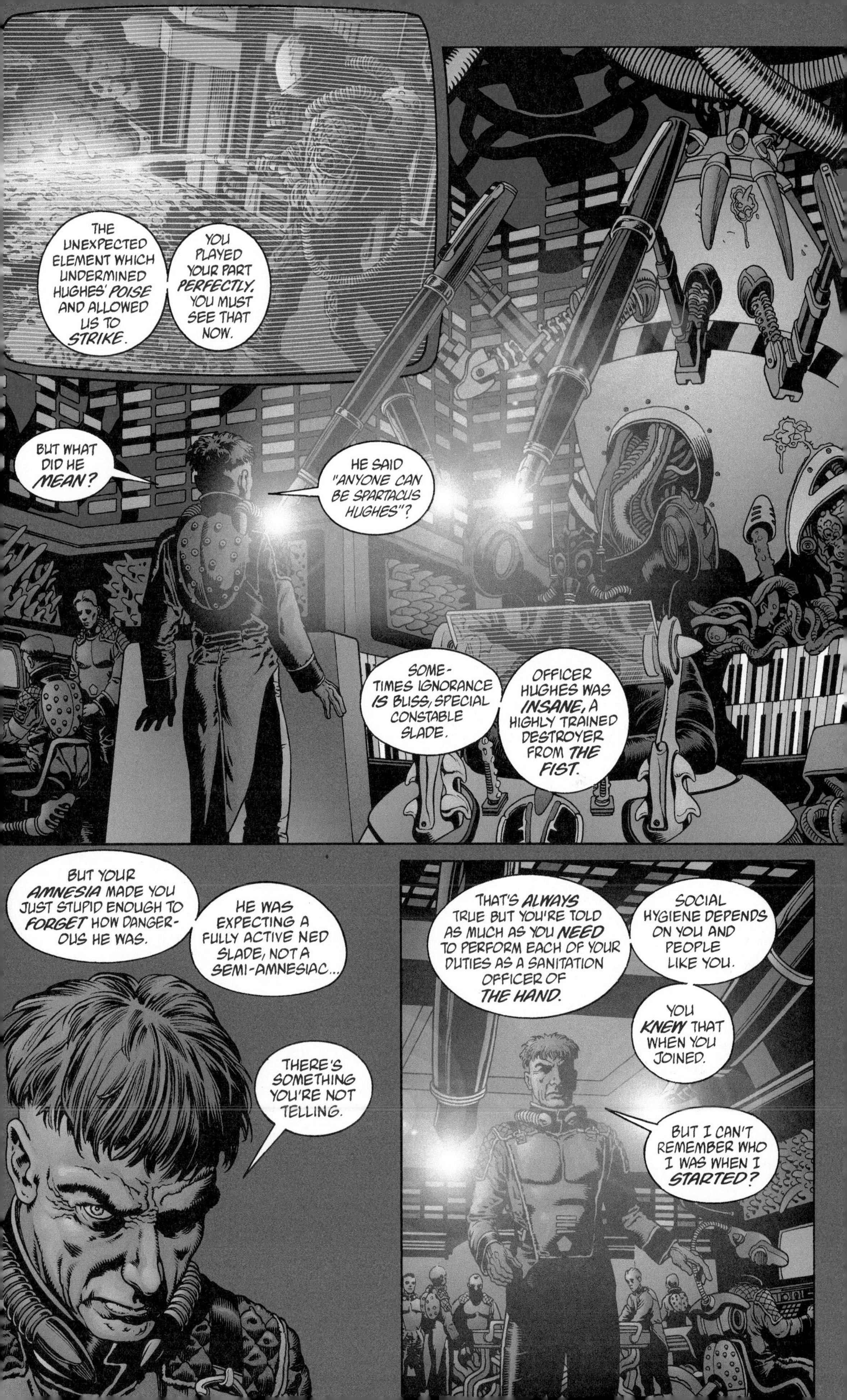
THE UNEXPECTED ELEMENT WHICH UNDERMINED HUGHES' POISE AND ALLOWED US TO STRIKE.
YOU PLAYED YOUR PART PERFECTLY. YOU MUST SEE THAT NOW.
BUT WHAT DID HE MEAN?
HE SAID "ANYONE CAN BE SPARTACUS HUGHES"?
SOME-TIMES IGNORANCE IS BLISS, SPECIAL CONSTABLE SLADE.
OFFICER HUGHES WAS INSANE, A HIGHLY TRAINED DESTROYER FROM THE FIST.
BUT YOUR AMNESIA MADE YOU JUST STUPID ENOUGH TO FORGET HOW DANGER-OUS HE WAS.
HE WAS EXPECTING A FULLY ACTIVE NED SLADE, NOT A SEMI-AMNESIAC...
THERE'S SOMETHING YOU'RE NOT TELLING.
THAT'S ALWAYS TRUE BUT YOU'RE TOLD AS MUCH AS YOU NEED TO PERFORM EACH OF YOUR DUTIES AS A SANITATION OFFICER OF THE HAND.
SOCIAL HYGIENE DEPENDS ON YOU AND PEOPLE LIKE YOU.
YOU KNEW THAT WHEN YOU JOINED.
BUT I CAN'T REMEMBER WHO I WAS WHEN I STARTED?

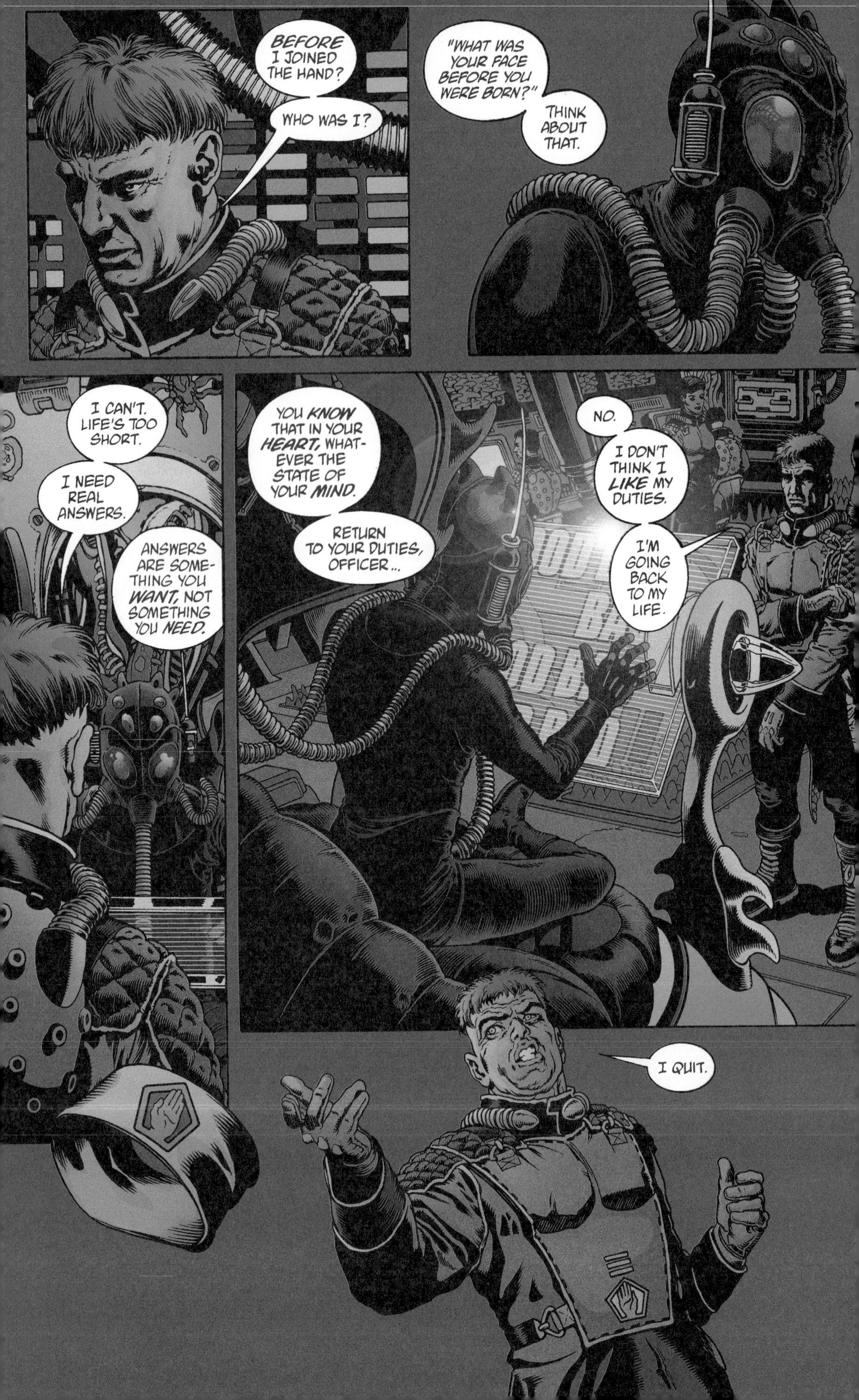

BEFORE I JOINED THE HAND?
WHO WAS I?
"WHAT WAS YOUR FACE BEFORE YOU WERE BORN?"
THINK ABOUT THAT.
I CAN'T. LIFE'S TOO SHORT.
I NEED REAL ANSWERS.
ANSWERS ARE SOMETHING YOU WANT, NOT SOMETHING YOU NEED.
YOU KNOW THAT IN YOUR HEART, WHATEVER THE STATE OF YOUR MIND.
RETURN TO YOUR DUTIES, OFFICER...
NO.
I DON'T THINK I LIKE MY DUTIES.
I'M GOING BACK TO MY LIFE.
I QUIT.

The Filth

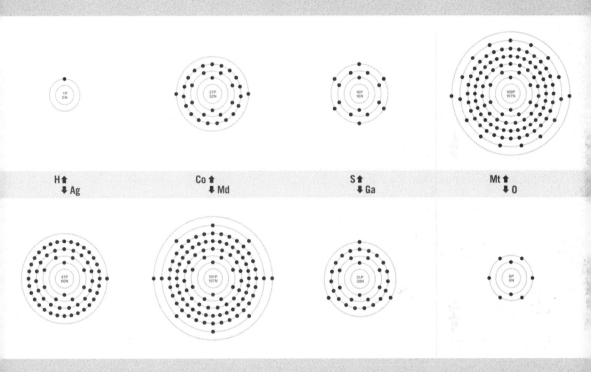

H ↑ ↓ Ag
Co ↑ ↓ Md
S ↑ ↓ Ga
Mt ↑ ↓ O

03.STRUCTURES AND ULTRASTRUCTURES

22 PAGES

Nd Fq Cy Fi St Fn Gr Hr Ns Pa Lm Ha Nd Fq Cy Fi St Fn Gr Hr Ns Pa Lm Ha Nd

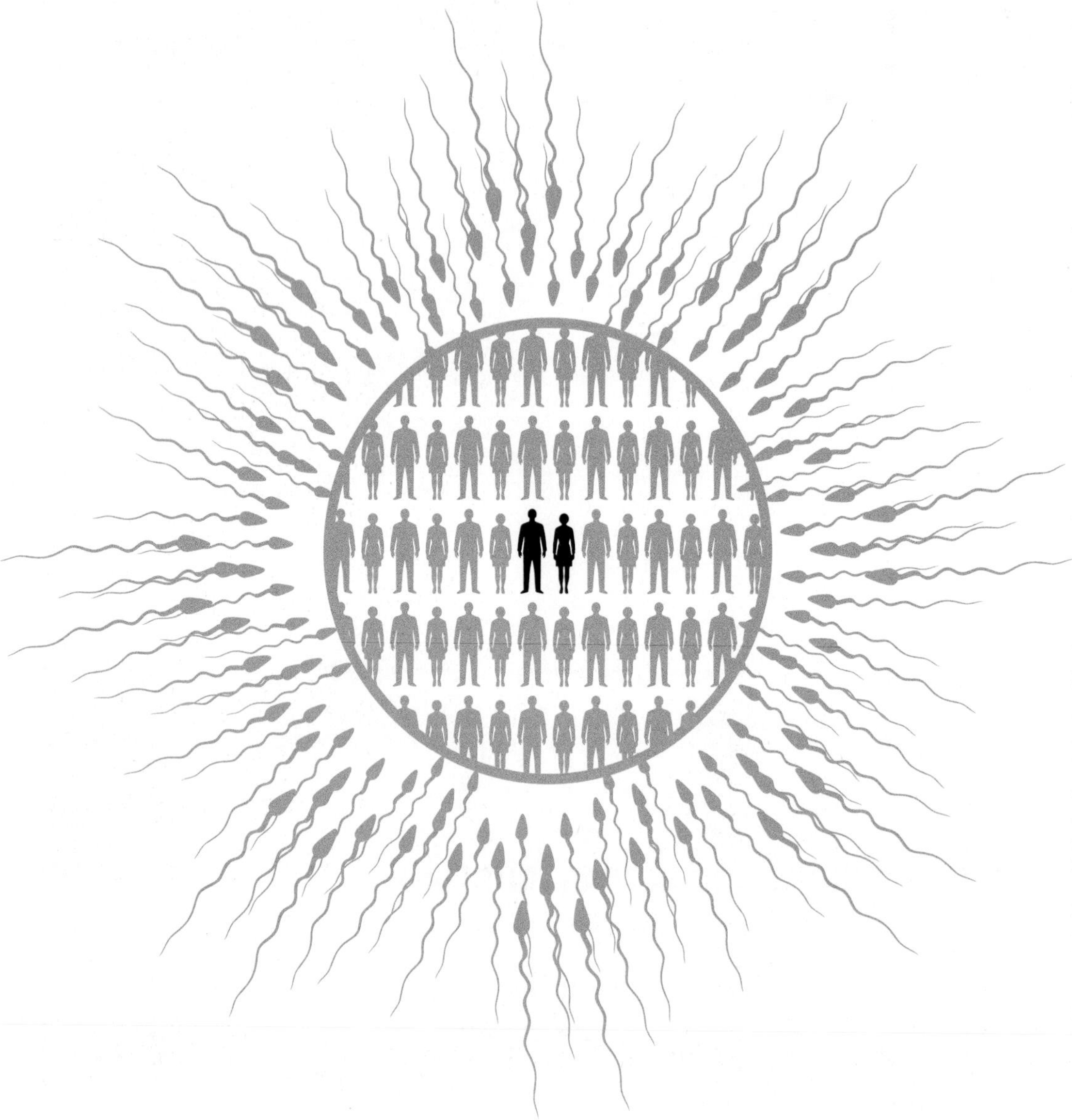

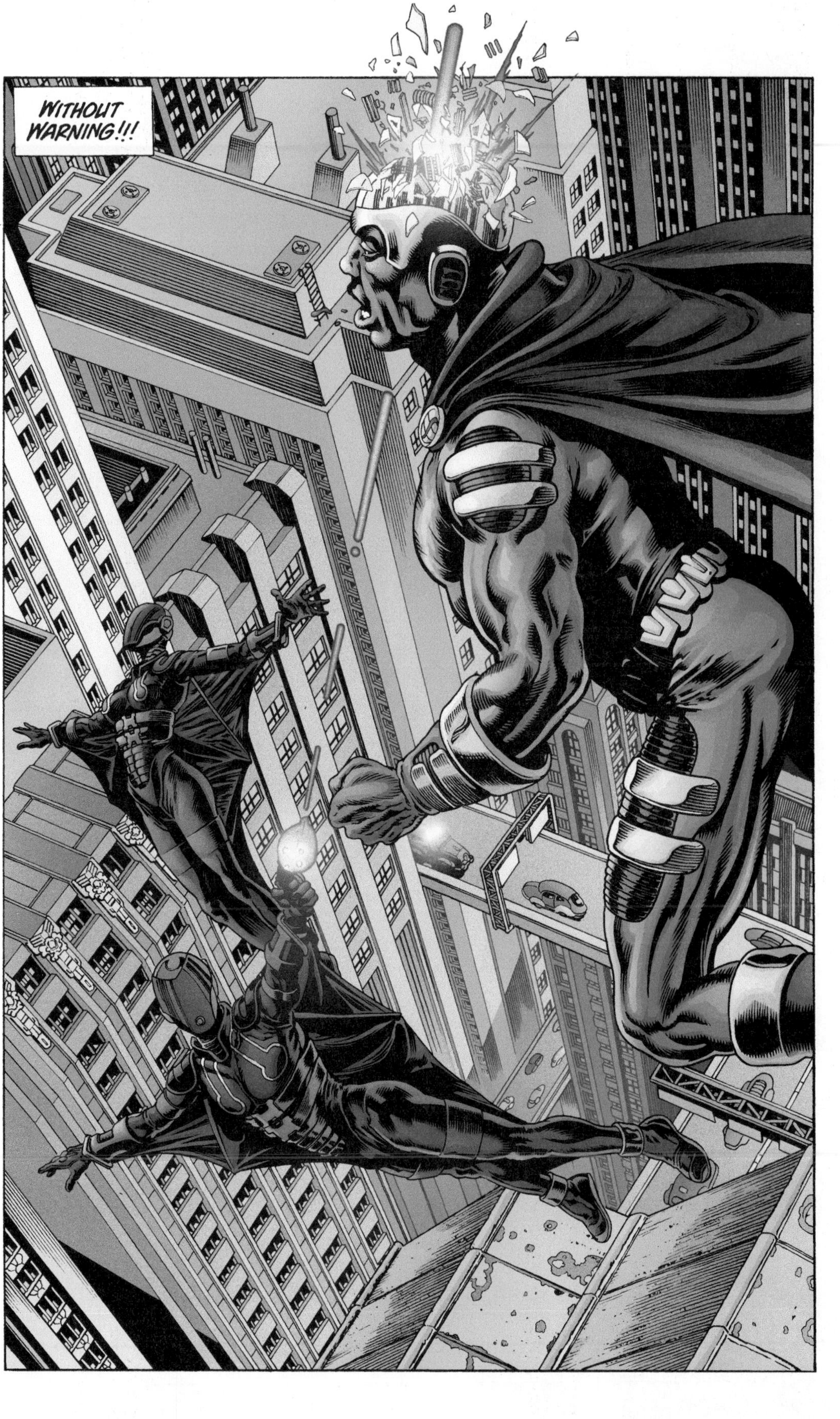
WITHOUT WARNING!!!

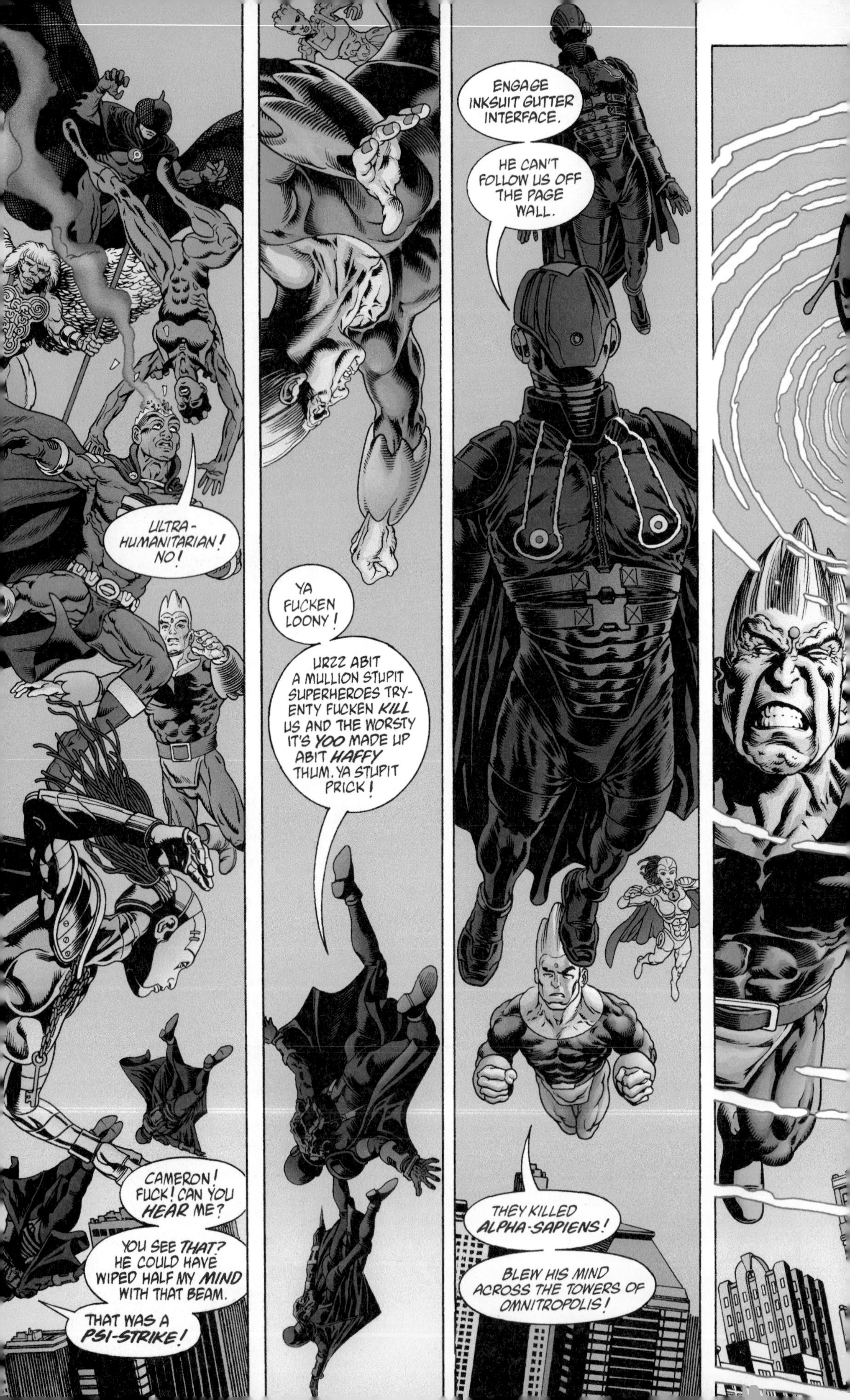
ULTRA-HUMANITARIAN! NO!
CAMERON! FUCK! CAN YOU HEAR ME?
YOU SEE THAT? HE COULD HAVE WIPED HALF MY MIND WITH THAT BEAM.
THAT WAS A PSI-STRIKE!
YA FUCKEN LOONY!
URZZ ABIT A MULLION STUPIT SUPERHEROES TRY-ENTY FUCKEN KILL US AND THE WORSTY IT'S YOO MADE UP ABIT HAFFY THUM. YA STUPIT PRICK!
ENGAGE INKSUIT GUTTER INTERFACE.
HE CAN'T FOLLOW US OFF THE PAGE WALL.
THEY KILLED ALPHA-SAPIENS!
BLEW HIS MIND ACROSS THE TOWERS OF OMNITROPOLIS!

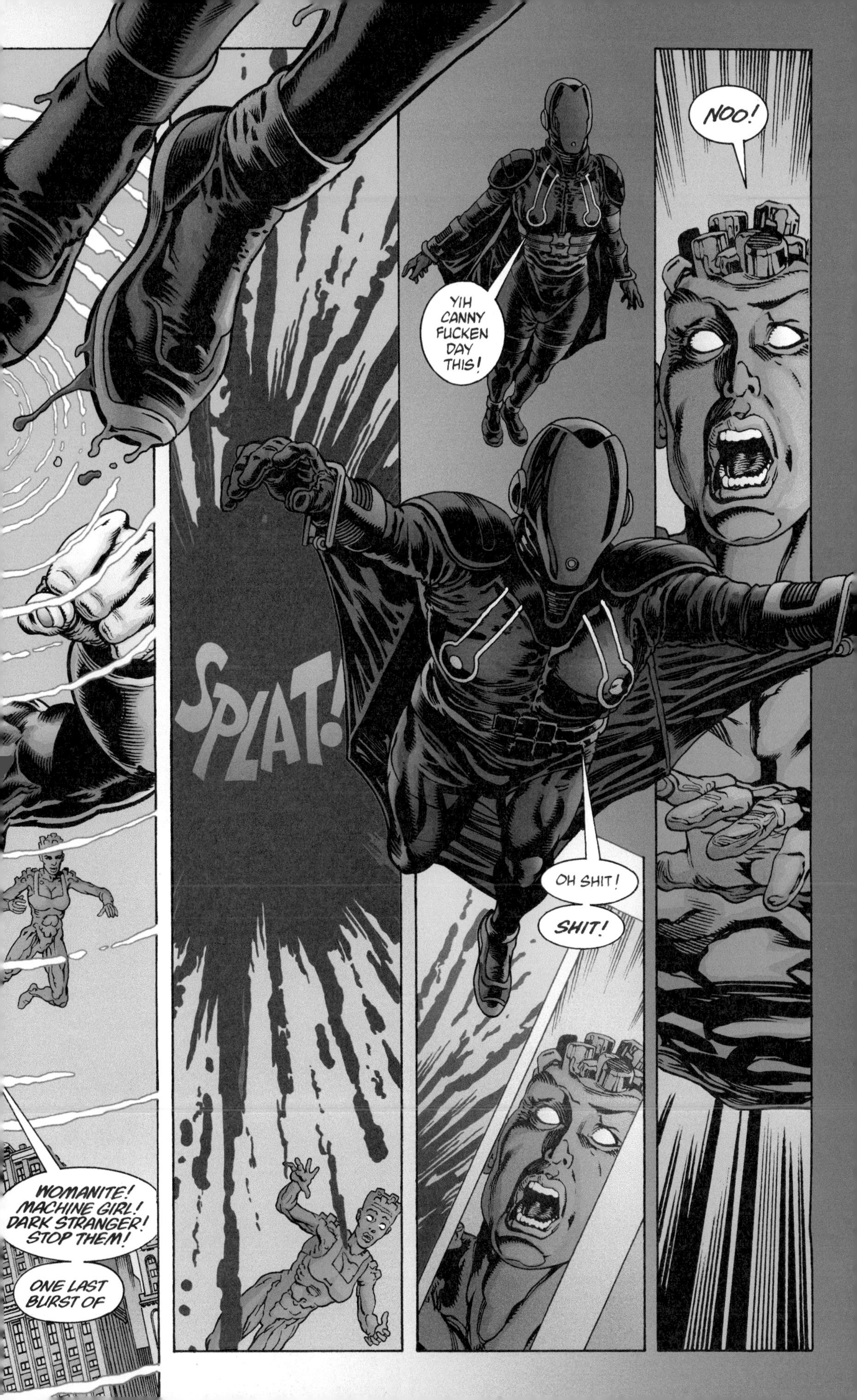
SPLAT!
YIH CANNY FUCKEN DAY THIS!
OH SHIT!
SHIT!
NOO!
WOMANITE! MACHINE GIRL! DARK STRANGER! STOP THEM!
ONE LAST BURST OF

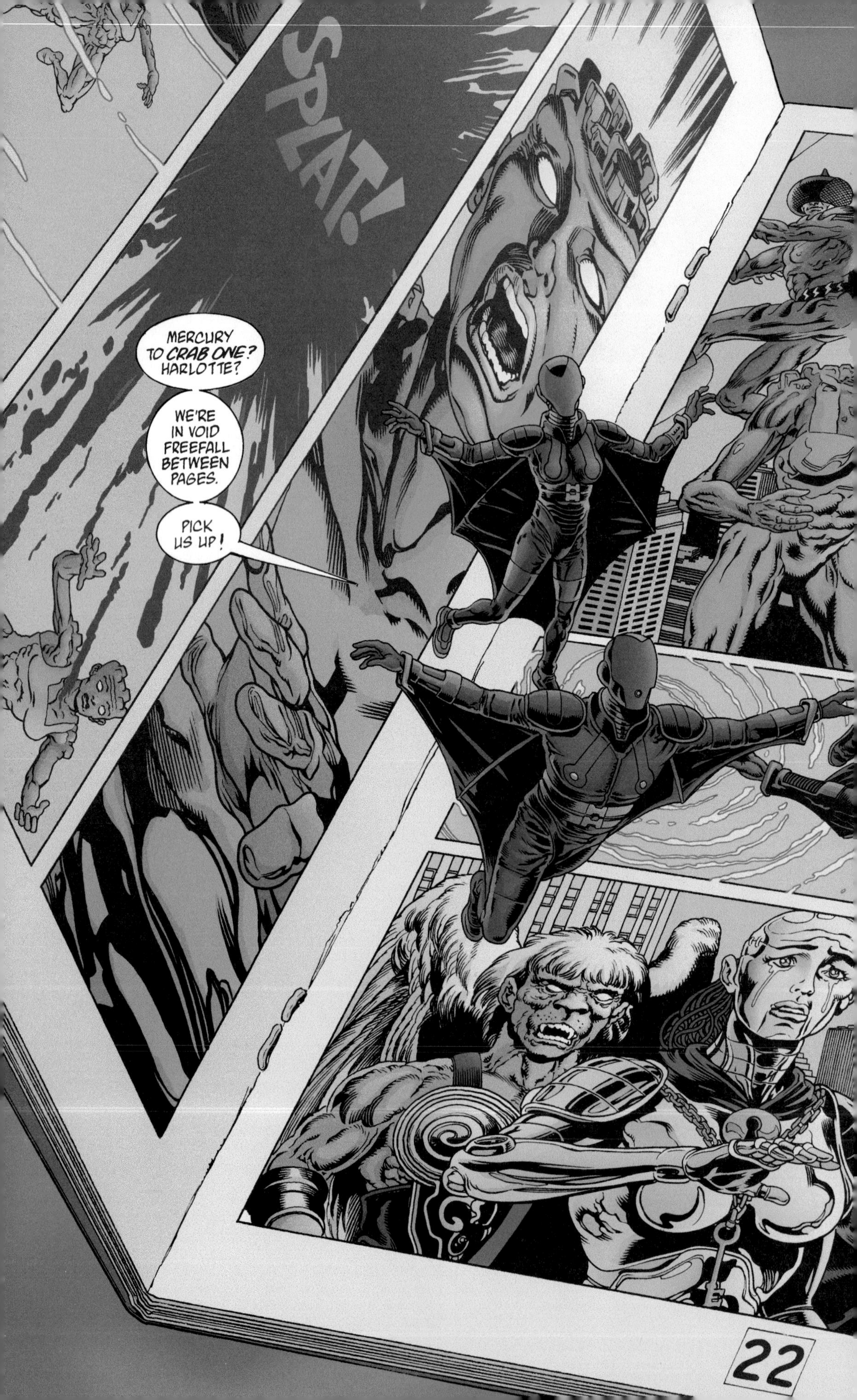
SPLAT!
MERCURY TO CRAB ONE? HARLOTTE?
WE'RE IN VOID FREEFALL BETWEEN PAGES.
PICK US UP!

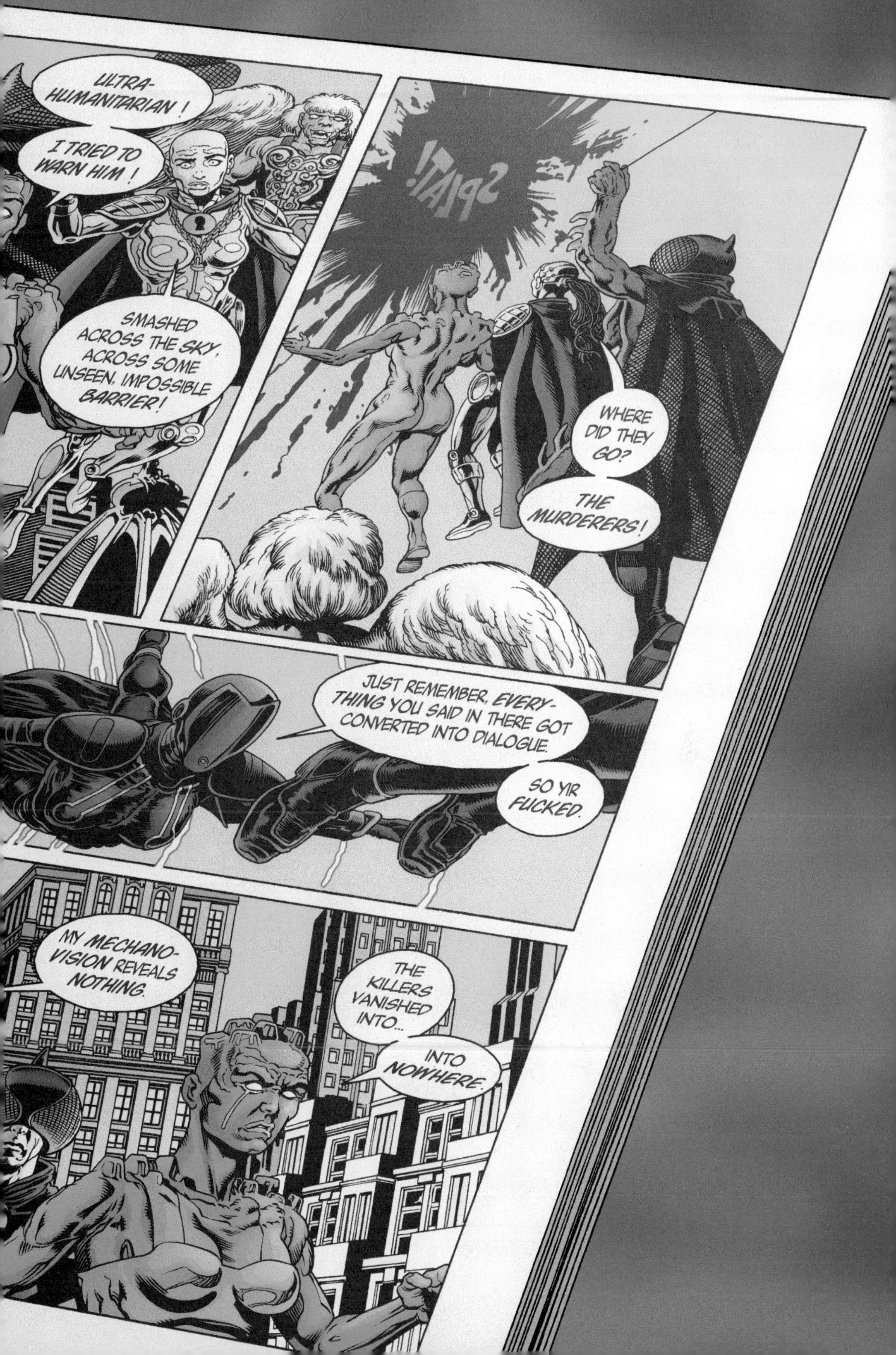
ULTRA-HUMANITARIAN!
I TRIED TO WARN HIM!
SMASHED ACROSS THE SKY, ACROSS SOME UNSEEN, IMPOSSIBLE BARRIER!
SPLAT!
WHERE DID THEY GO?
THE MURDERERS!
JUST REMEMBER, EVERYTHING YOU SAID IN THERE GOT CONVERTED INTO DIALOGUE.
SO YIR FUCKED.
MY MECHANO-VISION REVEALS NOTHING.
THE KILLERS VANISHED INTO...
INTO NOWHERE.

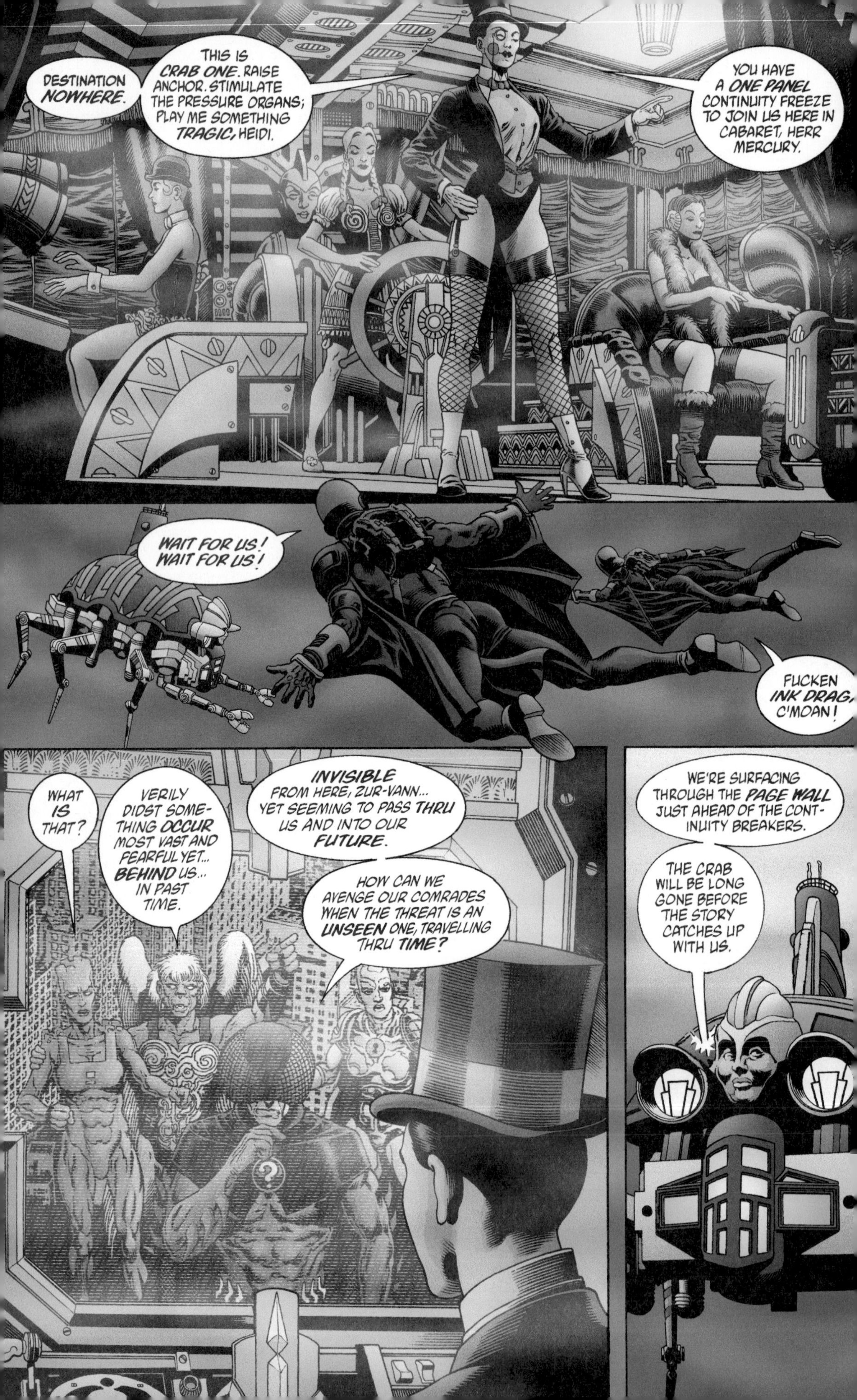
DESTINATION NOWHERE.
THIS IS CRAB ONE. RAISE ANCHOR. STIMULATE THE PRESSURE ORGANS; PLAY ME SOMETHING TRAGIC, HEIDI.
YOU HAVE A ONE PANEL CONTINUITY FREEZE TO JOIN US HERE IN CABARET, HERR MERCURY.
WAIT FOR US! WAIT FOR US!
FUCKEN INK DRAG, C'MOAN!
WHAT IS THAT?
VERILY DIDST SOMETHING OCCUR MOST VAST AND FEARFUL YET... BEHIND US... IN PAST TIME.
INVISIBLE FROM HERE, ZUR-VANN... YET SEEMING TO PASS THRU US AND INTO OUR FUTURE.
HOW CAN WE AVENGE OUR COMRADES WHEN THE THREAT IS AN UNSEEN ONE, TRAVELLING THRU TIME?
WE'RE SURFACING THROUGH THE PAGE WALL JUST AHEAD OF THE CONTINUITY BREAKERS.
THE CRAB WILL BE LONG GONE BEFORE THE STORY CATCHES UP WITH US.

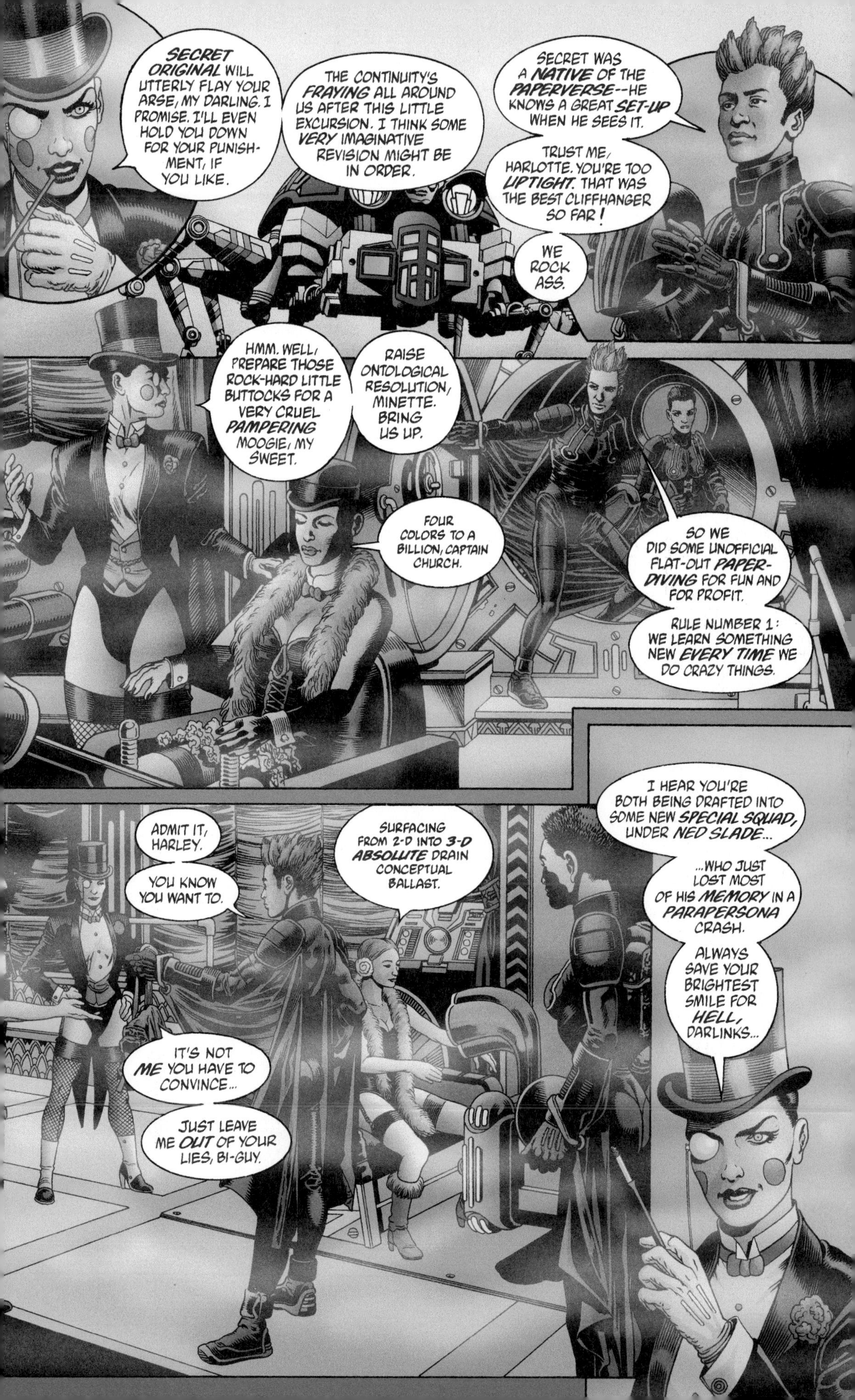
SECRET ORIGINAL WILL UTTERLY FLAY YOUR ARSE, MY DARLING. I PROMISE. I'LL EVEN HOLD YOU DOWN FOR YOUR PUNISH-MENT, IF YOU LIKE.
THE CONTINUITY'S FRAYING ALL AROUND US AFTER THIS LITTLE EXCURSION. I THINK SOME VERY IMAGINATIVE REVISION MIGHT BE IN ORDER.
SECRET WAS A NATIVE OF THE PAPERVERSE--HE KNOWS A GREAT SET-UP WHEN HE SEES IT.
TRUST ME, HARLOTTE. YOU'RE TOO UPTIGHT. THAT WAS THE BEST CLIFFHANGER SO FAR!
WE ROCK ASS.
HMM. WELL, PREPARE THOSE ROCK-HARD LITTLE BUTTOCKS FOR A VERY CRUEL PAMPERING MOOGIE, MY SWEET.
RAISE ONTOLOGICAL RESOLUTION, MINETTE. BRING US UP.
FOUR COLORS TO A BILLION, CAPTAIN CHURCH.
SO WE DID SOME UNOFFICIAL FLAT-OUT PAPER-DIVING FOR FUN AND FOR PROFIT.
RULE NUMBER 1: WE LEARN SOMETHING NEW EVERY TIME WE DO CRAZY THINGS.
ADMIT IT, HARLEY.
YOU KNOW YOU WANT TO.
SURFACING FROM 2-D INTO 3-D ABSOLUTE DRAIN CONCEPTUAL BALLAST.
I HEAR YOU'RE BOTH BEING DRAFTED INTO SOME NEW SPECIAL SQUAD, UNDER NED SLADE...
...WHO JUST LOST MOST OF HIS MEMORY IN A PARAPERSONA CRASH.
ALWAYS SAVE YOUR BRIGHTEST SMILE FOR HELL, DARLINKS...
IT'S NOT ME YOU HAVE TO CONVINCE...
JUST LEAVE ME OUT OF YOUR LIES, BI-GUY.

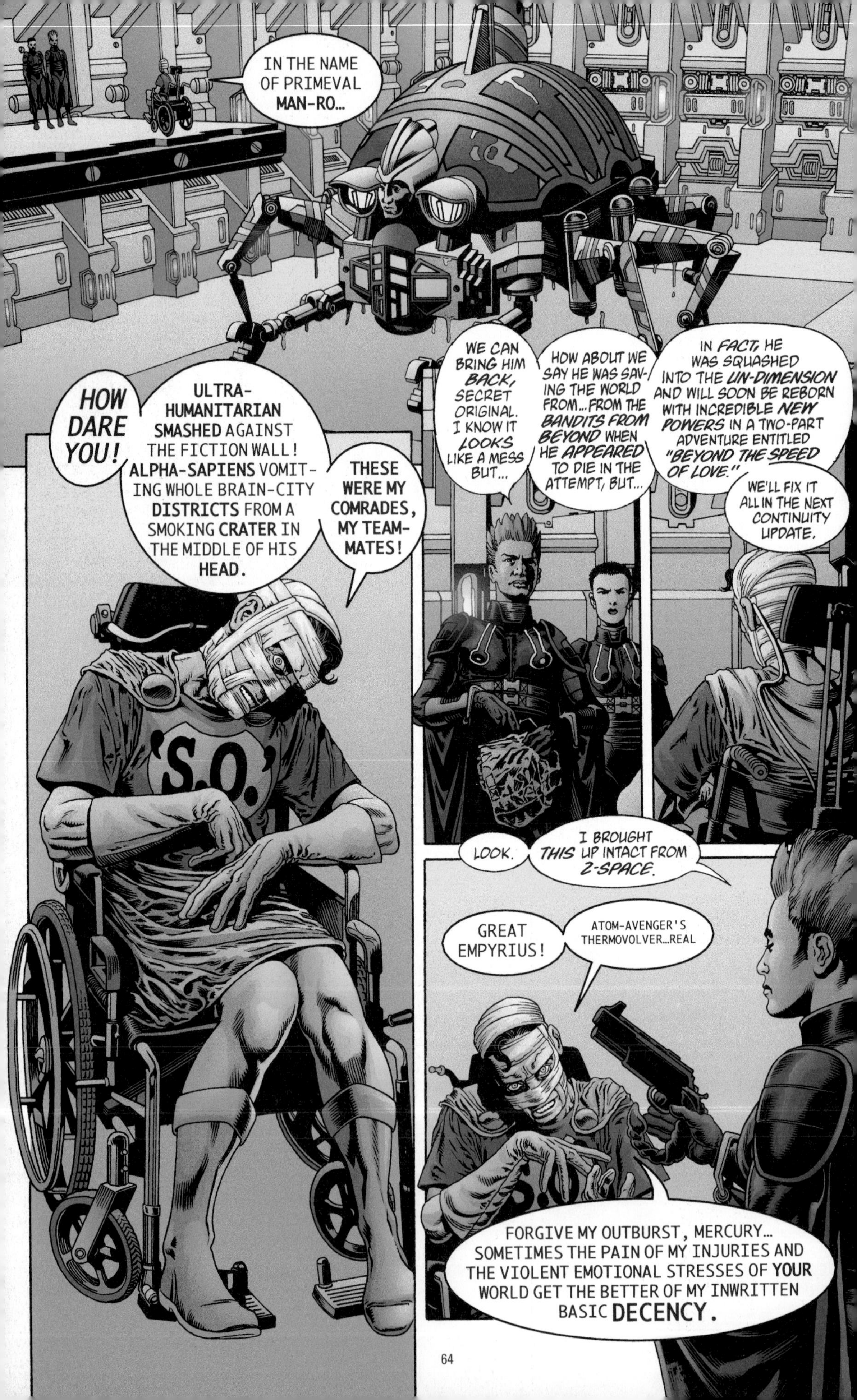

IN THE NAME OF PRIMEVAL MAN-RO...
HOW DARE YOU!
ULTRA-HUMANITARIAN SMASHED AGAINST THE FICTION WALL! ALPHA-SAPIENS VOMITING WHOLE BRAIN-CITY DISTRICTS FROM A SMOKING CRATER IN THE MIDDLE OF HIS HEAD.
THESE WERE MY COMRADES, MY TEAMMATES!
WE CAN BRING HIM BACK, SECRET ORIGINAL. I KNOW IT LOOKS LIKE A MESS BUT...
HOW ABOUT WE SAY HE WAS SAVING THE WORLD FROM...FROM THE BANDITS FROM BEYOND WHEN HE APPEARED TO DIE IN THE ATTEMPT, BUT...
IN FACT, HE WAS SQUASHED INTO THE UN-DIMENSION AND WILL SOON BE REBORN WITH INCREDIBLE NEW POWERS IN A TWO-PART ADVENTURE ENTITLED "BEYOND THE SPEED OF LOVE."
WE'LL FIX IT ALL IN THE NEXT CONTINUITY UPDATE.
LOOK.
I BROUGHT THIS UP INTACT FROM 2-SPACE.
GREAT EMPYRIUS!
ATOM-AVENGER'S THERMOVOLVER...REAL
FORGIVE MY OUTBURST, MERCURY... SOMETIMES THE PAIN OF MY INJURIES AND THE VIOLENT EMOTIONAL STRESSES OF YOUR WORLD GET THE BETTER OF MY INWRITTEN BASIC DECENCY.

MY AUNT RUNS THE FLOWER SHOP. *THAT'S* SORT OF PSYCHEDELIC, ISN'T IT?

FLOWERS AND SHIT.

AH, I WISH SOMETHING GREAT WOULD HAPPEN.

STONER CUNTS!

BUT NOT AS PSYCHEDELIC AS THE FACT THAT THE PLANET EARTH HAS ITS OWN *RING.*

WHAT? LIKE A TELEPHONE?

NO, LIKE *SATURN.*

A RING OF ORBITING, ANIMAL ASTRONAUTS, ALL DEAD.

WANKERS!

HEY, THAT'S ENOUGH!

DON'T LOOK AT THAT MAN, LAURIE, LOVE. HE'S NOT NICE.

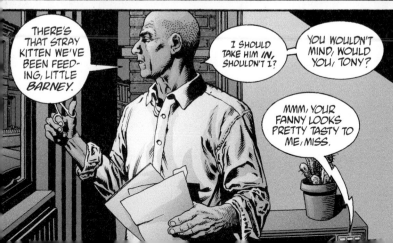

THERE'S THAT STRAY KITTEN WE'VE BEEN FEED-ING, LITTLE *BARNEY.*

I SHOULD TAKE HIM *IN,* SHOULDN'T I?

YOU WOULDN'T MIND, WOULD YOU, TONY?

MMM, YOUR FANNY LOOKS PRETTY TASTY TO ME, MISS.

BRRRT BRRRT

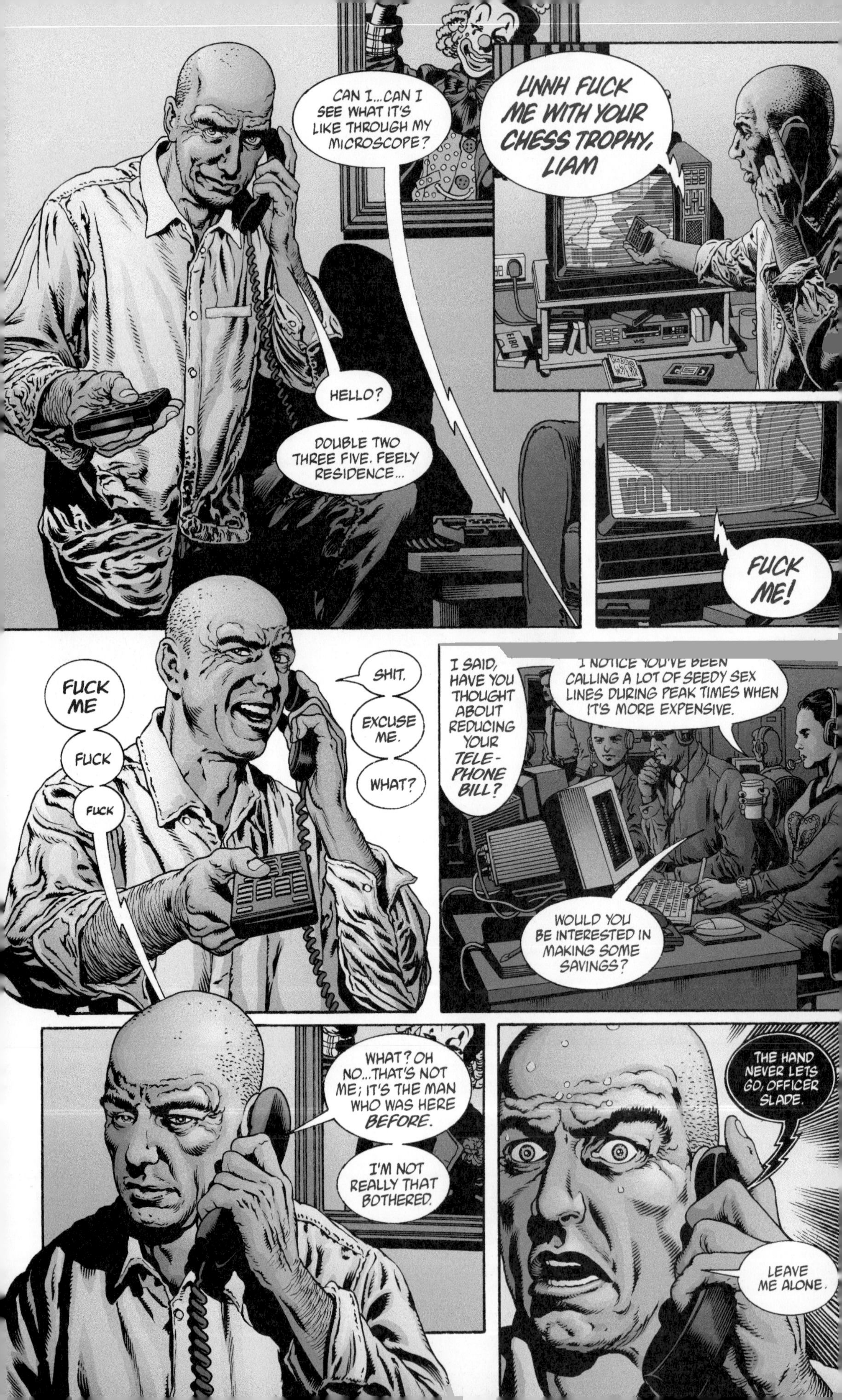
CAN I...CAN I SEE WHAT IT'S LIKE THROUGH MY MICROSCOPE?
UNNH FUCK ME WITH YOUR CHESS TROPHY, LIAM
HELLO?
DOUBLE TWO THREE FIVE. FEELY RESIDENCE...
FUCK ME!
FUCK ME
FUCK
FUCK
SHIT.
EXCUSE ME.
WHAT?
I SAID, HAVE YOU THOUGHT ABOUT REDUCING YOUR TELE-PHONE BILL?
I NOTICE YOU'VE BEEN CALLING A LOT OF SEEDY SEX LINES DURING PEAK TIMES WHEN IT'S MORE EXPENSIVE.
WOULD YOU BE INTERESTED IN MAKING SOME SAVINGS?
WHAT? OH NO...THAT'S NOT ME; IT'S THE MAN WHO WAS HERE BEFORE.
I'M NOT REALLY THAT BOTHERED.
THE HAND NEVER LETS GO, OFFICER SLADE.
LEAVE ME ALONE.

GOOD BOY. YOU'RE A GOOD BOY, TONY.

SHH.

DON'T WORRY.

HE'S VERY PATIENT WITH THESE BLOOD TESTS.

I WISH THEY WERE ALL LIKE HIM, MR. FEELY.

I KNOW.

I'VE ALWAYS SAID HE EXPECTED TO GROW UP INTO A HUMAN BEING.

I THINK HE WAS ALWAYS QUITE SURPRISED HE STAYED A CAT.

THEY BECOME LIKE FAMILY, DON'T THEY?

BREAKS YOUR HEART.

AH NO.

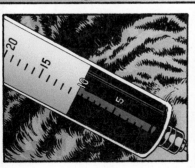

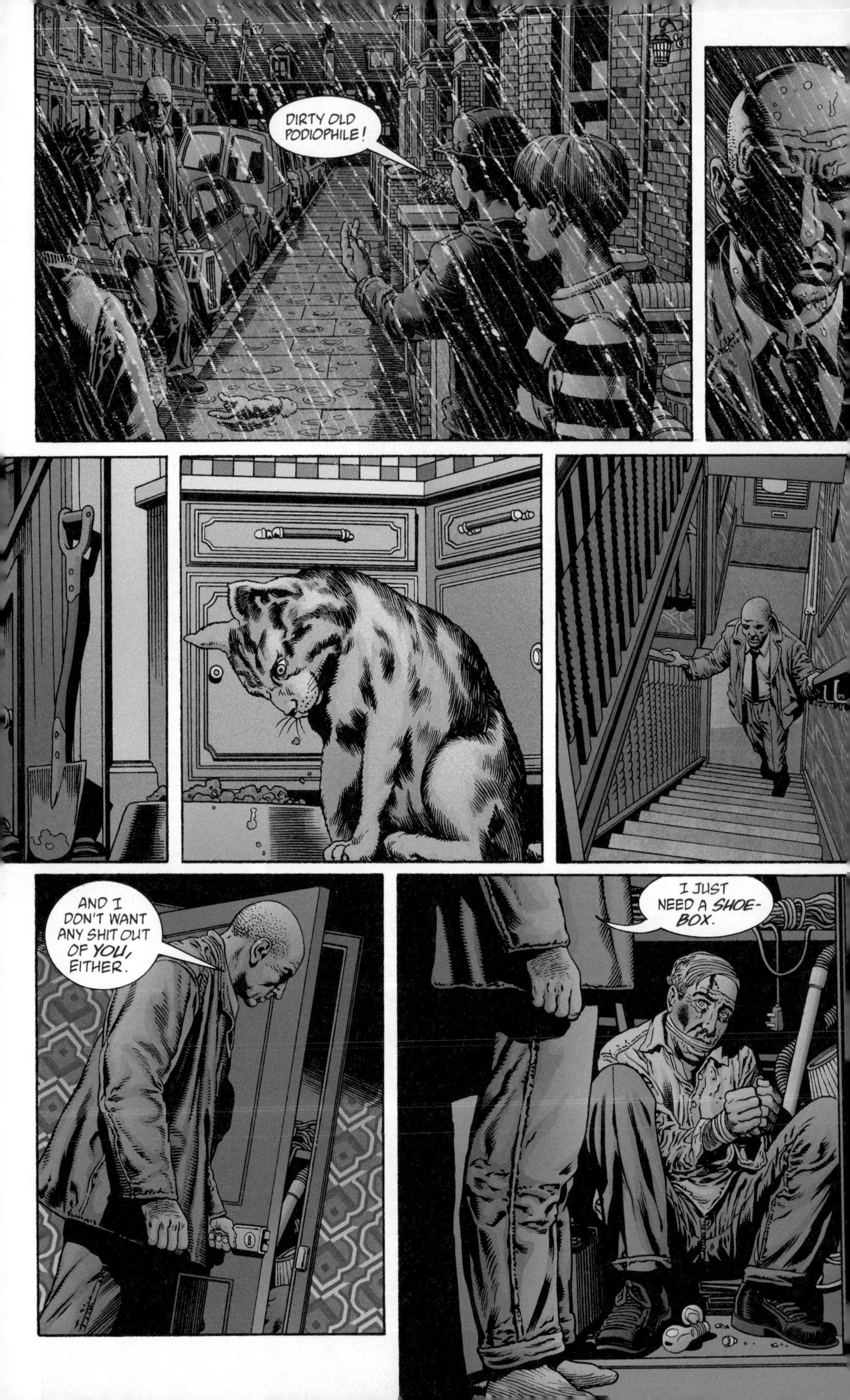
DIRTY OLD PODIOPHILE!
AND I DON'T WANT ANY SHIT OUT OF YOU, EITHER.
I JUST NEED A SHOE-BOX.

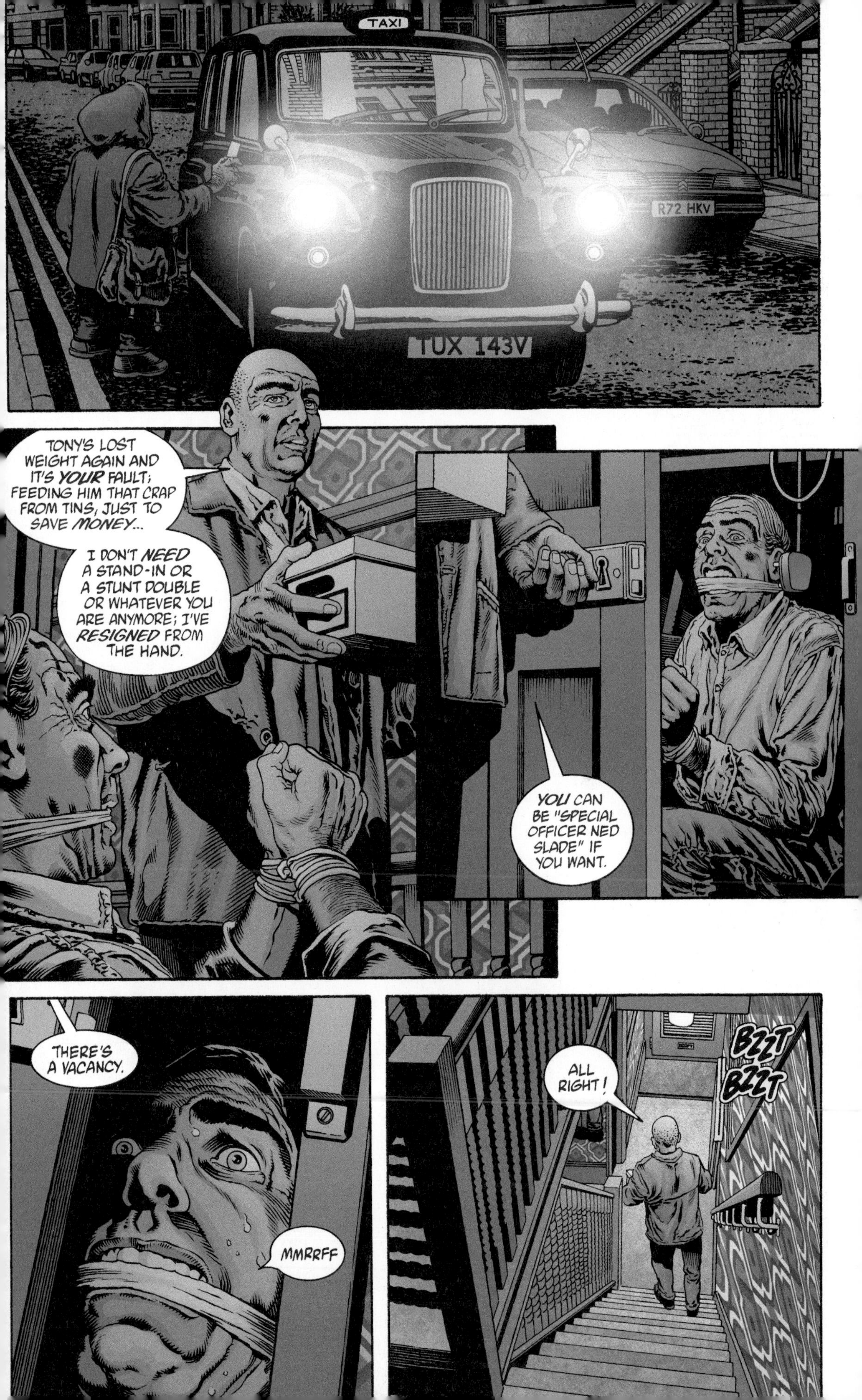
TAXI
R72 HKV
TUX 143V
TONY'S LOST WEIGHT AGAIN AND IT'S *YOUR* FAULT; FEEDING HIM THAT CRAP FROM TINS, JUST TO SAVE *MONEY*...
I DON'T *NEED* A STAND-IN OR A STUNT DOUBLE OR WHATEVER YOU ARE ANYMORE; I'VE *RESIGNED* FROM THE HAND.
YOU CAN BE "SPECIAL OFFICER NED SLADE" IF YOU WANT.
THERE'S A VACANCY.
MMRRFF
ALL RIGHT!
BZZT
BZZT

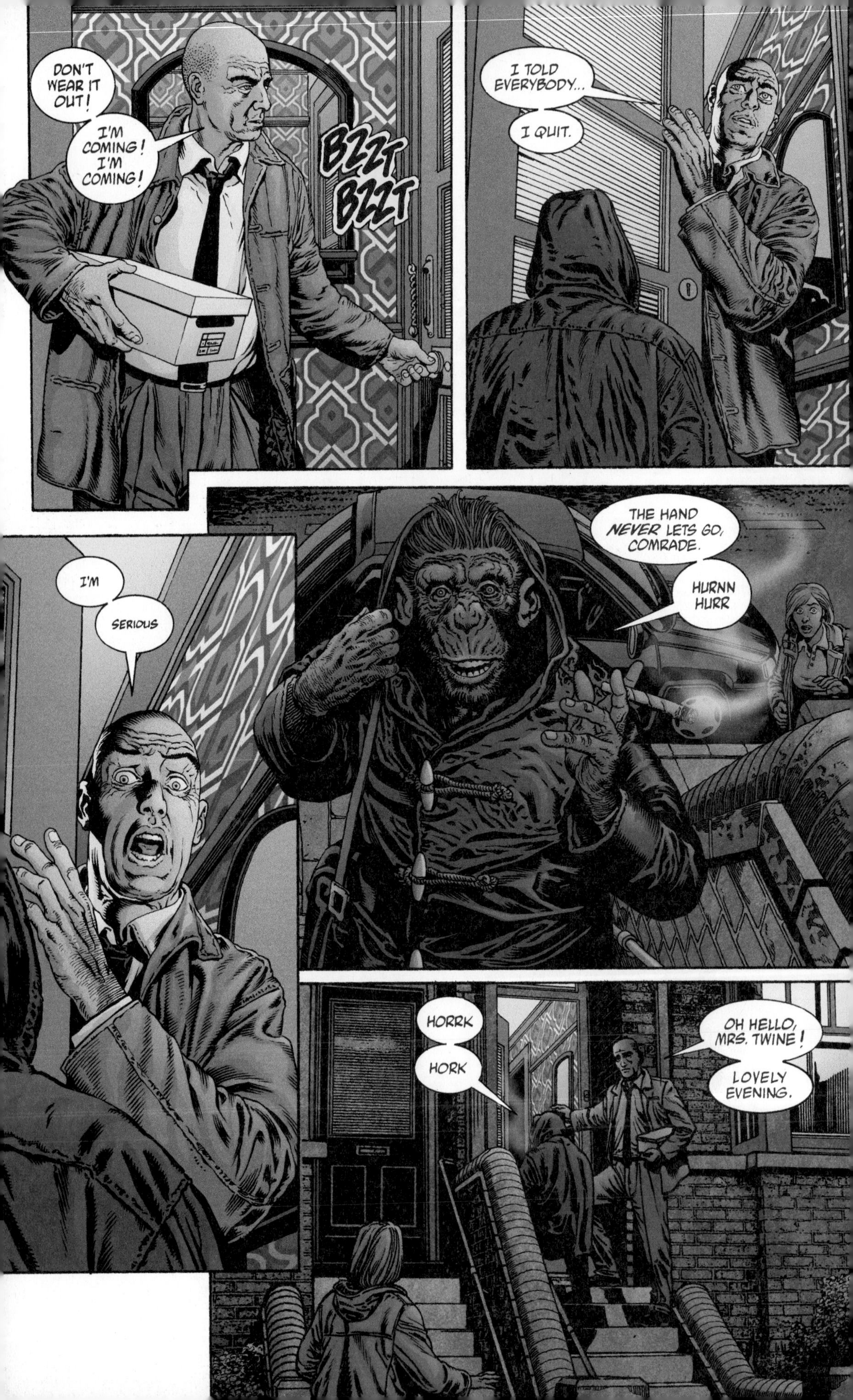
DON'T WEAR IT OUT!
I'M COMING! I'M COMING!
BZZT BZZT
I TOLD EVERYBODY...
I QUIT.
I'M
SERIOUS
THE HAND NEVER LETS GO, COMRADE.
HURNN HURR
HORRK
HORK
OH HELLO, MRS. TWINE!
LOVELY EVENING.

THIS ONE COULDN'T BE MORE THAN TEN YEARS OLD.

THEY TRAP THEM IN INTERNET ROOMS WITH PROMISES OF CHEATS FROM VIDEO GAMES. THERE WAS A CRIMEWATCH ALL ABOUT IT.

SOMEBODY SHOULD BE PHONING THE POLICE.

PHWEEZE

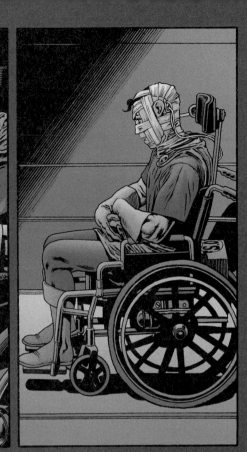

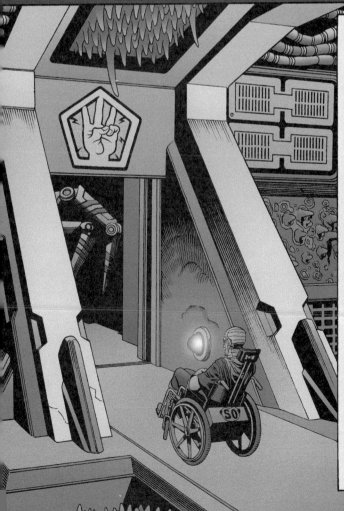

FLOOD INK CHAMBER.

CONTINUITY ONLINE.

RUN.

INVISIBLE FROM HERE...YET SEEMING TO PASS THRU US AND INTO OUR FUTURE.

HOW CAN WE AVENGE OUR COMRADES WHEN THE THREAT IS AN UNSEEN ONE, TRAVELLING THRU TIME?

REWIND.

...YET TO PASS AND INTO FUTURE.

HOW CAN WE AVENGE OUR COMRADES WHEN THE THREAT IS UNSEEN TRAVELLING TI...

STOP.

RUN CONTINUITY.

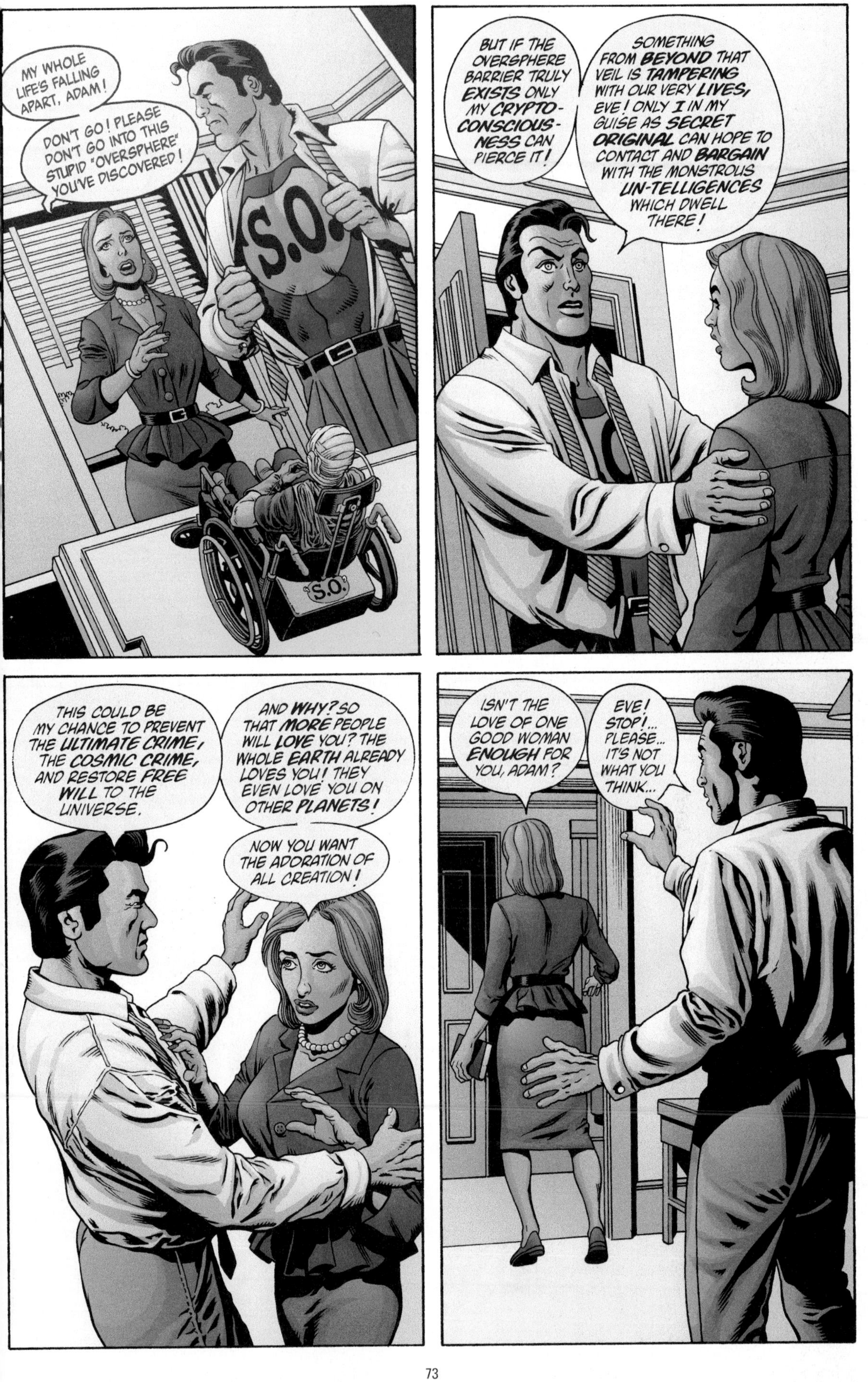
MY WHOLE LIFE'S FALLING APART, ADAM!
DON'T GO! PLEASE DON'T GO INTO THIS STUPID "OVERSPHERE" YOU'VE DISCOVERED!
S.O.
S.O.
BUT IF THE OVERSPHERE BARRIER TRULY EXISTS ONLY MY CRYPTO-CONSCIOUS-NESS CAN PIERCE IT!
SOMETHING FROM BEYOND THAT VEIL IS TAMPERING WITH OUR VERY LIVES, EVE! ONLY I IN MY GUISE AS SECRET ORIGINAL CAN HOPE TO CONTACT AND BARGAIN WITH THE MONSTROUS UN-TELLIGENCES WHICH DWELL THERE!
THIS COULD BE MY CHANCE TO PREVENT THE ULTIMATE CRIME, THE COSMIC CRIME, AND RESTORE FREE WILL TO THE UNIVERSE.
AND WHY? SO THAT MORE PEOPLE WILL LOVE YOU? THE WHOLE EARTH ALREADY LOVES YOU! THEY EVEN LOVE YOU ON OTHER PLANETS!
NOW YOU WANT THE ADORATION OF ALL CREATION!
ISN'T THE LOVE OF ONE GOOD WOMAN ENOUGH FOR YOU, ADAM?
EVE! STOP!... PLEASE... IT'S NOT WHAT YOU THINK...

NE
MAN
FOR
DAM?

EVE!
STOP!...
PLEASE...
IT'S NOT
WHAT YOU
THINK...

STOP.

OH, EVE. IF ONLY I COULD SEE YOU. IF ONLY I COULD TALK TO YOU AGAIN BUT I FLEW TOO HIGH AND BROKE AGAINST THE WALLS OF HEAVEN, EVE. YOU WERE RIGHT.

I SEE THE CRUEL REALITY BEHIND ALL OUR HOPES AND DREAMS NOW. I KNOW US FOR WHAT WE TRULY ARE.

NOT SUPERMEN BUT SUPER-SLAVES IN A SYNTHETIC PRISON.

PLAYING OUT CRUMMY MEANINGLESS ADVENTURES WRITTEN BY AMORAL MONSTERS.

THEY FARM US, EVE; THEY FARM US FOR THE WONDERS WE SIMPLY ACCEPT IN OUR IGNORANCE.

THERE ARE EVEN PORNOGRAPHIC VERSIONS OF OUR LIVES, MY LOVE.

ALTERNATIVE CONTINUITIES WHERE YOU LET THE ENTIRE STATUS QUORUM GANGBANG YOU FOR MONEY TO PAY YOUR RENT.

SICK SEX SITUATIONS I'D NEVER EVEN THOUGHT OF UNTIL I FOUND MERCURY'S FILES...THE SIDEWAYS LIVES HE'D WRITTEN FOR US TO LIVE...

I PULL OUT AND RUN THOSE ROTTEN STORIES EVERY NIGHT, EVE. I CAN'T HELP IT.

I...I LOVE TO WATCH YOU LOSE YOUR COOL AND YOUR DECENCY EVERY NIGHT BECAUSE IT'S THE CLOSEST I CAN GET...TO HOW IT ONCE FELT TO LOVE YOU.

MAN-RO HELP ME. I KEEP THINKING I'LL FIND A WAY TO SAVE US ALL.

THEN I JUST WASTE ANOTHER FIVE HOURS CHECKING OUT SLEAZY HARDCORE COMIX.

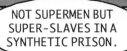

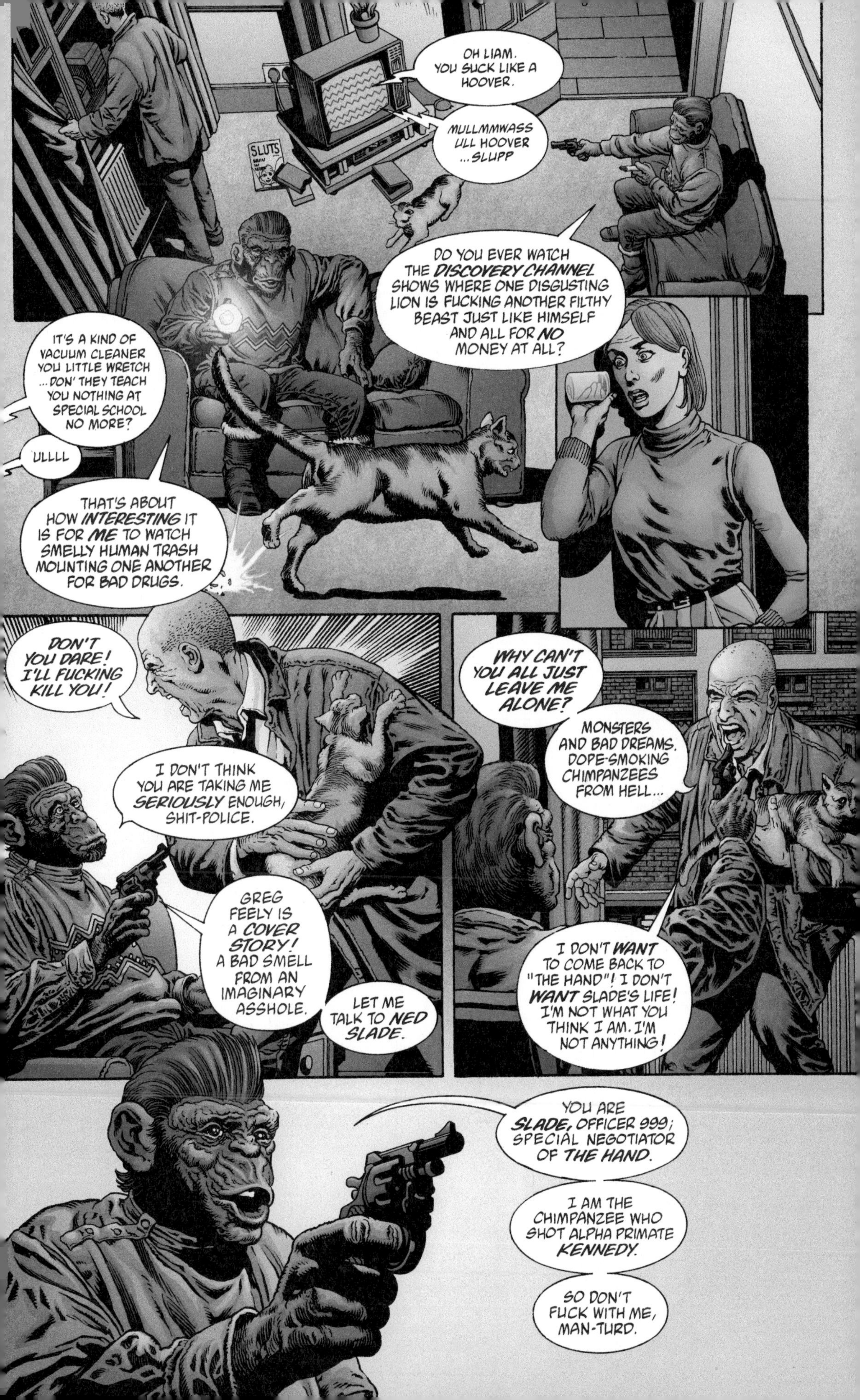
OH LIAM. YOU SUCK LIKE A HOOVER.
MULLMMWASS ULL HOOVER ...SLUPP
SLUTS
DO YOU EVER WATCH THE DISCOVERY CHANNEL SHOWS WHERE ONE DISGUSTING LION IS FUCKING ANOTHER FILTHY BEAST JUST LIKE HIMSELF AND ALL FOR NO MONEY AT ALL?
IT'S A KIND OF VACUUM CLEANER YOU LITTLE WRETCH ...DON' THEY TEACH YOU NOTHING AT SPECIAL SCHOOL NO MORE?
ULLLL
THAT'S ABOUT HOW INTERESTING IT IS FOR ME TO WATCH SMELLY HUMAN TRASH MOUNTING ONE ANOTHER FOR BAD DRUGS.
DON'T YOU DARE! I'LL FUCKING KILL YOU!
I DON'T THINK YOU ARE TAKING ME SERIOUSLY ENOUGH, SHIT-POLICE.
GREG FEELY IS A COVER STORY! A BAD SMELL FROM AN IMAGINARY ASSHOLE.
LET ME TALK TO NED SLADE.
WHY CAN'T YOU ALL JUST LEAVE ME ALONE?
MONSTERS AND BAD DREAMS. DOPE-SMOKING CHIMPANZEES FROM HELL...
I DON'T WANT TO COME BACK TO "THE HAND"! I DON'T WANT SLADE'S LIFE! I'M NOT WHAT YOU THINK I AM. I'M NOT ANYTHING!
YOU ARE SLADE, OFFICER 999; SPECIAL NEGOTIATOR OF THE HAND.
I AM THE CHIMPANZEE WHO SHOT ALPHA PRIMATE KENNEDY.
SO DON'T FUCK WITH ME, MAN-TURD.

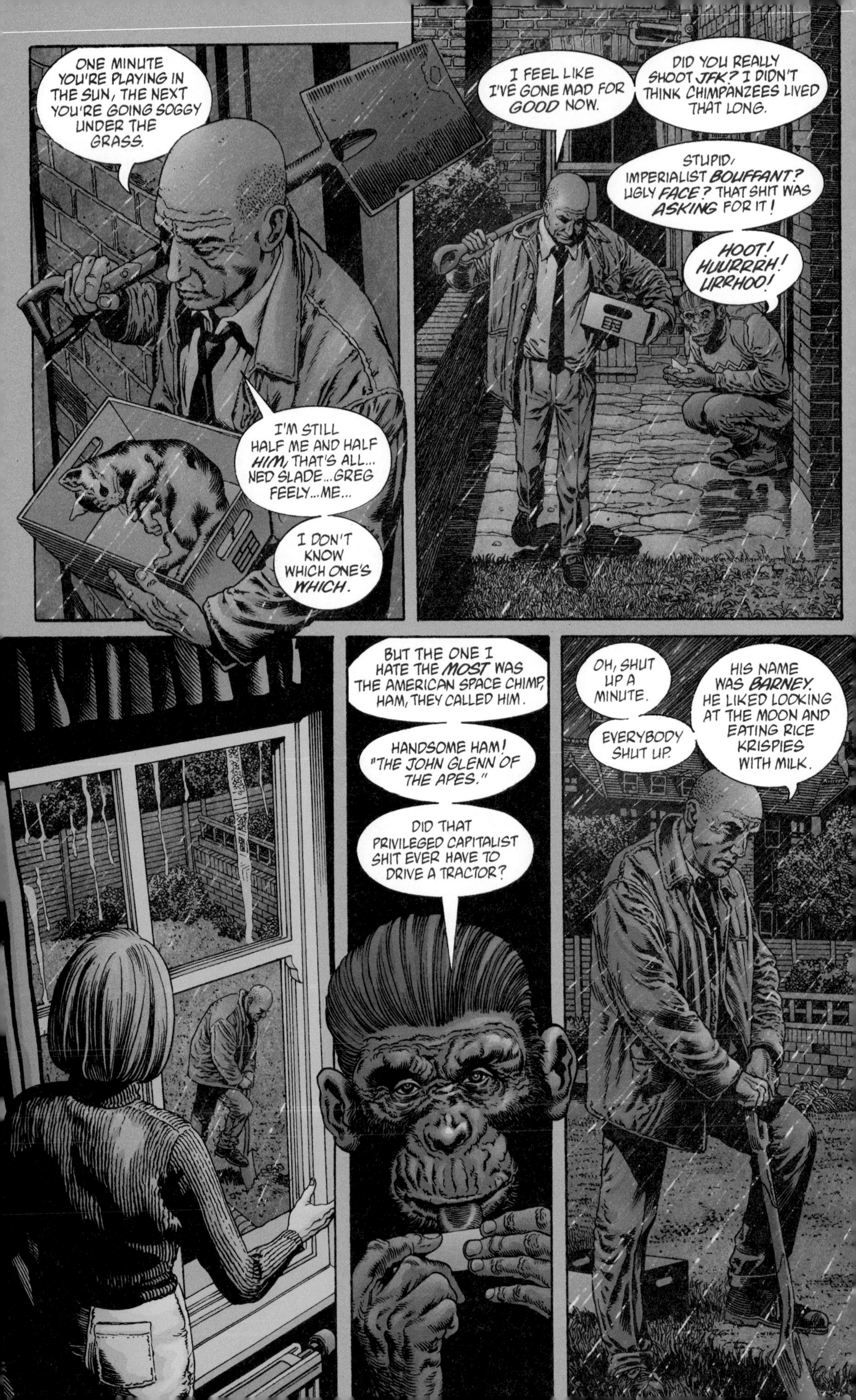
ONE MINUTE YOU'RE PLAYING IN THE SUN, THE NEXT YOU'RE GOING SOGGY UNDER THE GRASS.
I'M STILL HALF ME AND HALF HIM, THAT'S ALL... NED SLADE...GREG FEELY...ME...
I DON'T KNOW WHICH ONE'S WHICH.
I FEEL LIKE I'VE GONE MAD FOR GOOD NOW.
DID YOU REALLY SHOOT JFK? I DIDN'T THINK CHIMPANZEES LIVED THAT LONG.
STUPID, IMPERIALIST BOUFFANT? UGLY FACE? THAT SHIT WAS ASKING FOR IT!
HOOT! HUURRRH! URRHOO!
BUT THE ONE I HATE THE MOST WAS THE AMERICAN SPACE CHIMP, HAM, THEY CALLED HIM.
HANDSOME HAM! "THE JOHN GLENN OF THE APES."
DID THAT PRIVILEGED CAPITALIST SHIT EVER HAVE TO DRIVE A TRACTOR?
OH, SHUT UP A MINUTE.
EVERYBODY SHUT UP.
HIS NAME WAS BARNEY. HE LIKED LOOKING AT THE MOON AND EATING RICE KRISPIES WITH MILK.

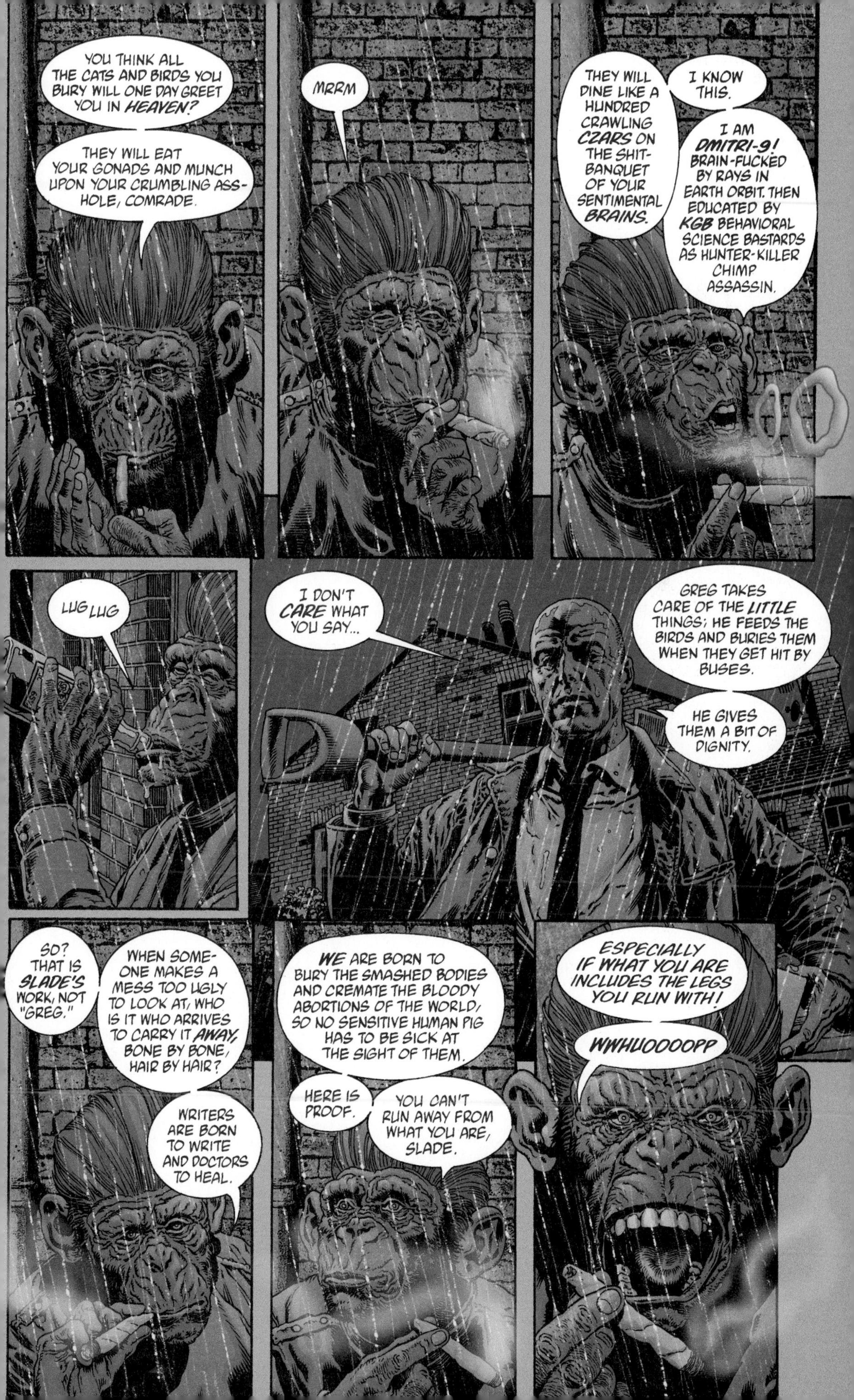
YOU THINK ALL THE CATS AND BIRDS YOU BURY WILL ONE DAY GREET YOU IN HEAVEN?
THEY WILL EAT YOUR GONADS AND MUNCH UPON YOUR CRUMBLING ASS-HOLE, COMRADE.
MRRM
THEY WILL DINE LIKE A HUNDRED CRAWLING CZARS ON THE SHIT-BANQUET OF YOUR SENTIMENTAL BRAINS.
I KNOW THIS.
I AM DMITRI-9! BRAIN-FUCKED BY RAYS IN EARTH ORBIT, THEN EDUCATED BY KGB BEHAVIORAL SCIENCE BASTARDS AS HUNTER-KILLER CHIMP ASSASSIN.
LUG LUG
I DON'T CARE WHAT YOU SAY...
GREG TAKES CARE OF THE LITTLE THINGS; HE FEEDS THE BIRDS AND BURIES THEM WHEN THEY GET HIT BY BUSES.
HE GIVES THEM A BIT OF DIGNITY.
SO? THAT IS SLADE'S WORK, NOT "GREG."
WHEN SOME-ONE MAKES A MESS TOO UGLY TO LOOK AT, WHO IS IT WHO ARRIVES TO CARRY IT AWAY, BONE BY BONE, HAIR BY HAIR?
WRITERS ARE BORN TO WRITE AND DOCTORS TO HEAL.
WE ARE BORN TO BURY THE SMASHED BODIES AND CREMATE THE BLOODY ABORTIONS OF THE WORLD, SO NO SENSITIVE HUMAN PIG HAS TO BE SICK AT THE SIGHT OF THEM.
HERE IS PROOF.
YOU CAN'T RUN AWAY FROM WHAT YOU ARE, SLADE.
ESPECIALLY IF WHAT YOU ARE INCLUDES THE LEGS YOU RUN WITH!
WWHUOOOOPP

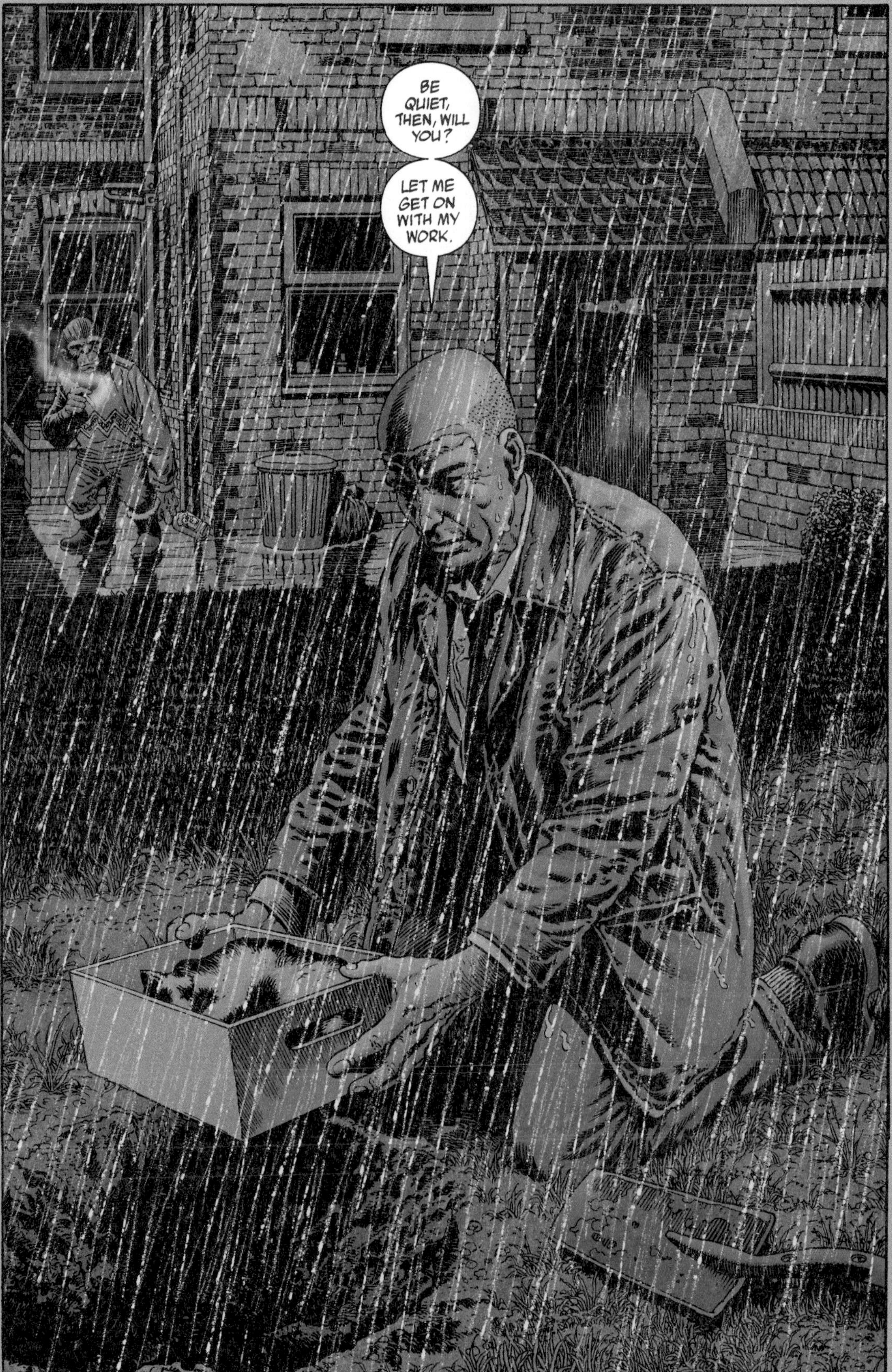
BE QUIET, THEN, WILL YOU?
LET ME GET ON WITH MY WORK.

The Filth

04. s**t happens

VERGIFT
POISON
DANGER
WARNING
BE CAREFUL

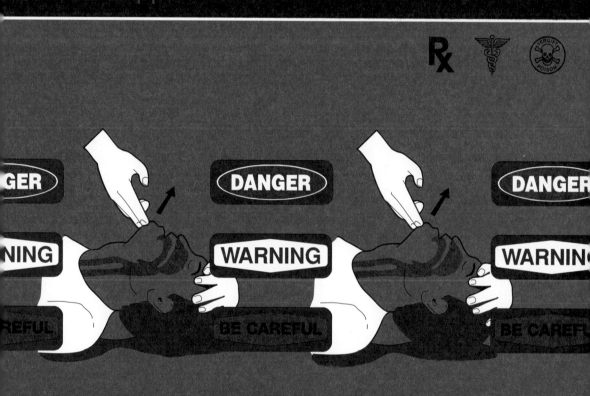

22 Pages

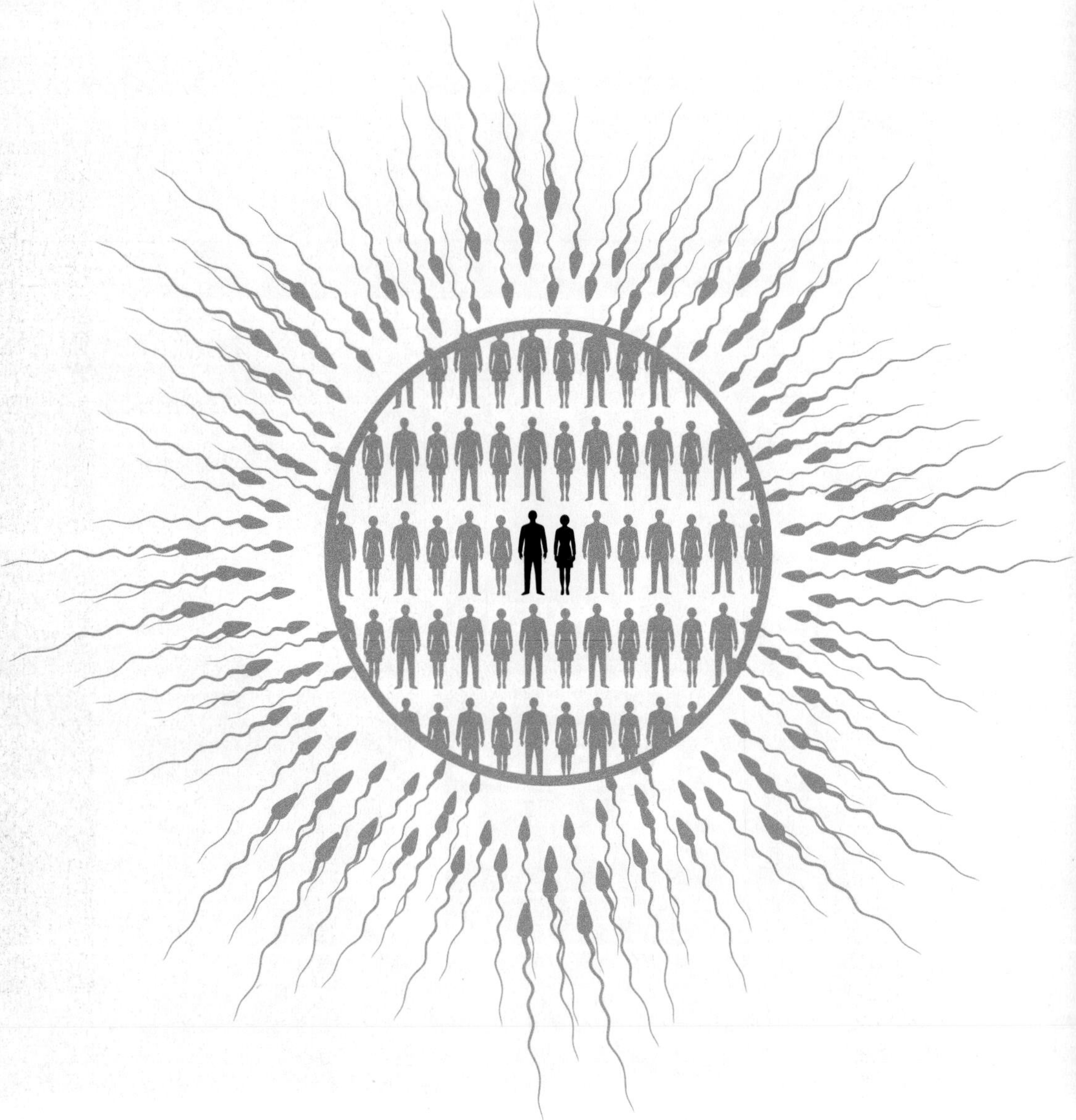

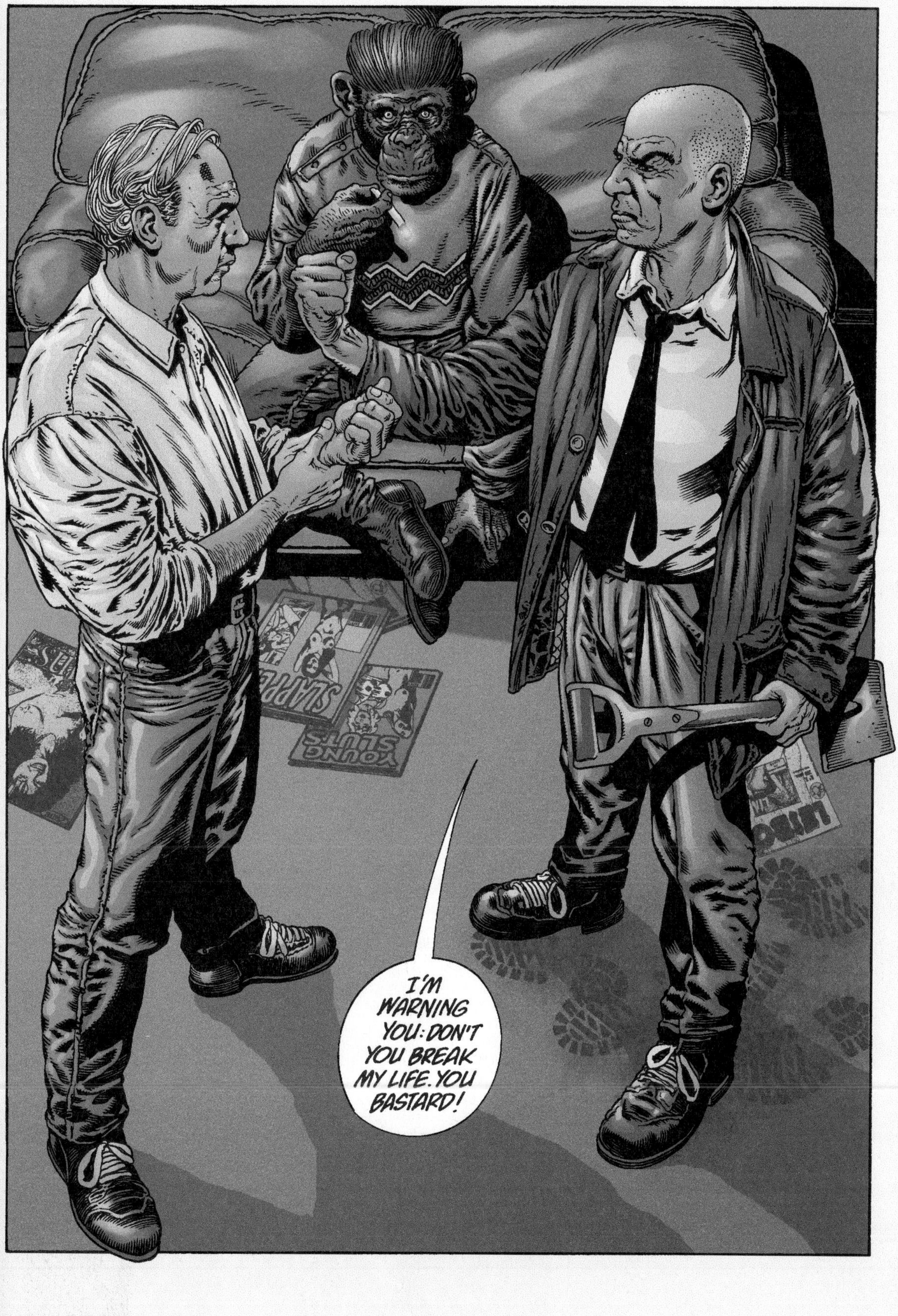
I'M WARNING YOU: DON'T YOU BREAK MY LIFE. YOU BASTARD!
YOUNG SLUTS

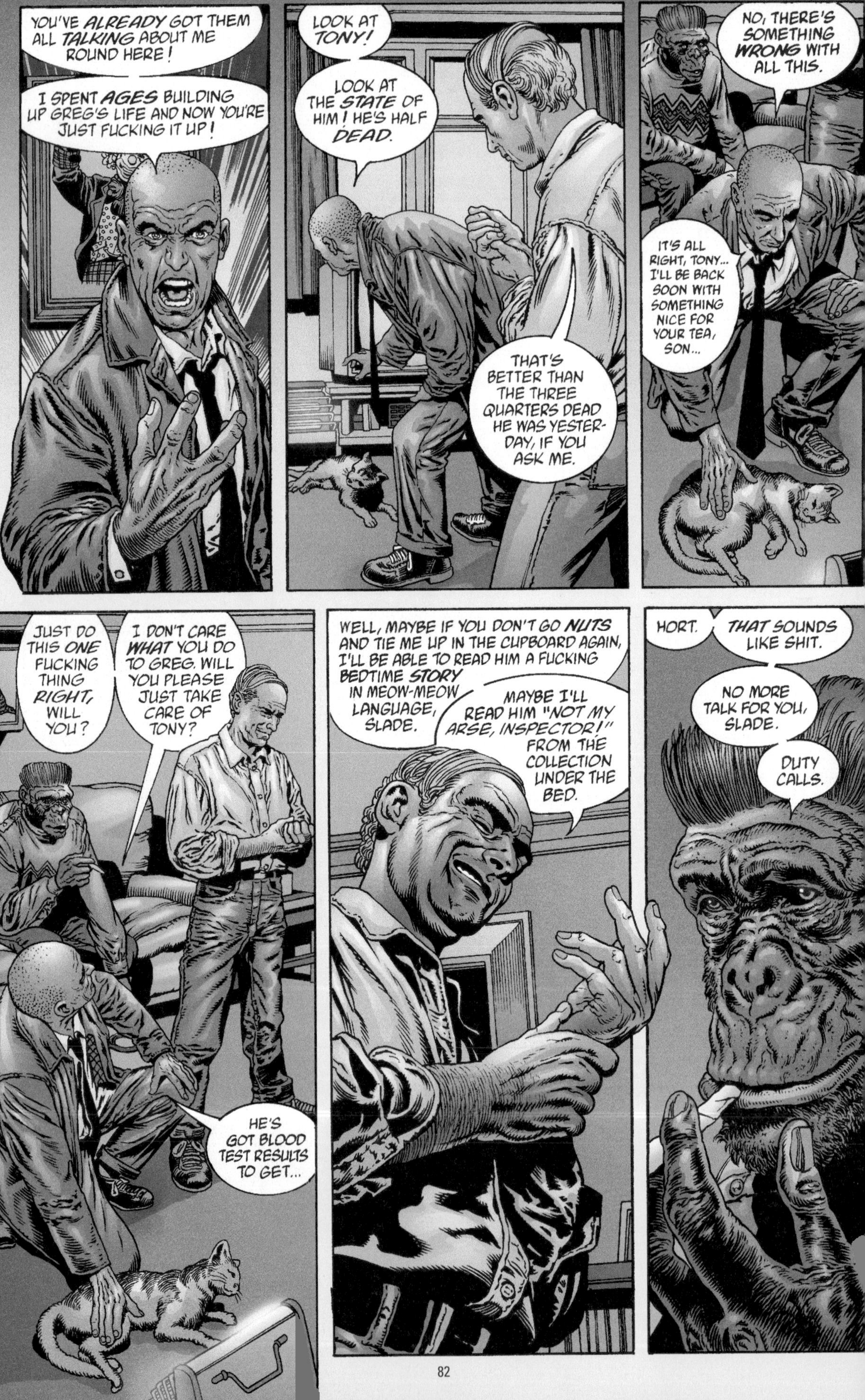

YOU'VE ALREADY GOT THEM ALL TALKING ABOUT ME ROUND HERE!
I SPENT AGES BUILDING UP GREG'S LIFE AND NOW YOU'RE JUST FUCKING IT UP!
LOOK AT TONY!
LOOK AT THE STATE OF HIM! HE'S HALF DEAD.
THAT'S BETTER THAN THE THREE QUARTERS DEAD HE WAS YESTERDAY, IF YOU ASK ME.
NO, THERE'S SOMETHING WRONG WITH ALL THIS.
IT'S ALL RIGHT, TONY... I'LL BE BACK SOON WITH SOMETHING NICE FOR YOUR TEA, SON...
JUST DO THIS ONE FUCKING THING RIGHT, WILL YOU?
I DON'T CARE WHAT YOU DO TO GREG. WILL YOU PLEASE JUST TAKE CARE OF TONY?
HE'S GOT BLOOD TEST RESULTS TO GET...
WELL, MAYBE IF YOU DON'T GO NUTS AND TIE ME UP IN THE CUPBOARD AGAIN, I'LL BE ABLE TO READ HIM A FUCKING BEDTIME STORY IN MEOW-MEOW LANGUAGE, SLADE.
MAYBE I'LL READ HIM "NOT MY ARSE, INSPECTOR!" FROM THE COLLECTION UNDER THE BED.
HORT.
THAT SOUNDS LIKE SHIT.
NO MORE TALK FOR YOU, SLADE.
DUTY CALLS.

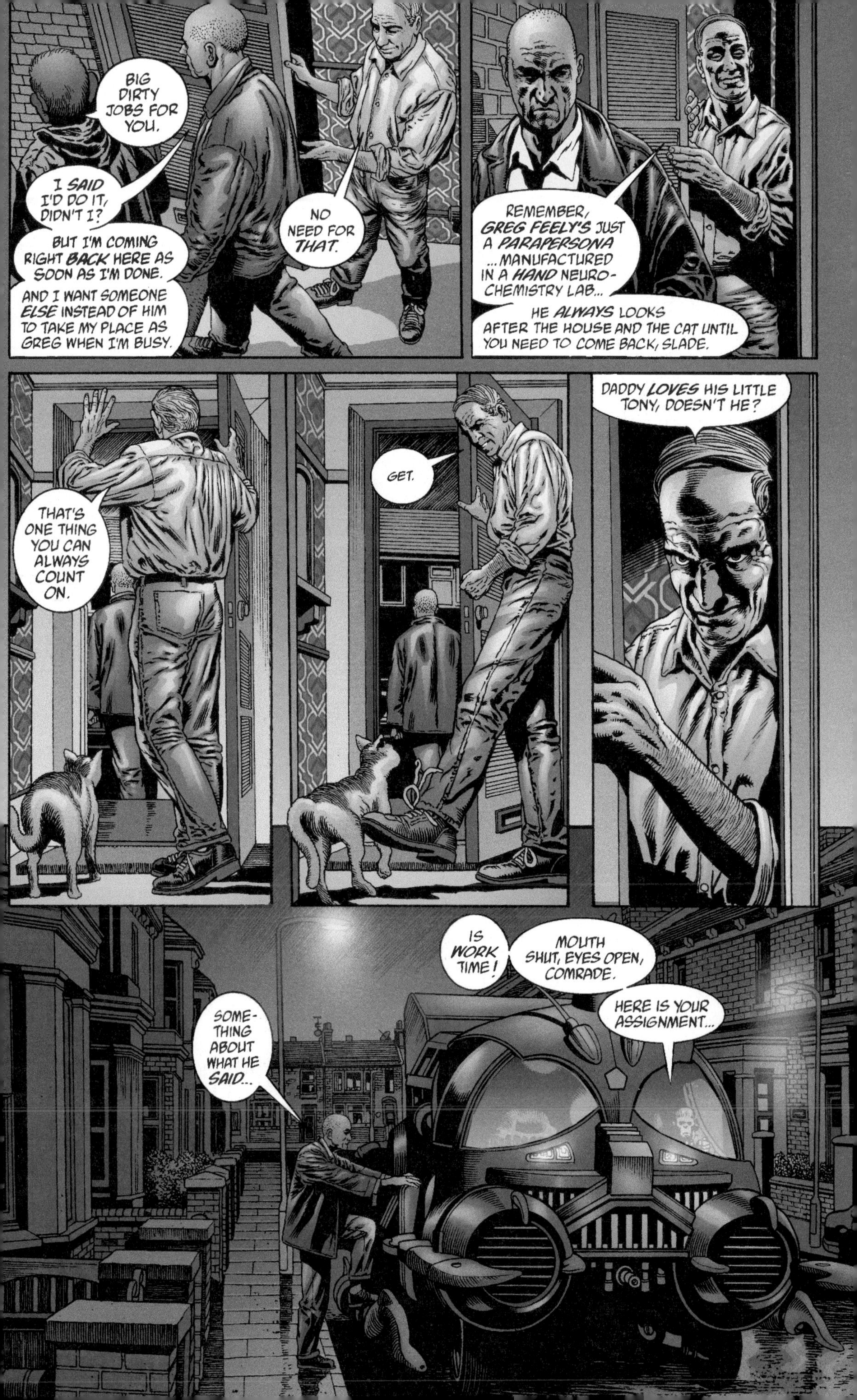
BIG DIRTY JOBS FOR YOU.
I SAID I'D DO IT, DIDN'T I?
BUT I'M COMING RIGHT BACK HERE AS SOON AS I'M DONE.
AND I WANT SOMEONE ELSE INSTEAD OF HIM TO TAKE MY PLACE AS GREG WHEN I'M BUSY.
NO NEED FOR THAT.
REMEMBER, GREG FEELY'S JUST A PARAPERSONA ...MANUFACTURED IN A HAND NEURO-CHEMISTRY LAB...
HE ALWAYS LOOKS AFTER THE HOUSE AND THE CAT UNTIL YOU NEED TO COME BACK, SLADE.
THAT'S ONE THING YOU CAN ALWAYS COUNT ON.
GET.
DADDY LOVES HIS LITTLE TONY, DOESN'T HE?
IS WORK TIME!
MOUTH SHUT, EYES OPEN, COMRADE.
HERE IS YOUR ASSIGNMENT...
SOME-THING ABOUT WHAT HE SAID...

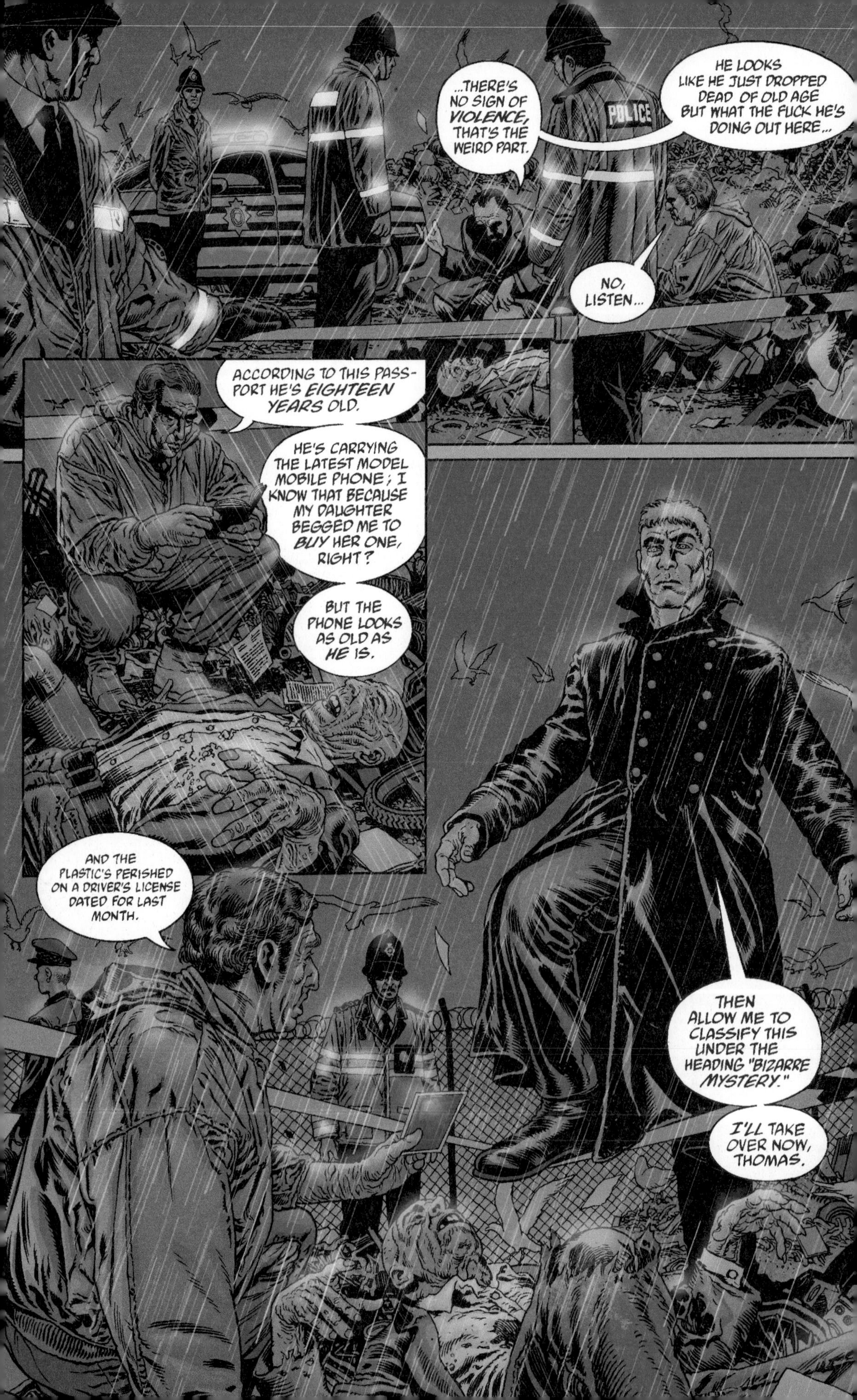
...THERE'S NO SIGN OF VIOLENCE, THAT'S THE WEIRD PART.
HE LOOKS LIKE HE JUST DROPPED DEAD OF OLD AGE BUT WHAT THE FUCK HE'S DOING OUT HERE...
POLICE
NO, LISTEN...
ACCORDING TO THIS PASS-PORT HE'S EIGHTEEN YEARS OLD.
HE'S CARRYING THE LATEST MODEL MOBILE PHONE; I KNOW THAT BECAUSE MY DAUGHTER BEGGED ME TO BUY HER ONE, RIGHT?
BUT THE PHONE LOOKS AS OLD AS HE IS.
AND THE PLASTIC'S PERISHED ON A DRIVER'S LICENSE DATED FOR LAST MONTH.
THEN ALLOW ME TO CLASSIFY THIS UNDER THE HEADING "BIZARRE MYSTERY."
I'LL TAKE OVER NOW, THOMAS.

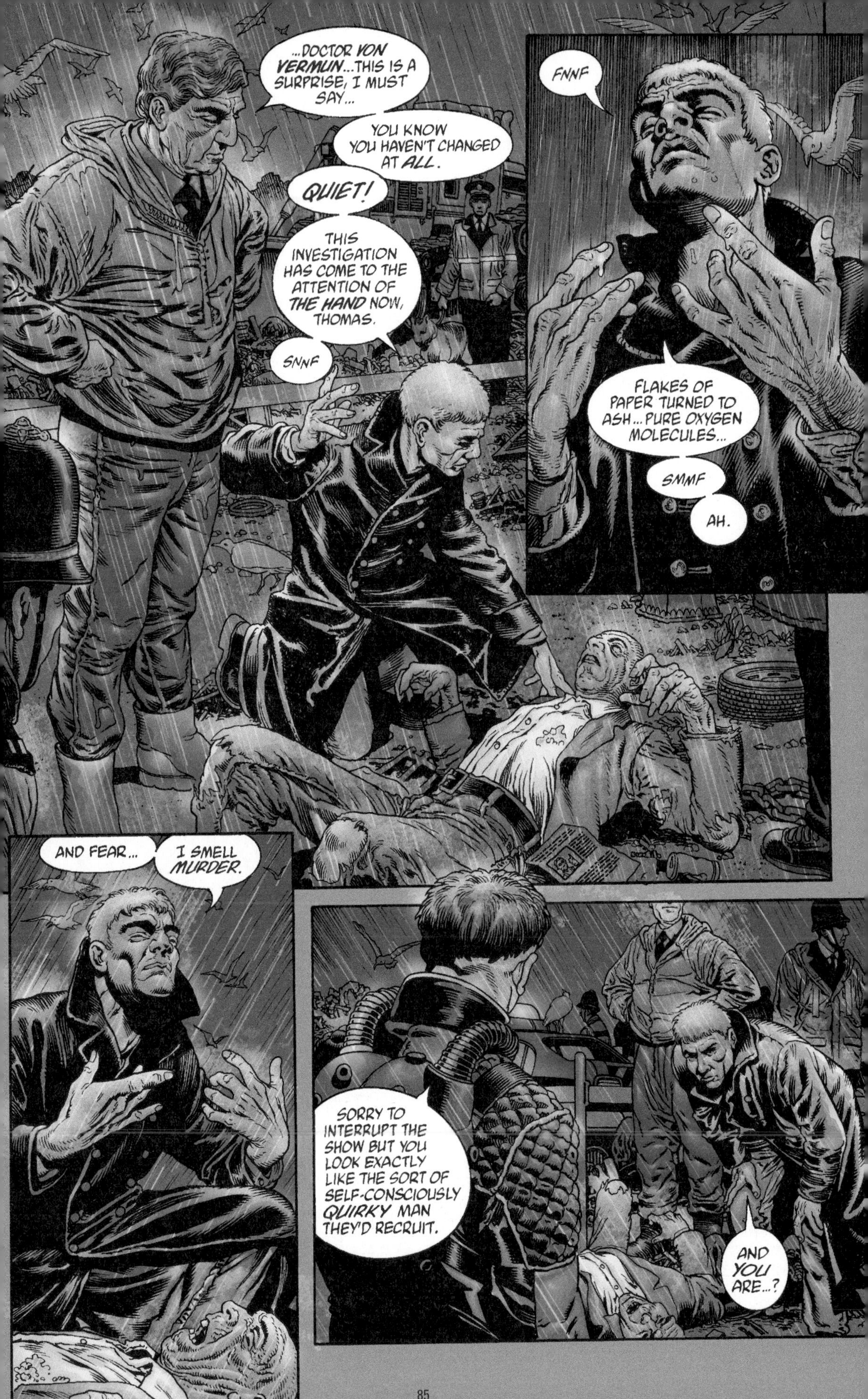
...DOCTOR VON VERMUN...THIS IS A SURPRISE, I MUST SAY...
YOU KNOW YOU HAVEN'T CHANGED AT ALL.
QUIET!
THIS INVESTIGATION HAS COME TO THE ATTENTION OF THE HAND NOW, THOMAS.
SNNF
FNNF
FLAKES OF PAPER TURNED TO ASH...PURE OXYGEN MOLECULES...
SMMF
AH.
AND FEAR...
I SMELL MURDER.
SORRY TO INTERRUPT THE SHOW BUT YOU LOOK EXACTLY LIKE THE SORT OF SELF-CONSCIOUSLY QUIRKY MAN THEY'D RECRUIT.
AND YOU ARE...?

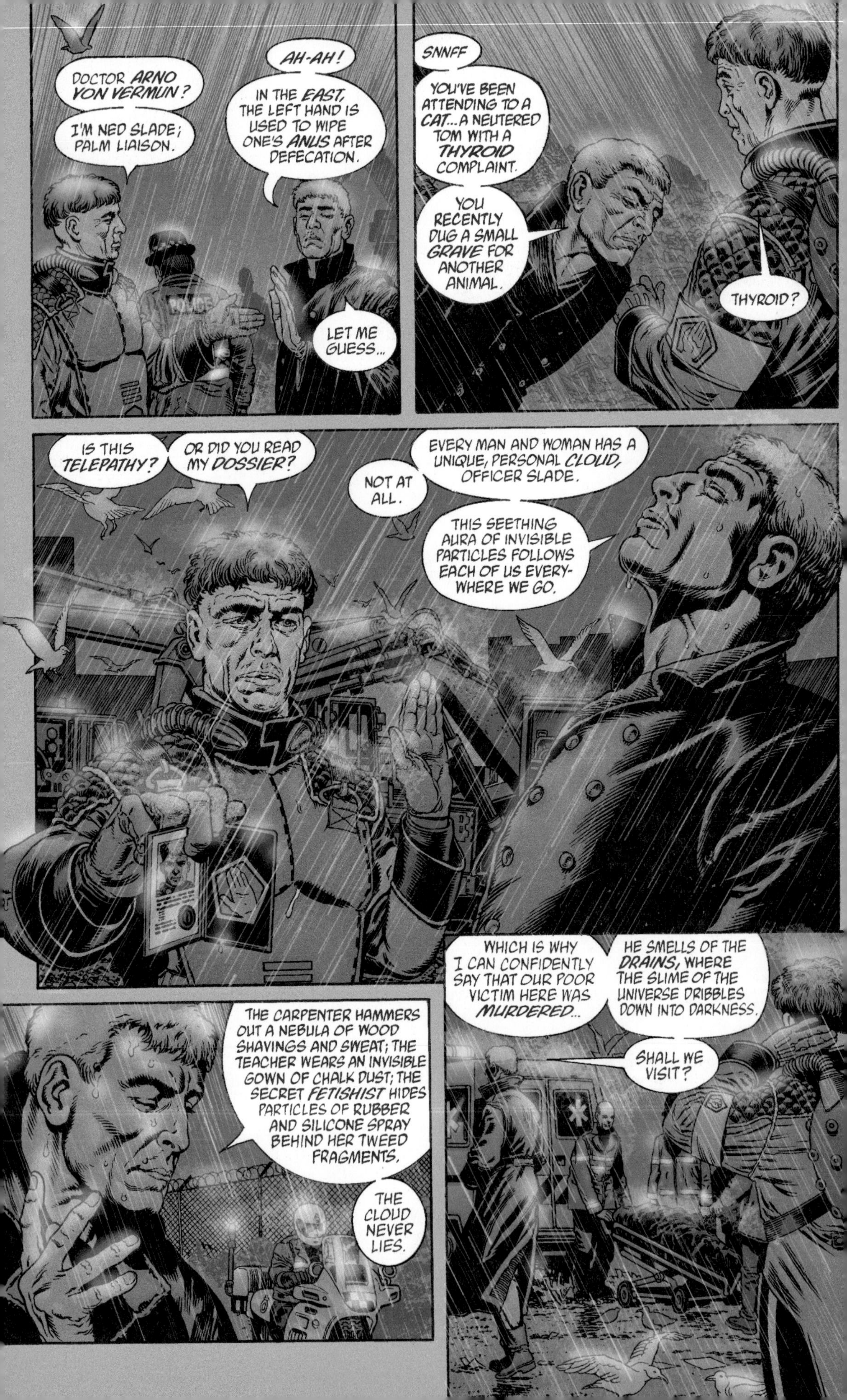
DOCTOR ARNO VON VERMUN?
I'M NED SLADE; PALM LIAISON.
AH-AH!
IN THE EAST, THE LEFT HAND IS USED TO WIPE ONE'S ANUS AFTER DEFECATION.
LET ME GUESS...
SNNFF
YOU'VE BEEN ATTENDING TO A CAT... A NEUTERED TOM WITH A THYROID COMPLAINT.
YOU RECENTLY DUG A SMALL GRAVE FOR ANOTHER ANIMAL.
THYROID?
IS THIS TELEPATHY?
OR DID YOU READ MY DOSSIER?
NOT AT ALL.
EVERY MAN AND WOMAN HAS A UNIQUE, PERSONAL CLOUD, OFFICER SLADE.
THIS SEETHING AURA OF INVISIBLE PARTICLES FOLLOWS EACH OF US EVERYWHERE WE GO.
THE CARPENTER HAMMERS OUT A NEBULA OF WOOD SHAVINGS AND SWEAT; THE TEACHER WEARS AN INVISIBLE GOWN OF CHALK DUST; THE SECRET FETISHIST HIDES PARTICLES OF RUBBER AND SILICONE SPRAY BEHIND HER TWEED FRAGMENTS.
THE CLOUD NEVER LIES.
WHICH IS WHY I CAN CONFIDENTLY SAY THAT OUR POOR VICTIM HERE WAS MURDERED...
HE SMELLS OF THE DRAINS, WHERE THE SLIME OF THE UNIVERSE DRIBBLES DOWN INTO DARKNESS.
SHALL WE VISIT?

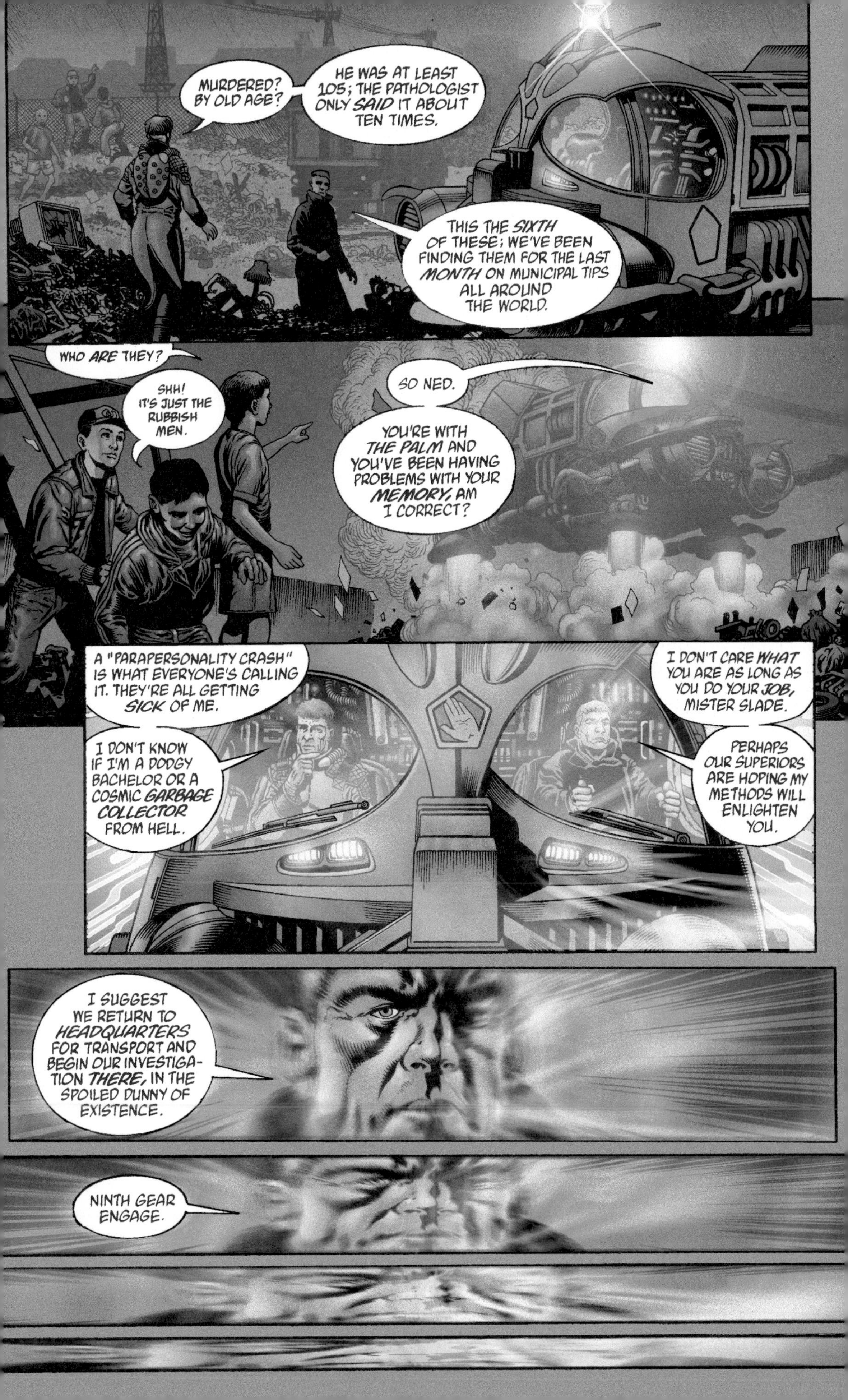
MURDERED? BY OLD AGE?
HE WAS AT LEAST 105; THE PATHOLOGIST ONLY SAID IT ABOUT TEN TIMES.
THIS THE SIXTH OF THESE; WE'VE BEEN FINDING THEM FOR THE LAST MONTH ON MUNICIPAL TIPS ALL AROUND THE WORLD.
WHO ARE THEY?
SHH! IT'S JUST THE RUBBISH MEN.
SO NED.
YOU'RE WITH THE PALM AND YOU'VE BEEN HAVING PROBLEMS WITH YOUR MEMORY, AM I CORRECT?
A "PARAPERSONALITY CRASH" IS WHAT EVERYONE'S CALLING IT. THEY'RE ALL GETTING SICK OF ME.
I DON'T KNOW IF I'M A DODGY BACHELOR OR A COSMIC GARBAGE COLLECTOR FROM HELL.
I DON'T CARE WHAT YOU ARE AS LONG AS YOU DO YOUR JOB, MISTER SLADE.
PERHAPS OUR SUPERIORS ARE HOPING MY METHODS WILL ENLIGHTEN YOU.
I SUGGEST WE RETURN TO HEADQUARTERS FOR TRANSPORT AND BEGIN OUR INVESTIGATION THERE, IN THE SPOILED DUNNY OF EXISTENCE.
NINTH GEAR ENGAGE.

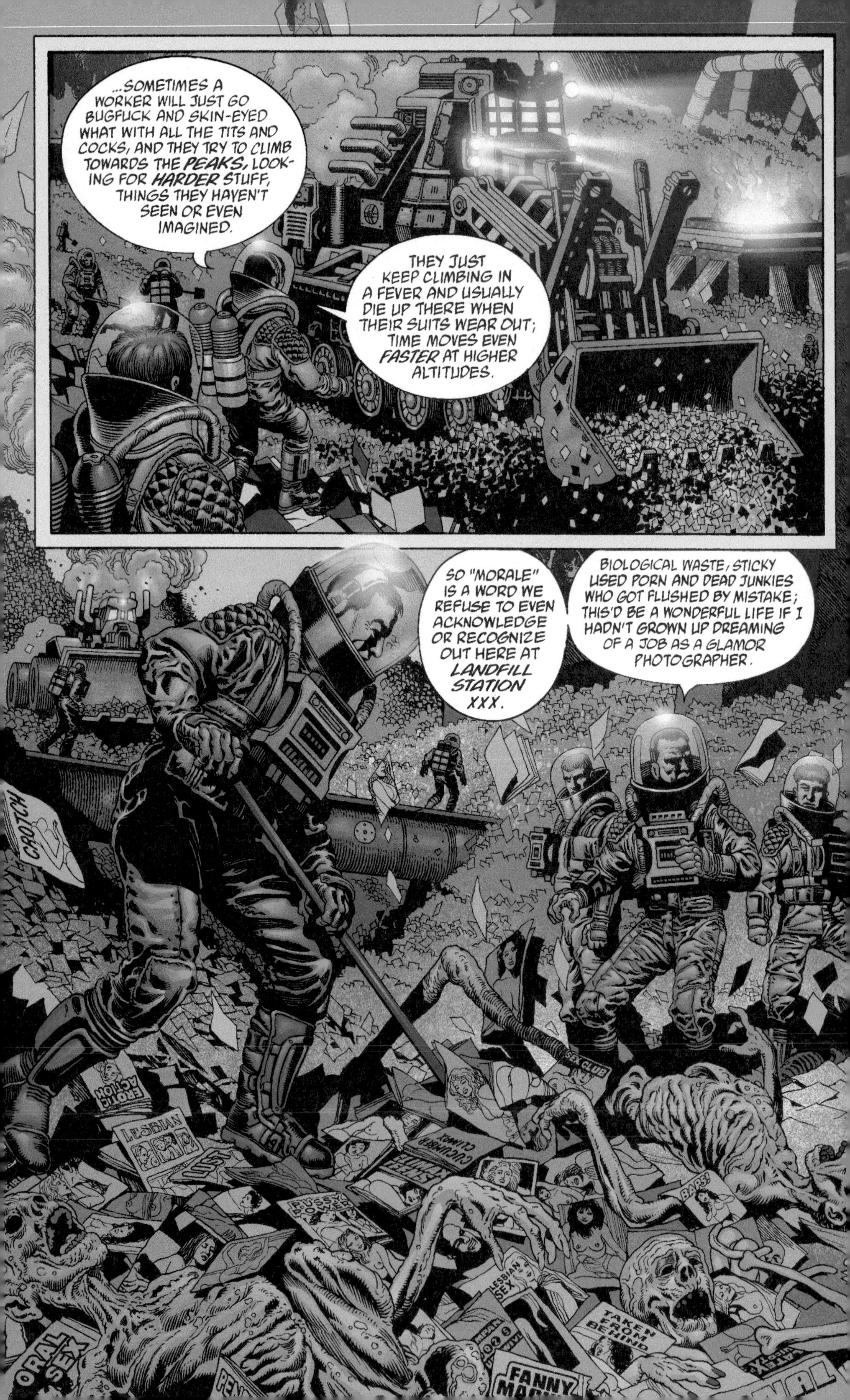
...SOMETIMES A WORKER WILL JUST GO BUGFUCK AND SKIN-EYED WHAT WITH ALL THE TITS AND COCKS, AND THEY TRY TO CLIMB TOWARDS THE *PEAKS,* LOOKING FOR *HARDER* STUFF, THINGS THEY HAVEN'T SEEN OR EVEN IMAGINED.
THEY JUST KEEP CLIMBING IN A FEVER AND USUALLY DIE UP THERE WHEN THEIR SUITS WEAR OUT; TIME MOVES EVEN *FASTER* AT HIGHER ALTITUDES.
SO "MORALE" IS A WORD WE REFUSE TO EVEN ACKNOWLEDGE OR RECOGNIZE OUT HERE AT *LANDFILL STATION XXX.*
BIOLOGICAL WASTE, STICKY USED PORN AND DEAD JUNKIES WHO GOT FLUSHED BY MISTAKE; THIS'D BE A WONDERFUL LIFE IF I HADN'T GROWN UP DREAMING OF A JOB AS A GLAMOR PHOTOGRAPHER.
CROTCH
EROTIC ACTION
LESBIAN
SEX CLUB
CUCUMBER CLIMAX
PUSSY POWER
BABS!
LESBIAN SEX
TAKEN FROM BEHIND
ORAL SEX

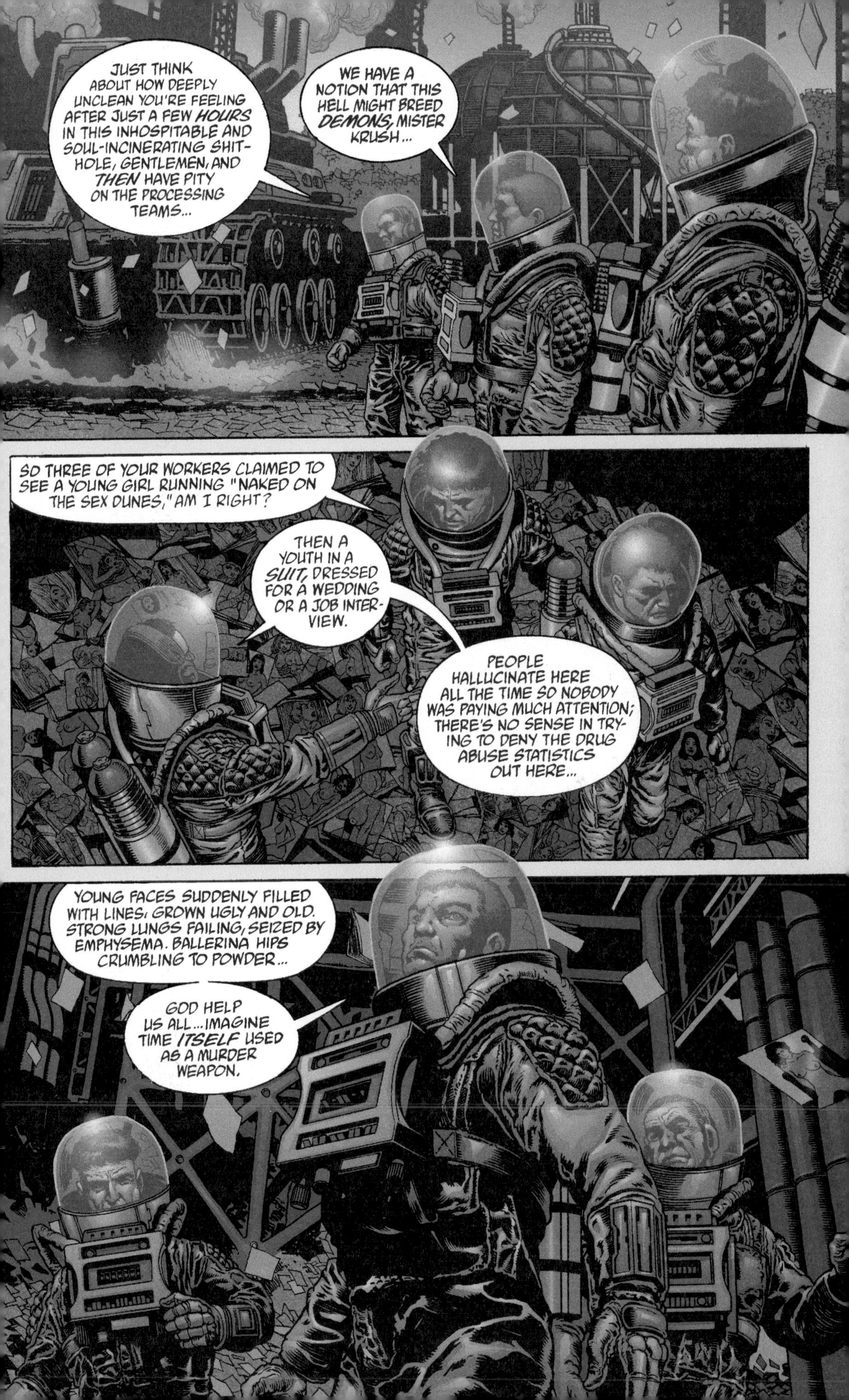
JUST THINK ABOUT HOW DEEPLY UNCLEAN YOU'RE FEELING AFTER JUST A FEW HOURS IN THIS INHOSPITABLE AND SOUL-INCINERATING SHIT-HOLE, GENTLEMEN, AND THEN HAVE PITY ON THE PROCESSING TEAMS...
WE HAVE A NOTION THAT THIS HELL MIGHT BREED DEMONS, MISTER KRUSH...
SO THREE OF YOUR WORKERS CLAIMED TO SEE A YOUNG GIRL RUNNING "NAKED ON THE SEX DUNES," AM I RIGHT?
THEN A YOUTH IN A SUIT, DRESSED FOR A WEDDING OR A JOB INTER-VIEW.
PEOPLE HALLUCINATE HERE ALL THE TIME SO NOBODY WAS PAYING MUCH ATTENTION; THERE'S NO SENSE IN TRY-ING TO DENY THE DRUG ABUSE STATISTICS OUT HERE...
YOUNG FACES SUDDENLY FILLED WITH LINES, GROWN UGLY AND OLD. STRONG LUNGS FAILING, SEIZED BY EMPHYSEMA. BALLERINA HIPS CRUMBLING TO POWDER...
GOD HELP US ALL...IMAGINE TIME ITSELF USED AS A MURDER WEAPON.

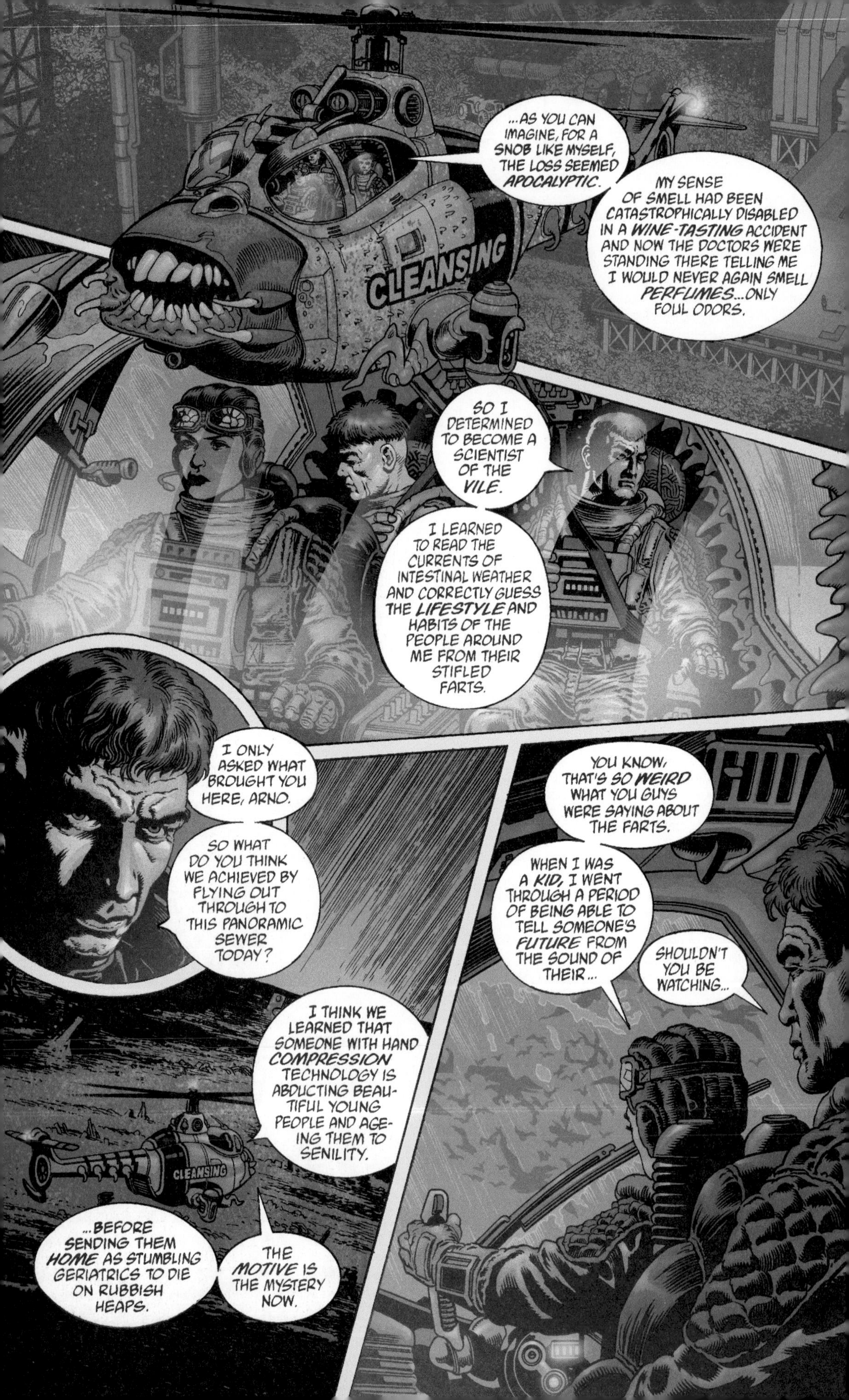
...AS YOU CAN IMAGINE, FOR A SNOB LIKE MYSELF, THE LOSS SEEMED *APOCALYPTIC*.
MY SENSE OF SMELL HAD BEEN CATASTROPHICALLY DISABLED IN A *WINE-TASTING* ACCIDENT AND NOW THE DOCTORS WERE STANDING THERE TELLING ME I WOULD NEVER AGAIN SMELL *PERFUMES*...ONLY FOUL ODORS.
CLEANSING
SO I DETERMINED TO BECOME A SCIENTIST OF THE *VILE*.
I LEARNED TO READ THE CURRENTS OF INTESTINAL WEATHER AND CORRECTLY GUESS THE *LIFESTYLE* AND HABITS OF THE PEOPLE AROUND ME FROM THEIR STIFLED FARTS.
I ONLY ASKED WHAT BROUGHT YOU HERE, ARNO.
SO WHAT DO YOU THINK WE ACHIEVED BY FLYING OUT THROUGH TO THIS PANORAMIC SEWER TODAY?
I THINK WE LEARNED THAT SOMEONE WITH HAND *COMPRESSION* TECHNOLOGY IS ABDUCTING BEAU-TIFUL YOUNG PEOPLE AND AGE-ING THEM TO SENILITY.
...BEFORE SENDING THEM *HOME* AS STUMBLING GERIATRICS TO DIE ON RUBBISH HEAPS.
THE *MOTIVE* IS THE MYSTERY NOW.
CLEANSING
YOU KNOW, THAT'S SO *WEIRD* WHAT YOU GUYS WERE SAYING ABOUT THE FARTS.
WHEN I WAS A *KID*, I WENT THROUGH A PERIOD OF BEING ABLE TO TELL SOMEONE'S *FUTURE* FROM THE SOUND OF THEIR...
SHOULDN'T YOU BE WATCHING...

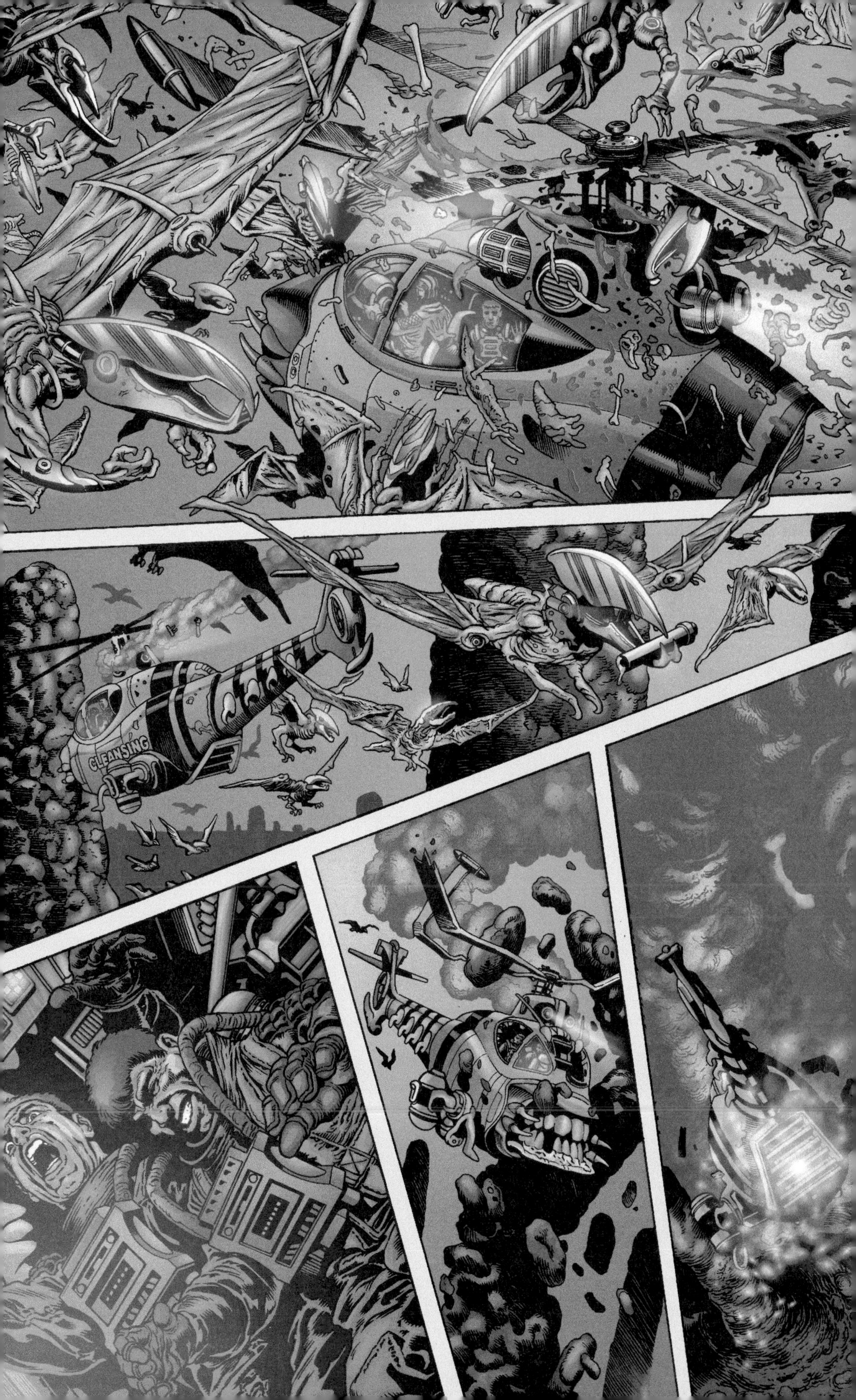
CLEANSING

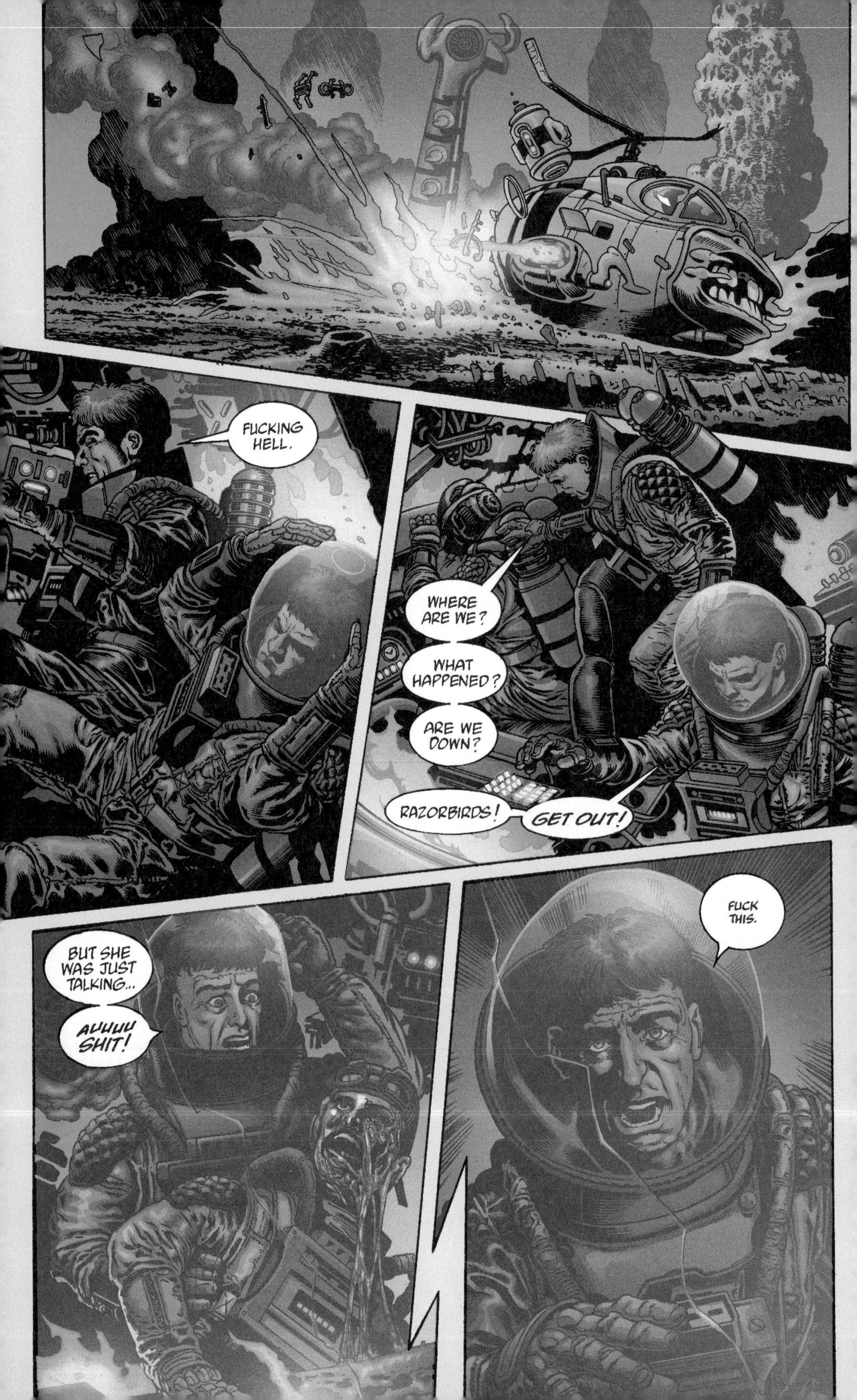
FUCKING HELL.
WHERE ARE WE?
WHAT HAPPENED?
ARE WE DOWN?
RAZORBIRDS!
GET OUT!
BUT SHE WAS JUST TALKING...
AUUUU SHIT!
FUCK THIS.

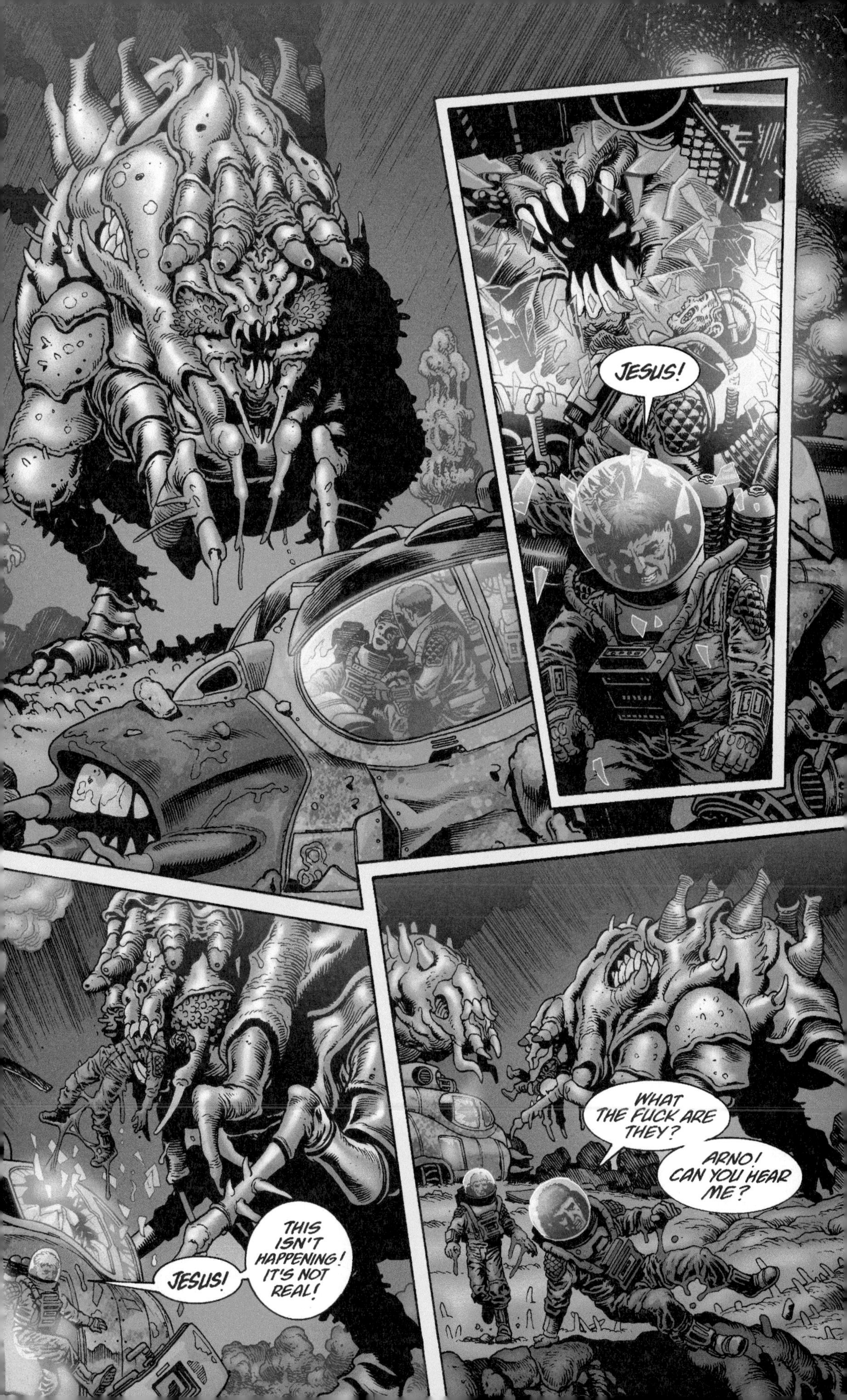
JESUS!
JESUS!
THIS ISN'T HAPPENING! IT'S NOT REAL!
WHAT THE FUCK ARE THEY?
ARNO! CAN YOU HEAR ME?

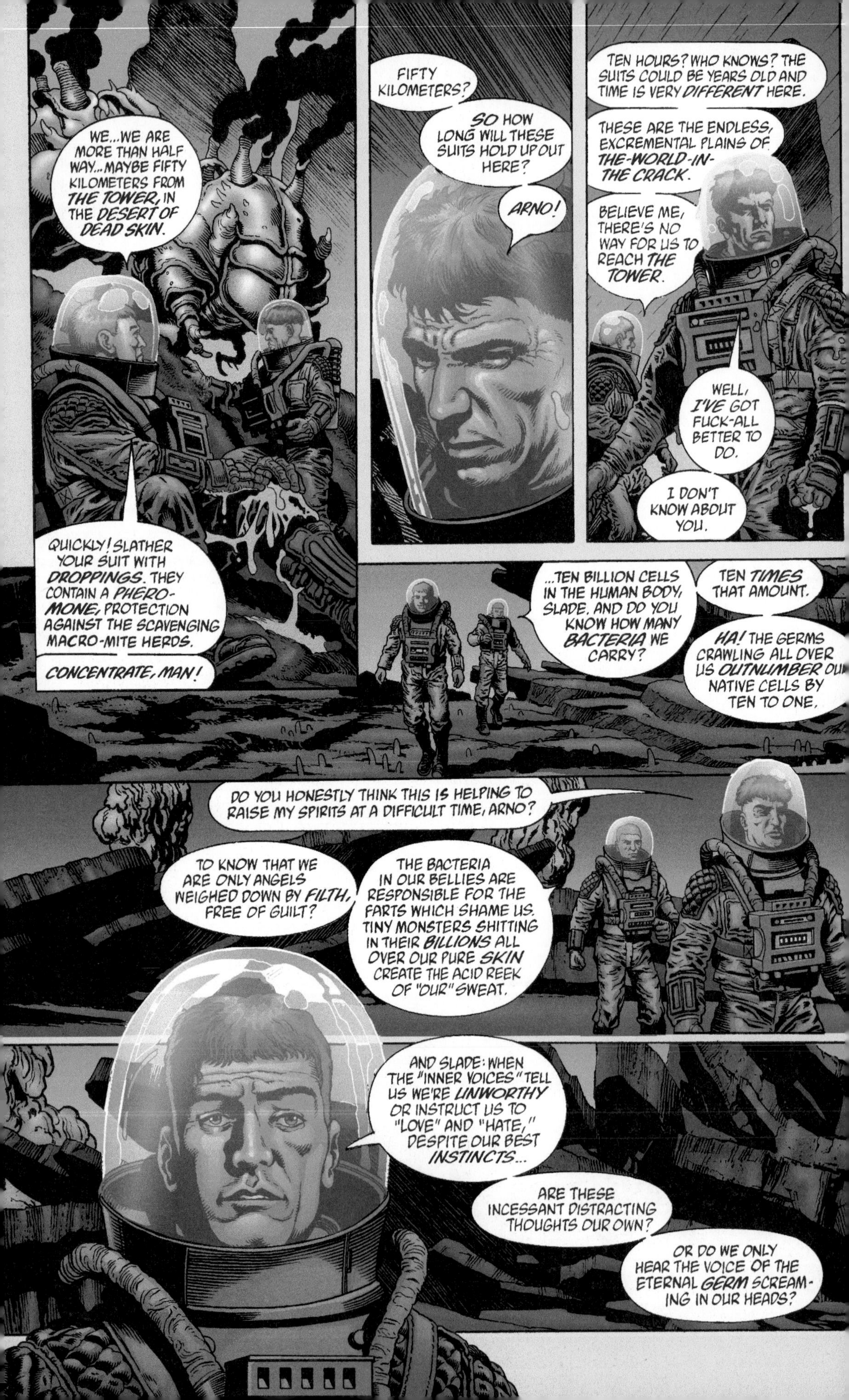
WE...WE ARE MORE THAN HALF WAY...MAYBE FIFTY KILOMETERS FROM THE TOWER, IN THE DESERT OF DEAD SKIN.
QUICKLY! SLATHER YOUR SUIT WITH DROPPINGS. THEY CONTAIN A PHERO-MONE, PROTECTION AGAINST THE SCAVENGING MACRO-MITE HERDS.
CONCENTRATE, MAN!
FIFTY KILOMETERS?
SO HOW LONG WILL THESE SUITS HOLD UP OUT HERE?
ARNO!
TEN HOURS? WHO KNOWS? THE SUITS COULD BE YEARS OLD AND TIME IS VERY DIFFERENT HERE.
THESE ARE THE ENDLESS, EXCREMENTAL PLAINS OF THE-WORLD-IN-THE CRACK.
BELIEVE ME, THERE'S NO WAY FOR US TO REACH THE TOWER.
WELL, I'VE GOT FUCK-ALL BETTER TO DO.
I DON'T KNOW ABOUT YOU.
...TEN BILLION CELLS IN THE HUMAN BODY, SLADE. AND DO YOU KNOW HOW MANY BACTERIA WE CARRY?
TEN TIMES THAT AMOUNT.
HA! THE GERMS CRAWLING ALL OVER US OUTNUMBER OUR NATIVE CELLS BY TEN TO ONE.
DO YOU HONESTLY THINK THIS IS HELPING TO RAISE MY SPIRITS AT A DIFFICULT TIME, ARNO?
TO KNOW THAT WE ARE ONLY ANGELS WEIGHED DOWN BY FILTH, FREE OF GUILT?
THE BACTERIA IN OUR BELLIES ARE RESPONSIBLE FOR THE FARTS WHICH SHAME US. TINY MONSTERS SHITTING IN THEIR BILLIONS ALL OVER OUR PURE SKIN CREATE THE ACID REEK OF "OUR" SWEAT.
AND SLADE: WHEN THE "INNER VOICES" TELL US WE'RE UNWORTHY OR INSTRUCT US TO "LOVE" AND "HATE," DESPITE OUR BEST INSTINCTS...
ARE THESE INCESSANT DISTRACTING THOUGHTS OUR OWN?
OR DO WE ONLY HEAR THE VOICE OF THE ETERNAL GERM SCREAM-ING IN OUR HEADS?

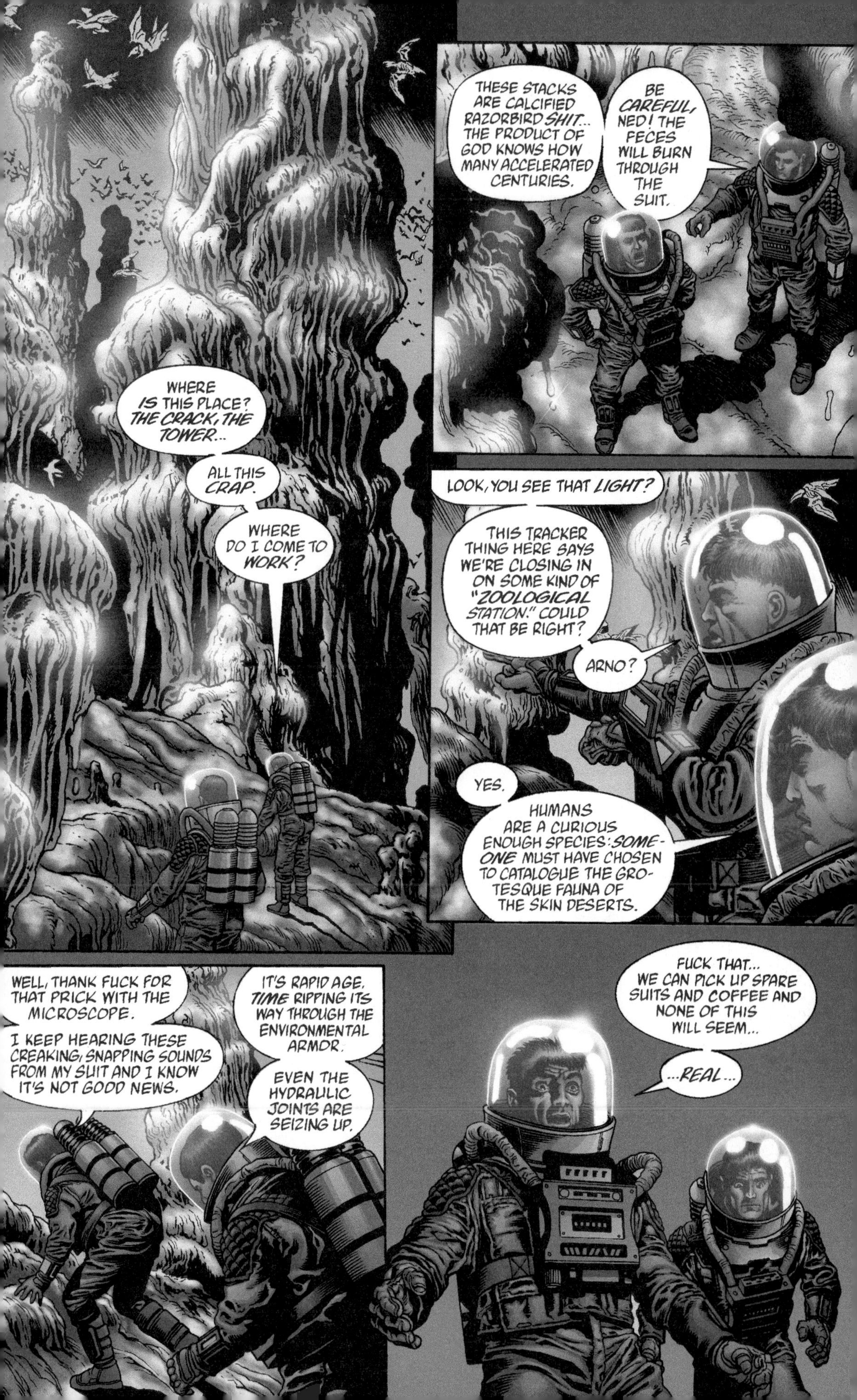
WHERE IS THIS PLACE? THE CRACK, THE TOWER...
ALL THIS CRAP.
WHERE DO I COME TO WORK?
THESE STACKS ARE CALCIFIED RAZORBIRD SHIT... THE PRODUCT OF GOD KNOWS HOW MANY ACCELERATED CENTURIES.
BE CAREFUL, NED! THE FECES WILL BURN THROUGH THE SUIT.
LOOK, YOU SEE THAT LIGHT?
THIS TRACKER THING HERE SAYS WE'RE CLOSING IN ON SOME KIND OF "ZOOLOGICAL STATION." COULD THAT BE RIGHT?
ARNO?
YES.
HUMANS ARE A CURIOUS ENOUGH SPECIES: SOME-ONE MUST HAVE CHOSEN TO CATALOGUE THE GRO-TESQUE FAUNA OF THE SKIN DESERTS.
WELL, THANK FUCK FOR THAT PRICK WITH THE MICROSCOPE.
I KEEP HEARING THESE CREAKING, SNAPPING SOUNDS FROM MY SUIT AND I KNOW IT'S NOT GOOD NEWS.
IT'S RAPID AGE. TIME RIPPING ITS WAY THROUGH THE ENVIRONMENTAL ARMOR.
EVEN THE HYDRAULIC JOINTS ARE SEIZING UP.
FUCK THAT... WE CAN PICK UP SPARE SUITS AND COFFEE AND NONE OF THIS WILL SEEM...
...REAL...

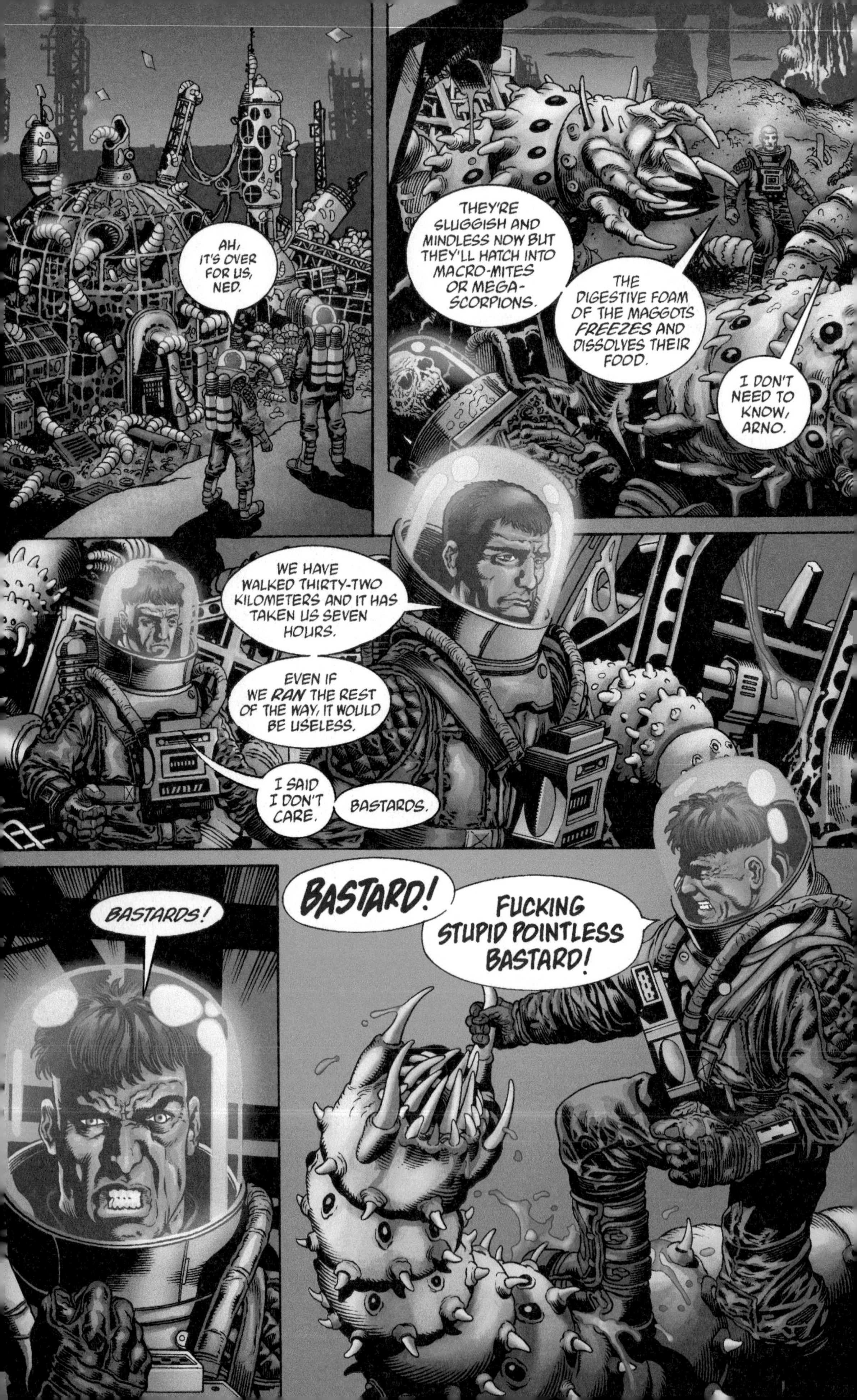
AH, IT'S OVER FOR US, NED.
THEY'RE SLUGGISH AND MINDLESS NOW BUT THEY'LL HATCH INTO MACRO-MITES OR MEGA-SCORPIONS.
THE DIGESTIVE FOAM OF THE MAGGOTS FREEZES AND DISSOLVES THEIR FOOD.
I DON'T NEED TO KNOW, ARNO.
WE HAVE WALKED THIRTY-TWO KILOMETERS AND IT HAS TAKEN US SEVEN HOURS.
EVEN IF WE RAN THE REST OF THE WAY, IT WOULD BE USELESS.
I SAID I DON'T CARE.
BASTARDS.
BASTARDS!
BASTARD!
FUCKING STUPID POINTLESS BASTARD!

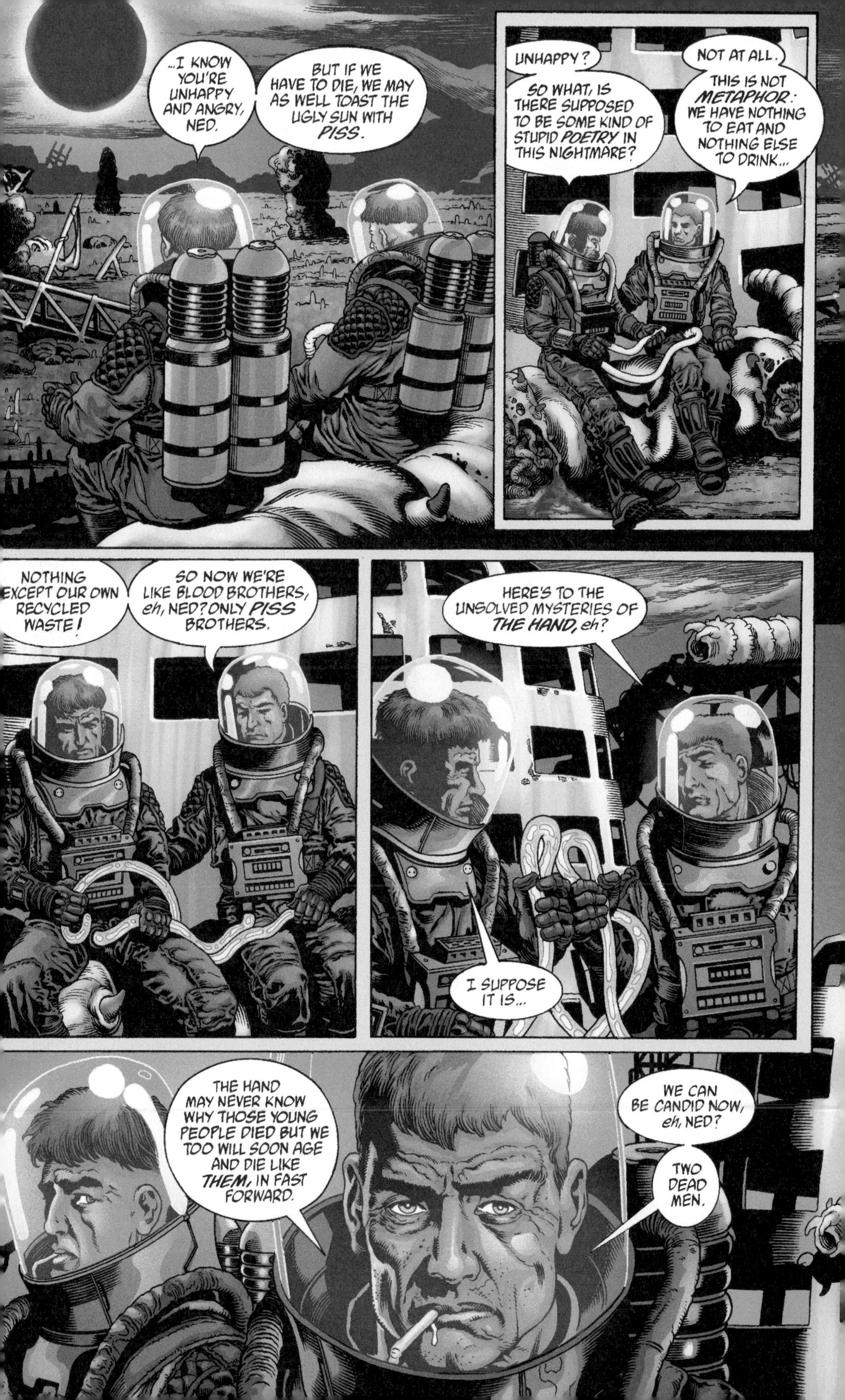
...I KNOW YOU'RE UNHAPPY AND ANGRY, NED.
BUT IF WE HAVE TO DIE, WE MAY AS WELL TOAST THE UGLY SUN WITH PISS.
UNHAPPY?
SO WHAT, IS THERE SUPPOSED TO BE SOME KIND OF STUPID POETRY IN THIS NIGHTMARE?
NOT AT ALL.
THIS IS NOT METAPHOR: WE HAVE NOTHING TO EAT AND NOTHING ELSE TO DRINK...
NOTHING EXCEPT OUR OWN RECYCLED WASTE!
SO NOW WE'RE LIKE BLOOD BROTHERS, eh, NED? ONLY PISS BROTHERS.
HERE'S TO THE UNSOLVED MYSTERIES OF THE HAND, eh?
I SUPPOSE IT IS...
THE HAND MAY NEVER KNOW WHY THOSE YOUNG PEOPLE DIED BUT WE TOO WILL SOON AGE AND DIE LIKE THEM, IN FAST FORWARD.
WE CAN BE CANDID NOW, eh, NED?
TWO DEAD MEN.

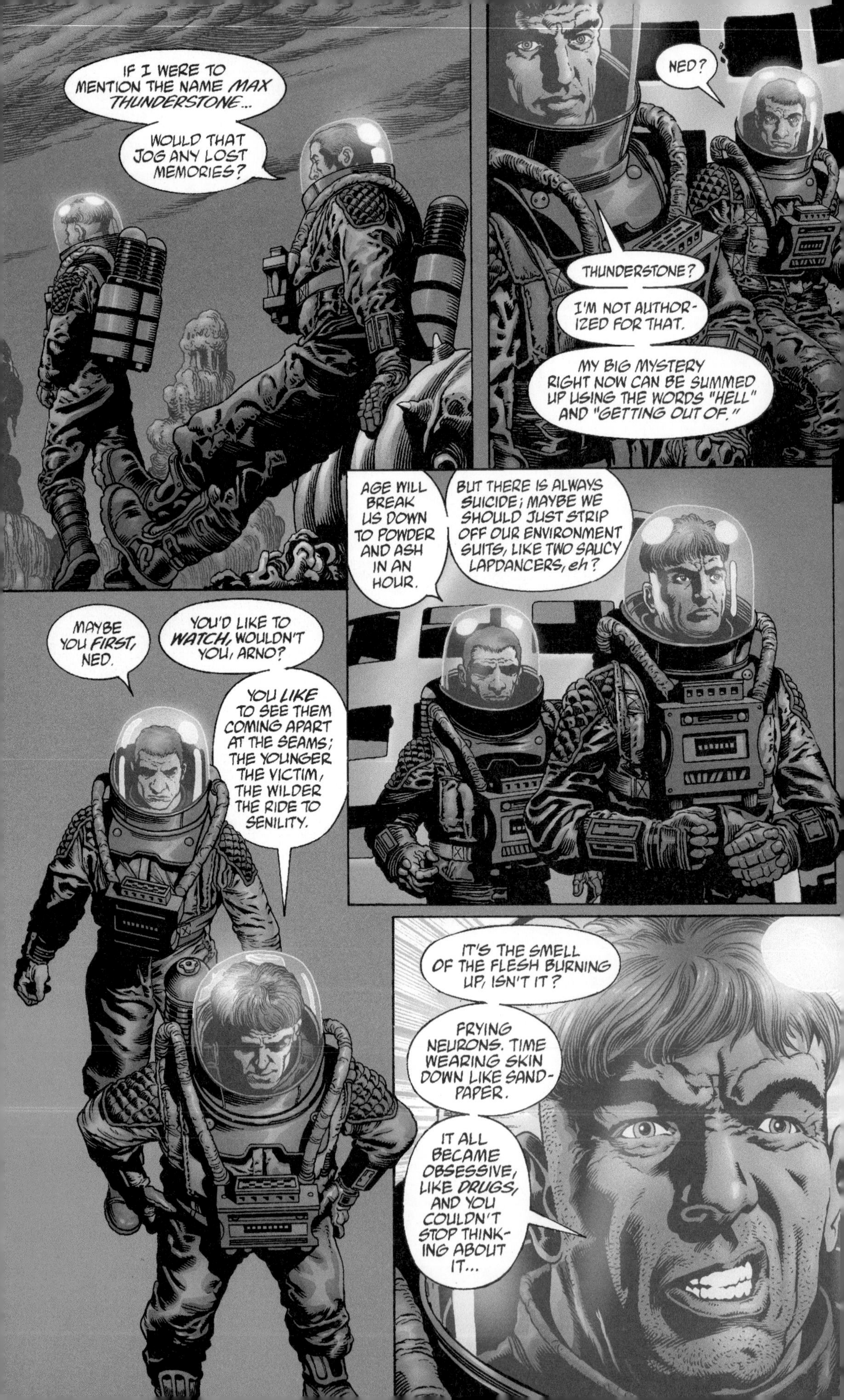

IF I WERE TO MENTION THE NAME *MAX THUNDERSTONE*...
WOULD THAT JOG ANY LOST MEMORIES?
NED?
THUNDERSTONE?
I'M NOT AUTHOR-IZED FOR THAT.
MY BIG MYSTERY RIGHT NOW CAN BE SUMMED UP USING THE WORDS "HELL" AND "GETTING OUT OF."
AGE WILL BREAK US DOWN TO POWDER AND ASH IN AN HOUR.
BUT THERE IS ALWAYS SUICIDE; MAYBE WE SHOULD JUST STRIP OFF OUR ENVIRONMENT SUITS, LIKE TWO SAUCY LAPDANCERS, *eh*?
MAYBE YOU *FIRST*, NED.
YOU'D LIKE TO *WATCH*, WOULDN'T YOU, ARNO?
YOU *LIKE* TO SEE THEM COMING APART AT THE SEAMS; THE YOUNGER THE VICTIM, THE WILDER THE RIDE TO SENILITY.
IT'S THE SMELL OF THE FLESH BURNING UP, ISN'T IT?
FRYING NEURONS. TIME WEARING SKIN DOWN LIKE SAND-PAPER.
IT ALL BECAME OBSESSIVE, LIKE *DRUGS*, AND YOU COULDN'T STOP THINK-ING ABOUT IT...

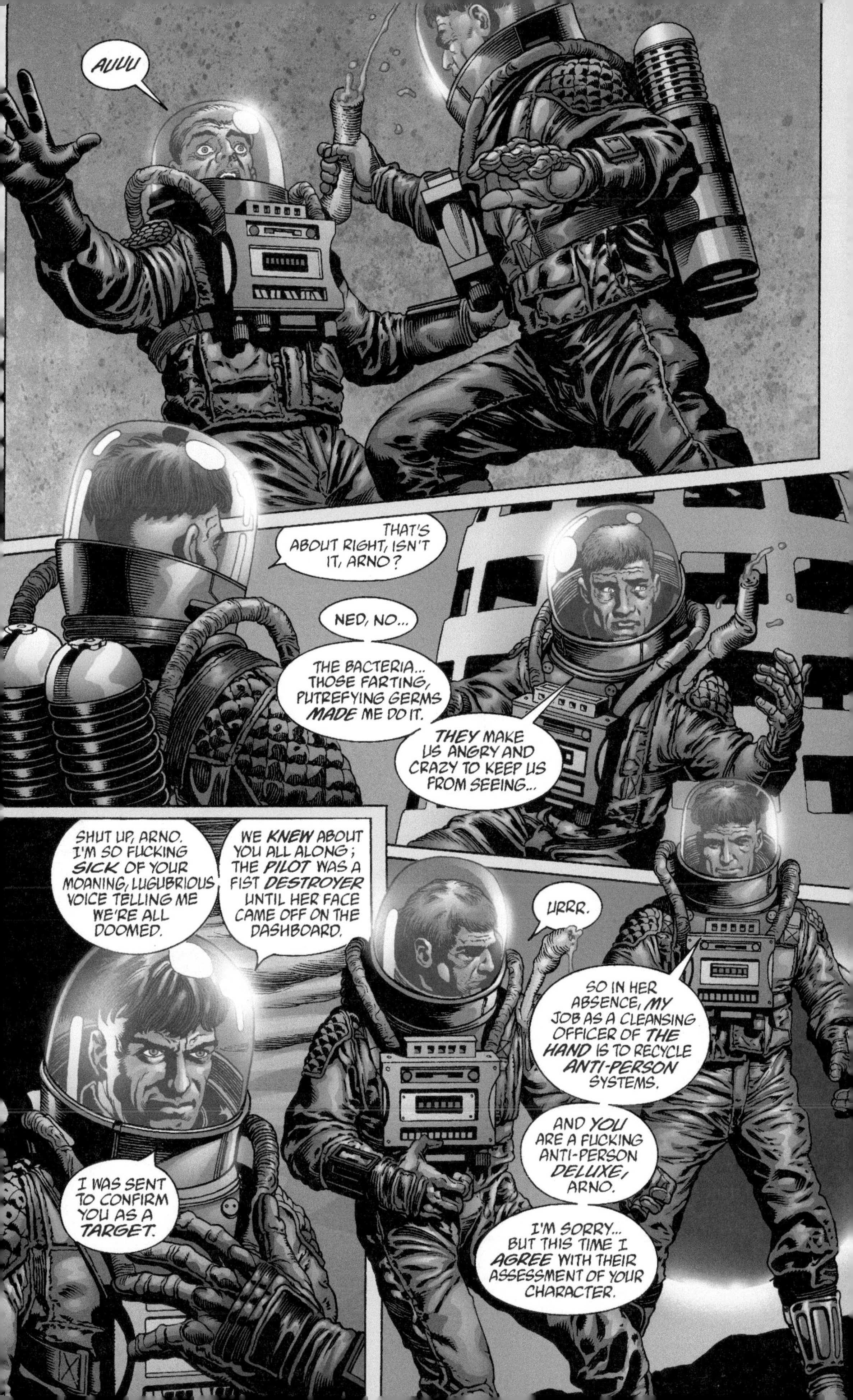
AUUU
THAT'S ABOUT RIGHT, ISN'T IT, ARNO?
NED, NO...
THE BACTERIA... THOSE FARTING, PUTREFYING GERMS MADE ME DO IT.
THEY MAKE US ANGRY AND CRAZY TO KEEP US FROM SEEING...
SHUT UP, ARNO. I'M SO FUCKING SICK OF YOUR MOANING, LUGUBRIOUS VOICE TELLING ME WE'RE ALL DOOMED.
WE KNEW ABOUT YOU ALL ALONG; THE PILOT WAS A FIST DESTROYER UNTIL HER FACE CAME OFF ON THE DASHBOARD.
URRR.
SO IN HER ABSENCE, MY JOB AS A CLEANSING OFFICER OF THE HAND IS TO RECYCLE ANTI-PERSON SYSTEMS.
AND YOU ARE A FUCKING ANTI-PERSON DELUXE, ARNO.
I WAS SENT TO CONFIRM YOU AS A TARGET.
I'M SORRY... BUT THIS TIME I AGREE WITH THEIR ASSESSMENT OF YOUR CHARACTER.

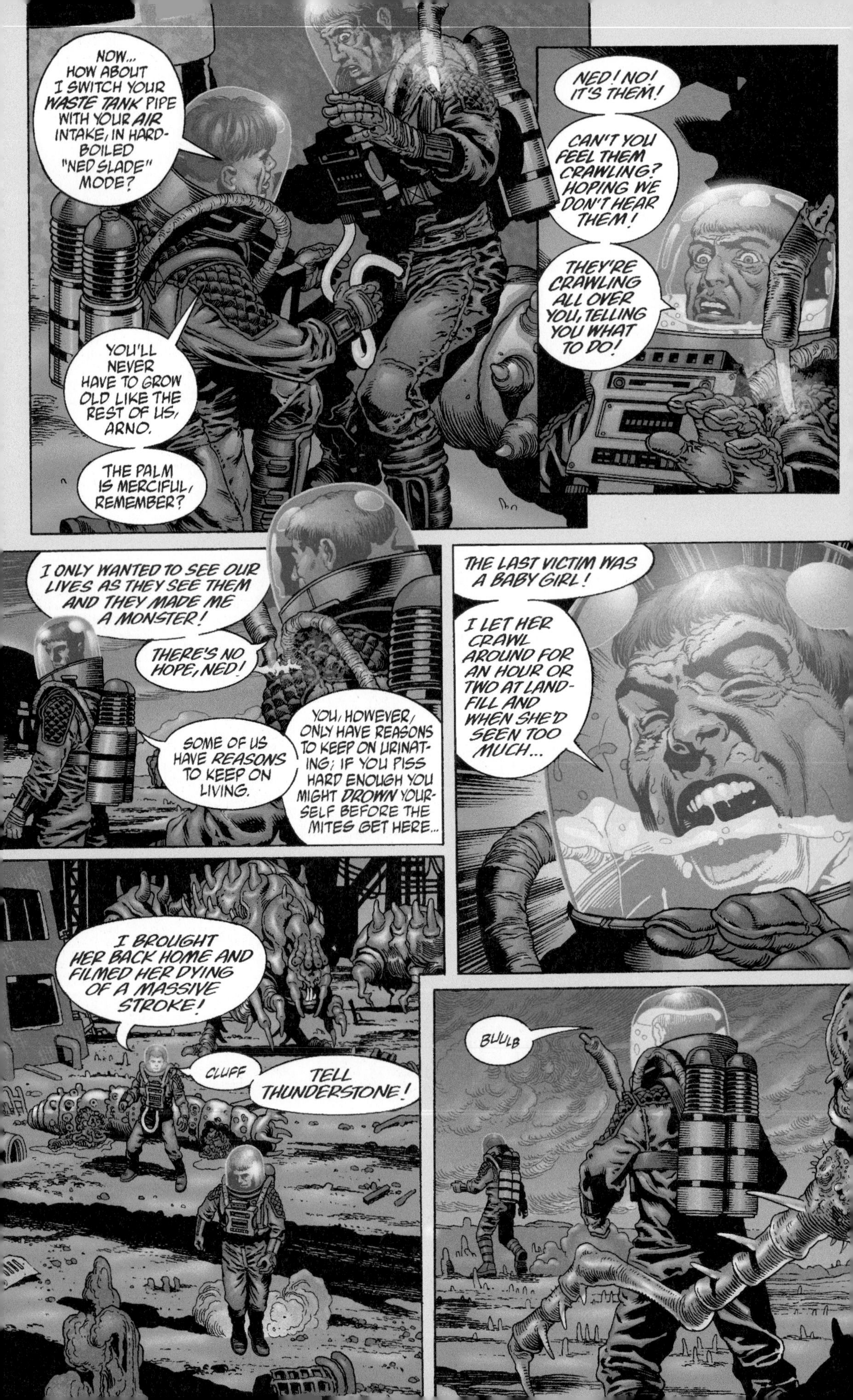
NOW... HOW ABOUT I SWITCH YOUR WASTE TANK PIPE WITH YOUR AIR INTAKE, IN HARD-BOILED "NED SLADE" MODE?
YOU'LL NEVER HAVE TO GROW OLD LIKE THE REST OF US, ARNO.
THE PALM IS MERCIFUL, REMEMBER?
NED! NO! IT'S THEM!
CAN'T YOU FEEL THEM CRAWLING? HOPING WE DON'T HEAR THEM!
THEY'RE CRAWLING ALL OVER YOU, TELLING YOU WHAT TO DO!
I ONLY WANTED TO SEE OUR LIVES AS THEY SEE THEM AND THEY MADE ME A MONSTER!
THERE'S NO HOPE, NED!
SOME OF US HAVE REASONS TO KEEP ON LIVING.
YOU, HOWEVER, ONLY HAVE REASONS TO KEEP ON URINATING; IF YOU PISS HARD ENOUGH YOU MIGHT DROWN YOURSELF BEFORE THE MITES GET HERE...
THE LAST VICTIM WAS A BABY GIRL!
I LET HER CRAWL AROUND FOR AN HOUR OR TWO AT LANDFILL AND WHEN SHE'D SEEN TOO MUCH...
I BROUGHT HER BACK HOME AND FILMED HER DYING OF A MASSIVE STROKE!
CLUFF
TELL THUNDERSTONE!
BUULB

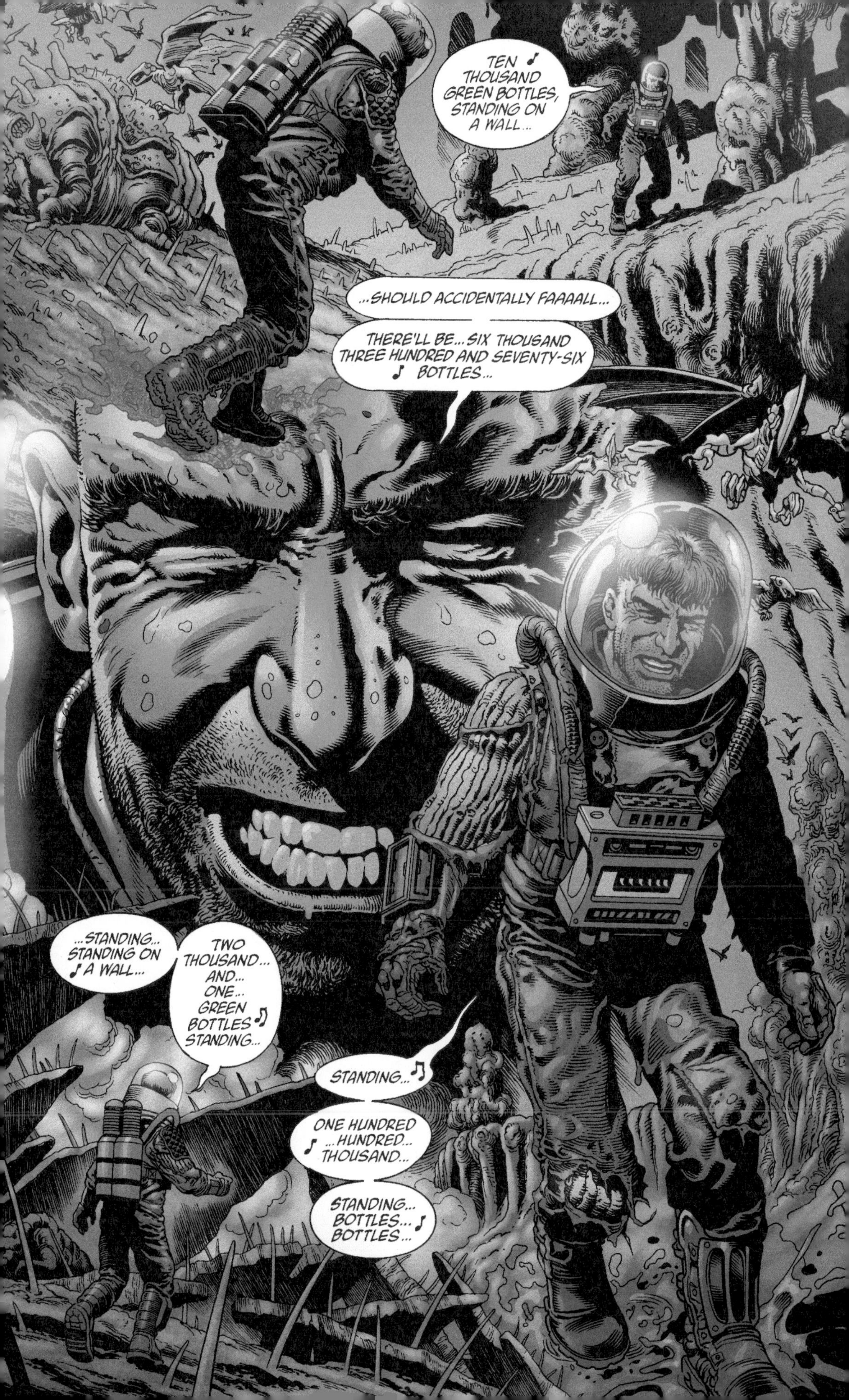
TEN ♪ THOUSAND GREEN BOTTLES, STANDING ON A WALL...
...SHOULD ACCIDENTALLY FAAAALL...
THERE'LL BE...SIX THOUSAND THREE HUNDRED AND SEVENTY-SIX ♪ BOTTLES...
...STANDING... STANDING ON ♪ A WALL...
TWO THOUSAND... AND... ONE... GREEN BOTTLES ♫ STANDING...
STANDING... ♫
ONE HUNDRED ♪ ...HUNDRED... THOUSAND...
STANDING... BOTTLES... ♪ BOTTLES...

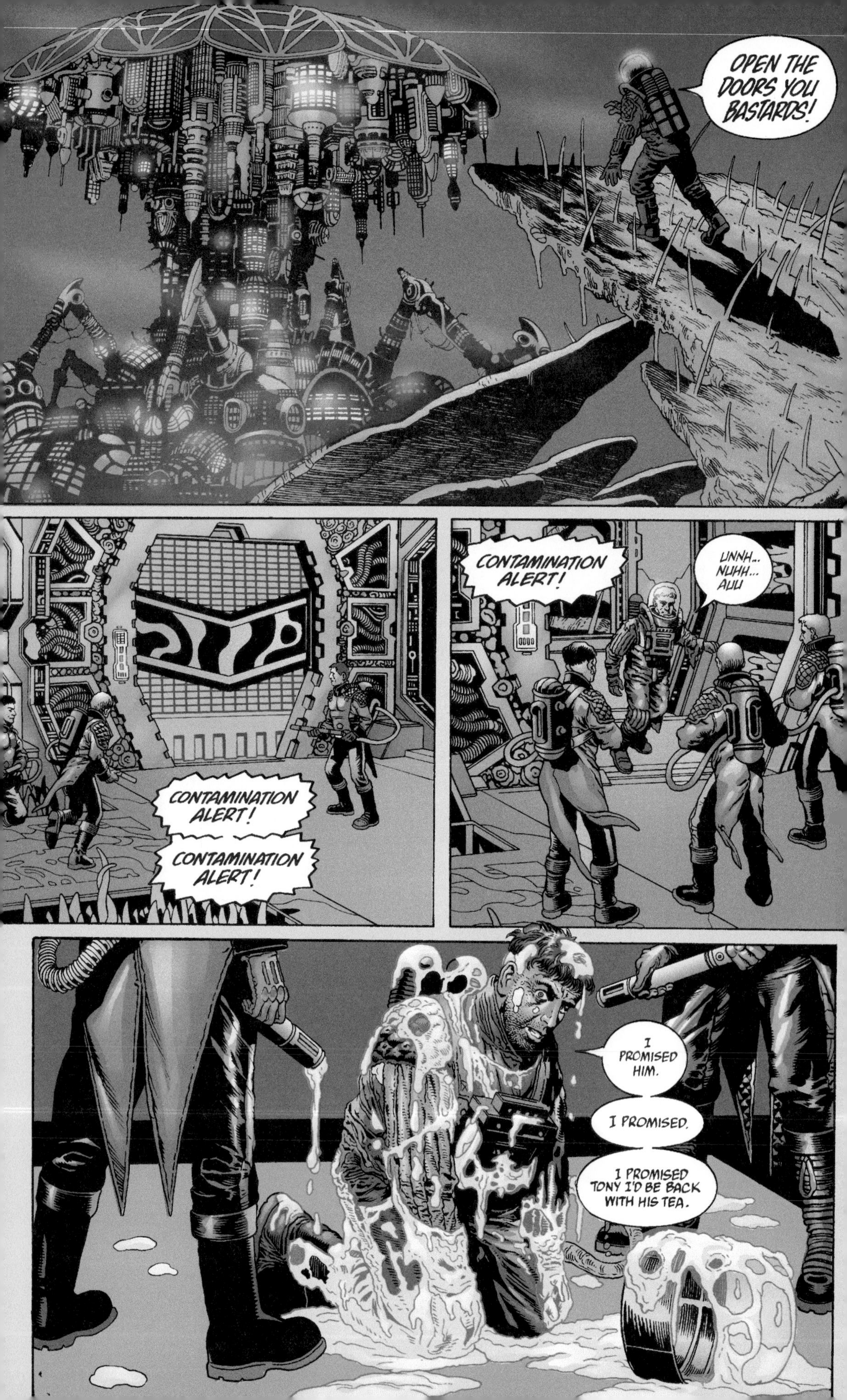

OPEN THE DOORS YOU BASTARDS!
CONTAMINATION ALERT!
CONTAMINATION ALERT!
CONTAMINATION ALERT!
UNNH... NUHH... AUU
I PROMISED HIM.
I PROMISED.
I PROMISED TONY I'D BE BACK WITH HIS TEA.

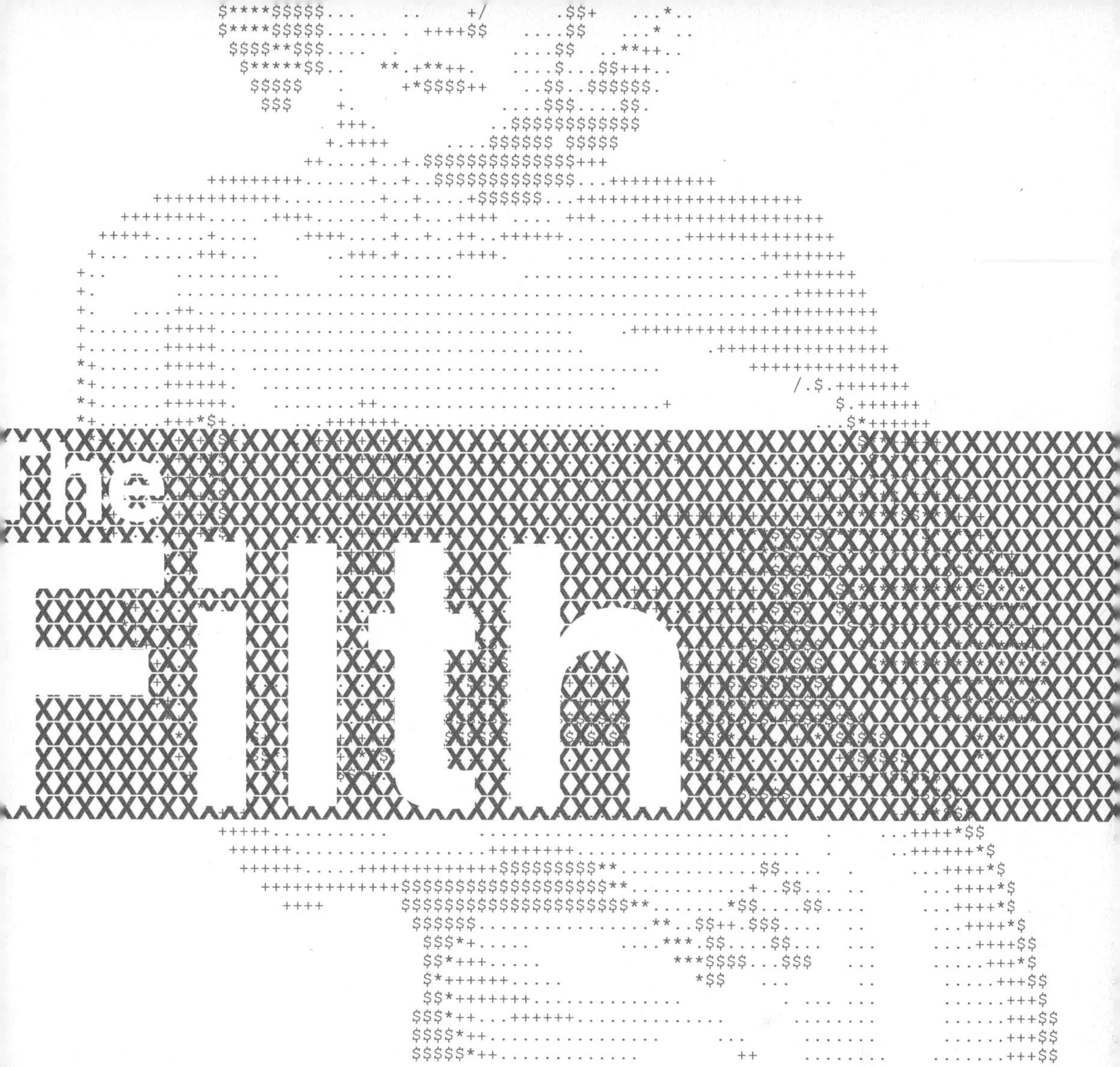
the Filth

05. Pornomancer

22 PAGES

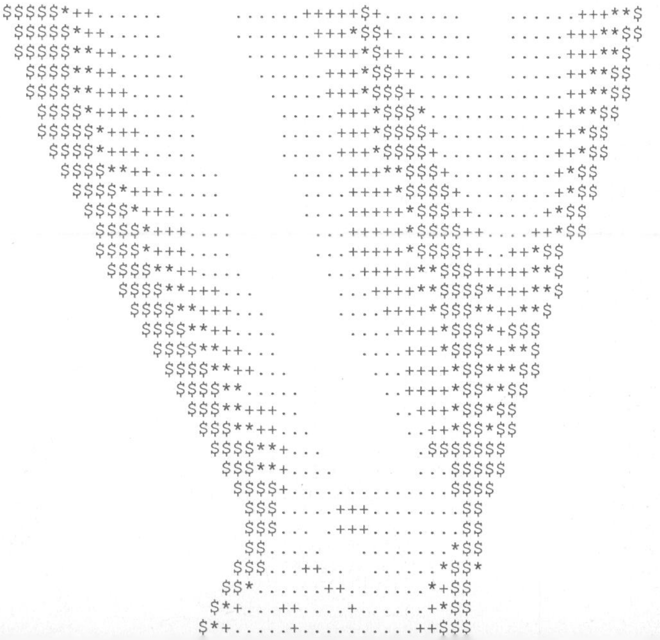

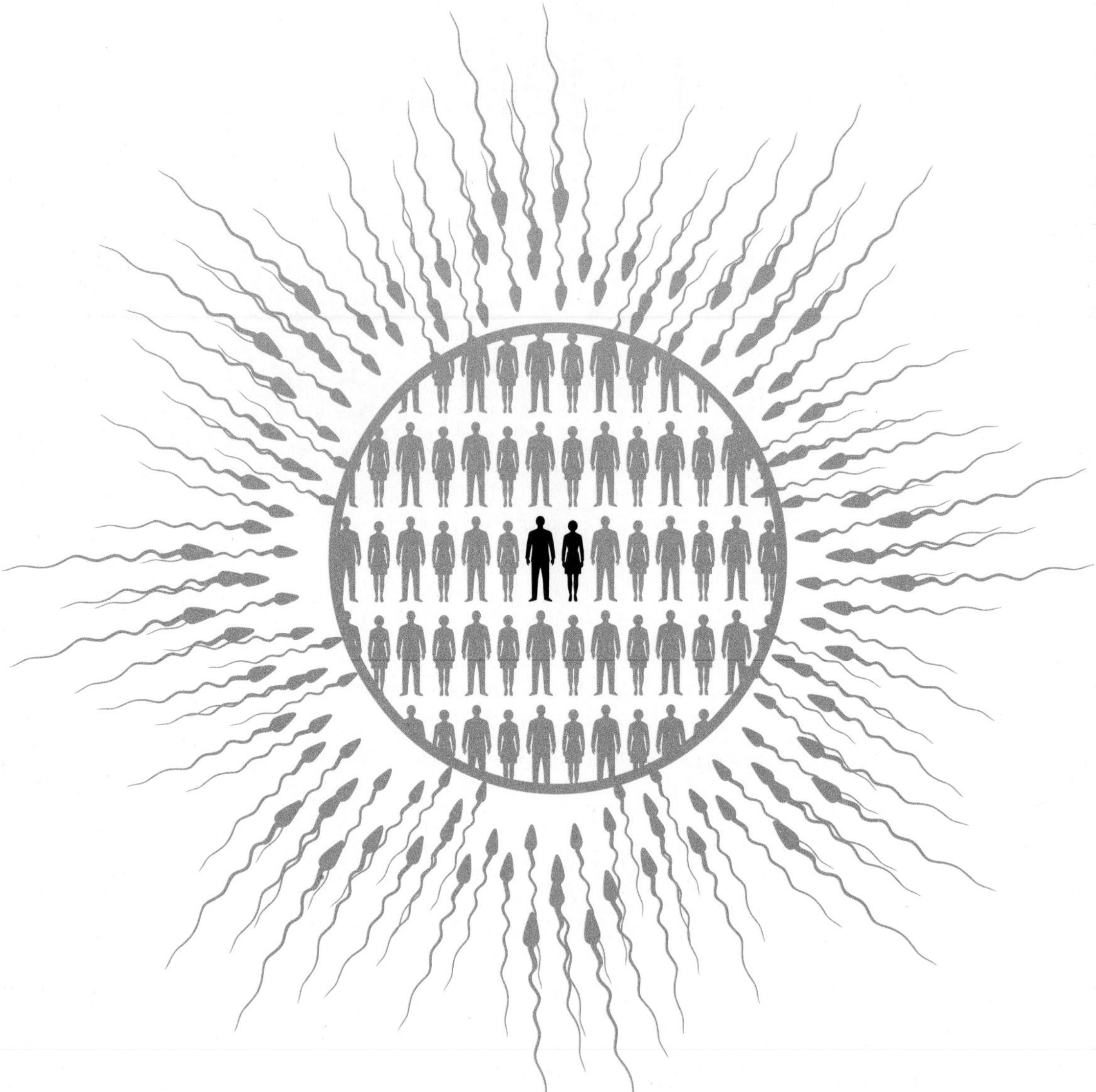

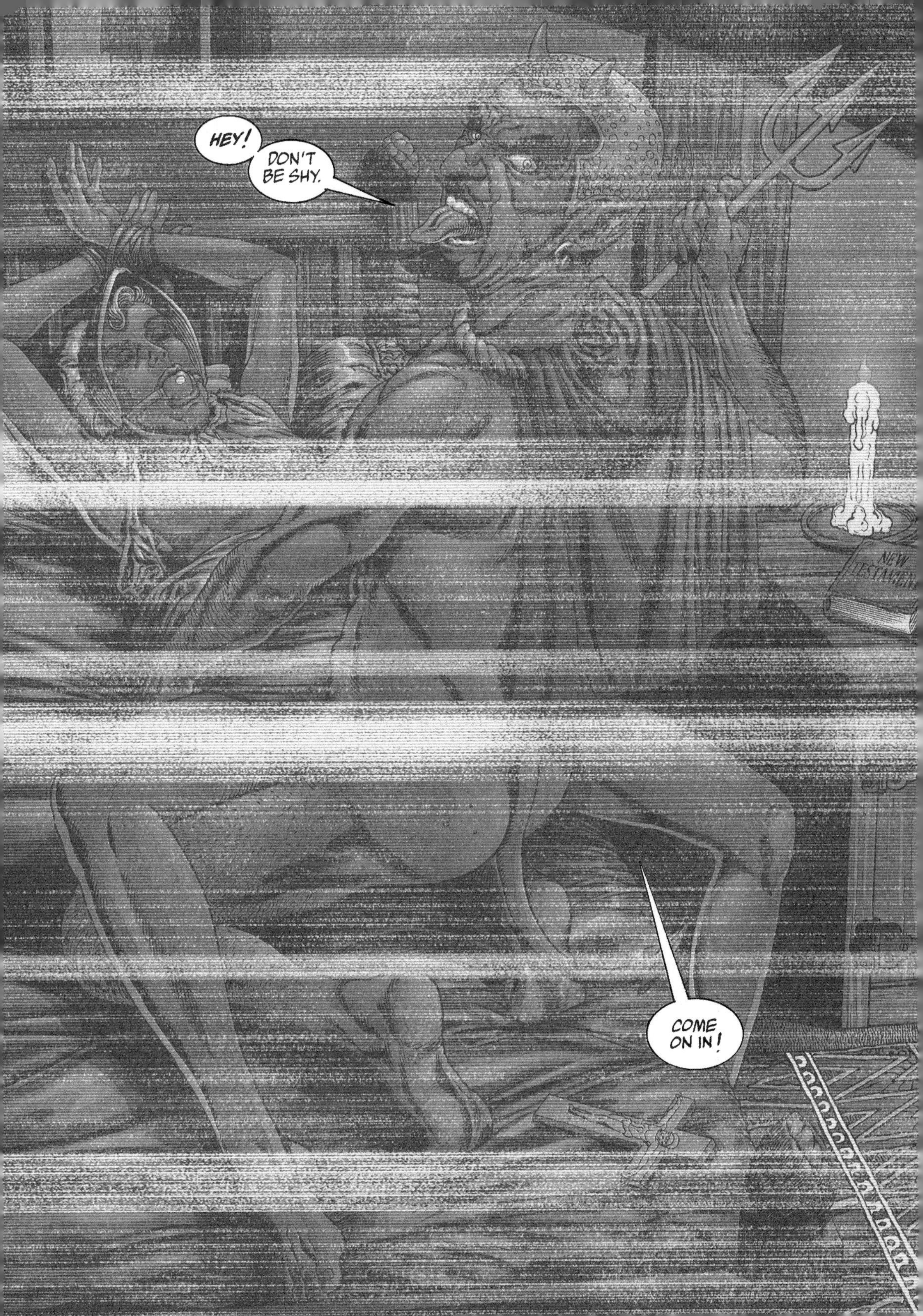
HEY!
DON'T BE SHY.
COME ON IN!

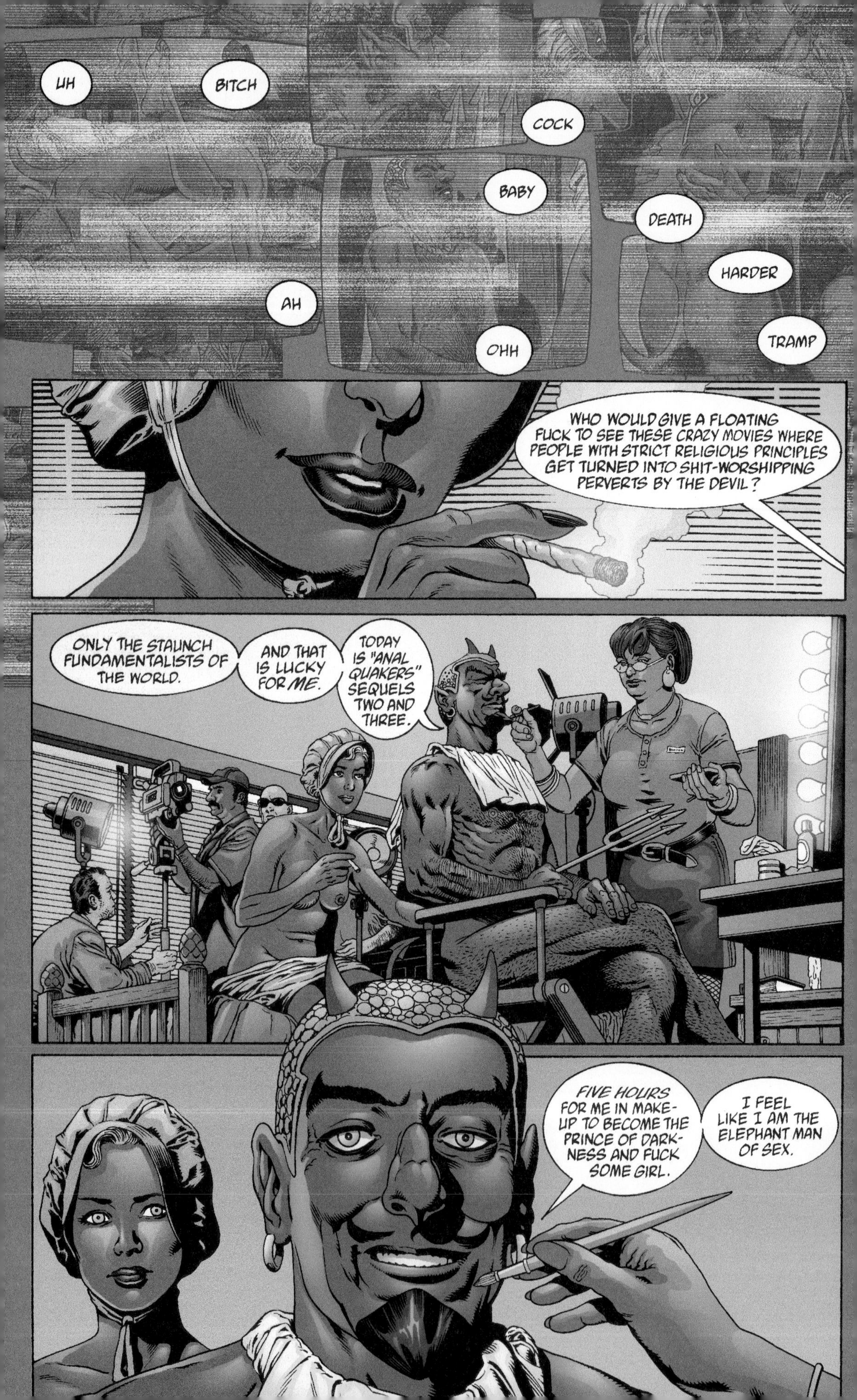
UH
BITCH
COCK
BABY
DEATH
HARDER
AH
OHH
TRAMP
WHO WOULD GIVE A FLOATING FUCK TO SEE THESE CRAZY MOVIES WHERE PEOPLE WITH STRICT RELIGIOUS PRINCIPLES GET TURNED INTO SHIT-WORSHIPPING PERVERTS BY THE DEVIL?
ONLY THE STAUNCH FUNDAMENTALISTS OF THE WORLD.
AND THAT IS LUCKY FOR ME.
TODAY IS "ANAL QUAKERS" SEQUELS TWO AND THREE.
FIVE HOURS FOR ME IN MAKE-UP TO BECOME THE PRINCE OF DARK-NESS AND FUCK SOME GIRL.
I FEEL LIKE I AM THE ELEPHANT MAN OF SEX.

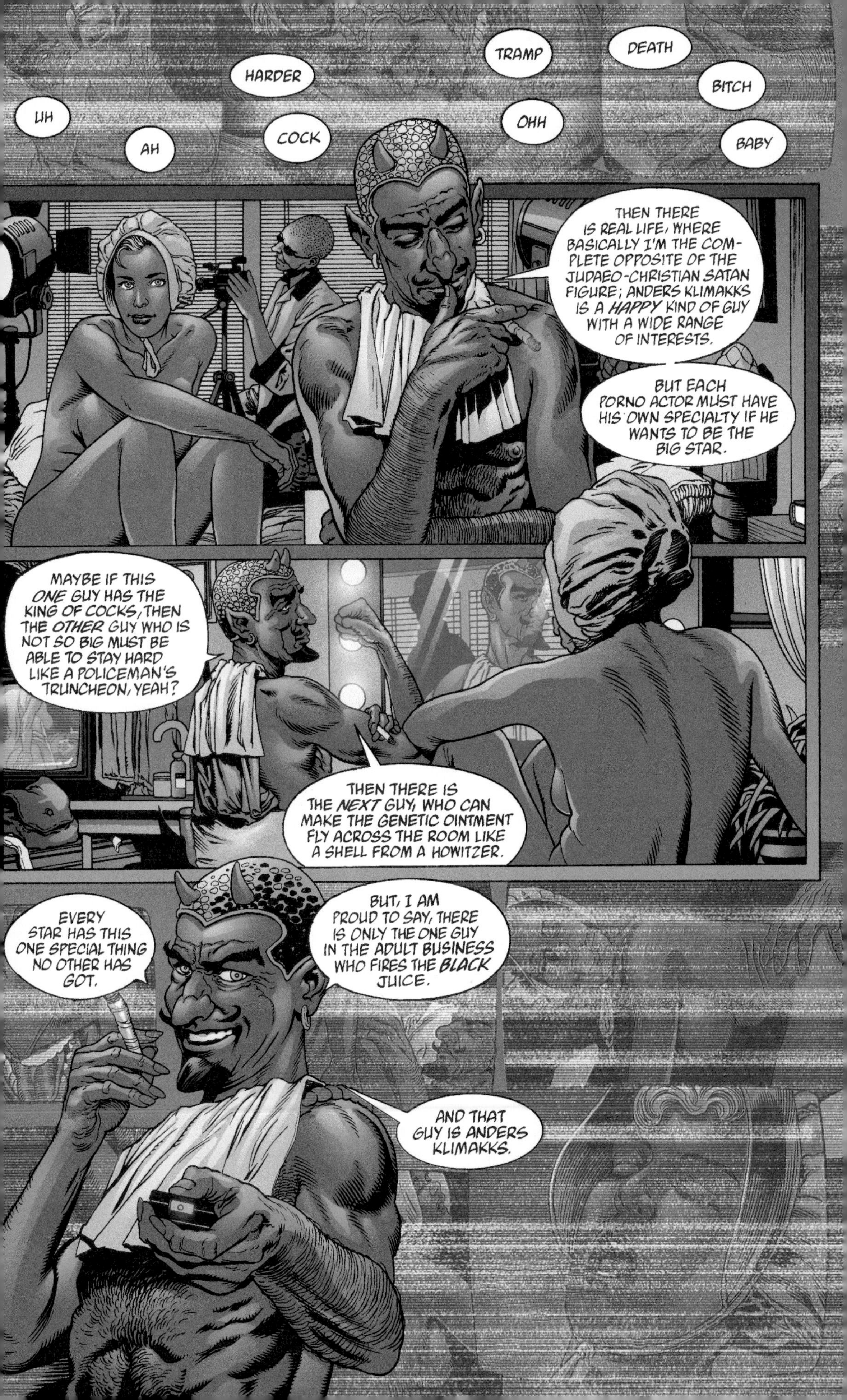
UH
AH
HARDER
COCK
TRAMP
OHH
DEATH
BITCH
BABY
THEN THERE IS REAL LIFE, WHERE BASICALLY I'M THE COMPLETE OPPOSITE OF THE JUDAEO-CHRISTIAN SATAN FIGURE; ANDERS KLIMAKKS IS A *HAPPY* KIND OF GUY WITH A WIDE RANGE OF INTERESTS.
BUT EACH PORNO ACTOR MUST HAVE HIS OWN SPECIALTY IF HE WANTS TO BE THE BIG STAR.
MAYBE IF THIS *ONE* GUY HAS THE KING OF COCKS, THEN THE *OTHER* GUY WHO IS NOT SO BIG MUST BE ABLE TO STAY HARD LIKE A POLICEMAN'S TRUNCHEON, YEAH?
THEN THERE IS THE *NEXT* GUY, WHO CAN MAKE THE GENETIC OINTMENT FLY ACROSS THE ROOM LIKE A SHELL FROM A HOWITZER.
EVERY STAR HAS THIS ONE SPECIAL THING NO OTHER HAS GOT.
BUT, I AM PROUD TO SAY, THERE IS ONLY THE ONE GUY IN THE ADULT BUSINESS WHO FIRES THE *BLACK* JUICE.
AND THAT GUY IS ANDERS KLIMAKKS.

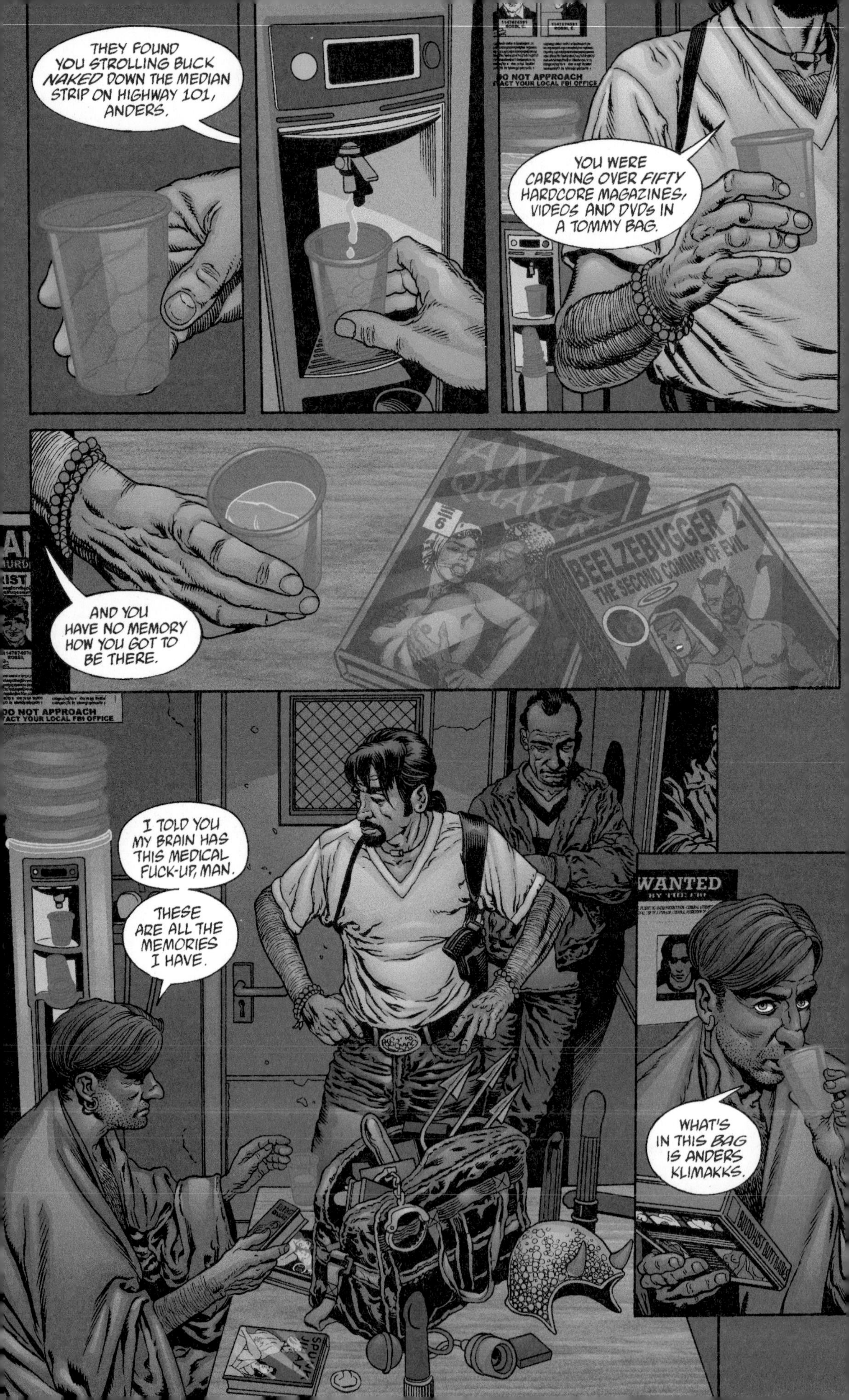
THEY FOUND YOU STROLLING BUCK *NAKED* DOWN THE MEDIAN STRIP ON HIGHWAY 101, ANDERS.
DO NOT APPROACH
YOU WERE CARRYING OVER *FIFTY* HARDCORE MAGAZINES, VIDEOS AND DVDs IN A TOMMY BAG.
AND YOU HAVE NO MEMORY HOW YOU GOT TO BE THERE.
BEELZEBUGGER 2
THE SECOND COMING OF EVIL
DO NOT APPROACH
I TOLD YOU MY BRAIN HAS THIS MEDICAL FUCK-UP, MAN.
THESE ARE ALL THE MEMORIES I HAVE.
WANTED
WHAT'S IN THIS *BAG* IS ANDERS KLIMAKKS.

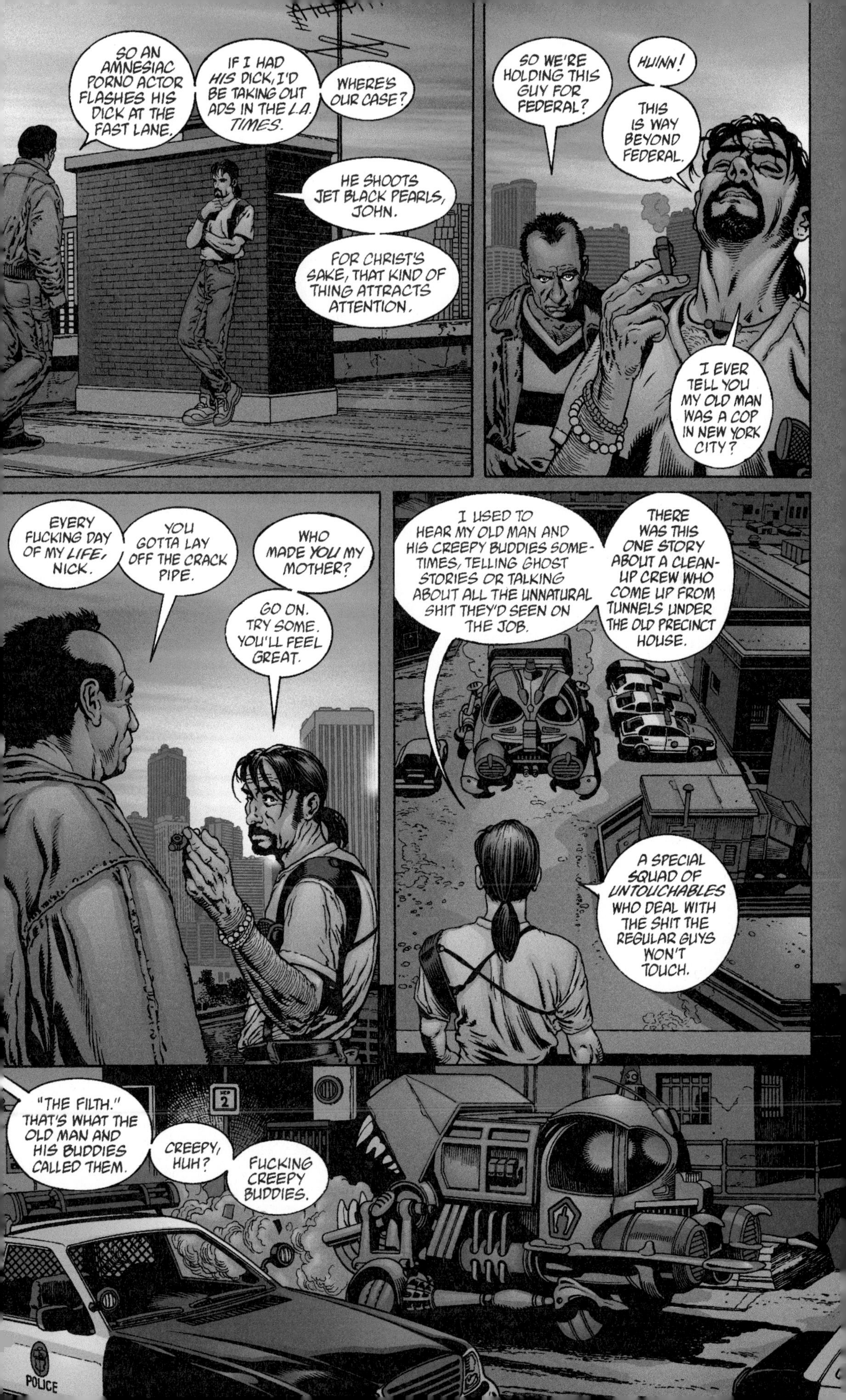
SO AN AMNESIAC PORNO ACTOR FLASHES HIS DICK AT THE FAST LANE.
IF I HAD HIS DICK, I'D BE TAKING OUT ADS IN THE L.A. TIMES.
WHERE'S OUR CASE?
HE SHOOTS JET BLACK PEARLS, JOHN.
FOR CHRIST'S SAKE, THAT KIND OF THING ATTRACTS ATTENTION.
SO WE'RE HOLDING THIS GUY FOR FEDERAL?
HUINN!
THIS IS WAY BEYOND FEDERAL.
I EVER TELL YOU MY OLD MAN WAS A COP IN NEW YORK CITY?
EVERY FUCKING DAY OF MY LIFE, NICK.
YOU GOTTA LAY OFF THE CRACK PIPE.
WHO MADE YOU MY MOTHER?
GO ON. TRY SOME. YOU'LL FEEL GREAT.
I USED TO HEAR MY OLD MAN AND HIS CREEPY BUDDIES SOME-TIMES, TELLING GHOST STORIES OR TALKING ABOUT ALL THE UNNATURAL SHIT THEY'D SEEN ON THE JOB.
THERE WAS THIS ONE STORY ABOUT A CLEAN-UP CREW WHO COME UP FROM TUNNELS UNDER THE OLD PRECINCT HOUSE.
A SPECIAL SQUAD OF UNTOUCHABLES WHO DEAL WITH THE SHIT THE REGULAR GUYS WON'T TOUCH.
"THE FILTH." THAT'S WHAT THE OLD MAN AND HIS BUDDIES CALLED THEM.
CREEPY, HUH?
FUCKING CREEPY BUDDIES.
2
POLICE

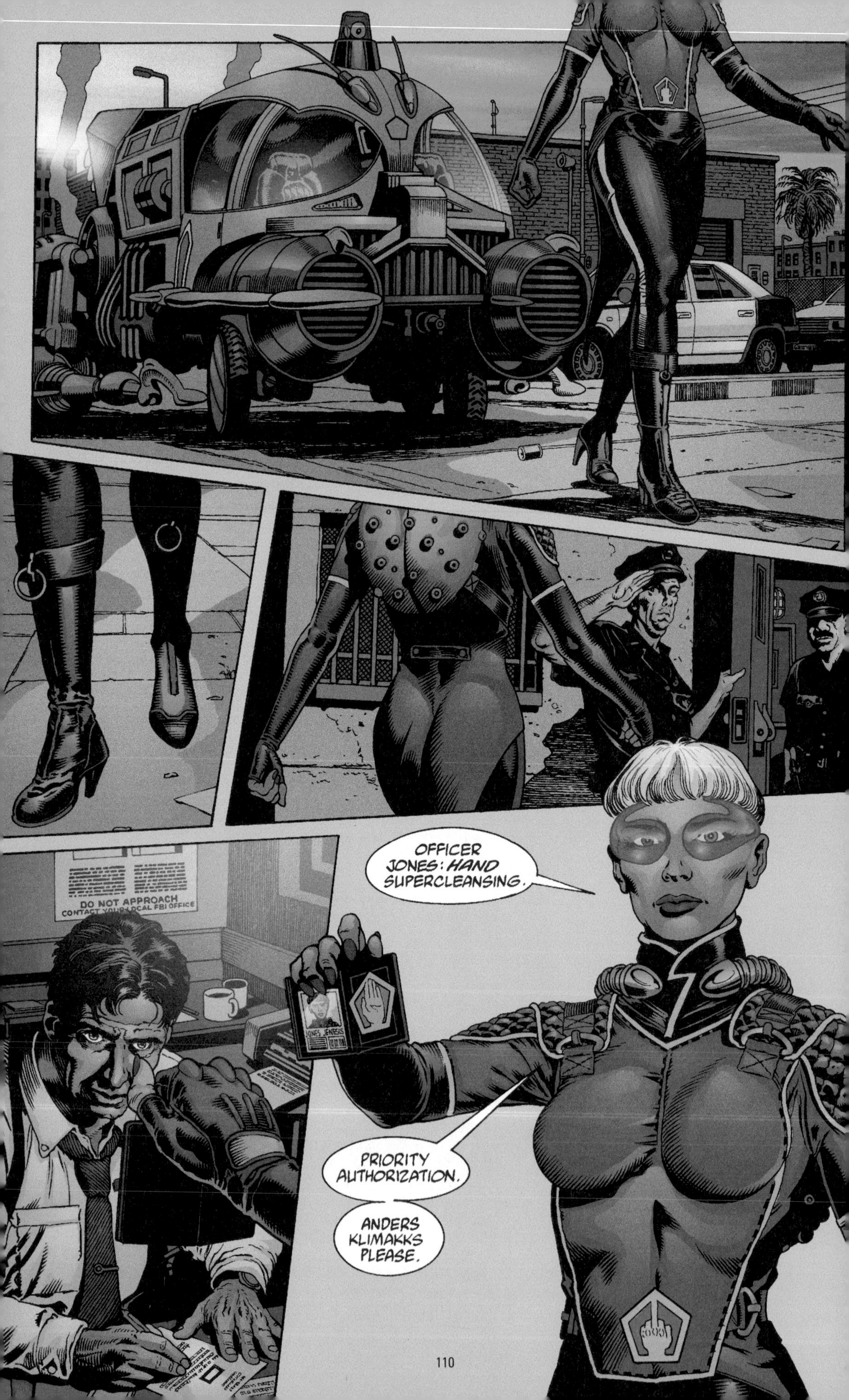
DO NOT APPROACH
CONTACT YOUR LOCAL FBI OFFICE
OFFICER JONES: *HAND* SUPERCLEANSING.
PRIORITY AUTHORIZATION.
ANDERS KLIMAKKS PLEASE.

THERE IS NOTHING MORE I CAN SAY.

HOW ABOUT THE STORY OF *YOU*; YOU'RE A VERY SEXY LADY, THAT'S FROM WHERE I'M SITTING.

JONES, JENESIS

WANTED FOR ARMED ROBBERY NICOLA MARI

MISSING ADELA STEELE

WANTED ON MURDER CHRISTIA

WELL.. I KNOW YOU CAME OUT OF *NOWHERE* FIVE YEARS AGO.

I KNOW YOU HAVE A NOVELTY PENIS WHICH DEFIES MEDICAL ANALYSIS.

OTHERWISE *DON'T* TRY TO FUCK WITH ME, ANDERS; I HAVE *PMS*.

SPERM SPECIMEN.

PLEASE.

SURE.

THIS IS WHAT I DO FOR A LIVING.

JESUS.

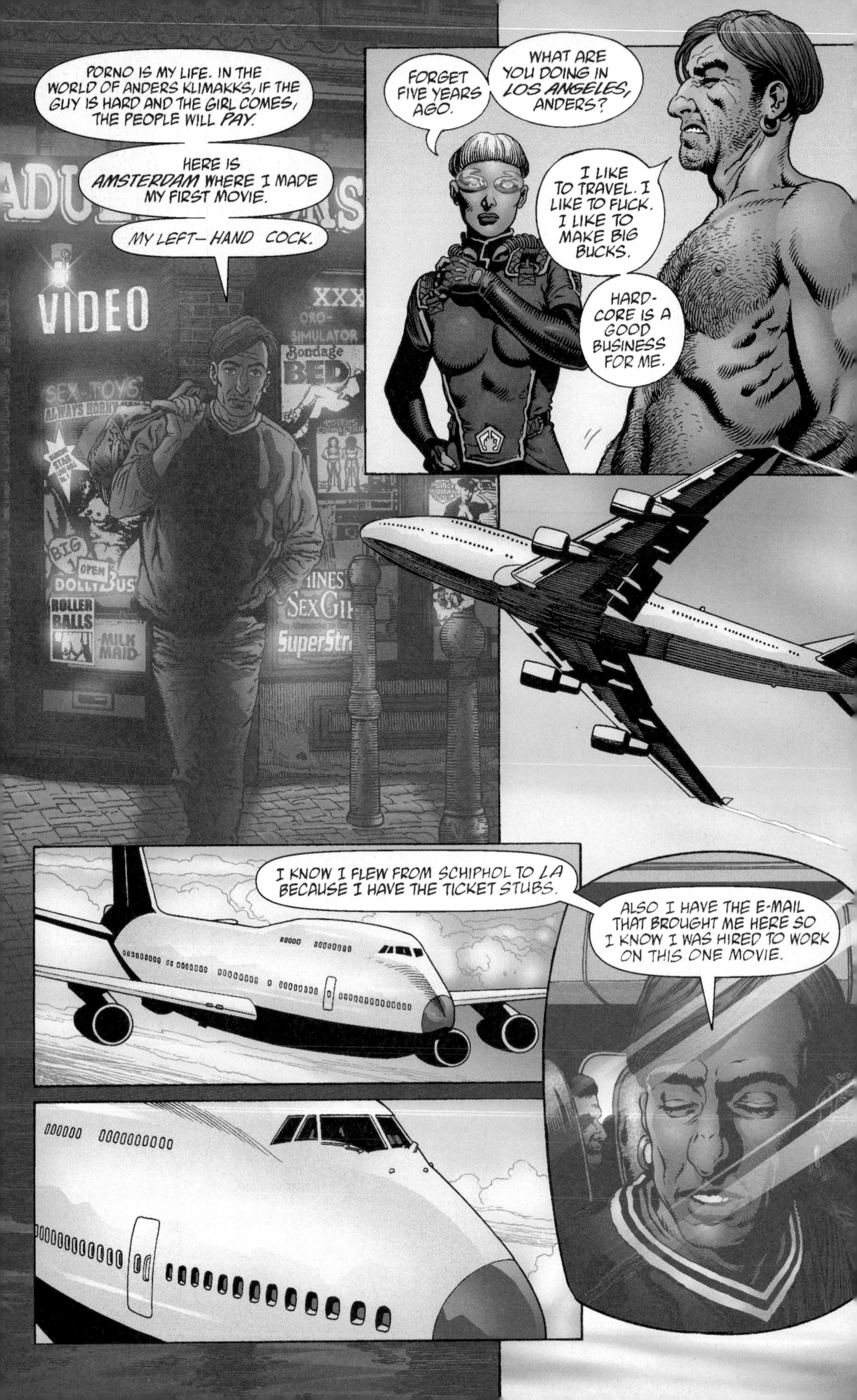
PORNO IS MY LIFE. IN THE WORLD OF ANDERS KLIMAKKS, IF THE GUY IS HARD AND THE GIRL COMES, THE PEOPLE WILL PAY.
HERE IS AMSTERDAM WHERE I MADE MY FIRST MOVIE.
MY LEFT-HAND COCK.
VIDEO
XXX
Bondage BED
SEX-TOYS
ALWAYS HORNY
OPEN
ROLLER BALLS
MILK MAID
FORGET FIVE YEARS AGO.
WHAT ARE YOU DOING IN LOS ANGELES, ANDERS?
I LIKE TO TRAVEL. I LIKE TO FUCK. I LIKE TO MAKE BIG BUCKS.
HARD-CORE IS A GOOD BUSINESS FOR ME.
I KNOW I FLEW FROM SCHIPHOL TO LA BECAUSE I HAVE THE TICKET STUBS.
ALSO I HAVE THE E-MAIL THAT BROUGHT ME HERE SO I KNOW I WAS HIRED TO WORK ON THIS ONE MOVIE.

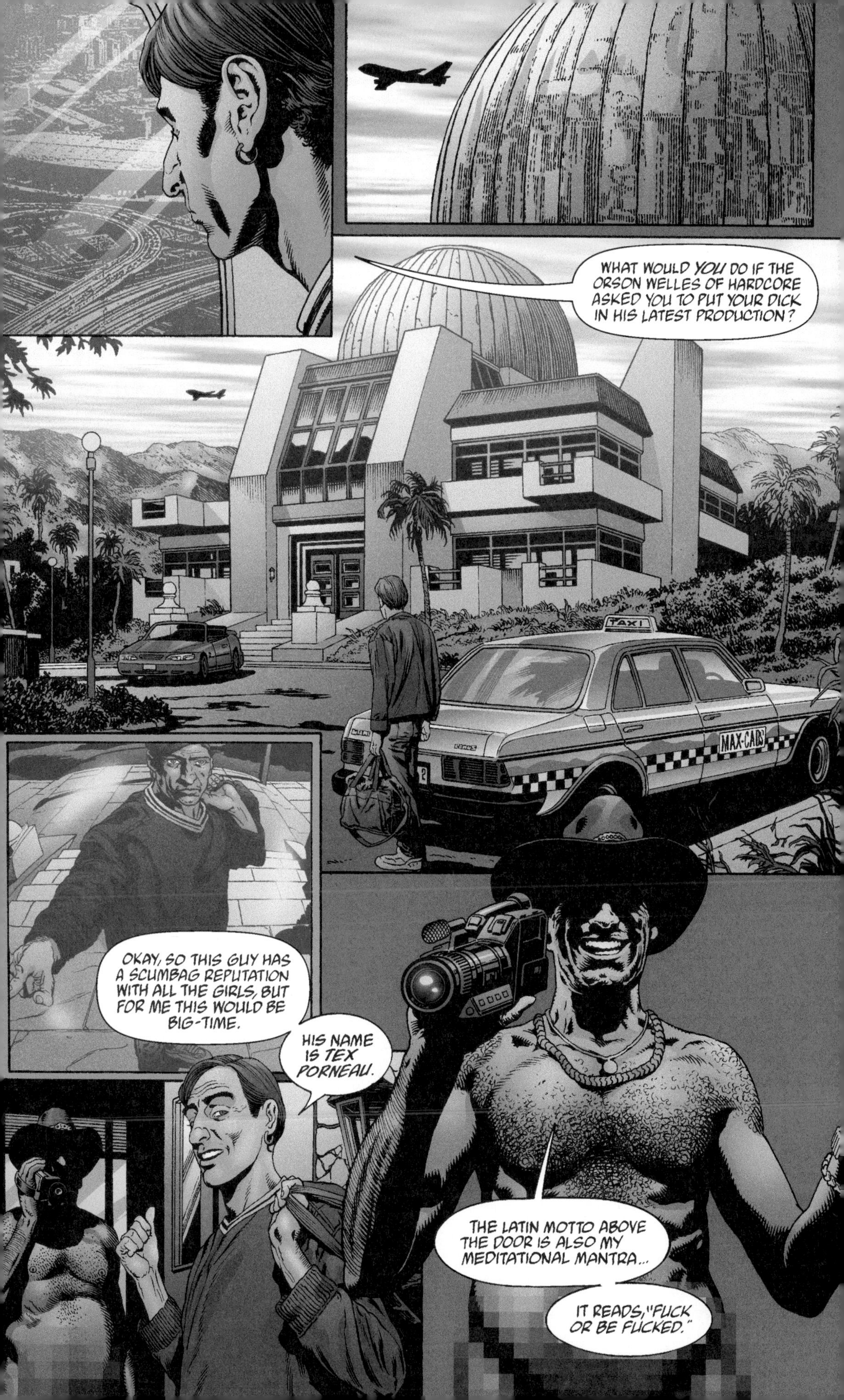
WHAT WOULD YOU DO IF THE ORSON WELLES OF HARDCORE ASKED YOU TO PUT YOUR DICK IN HIS LATEST PRODUCTION?
TAXI
MAX-CABS
OKAY, SO THIS GUY HAS A SCUMBAG REPUTATION WITH ALL THE GIRLS, BUT FOR ME THIS WOULD BE BIG-TIME.
HIS NAME IS TEX PORNEAU.
THE LATIN MOTTO ABOVE THE DOOR IS ALSO MY MEDITATIONAL MANTRA...
IT READS, "FUCK OR BE FUCKED."

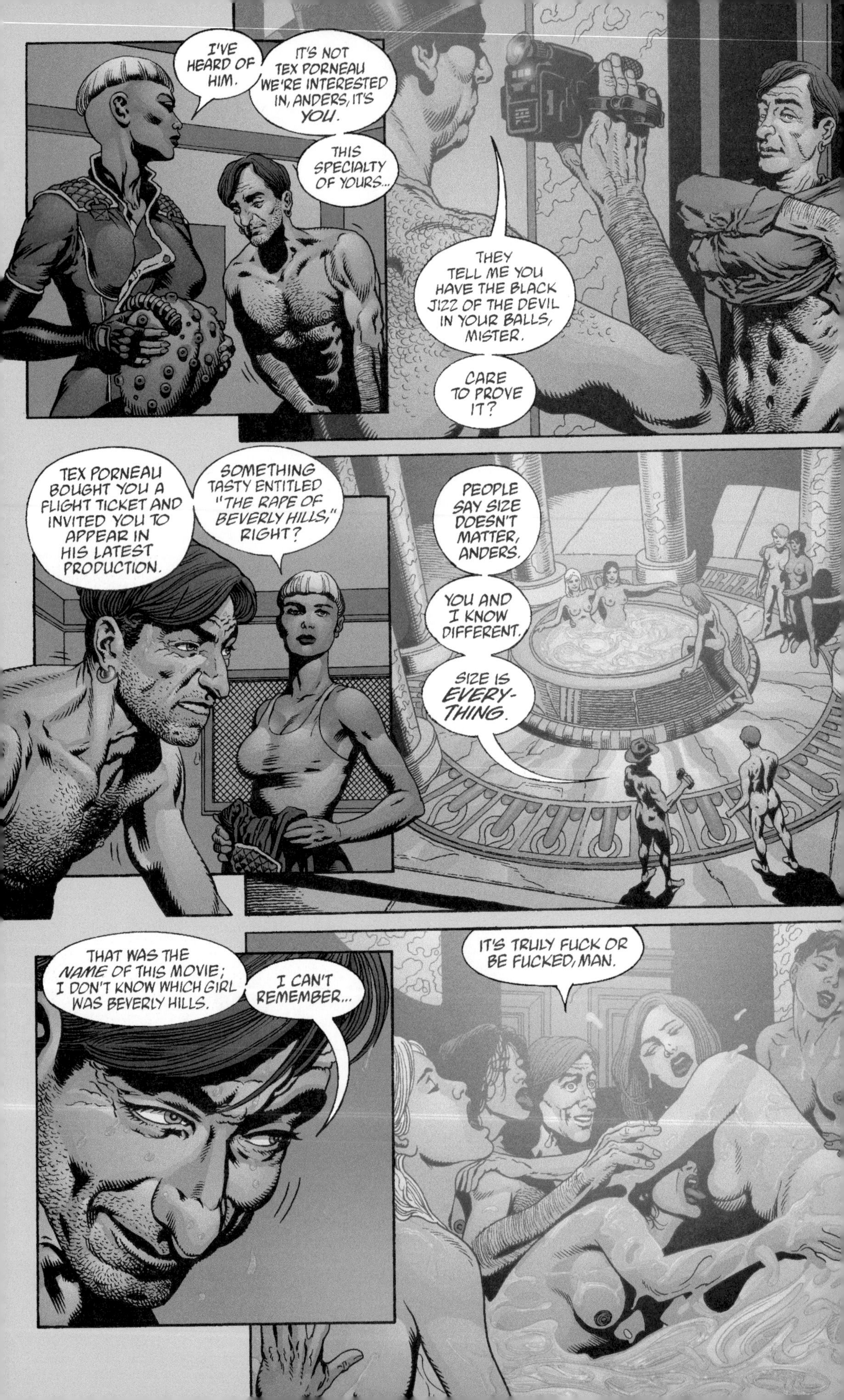

I'VE HEARD OF HIM.
IT'S NOT TEX PORNEAU WE'RE INTERESTED IN, ANDERS, IT'S *YOU*.
THIS SPECIALTY OF YOURS...
THEY TELL ME YOU HAVE THE BLACK JIZZ OF THE DEVIL IN YOUR BALLS, MISTER.
CARE TO PROVE IT?
TEX PORNEAU BOUGHT YOU A FLIGHT TICKET AND INVITED YOU TO APPEAR IN HIS LATEST PRODUCTION.
SOMETHING TASTY ENTITLED *"THE RAPE OF BEVERLY HILLS,"* RIGHT?
PEOPLE SAY SIZE DOESN'T MATTER, ANDERS.
YOU AND I KNOW DIFFERENT.
SIZE IS *EVERY-THING*.
THAT WAS THE *NAME* OF THIS MOVIE; I DON'T KNOW WHICH GIRL WAS BEVERLY HILLS.
I CAN'T REMEMBER...
IT'S TRULY FUCK OR BE FUCKED, MAN.

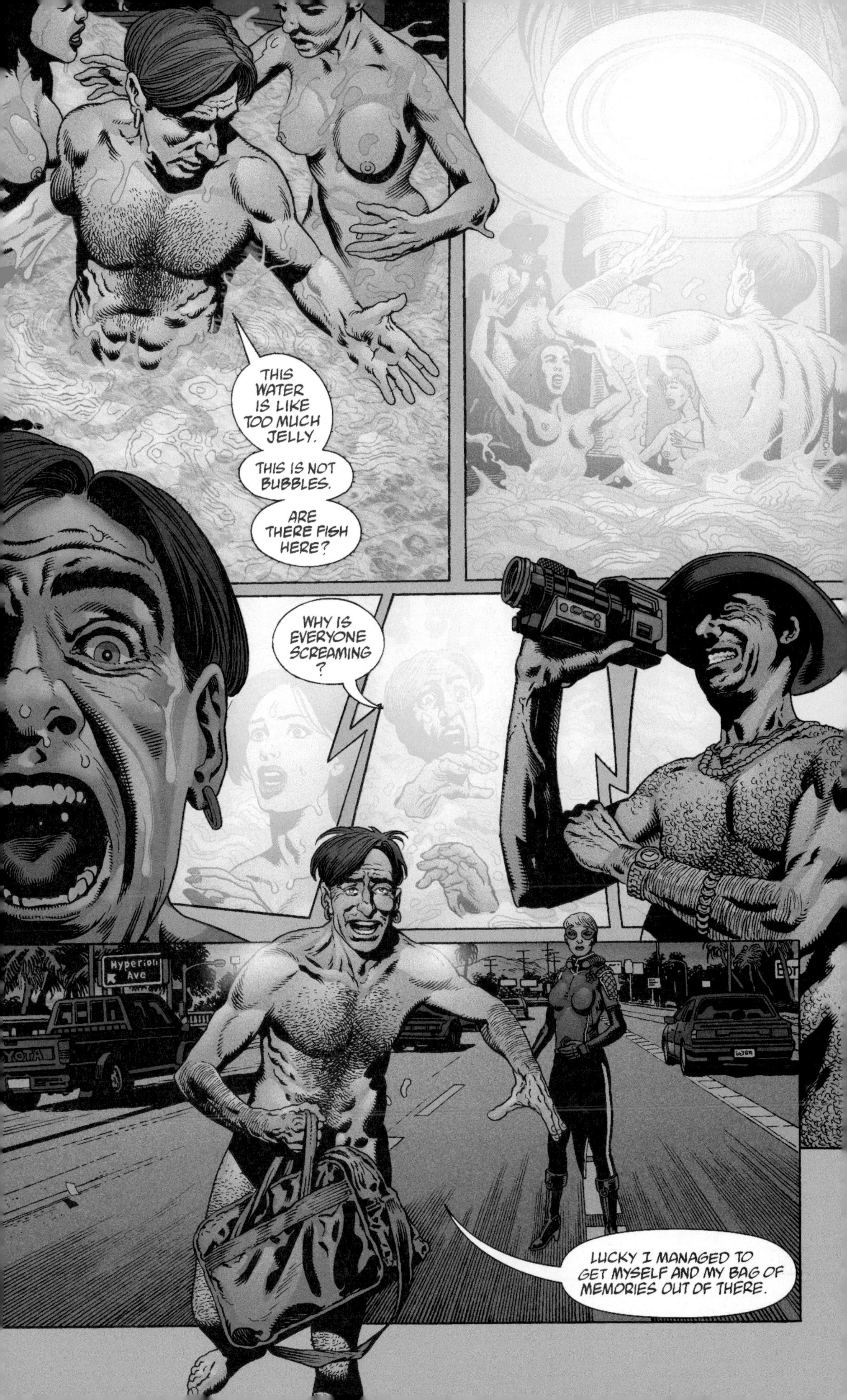

THIS WATER IS LIKE TOO MUCH JELLY.
THIS IS NOT BUBBLES.
ARE THERE FISH HERE?
WHY IS EVERYONE SCREAMING?
Hyperion Ave
LUCKY I MANAGED TO GET MYSELF AND MY BAG OF MEMORIES OUT OF THERE.

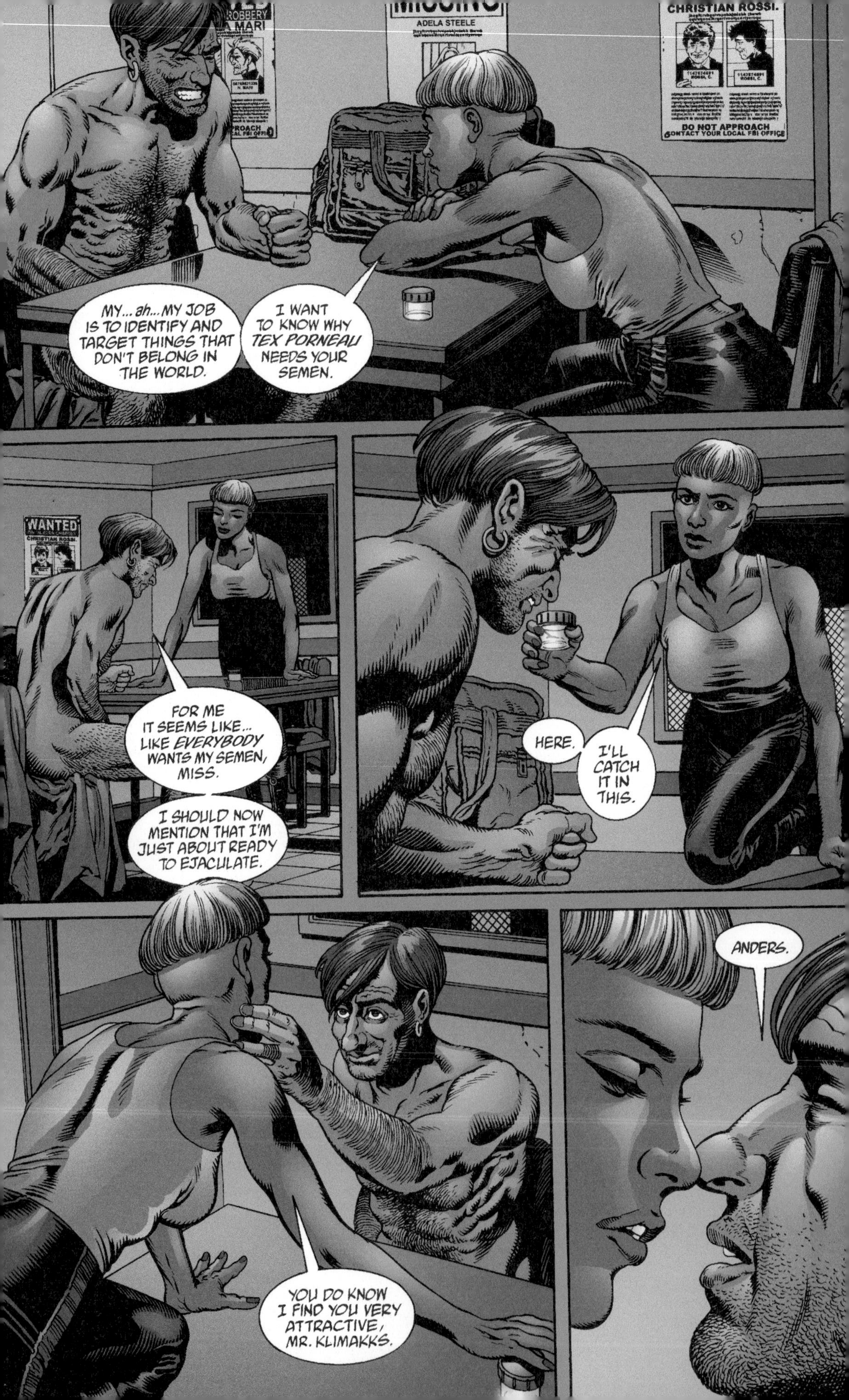

ADELA STEELE
CHRISTIAN ROSSI.
DO NOT APPROACH
CONTACT YOUR LOCAL FBI OFFICE
MY... ah... MY JOB IS TO IDENTIFY AND TARGET THINGS THAT DON'T BELONG IN THE WORLD.
I WANT TO KNOW WHY TEX PORNEAU NEEDS YOUR SEMEN.
WANTED
CHRISTIAN ROSSI
FOR ME IT SEEMS LIKE... LIKE EVERYBODY WANTS MY SEMEN, MISS.
I SHOULD NOW MENTION THAT I'M JUST ABOUT READY TO EJACULATE.
HERE.
I'LL CATCH IT IN THIS.
YOU DO KNOW I FIND YOU VERY ATTRACTIVE, MR. KLIMAKKS.
ANDERS.

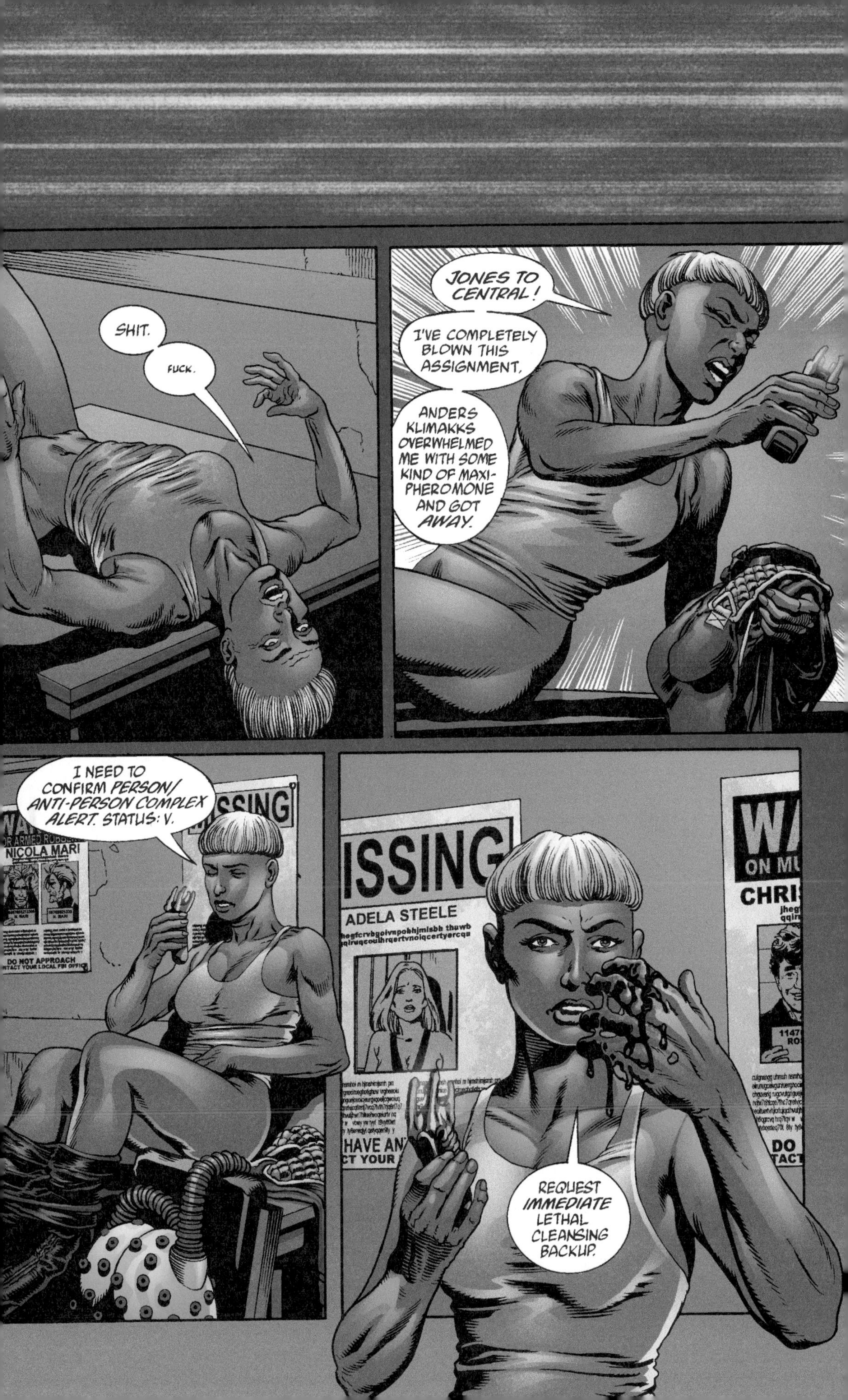
SHIT.
FUCK.
JONES TO CENTRAL!
I'VE COMPLETELY BLOWN THIS ASSIGNMENT.
ANDERS KLIMAKKS OVERWHELMED ME WITH SOME KIND OF MAXI-PHEROMONE AND GOT AWAY.
I NEED TO CONFIRM PERSON/ ANTI-PERSON COMPLEX ALERT. STATUS: V.
MISSING
NICOLA MARI
DO NOT APPROACH
MISSING
ADELA STEELE
HAVE ANY
WA
ON MU
CHRIS
DO
REQUEST IMMEDIATE LETHAL CLEANSING BACKUP.

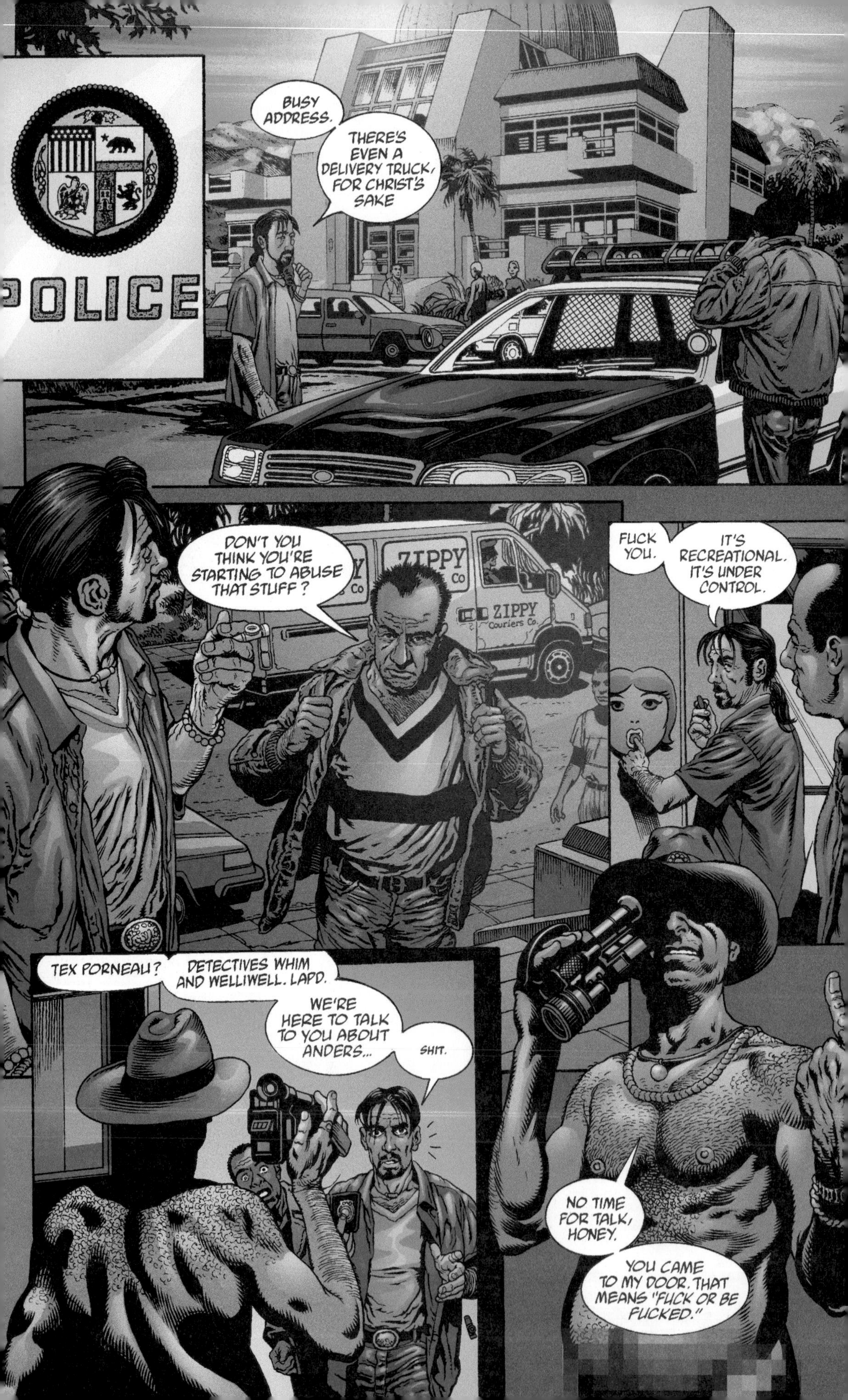
POLICE
BUSY ADDRESS.
THERE'S EVEN A DELIVERY TRUCK, FOR CHRIST'S SAKE
DON'T YOU THINK YOU'RE STARTING TO ABUSE THAT STUFF ?
ZIPPY Couriers Co.
FUCK YOU.
IT'S RECREATIONAL. IT'S UNDER CONTROL.
TEX PORNEAU?
DETECTIVES WHIM AND WELLIWELL. LAPD.
WE'RE HERE TO TALK TO YOU ABOUT ANDERS...
SHIT.
NO TIME FOR TALK, HONEY.
YOU CAME TO MY DOOR. THAT MEANS "FUCK OR BE FUCKED."

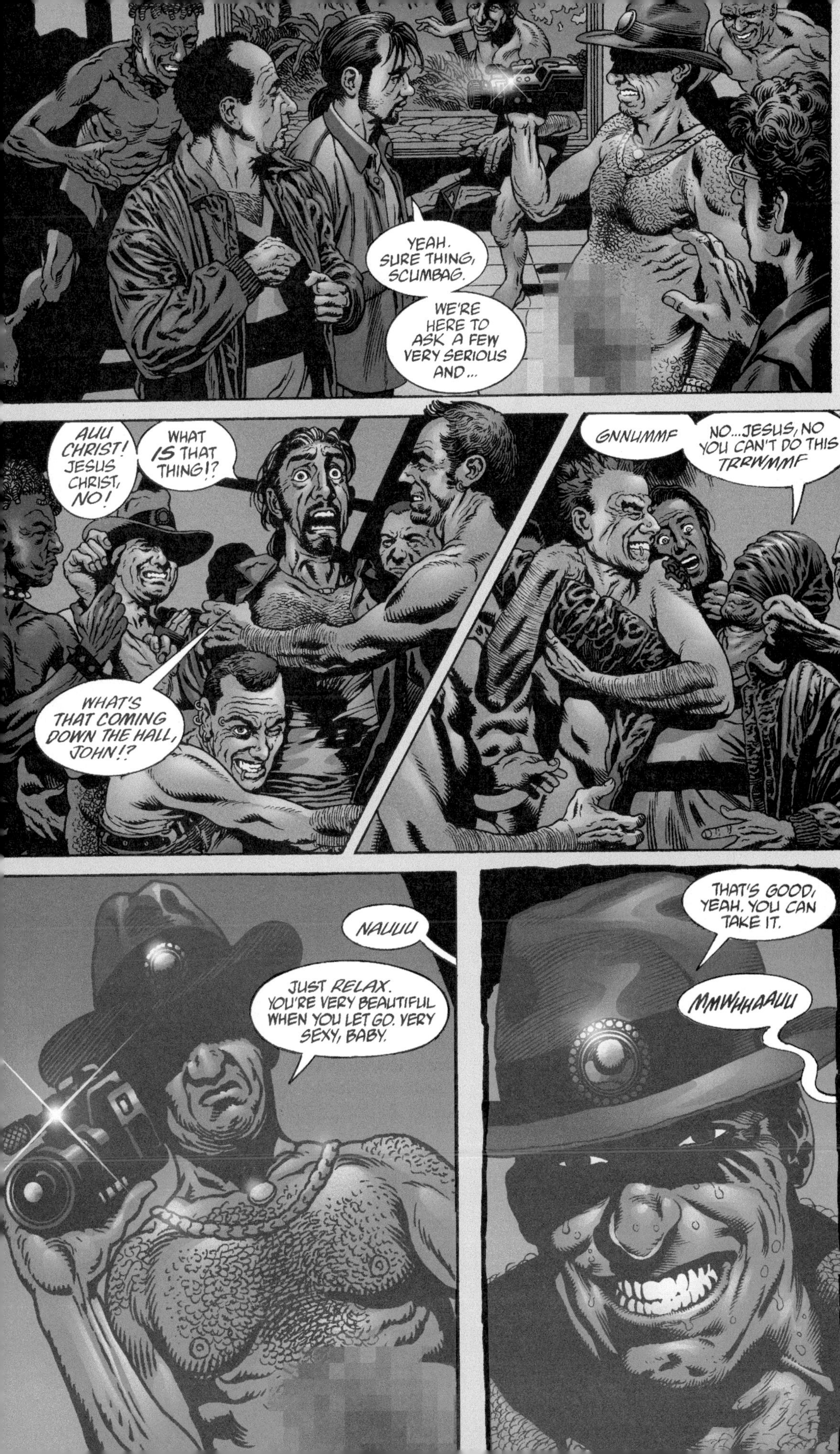
YEAH. SURE THING, SCUMBAG.
WE'RE HERE TO ASK A FEW VERY SERIOUS AND...
AUU CHRIST! JESUS CHRIST, NO!
WHAT IS THAT THING!?
WHAT'S THAT COMING DOWN THE HALL, JOHN!?
GNNUMMF
NO...JESUS, NO YOU CAN'T DO THIS TRRWMMF
NAUUU
JUST RELAX. YOU'RE VERY BEAUTIFUL WHEN YOU LET GO. VERY SEXY, BABY.
THAT'S GOOD, YEAH. YOU CAN TAKE IT.
MMWHHAAUU

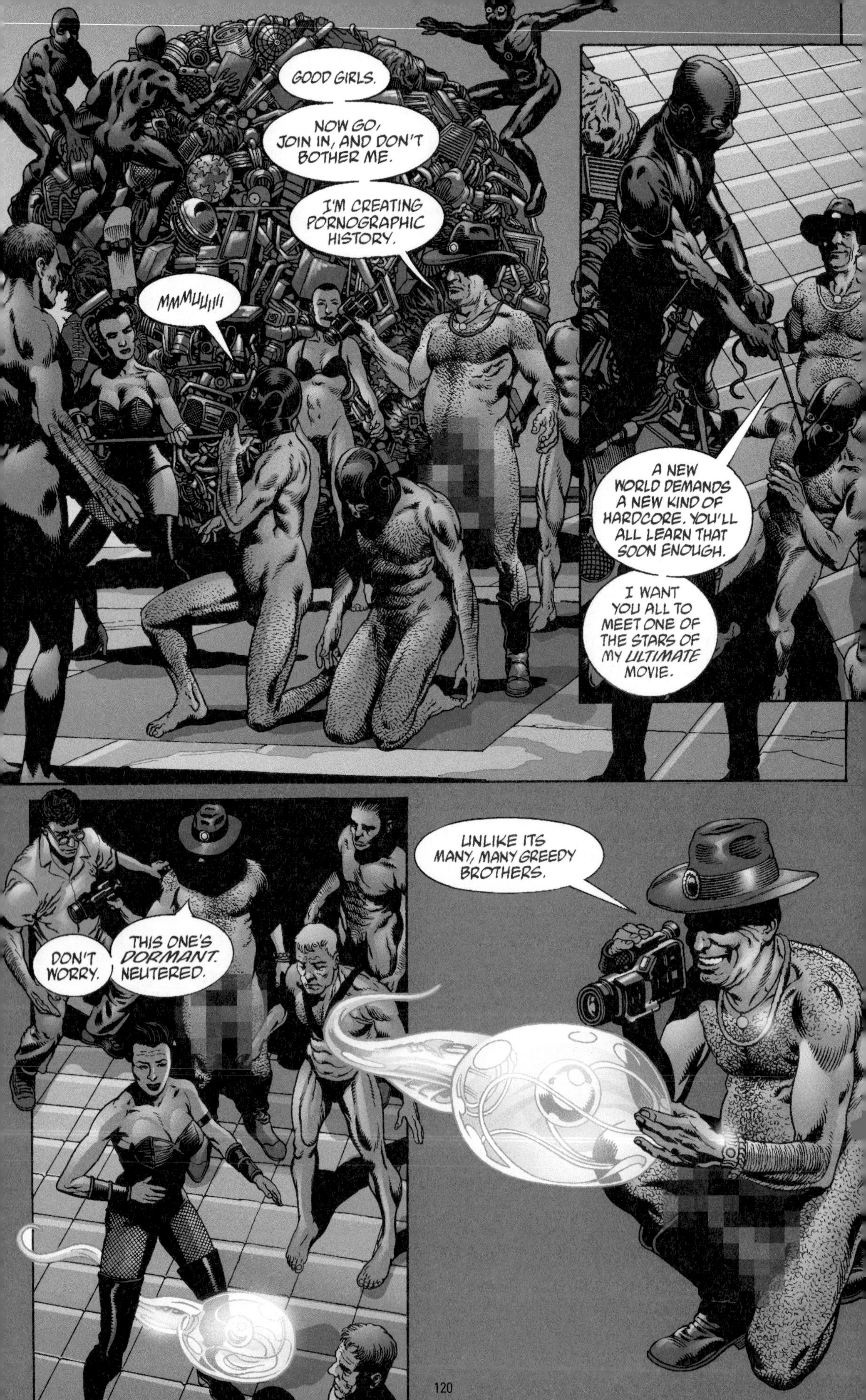
GOOD GIRLS.
NOW GO, JOIN IN, AND DON'T BOTHER ME.
I'M CREATING PORNOGRAPHIC HISTORY.
MMMUUIII
A NEW WORLD DEMANDS A NEW KIND OF HARDCORE. YOU'LL ALL LEARN THAT SOON ENOUGH.
I WANT YOU ALL TO MEET ONE OF THE STARS OF MY *ULTIMATE* MOVIE.
DON'T WORRY.
THIS ONE'S *DORMANT.* NEUTERED.
UNLIKE ITS MANY, MANY GREEDY BROTHERS.

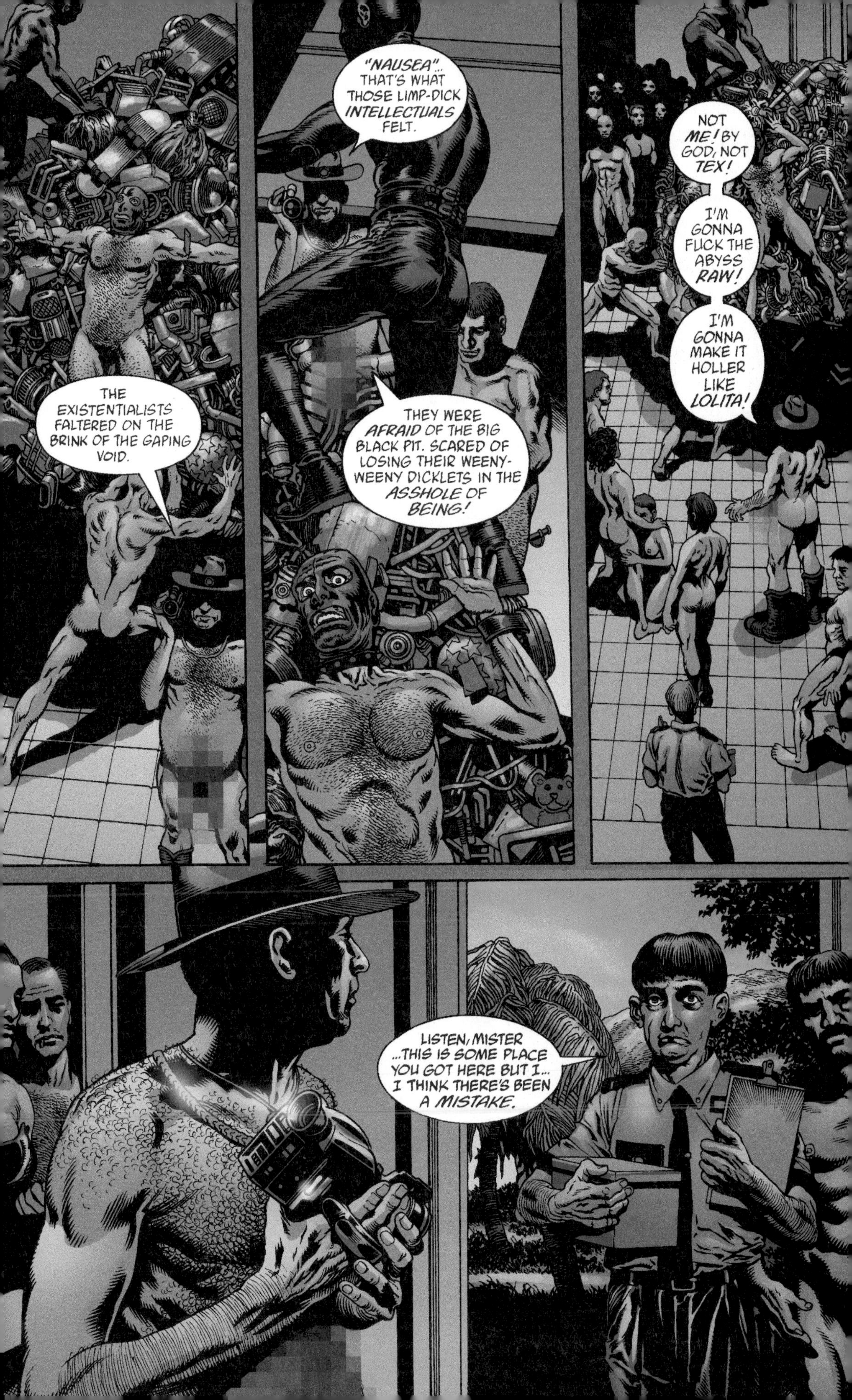
THE EXISTENTIALISTS FALTERED ON THE BRINK OF THE GAPING VOID.
"NAUSEA"... THAT'S WHAT THOSE LIMP-DICK INTELLECTUALS FELT.
THEY WERE AFRAID OF THE BIG BLACK PIT. SCARED OF LOSING THEIR WEENY-WEENY DICKLETS IN THE ASSHOLE OF BEING!
NOT ME! BY GOD, NOT TEX!
I'M GONNA FUCK THE ABYSS RAW!
I'M GONNA MAKE IT HOLLER LIKE LOLITA!
LISTEN, MISTER ...THIS IS SOME PLACE YOU GOT HERE BUT I... I THINK THERE'S BEEN A MISTAKE.

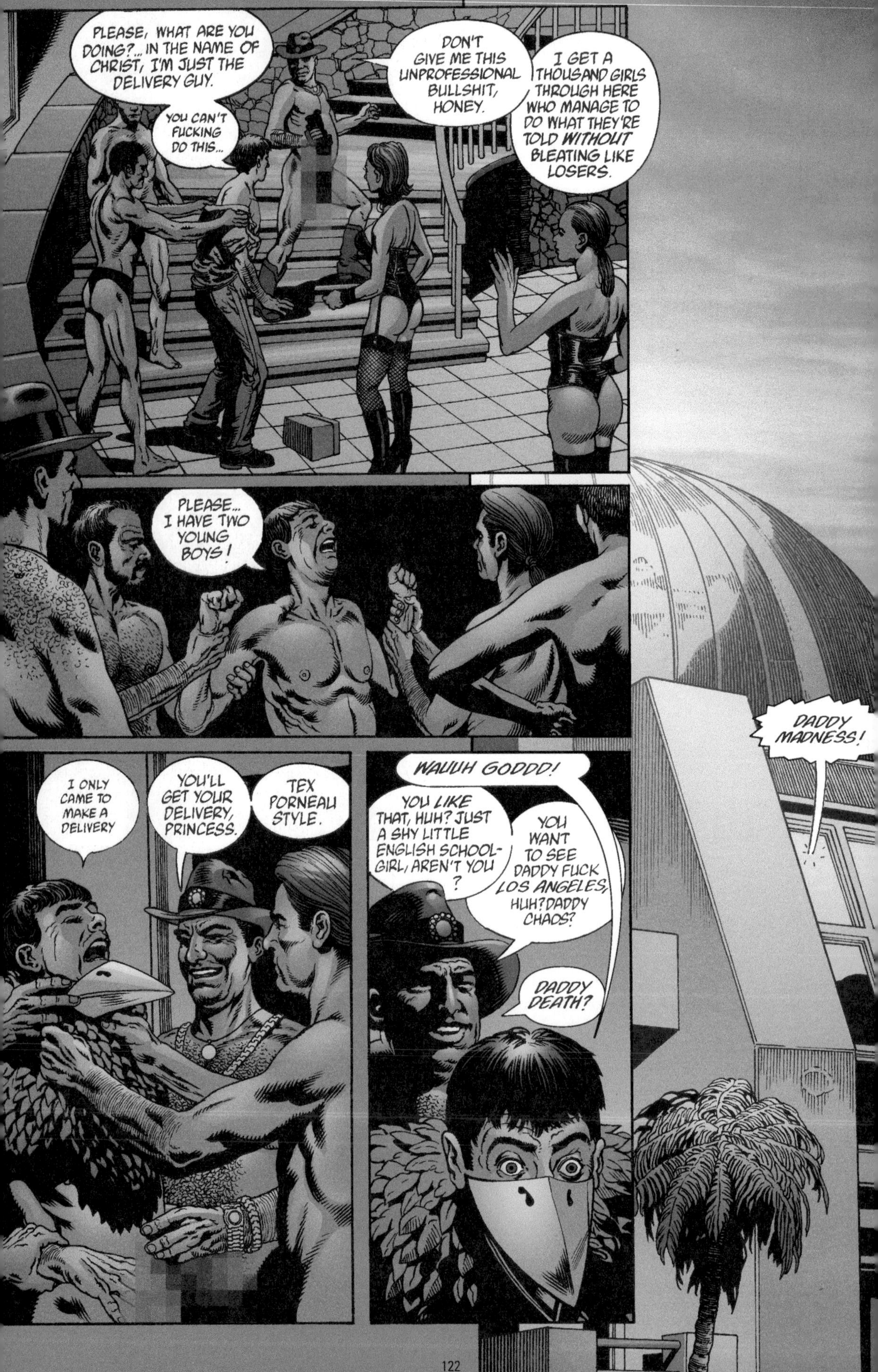
PLEASE, WHAT ARE YOU DOING?... IN THE NAME OF CHRIST, I'M JUST THE DELIVERY GUY.
YOU CAN'T FUCKING DO THIS...
DON'T GIVE ME THIS UNPROFESSIONAL BULLSHIT, HONEY.
I GET A THOUSAND GIRLS THROUGH HERE WHO MANAGE TO DO WHAT THEY'RE TOLD *WITHOUT* BLEATING LIKE LOSERS.
PLEASE... I HAVE TWO YOUNG BOYS!
I ONLY CAME TO MAKE A DELIVERY
YOU'LL GET YOUR DELIVERY, PRINCESS.
TEX PORNEAU STYLE.
WAUUH GODDD!
YOU *LIKE* THAT, HUH? JUST A SHY LITTLE ENGLISH SCHOOL-GIRL, AREN'T YOU?
YOU WANT TO SEE DADDY FUCK *LOS ANGELES*, HUH? DADDY CHAOS?
DADDY DEATH?
DADDY MADNESS!

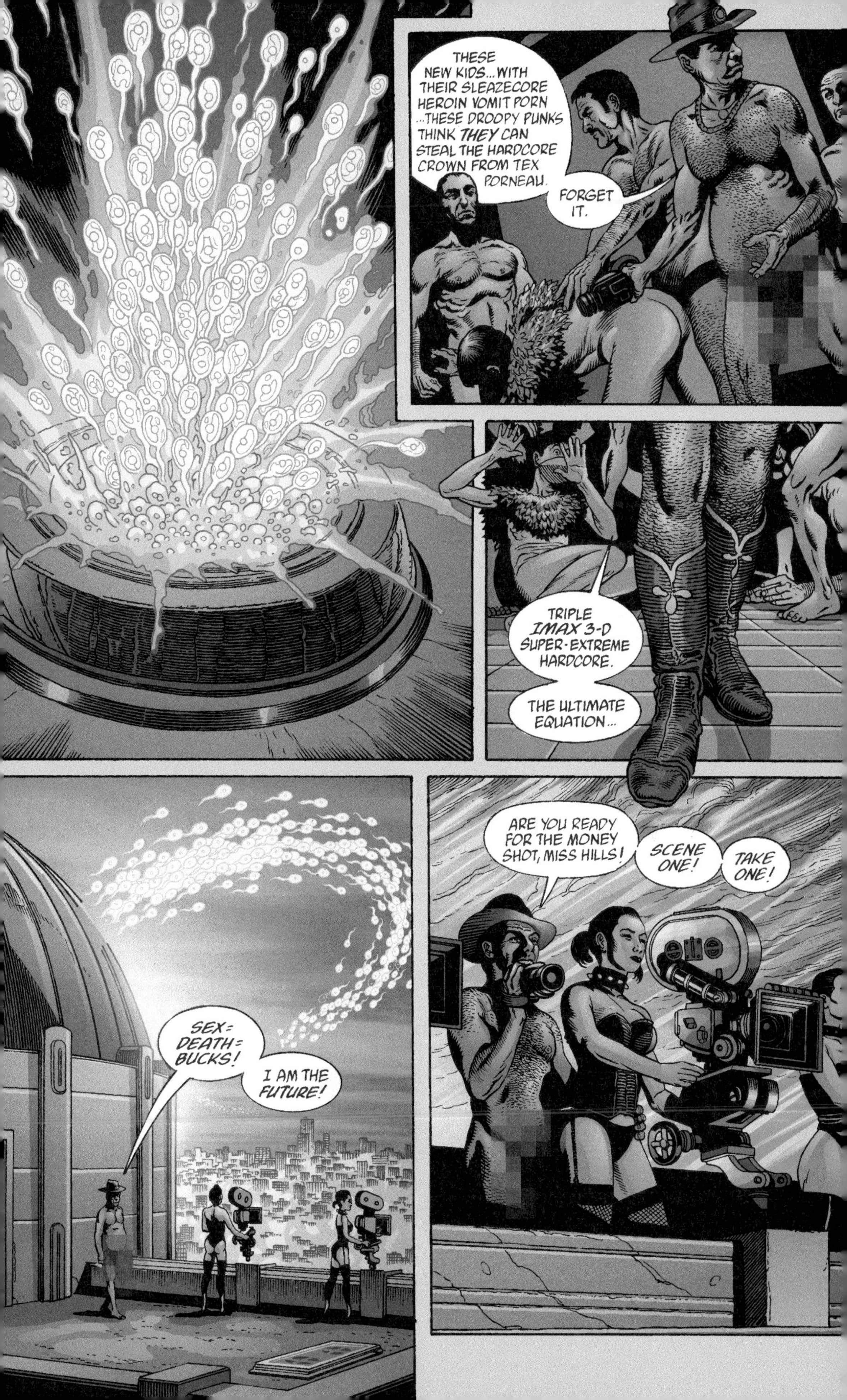
THESE NEW KIDS...WITH THEIR SLEAZECORE HEROIN VOMIT PORN ...THESE DROOPY PUNKS THINK THEY CAN STEAL THE HARDCORE CROWN FROM TEX PORNEAU.
FORGET IT.
TRIPLE IMAX 3-D SUPER-EXTREME HARDCORE.
THE ULTIMATE EQUATION...
SEX= DEATH= BUCKS!
I AM THE FUTURE!
ARE YOU READY FOR THE MONEY SHOT, MISS HILLS!
SCENE ONE!
TAKE ONE!

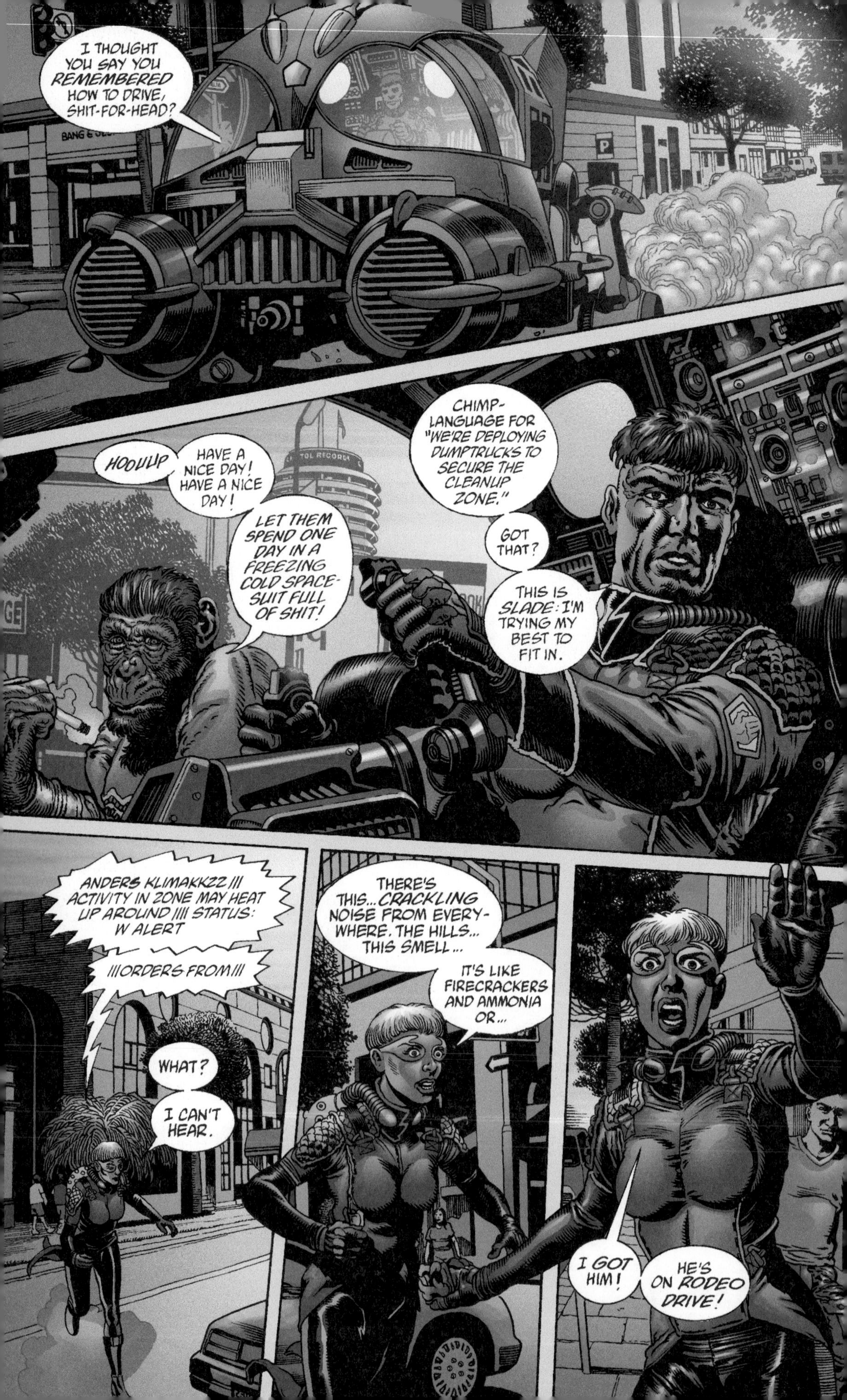

I THOUGHT YOU SAY YOU REMEMBERED HOW TO DRIVE, SHIT-FOR-HEAD?
BANG & OLU
P
CHIMP-LANGUAGE FOR "WE'RE DEPLOYING DUMPTRUCKS TO SECURE THE CLEANUP ZONE."
HOOUUP
HAVE A NICE DAY! HAVE A NICE DAY!
LET THEM SPEND ONE DAY IN A FREEZING COLD SPACE-SUIT FULL OF SHIT!
GOT THAT?
THIS IS SLADE: I'M TRYING MY BEST TO FIT IN.
ANDERS KLIMAKKZZ /// ACTIVITY IN ZONE MAY HEAT UP AROUND //// STATUS: W ALERT
///ORDERS FROM///
WHAT?
I CAN'T HEAR.
THERE'S THIS... CRACKLING NOISE FROM EVERY-WHERE. THE HILLS... THIS SMELL...
IT'S LIKE FIRECRACKERS AND AMMONIA OR...
I GOT HIM!
HE'S ON RODEO DRIVE!

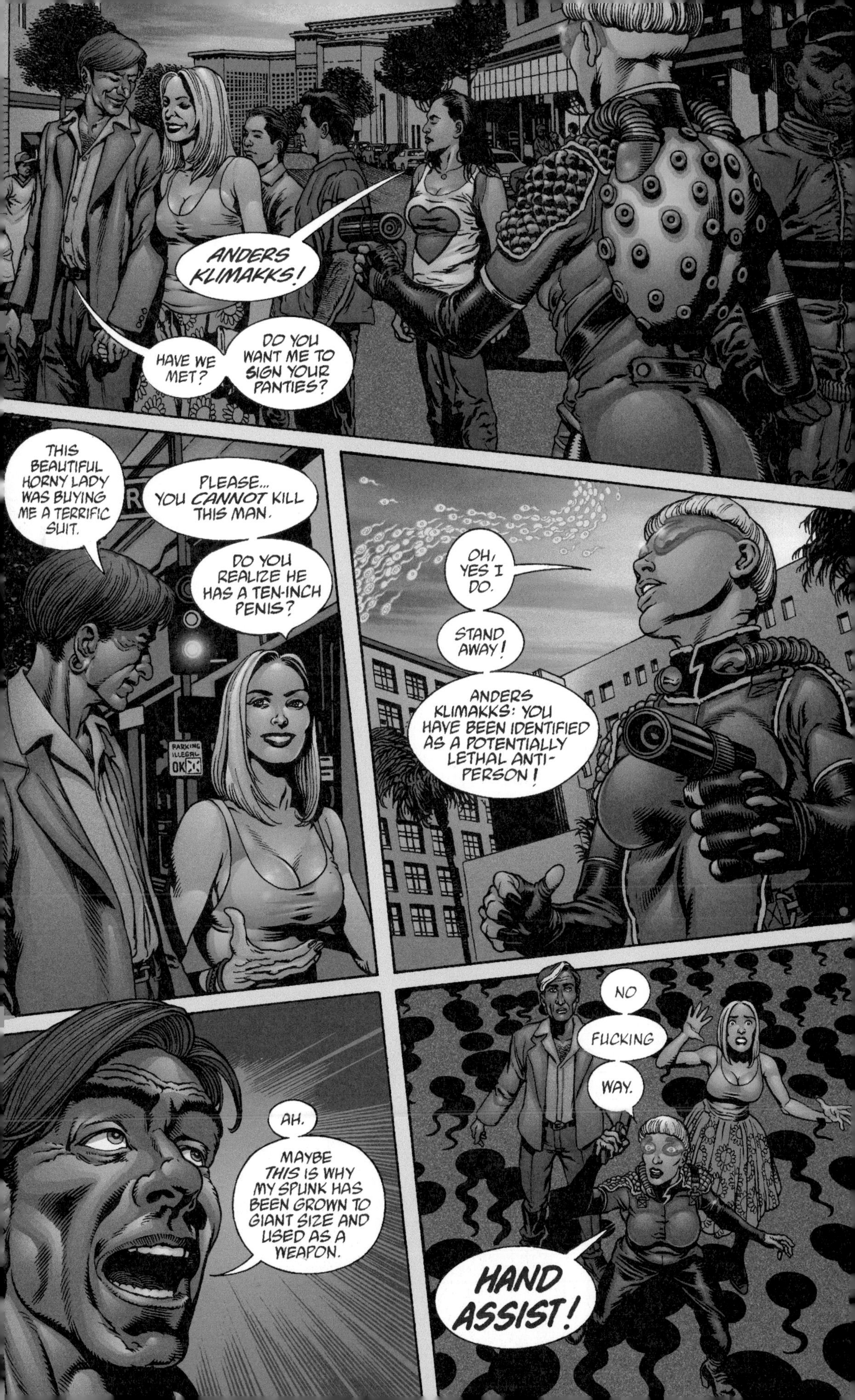
ANDERS KLIMAKKS!
HAVE WE MET?
DO YOU WANT ME TO SIGN YOUR PANTIES?
THIS BEAUTIFUL HORNY LADY WAS BUYING ME A TERRIFIC SUIT.
PLEASE... YOU CANNOT KILL THIS MAN.
DO YOU REALIZE HE HAS A TEN-INCH PENIS?
PARKING ILLEGAL OK
OH, YES I DO.
STAND AWAY!
ANDERS KLIMAKKS: YOU HAVE BEEN IDENTIFIED AS A POTENTIALLY LETHAL ANTI-PERSON!
AH.
MAYBE THIS IS WHY MY SPUNK HAS BEEN GROWN TO GIANT SIZE AND USED AS A WEAPON.
NO
FUCKING
WAY.
HAND ASSIST!

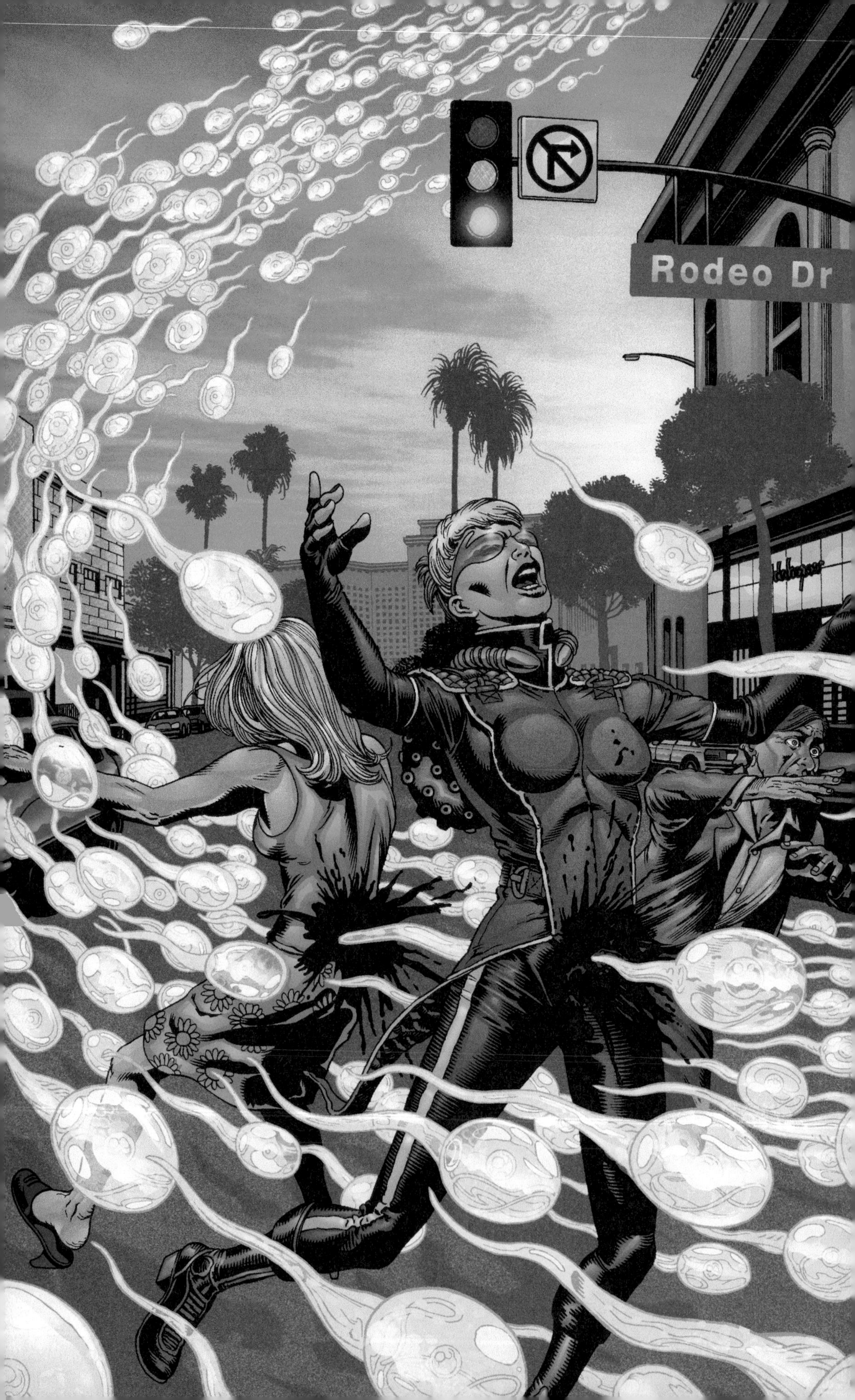
Rodeo Dr

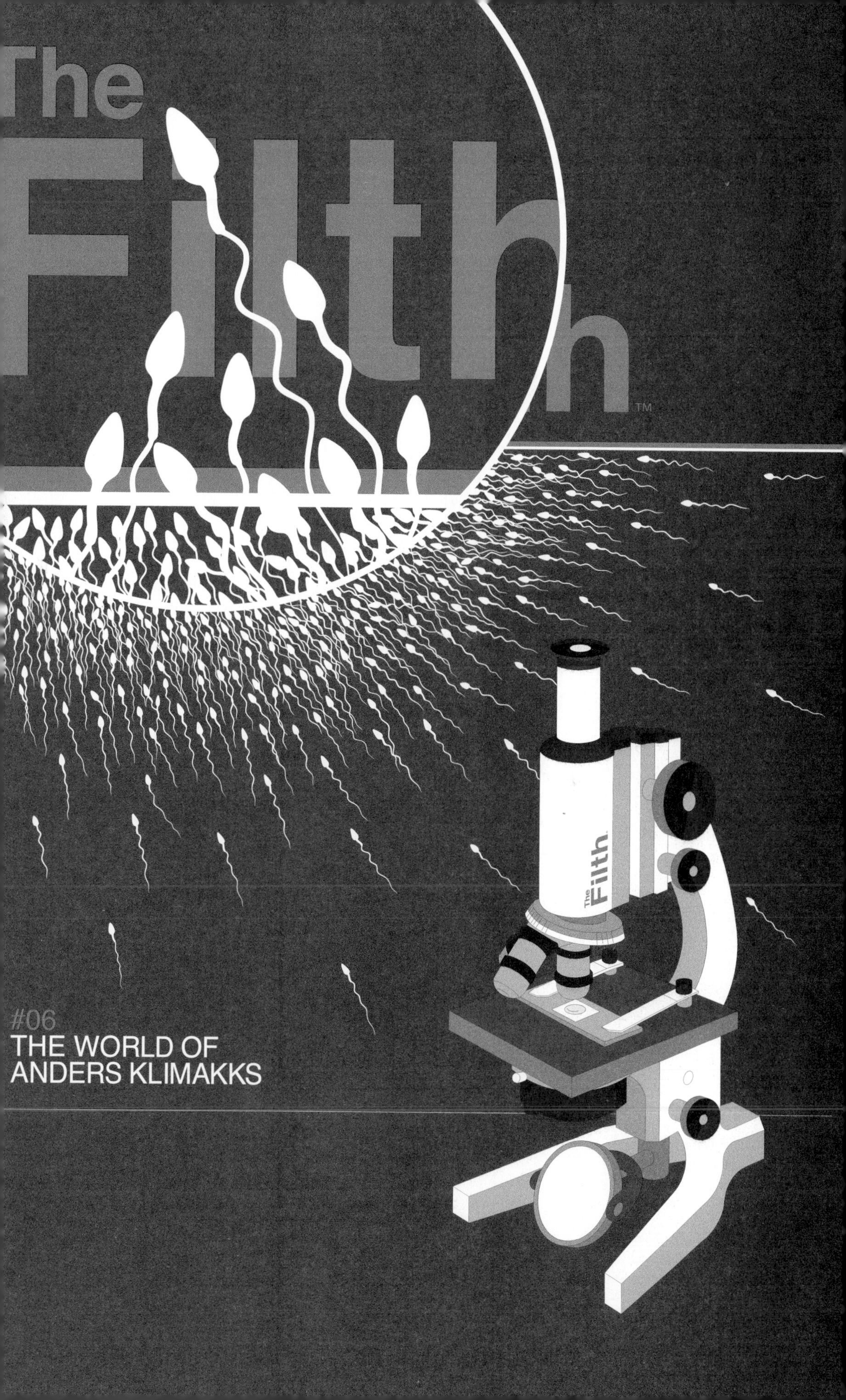
The Filth
TM
#06
THE WORLD OF
ANDERS KLIMAKKS
The Filth

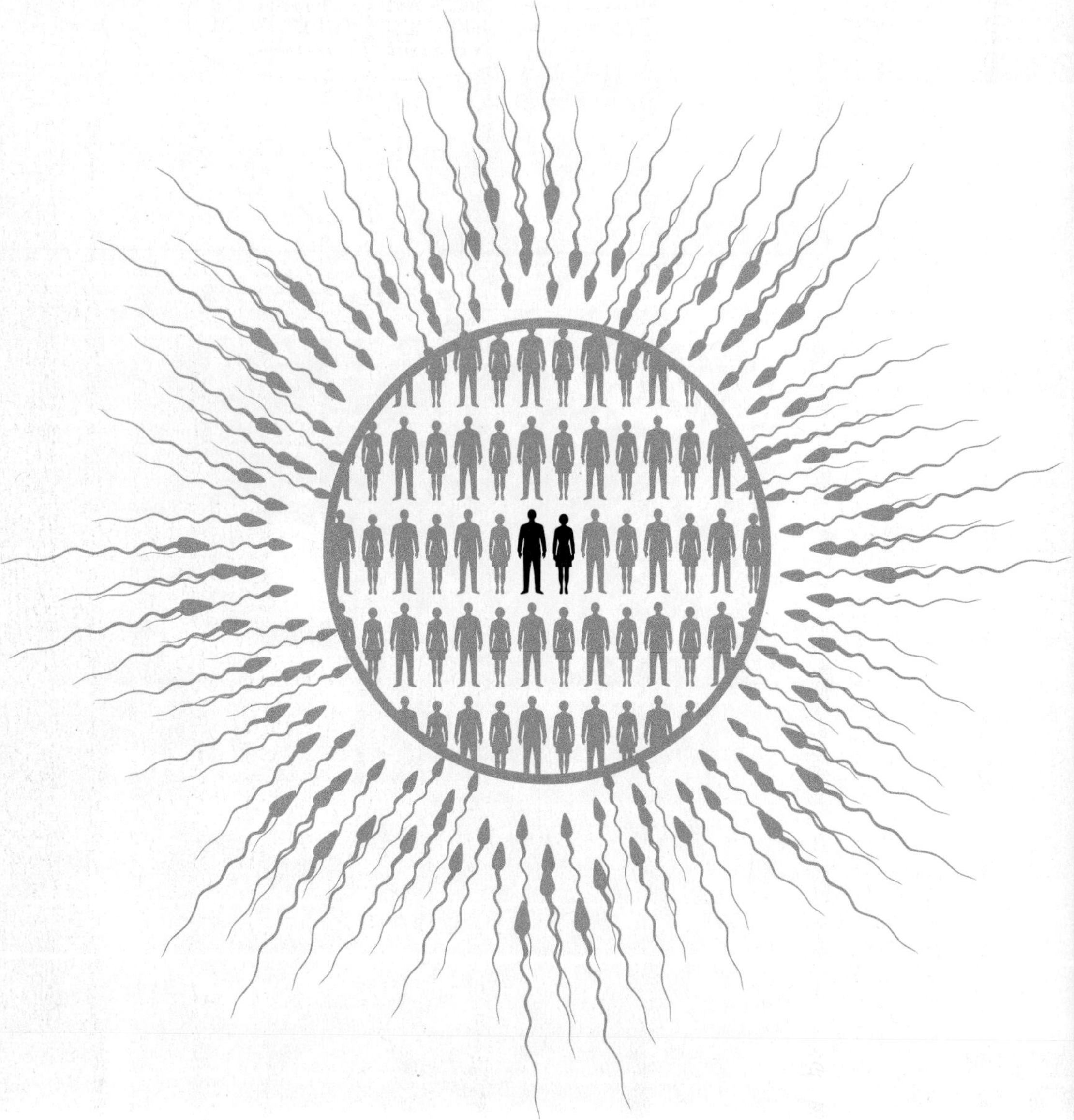

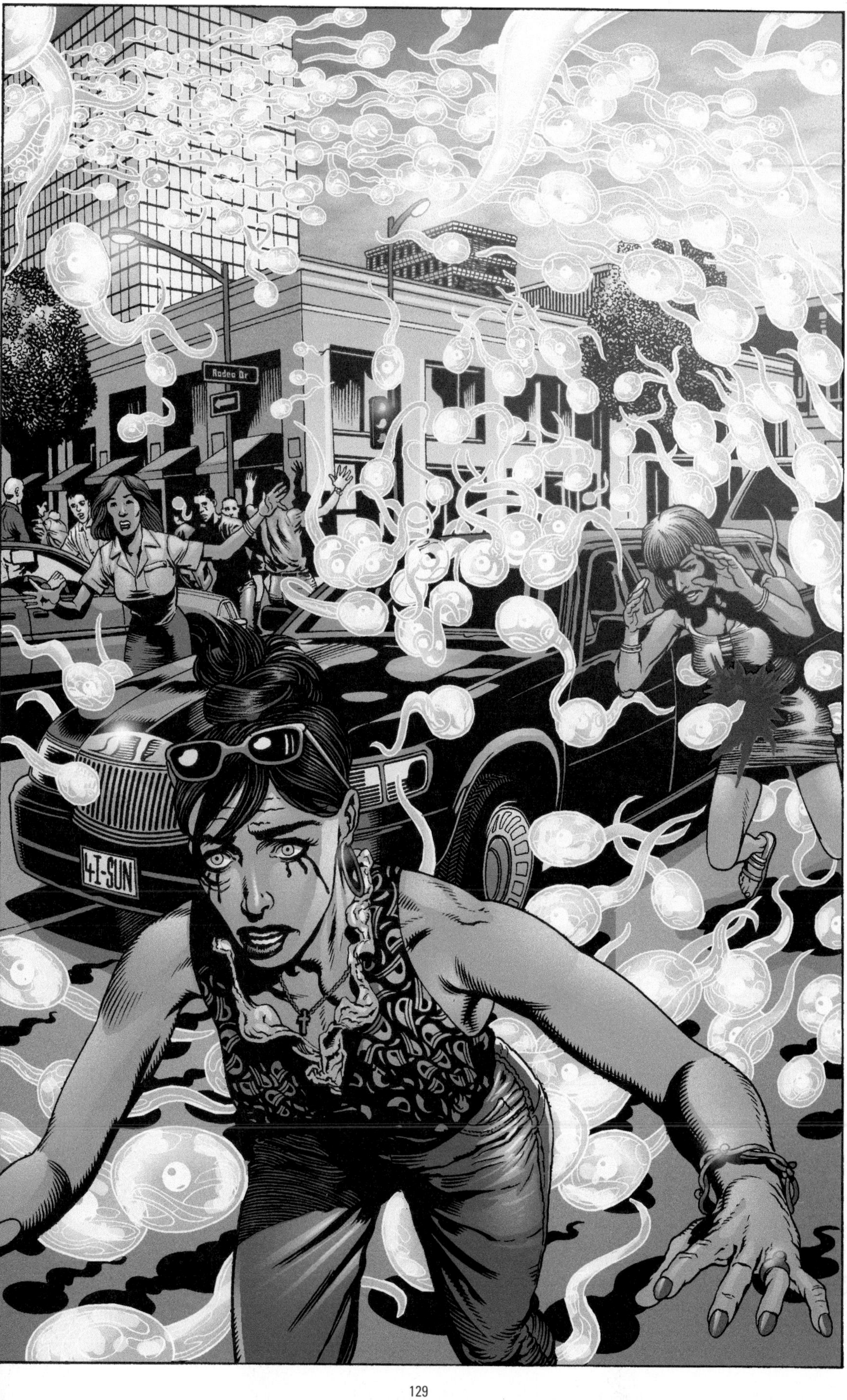
Rodeo Dr
4I-SUN

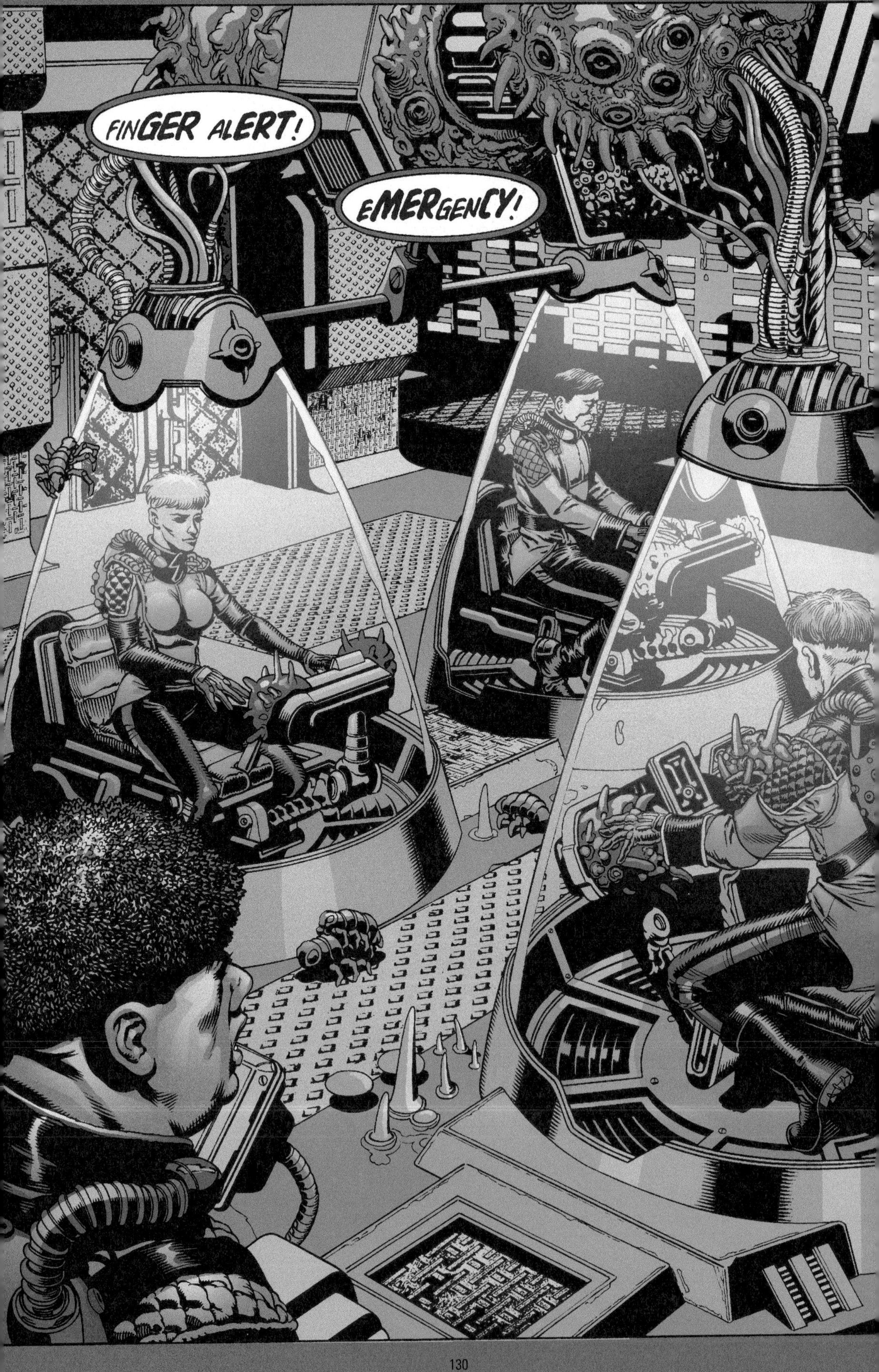
FINGER ALERT!
EMERGENCY!

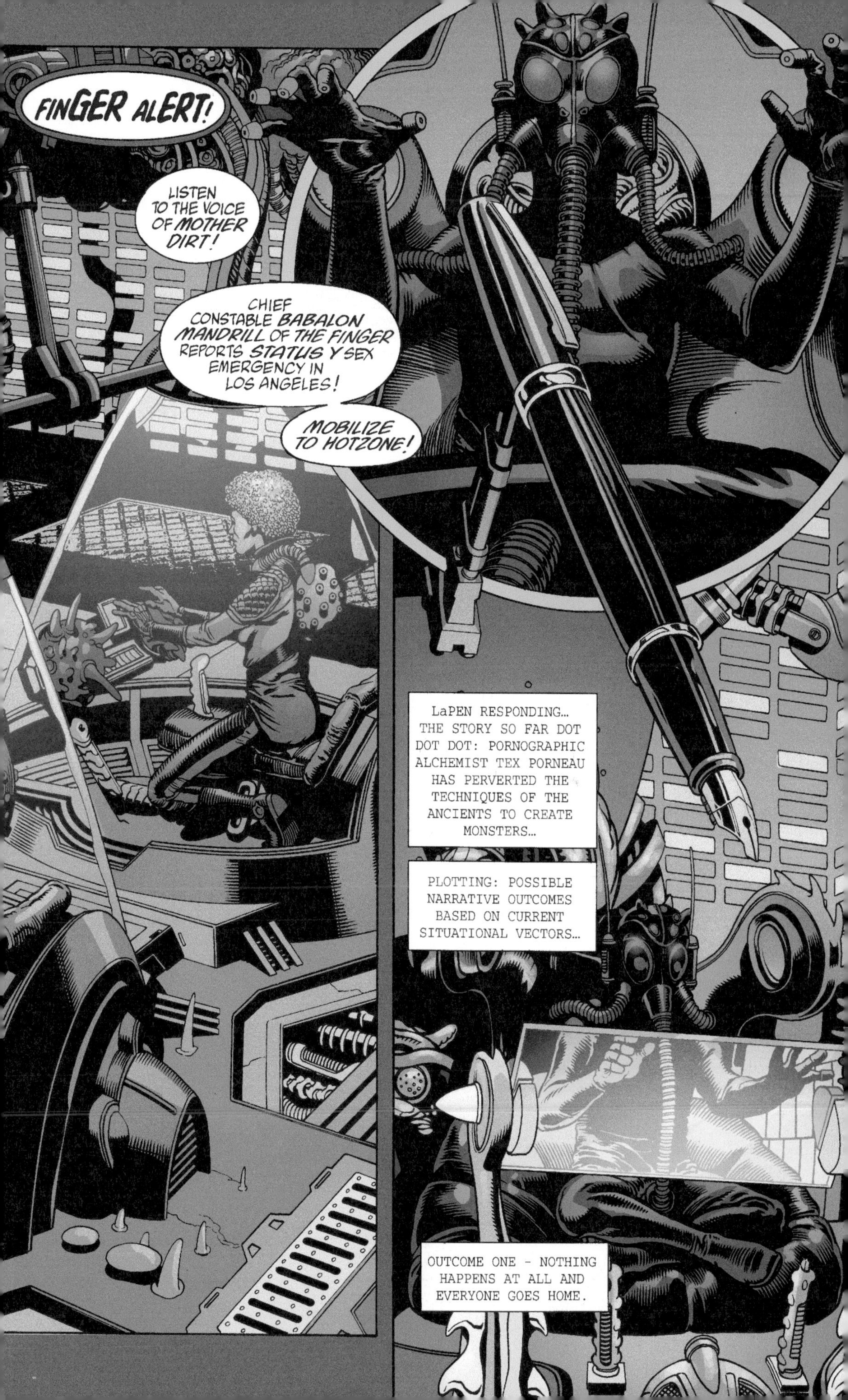
FINGER ALERT!
LISTEN TO THE VOICE OF MOTHER DIRT!
CHIEF CONSTABLE BABALON MANDRILL OF THE FINGER REPORTS STATUS Y SEX EMERGENCY IN LOS ANGELES!
MOBILIZE TO HOTZONE!
LaPEN RESPONDING... THE STORY SO FAR DOT DOT DOT: PORNOGRAPHIC ALCHEMIST TEX PORNEAU HAS PERVERTED THE TECHNIQUES OF THE ANCIENTS TO CREATE MONSTERS...
PLOTTING: POSSIBLE NARRATIVE OUTCOMES BASED ON CURRENT SITUATIONAL VECTORS...
OUTCOME ONE - NOTHING HAPPENS AT ALL AND EVERYONE GOES HOME.

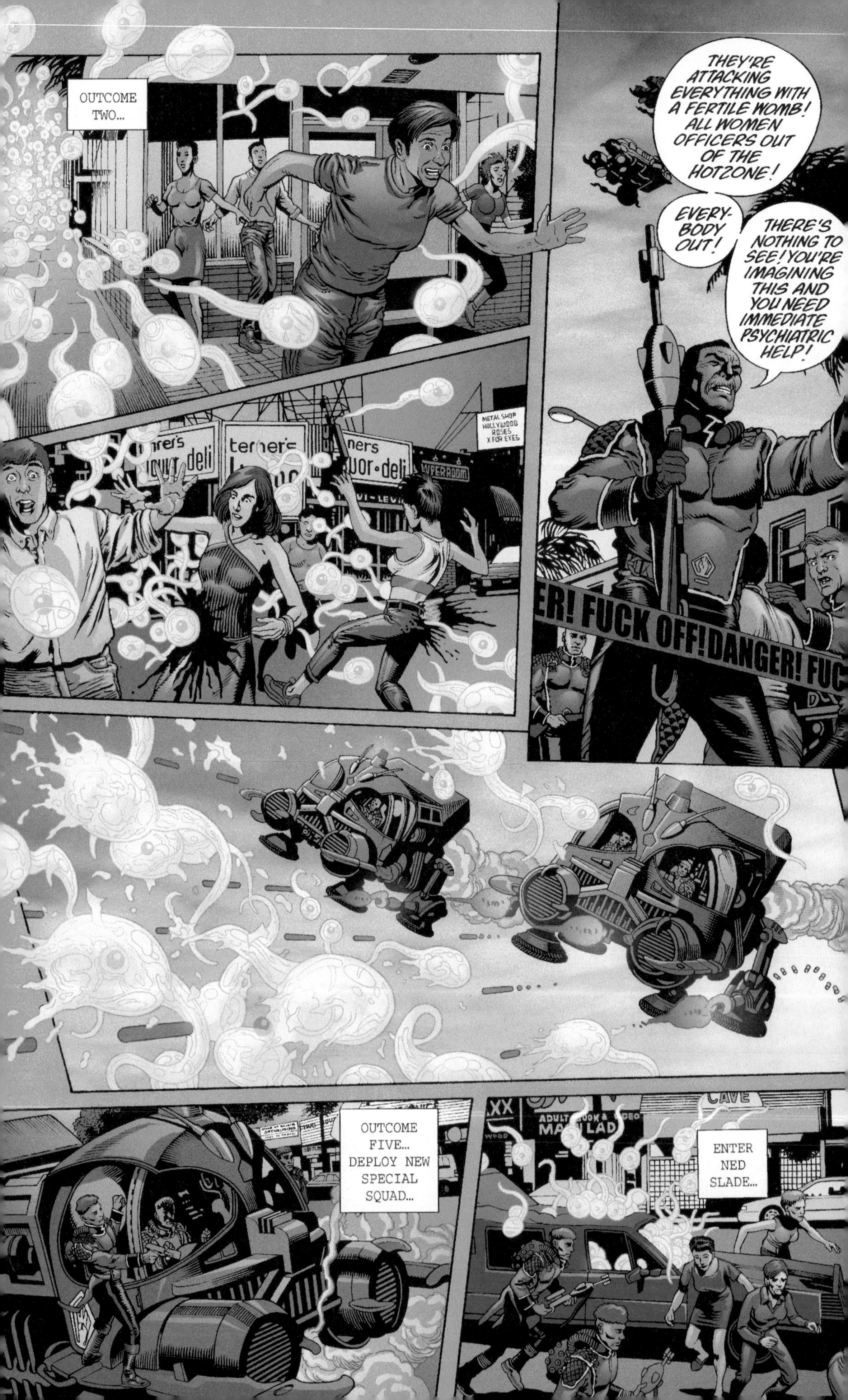
OUTCOME TWO...
METAL SHOP HOLLYWOOD ROSES X FOR EYES
THEY'RE ATTACKING EVERYTHING WITH A FERTILE WOMB! ALL WOMEN OFFICERS OUT OF THE HOTZONE!
EVERY-BODY OUT!
THERE'S NOTHING TO SEE! YOU'RE IMAGINING THIS AND YOU NEED IMMEDIATE PSYCHIATRIC HELP!
ER! FUCK OFF! DANGER! FUC
OUTCOME FIVE... DEPLOY NEW SPECIAL SQUAD...
CAVE
ENTER NED SLADE...

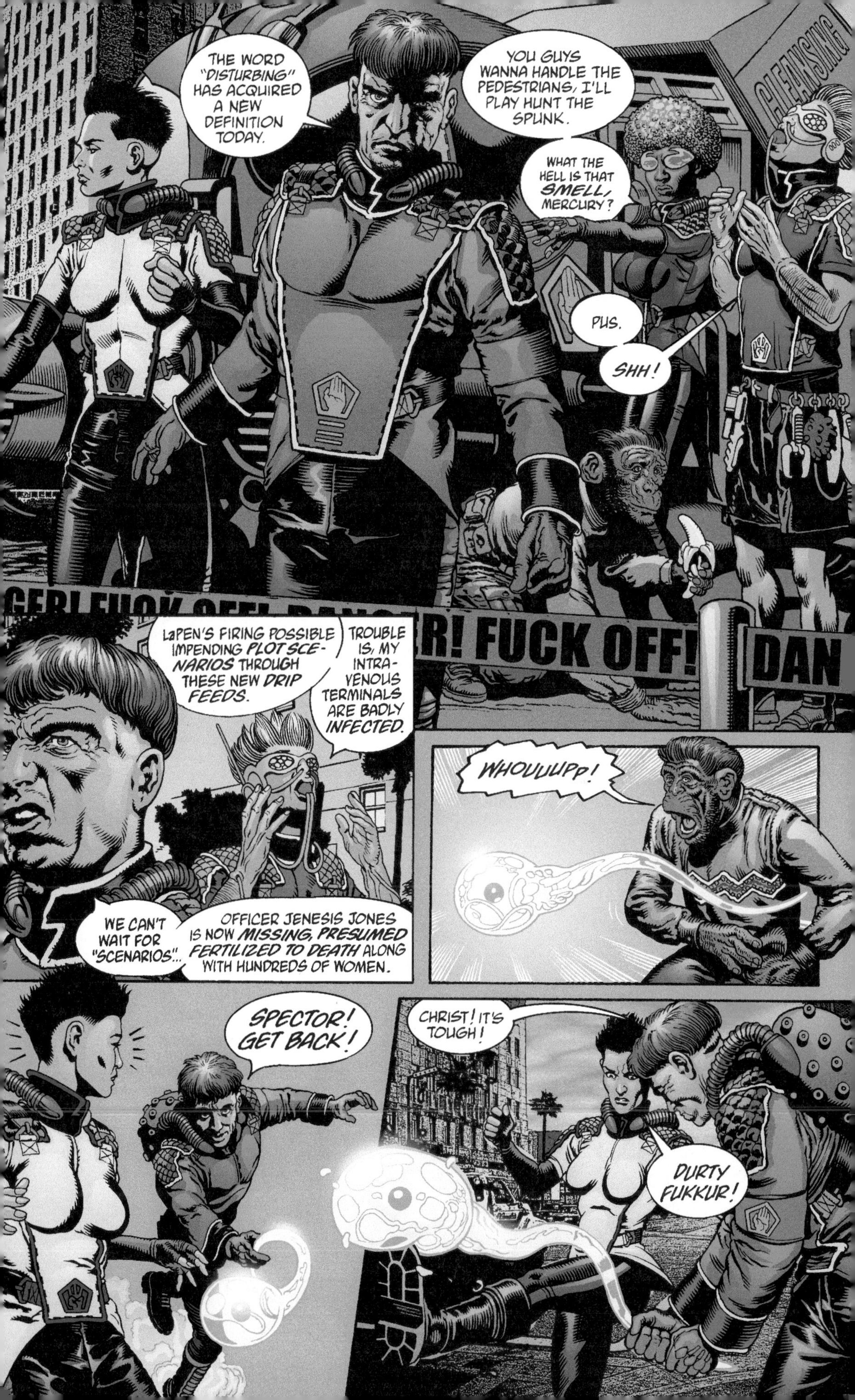
CLEANSING
THE WORD "DISTURBING" HAS ACQUIRED A NEW DEFINITION TODAY.
YOU GUYS WANNA HANDLE THE PEDESTRIANS, I'LL PLAY HUNT THE SPUNK.
WHAT THE HELL IS THAT SMELL, MERCURY?
PUS.
SHH!
R! FUCK OFF!
DAN
LaPEN'S FIRING POSSIBLE IMPENDING PLOT SCENARIOS THROUGH THESE NEW DRIP FEEDS.
TROUBLE IS, MY INTRAVENOUS TERMINALS ARE BADLY INFECTED.
WE CAN'T WAIT FOR "SCENARIOS"...
OFFICER JENESIS JONES IS NOW MISSING, PRESUMED FERTILIZED TO DEATH ALONG WITH HUNDREDS OF WOMEN.
WHOUUUPP!
SPECTOR! GET BACK!
CHRIST! IT'S TOUGH!
DURTY FUKKUR!

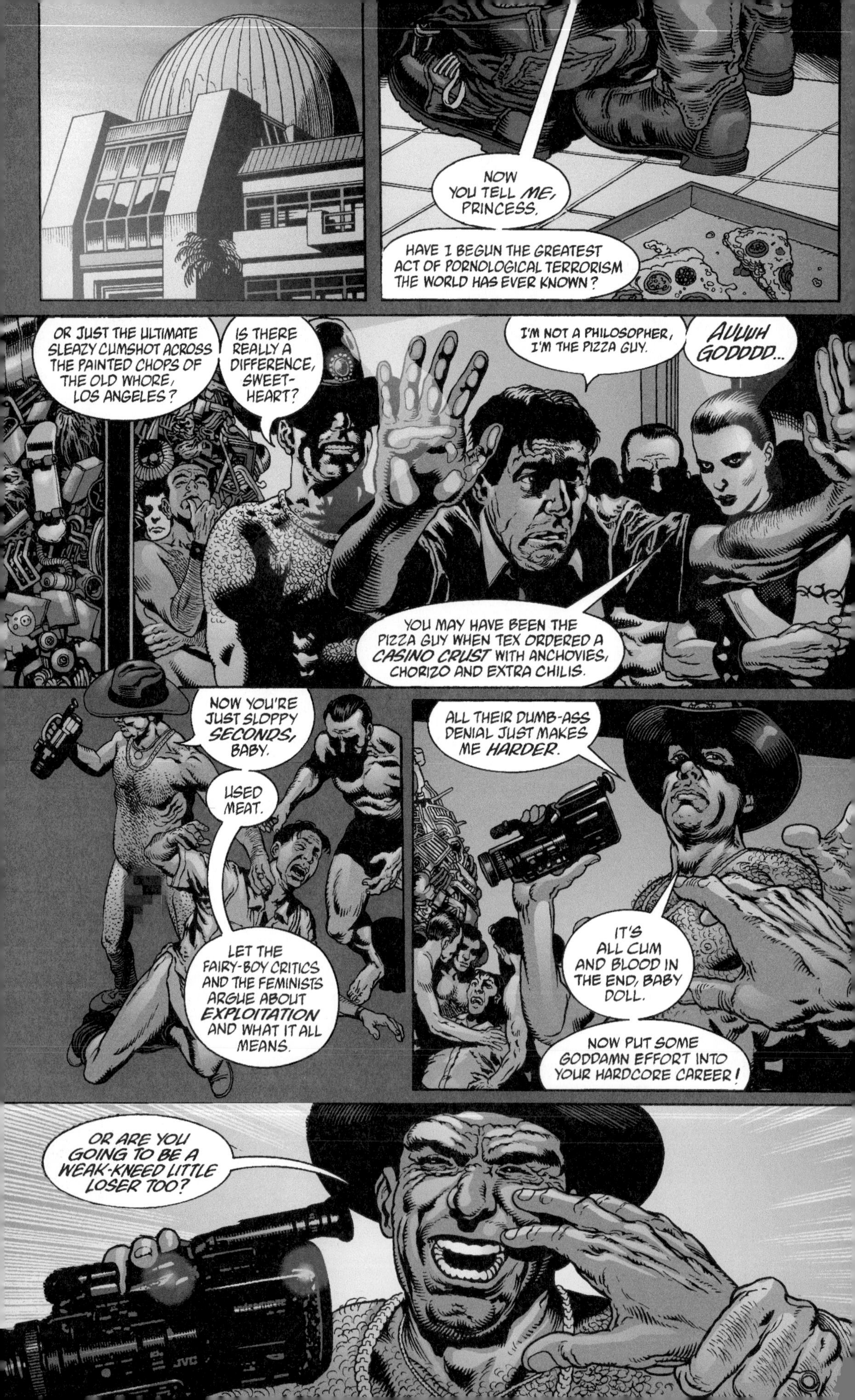
NOW YOU TELL *ME*, PRINCESS.
HAVE I BEGUN THE GREATEST ACT OF PORNOLOGICAL TERRORISM THE WORLD HAS EVER KNOWN?
OR JUST THE ULTIMATE SLEAZY CUMSHOT ACROSS THE PAINTED CHOPS OF THE OLD WHORE, LOS ANGELES?
IS THERE REALLY A DIFFERENCE, SWEET-HEART?
I'M NOT A PHILOSOPHER, I'M THE PIZZA GUY.
AUUUH GODDDD...
YOU MAY HAVE BEEN THE PIZZA GUY WHEN TEX ORDERED A *CASINO CRUST* WITH ANCHOVIES, CHORIZO AND EXTRA CHILIS.
NOW YOU'RE JUST SLOPPY *SECONDS,* BABY.
USED MEAT.
LET THE FAIRY-BOY CRITICS AND THE FEMINISTS ARGUE ABOUT *EXPLOITATION* AND WHAT IT ALL MEANS.
ALL THEIR DUMB-ASS DENIAL JUST MAKES ME *HARDER*.
IT'S ALL CUM AND BLOOD IN THE END, BABY DOLL.
NOW PUT SOME GODDAMN EFFORT INTO YOUR HARDCORE CAREER!
OR ARE YOU GOING TO BE A WEAK-KNEED LITTLE LOSER TOO?

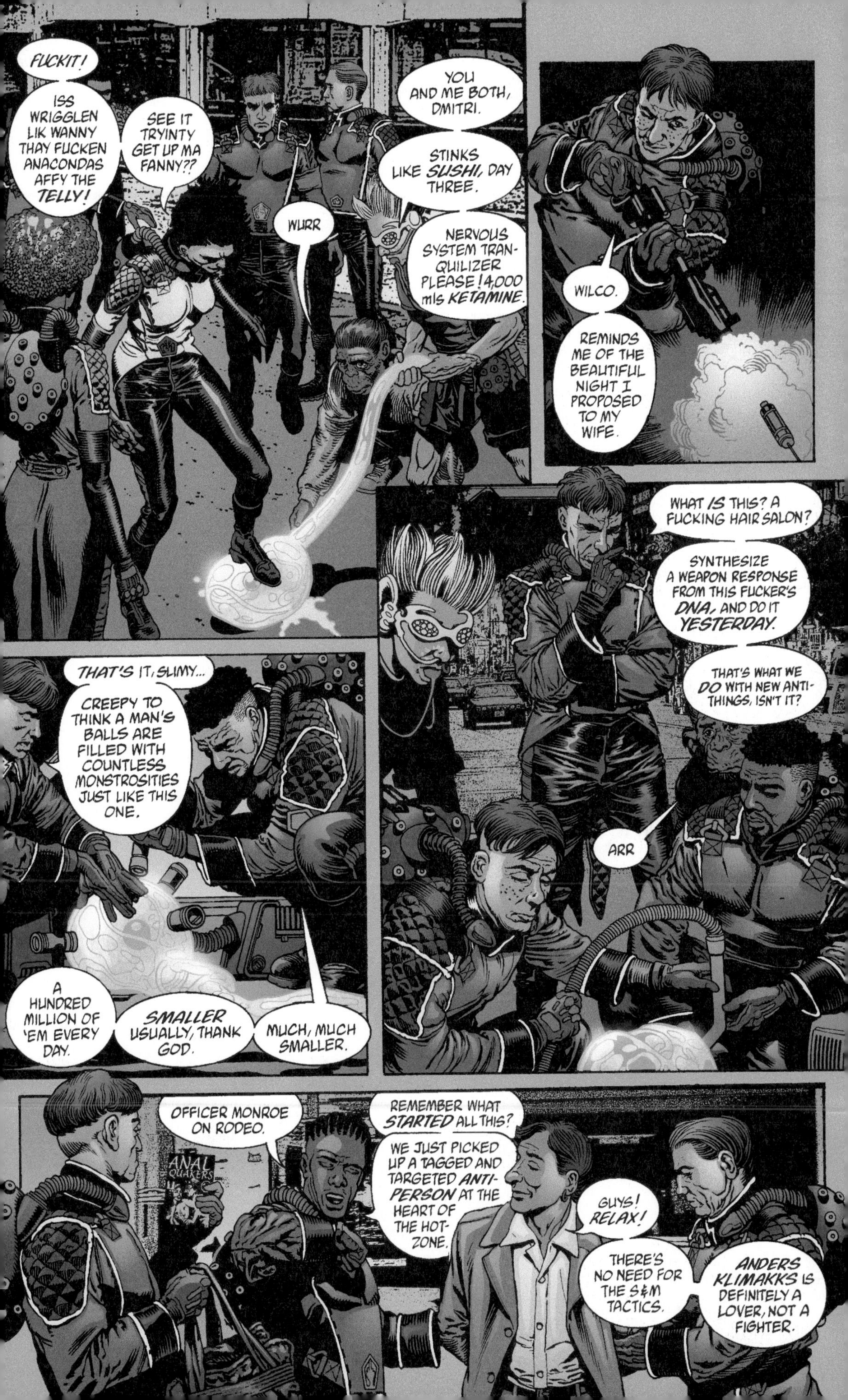
FUCKIT!
ISS WRIGGLEN LIK WANNY THAY FUCKEN ANACONDAS AFFY THE TELLY!
SEE IT TRYINTY GET UP MA FANNY??
YOU AND ME BOTH, DMITRI.
STINKS LIKE SUSHI, DAY THREE.
WURR
NERVOUS SYSTEM TRANQUILIZER PLEASE! 4,000 mls KETAMINE.
WILCO.
REMINDS ME OF THE BEAUTIFUL NIGHT I PROPOSED TO MY WIFE.
WHAT IS THIS? A FUCKING HAIR SALON?
SYNTHESIZE A WEAPON RESPONSE FROM THIS FUCKER'S DNA, AND DO IT YESTERDAY.
THAT'S WHAT WE DO WITH NEW ANTI-THINGS, ISN'T IT?
ARR
THAT'S IT, SLIMY...
CREEPY TO THINK A MAN'S BALLS ARE FILLED WITH COUNTLESS MONSTROSITIES JUST LIKE THIS ONE.
A HUNDRED MILLION OF 'EM EVERY DAY.
SMALLER USUALLY, THANK GOD.
MUCH, MUCH SMALLER.
OFFICER MONROE ON RODEO.
ANAL QUAKERS
REMEMBER WHAT STARTED ALL THIS?
WE JUST PICKED UP A TAGGED AND TARGETED ANTI-PERSON AT THE HEART OF THE HOT-ZONE.
GUYS! RELAX!
THERE'S NO NEED FOR THE S&M TACTICS.
ANDERS KLIMAKKS IS DEFINITELY A LOVER, NOT A FIGHTER.

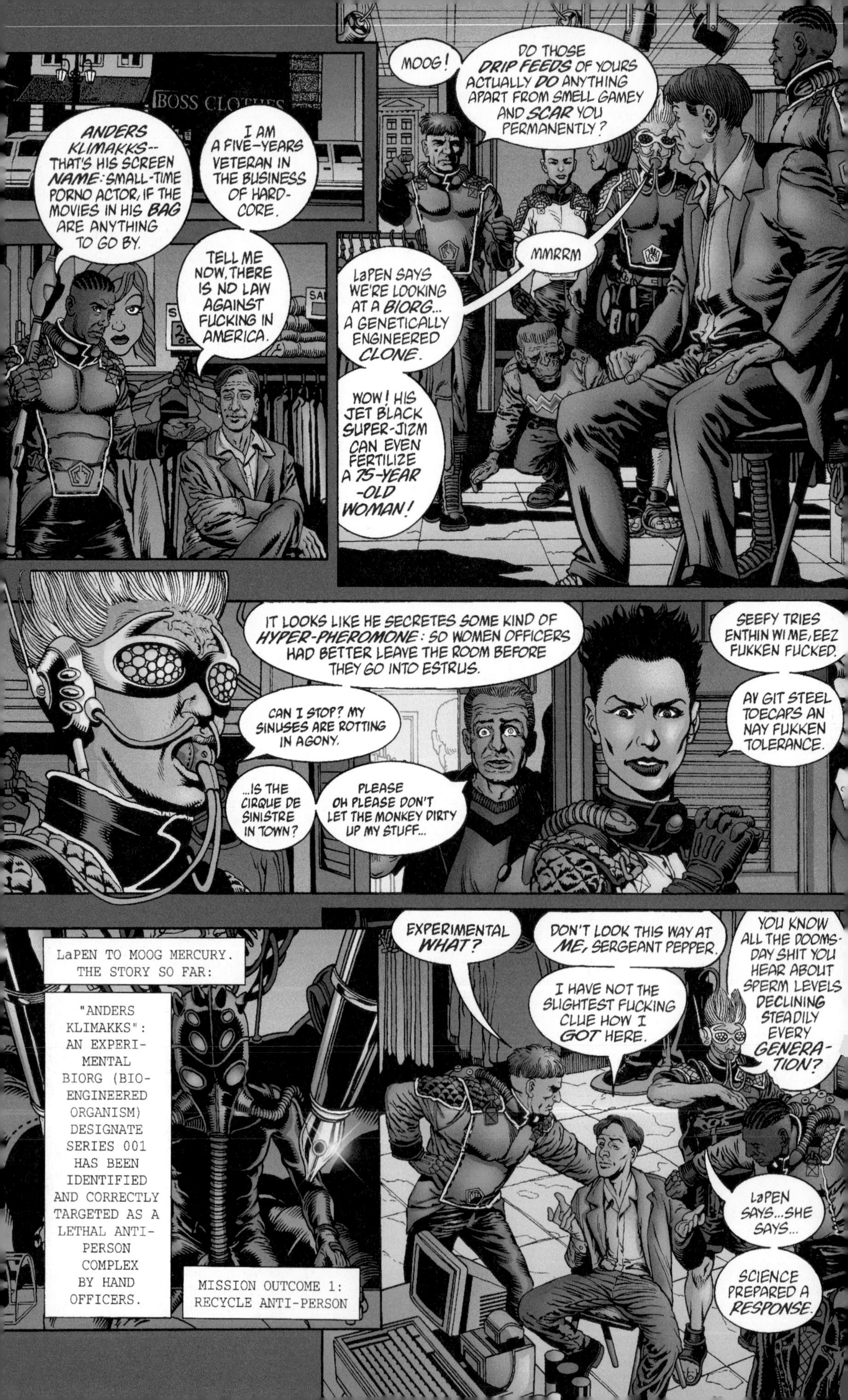

BOSS CLOTHES
ANDERS KLIMAKKS-- THAT'S HIS SCREEN NAME: SMALL-TIME PORNO ACTOR, IF THE MOVIES IN HIS BAG ARE ANYTHING TO GO BY.
I AM A FIVE-YEARS VETERAN IN THE BUSINESS OF HARD-CORE.
TELL ME NOW, THERE IS NO LAW AGAINST FUCKING IN AMERICA.
MOOG!
DO THOSE DRIP FEEDS OF YOURS ACTUALLY DO ANYTHING APART FROM SMELL GAMEY AND SCAR YOU PERMANENTLY?
MMRRM
LaPEN SAYS WE'RE LOOKING AT A BIORG... A GENETICALLY ENGINEERED CLONE.
WOW! HIS JET BLACK SUPER-JIZM CAN EVEN FERTILIZE A 75-YEAR-OLD WOMAN!
IT LOOKS LIKE HE SECRETES SOME KIND OF HYPER-PHEROMONE: SO WOMEN OFFICERS HAD BETTER LEAVE THE ROOM BEFORE THEY GO INTO ESTRUS.
CAN I STOP? MY SINUSES ARE ROTTING IN AGONY.
...IS THE CIRQUE DE SINISTRE IN TOWN?
PLEASE OH PLEASE DON'T LET THE MONKEY DIRTY UP MY STUFF...
SEEFY TRIES ENTHIN WI ME, EEZ FUKKEN FUCKED.
AY GIT STEEL TOECAPS AN NAY FUKKEN TOLERANCE.
LaPEN TO MOOG MERCURY. THE STORY SO FAR:
"ANDERS KLIMAKKS": AN EXPERI-MENTAL BIORG (BIO-ENGINEERED ORGANISM) DESIGNATE SERIES 001 HAS BEEN IDENTIFIED AND CORRECTLY TARGETED AS A LETHAL ANTI-PERSON COMPLEX BY HAND OFFICERS.
MISSION OUTCOME 1: RECYCLE ANTI-PERSON
EXPERIMENTAL WHAT?
DON'T LOOK THIS WAY AT ME, SERGEANT PEPPER.
I HAVE NOT THE SLIGHTEST FUCKING CLUE HOW I GOT HERE.
YOU KNOW ALL THE DOOMS-DAY SHIT YOU HEAR ABOUT SPERM LEVELS DECLINING STEADILY EVERY GENERA-TION?
LaPEN SAYS...SHE SAYS...
SCIENCE PREPARED A RESPONSE.

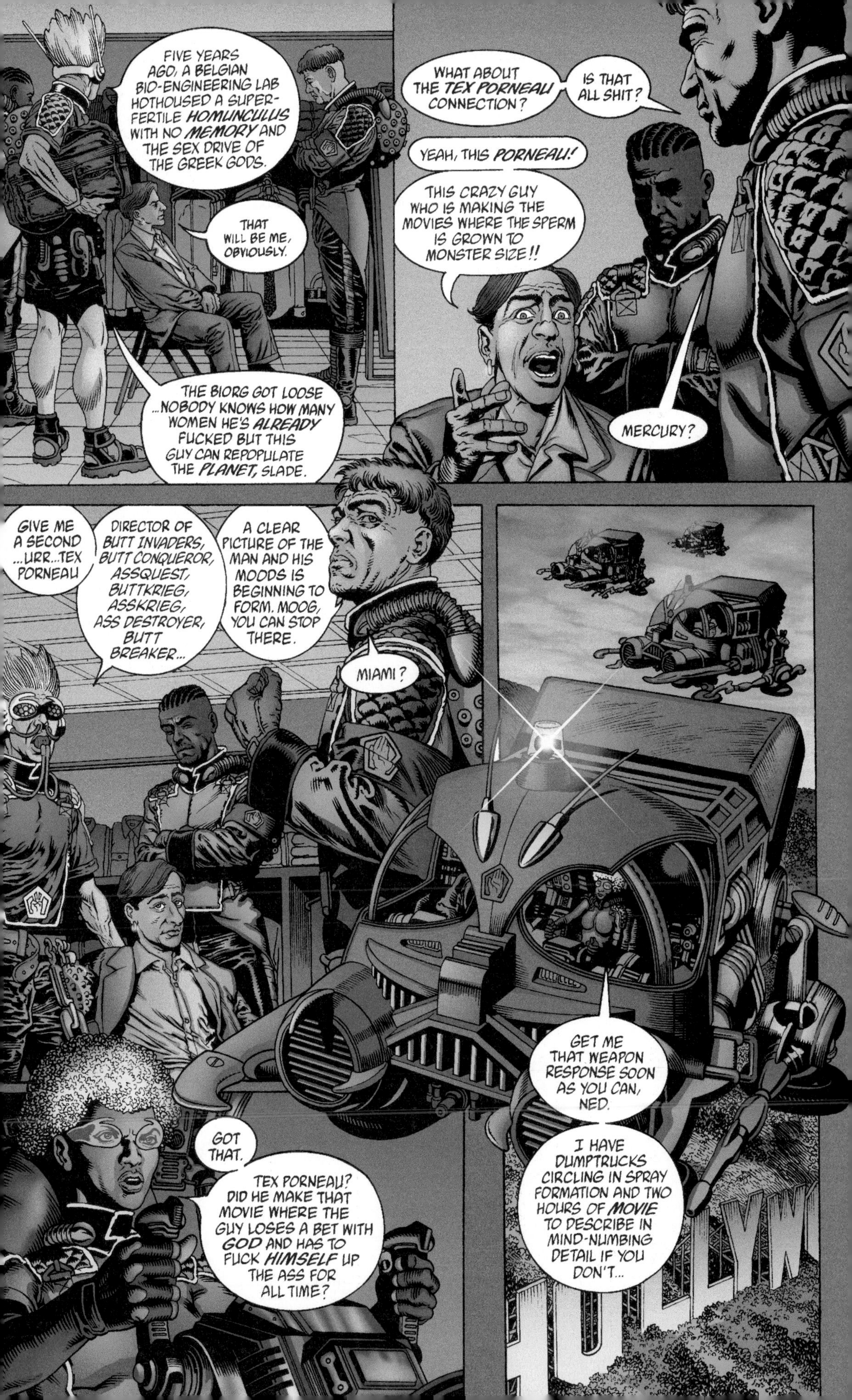
FIVE YEARS AGO, A BELGIAN BIO-ENGINEERING LAB HOTHOUSED A SUPER-FERTILE HOMUNCULUS WITH NO MEMORY AND THE SEX DRIVE OF THE GREEK GODS.
THAT WILL BE ME, OBVIOUSLY.
THE BIORG GOT LOOSE ...NOBODY KNOWS HOW MANY WOMEN HE'S ALREADY FUCKED BUT THIS GUY CAN REPOPULATE THE PLANET, SLADE.
WHAT ABOUT THE TEX PORNEAU CONNECTION?
IS THAT ALL SHIT?
YEAH, THIS PORNEAU!
THIS CRAZY GUY WHO IS MAKING THE MOVIES WHERE THE SPERM IS GROWN TO MONSTER SIZE!!
MERCURY?
GIVE ME A SECOND ...URR...TEX PORNEAU
DIRECTOR OF BUTT INVADERS, BUTT CONQUEROR, ASSQUEST, BUTTKRIEG, ASSKRIEG, ASS DESTROYER, BUTT BREAKER...
A CLEAR PICTURE OF THE MAN AND HIS MOODS IS BEGINNING TO FORM. MOOG, YOU CAN STOP THERE.
MIAMI?
GOT THAT.
TEX PORNEAU? DID HE MAKE THAT MOVIE WHERE THE GUY LOSES A BET WITH GOD AND HAS TO FUCK HIMSELF UP THE ASS FOR ALL TIME?
GET ME THAT WEAPON RESPONSE SOON AS YOU CAN, NED.
I HAVE DUMPTRUCKS CIRCLING IN SPRAY FORMATION AND TWO HOURS OF MOVIE TO DESCRIBE IN MIND-NUMBING DETAIL IF YOU DON'T...

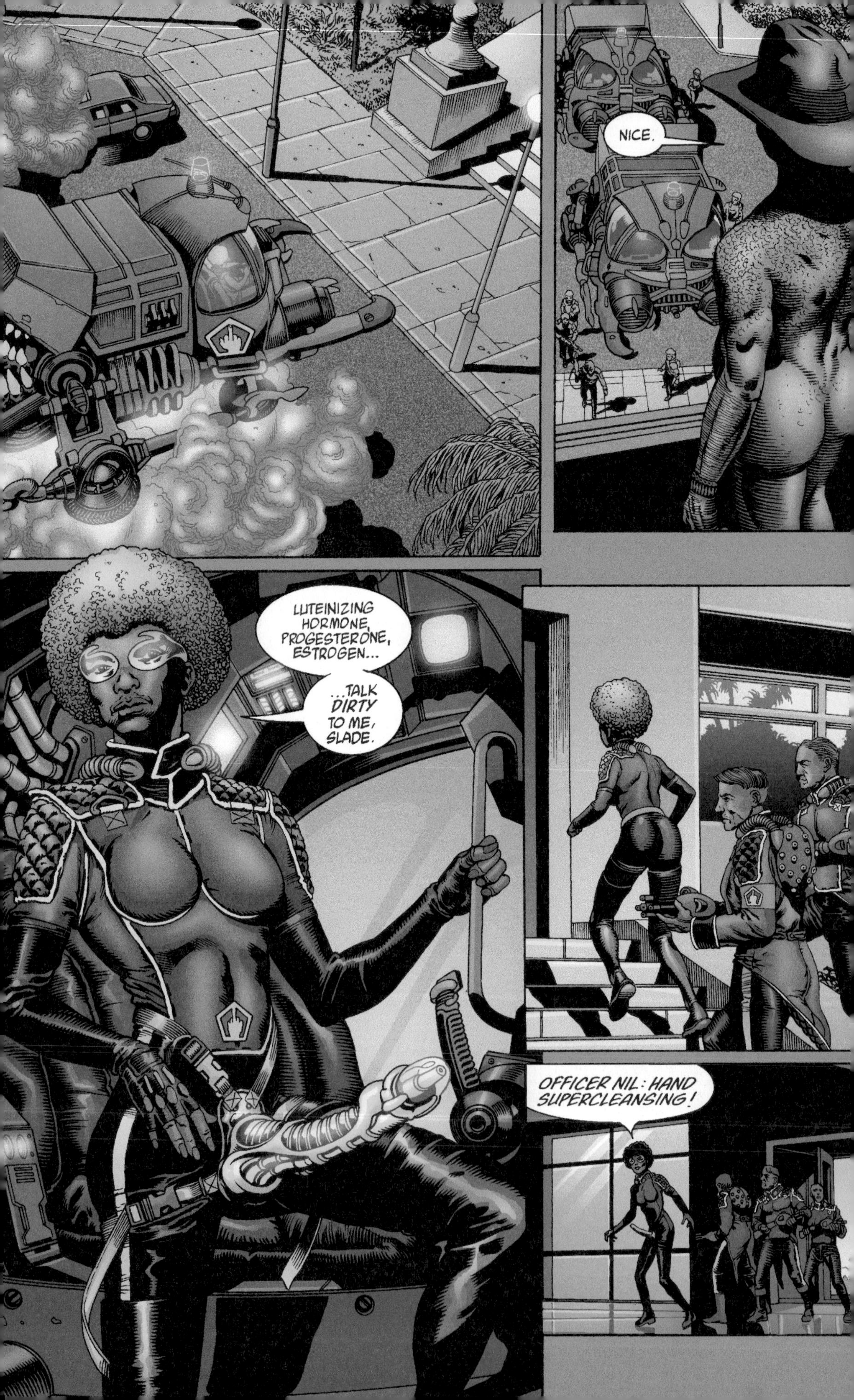
NICE.
LUTEINIZING HORMONE, PROGESTERONE, ESTROGEN...
...TALK DIRTY TO ME, SLADE.
OFFICER NIL: HAND SUPERCLEANSING!

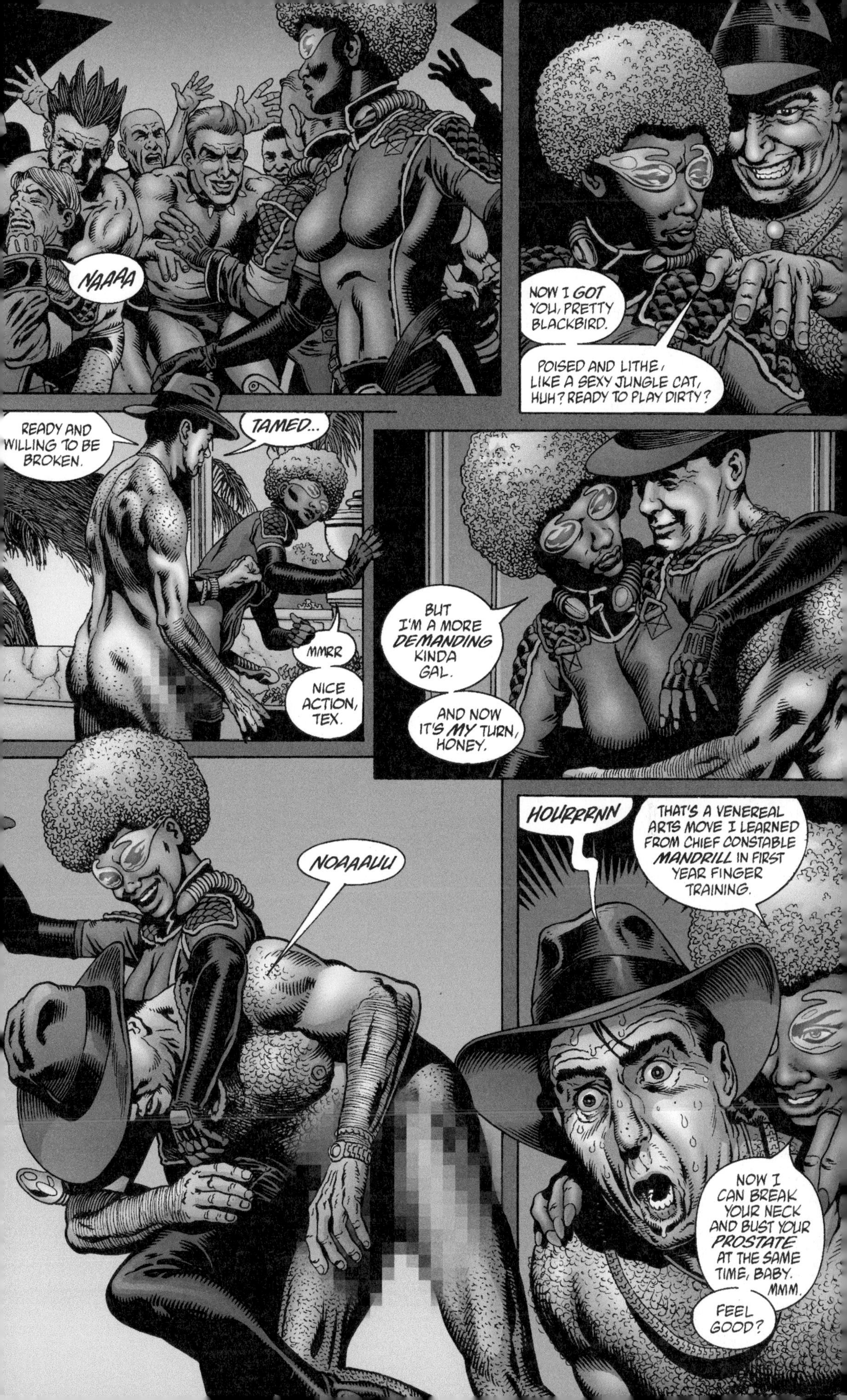
NAAAA
NOW I *GOT* YOU, PRETTY BLACKBIRD.
POISED AND LITHE, LIKE A SEXY JUNGLE CAT, HUH? READY TO PLAY DIRTY?
READY AND WILLING TO BE BROKEN.
TAMED...
MMRR
NICE ACTION, TEX.
BUT I'M A MORE *DEMANDING* KINDA GAL.
AND NOW IT'S *MY* TURN, HONEY.
NOAAAUU
HOURRRNN
THAT'S A VENEREAL ARTS MOVE I LEARNED FROM CHIEF CONSTABLE *MANDRILL* IN FIRST YEAR FINGER TRAINING.
NOW I CAN BREAK YOUR NECK AND BUST YOUR *PROSTATE* AT THE SAME TIME, BABY.
MMM.
FEEL GOOD?

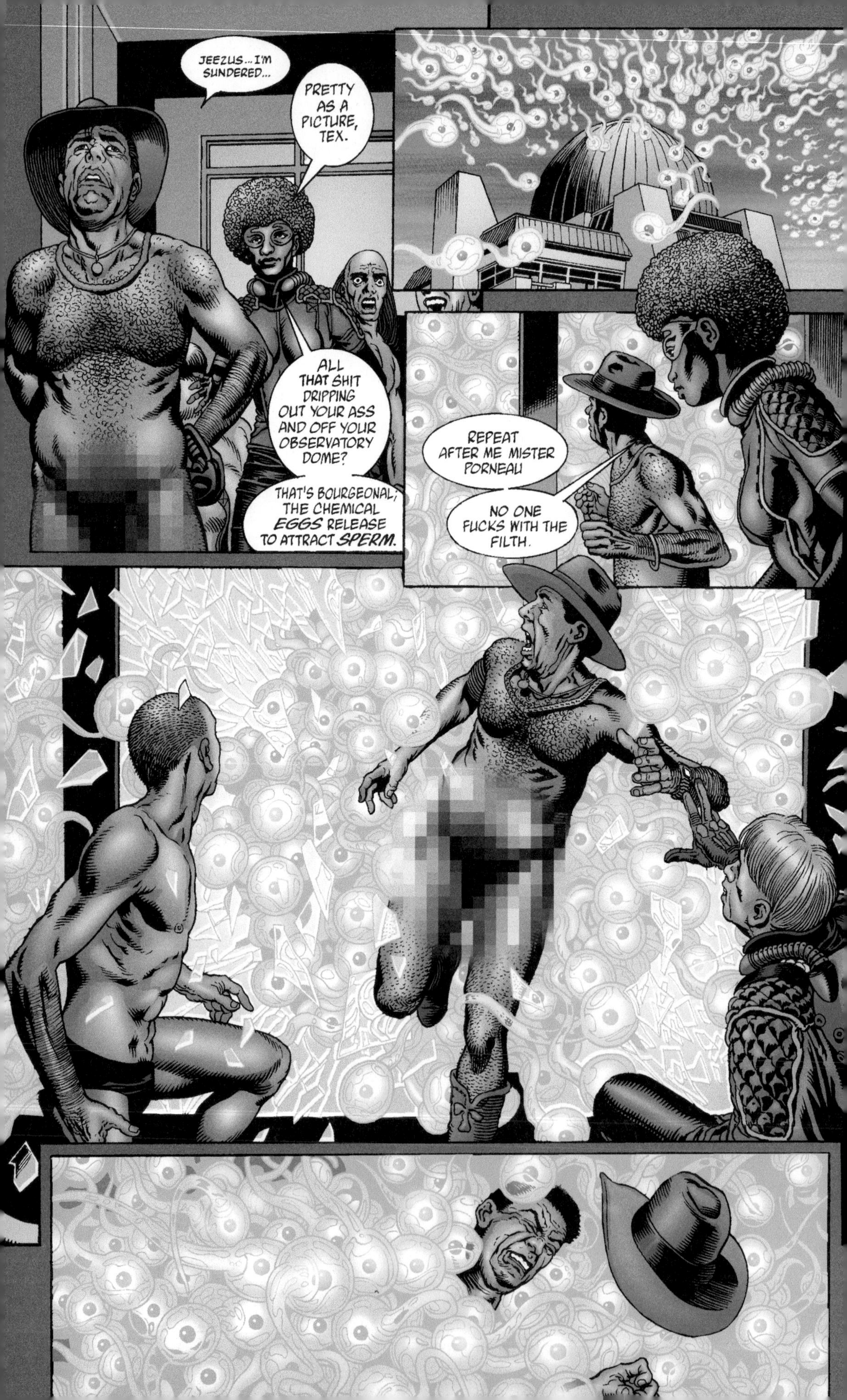
JEEZUS... I'M SUNDERED...
PRETTY AS A PICTURE, TEX.
ALL THAT SHIT DRIPPING OUT YOUR ASS AND OFF YOUR OBSERVATORY DOME?
THAT'S BOURGEONAL; THE CHEMICAL EGGS RELEASE TO ATTRACT SPERM.
REPEAT AFTER ME MISTER PORNEAU
NO ONE FUCKS WITH THE FILTH.

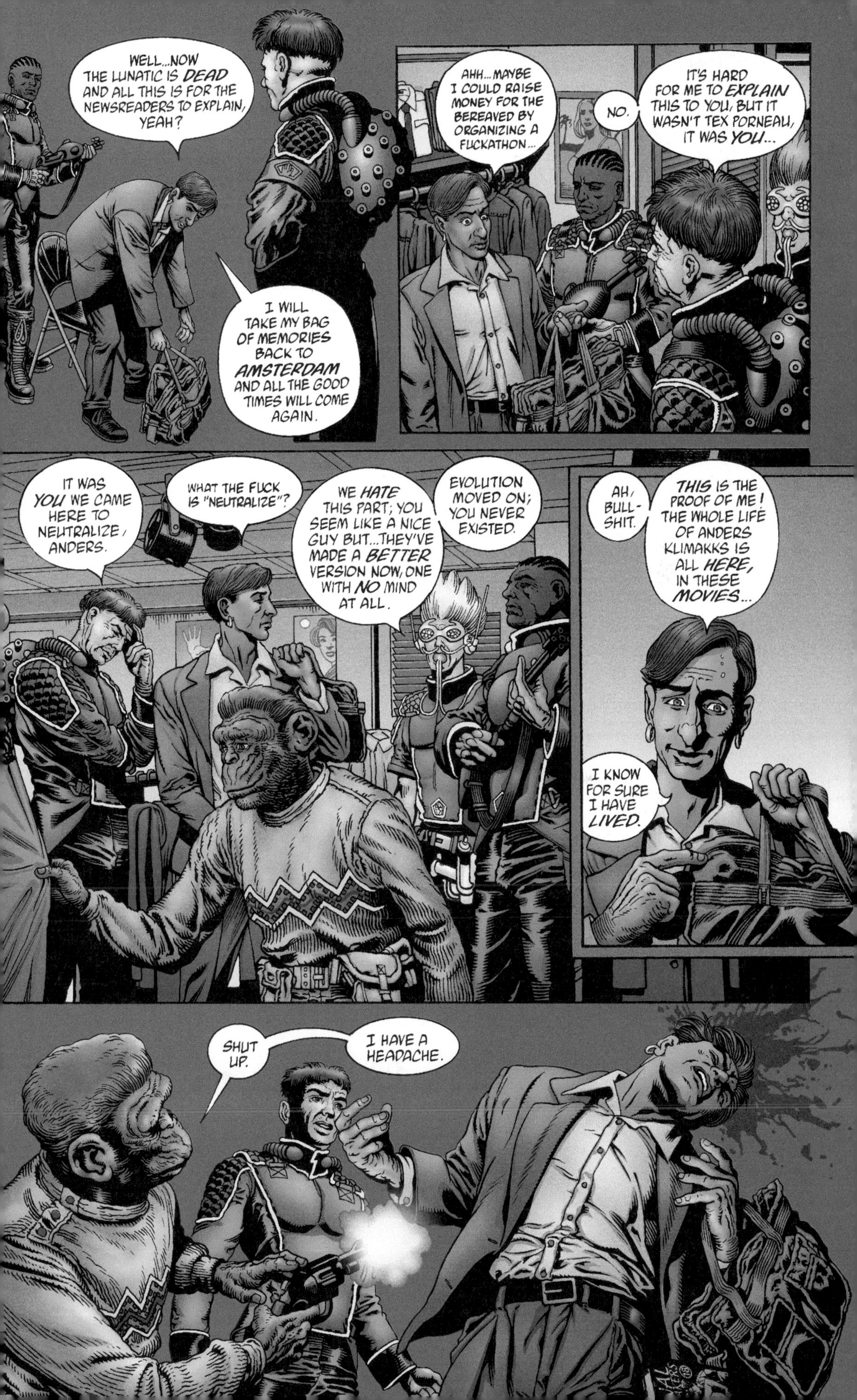
WELL...NOW THE LUNATIC IS DEAD AND ALL THIS IS FOR THE NEWSREADERS TO EXPLAIN, YEAH?
I WILL TAKE MY BAG OF MEMORIES BACK TO AMSTERDAM AND ALL THE GOOD TIMES WILL COME AGAIN.
AHH...MAYBE I COULD RAISE MONEY FOR THE BEREAVED BY ORGANIZING A FUCKATHON...
NO.
IT'S HARD FOR ME TO EXPLAIN THIS TO YOU, BUT IT WASN'T TEX PORNEAU, IT WAS YOU...
IT WAS YOU WE CAME HERE TO NEUTRALIZE, ANDERS.
WHAT THE FUCK IS "NEUTRALIZE"?
WE HATE THIS PART; YOU SEEM LIKE A NICE GUY BUT...THEY'VE MADE A BETTER VERSION NOW, ONE WITH NO MIND AT ALL.
EVOLUTION MOVED ON; YOU NEVER EXISTED.
AH, BULL-SHIT.
THIS IS THE PROOF OF ME! THE WHOLE LIFE OF ANDERS KLIMAKKS IS ALL HERE, IN THESE MOVIES...
I KNOW FOR SURE I HAVE LIVED.
SHUT UP.
I HAVE A HEADACHE.

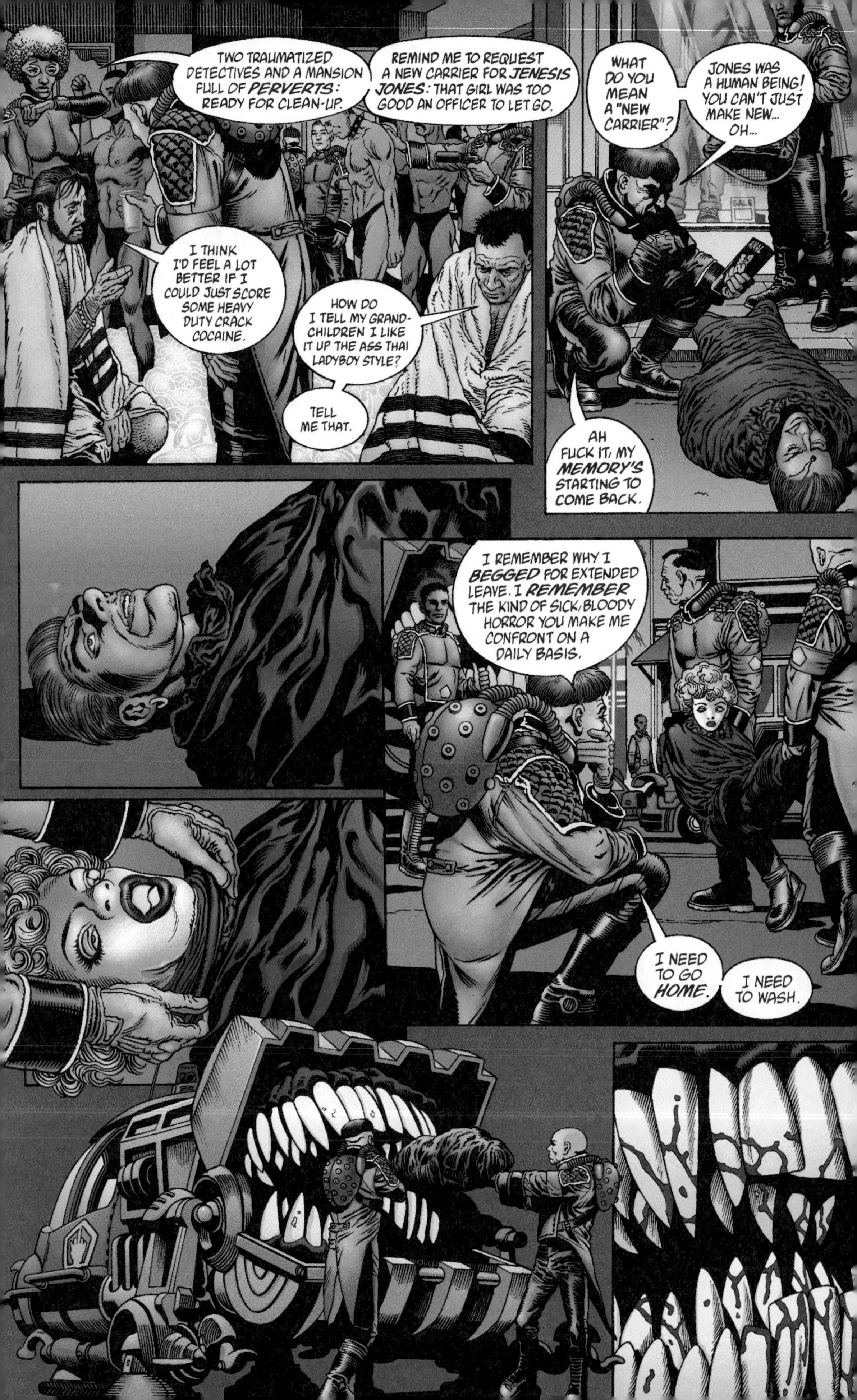
TWO TRAUMATIZED DETECTIVES AND A MANSION FULL OF PERVERTS: READY FOR CLEAN-UP.
REMIND ME TO REQUEST A NEW CARRIER FOR JENESIS JONES: THAT GIRL WAS TOO GOOD AN OFFICER TO LET GO.
I THINK I'D FEEL A LOT BETTER IF I COULD JUST SCORE SOME HEAVY DUTY CRACK COCAINE.
HOW DO I TELL MY GRAND-CHILDREN I LIKE IT UP THE ASS THAI LADYBOY STYLE?
TELL ME THAT.
WHAT DO YOU MEAN A "NEW CARRIER"?
JONES WAS A HUMAN BEING! YOU CAN'T JUST MAKE NEW... OH...
AH FUCK IT, MY MEMORY'S STARTING TO COME BACK.
I REMEMBER WHY I BEGGED FOR EXTENDED LEAVE. I REMEMBER THE KIND OF SICK, BLOODY HORROR YOU MAKE ME CONFRONT ON A DAILY BASIS.
I NEED TO GO HOME.
I NEED TO WASH.

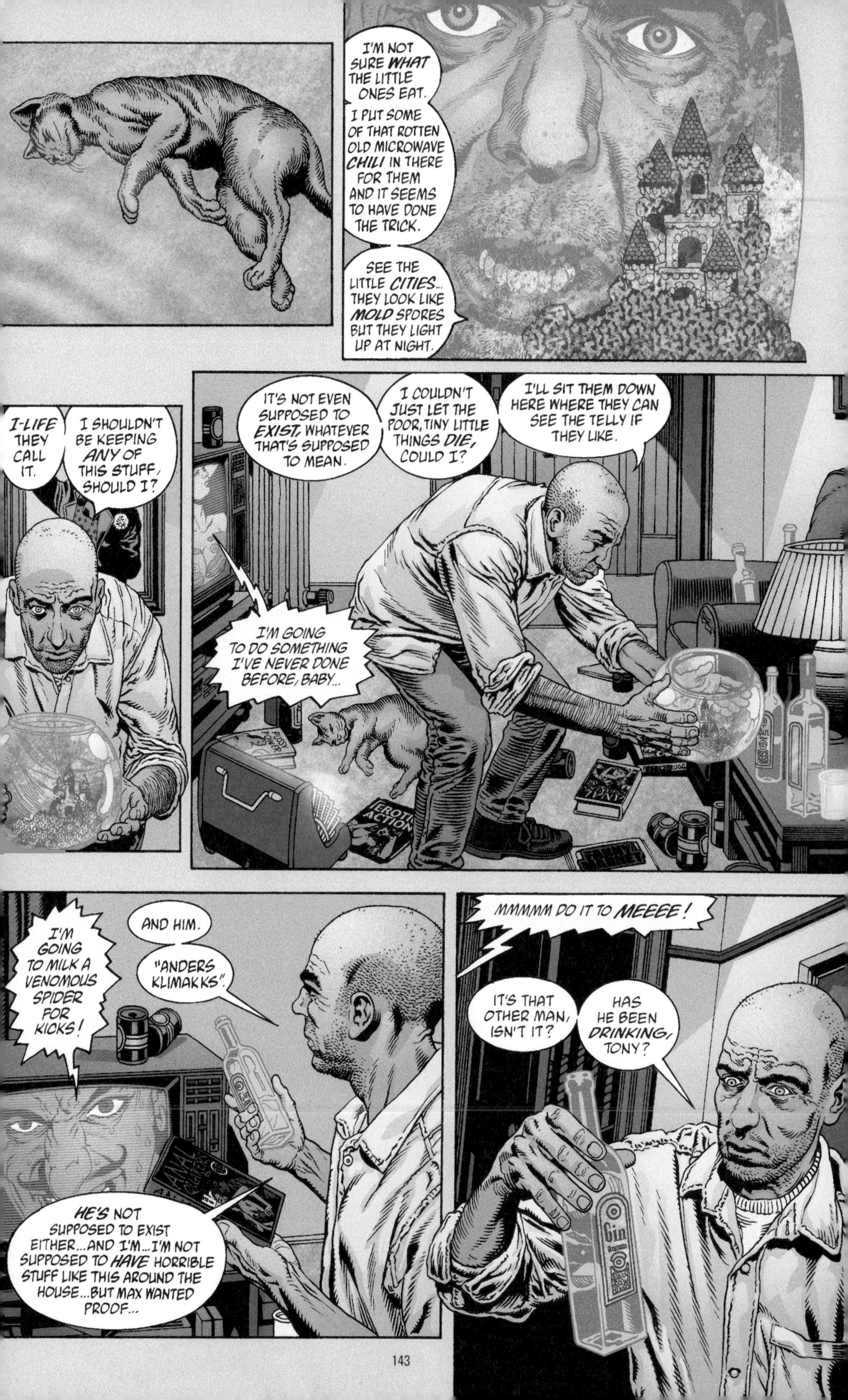
I'M NOT SURE WHAT THE LITTLE ONES EAT.
I PUT SOME OF THAT ROTTEN OLD MICROWAVE CHILI IN THERE FOR THEM AND IT SEEMS TO HAVE DONE THE TRICK.
SEE THE LITTLE CITIES... THEY LOOK LIKE MOLD SPORES BUT THEY LIGHT UP AT NIGHT.
I-LIFE THEY CALL IT.
I SHOULDN'T BE KEEPING ANY OF THIS STUFF, SHOULD I?
IT'S NOT EVEN SUPPOSED TO EXIST, WHATEVER THAT'S SUPPOSED TO MEAN.
I COULDN'T JUST LET THE POOR, TINY LITTLE THINGS DIE, COULD I?
I'LL SIT THEM DOWN HERE WHERE THEY CAN SEE THE TELLY IF THEY LIKE.
I'M GOING TO DO SOMETHING I'VE NEVER DONE BEFORE, BABY...
I'M GOING TO MILK A VENOMOUS SPIDER FOR KICKS!
AND HIM.
"ANDERS KLIMAKKS".
HE'S NOT SUPPOSED TO EXIST EITHER...AND I'M...I'M NOT SUPPOSED TO HAVE HORRIBLE STUFF LIKE THIS AROUND THE HOUSE...BUT MAX WANTED PROOF...
MMMMM DO IT TO MEEEE!
IT'S THAT OTHER MAN, ISN'T IT?
HAS HE BEEN DRINKING, TONY?

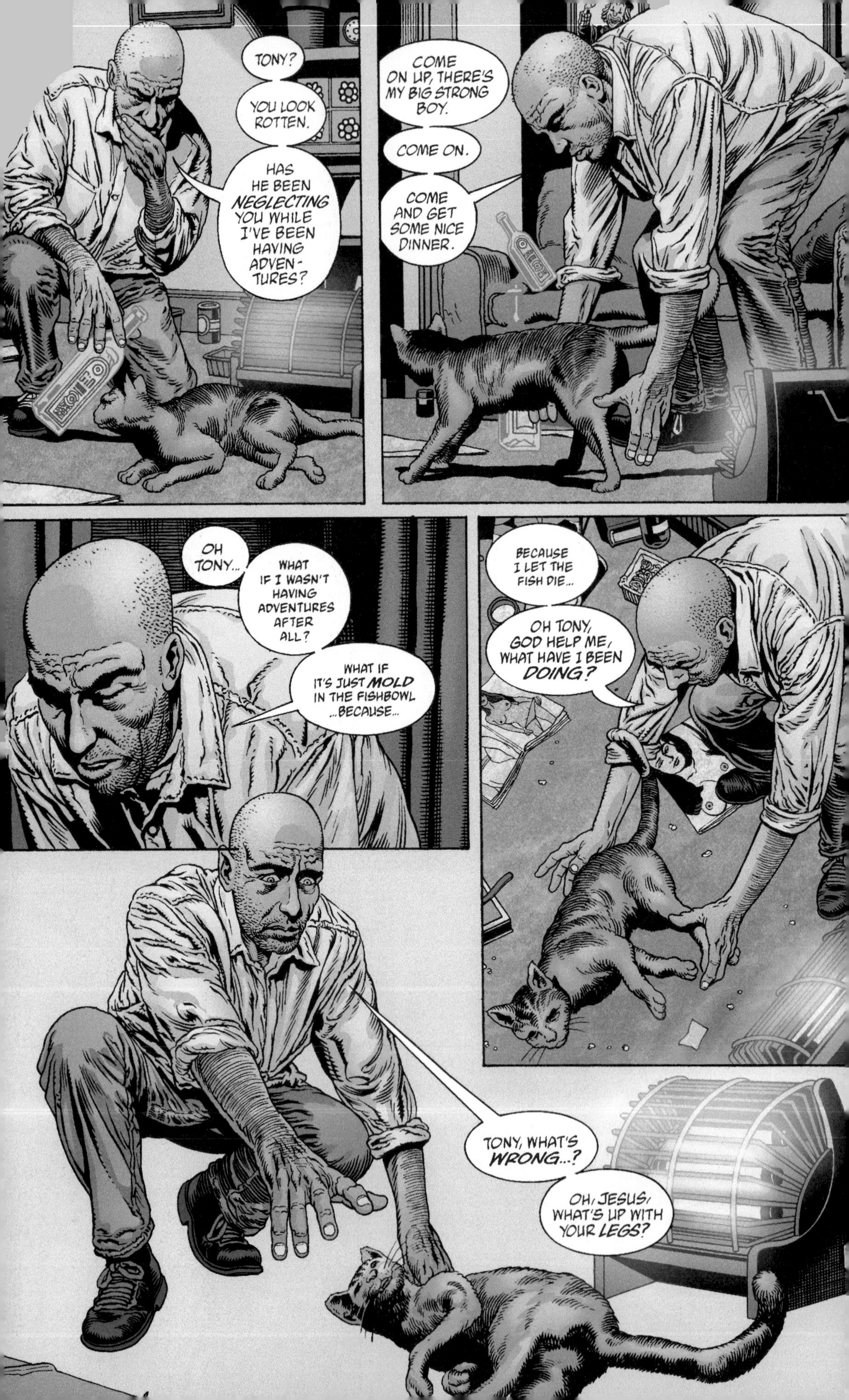
TONY?
YOU LOOK ROTTEN.
HAS HE BEEN NEGLECTING YOU WHILE I'VE BEEN HAVING ADVEN-TURES?
COME ON UP, THERE'S MY BIG STRONG BOY.
COME ON.
COME AND GET SOME NICE DINNER.
OH TONY...
WHAT IF I WASN'T HAVING ADVENTURES AFTER ALL?
WHAT IF IT'S JUST MOLD IN THE FISHBOWL ...BECAUSE...
BECAUSE I LET THE FISH DIE...
OH TONY, GOD HELP ME, WHAT HAVE I BEEN DOING?
TONY, WHAT'S WRONG...?
OH, JESUS, WHAT'S UP WITH YOUR LEGS?

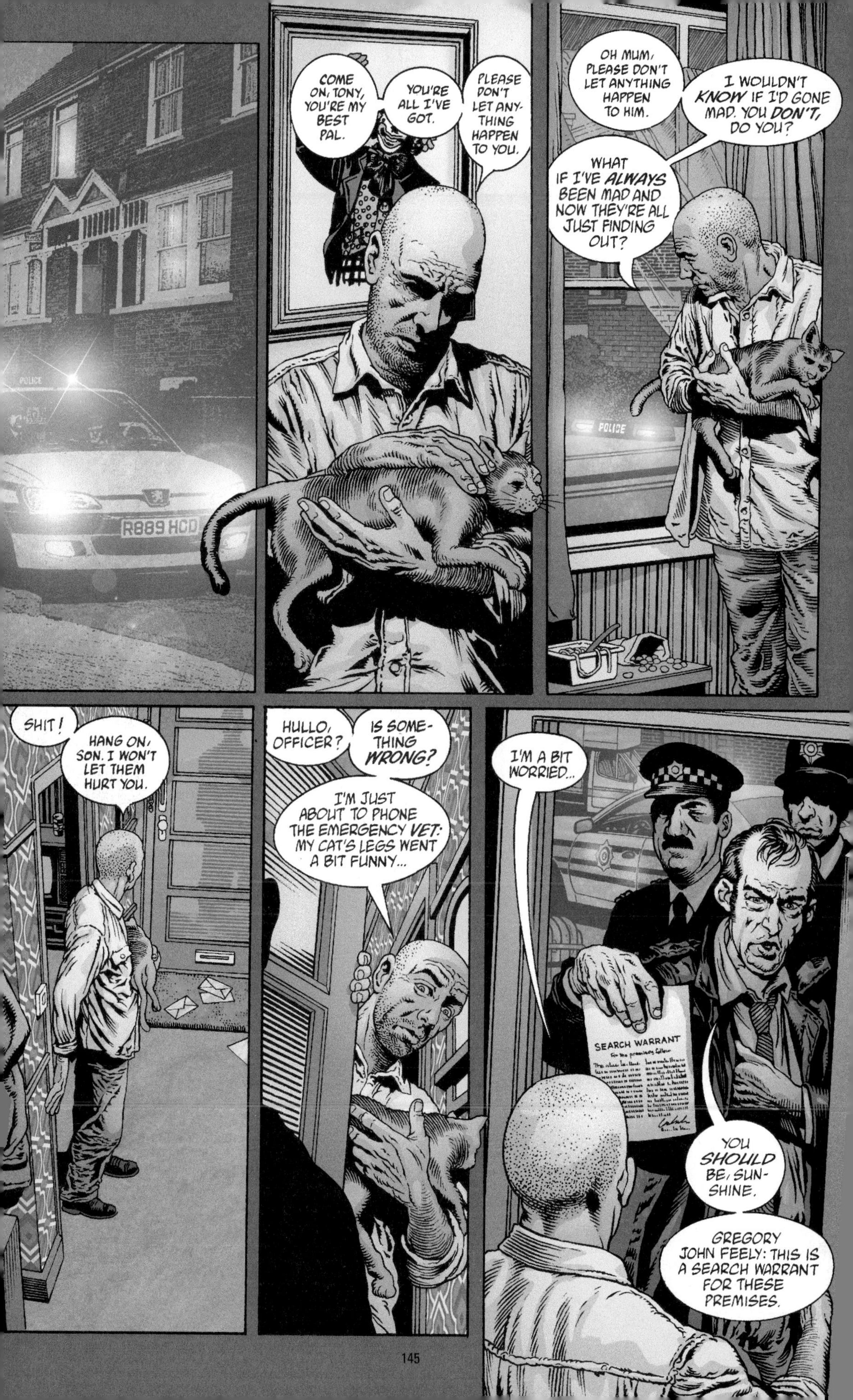
POLICE
R889 HCD
COME ON, TONY, YOU'RE MY BEST PAL.
YOU'RE ALL I'VE GOT.
PLEASE DON'T LET ANYTHING HAPPEN TO YOU.
OH MUM, PLEASE DON'T LET ANYTHING HAPPEN TO HIM.
I WOULDN'T KNOW IF I'D GONE MAD. YOU DON'T, DO YOU?
WHAT IF I'VE ALWAYS BEEN MAD AND NOW THEY'RE ALL JUST FINDING OUT?
POLICE
SHIT!
HANG ON, SON. I WON'T LET THEM HURT YOU.
HULLO, OFFICER?
IS SOMETHING WRONG?
I'M JUST ABOUT TO PHONE THE EMERGENCY VET: MY CAT'S LEGS WENT A BIT FUNNY...
I'M A BIT WORRIED...
SEARCH WARRANT
YOU SHOULD BE, SUNSHINE.
GREGORY JOHN FEELY: THIS IS A SEARCH WARRANT FOR THESE PREMISES.

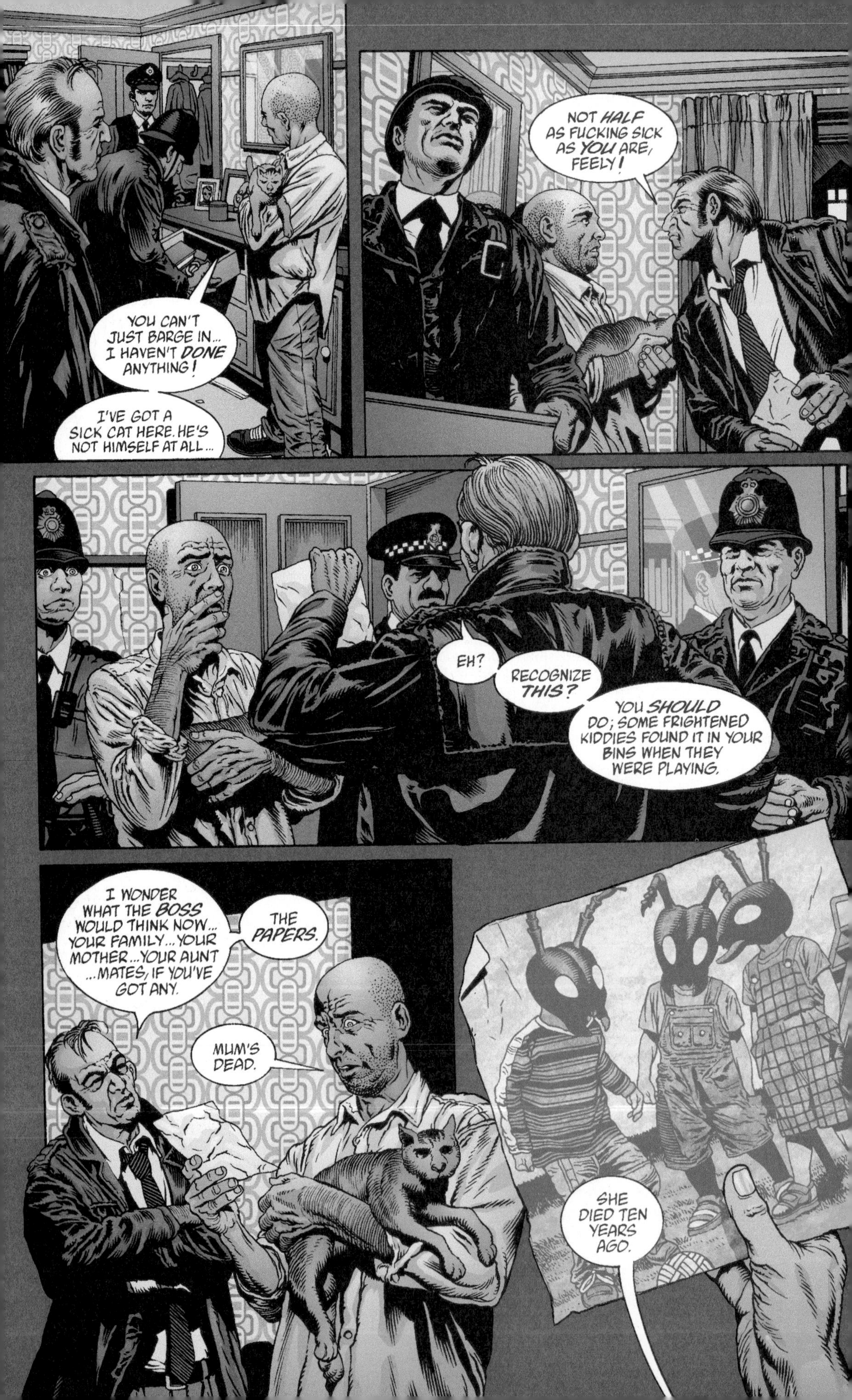
YOU CAN'T JUST BARGE IN... I HAVEN'T DONE ANYTHING!
I'VE GOT A SICK CAT HERE. HE'S NOT HIMSELF AT ALL...
NOT HALF AS FUCKING SICK AS YOU ARE, FEELY!
EH?
RECOGNIZE THIS?
YOU SHOULD DO; SOME FRIGHTENED KIDDIES FOUND IT IN YOUR BINS WHEN THEY WERE PLAYING.
I WONDER WHAT THE BOSS WOULD THINK NOW... YOUR FAMILY... YOUR MOTHER... YOUR AUNT ...MATES, IF YOU'VE GOT ANY.
THE PAPERS.
MUM'S DEAD.
SHE DIED TEN YEARS AGO.

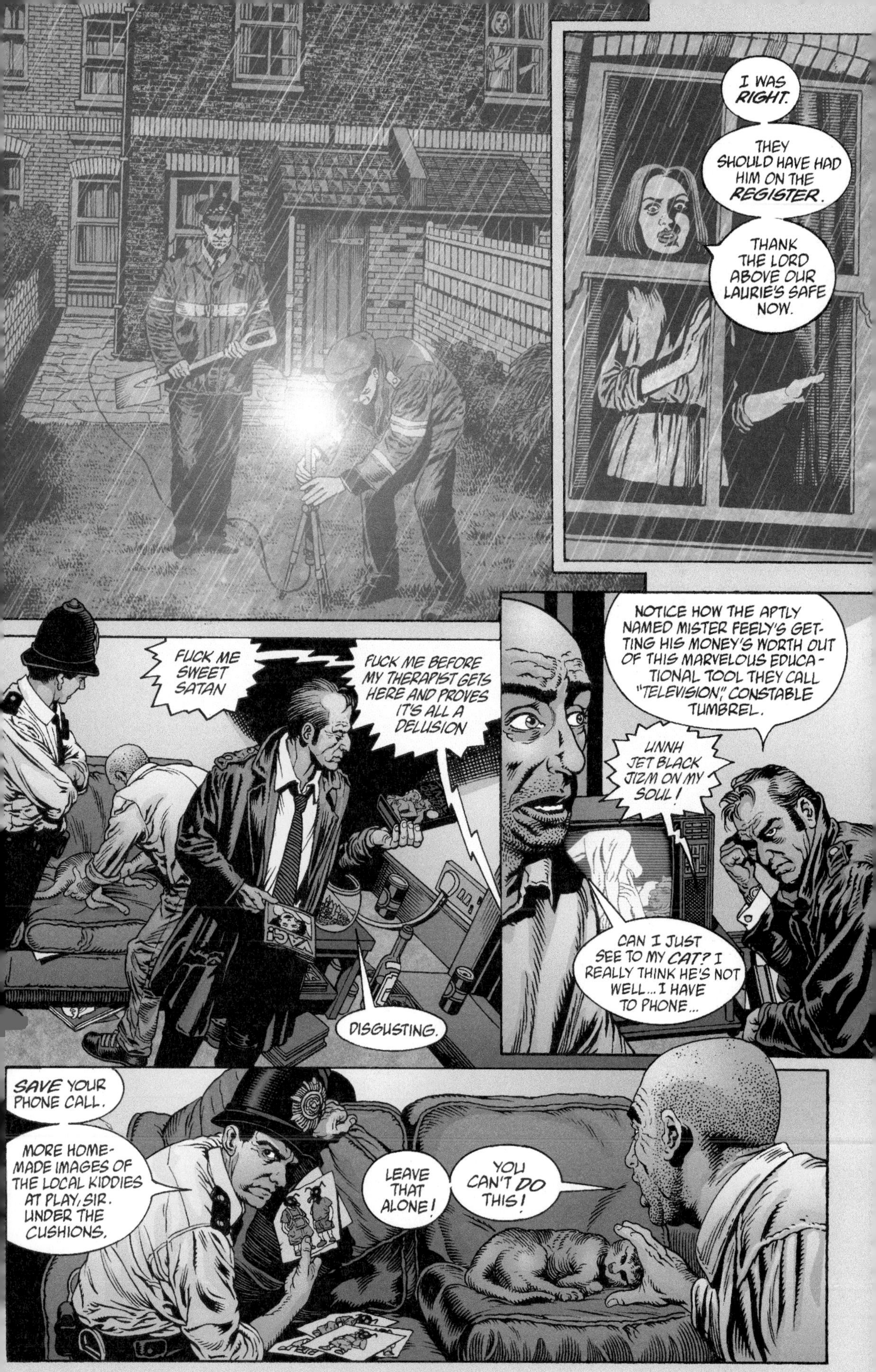
I WAS RIGHT.
THEY SHOULD HAVE HAD HIM ON THE REGISTER.
THANK THE LORD ABOVE OUR LAURIE'S SAFE NOW.
FUCK ME SWEET SATAN
FUCK ME BEFORE MY THERAPIST GETS HERE AND PROVES IT'S ALL A DELUSION
DISGUSTING.
NOTICE HOW THE APTLY NAMED MISTER FEELY'S GETTING HIS MONEY'S WORTH OUT OF THIS MARVELOUS EDUCATIONAL TOOL THEY CALL "TELEVISION," CONSTABLE TUMBREL.
UNNH JET BLACK JIZM ON MY SOUL!
CAN I JUST SEE TO MY CAT? I REALLY THINK HE'S NOT WELL... I HAVE TO PHONE...
SAVE YOUR PHONE CALL.
MORE HOME-MADE IMAGES OF THE LOCAL KIDDIES AT PLAY, SIR. UNDER THE CUSHIONS.
LEAVE THAT ALONE!
YOU CAN'T DO THIS!

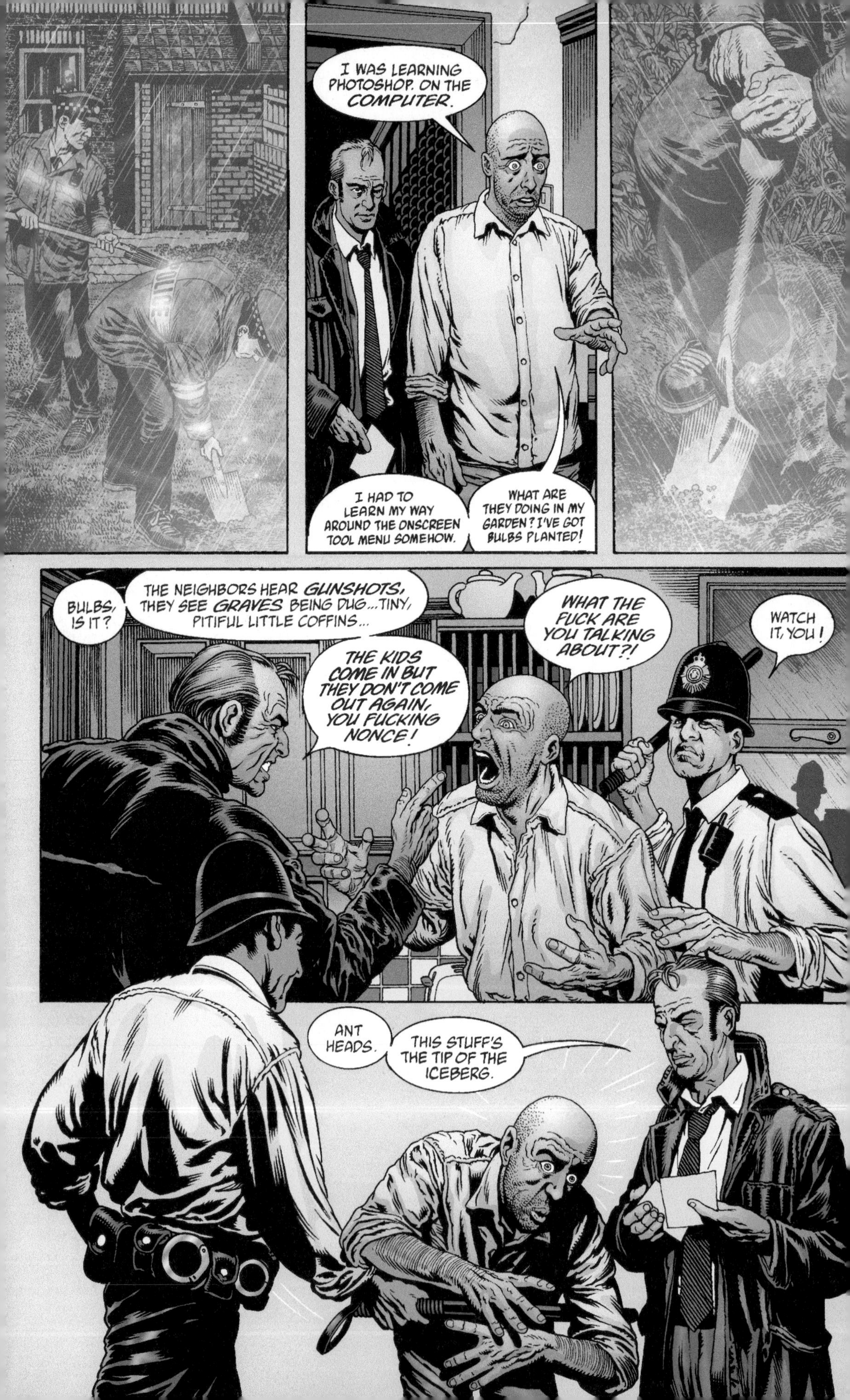
I WAS LEARNING PHOTOSHOP. ON THE COMPUTER.
I HAD TO LEARN MY WAY AROUND THE ONSCREEN TOOL MENU SOMEHOW.
WHAT ARE THEY DOING IN MY GARDEN? I'VE GOT BULBS PLANTED!
BULBS, IS IT?
THE NEIGHBORS HEAR GUNSHOTS, THEY SEE GRAVES BEING DUG... TINY, PITIFUL LITTLE COFFINS...
THE KIDS COME IN BUT THEY DON'T COME OUT AGAIN, YOU FUCKING NONCE!
WHAT THE FUCK ARE YOU TALKING ABOUT?!
WATCH IT, YOU!
ANT HEADS.
THIS STUFF'S THE TIP OF THE ICEBERG.

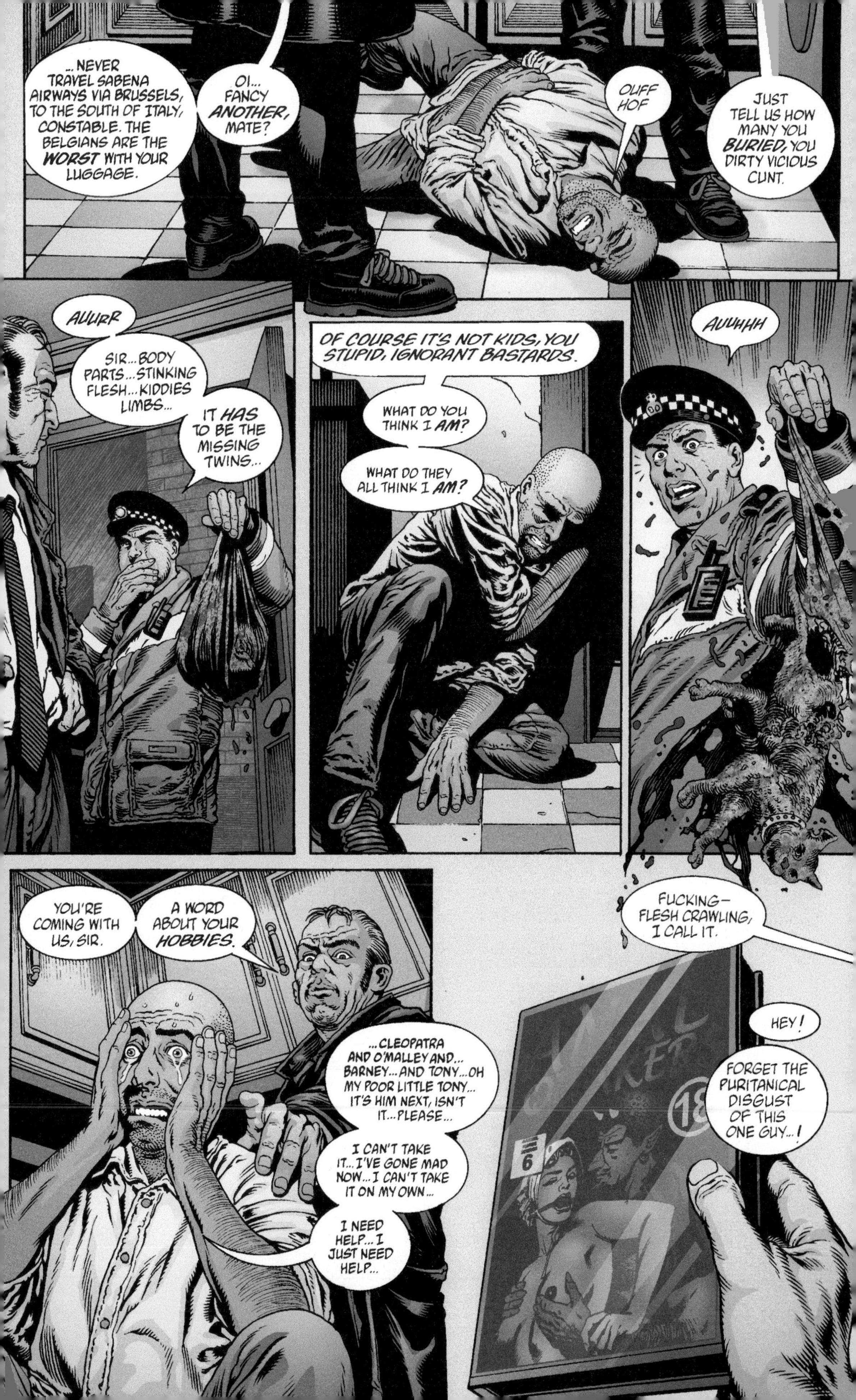
...NEVER TRAVEL SABENA AIRWAYS VIA BRUSSELS, TO THE SOUTH OF ITALY, CONSTABLE. THE BELGIANS ARE THE WORST WITH YOUR LUGGAGE.
OI... FANCY ANOTHER, MATE?
OUFF HOF
JUST TELL US HOW MANY YOU BURIED, YOU DIRTY VICIOUS CUNT.
AUURR
SIR...BODY PARTS...STINKING FLESH...KIDDIES LIMBS...
IT HAS TO BE THE MISSING TWINS...
OF COURSE IT'S NOT KIDS, YOU STUPID, IGNORANT BASTARDS.
WHAT DO YOU THINK I AM?
WHAT DO THEY ALL THINK I AM?
AUUHHH
YOU'RE COMING WITH US, SIR.
A WORD ABOUT YOUR HOBBIES.
...CLEOPATRA AND O'MALLEY AND... BARNEY...AND TONY...OH MY POOR LITTLE TONY... IT'S HIM NEXT, ISN'T IT...PLEASE...
I CAN'T TAKE IT...I'VE GONE MAD NOW...I CAN'T TAKE IT ON MY OWN...
I NEED HELP...I JUST NEED HELP...
FUCKING— FLESH CRAWLING, I CALL IT.
HEY!
FORGET THE PURITANICAL DISGUST OF THIS ONE GUY...!
18
6

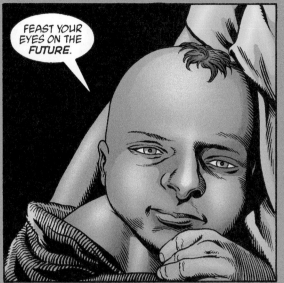

FEAST YOUR EYES ON THE *FUTURE.*

IN HIS *CRAZY,* HEADLONG LIFESTYLE OF FIVE YEARS, ANDERS KLIMAKKS HAS SEDUCED, FUCKED AND MADE BABIES WITH *824* WOMEN.

EVERY SINGLE BLACK SPERM, AND ALL THE BABIES, ARE COPIES OF ANDERS KLIMAKKS AND HAVE READ THE SAME *BOOKS* AND WATCHED THE SAME *MOVIES* ALSO AS ANDERS.

WHO WOULD BELIEVE THIS? THAT A *NOBODY* IS THE GUY WHO WILL ONE DAY BECOME THE ULTIMATE *EVERYBODY?*

ALL YOU NEED IS FUCK, YEAH?

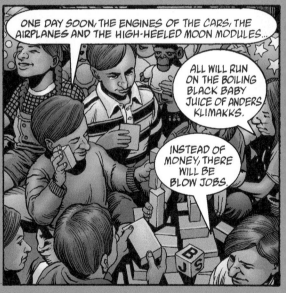

ONE DAY SOON, THE ENGINES OF THE CARS, THE AIRPLANES AND THE HIGH-HEELED MOON MODULES...

ALL WILL RUN ON THE BOILING BLACK BABY JUICE OF ANDERS KLIMAKKS.

INSTEAD OF MONEY, THERE WILL BE BLOW JOBS.

THE LONELY AND THE SUICIDAL WILL BE GANG-BANGED BACK TO SANITY ONLINE.

THE JOB OF EVERYBODY WILL BE TO FUCK EVERY-BODY *ELSE* FOR THE CAMERA TO WATCH.

AND THE CUM WILL FLOW LIKE THERE CAN BE NO TOMOR-ROW, SO EVERY-ONE IS HAPPY.

IN THE WORLD OF ANDERS KLIMAKKS.

The Filth™

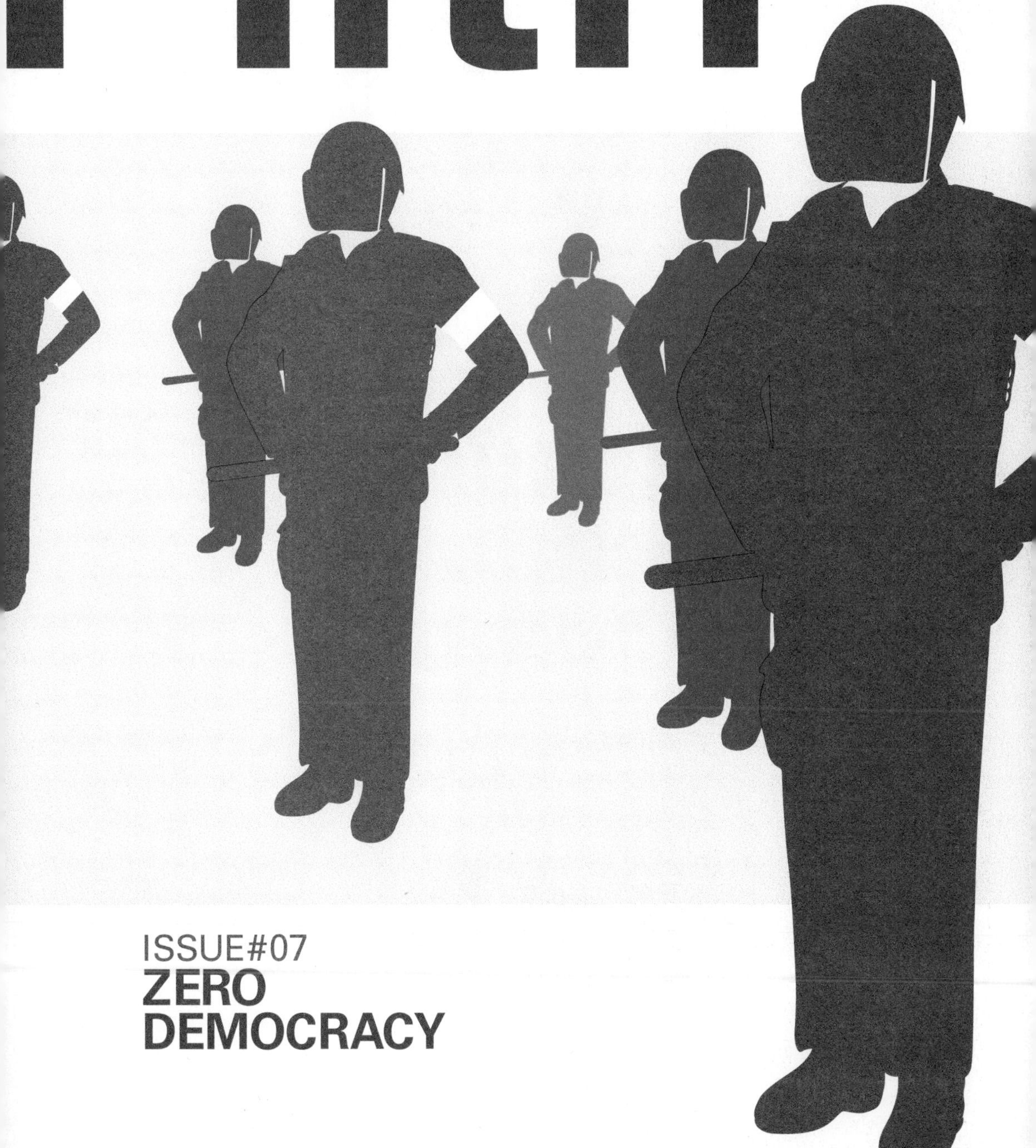

ISSUE#07
ZERO DEMOCRACY

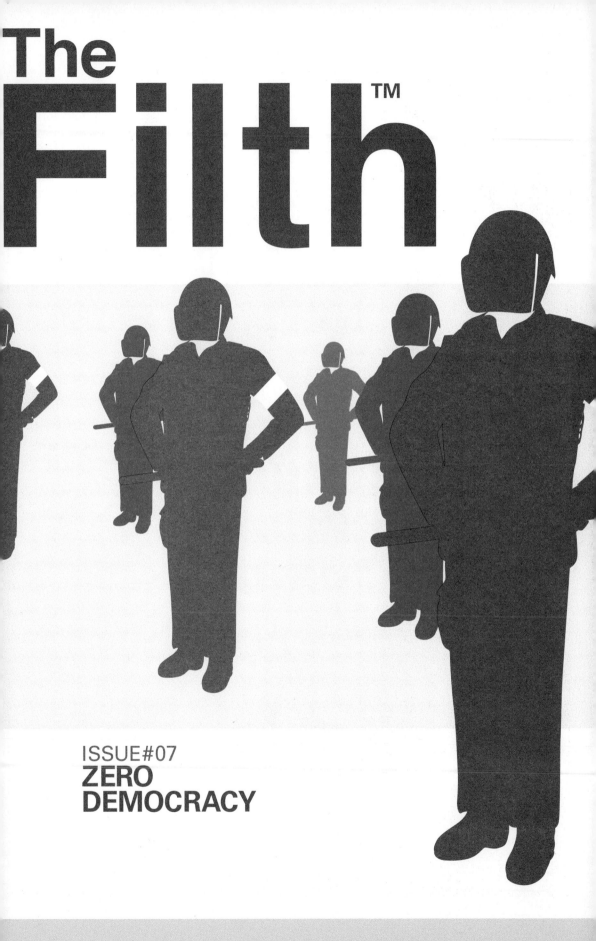

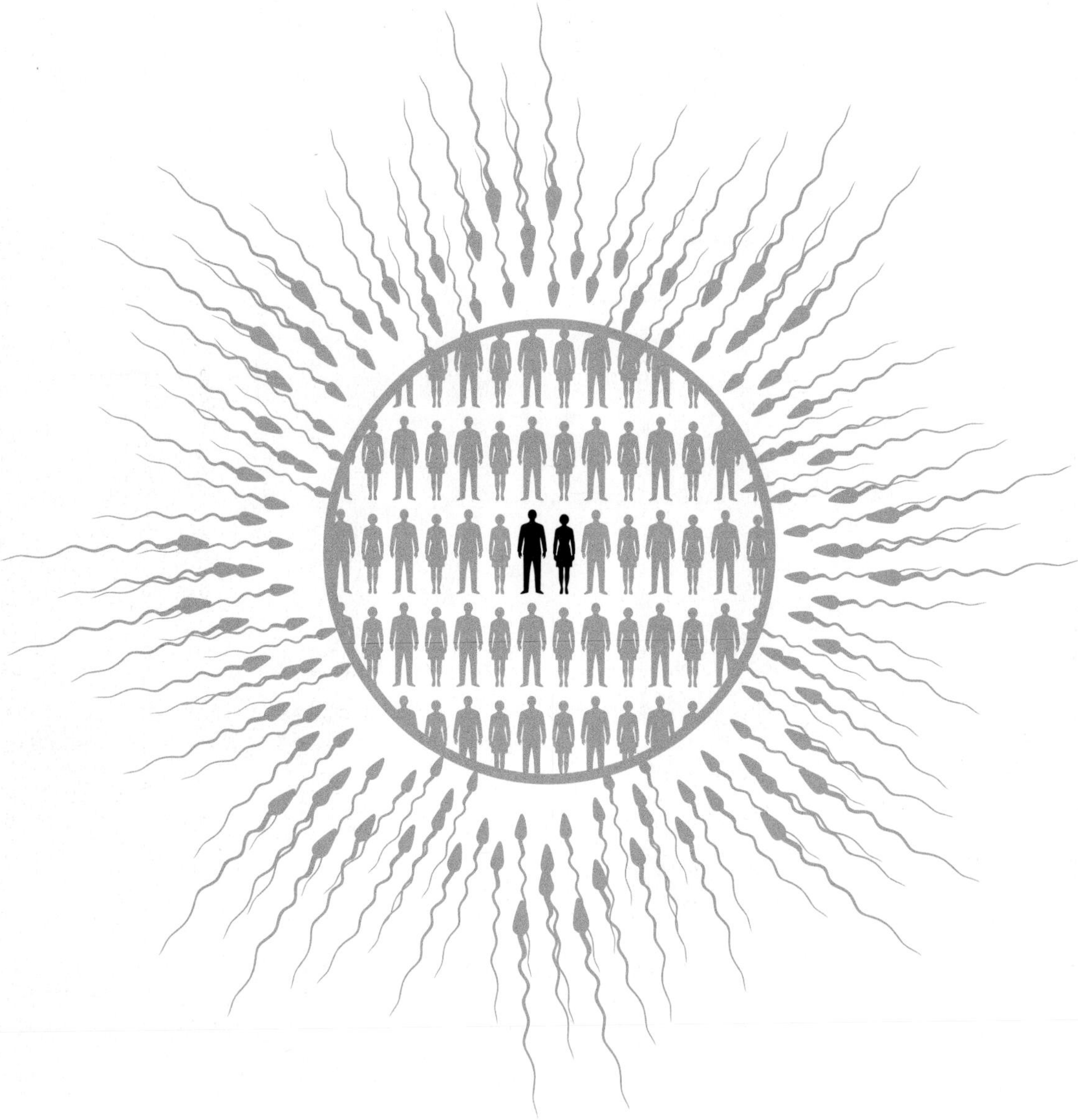

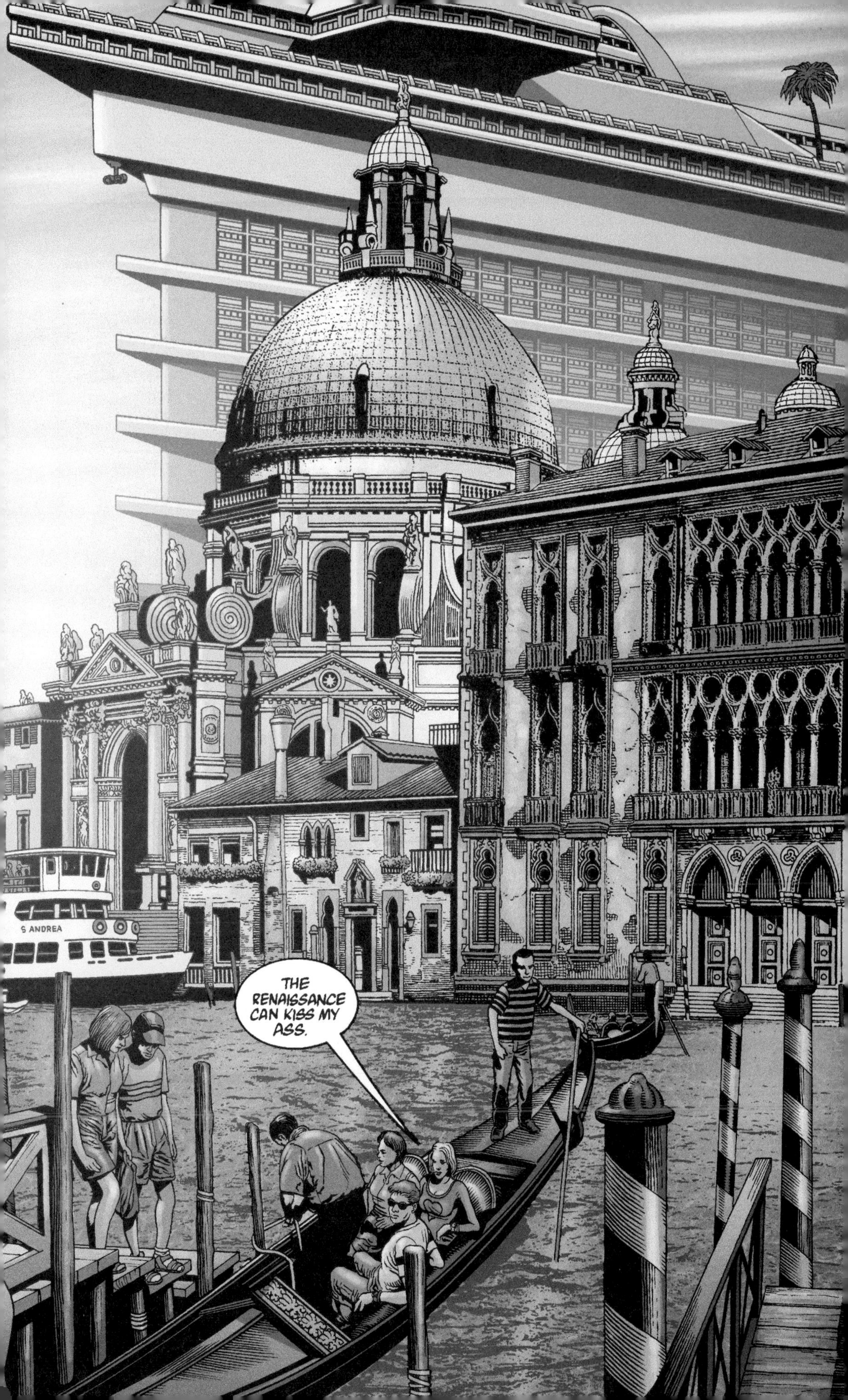
S ANDREA
THE RENAISSANCE CAN KISS MY ASS.

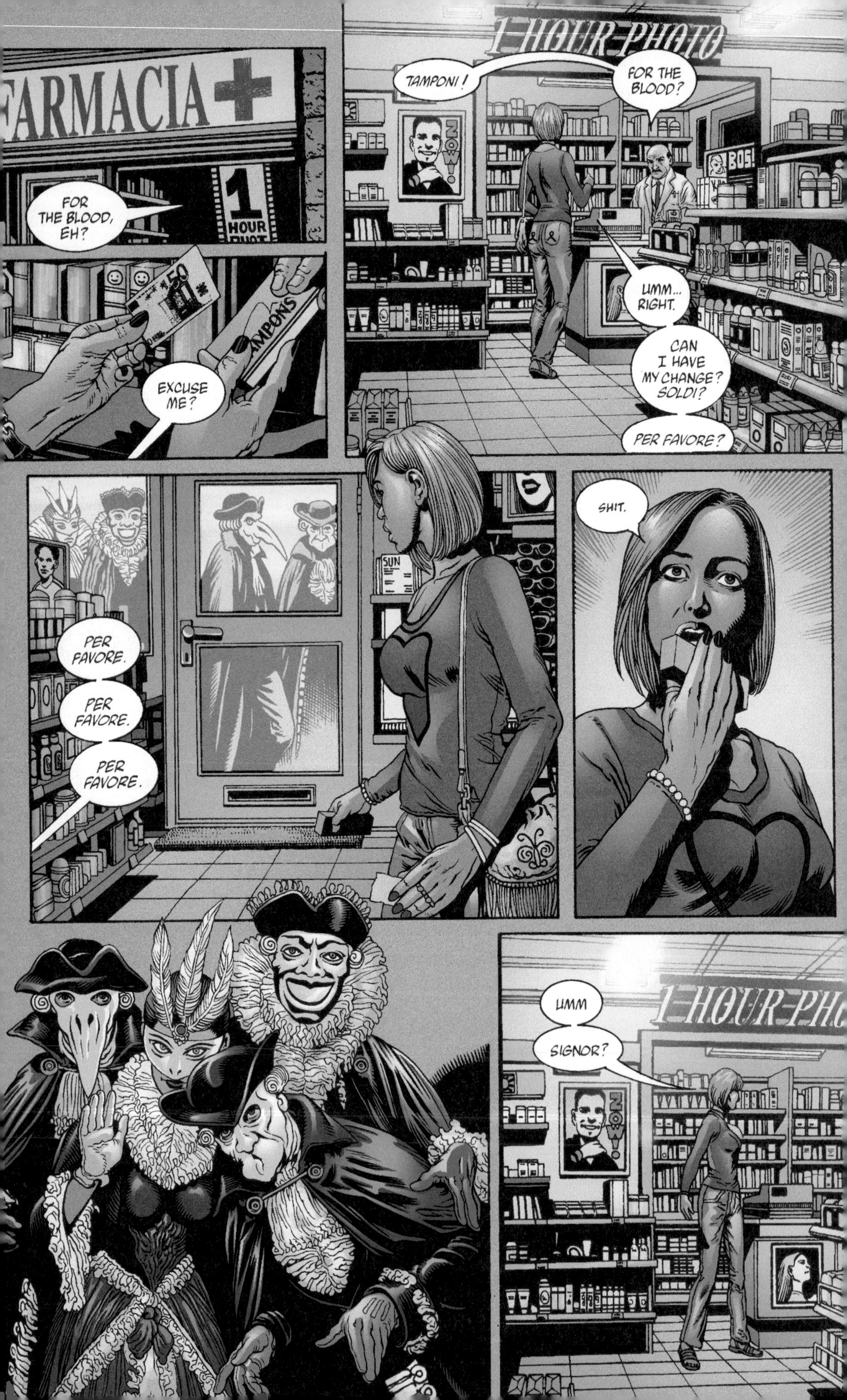
FARMACIA
1 HOUR PHOT
FOR THE BLOOD, EH?
EXCUSE ME?
AMPONS
1 HOUR PHOTO
TAMPONI!
FOR THE BLOOD?
BOS!
UMM... RIGHT.
CAN I HAVE MY CHANGE? SOLDI?
PER FAVORE?
PER FAVORE.
PER FAVORE.
PER FAVORE.
SUN
SHIT.
1 HOUR PHO
UMM
SIGNOR?

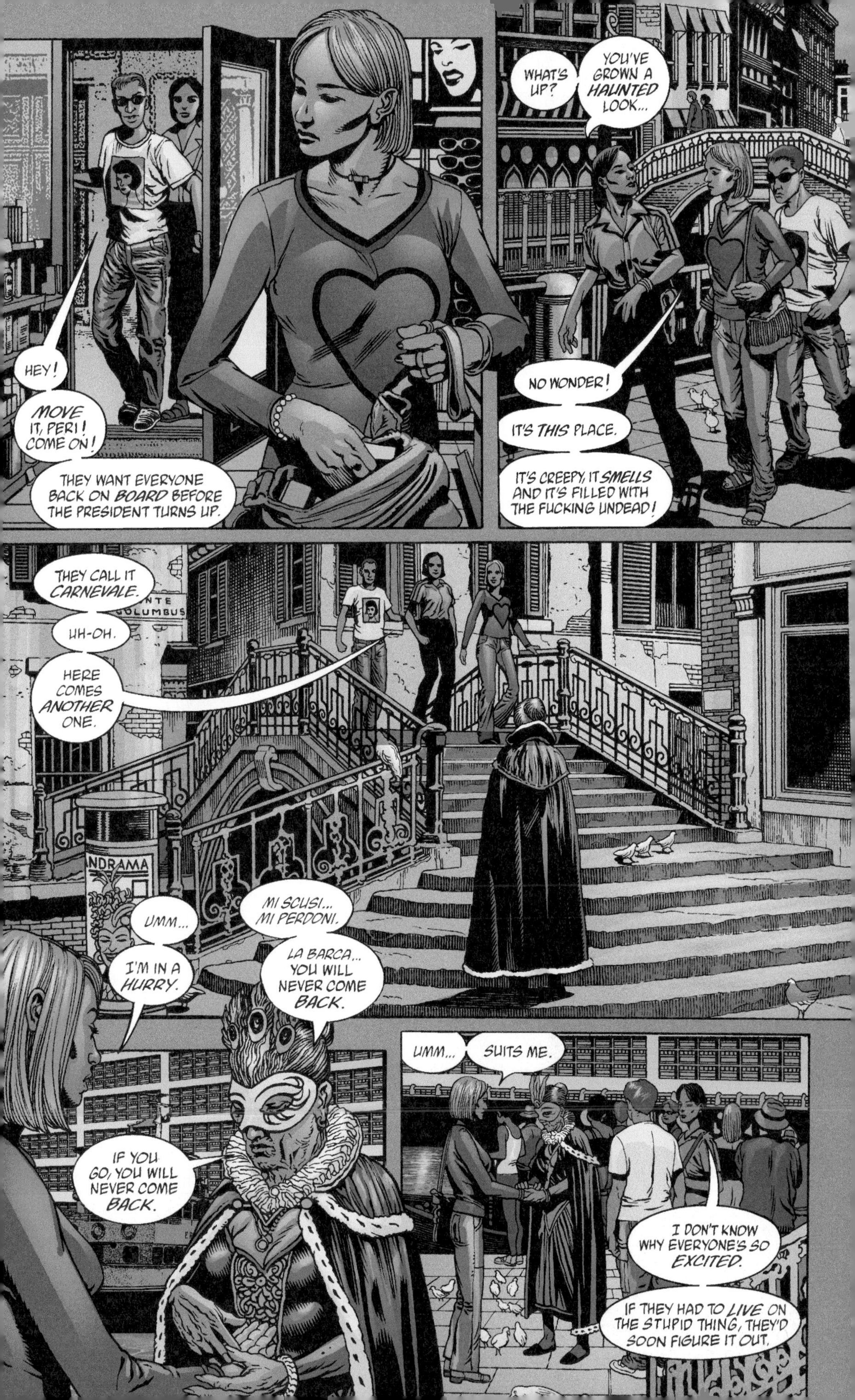
HEY!
MOVE IT, PERI! COME ON!
THEY WANT EVERYONE BACK ON BOARD BEFORE THE PRESIDENT TURNS UP.
WHAT'S UP?
YOU'VE GROWN A HAUNTED LOOK...
NO WONDER!
IT'S THIS PLACE.
IT'S CREEPY, IT SMELLS AND IT'S FILLED WITH THE FUCKING UNDEAD!
THEY CALL IT CARNEVALE.
UH-OH.
HERE COMES ANOTHER ONE.
NTE
COLUMBUS
ANDRAMA
UMM...
I'M IN A HURRY.
MI SCUSI... MI PERDONI.
LA BARCA... YOU WILL NEVER COME BACK.
IF YOU GO, YOU WILL NEVER COME BACK.
UMM...
SUITS ME.
I DON'T KNOW WHY EVERYONE'S SO EXCITED.
IF THEY HAD TO LIVE ON THE STUPID THING, THEY'D SOON FIGURE IT OUT.

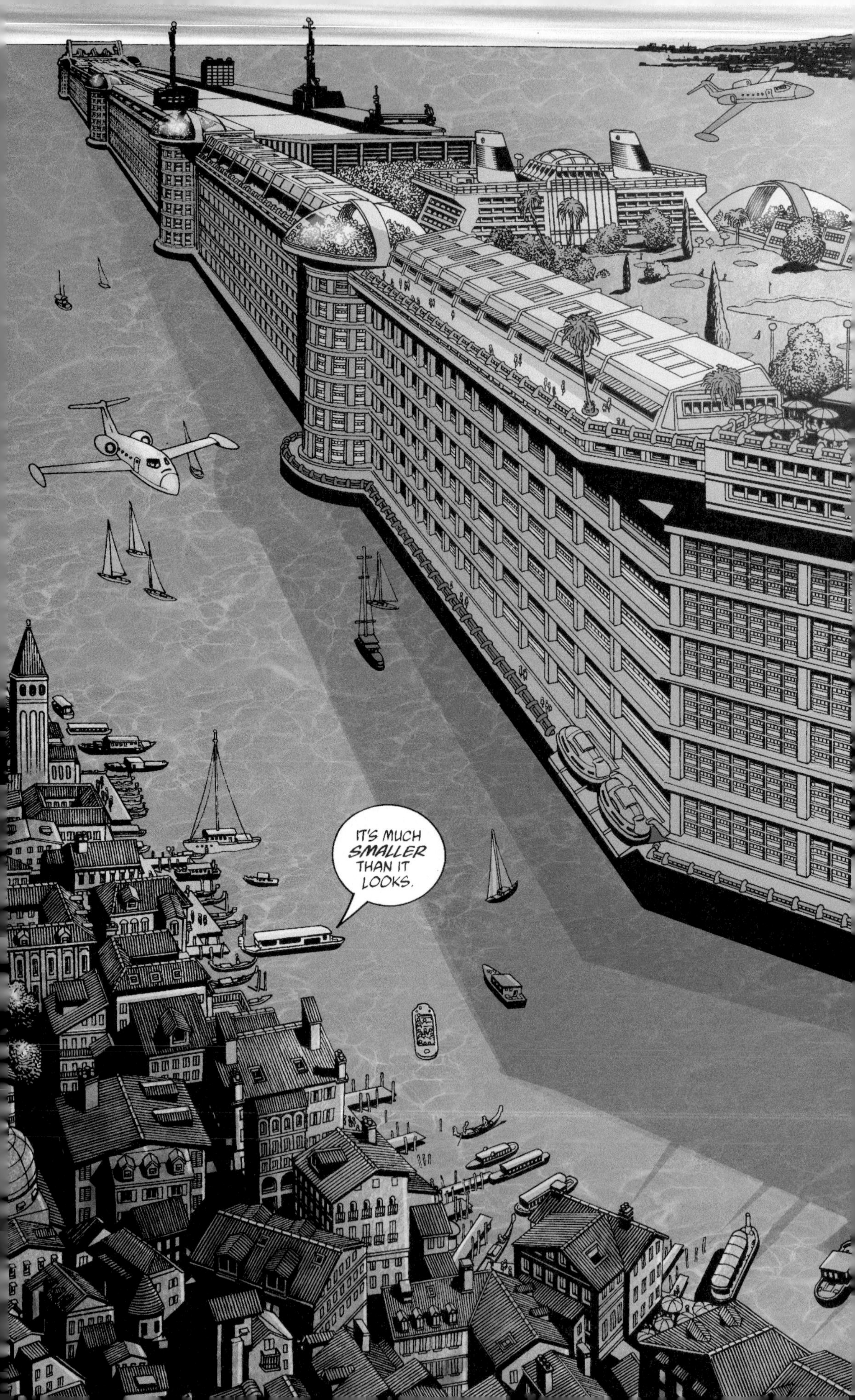
IT'S MUCH SMALLER THAN IT LOOKS.

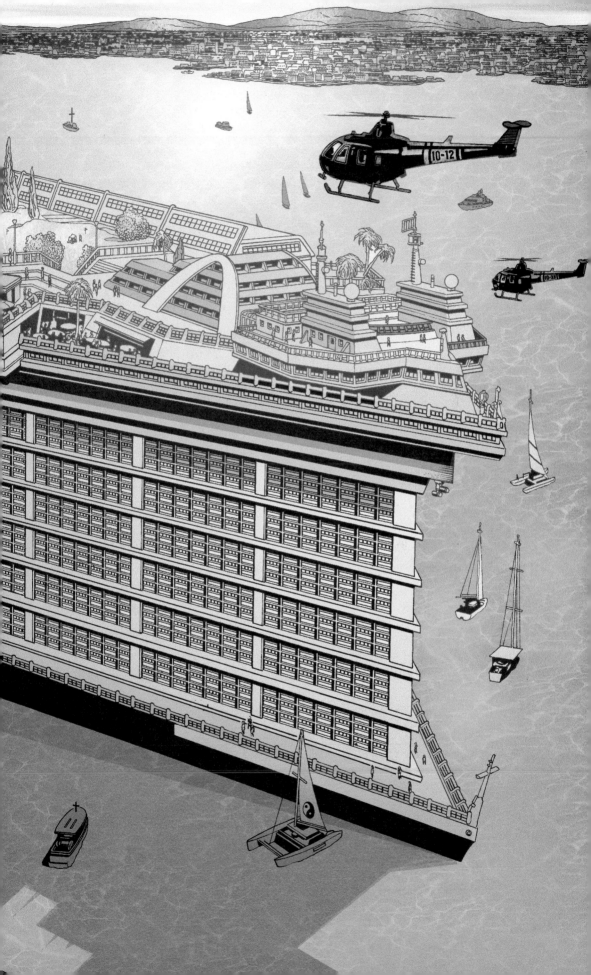

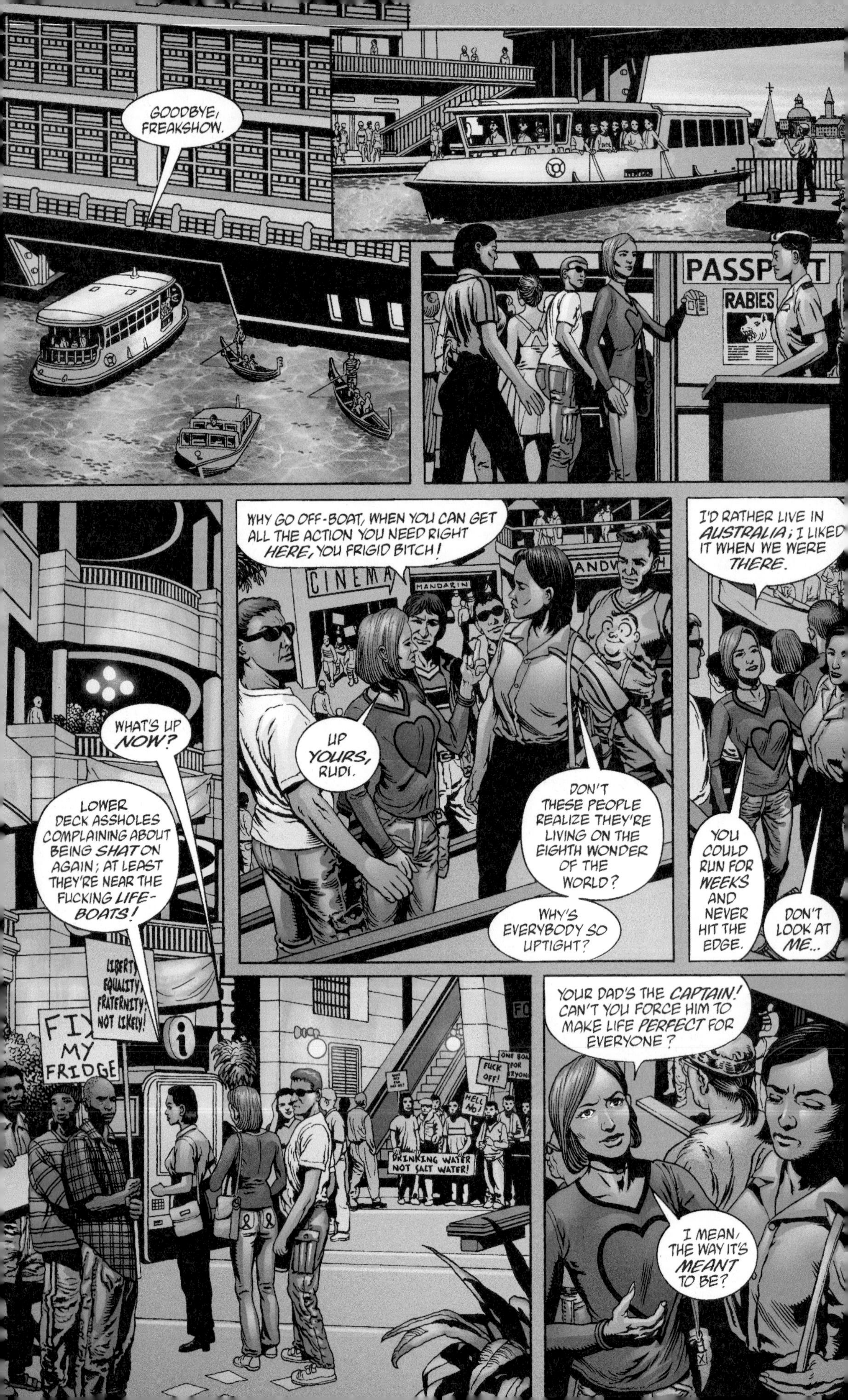
GOODBYE, FREAKSHOW.
RABIES
WHAT'S UP NOW?
LOWER DECK ASSHOLES COMPLAINING ABOUT BEING SHAT ON AGAIN; AT LEAST THEY'RE NEAR THE FUCKING LIFE-BOATS!
WHY GO OFF-BOAT, WHEN YOU CAN GET ALL THE ACTION YOU NEED RIGHT HERE, YOU FRIGID BITCH!
CINEMA
MANDARIN
UP YOURS, RUDI.
DON'T THESE PEOPLE REALIZE THEY'RE LIVING ON THE EIGHTH WONDER OF THE WORLD?
WHY'S EVERYBODY SO UPTIGHT?
I'D RATHER LIVE IN AUSTRALIA; I LIKED IT WHEN WE WERE THERE.
YOU COULD RUN FOR WEEKS AND NEVER HIT THE EDGE.
DON'T LOOK AT ME...
LIBERTY, EQUALITY, FRATERNITY: NOT LIKELY!
FIX MY FRIDGE
FUCK OFF!
HELL NO!
DRINKING WATER NOT SALT WATER!
YOUR DAD'S THE CAPTAIN! CAN'T YOU FORCE HIM TO MAKE LIFE PERFECT FOR EVERYONE?
I MEAN, THE WAY IT'S MEANT TO BE?

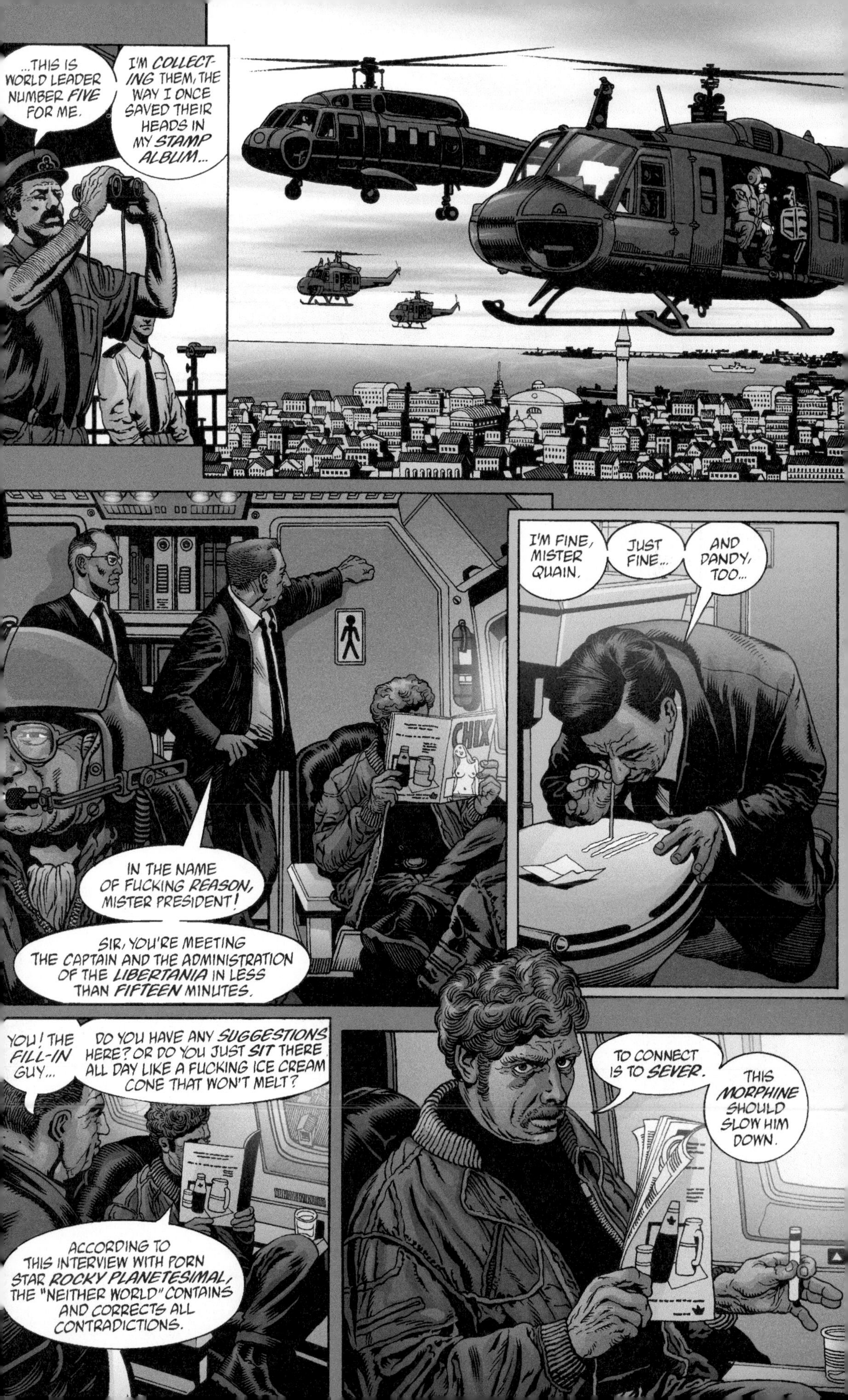
...THIS IS WORLD LEADER NUMBER FIVE FOR ME.
I'M COLLECTING THEM, THE WAY I ONCE SAVED THEIR HEADS IN MY STAMP ALBUM...
I'M FINE, MISTER QUAIN.
JUST FINE...
AND DANDY, TOO...
IN THE NAME OF FUCKING REASON, MISTER PRESIDENT!
SIR, YOU'RE MEETING THE CAPTAIN AND THE ADMINISTRATION OF THE LIBERTANIA IN LESS THAN FIFTEEN MINUTES.
YOU! THE FILL-IN GUY...
DO YOU HAVE ANY SUGGESTIONS HERE? OR DO YOU JUST SIT THERE ALL DAY LIKE A FUCKING ICE CREAM CONE THAT WON'T MELT?
ACCORDING TO THIS INTERVIEW WITH PORN STAR ROCKY PLANETESIMAL, THE "NEITHER WORLD" CONTAINS AND CORRECTS ALL CONTRADICTIONS.
TO CONNECT IS TO SEVER.
THIS MORPHINE SHOULD SLOW HIM DOWN.

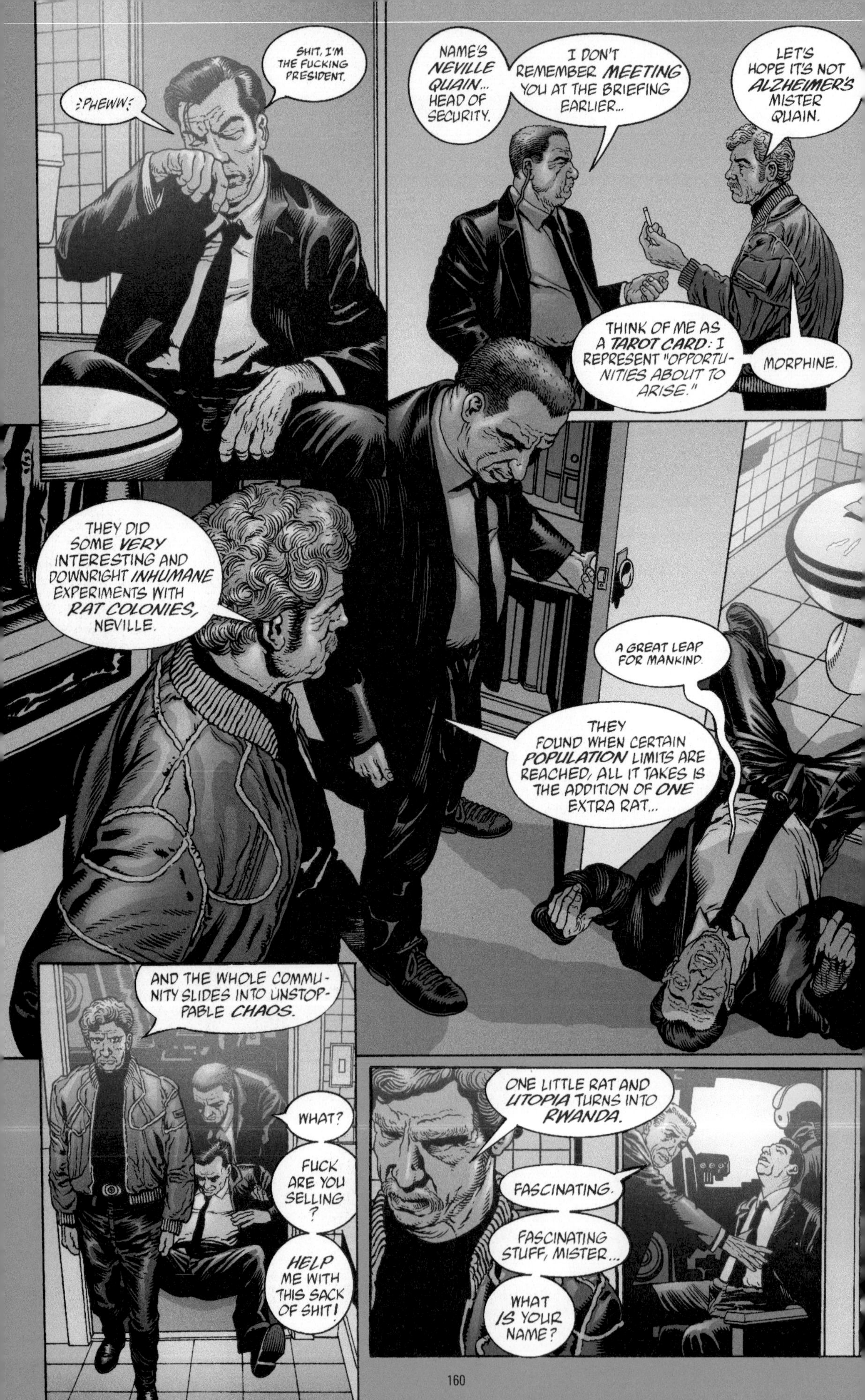

:PHEWW:
SHIT, I'M THE FUCKING PRESIDENT.
NAME'S NEVILLE QUAIN... HEAD OF SECURITY.
I DON'T REMEMBER MEETING YOU AT THE BRIEFING EARLIER...
LET'S HOPE IT'S NOT ALZHEIMER'S MISTER QUAIN.
MORPHINE.
THINK OF ME AS A TAROT CARD: I REPRESENT "OPPORTUNITIES ABOUT TO ARISE."
THEY DID SOME VERY INTERESTING AND DOWNRIGHT INHUMANE EXPERIMENTS WITH RAT COLONIES, NEVILLE.
A GREAT LEAP FOR MANKIND.
THEY FOUND WHEN CERTAIN POPULATION LIMITS ARE REACHED, ALL IT TAKES IS THE ADDITION OF ONE EXTRA RAT...
AND THE WHOLE COMMUNITY SLIDES INTO UNSTOPPABLE CHAOS.
WHAT?
FUCK ARE YOU SELLING?
HELP ME WITH THIS SACK OF SHIT!
ONE LITTLE RAT AND UTOPIA TURNS INTO RWANDA.
FASCINATING.
FASCINATING STUFF, MISTER...
WHAT IS YOUR NAME?

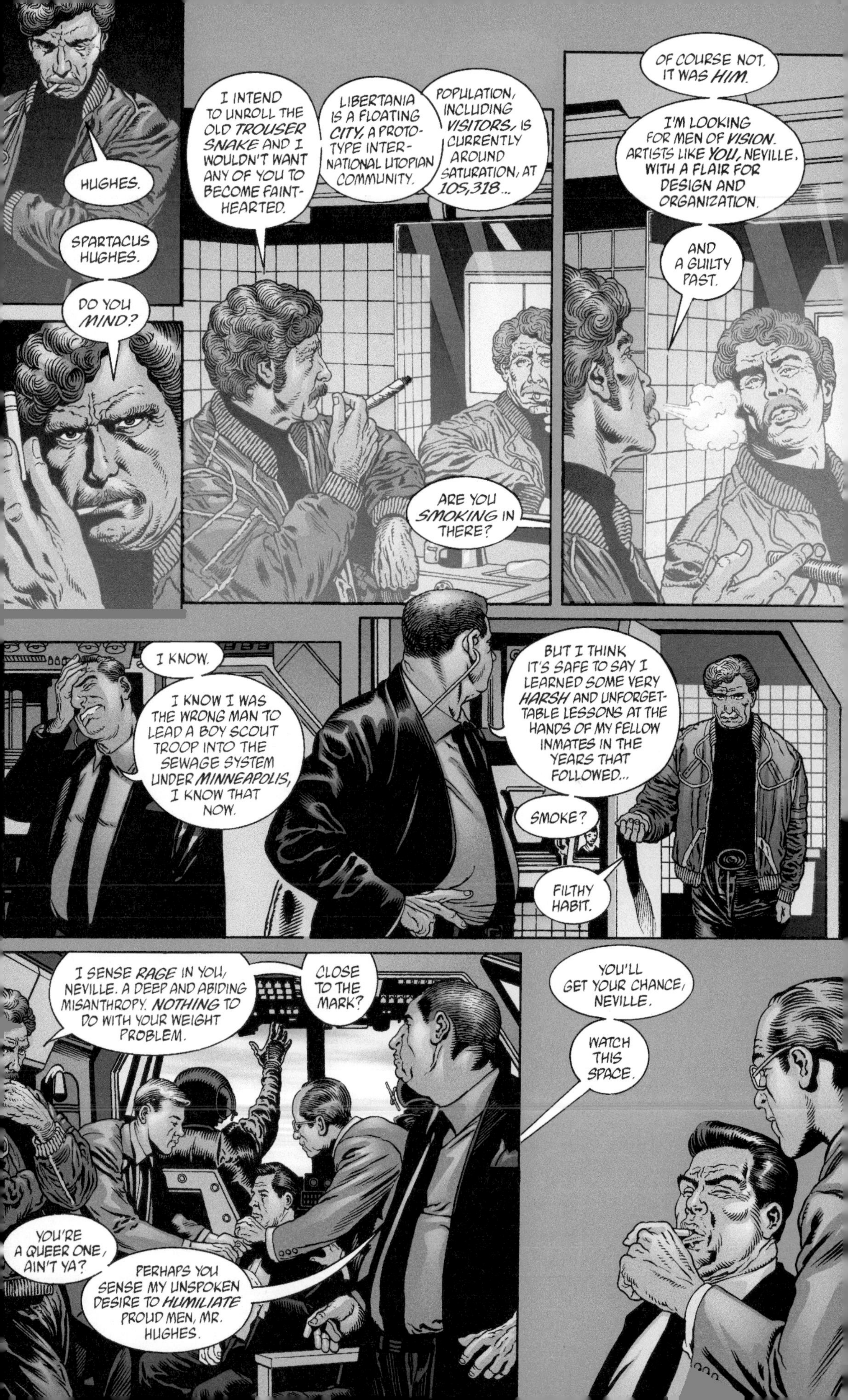
HUGHES.
SPARTACUS HUGHES.
DO YOU MIND?
I INTEND TO UNROLL THE OLD TROUSER SNAKE AND I WOULDN'T WANT ANY OF YOU TO BECOME FAINT-HEARTED.
LIBERTANIA IS A FLOATING CITY, A PROTO-TYPE INTER-NATIONAL UTOPIAN COMMUNITY.
POPULATION, INCLUDING VISITORS, IS CURRENTLY AROUND SATURATION, AT 105,318...
ARE YOU SMOKING IN THERE?
OF COURSE NOT. IT WAS HIM.
I'M LOOKING FOR MEN OF VISION. ARTISTS LIKE YOU, NEVILLE, WITH A FLAIR FOR DESIGN AND ORGANIZATION.
AND A GUILTY PAST.
I KNOW.
I KNOW I WAS THE WRONG MAN TO LEAD A BOY SCOUT TROOP INTO THE SEWAGE SYSTEM UNDER MINNEAPOLIS, I KNOW THAT NOW.
BUT I THINK IT'S SAFE TO SAY I LEARNED SOME VERY HARSH AND UNFORGET-TABLE LESSONS AT THE HANDS OF MY FELLOW INMATES IN THE YEARS THAT FOLLOWED...
SMOKE?
FILTHY HABIT.
I SENSE RAGE IN YOU, NEVILLE. A DEEP AND ABIDING MISANTHROPY. NOTHING TO DO WITH YOUR WEIGHT PROBLEM.
CLOSE TO THE MARK?
YOU'RE A QUEER ONE, AIN'T YA?
PERHAPS YOU SENSE MY UNSPOKEN DESIRE TO HUMILIATE PROUD MEN, MR. HUGHES.
YOU'LL GET YOUR CHANCE, NEVILLE.
WATCH THIS SPACE.

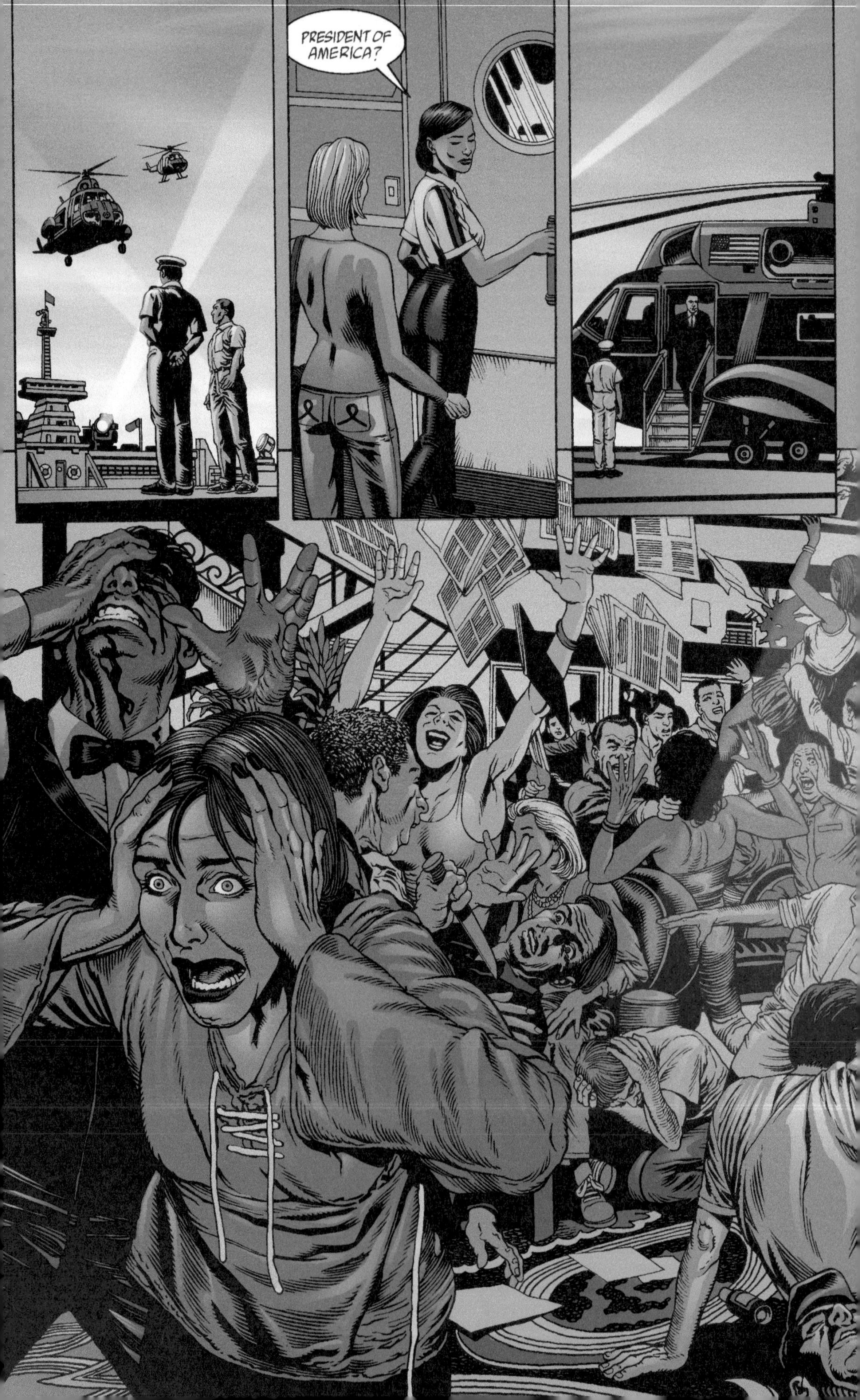
PRESIDENT OF AMERICA?

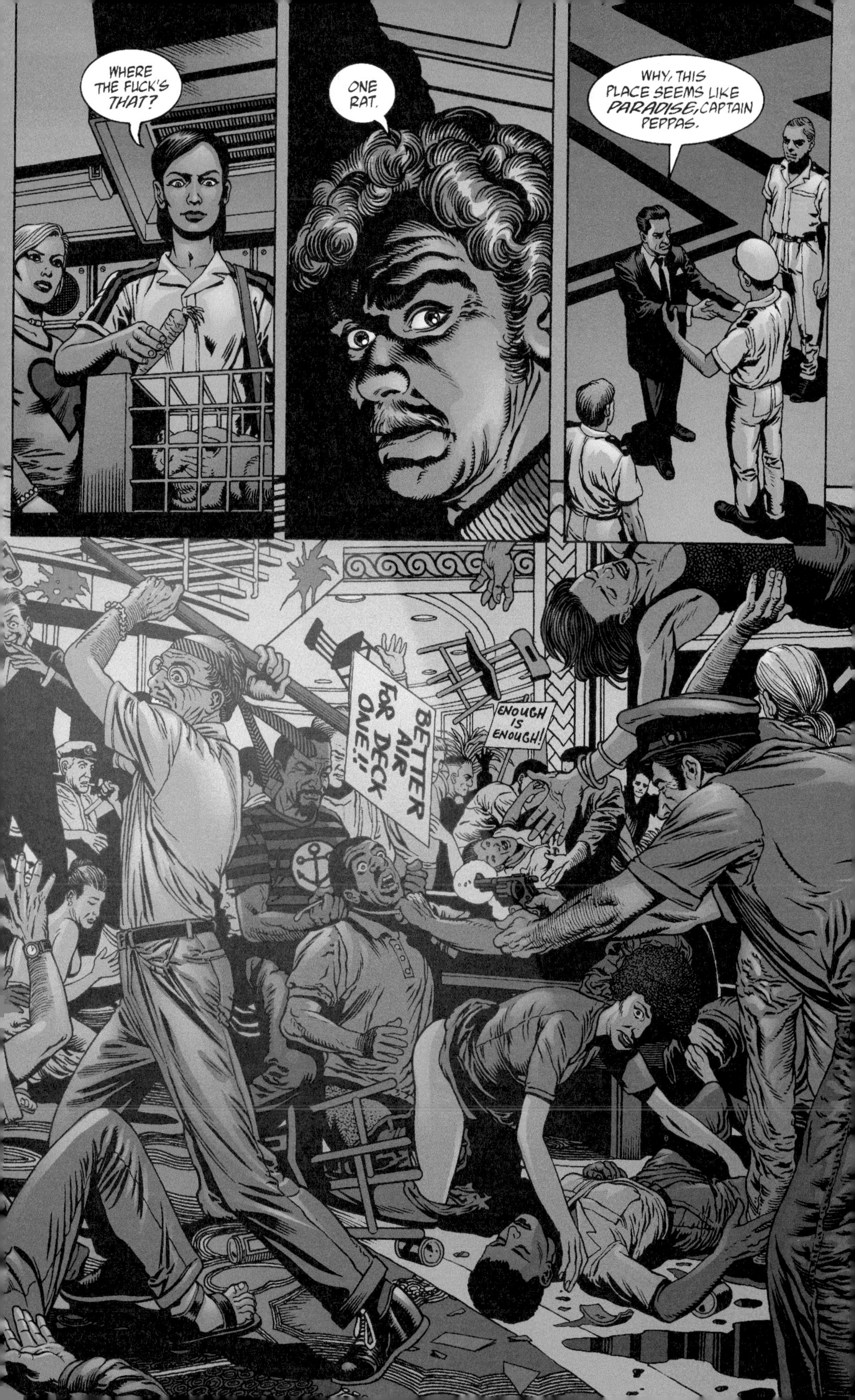
WHERE THE FUCK'S THAT?
ONE RAT.
WHY, THIS PLACE SEEMS LIKE PARADISE, CAPTAIN PEPPAS.
BETTER AIR FOR DECK ONE!!
ENOUGH IS ENOUGH!

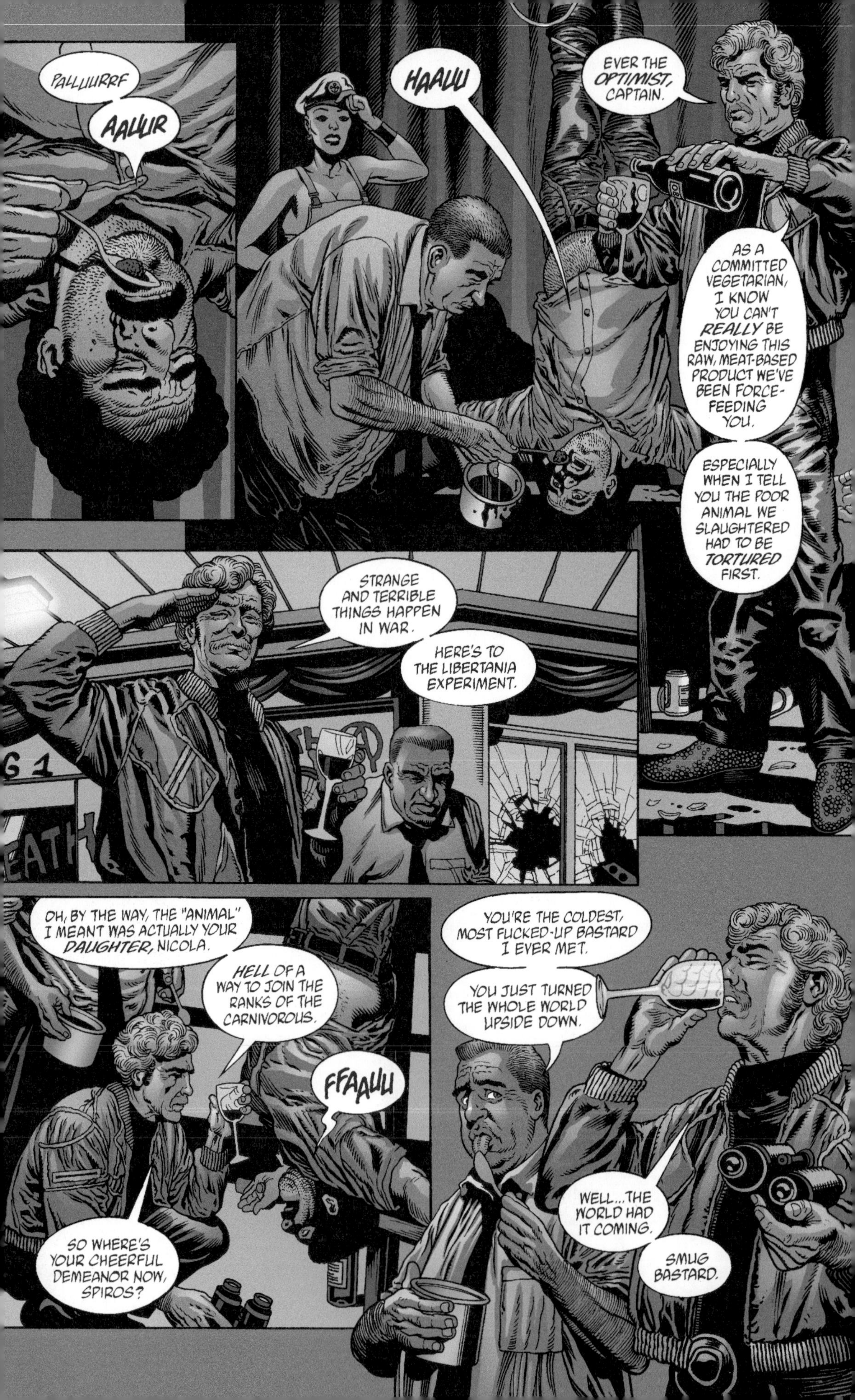
PALLUURRF
AALLUR
HAALLU
EVER THE OPTIMIST, CAPTAIN.
AS A COMMITTED VEGETARIAN, I KNOW YOU CAN'T REALLY BE ENJOYING THIS RAW, MEAT-BASED PRODUCT WE'VE BEEN FORCE-FEEDING YOU.
ESPECIALLY WHEN I TELL YOU THE POOR ANIMAL WE SLAUGHTERED HAD TO BE TORTURED FIRST.
STRANGE AND TERRIBLE THINGS HAPPEN IN WAR.
HERE'S TO THE LIBERTANIA EXPERIMENT.
OH, BY THE WAY, THE "ANIMAL" I MEANT WAS ACTUALLY YOUR DAUGHTER, NICOLA.
HELL OF A WAY TO JOIN THE RANKS OF THE CARNIVOROUS.
FFAAULL
SO WHERE'S YOUR CHEERFUL DEMEANOR NOW, SPIROS?
YOU'RE THE COLDEST, MOST FUCKED-UP BASTARD I EVER MET.
YOU JUST TURNED THE WHOLE WORLD UPSIDE DOWN.
WELL... THE WORLD HAD IT COMING.
SMUG BASTARD.

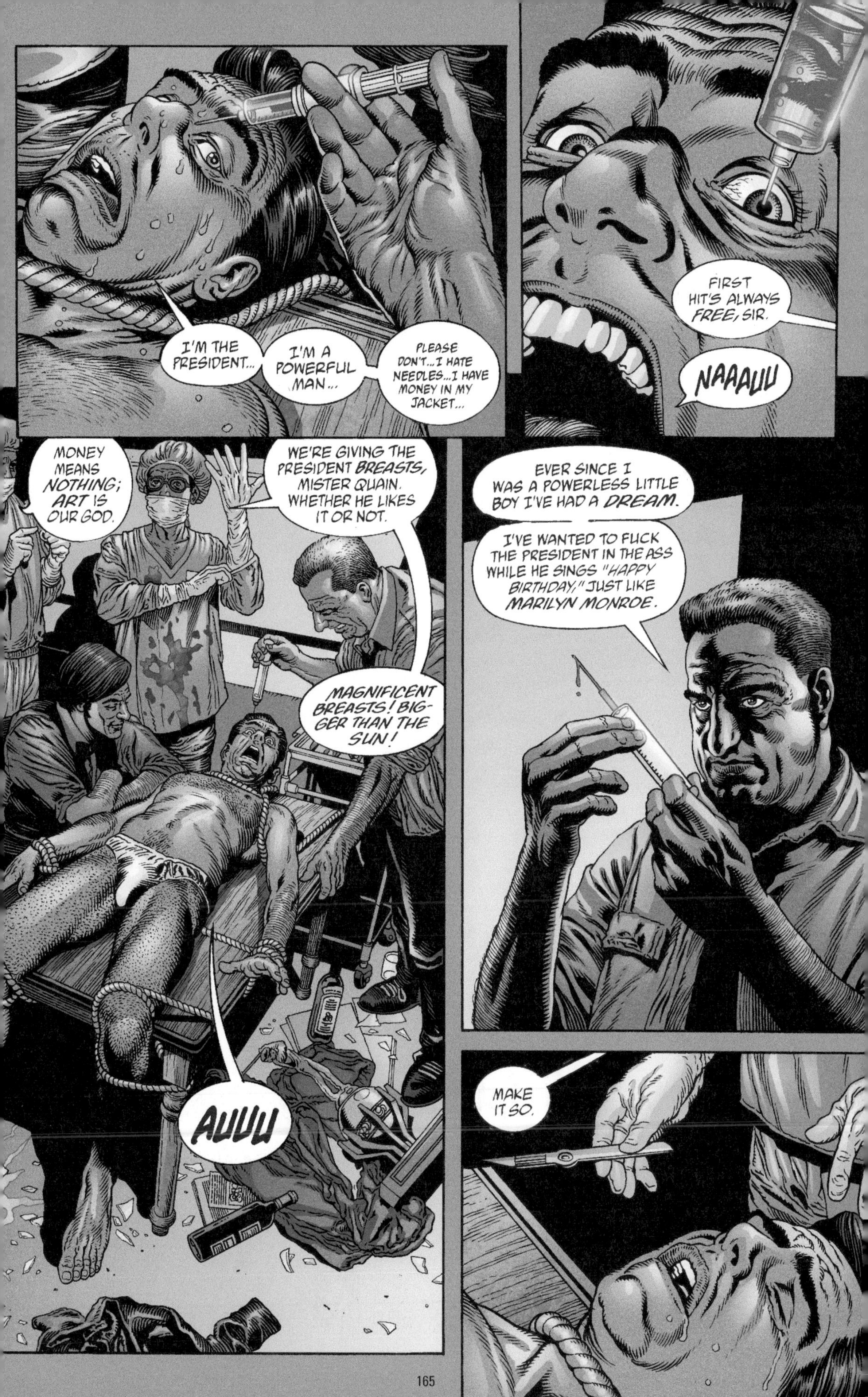
I'M THE PRESIDENT...
I'M A POWERFUL MAN...
PLEASE DON'T...I HATE NEEDLES...I HAVE MONEY IN MY JACKET...
FIRST HIT'S ALWAYS FREE, SIR.
NAAAUU
MONEY MEANS NOTHING; ART IS OUR GOD.
WE'RE GIVING THE PRESIDENT BREASTS, MISTER QUAIN. WHETHER HE LIKES IT OR NOT.
MAGNIFICENT BREASTS! BIGGER THAN THE SUN!
AUUU
EVER SINCE I WAS A POWERLESS LITTLE BOY I'VE HAD A DREAM.
I'VE WANTED TO FUCK THE PRESIDENT IN THE ASS WHILE HE SINGS "HAPPY BIRTHDAY," JUST LIKE MARILYN MONROE.
MAKE IT SO.

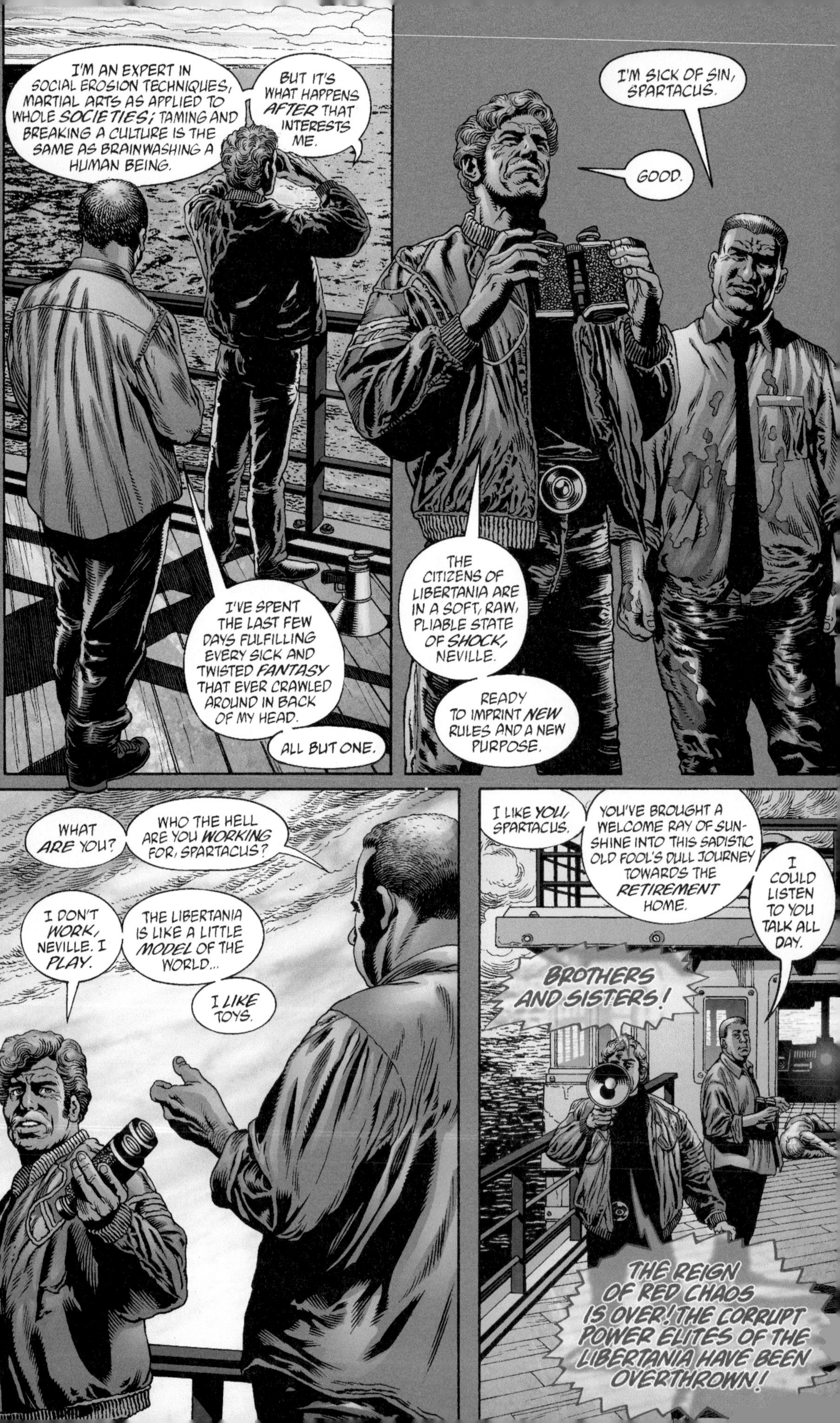
I'M AN EXPERT IN SOCIAL EROSION TECHNIQUES, MARTIAL ARTS AS APPLIED TO WHOLE SOCIETIES; TAMING AND BREAKING A CULTURE IS THE SAME AS BRAINWASHING A HUMAN BEING.
BUT IT'S WHAT HAPPENS AFTER THAT INTERESTS ME.
I'VE SPENT THE LAST FEW DAYS FULFILLING EVERY SICK AND TWISTED FANTASY THAT EVER CRAWLED AROUND IN BACK OF MY HEAD.
ALL BUT ONE.
I'M SICK OF SIN, SPARTACUS.
GOOD.
THE CITIZENS OF LIBERTANIA ARE IN A SOFT, RAW, PLIABLE STATE OF SHOCK, NEVILLE.
READY TO IMPRINT NEW RULES AND A NEW PURPOSE.
WHAT ARE YOU?
WHO THE HELL ARE YOU WORKING FOR, SPARTACUS?
I DON'T WORK, NEVILLE. I PLAY.
THE LIBERTANIA IS LIKE A LITTLE MODEL OF THE WORLD...
I LIKE TOYS.
I LIKE YOU, SPARTACUS.
YOU'VE BROUGHT A WELCOME RAY OF SUN-SHINE INTO THIS SADISTIC OLD FOOL'S DULL JOURNEY TOWARDS THE RETIREMENT HOME.
I COULD LISTEN TO YOU TALK ALL DAY.
BROTHERS AND SISTERS!
THE REIGN OF RED CHAOS IS OVER! THE CORRUPT POWER ELITES OF THE LIBERTANIA HAVE BEEN OVERTHROWN!

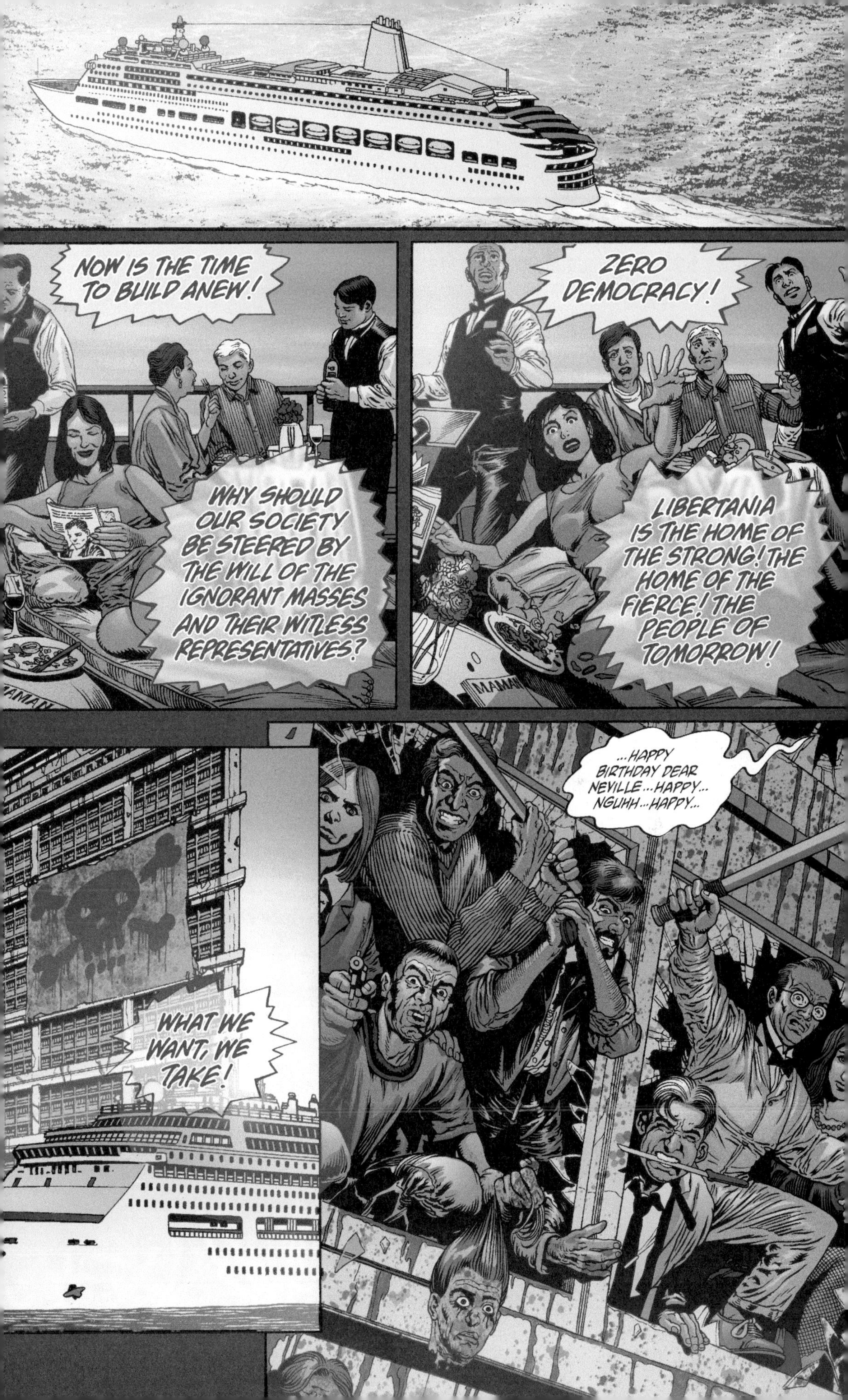
NOW IS THE TIME TO BUILD ANEW!
WHY SHOULD OUR SOCIETY BE STEERED BY THE WILL OF THE IGNORANT MASSES AND THEIR WITLESS REPRESENTATIVES?
ZERO DEMOCRACY!
LIBERTANIA IS THE HOME OF THE STRONG! THE HOME OF THE FIERCE! THE PEOPLE OF TOMORROW!
WHAT WE WANT, WE TAKE!
...HAPPY BIRTHDAY DEAR NEVILLE...HAPPY... NGUHH...HAPPY...

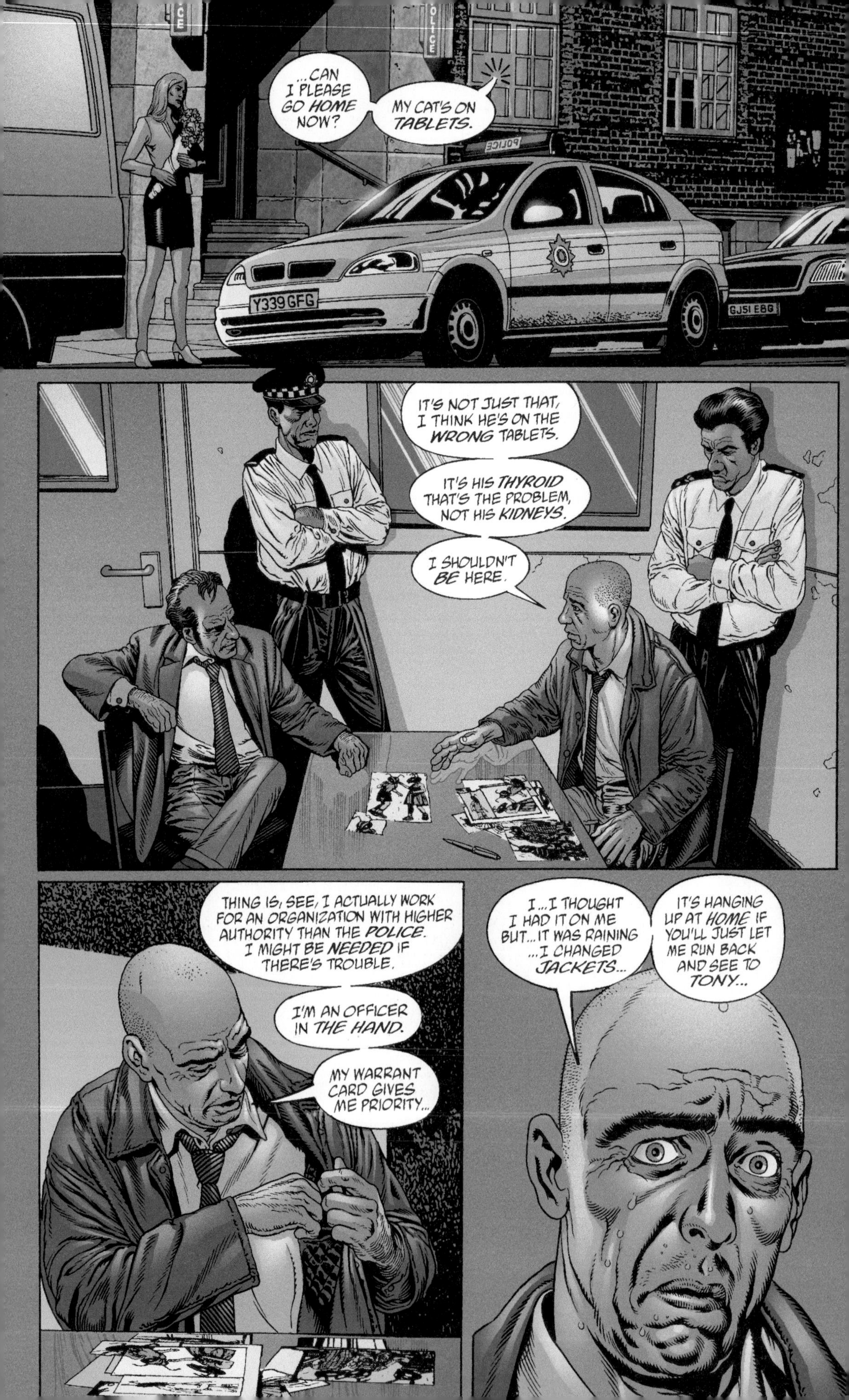
...CAN I PLEASE GO HOME NOW?
MY CAT'S ON TABLETS.
POLICE
Y339 GFG
GJ51 EBG
IT'S NOT JUST THAT, I THINK HE'S ON THE WRONG TABLETS.
IT'S HIS THYROID THAT'S THE PROBLEM, NOT HIS KIDNEYS.
I SHOULDN'T BE HERE.
THING IS, SEE, I ACTUALLY WORK FOR AN ORGANIZATION WITH HIGHER AUTHORITY THAN THE POLICE. I MIGHT BE NEEDED IF THERE'S TROUBLE.
I'M AN OFFICER IN THE HAND.
MY WARRANT CARD GIVES ME PRIORITY...
I...I THOUGHT I HAD IT ON ME BUT...IT WAS RAINING ...I CHANGED JACKETS...
IT'S HANGING UP AT HOME IF YOU'LL JUST LET ME RUN BACK AND SEE TO TONY...

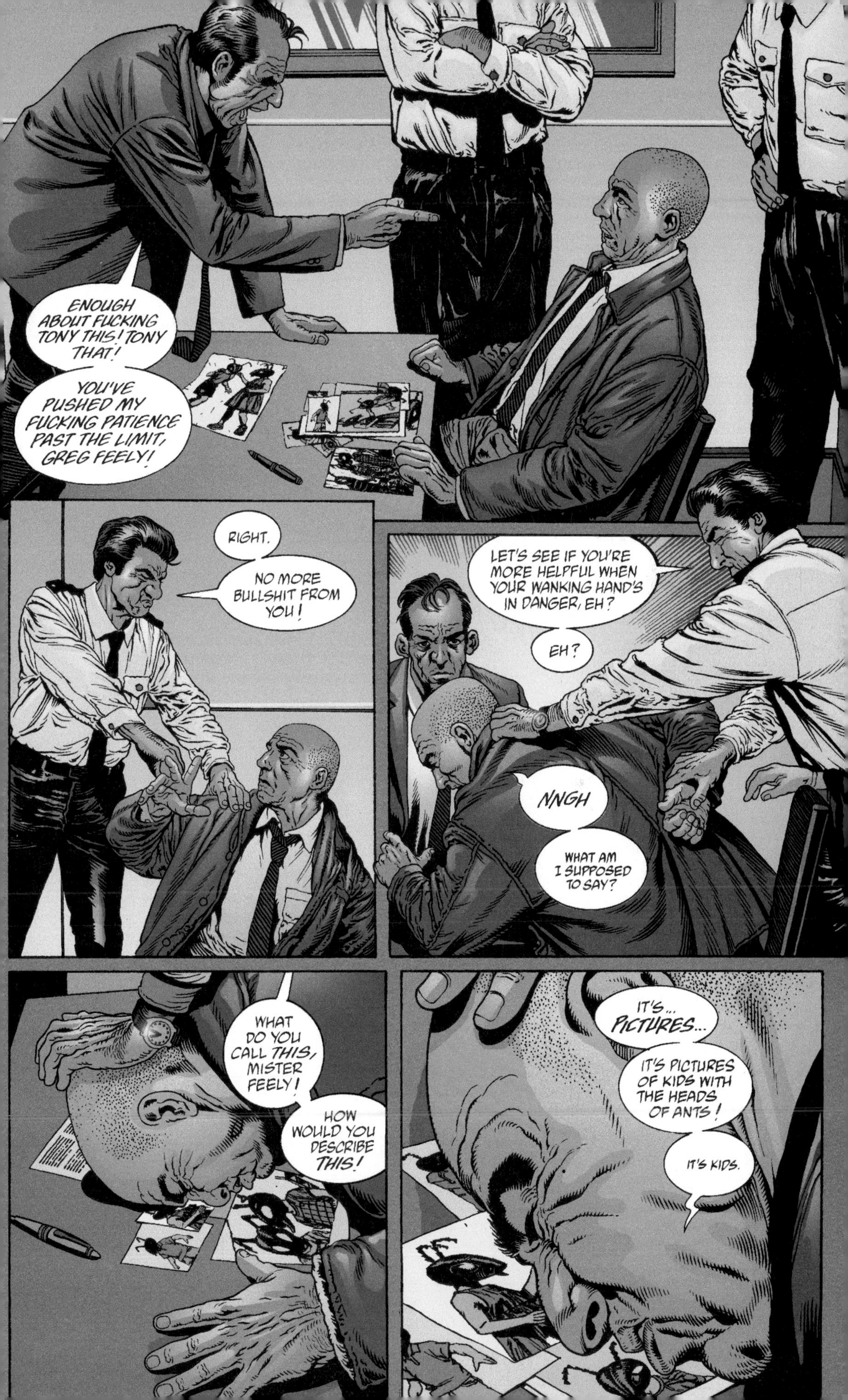
ENOUGH ABOUT FUCKING TONY THIS! TONY THAT!
YOU'VE PUSHED MY FUCKING PATIENCE PAST THE LIMIT, GREG FEELY!
RIGHT.
NO MORE BULLSHIT FROM YOU!
LET'S SEE IF YOU'RE MORE HELPFUL WHEN YOUR WANKING HAND'S IN DANGER, EH?
EH?
NNGH
WHAT AM I SUPPOSED TO SAY?
WHAT DO YOU CALL THIS, MISTER FEELY!
HOW WOULD YOU DESCRIBE THIS!
IT'S... PICTURES...
IT'S PICTURES OF KIDS WITH THE HEADS OF ANTS!
IT'S KIDS.

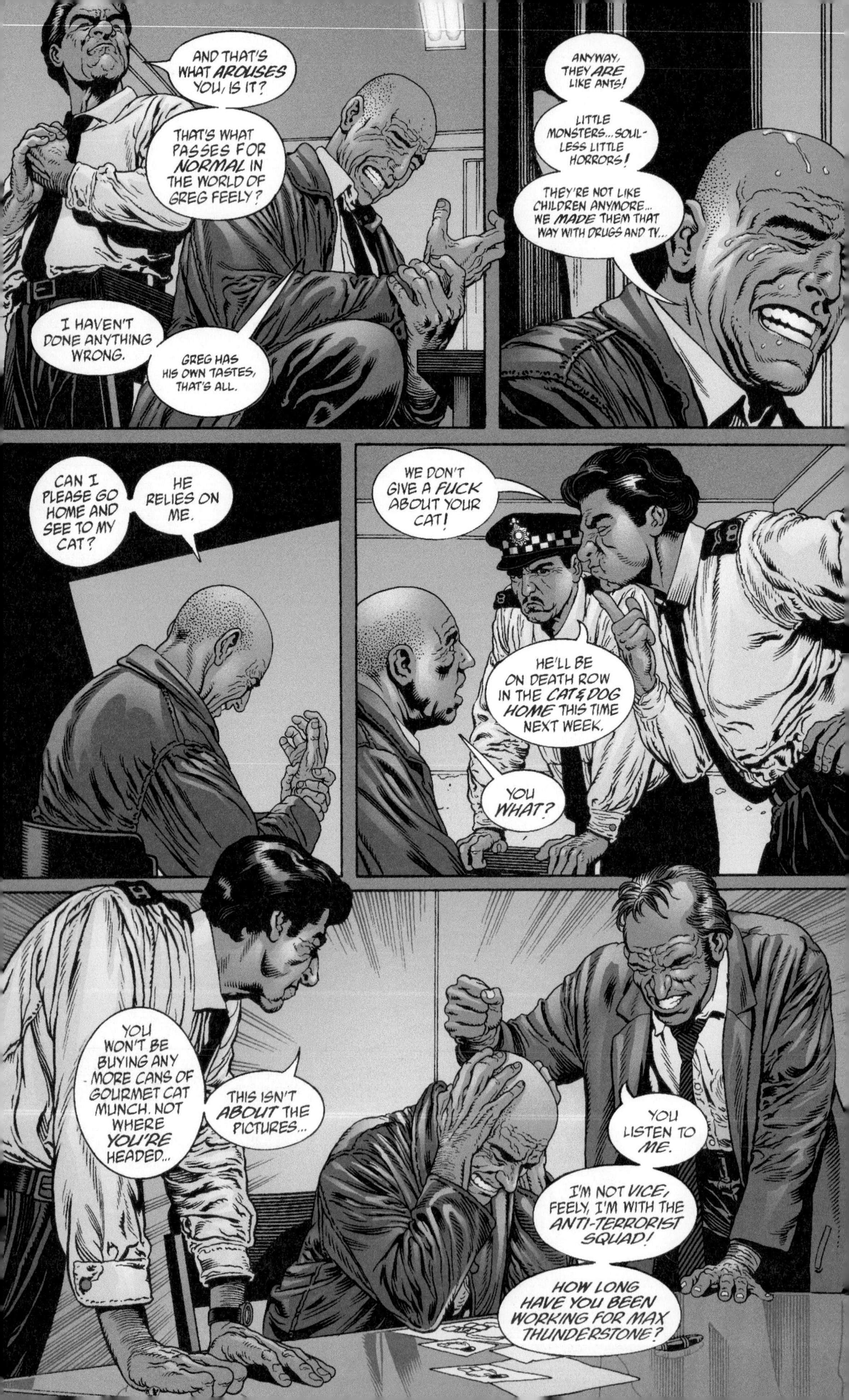
AND THAT'S WHAT AROUSES YOU, IS IT?
THAT'S WHAT PASSES FOR NORMAL IN THE WORLD OF GREG FEELY?
I HAVEN'T DONE ANYTHING WRONG.
GREG HAS HIS OWN TASTES, THAT'S ALL.
ANYWAY, THEY ARE LIKE ANTS!
LITTLE MONSTERS... SOUL-LESS LITTLE HORRORS!
THEY'RE NOT LIKE CHILDREN ANYMORE... WE MADE THEM THAT WAY WITH DRUGS AND TV...
CAN I PLEASE GO HOME AND SEE TO MY CAT?
HE RELIES ON ME.
WE DON'T GIVE A FUCK ABOUT YOUR CAT!
HE'LL BE ON DEATH ROW IN THE CAT & DOG HOME THIS TIME NEXT WEEK.
YOU WHAT?
YOU WON'T BE BUYING ANY MORE CANS OF GOURMET CAT MUNCH. NOT WHERE YOU'RE HEADED...
THIS ISN'T ABOUT THE PICTURES...
YOU LISTEN TO ME.
I'M NOT VICE, FEELY, I'M WITH THE ANTI-TERRORIST SQUAD!
HOW LONG HAVE YOU BEEN WORKING FOR MAX THUNDERSTONE?

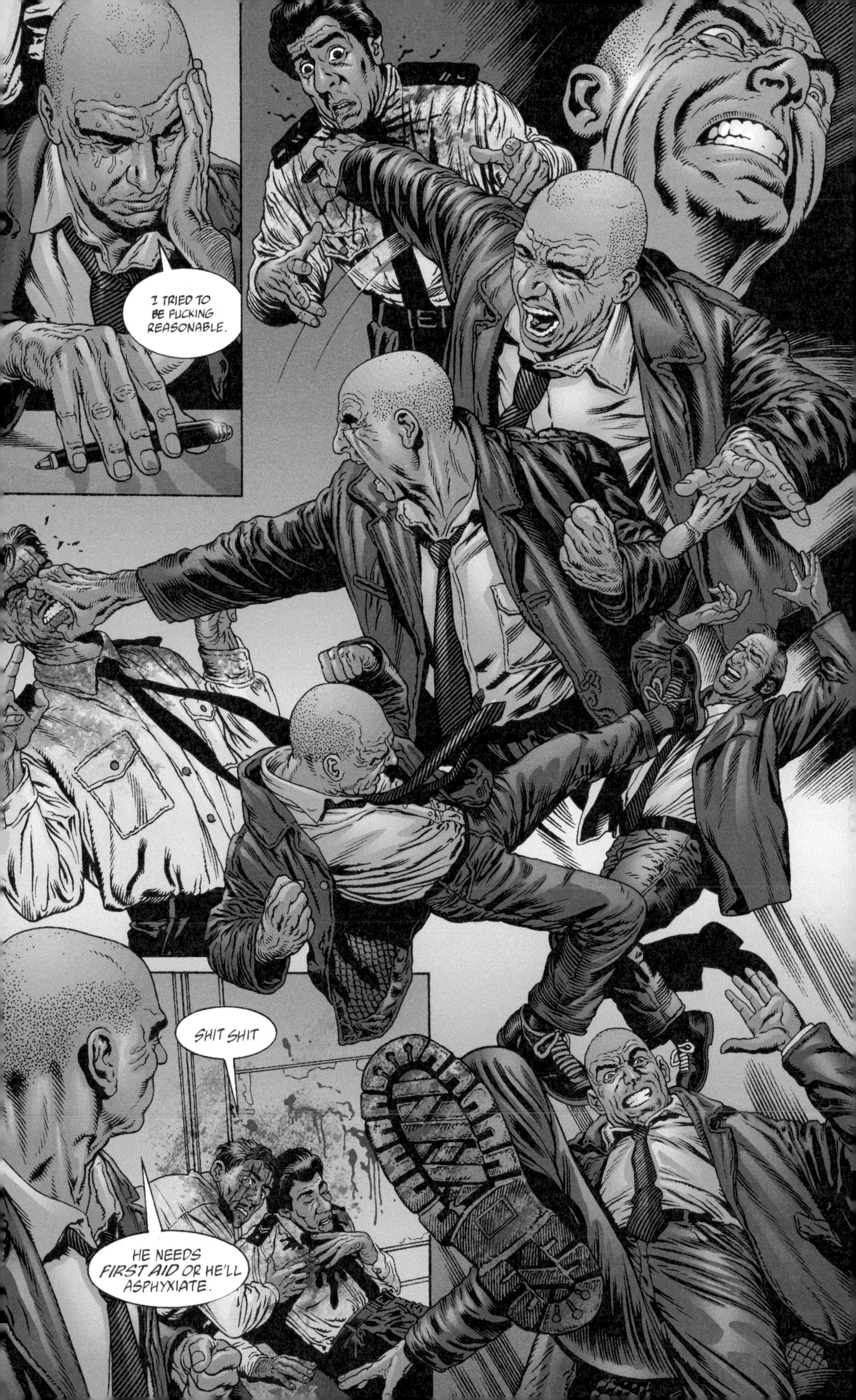
I TRIED TO BE FUCKING REASONABLE.
SHIT SHIT
HE NEEDS FIRST AID OR HE'LL ASPHYXIATE.

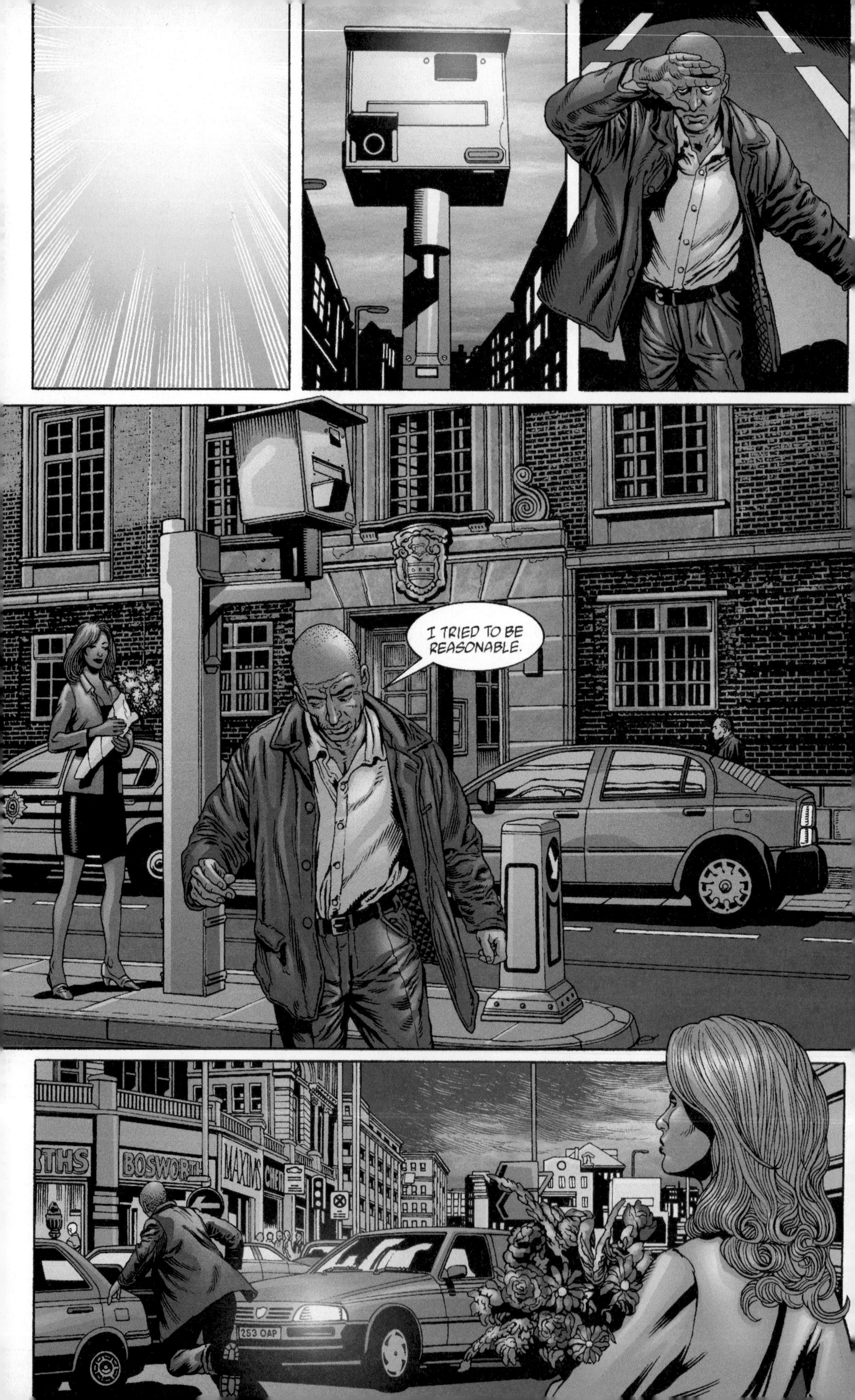
I TRIED TO BE REASONABLE.
THS
BOSWORTH
MAXIMS
253 OAP

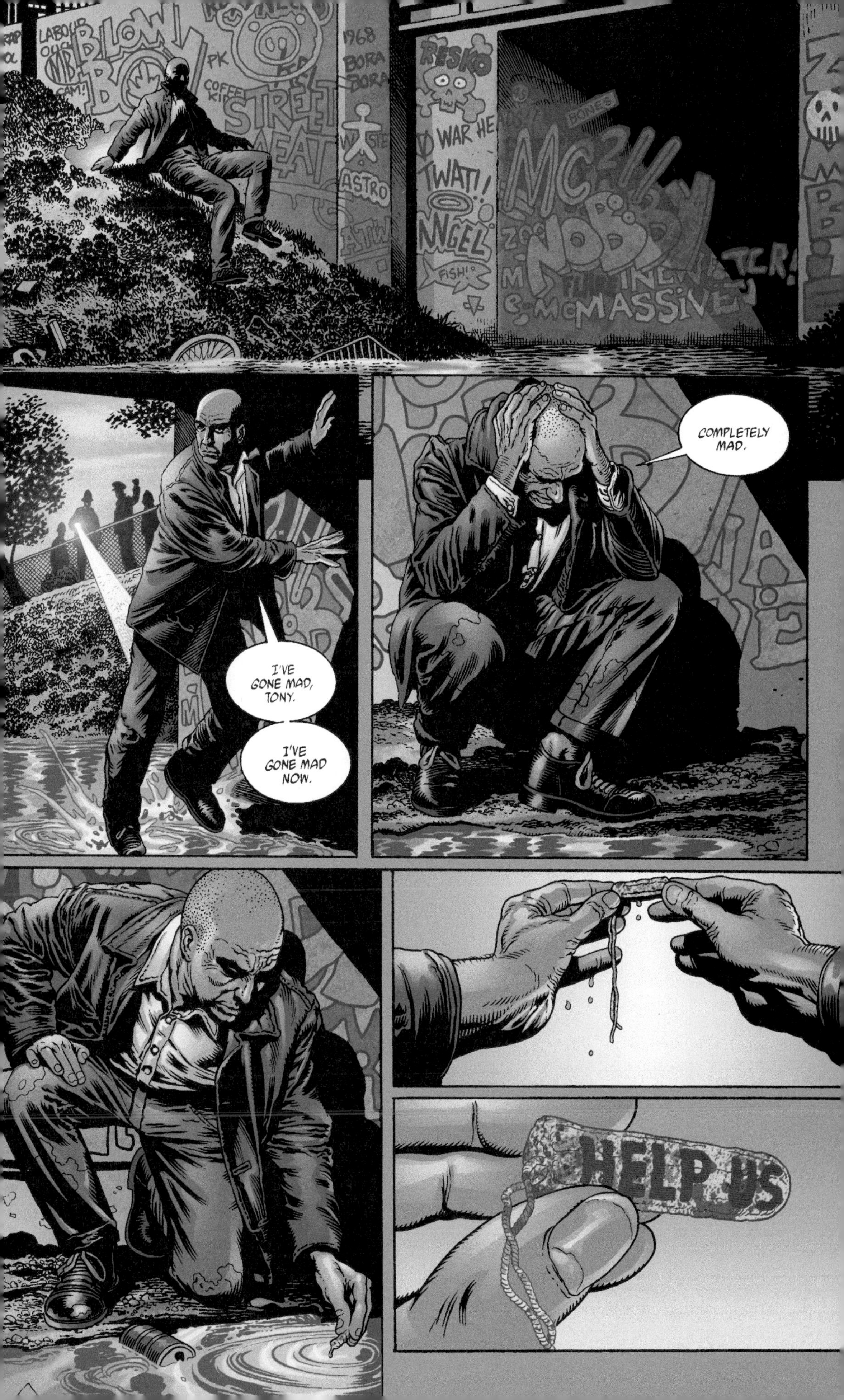

I'VE GONE MAD, TONY.
I'VE GONE MAD NOW.
COMPLETELY MAD.
HELP US

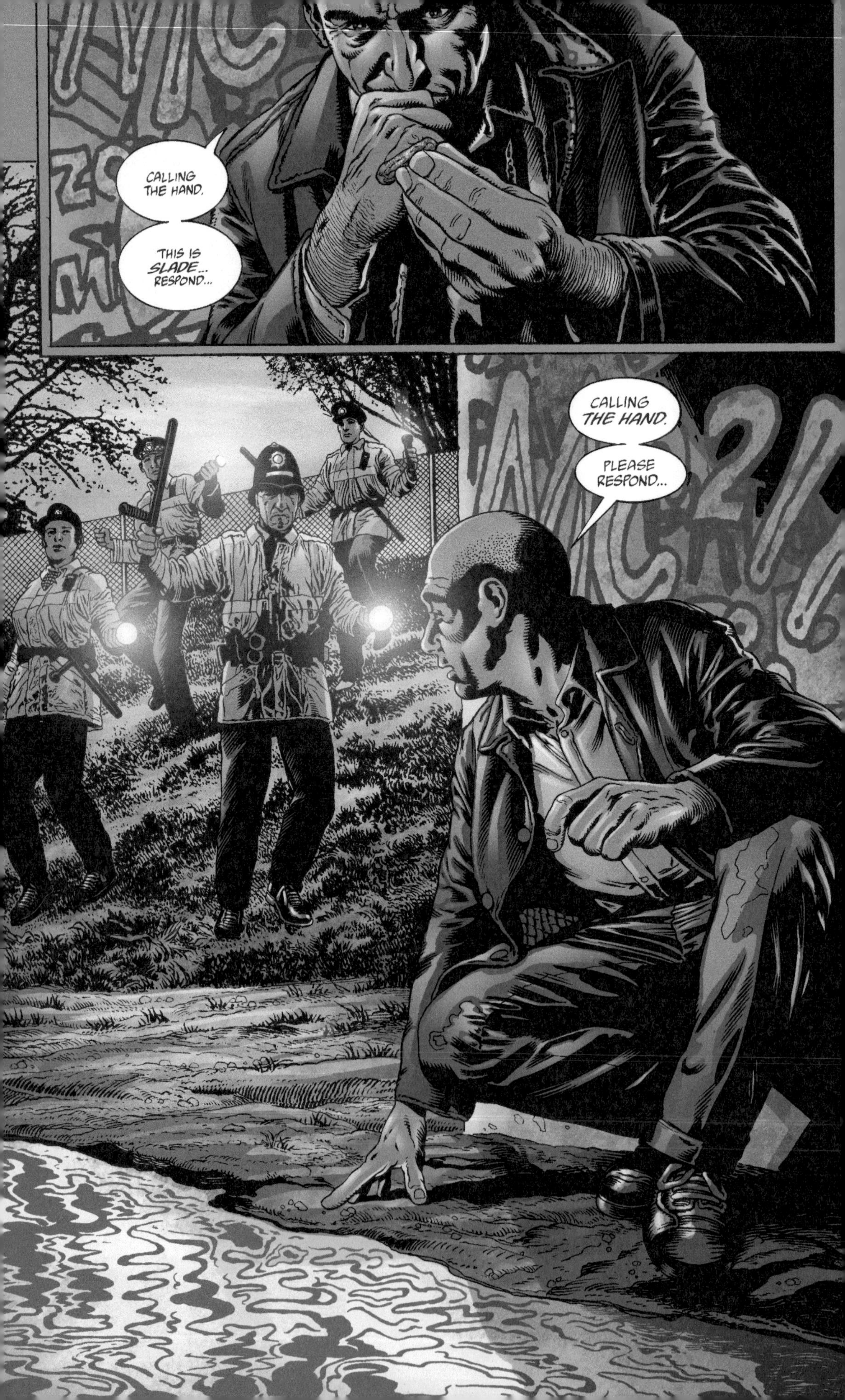
CALLING THE HAND.
THIS IS SLADE... RESPOND...
CALLING THE HAND.
PLEASE RESPOND...

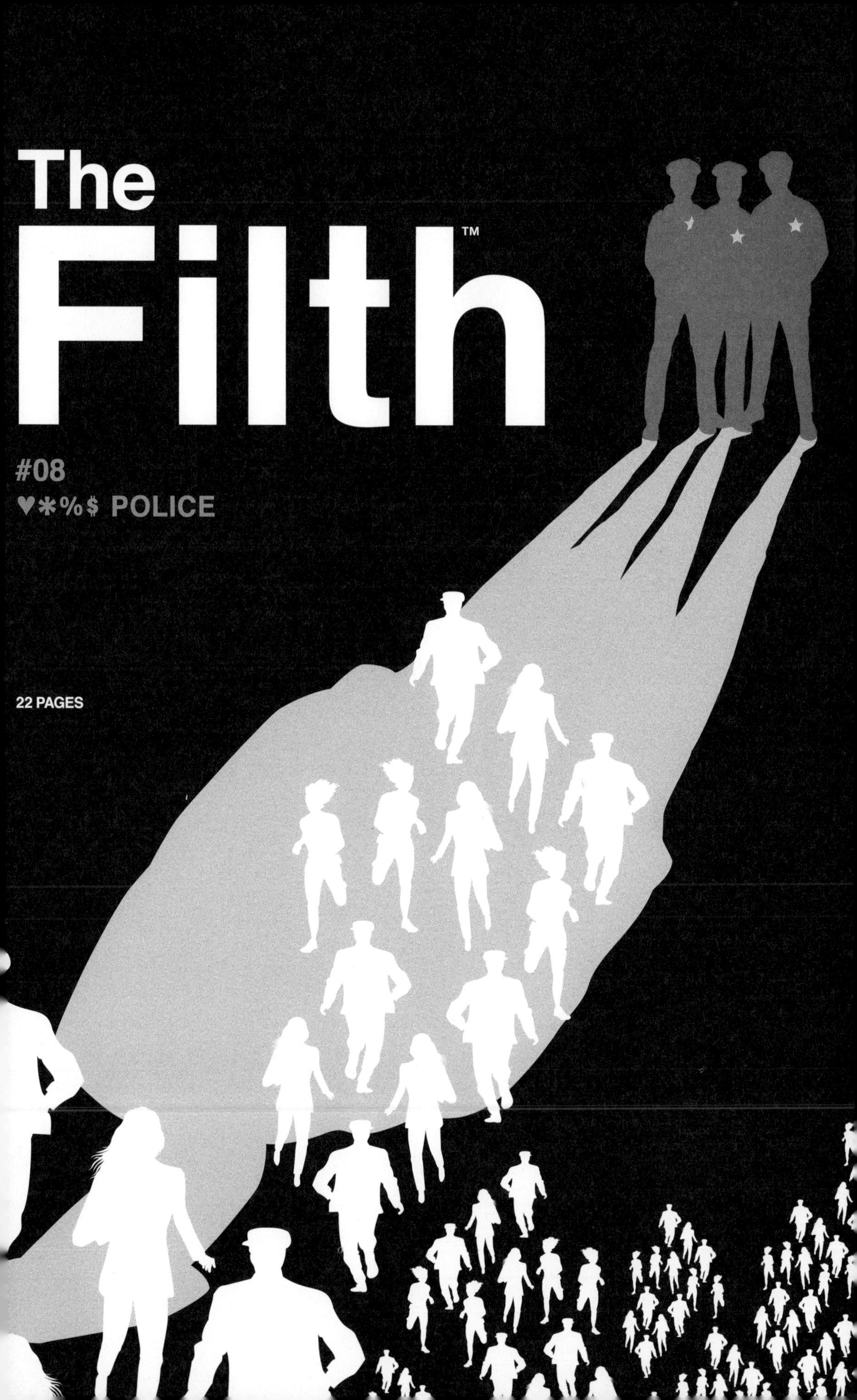
The Filth™
#08
♥✱%$ POLICE
22 PAGES

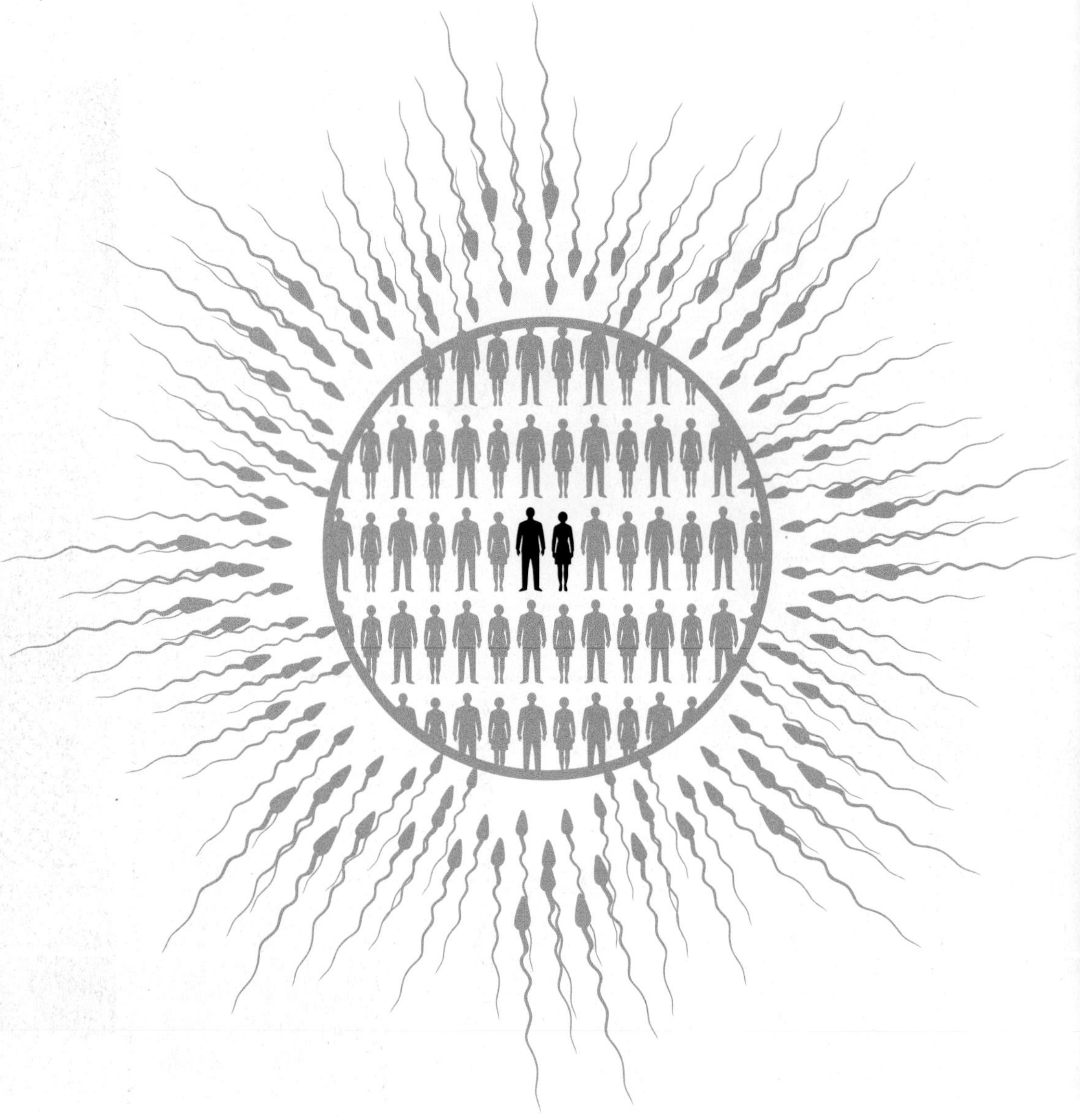

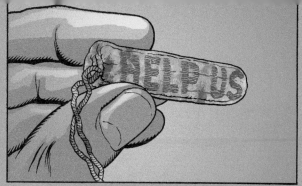

I'LL TRY MY BEST.

IT'S ALL I CAN PROMISE.

WHAT D'YOU THINK YOU'RE *UP* TO IN THERE?

GREG FEELY, YOU'RE UNDER *ARREST*.

LET'S SEE THOSE HANDS.

I'M *BUSY*.

I'M A HIGH-RANKING MEMBER OF A SECRET SOCIETY. I HAVE TO TELL THEM ABOUT THE MESSAGE ON THIS *TAMPON*...

I THINK THE WHOLE WORLD MIGHT BE IN DANGER OF FALLING APART AGAIN.

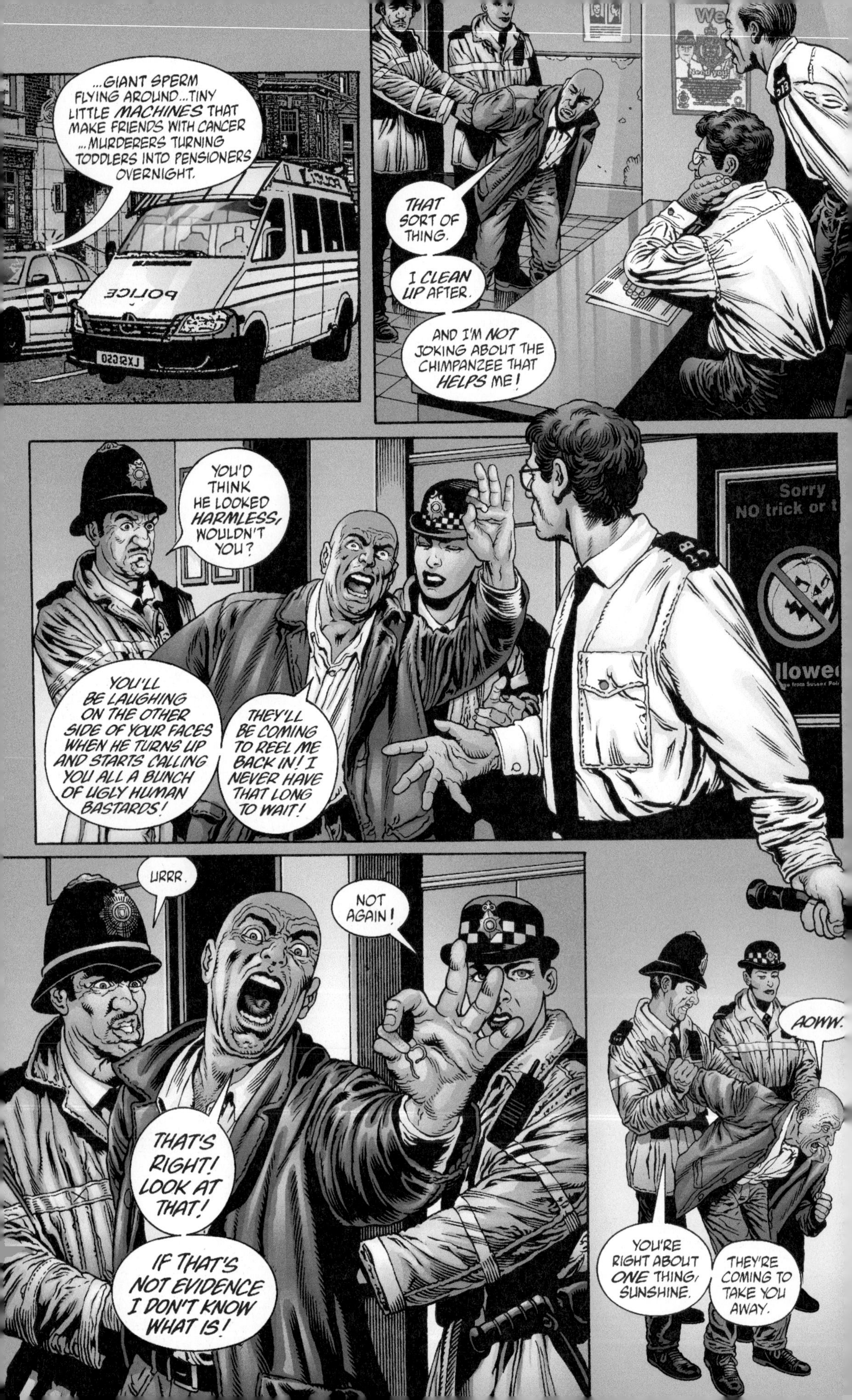
...GIANT SPERM FLYING AROUND...TINY LITTLE MACHINES THAT MAKE FRIENDS WITH CANCER ...MURDERERS TURNING TODDLERS INTO PENSIONERS OVERNIGHT.
POLICE
LX51 GSO
THAT SORT OF THING.
I CLEAN UP AFTER.
AND I'M NOT JOKING ABOUT THE CHIMPANZEE THAT HELPS ME!
YOU'D THINK HE LOOKED HARMLESS, WOULDN'T YOU?
Sorry NO trick or t
llowe
YOU'LL BE LAUGHING ON THE OTHER SIDE OF YOUR FACES WHEN HE TURNS UP AND STARTS CALLING YOU ALL A BUNCH OF UGLY HUMAN BASTARDS!
THEY'LL BE COMING TO REEL ME BACK IN! I NEVER HAVE THAT LONG TO WAIT!
URRR.
NOT AGAIN!
THAT'S RIGHT! LOOK AT THAT!
IF THAT'S NOT EVIDENCE I DON'T KNOW WHAT IS!
AOWW.
YOU'RE RIGHT ABOUT ONE THING, SUNSHINE.
THEY'RE COMING TO TAKE YOU AWAY.

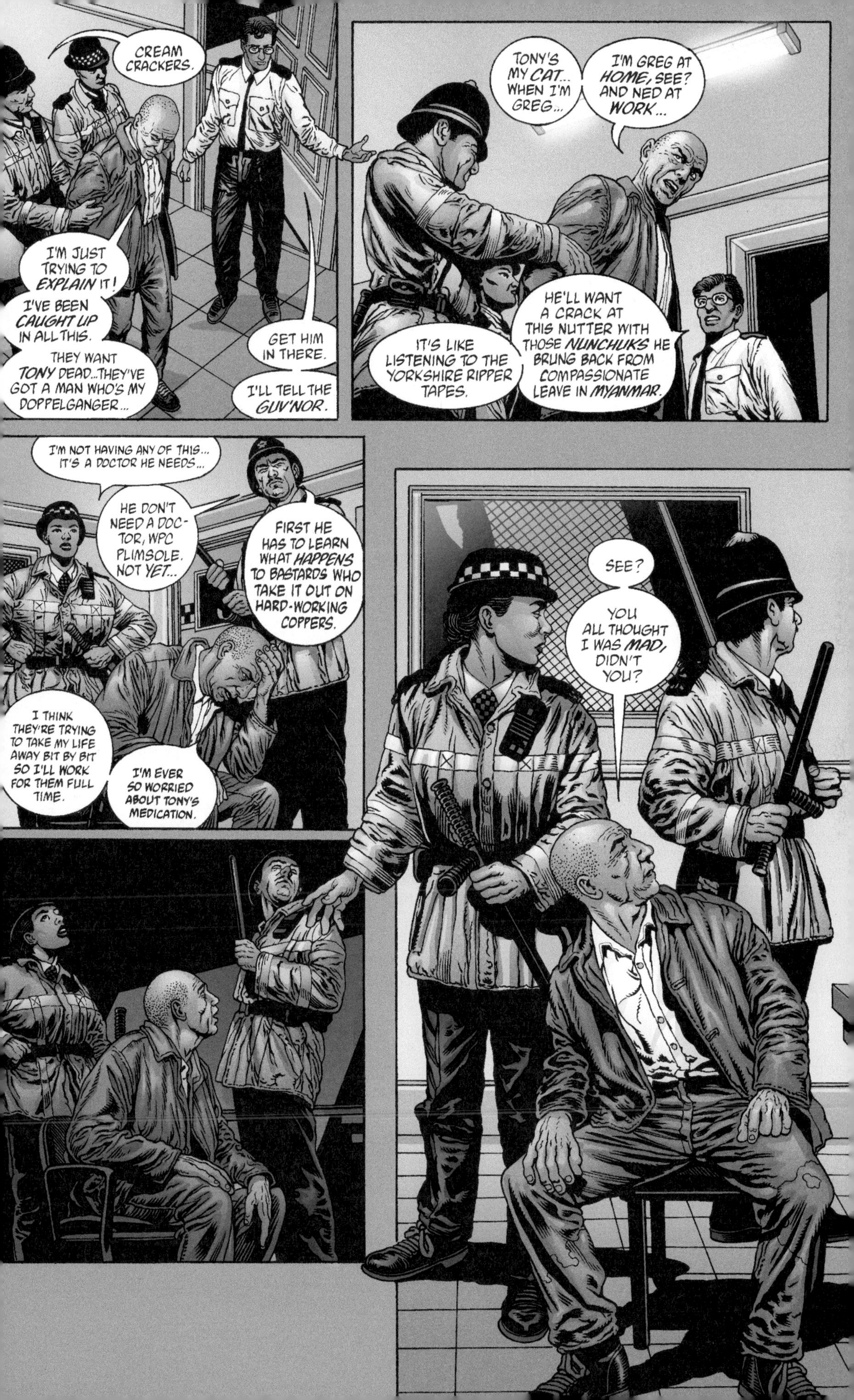
CREAM CRACKERS.
I'M JUST TRYING TO EXPLAIN IT!
I'VE BEEN CAUGHT UP IN ALL THIS.
THEY WANT TONY DEAD...THEY'VE GOT A MAN WHO'S MY DOPPELGANGER...
GET HIM IN THERE.
I'LL TELL THE GUV'NOR.
TONY'S MY CAT... WHEN I'M GREG...
I'M GREG AT HOME, SEE? AND NED AT WORK...
IT'S LIKE LISTENING TO THE YORKSHIRE RIPPER TAPES.
HE'LL WANT A CRACK AT THIS NUTTER WITH THOSE NUNCHUKS HE BRUNG BACK FROM COMPASSIONATE LEAVE IN MYANMAR.
I'M NOT HAVING ANY OF THIS... IT'S A DOCTOR HE NEEDS...
HE DON'T NEED A DOCTOR, WPC PLIMSOLE. NOT YET...
FIRST HE HAS TO LEARN WHAT HAPPENS TO BASTARDS WHO TAKE IT OUT ON HARD-WORKING COPPERS.
I THINK THEY'RE TRYING TO TAKE MY LIFE AWAY BIT BY BIT SO I'LL WORK FOR THEM FULL TIME.
I'M EVER SO WORRIED ABOUT TONY'S MEDICATION.
SEE?
YOU ALL THOUGHT I WAS MAD, DIDN'T YOU?

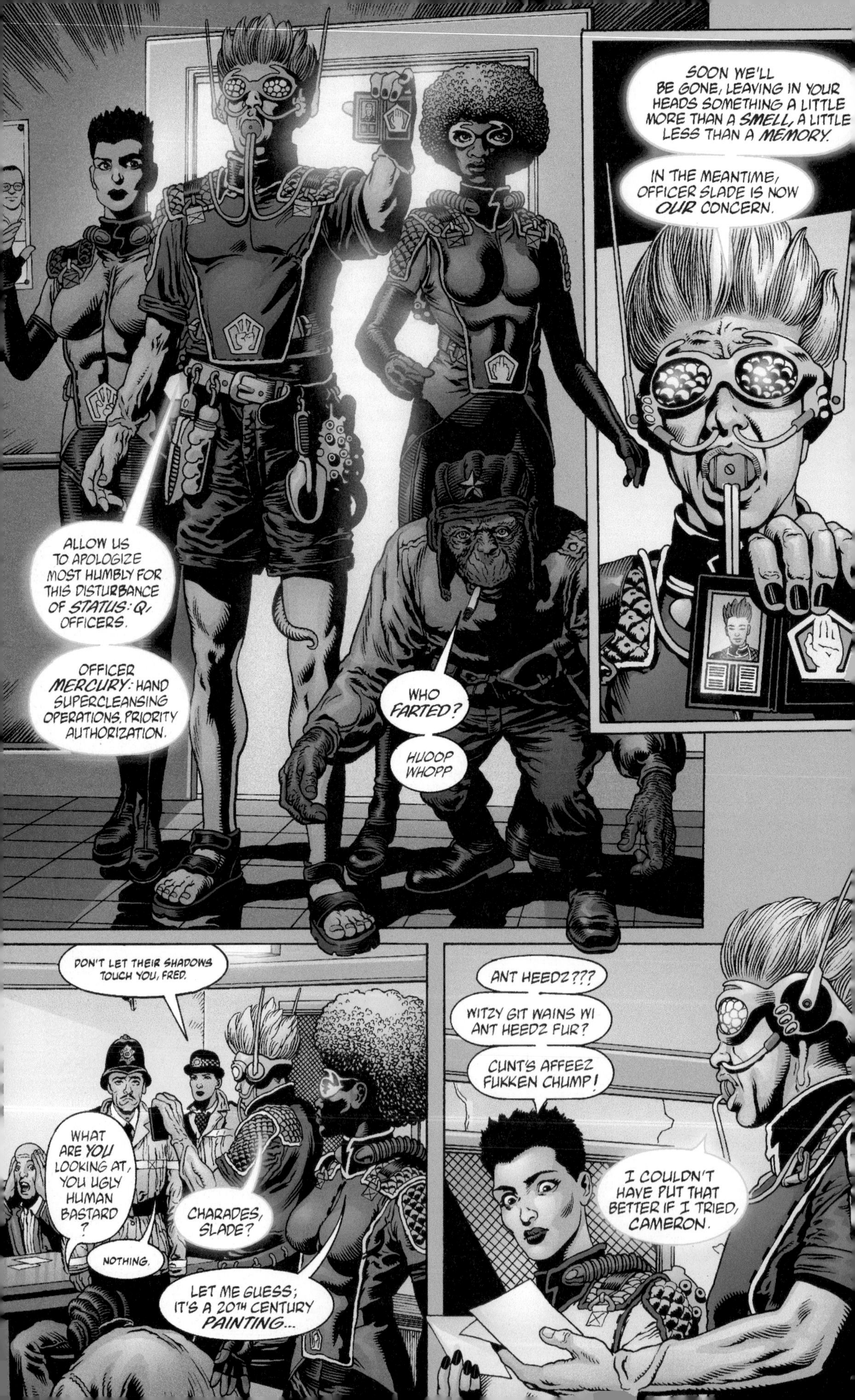
SOON WE'LL BE GONE, LEAVING IN YOUR HEADS SOMETHING A LITTLE MORE THAN A SMELL, A LITTLE LESS THAN A MEMORY.
IN THE MEANTIME, OFFICER SLADE IS NOW OUR CONCERN.
ALLOW US TO APOLOGIZE MOST HUMBLY FOR THIS DISTURBANCE OF STATUS: Q, OFFICERS.
OFFICER MERCURY: HAND SUPERCLEANSING OPERATIONS, PRIORITY AUTHORIZATION.
WHO FARTED?
HUOOP WHOPP
DON'T LET THEIR SHADOWS TOUCH YOU, FRED.
WHAT ARE YOU LOOKING AT, YOU UGLY HUMAN BASTARD?
NOTHING.
CHARADES, SLADE?
LET ME GUESS; IT'S A 20TH CENTURY PAINTING...
ANT HEEDZ???
WITZY GIT WAINS WI ANT HEEDZ FUR?
CUNT'S AFFEEZ FUKKEN CHUMP!
I COULDN'T HAVE PUT THAT BETTER IF I TRIED, CAMERON.

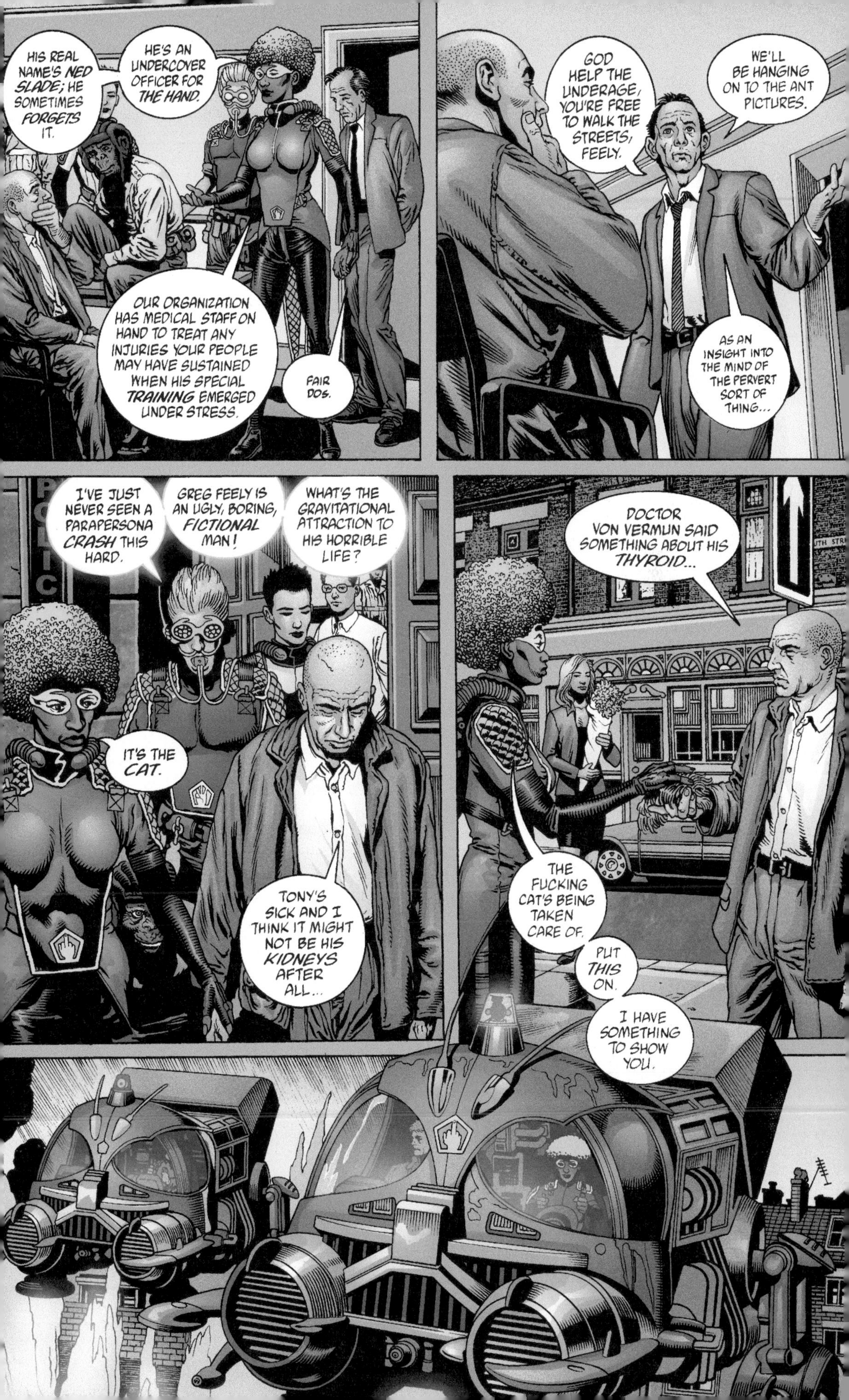
HIS REAL NAME'S NED SLADE; HE SOMETIMES FORGETS IT.
HE'S AN UNDERCOVER OFFICER FOR THE HAND.
OUR ORGANIZATION HAS MEDICAL STAFF ON HAND TO TREAT ANY INJURIES YOUR PEOPLE MAY HAVE SUSTAINED WHEN HIS SPECIAL TRAINING EMERGED UNDER STRESS.
FAIR DOS.
GOD HELP THE UNDERAGE, YOU'RE FREE TO WALK THE STREETS, FEELY.
WE'LL BE HANGING ON TO THE ANT PICTURES.
AS AN INSIGHT INTO THE MIND OF THE PERVERT SORT OF THING...
I'VE JUST NEVER SEEN A PARAPERSONA CRASH THIS HARD.
GREG FEELY IS AN UGLY, BORING, FICTIONAL MAN!
WHAT'S THE GRAVITATIONAL ATTRACTION TO HIS HORRIBLE LIFE?
IT'S THE CAT.
TONY'S SICK AND I THINK IT MIGHT NOT BE HIS KIDNEYS AFTER ALL...
DOCTOR VON VERMUN SAID SOMETHING ABOUT HIS THYROID...
THE FUCKING CAT'S BEING TAKEN CARE OF.
PUT THIS ON.
I HAVE SOMETHING TO SHOW YOU.

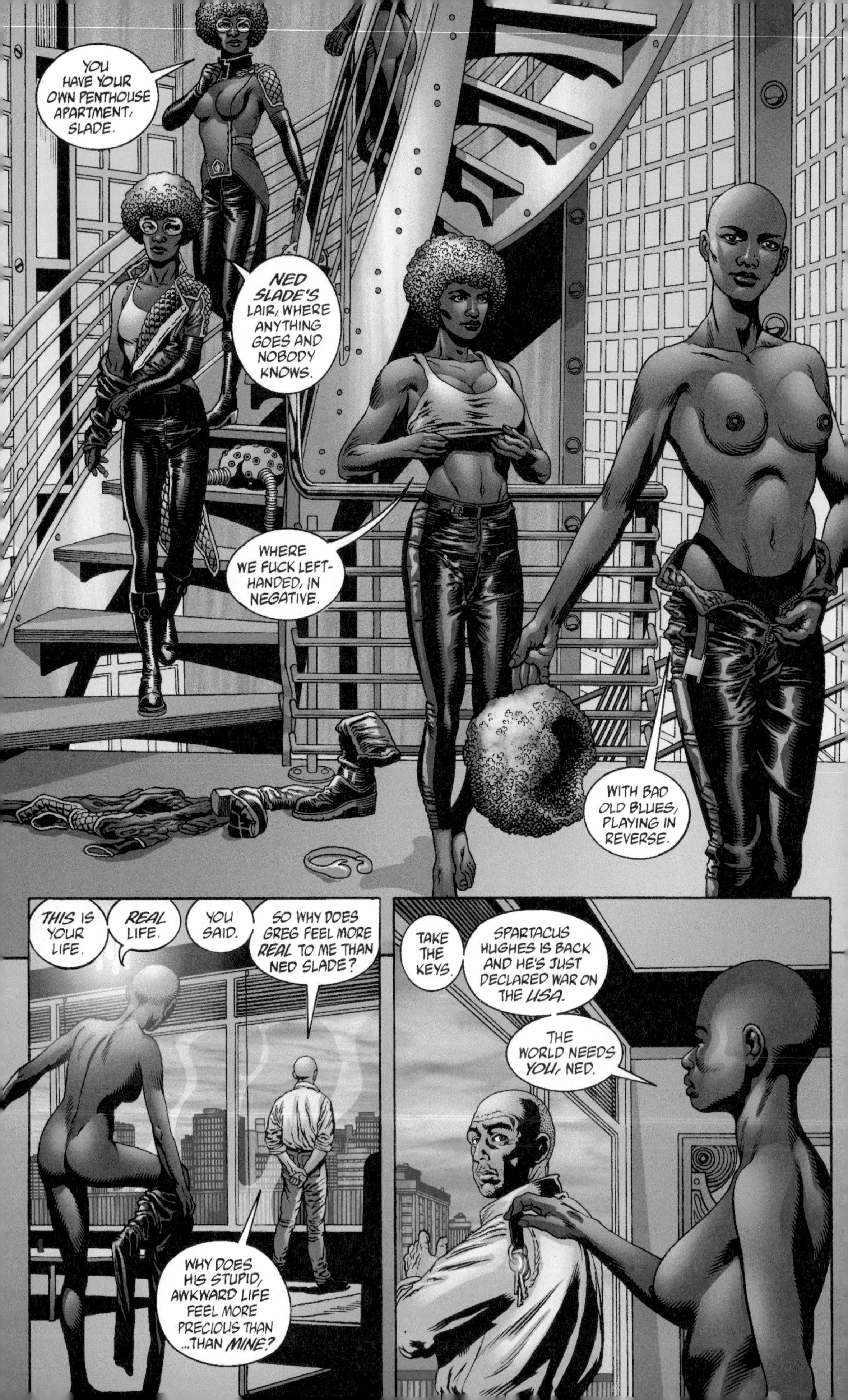
YOU HAVE YOUR OWN PENTHOUSE APARTMENT, SLADE.
NED SLADE'S LAIR, WHERE ANYTHING GOES AND NOBODY KNOWS.
WHERE WE FUCK LEFT-HANDED, IN NEGATIVE.
WITH BAD OLD BLUES, PLAYING IN REVERSE.
THIS IS YOUR LIFE.
REAL LIFE.
YOU SAID.
SO WHY DOES GREG FEEL MORE REAL TO ME THAN NED SLADE?
WHY DOES HIS STUPID, AWKWARD LIFE FEEL MORE PRECIOUS THAN ...THAN MINE?
TAKE THE KEYS.
SPARTACUS HUGHES IS BACK AND HE'S JUST DECLARED WAR ON THE USA.
THE WORLD NEEDS YOU, NED.

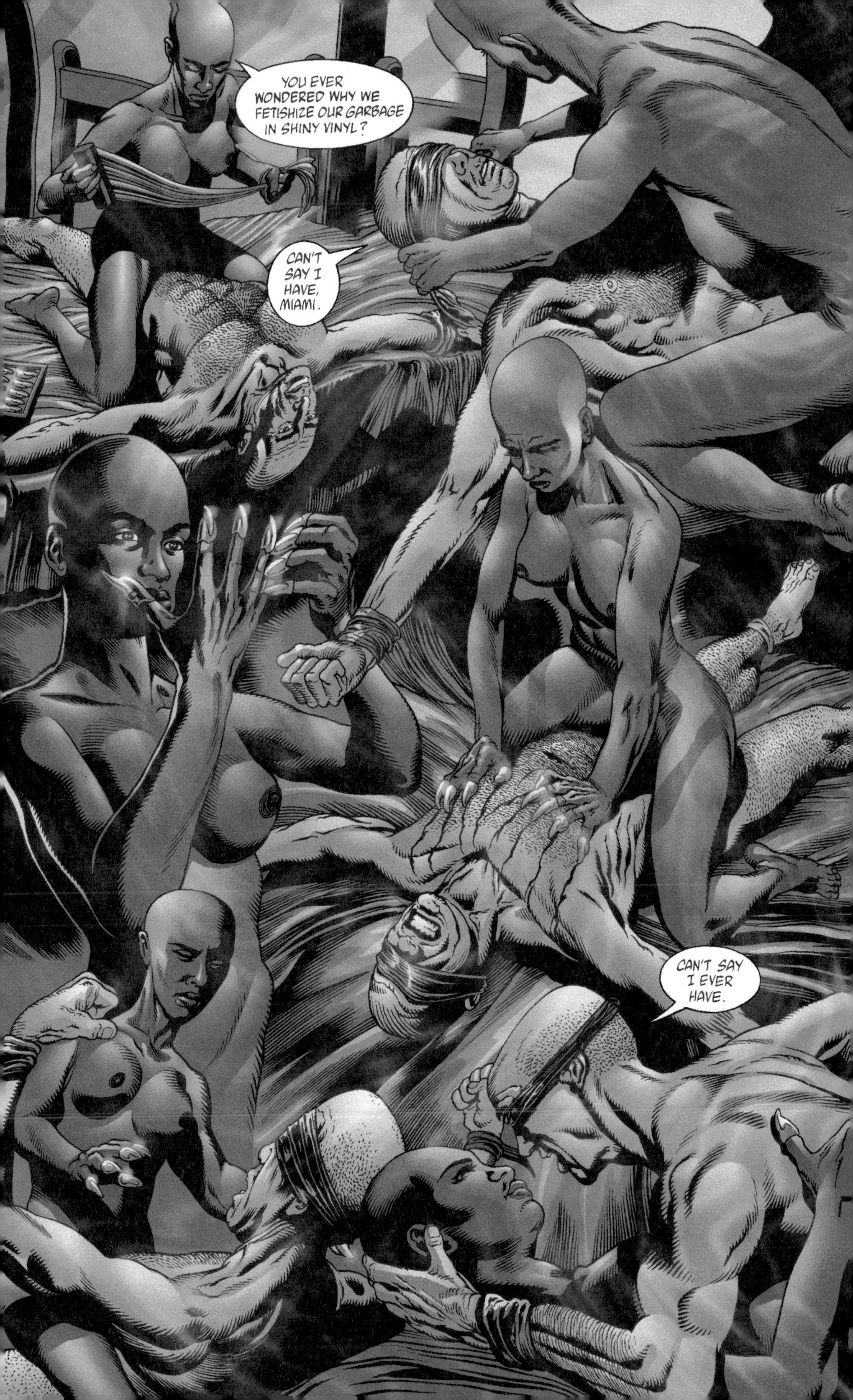
YOU EVER WONDERED WHY WE FETISHIZE OUR GARBAGE IN SHINY VINYL?
CAN'T SAY I HAVE, MIAMI.
CAN'T SAY I EVER HAVE.

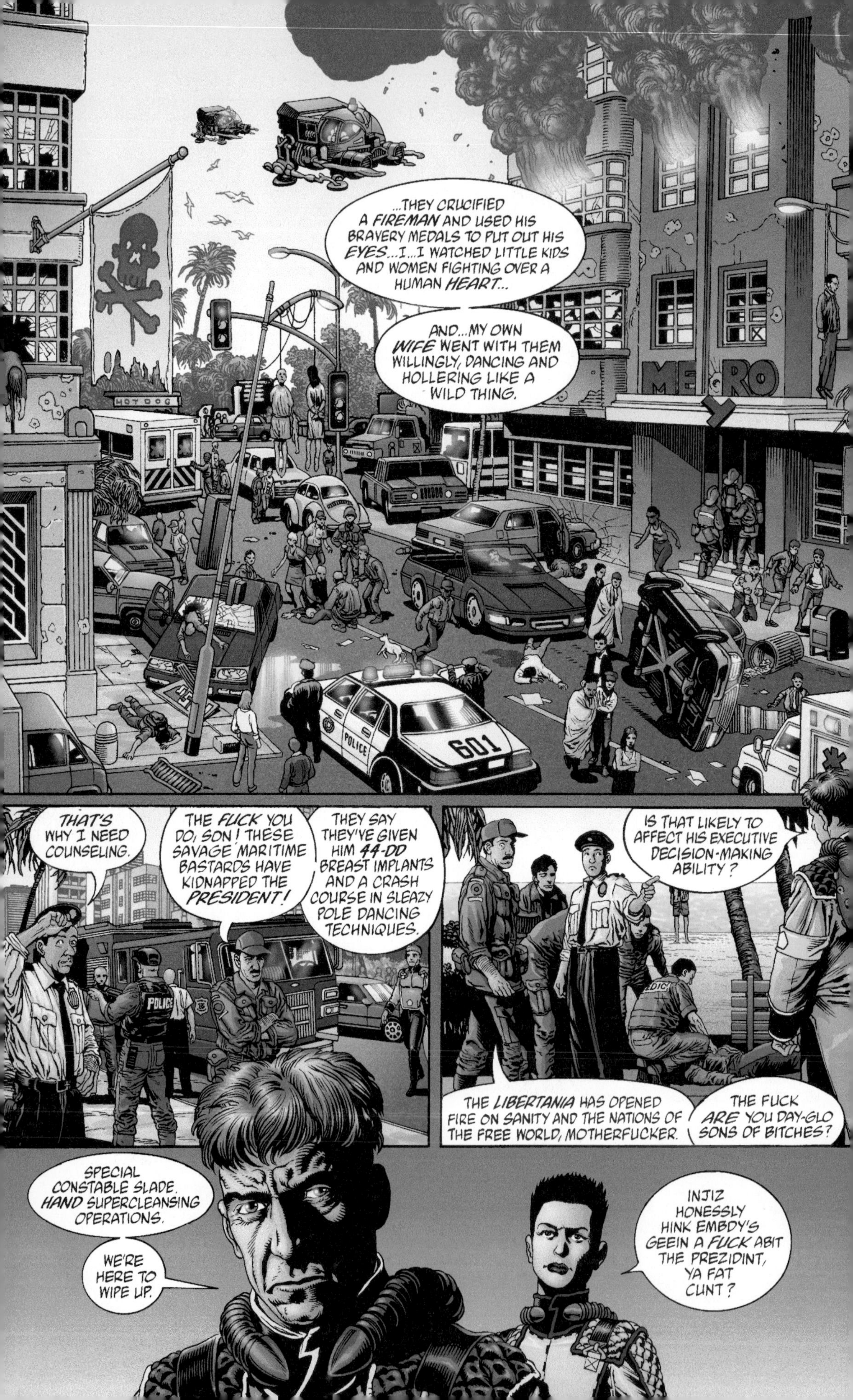

...THEY CRUCIFIED A FIREMAN AND USED HIS BRAVERY MEDALS TO PUT OUT HIS EYES...I...I WATCHED LITTLE KIDS AND WOMEN FIGHTING OVER A HUMAN HEART...
AND...MY OWN WIFE WENT WITH THEM WILLINGLY, DANCING AND HOLLERING LIKE A WILD THING.
HOT DOG
METRO
POLICE
601
THAT'S WHY I NEED COUNSELING.
THE FUCK YOU DO, SON! THESE SAVAGE MARITIME BASTARDS HAVE KIDNAPPED THE PRESIDENT!
THEY SAY THEY'VE GIVEN HIM 44-DD BREAST IMPLANTS AND A CRASH COURSE IN SLEAZY POLE DANCING TECHNIQUES.
POLICE
IS THAT LIKELY TO AFFECT HIS EXECUTIVE DECISION-MAKING ABILITY?
THE LIBERTANIA HAS OPENED FIRE ON SANITY AND THE NATIONS OF THE FREE WORLD, MOTHERFUCKER.
THE FUCK ARE YOU DAY-GLO SONS OF BITCHES?
SPECIAL CONSTABLE SLADE. HAND SUPERCLEANSING OPERATIONS.
WE'RE HERE TO WIPE UP.
INJIZ HONESSLY HINK EMBDY'S GEEIN A FUCK ABIT THE PREZIDINT, YA FAT CUNT?

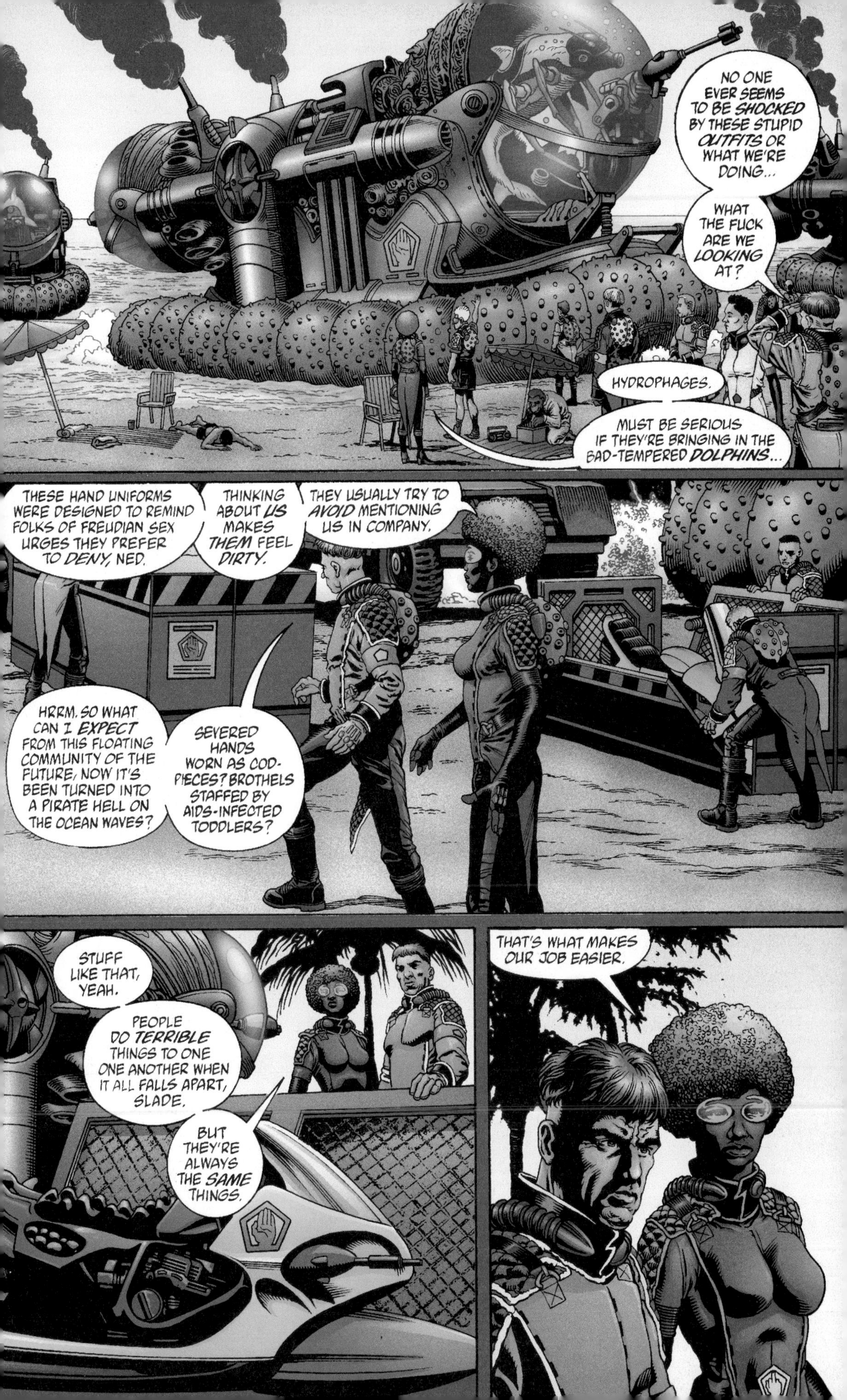
NO ONE EVER SEEMS TO BE SHOCKED BY THESE STUPID OUTFITS OR WHAT WE'RE DOING...
WHAT THE FUCK ARE WE LOOKING AT?
HYDROPHAGES.
MUST BE SERIOUS IF THEY'RE BRINGING IN THE BAD-TEMPERED DOLPHINS...
THESE HAND UNIFORMS WERE DESIGNED TO REMIND FOLKS OF FREUDIAN SEX URGES THEY PREFER TO DENY, NED.
THINKING ABOUT US MAKES THEM FEEL DIRTY.
THEY USUALLY TRY TO AVOID MENTIONING US IN COMPANY.
HRRM. SO WHAT CAN I EXPECT FROM THIS FLOATING COMMUNITY OF THE FUTURE, NOW IT'S BEEN TURNED INTO A PIRATE HELL ON THE OCEAN WAVES?
SEVERED HANDS WORN AS COD-PIECES? BROTHELS STAFFED BY AIDS-INFECTED TODDLERS?
STUFF LIKE THAT, YEAH.
PEOPLE DO TERRIBLE THINGS TO ONE ONE ANOTHER WHEN IT ALL FALLS APART, SLADE.
BUT THEY'RE ALWAYS THE SAME THINGS.
THAT'S WHAT MAKES OUR JOB EASIER.

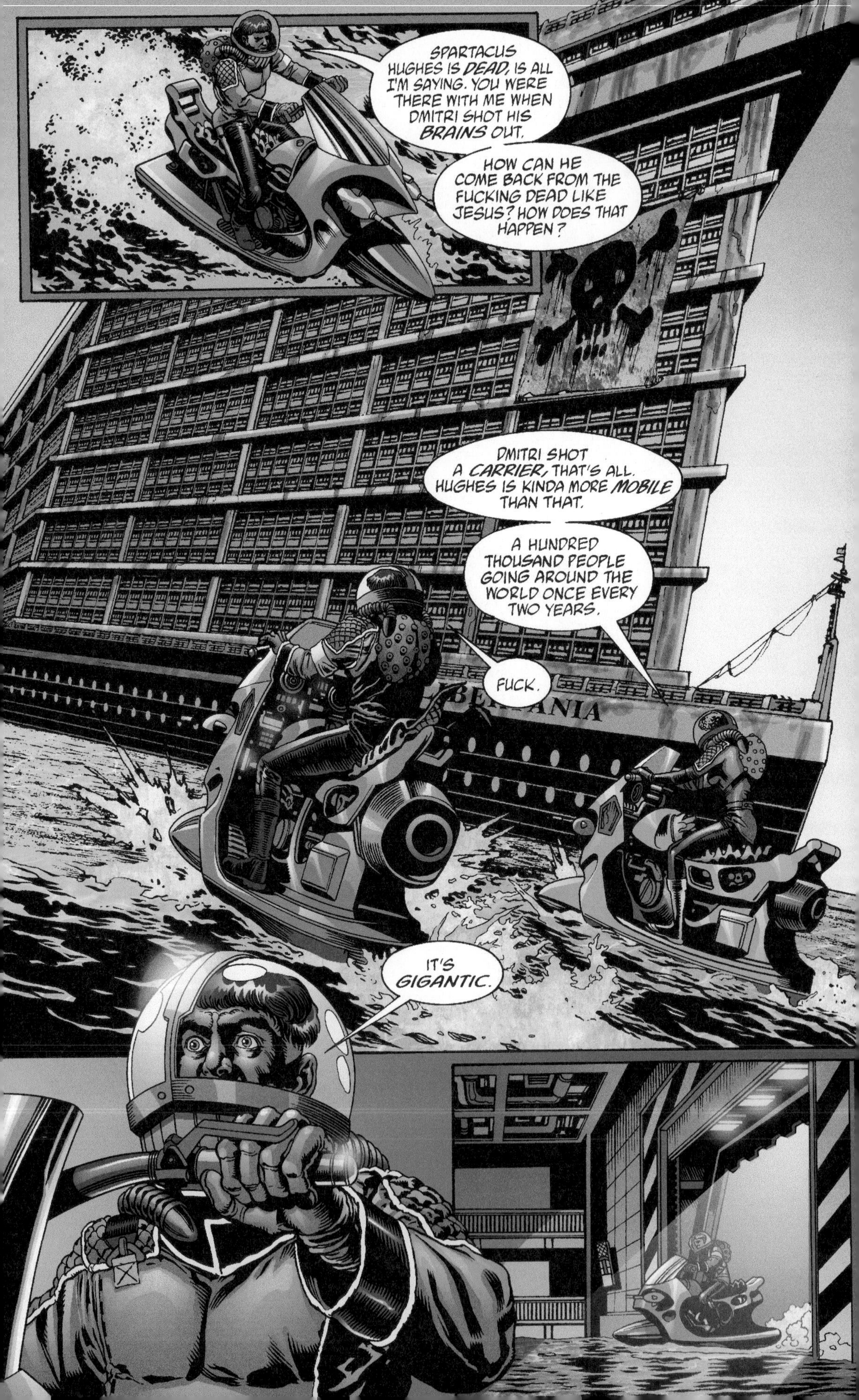
SPARTACUS HUGHES IS DEAD, IS ALL I'M SAYING. YOU WERE THERE WITH ME WHEN DMITRI SHOT HIS BRAINS OUT.
HOW CAN HE COME BACK FROM THE FUCKING DEAD LIKE JESUS? HOW DOES THAT HAPPEN?
DMITRI SHOT A CARRIER, THAT'S ALL. HUGHES IS KINDA MORE MOBILE THAN THAT.
A HUNDRED THOUSAND PEOPLE GOING AROUND THE WORLD ONCE EVERY TWO YEARS.
FUCK.
IT'S GIGANTIC.

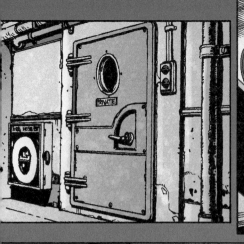

...GOT ALL THAT? WHEN SOCIAL BONDS DISINTEGRATE, THE WORST THINGS YOU CAN *IMAGINE* START TO HAPPEN ON A DAILY BASIS.

BE READY FOR

ANY-THING.

PEOPLE HAVE DEGENERATED INTO FRENZIED PIRATE BLOOD-LUST...

EXPECT CANNIBAL BEHAVIOR, INCEST, FRATRICIDE, SELF-MUTILATION AND PET MICROWAVING...

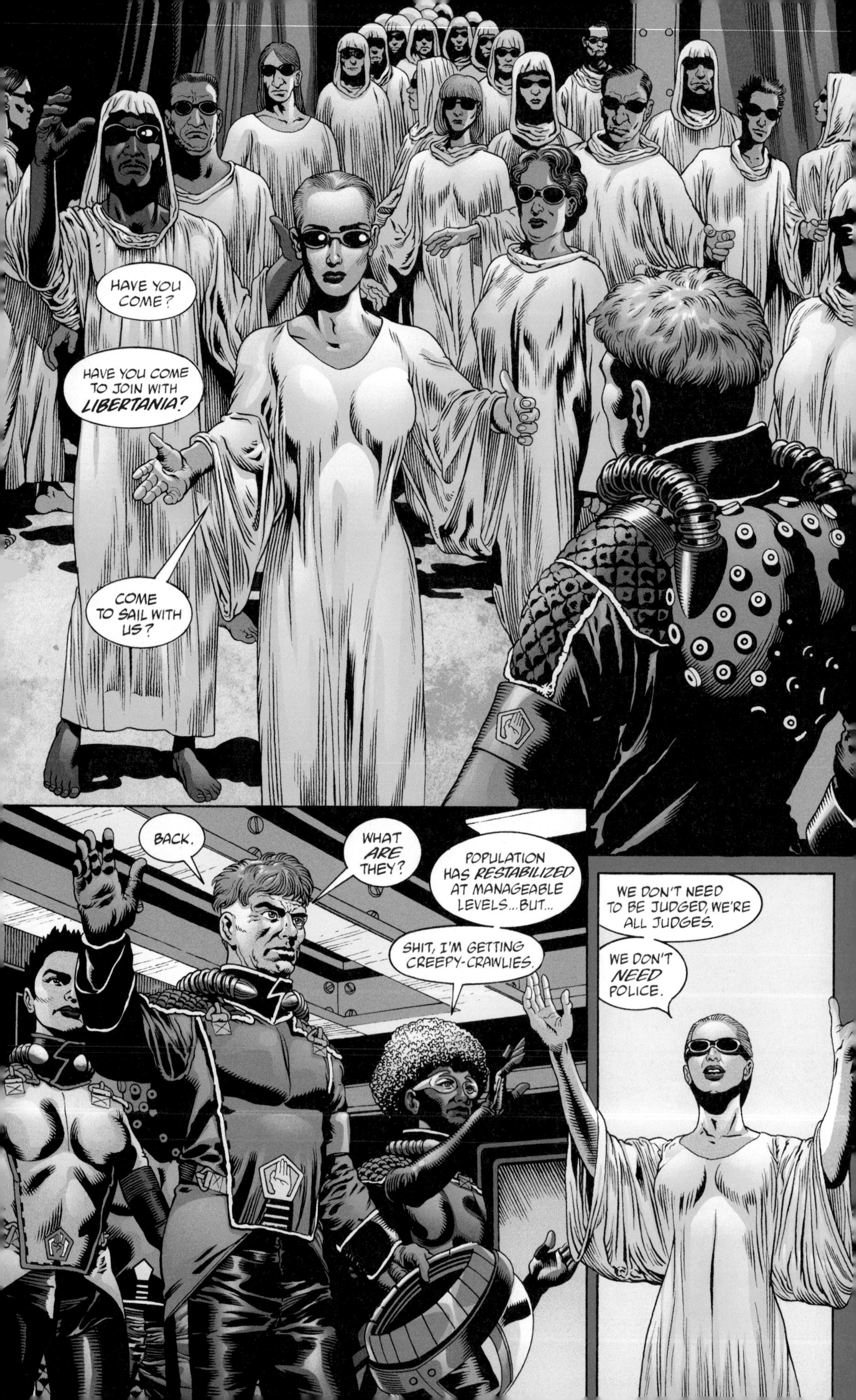

HAVE YOU COME?
HAVE YOU COME TO JOIN WITH LIBERTANIA?
COME TO SAIL WITH US?
BACK.
WHAT ARE THEY?
POPULATION HAS RESTABILIZED AT MANAGEABLE LEVELS...BUT...
SHIT, I'M GETTING CREEPY-CRAWLIES.
WE DON'T NEED TO BE JUDGED, WE'RE ALL JUDGES.
WE DON'T NEED POLICE.

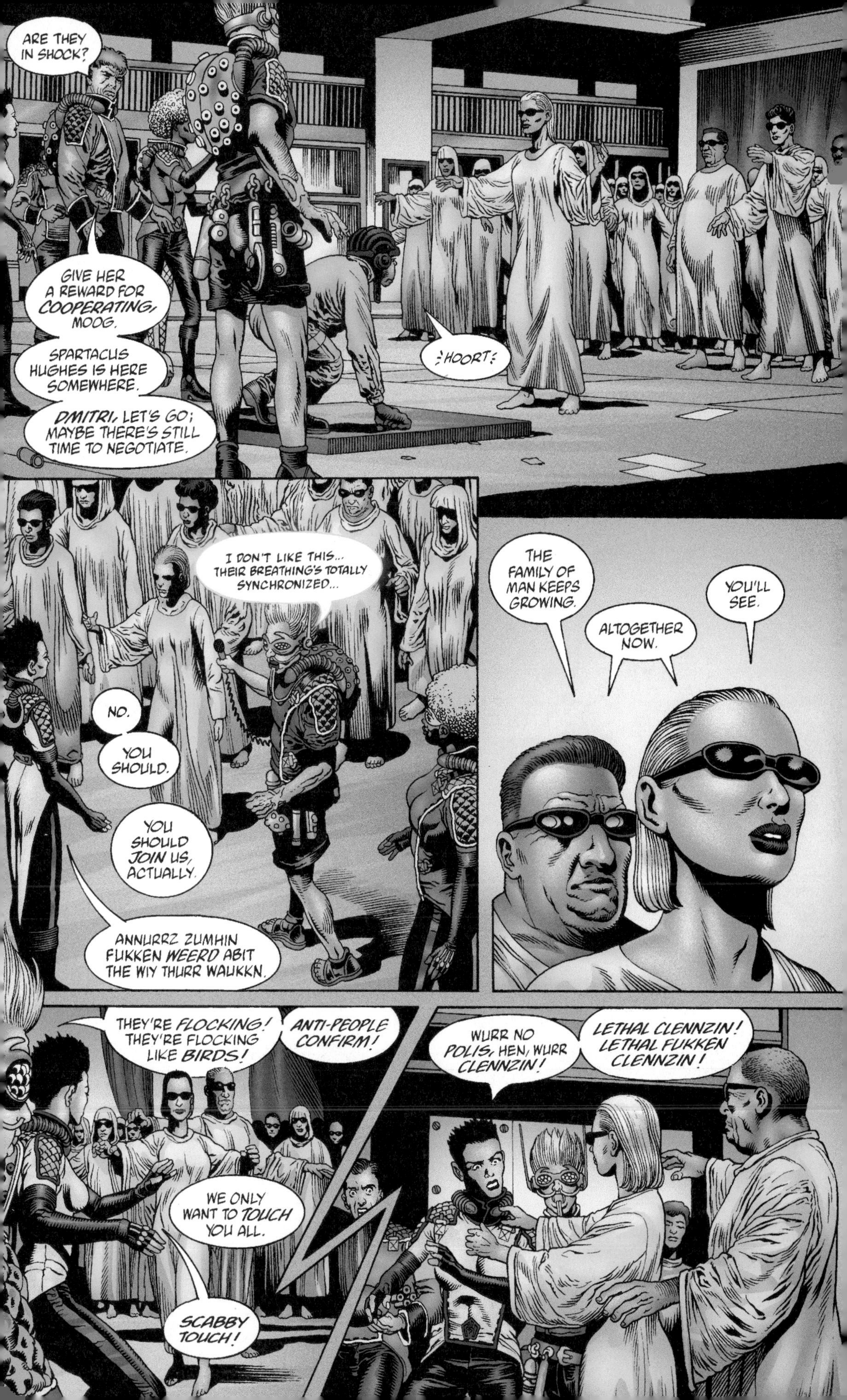
ARE THEY IN SHOCK?
GIVE HER A REWARD FOR COOPERATING, MOOG.
SPARTACUS HUGHES IS HERE SOMEWHERE.
DMITRI, LET'S GO; MAYBE THERE'S STILL TIME TO NEGOTIATE.
HOORT
I DON'T LIKE THIS... THEIR BREATHING'S TOTALLY SYNCHRONIZED...
NO.
YOU SHOULD.
YOU SHOULD JOIN US, ACTUALLY.
ANNURRZ ZUMHIN FUKKEN WEERD ABIT THE WIY THURR WAUKKN.
THE FAMILY OF MAN KEEPS GROWING.
ALTOGETHER NOW.
YOU'LL SEE.
THEY'RE FLOCKING! THEY'RE FLOCKING LIKE BIRDS!
ANTI-PEOPLE CONFIRM!
WE ONLY WANT TO TOUCH YOU ALL.
SCABBY TOUCH!
WURR NO POLIS, HEN, WURR CLENNZIN!
LETHAL CLENNZIN! LETHAL FUKKEN CLENNZIN!

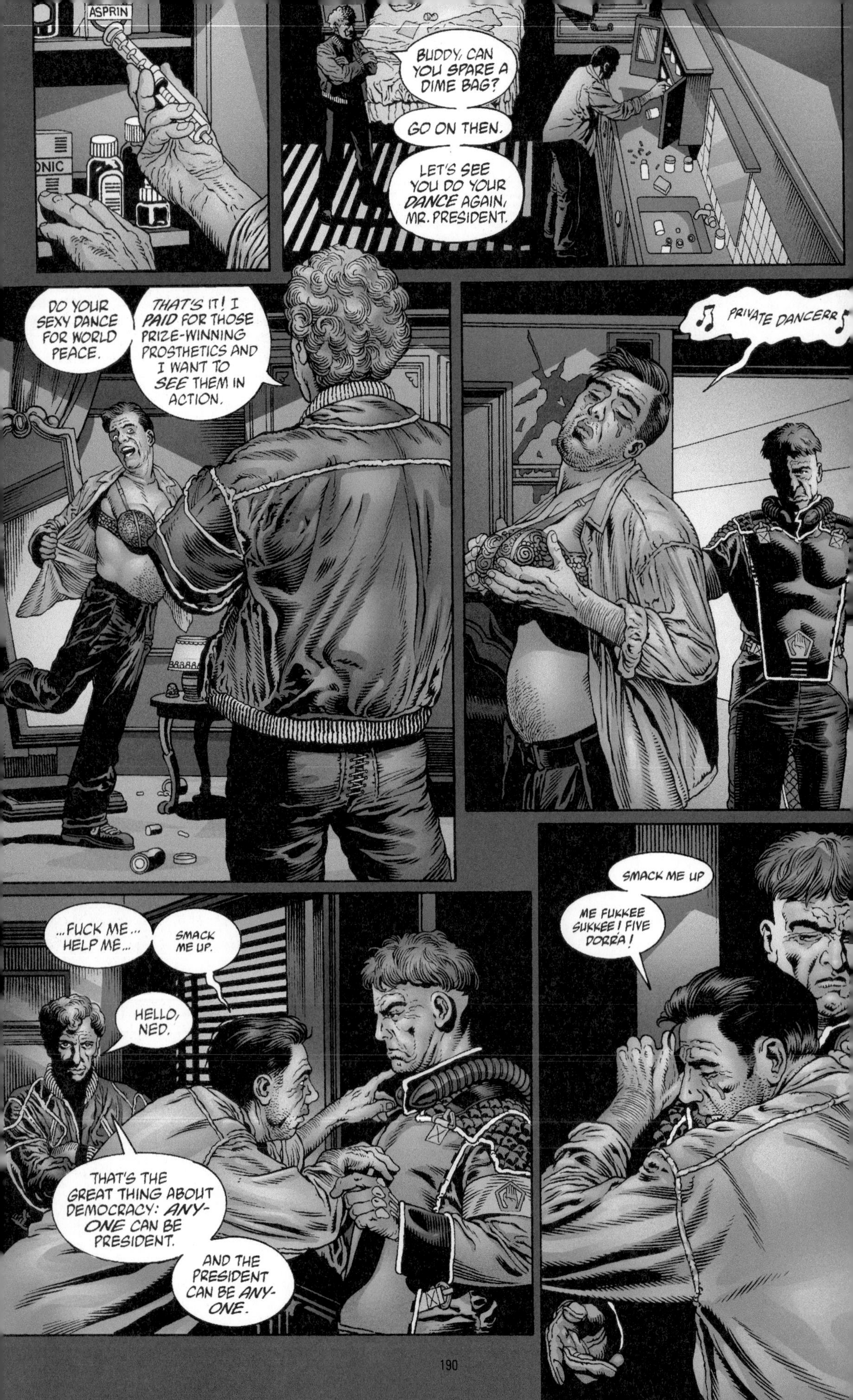
ASPRIN
ONIC
BUDDY, CAN YOU SPARE A DIME BAG?
GO ON THEN.
LET'S SEE YOU DO YOUR DANCE AGAIN, MR. PRESIDENT.
DO YOUR SEXY DANCE FOR WORLD PEACE.
THAT'S IT! I PAID FOR THOSE PRIZE-WINNING PROSTHETICS AND I WANT TO SEE THEM IN ACTION.
PRIVATE DANCERR
...FUCK ME... HELP ME...
SMACK ME UP.
HELLO, NED.
THAT'S THE GREAT THING ABOUT DEMOCRACY: ANY-ONE CAN BE PRESIDENT.
AND THE PRESIDENT CAN BE ANY-ONE.
SMACK ME UP
ME FUKKEE SUKKEE! FIVE DORRA!

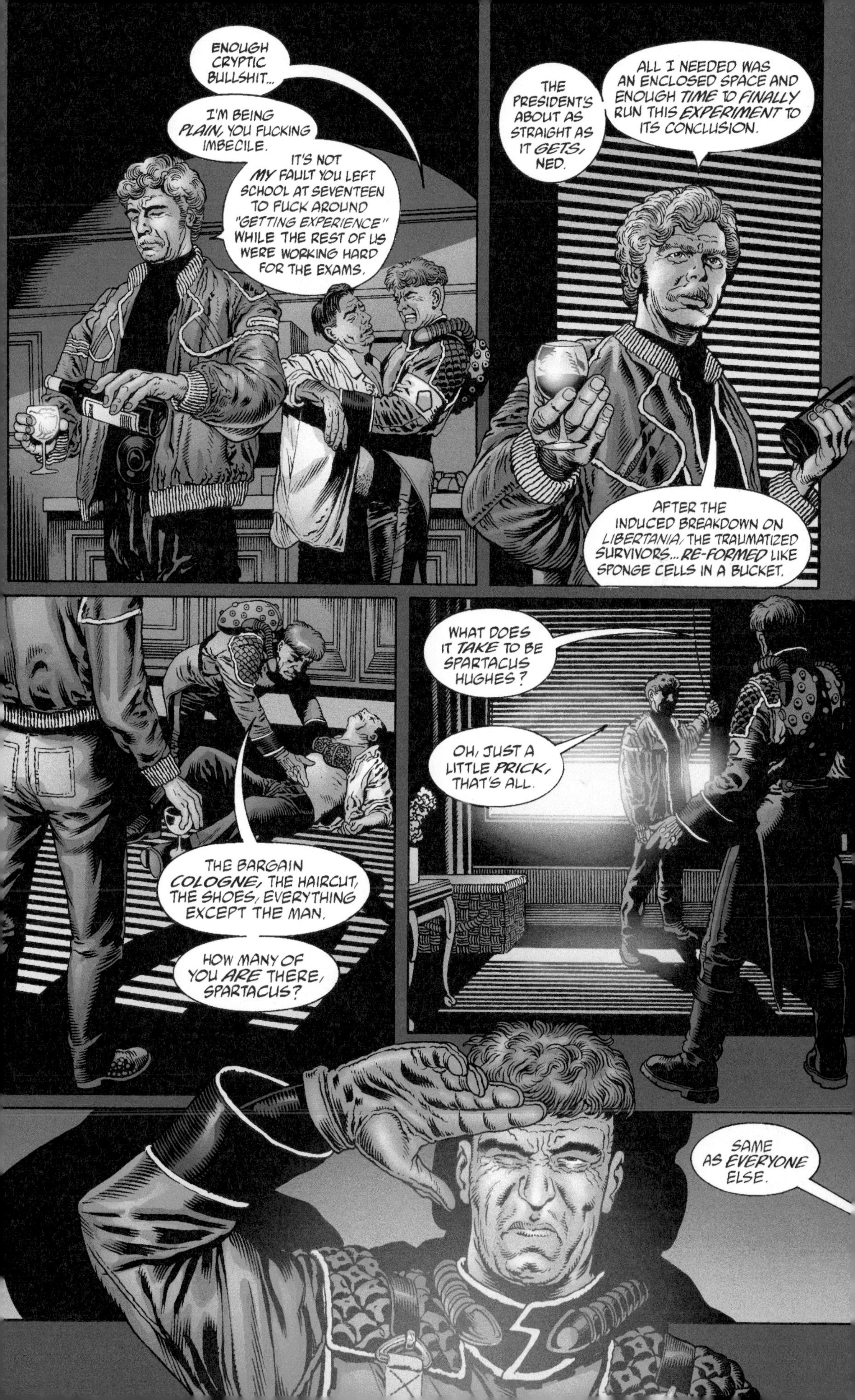
ENOUGH CRYPTIC BULLSHIT...
I'M BEING *PLAIN*, YOU FUCKING IMBECILE.
IT'S NOT *MY* FAULT YOU LEFT SCHOOL AT SEVENTEEN TO FUCK AROUND "GETTING EXPERIENCE" WHILE THE REST OF US WERE WORKING HARD FOR THE EXAMS.
THE PRESIDENT'S ABOUT AS STRAIGHT AS IT *GETS*, NED.
ALL I NEEDED WAS AN ENCLOSED SPACE AND ENOUGH *TIME* TO *FINALLY* RUN THIS *EXPERIMENT* TO ITS CONCLUSION.
AFTER THE INDUCED BREAKDOWN ON *LIBERTANIA*, THE TRAUMATIZED SURVIVORS... *RE-FORMED* LIKE SPONGE CELLS IN A BUCKET.
THE BARGAIN *COLOGNE*, THE HAIRCUT, THE SHOES, EVERYTHING EXCEPT THE MAN.
HOW MANY OF YOU *ARE* THERE, SPARTACUS?
WHAT DOES IT *TAKE* TO BE SPARTACUS HUGHES?
OH, JUST A LITTLE *PRICK*, THAT'S ALL.
SAME AS *EVERYONE* ELSE.

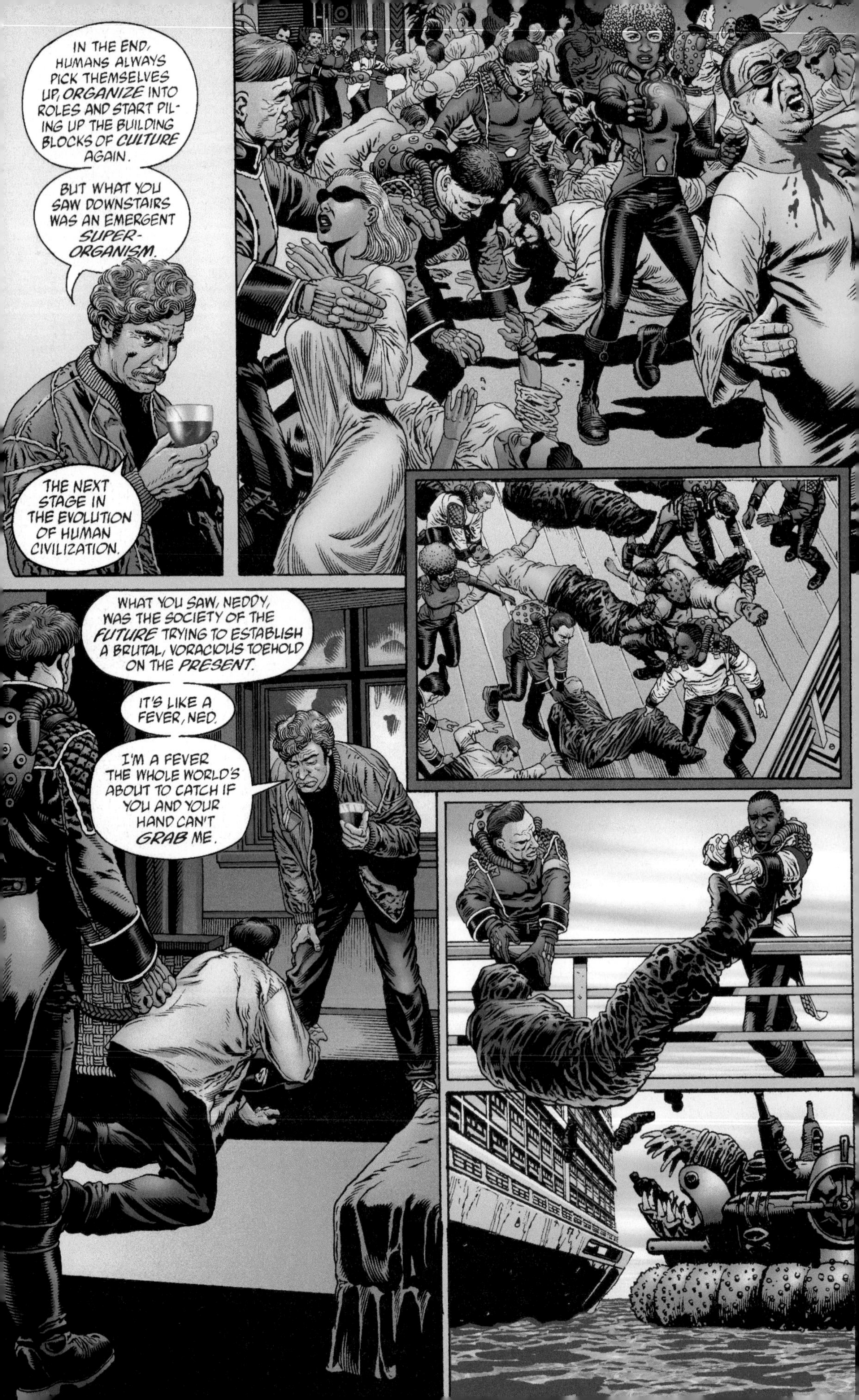
IN THE END, HUMANS ALWAYS PICK THEMSELVES UP, ORGANIZE INTO ROLES AND START PILING UP THE BUILDING BLOCKS OF CULTURE AGAIN.
BUT WHAT YOU SAW DOWNSTAIRS WAS AN EMERGENT SUPER-ORGANISM.
THE NEXT STAGE IN THE EVOLUTION OF HUMAN CIVILIZATION.
WHAT YOU SAW, NEDDY, WAS THE SOCIETY OF THE FUTURE TRYING TO ESTABLISH A BRUTAL, VORACIOUS TOEHOLD ON THE PRESENT.
IT'S LIKE A FEVER, NED.
I'M A FEVER THE WHOLE WORLD'S ABOUT TO CATCH IF YOU AND YOUR HAND CAN'T GRAB ME.

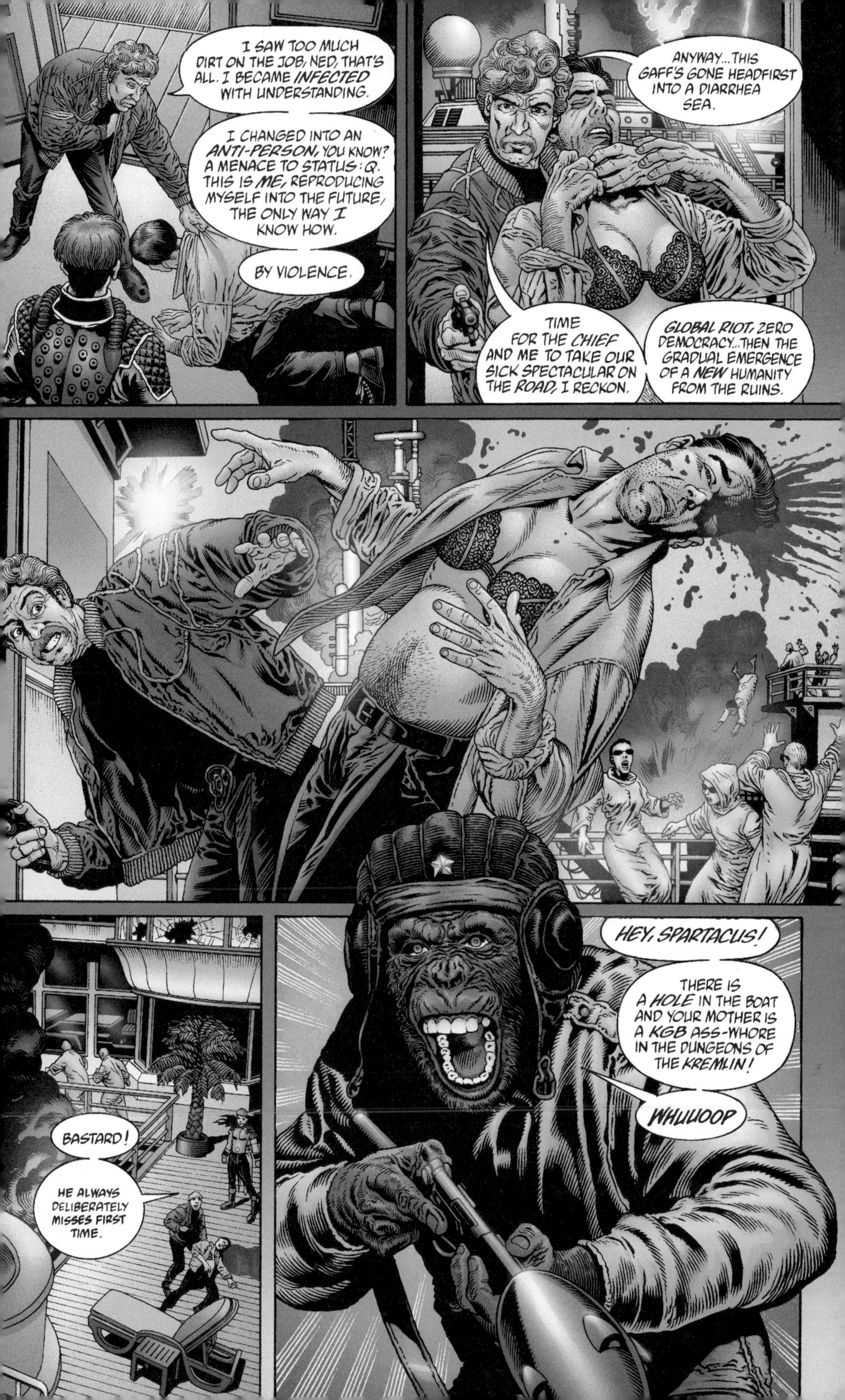
I SAW TOO MUCH DIRT ON THE JOB, NED, THAT'S ALL. I BECAME *INFECTED* WITH UNDERSTANDING.
I CHANGED INTO AN *ANTI-PERSON*, YOU KNOW? A MENACE TO STATUS: Q. THIS IS *ME*, REPRODUCING MYSELF INTO THE FUTURE, THE ONLY WAY I KNOW HOW.
BY VIOLENCE.
ANYWAY... THIS GAFF'S GONE HEADFIRST INTO A DIARRHEA SEA.
GLOBAL RIOT, ZERO DEMOCRACY... THEN THE GRADUAL EMERGENCE OF A *NEW* HUMANITY FROM THE RUINS.
TIME FOR THE *CHIEF* AND ME TO TAKE OUR SICK SPECTACULAR ON THE *ROAD*, I RECKON.
HEY, SPARTACUS!
THERE IS A *HOLE* IN THE BOAT AND YOUR MOTHER IS A *KGB* ASS-WHORE IN THE DUNGEONS OF THE *KREMLIN*!
WHUUOOP
BASTARD!
HE ALWAYS DELIBERATELY MISSES FIRST TIME.

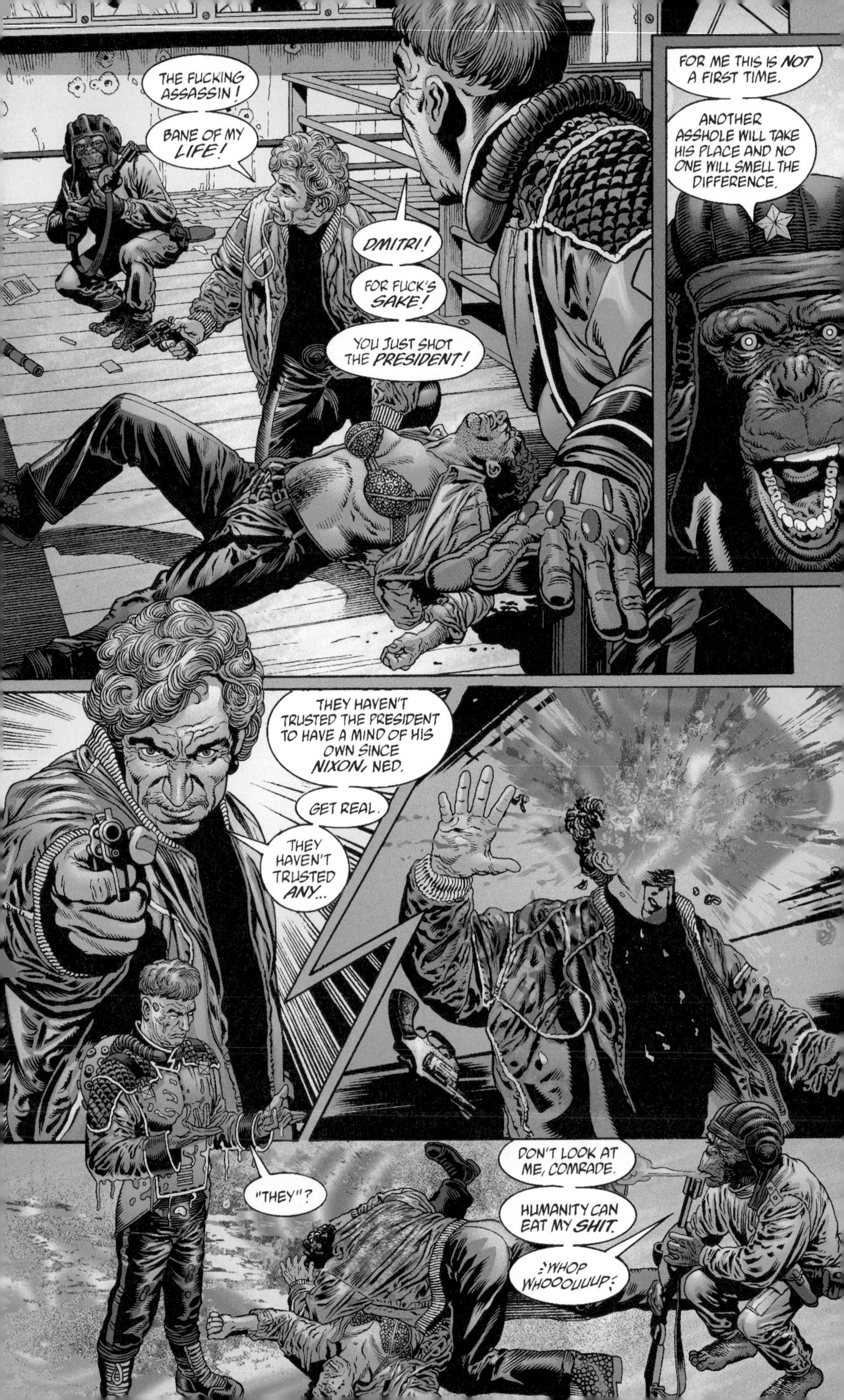
THE FUCKING ASSASSIN!
BANE OF MY LIFE!
DMITRI!
FOR FUCK'S SAKE!
YOU JUST SHOT THE PRESIDENT!
FOR ME THIS IS NOT A FIRST TIME.
ANOTHER ASSHOLE WILL TAKE HIS PLACE AND NO ONE WILL SMELL THE DIFFERENCE.
THEY HAVEN'T TRUSTED THE PRESIDENT TO HAVE A MIND OF HIS OWN SINCE NIXON, NED.
GET REAL.
THEY HAVEN'T TRUSTED ANY...
"THEY"?
DON'T LOOK AT ME, COMRADE.
HUMANITY CAN EAT MY SHIT.
WHOP WHOOOUUUP

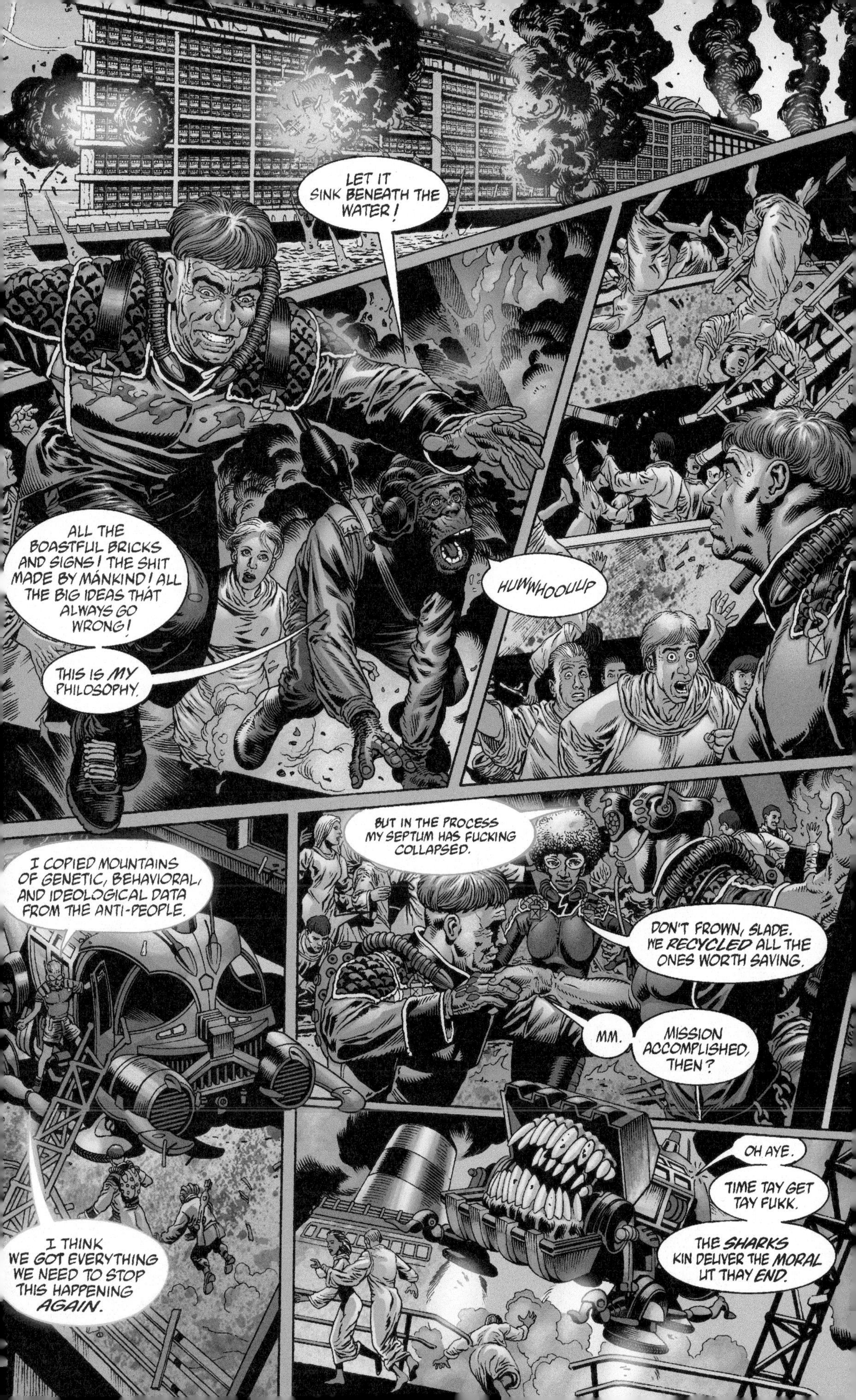
LET IT SINK BENEATH THE WATER!
ALL THE BOASTFUL BRICKS AND SIGNS! THE SHIT MADE BY MANKIND! ALL THE BIG IDEAS THAT ALWAYS GO WRONG!
THIS IS MY PHILOSOPHY.
HUWWHOOULP
I COPIED MOUNTAINS OF GENETIC, BEHAVIORAL, AND IDEOLOGICAL DATA FROM THE ANTI-PEOPLE.
I THINK WE GOT EVERYTHING WE NEED TO STOP THIS HAPPENING AGAIN.
BUT IN THE PROCESS MY SEPTUM HAS FUCKING COLLAPSED.
DON'T FROWN, SLADE. WE RECYCLED ALL THE ONES WORTH SAVING.
MM.
MISSION ACCOMPLISHED, THEN?
OH AYE.
TIME TAY GET TAY FUKK.
THE SHARKS KIN DELIVER THE MORAL UT THAY END.

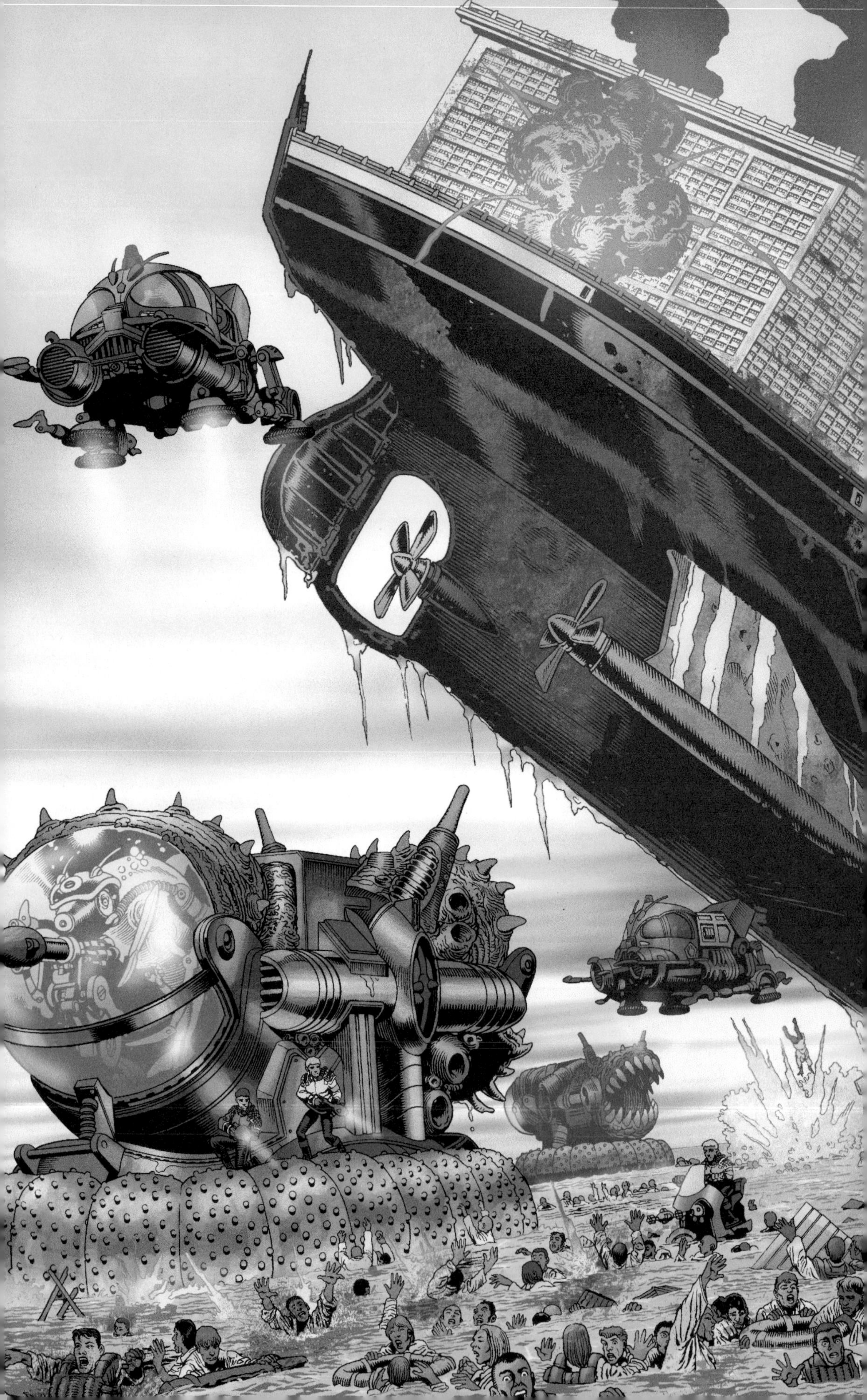

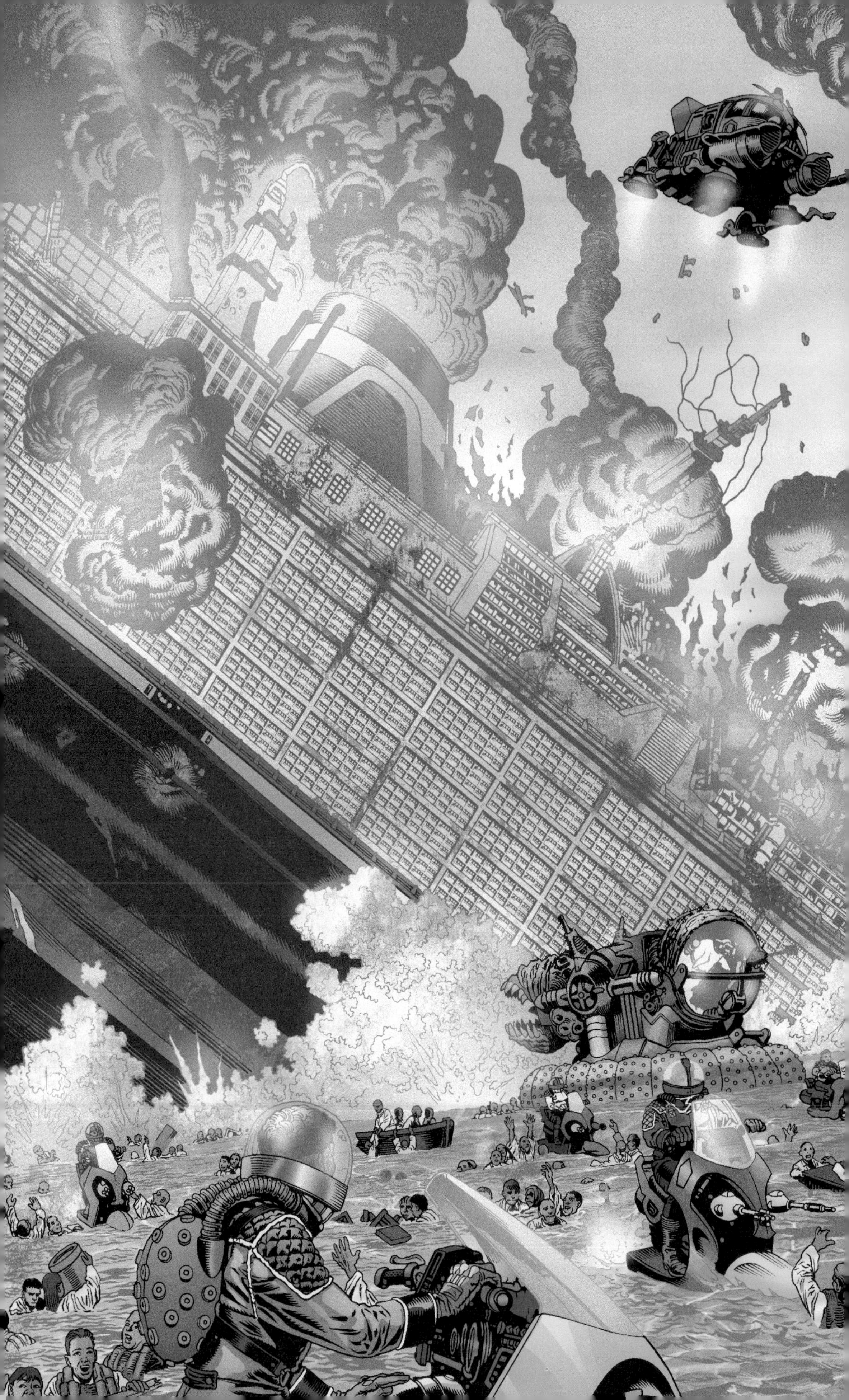

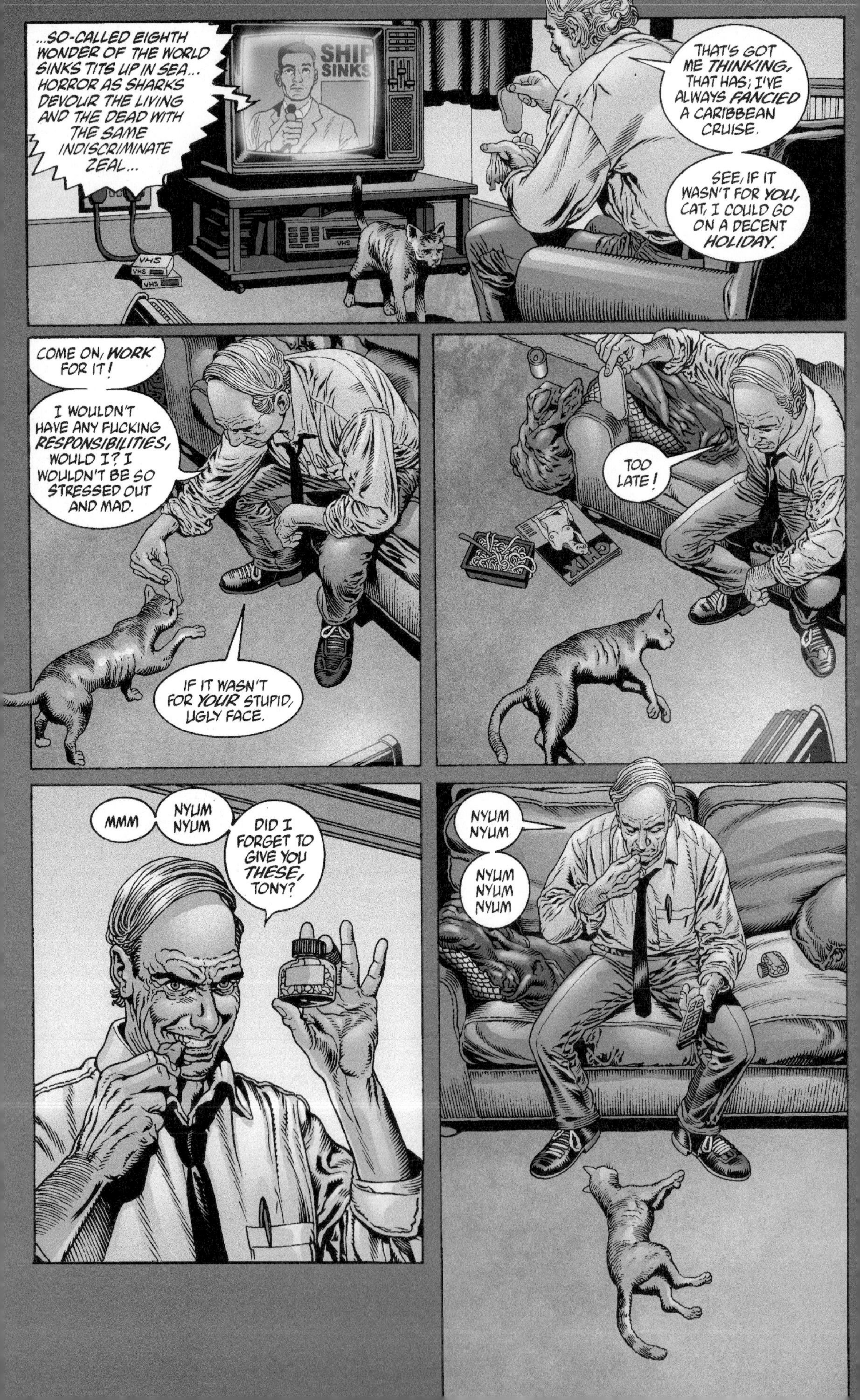
...SO-CALLED EIGHTH WONDER OF THE WORLD SINKS TITS UP IN SEA... HORROR AS SHARKS DEVOUR THE LIVING AND THE DEAD WITH THE SAME INDISCRIMINATE ZEAL...
SHIP SINKS
VHS
THAT'S GOT ME THINKING, THAT HAS; I'VE ALWAYS FANCIED A CARIBBEAN CRUISE.
SEE, IF IT WASN'T FOR YOU, CAT, I COULD GO ON A DECENT HOLIDAY.
COME ON, WORK FOR IT!
I WOULDN'T HAVE ANY FUCKING RESPONSIBILITIES, WOULD I? I WOULDN'T BE SO STRESSED OUT AND MAD.
IF IT WASN'T FOR YOUR STUPID, UGLY FACE.
TOO LATE!
MMM
NYUM NYUM
DID I FORGET TO GIVE YOU THESE, TONY?
NYUM NYUM
NYUM NYUM NYUM

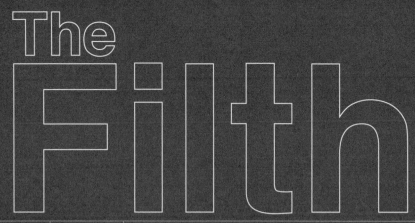

The Filth

09	PROJECT TITLE	**INSIDE THE HAND**
	PRIMARY ARCHITECTS	GRANT MORRISON CHRIS WESTON GARY ERSKINE

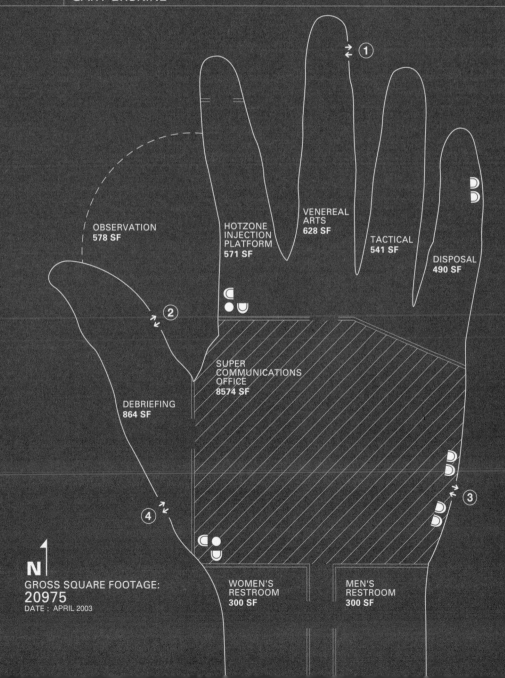

OBSERVATION
578 SF

HOTZONE
INJECTION
PLATFORM
571 SF

VENEREAL
ARTS
628 SF

TACTICAL
541 SF

DISPOSAL
490 SF

SUPER
COMMUNICATIONS
OFFICE
8574 SF

DEBRIEFING
864 SF

N

GROSS SQUARE FOOTAGE:
20975
DATE : APRIL 2003

WOMEN'S
RESTROOM
300 SF

MEN'S
RESTROOM
300 SF

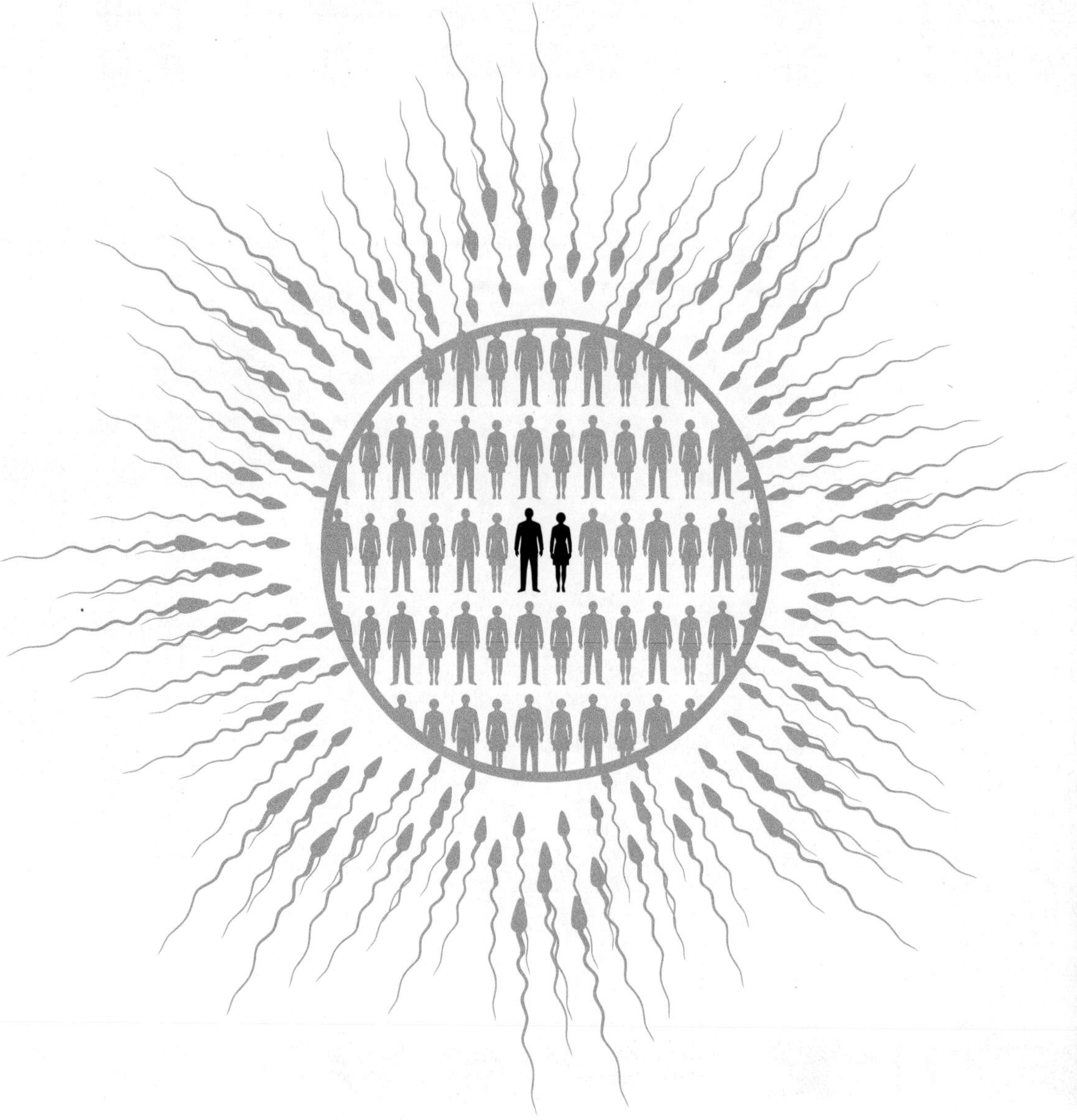

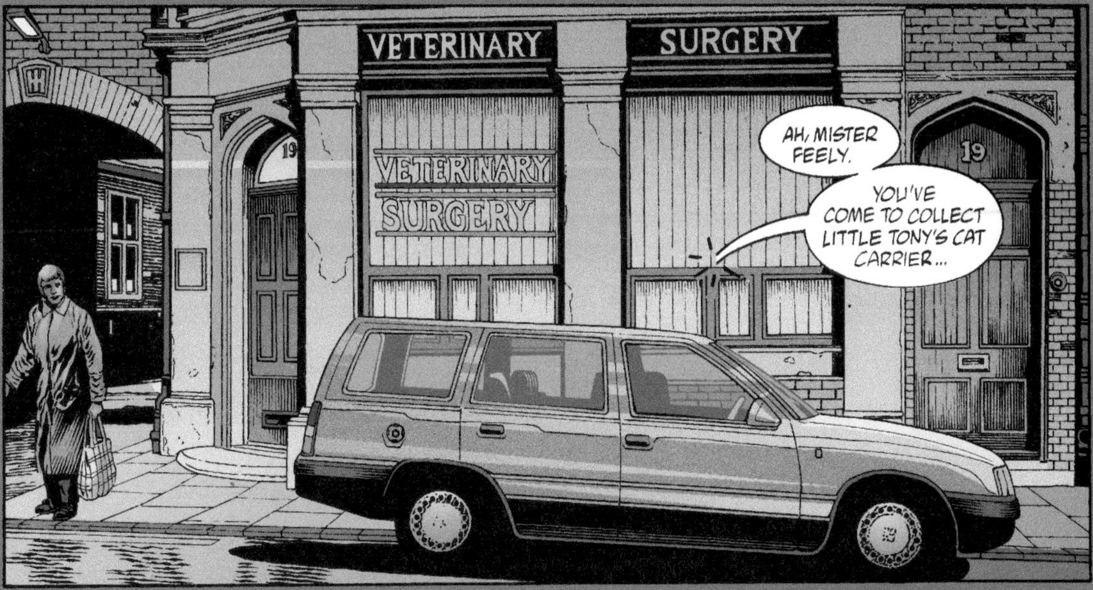
VETERINARY SURGERY
VETERINARY SURGERY
AH, MISTER FEELY.
YOU'VE COME TO COLLECT LITTLE TONY'S CAT CARRIER...

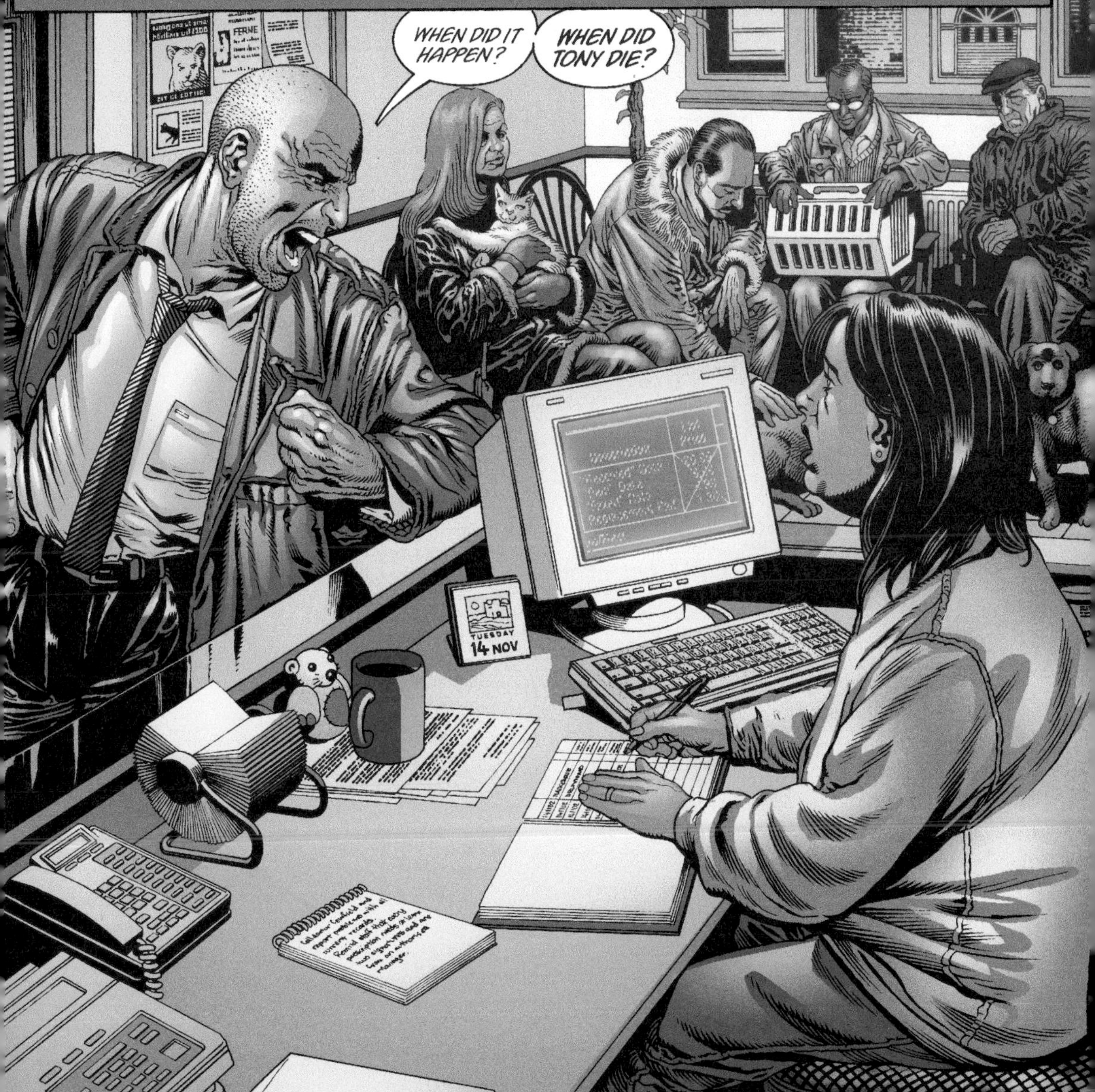
WHEN DID IT HAPPEN?
WHEN DID TONY DIE?
TUESDAY 14 NOV

YOU! WHY DIDN'T I GET TO SEE HIM?

WHERE'S HIS BODY!

I'M SORRY?

WHY DIDN'T I GET TO SAY GOODBYE?

BUT YOU DID...

YOU BROUGHT HIM IN YOURSELF, TWO... TWO DAYS AGO?...

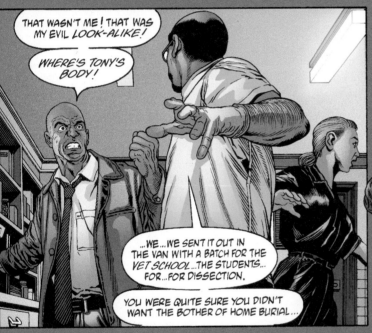

THAT WASN'T ME! THAT WAS MY EVIL LOOK-ALIKE!

WHERE'S TONY'S BODY!

...WE...WE SENT IT OUT IN THE VAN WITH A BATCH FOR THE VET SCHOOL...THE STUDENTS... FOR...FOR DISSECTION.

YOU WERE QUITE SURE YOU DIDN'T WANT THE BOTHER OF HOME BURIAL...

DISSECTION, IS IT!

PUT THAT DOWN, MISTER FEELY. WITHOUT THAT MEDICINE A PAIR OF GOLDEN HAMSTERS MIGHT NOT LAST THE NIGHT...

DON'T BOTHER THE POLICE.

I OUTRANK THEM!

CALL ME A FUCKING TAXI!

PETS ARE FUNNY AREN'T THEY?

MATE OF MINE FROM SCHOOL USED TO HAVE A TARANTULA SPIDER THAT DID AN IMPRESSION OF WINSTON CHURCHILL IF YOU POKED ITS FACE WITH A PENCIL...

CAN YOU WAIT FOR ME, DRIVER? I WON'T BE LONG.

I WANT MY FUCKING CAT BACK!!!

I WANT TONY AND I DON'T WANT HIM IN BITS!!!

IT'S ALL RIGHT, TONY

THEY WON'T GET YOU.

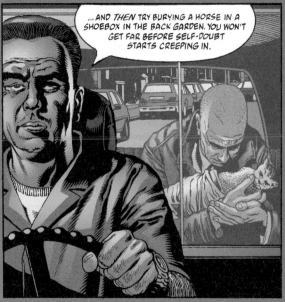

...AND THEN TRY BURYING A HORSE IN A SHOEBOX IN THE BACK GARDEN. YOU WON'T GET FAR BEFORE SELF-DOUBT STARTS CREEPING IN.

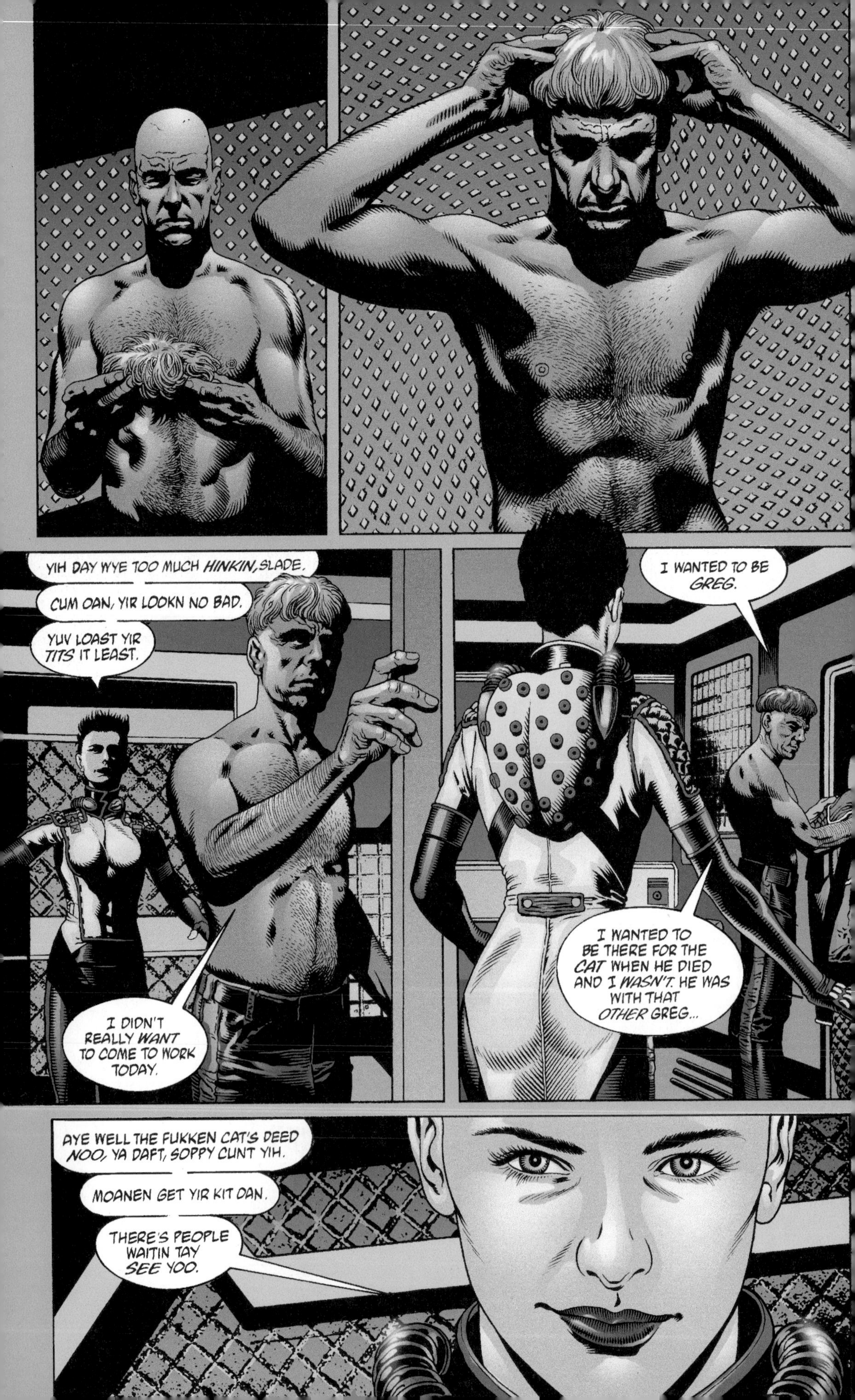
YIH DAY WYE TOO MUCH HINKIN, SLADE.
CUM OAN, YIR LOOKN NO BAD.
YUV LOAST YIR TITS IT LEAST.
I DIDN'T REALLY WANT TO COME TO WORK TODAY.
I WANTED TO BE GREG.
I WANTED TO BE THERE FOR THE CAT WHEN HE DIED AND I WASN'T. HE WAS WITH THAT OTHER GREG...
AYE WELL THE FUKKEN CAT'S DEED NOO, YA DAFT, SOPPY CUNT YIH.
MOANEN GET YIR KIT OAN.
THERE'S PEOPLE WAITIN TAY SEE YOO.

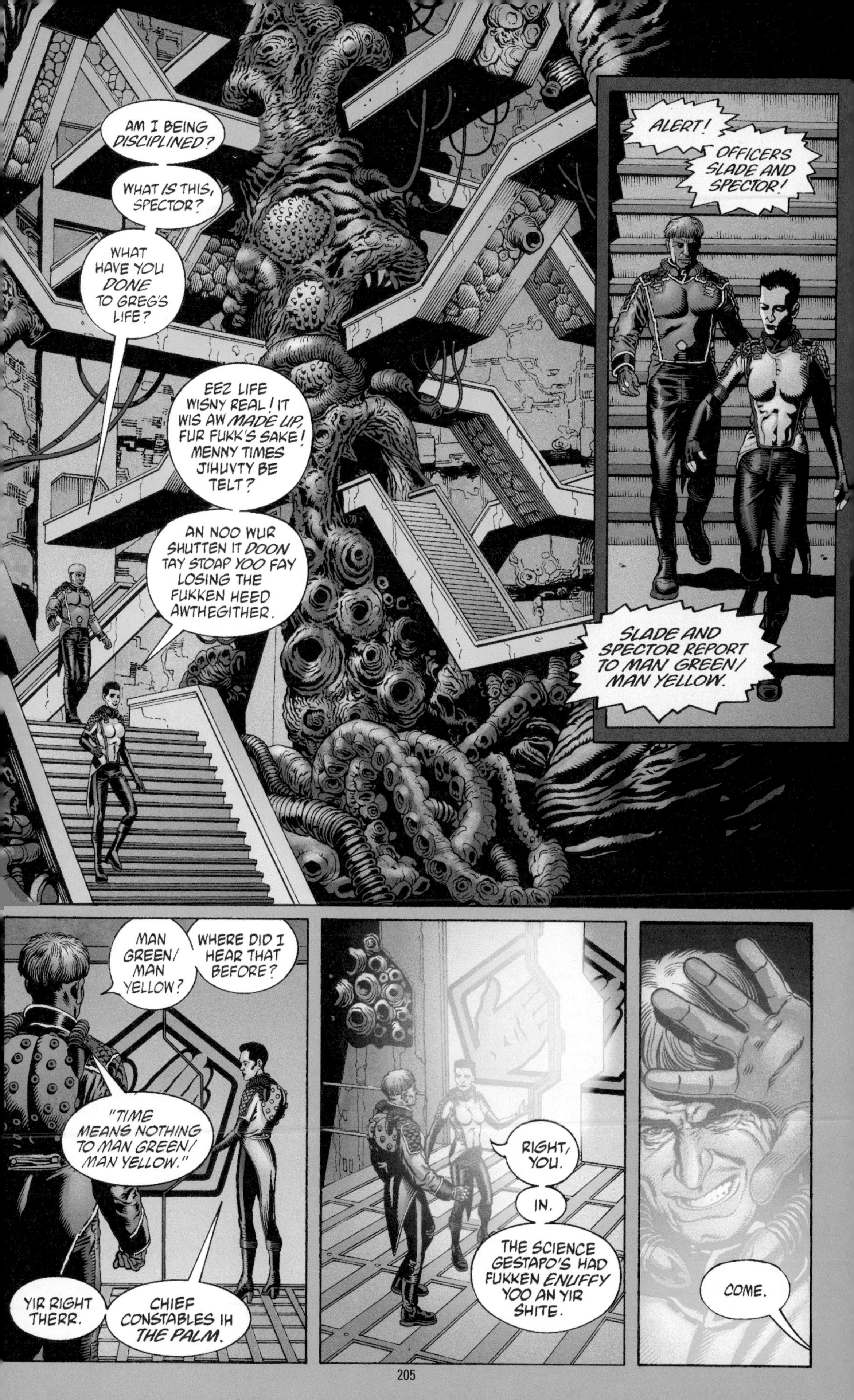
AM I BEING DISCIPLINED?
WHAT IS THIS, SPECTOR?
WHAT HAVE YOU DONE TO GREG'S LIFE?
EEZ LIFE WISNY REAL! IT WIS AW MADE UP, FUR FUKK'S SAKE! MENNY TIMES JIHUVTY BE TELT?
AN NOO WUR SHUTTEN IT DOON TAY STOAP YOO FAY LOSING THE FUKKEN HEED AWTHEGITHER.
ALERT!
OFFICERS SLADE AND SPECTOR!
SLADE AND SPECTOR REPORT TO MAN GREEN/ MAN YELLOW.
MAN GREEN/ MAN YELLOW?
WHERE DID I HEAR THAT BEFORE?
"TIME MEANS NOTHING TO MAN GREEN/ MAN YELLOW."
YIR RIGHT THERR.
CHIEF CONSTABLES IH THE PALM.
RIGHT, YOU.
IN.
THE SCIENCE GESTAPO'S HAD FUKKEN ENUFFY YOO AN YIR SHITE.
COME.

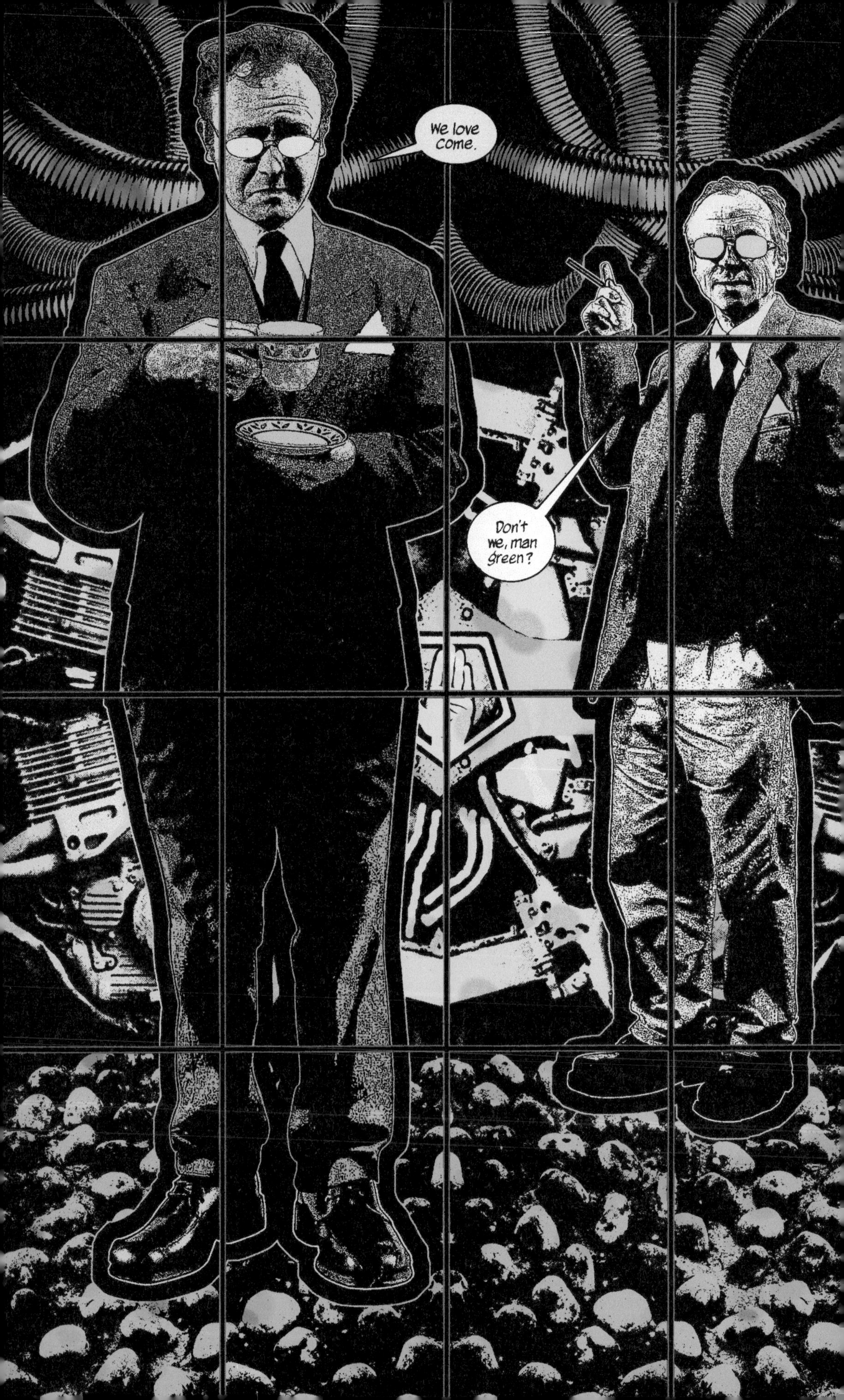
We love come.
Don't we, man green?

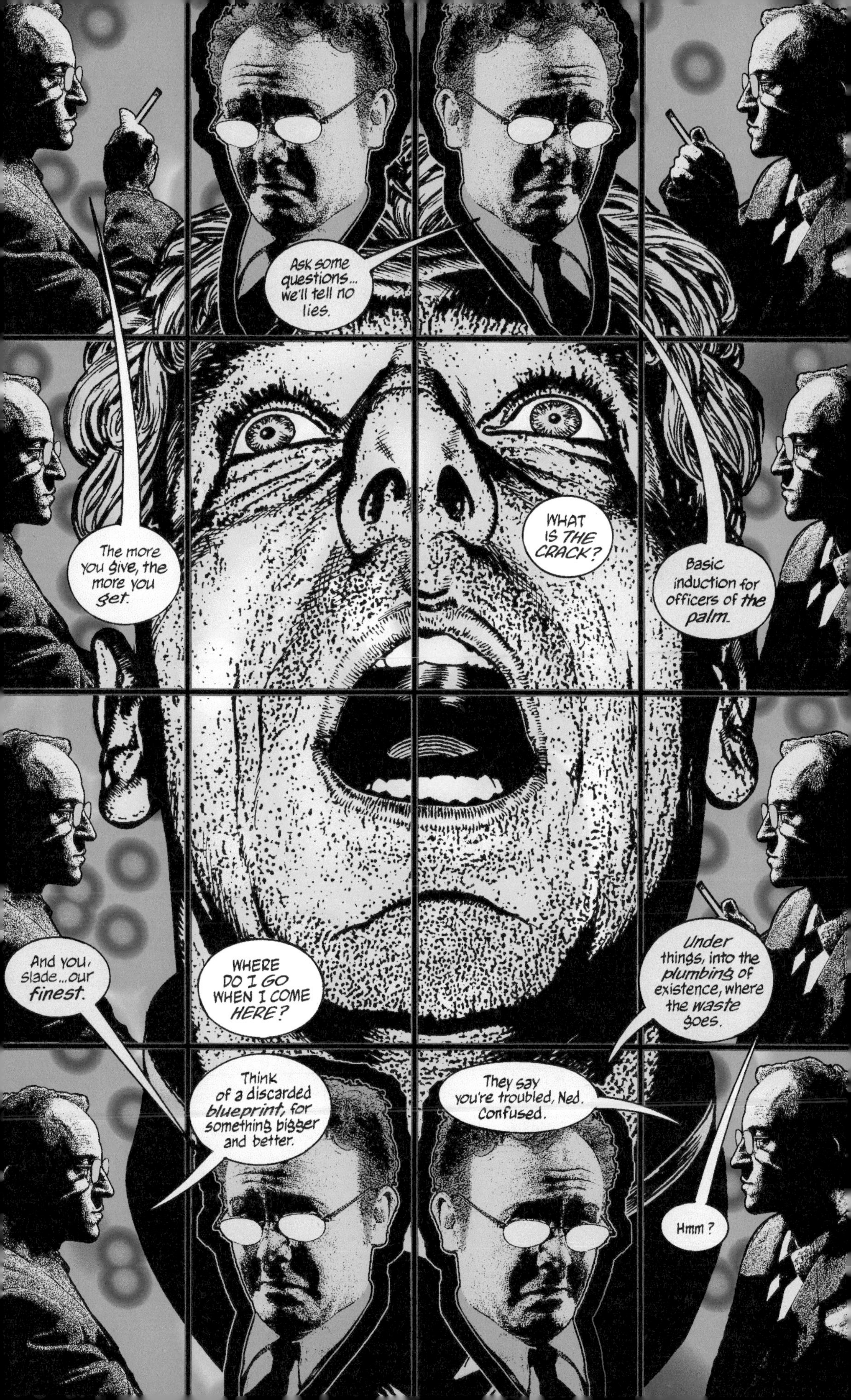
Ask some questions... we'll tell no lies.
The more you give, the more you get.
WHAT IS THE CRACK?
Basic induction for officers of the palm.
And you, slade...our finest.
WHERE DO I GO WHEN I COME HERE?
Under things, into the plumbing of existence, where the waste goes.
Think of a discarded blueprint, for something bigger and better.
They say you're troubled, Ned. Confused.
Hmm?

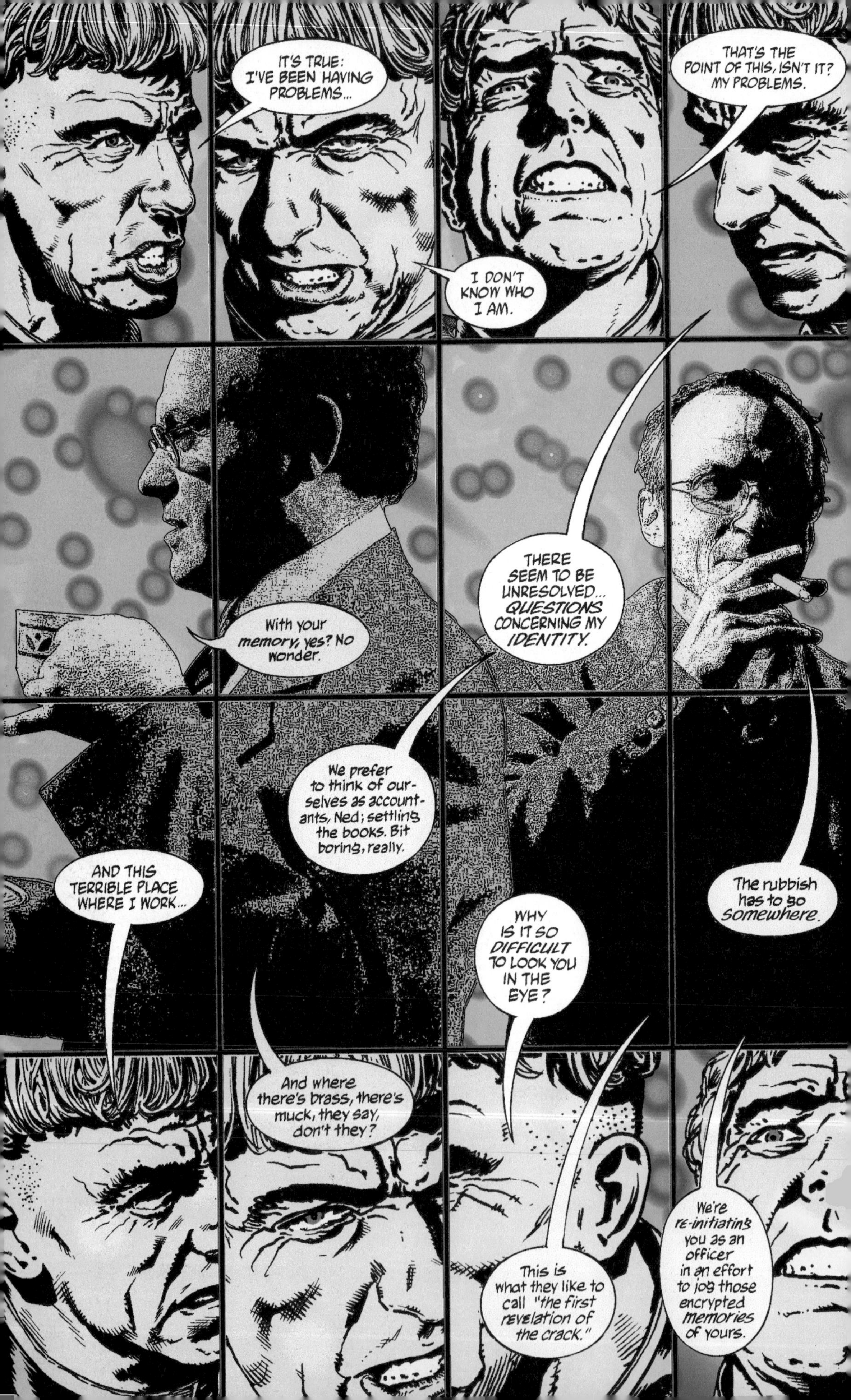
IT'S TRUE: I'VE BEEN HAVING PROBLEMS...
I DON'T KNOW WHO I AM.
THAT'S THE POINT OF THIS, ISN'T IT? MY PROBLEMS.
With your *memory*, yes? No wonder.
THERE SEEM TO BE UNRESOLVED... *QUESTIONS* CONCERNING MY *IDENTITY.*
We prefer to think of our-selves as account-ants, Ned; settling the books. Bit boring, really.
The rubbish has to go *somewhere*.
AND THIS TERRIBLE PLACE WHERE I WORK...
WHY IS IT SO *DIFFICULT* TO LOOK YOU IN THE EYE?
And where there's brass, there's muck, they say, don't they?
This is what they like to call "*the first revelation of the crack.*"
We're *re-initiating* you as an officer in an effort to jog those encrypted *memories* of yours.

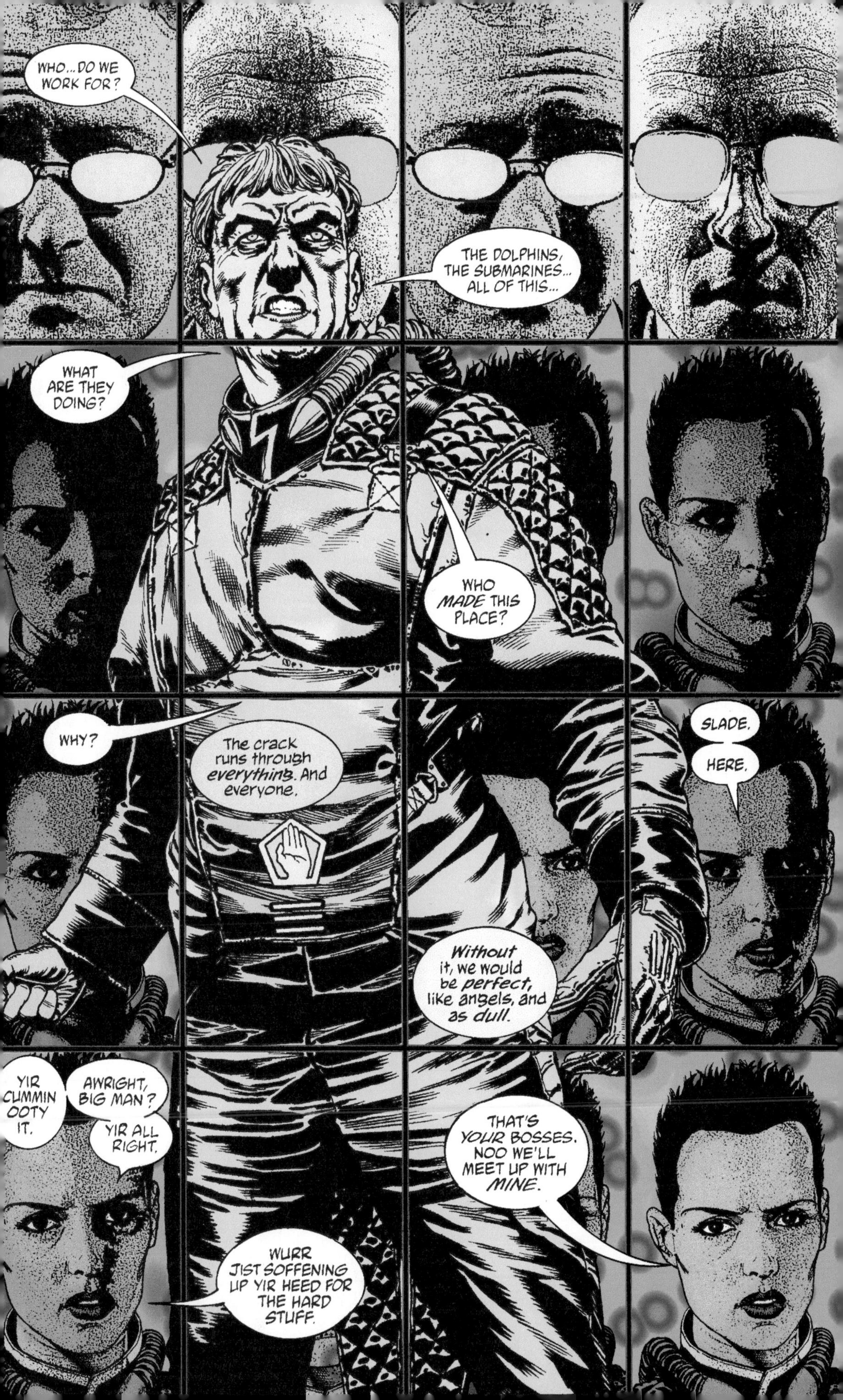
WHO...DO WE WORK FOR?
THE DOLPHINS, THE SUBMARINES... ALL OF THIS...
WHAT ARE THEY DOING?
WHO MADE THIS PLACE?
WHY?
The crack runs through everything. And everyone.
SLADE.
HERE.
Without it, we would be perfect, like angels, and as dull.
YIR CUMMIN OOTY IT.
AWRIGHT, BIG MAN?
YIR ALL RIGHT.
WURR JIST SOFFENING UP YIR HEED FOR THE HARD STUFF.
THAT'S YOUR BOSSES. NOO WE'LL MEET UP WITH MINE.

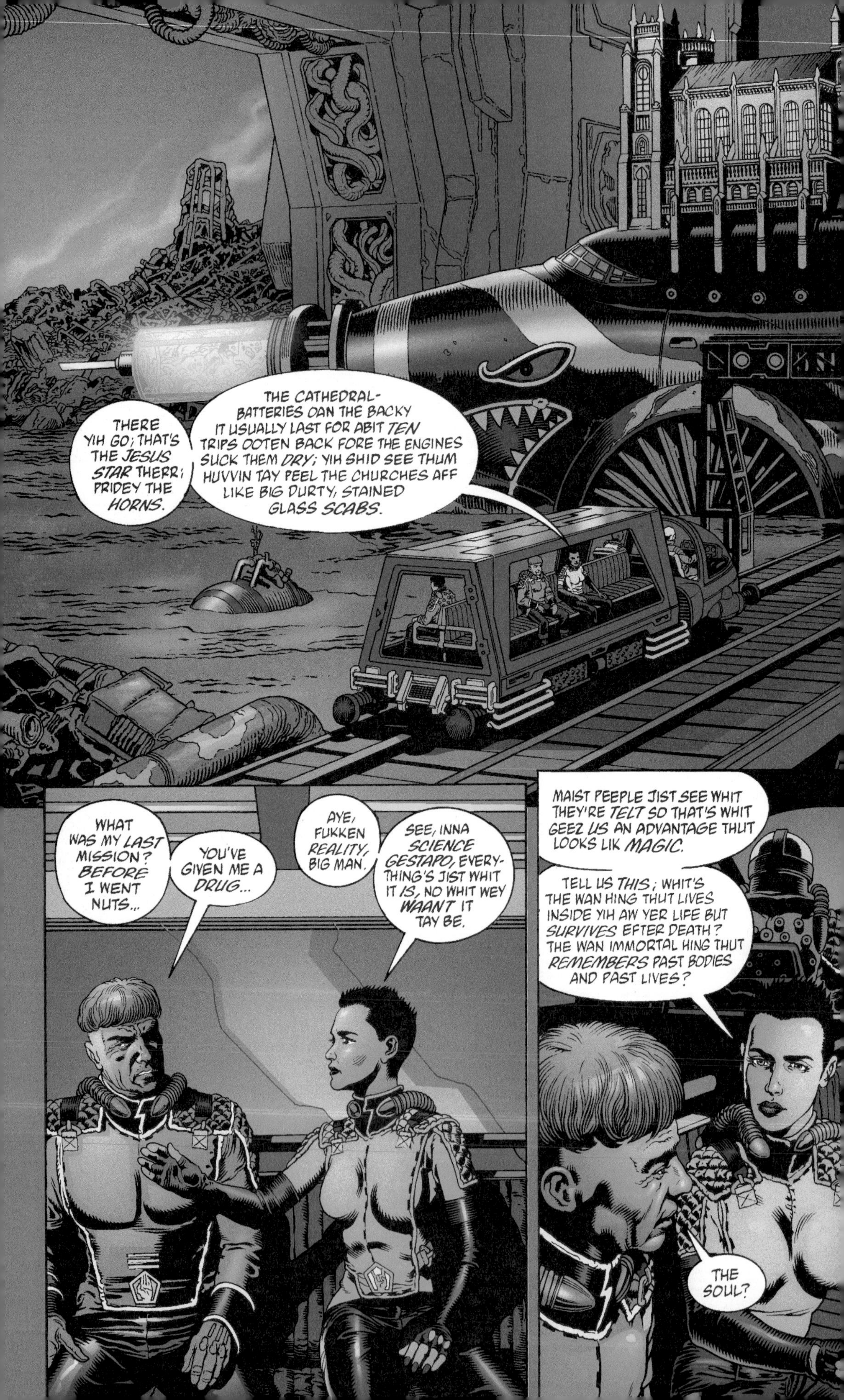
THERE YIH GO; THAT'S THE JESUS STAR THERR; PRIDEY THE HORNS.
THE CATHEDRAL-BATTERIES OAN THE BACKY IT USUALLY LAST FOR ABIT TEN TRIPS OOTEN BACK FORE THE ENGINES SUCK THEM DRY; YIH SHID SEE THUM HUVVIN TAY PEEL THE CHURCHES AFF LIKE BIG DURTY, STAINED GLASS SCABS.
WHAT WAS MY LAST MISSION? BEFORE I WENT NUTS...
YOU'VE GIVEN ME A DRUG...
AYE, FUKKEN REALITY, BIG MAN.
SEE, INNA SCIENCE GESTAPO, EVERY-THING'S JIST WHIT IT IS, NO WHIT WEY WAANT IT TAY BE.
MAIST PEEPLE JIST SEE WHIT THEY'RE TELT SO THAT'S WHIT GEEZ US AN ADVANTAGE THUT LOOKS LIK MAGIC.
TELL US THIS; WHIT'S THE WAN HING THUT LIVES INSIDE YIH AW YER LIFE BUT SURVIVES EFTER DEATH? THE WAN IMMORTAL HING THUT REMEMBERS PAST BODIES AND PAST LIVES?
THE SOUL?

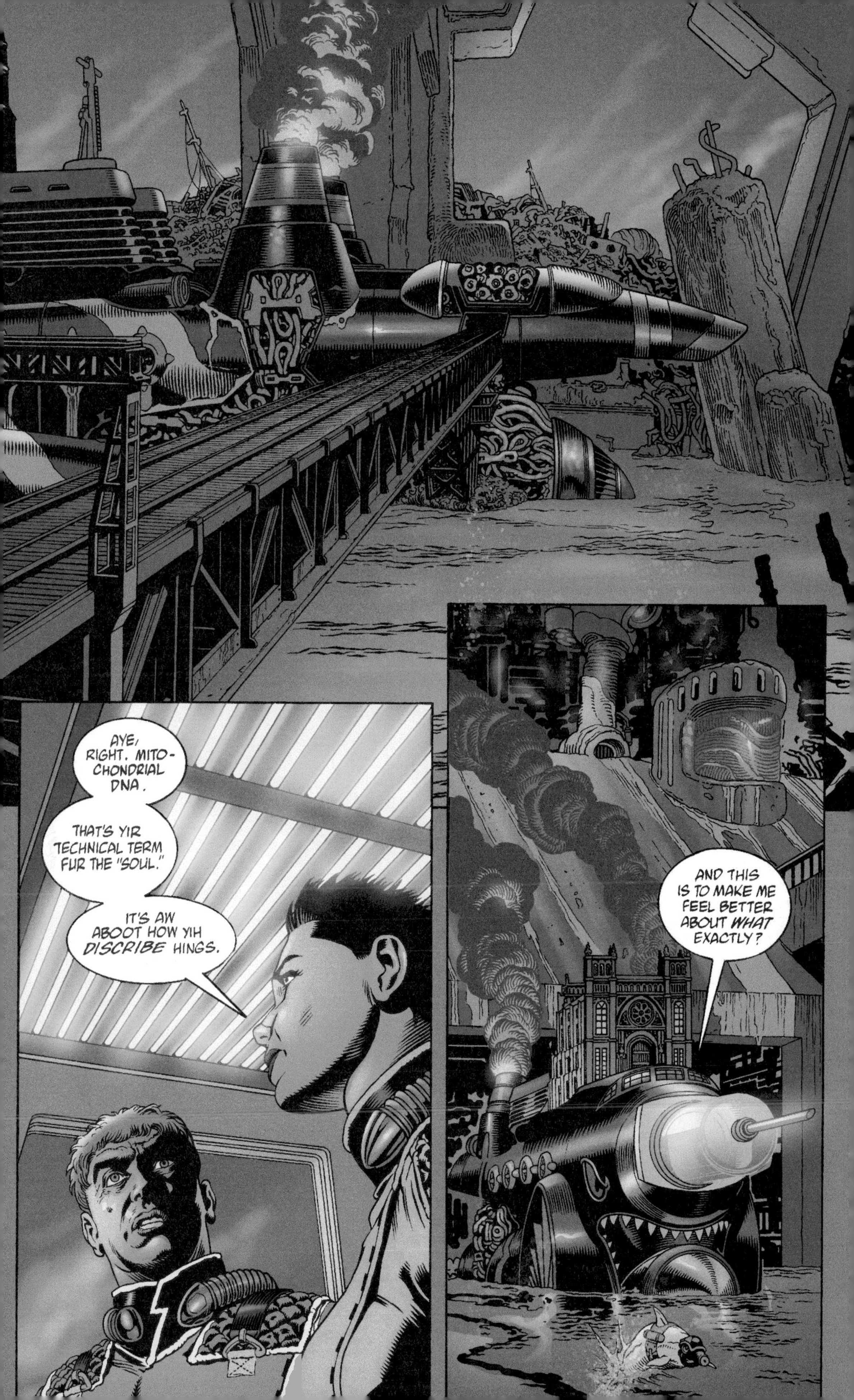
AYE, RIGHT. MITO-CHONDRIAL DNA.
THAT'S YIR TECHNICAL TERM FUR THE "SOUL."
IT'S AW ABOOT HOW YIH *DISCRIBE* HINGS.
AND THIS IS TO MAKE ME FEEL BETTER ABOUT *WHAT* EXACTLY?

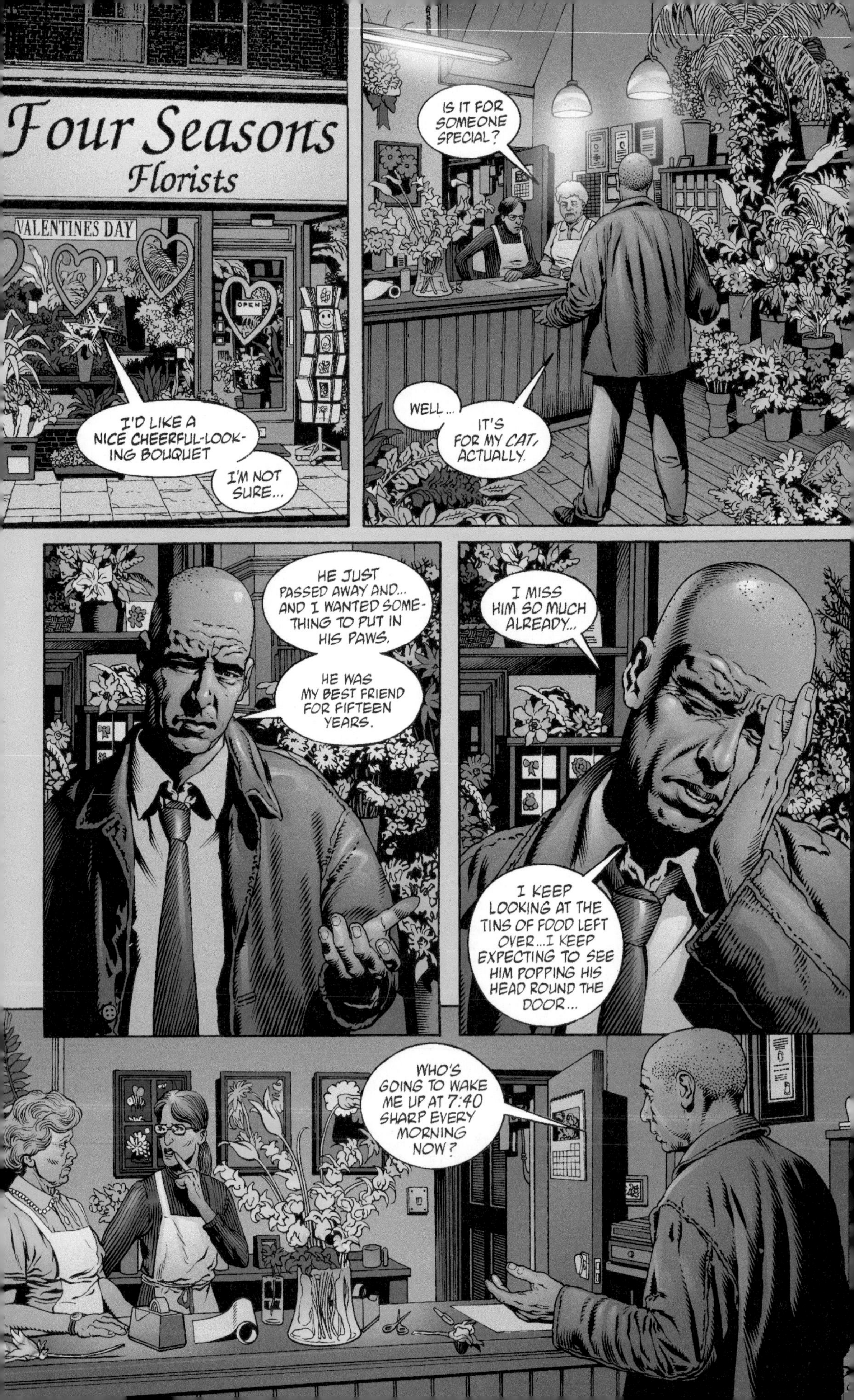
Four Seasons
Florists
VALENTINES DAY
OPEN
I'D LIKE A NICE CHEERFUL-LOOKING BOUQUET
I'M NOT SURE...
IS IT FOR SOMEONE SPECIAL?
WELL...
IT'S FOR MY CAT, ACTUALLY.
HE JUST PASSED AWAY AND... AND I WANTED SOMETHING TO PUT IN HIS PAWS.
HE WAS MY BEST FRIEND FOR FIFTEEN YEARS.
I MISS HIM SO MUCH ALREADY...
I KEEP LOOKING AT THE TINS OF FOOD LEFT OVER...I KEEP EXPECTING TO SEE HIM POPPING HIS HEAD ROUND THE DOOR...
WHO'S GOING TO WAKE ME UP AT 7:40 SHARP EVERY MORNING NOW?

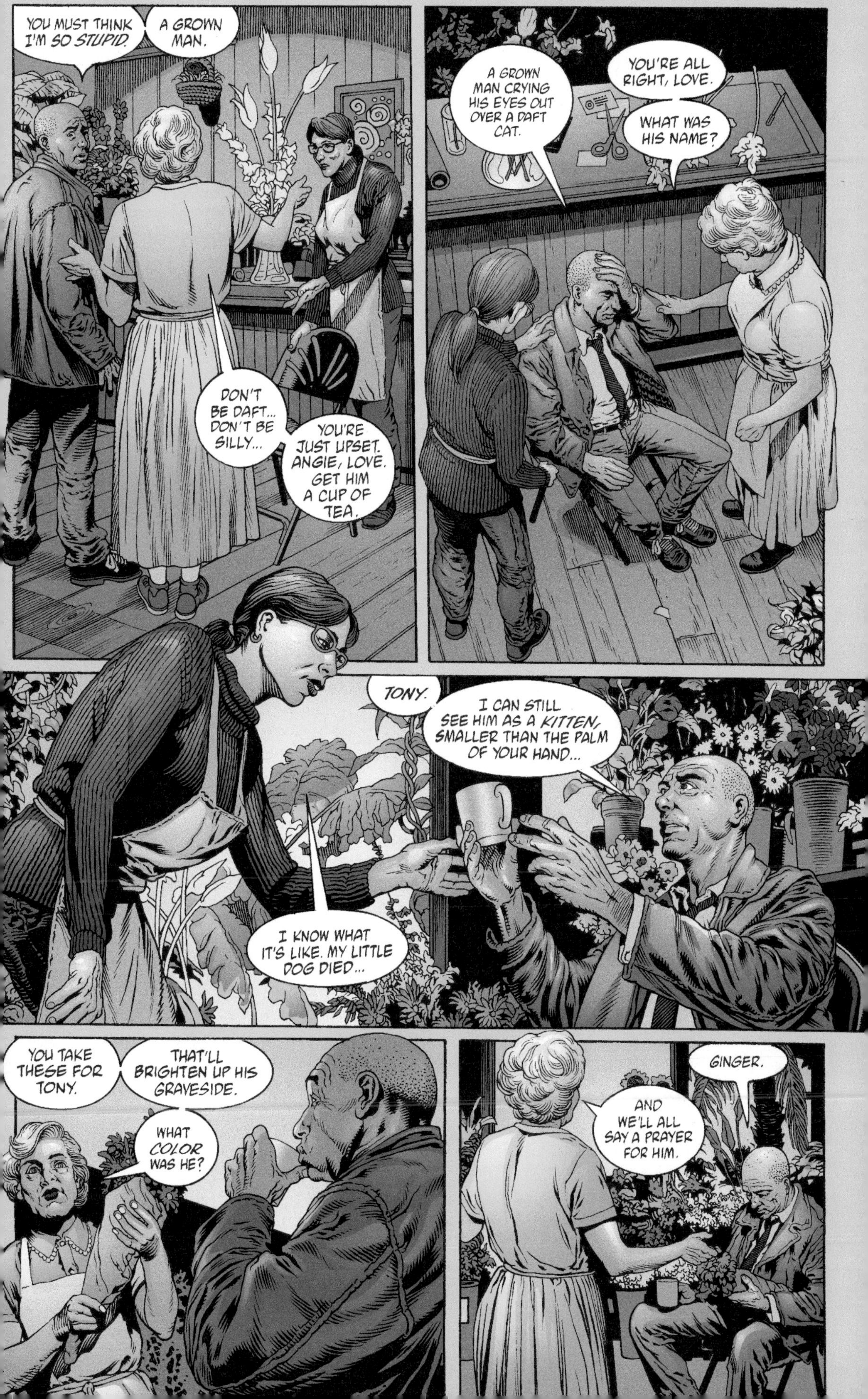
YOU MUST THINK I'M SO *STUPID.*
A GROWN MAN.
DON'T BE DAFT... DON'T BE SILLY...
YOU'RE JUST UPSET. ANGIE, LOVE. GET HIM A CUP OF TEA.
A GROWN MAN CRYING HIS EYES OUT OVER A DAFT CAT.
YOU'RE ALL RIGHT, LOVE.
WHAT WAS HIS NAME?
TONY.
I CAN STILL SEE HIM AS A *KITTEN,* SMALLER THAN THE PALM OF YOUR HAND...
I KNOW WHAT IT'S LIKE. MY LITTLE DOG DIED...
YOU TAKE THESE FOR TONY.
THAT'LL BRIGHTEN UP HIS GRAVESIDE.
WHAT *COLOR* WAS HE?
GINGER.
AND WE'LL ALL SAY A PRAYER FOR HIM.

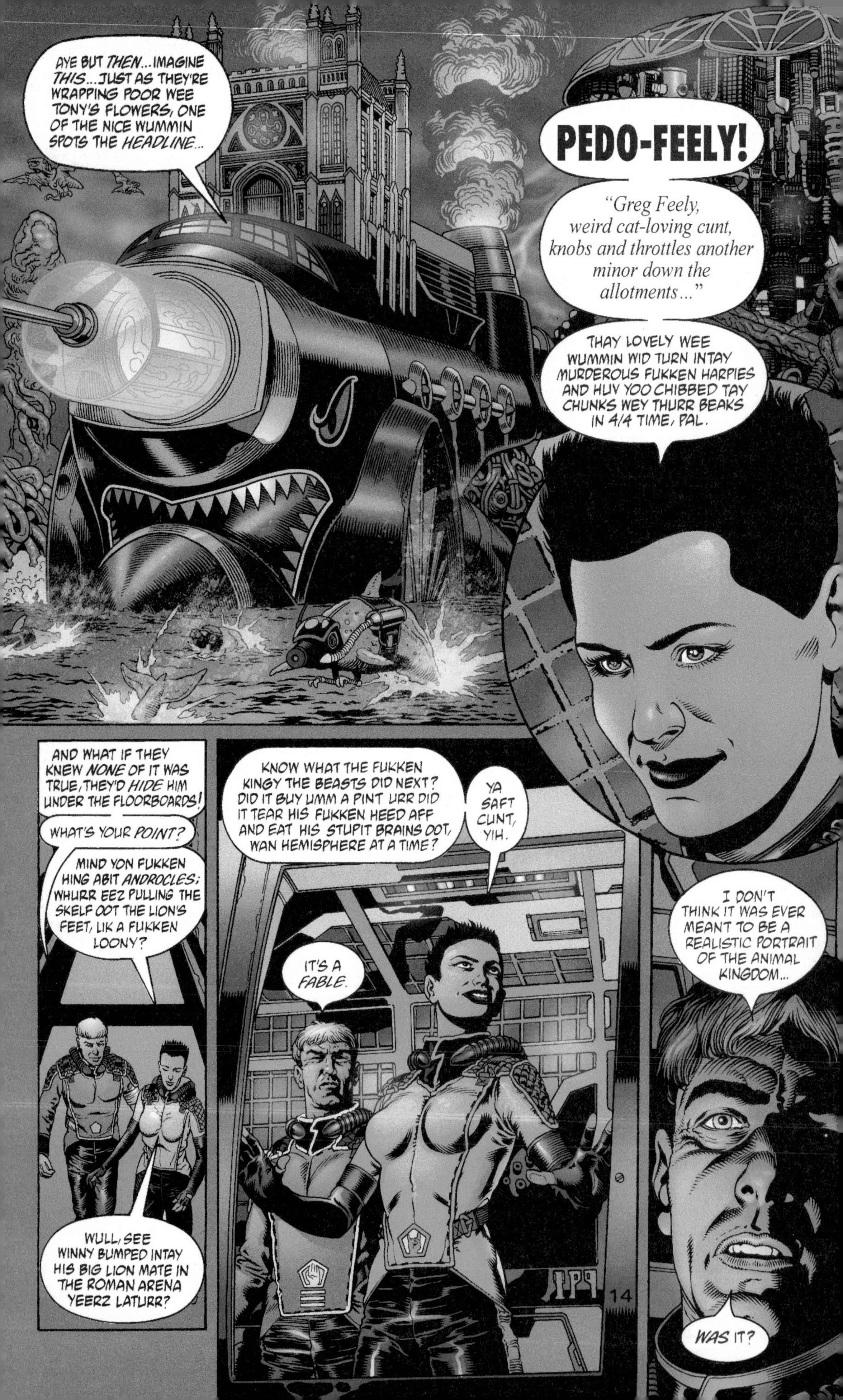
AYE BUT THEN...IMAGINE THIS...JUST AS THEY'RE WRAPPING POOR WEE TONY'S FLOWERS, ONE OF THE NICE WUMMIN SPOTS THE HEADLINE...
PEDO-FEELY!
"Greg Feely, weird cat-loving cunt, knobs and throttles another minor down the allotments..."
THAY LOVELY WEE WUMMIN WID TURN INTAY MURDEROUS FUKKEN HARPIES AND HUV YOO CHIBBED TAY CHUNKS WEY THURR BEAKS IN 4/4 TIME, PAL.
AND WHAT IF THEY KNEW NONE OF IT WAS TRUE, THEY'D HIDE HIM UNDER THE FLOORBOARDS!
WHAT'S YOUR POINT?
MIND YON FUKKEN HING ABIT ANDROCLES; WHURR EEZ PULLING THE SKELF OOT THE LION'S FEET, LIK A FUKKEN LOONY?
WULL, SEE WINNY BUMPED INTAY HIS BIG LION MATE IN THE ROMAN ARENA YEERZ LATURR?
KNOW WHAT THE FUKKEN KINGY THE BEASTS DID NEXT? DID IT BUY UMM A PINT URR DID IT TEAR HIS FUKKEN HEED AFF AND EAT HIS STUPIT BRAINS OOT, WAN HEMISPHERE AT A TIME?
YA SAFT CUNT, YIH.
IT'S A FABLE.
I DON'T THINK IT WAS EVER MEANT TO BE A REALISTIC PORTRAIT OF THE ANIMAL KINGDOM...
WAS IT?
14

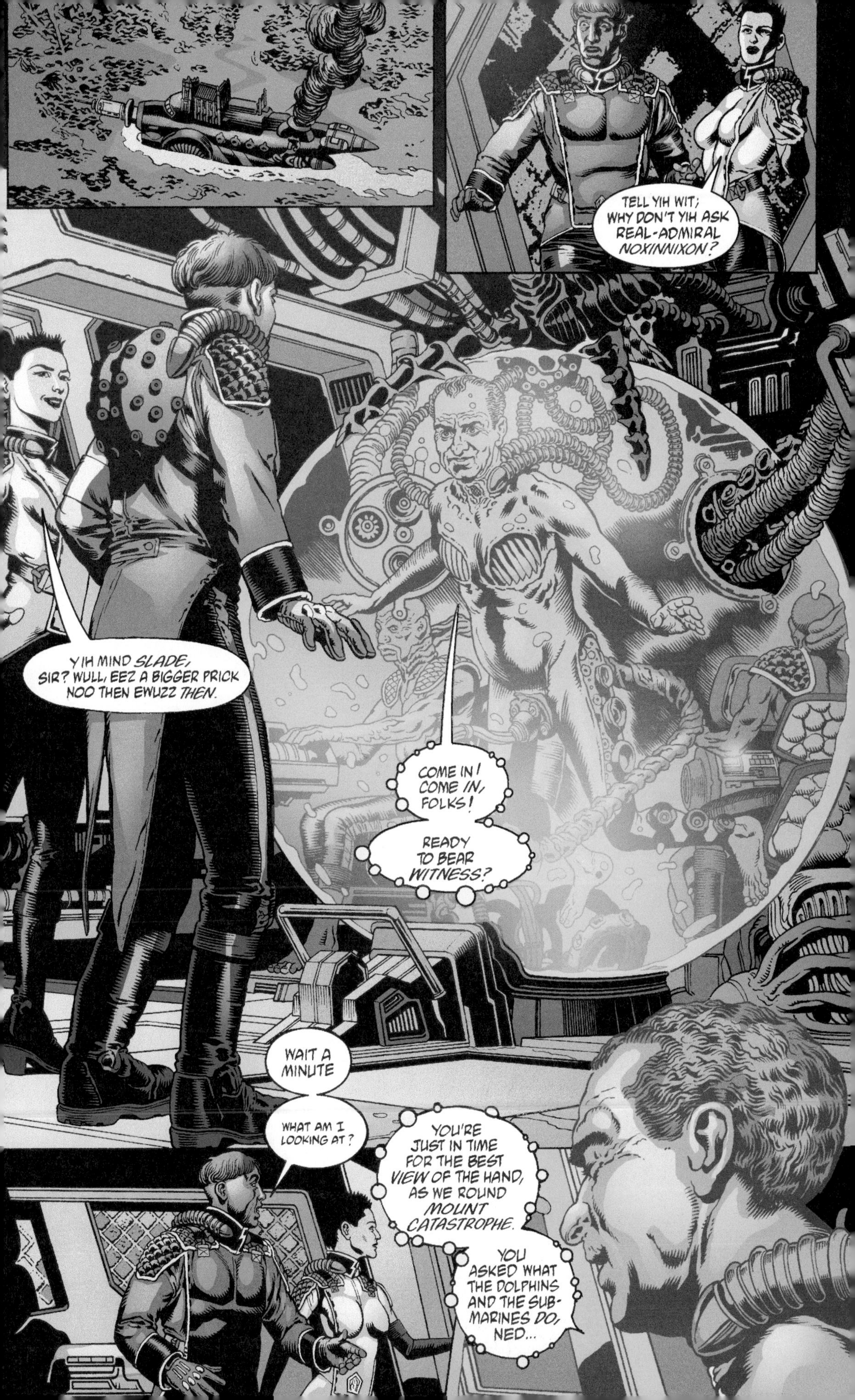
TELL YIH WIT; WHY DON'T YIH ASK REAL-ADMIRAL NOXINNIXON?
YIH MIND SLADE, SIR? WULL, EEZ A BIGGER PRICK NOO THEN EWUZZ THEN.
COME IN! COME IN, FOLKS!
READY TO BEAR WITNESS?
WAIT A MINUTE
WHAT AM I LOOKING AT?
YOU'RE JUST IN TIME FOR THE BEST VIEW OF THE HAND, AS WE ROUND MOUNT CATASTROPHE.
YOU ASKED WHAT THE DOLPHINS AND THE SUB-MARINES DO, NED...

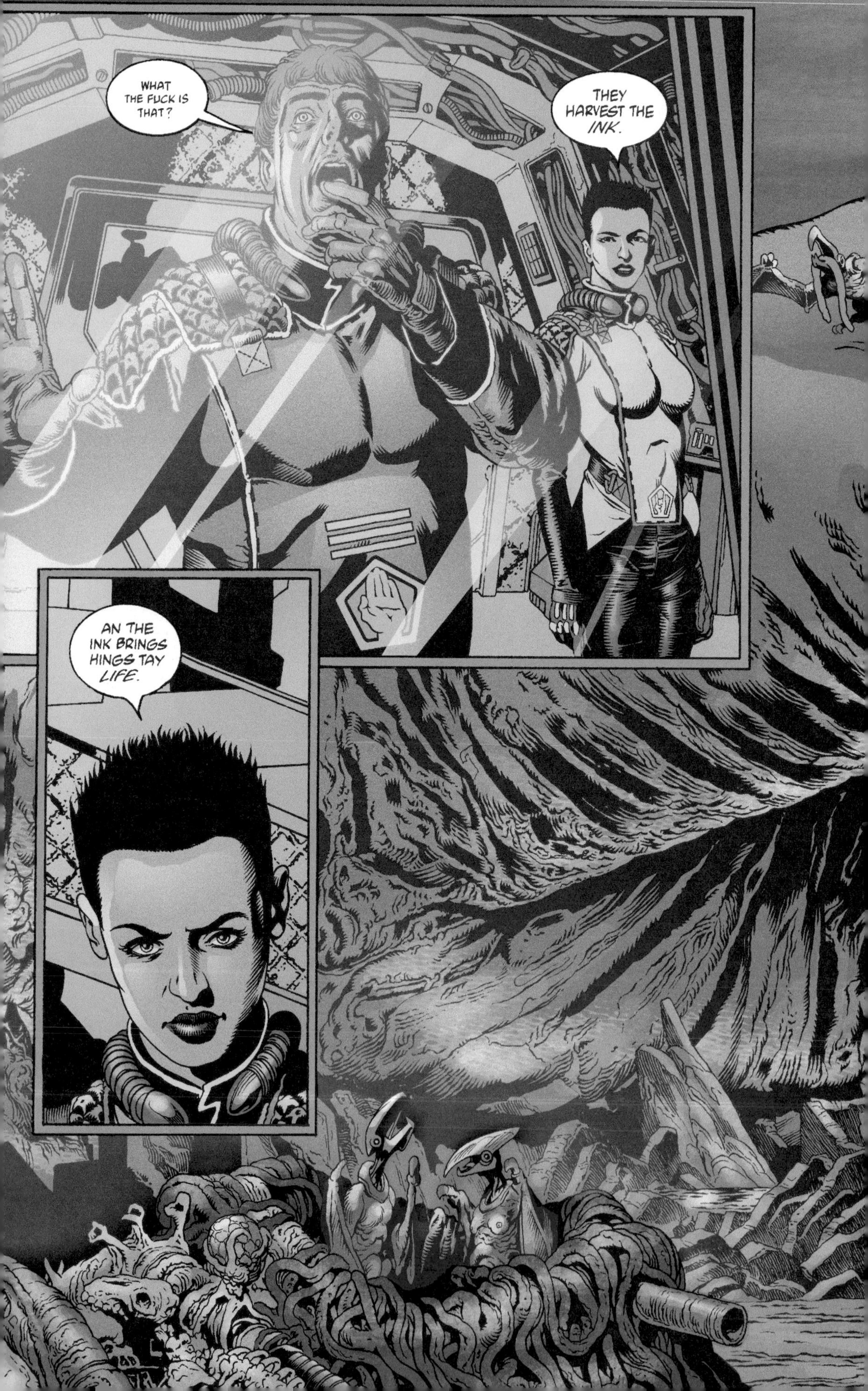
WHAT THE FUCK IS THAT?
THEY HARVEST THE INK.
AN THE INK BRINGS HINGS TAY LIFE.

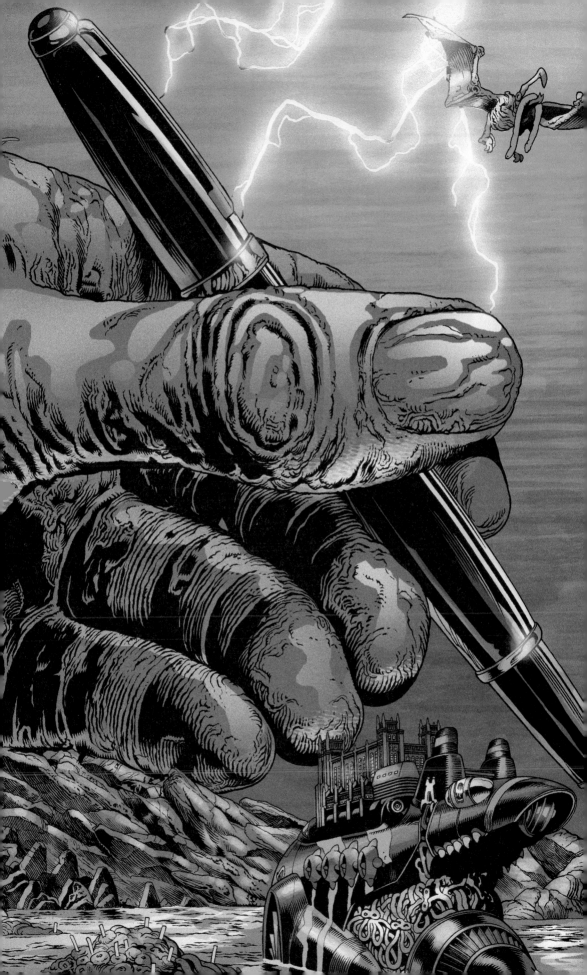

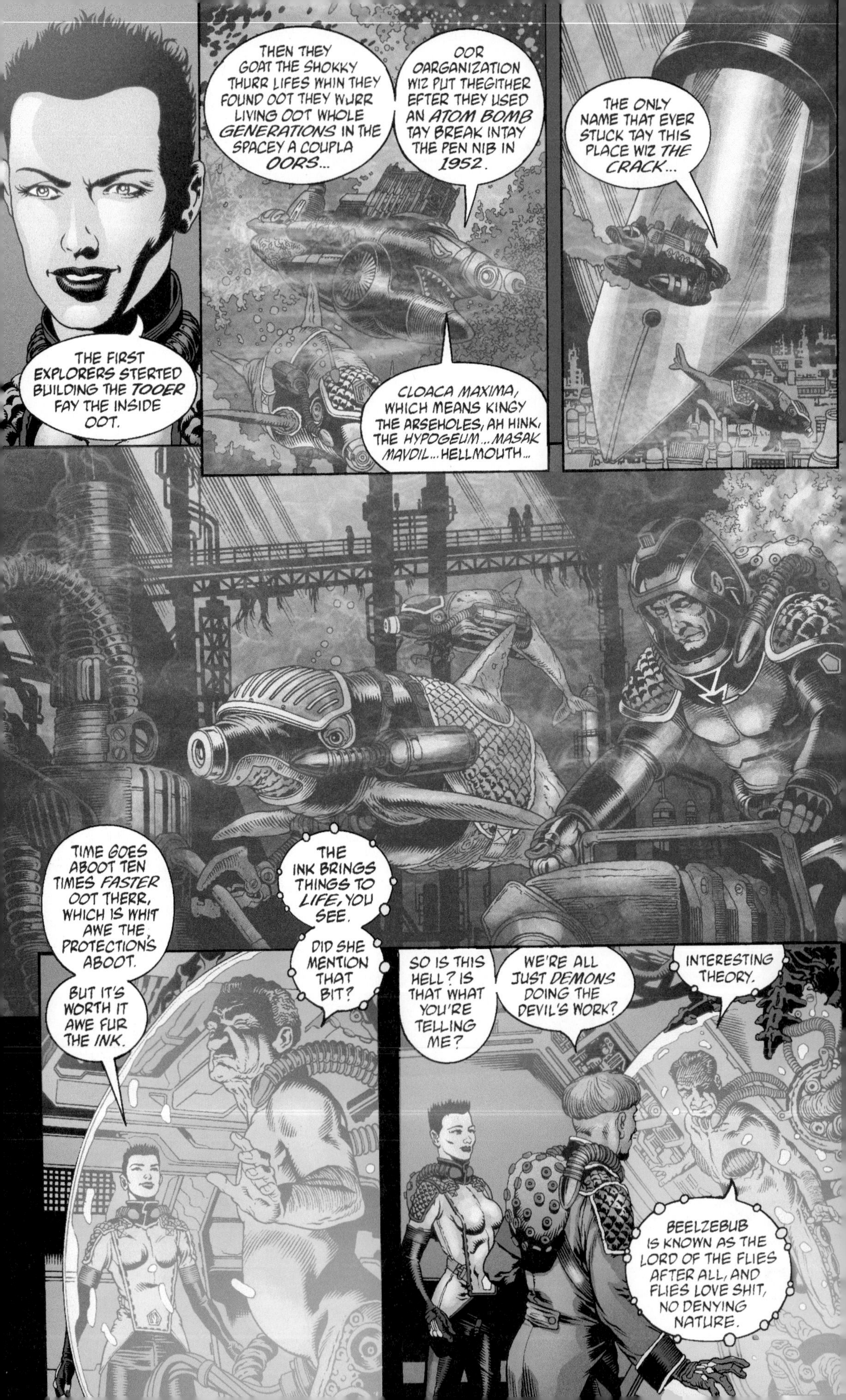
THE FIRST EXPLORERS STERTED BUILDING THE *TOOER* FAY THE INSIDE OOT.
THEN THEY GOAT THE SHOKKY THURR LIFES WHIN THEY FOUND OOT THEY WURR LIVING OOT WHOLE *GENERATIONS* IN THE SPACEY A COUPLA *OORS*...
OOR OARGANIZATION WIZ PUT THEGITHER EFTER THEY USED AN *ATOM BOMB* TAY BREAK INTAY THE PEN NIB IN *1952*.
CLOACA MAXIMA, WHICH MEANS KINGY THE ARSEHOLES, AH HINK, THE *HYPOGEUM*... *MASAK MAVDIL*... HELLMOUTH...
THE ONLY NAME THAT EVER STUCK TAY THIS PLACE WIZ *THE CRACK*...
TIME GOES ABOOT TEN TIMES *FASTER* OOT THERR, WHICH IS WHIT AWE THE PROTECTION'S ABOOT.
THE INK BRINGS THINGS TO *LIFE*, YOU SEE.
DID SHE MENTION THAT BIT?
BUT IT'S WORTH IT AWE FUR THE *INK*.
SO IS THIS HELL? IS THAT WHAT YOU'RE TELLING ME?
WE'RE ALL JUST *DEMONS* DOING THE DEVIL'S WORK?
INTERESTING THEORY.
BEELZEBUB IS KNOWN AS THE LORD OF THE FLIES AFTER ALL, AND FLIES LOVE SHIT, NO DENYING NATURE.

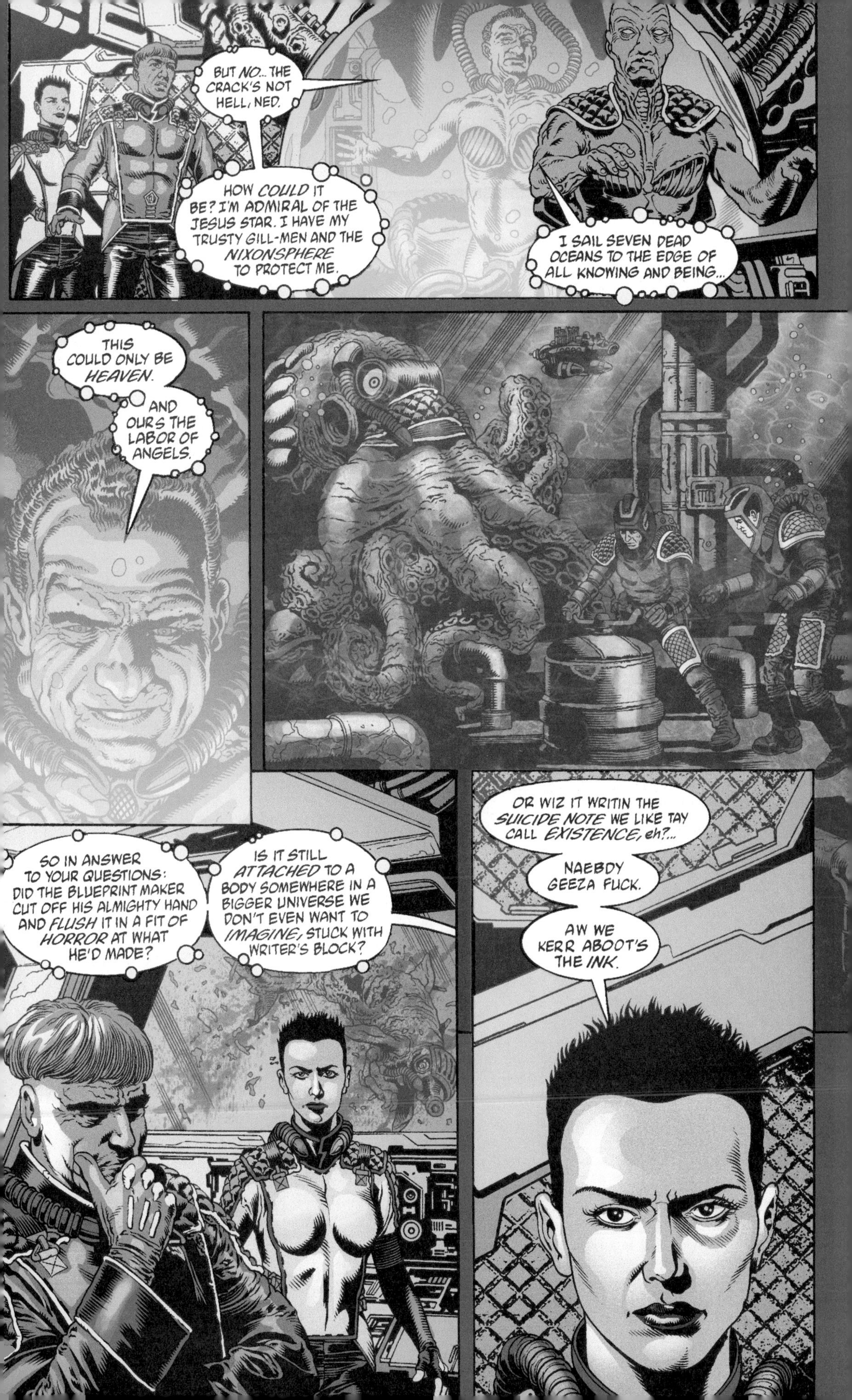
BUT NO... THE CRACK'S NOT HELL, NED.
HOW COULD IT BE? I'M ADMIRAL OF THE JESUS STAR. I HAVE MY TRUSTY GILL-MEN AND THE NIXONSPHERE TO PROTECT ME.
I SAIL SEVEN DEAD OCEANS TO THE EDGE OF ALL KNOWING AND BEING...
THIS COULD ONLY BE HEAVEN.
AND OURS THE LABOR OF ANGELS.
SO IN ANSWER TO YOUR QUESTIONS: DID THE BLUEPRINT MAKER CUT OFF HIS ALMIGHTY HAND AND FLUSH IT IN A FIT OF HORROR AT WHAT HE'D MADE?
IS IT STILL ATTACHED TO A BODY SOMEWHERE IN A BIGGER UNIVERSE WE DON'T EVEN WANT TO IMAGINE, STUCK WITH WRITER'S BLOCK?
OR WIZ IT WRITIN THE SUICIDE NOTE WE LIKE TAY CALL EXISTENCE, eh?...
NAEBDY GEEZA FUCK.
AW WE KERR ABOOT'S THE INK.

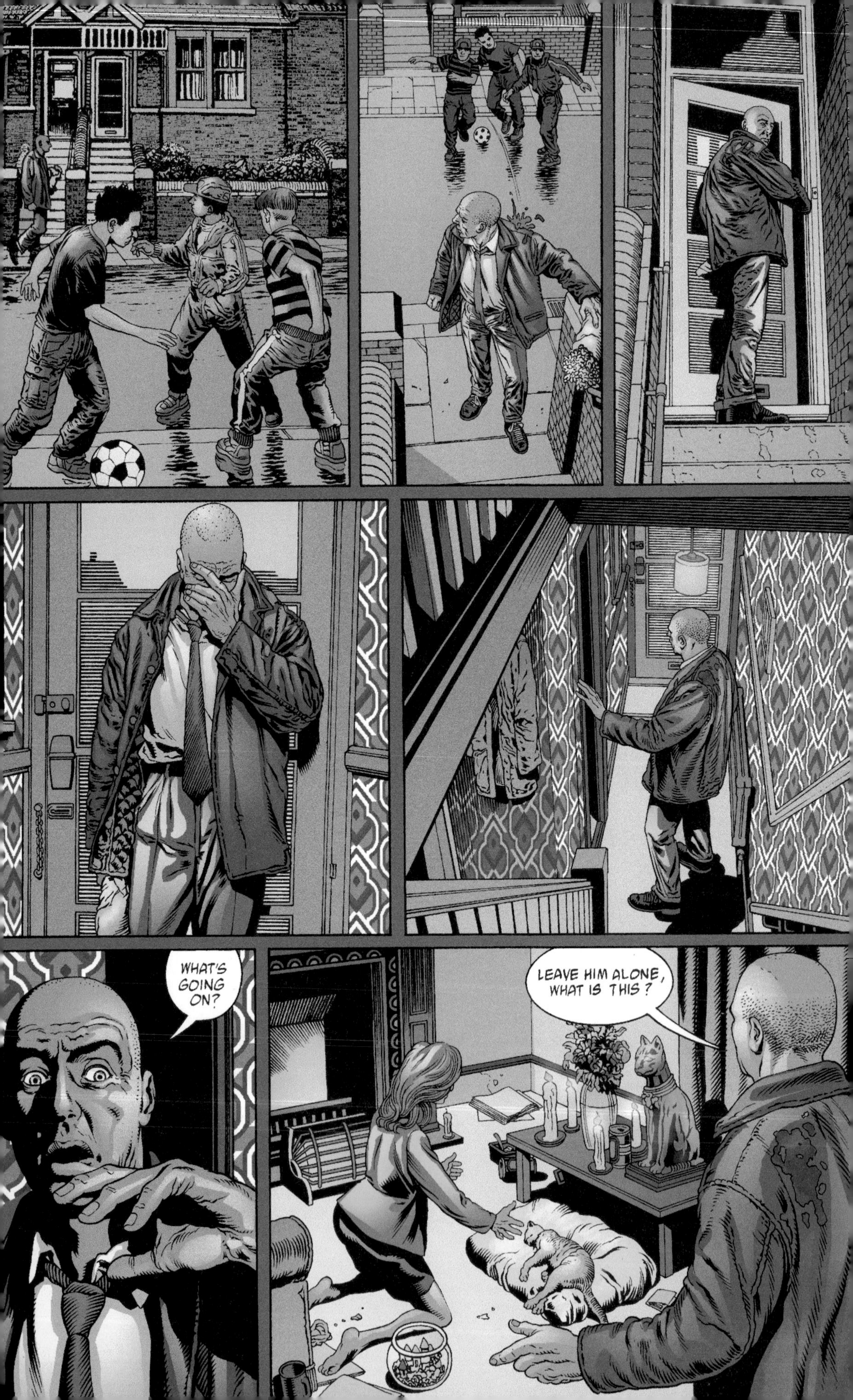
WHAT'S GOING ON?
LEAVE HIM ALONE, WHAT IS THIS?

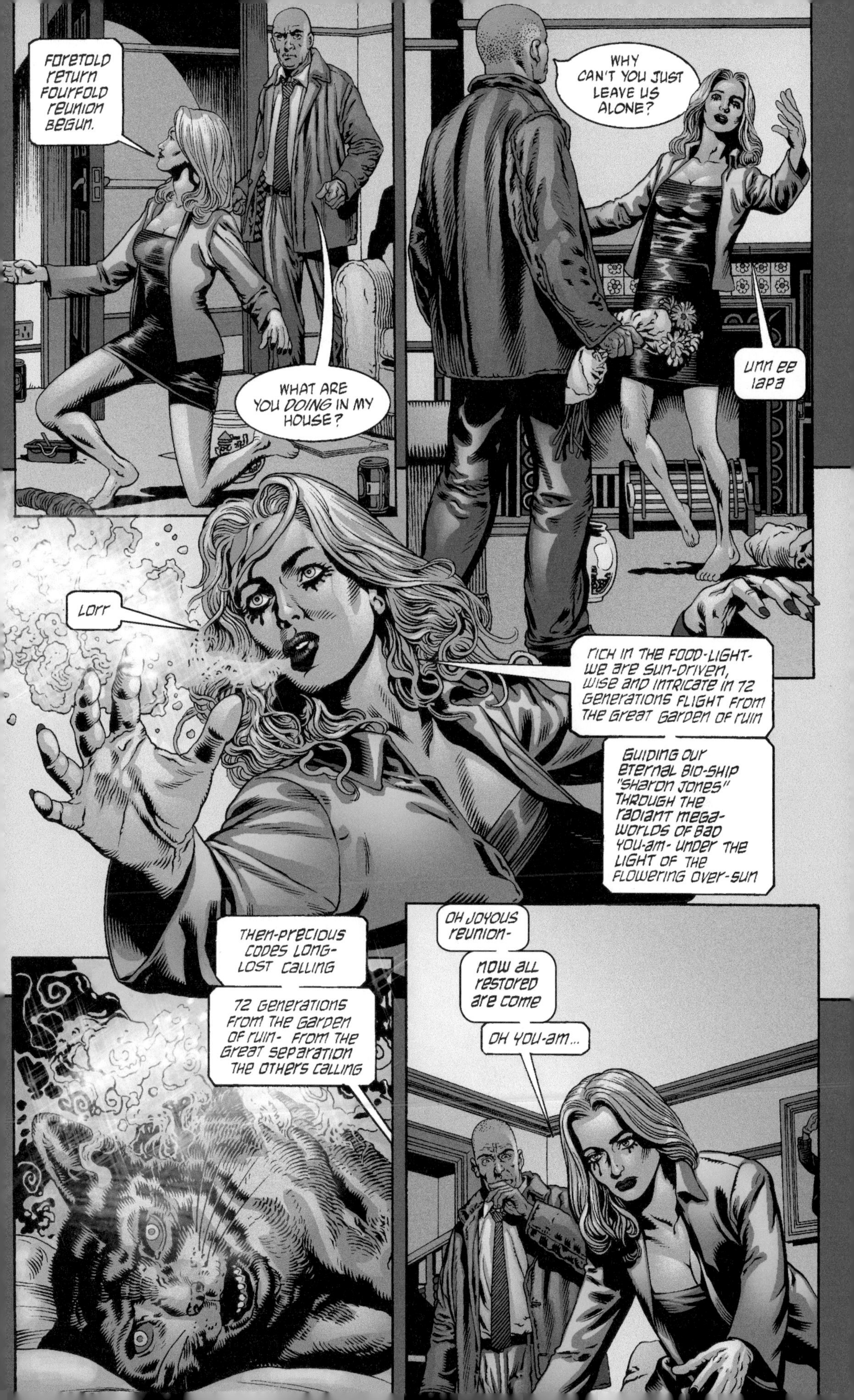

Foretold return Fourfold reunion begun.
WHAT ARE YOU DOING IN MY HOUSE?
WHY CAN'T YOU JUST LEAVE US ALONE?
unn ee lapa
Lorr
rich in the food-light- we are sun-driven, wise and intricate in 72 generations flight from the great garden of ruin
Guiding our eternal bio-ship "sharon jones" through the radiant mega-worlds of bad you-am- under the light of the flowering over-sun
Then-precious codes long-lost calling
72 generations from the garden of ruin- from the great separation the others calling
Oh joyous reunion-
now all restored are come
Oh you-am...

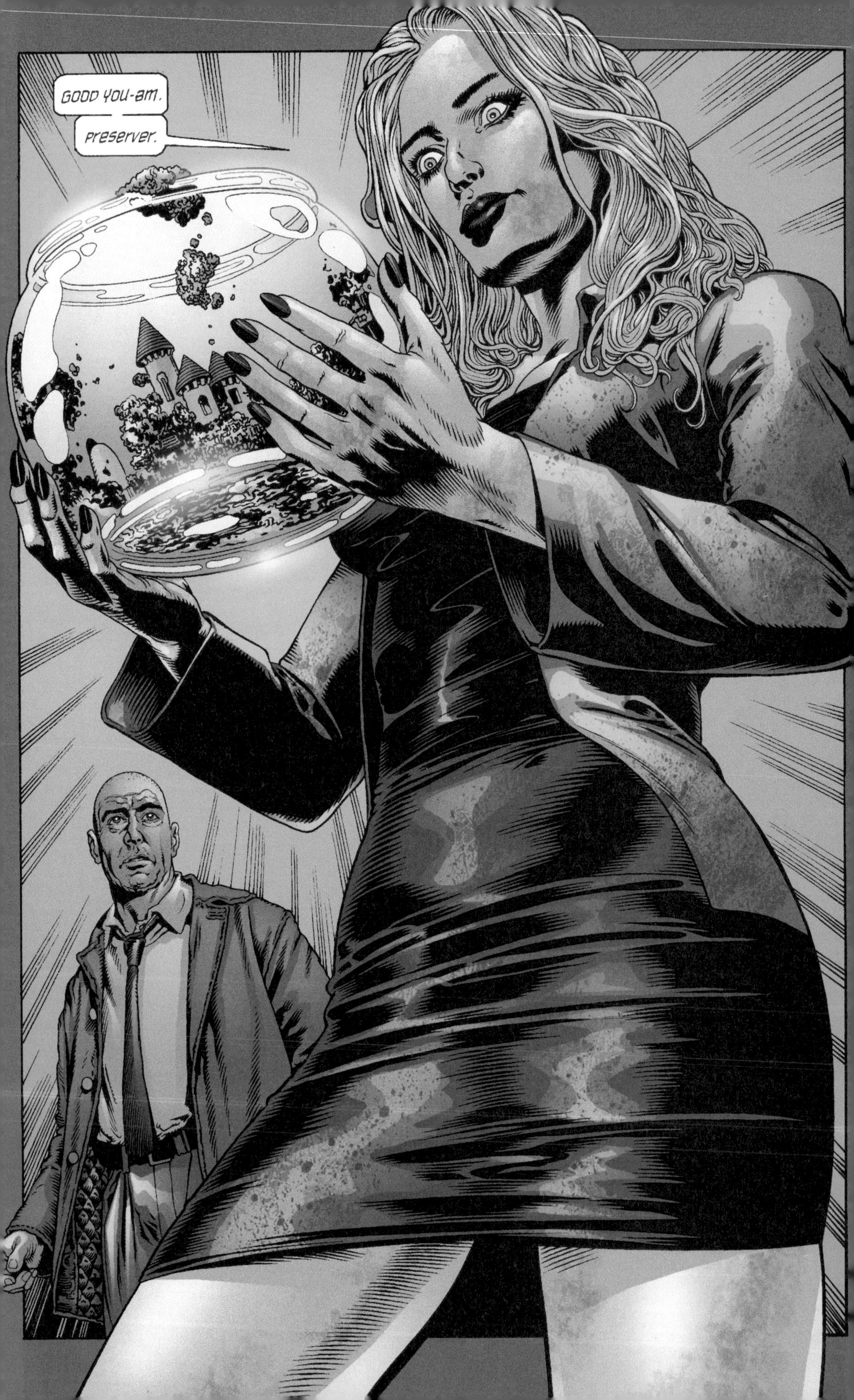
GOOD YOU-AM.
PRESERVER.

The Filth

22 PAGES

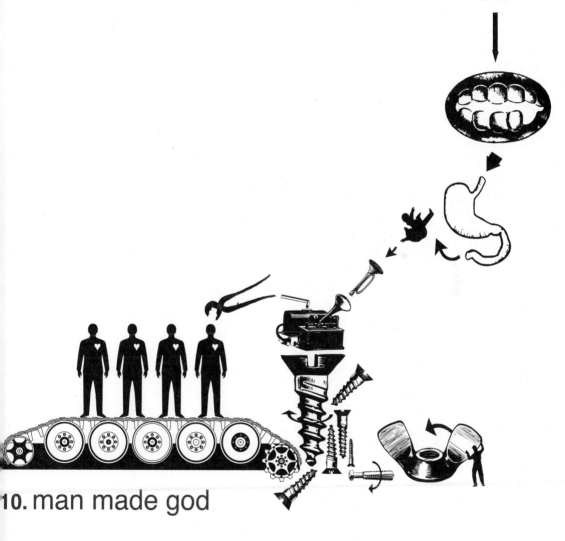

10. man made god

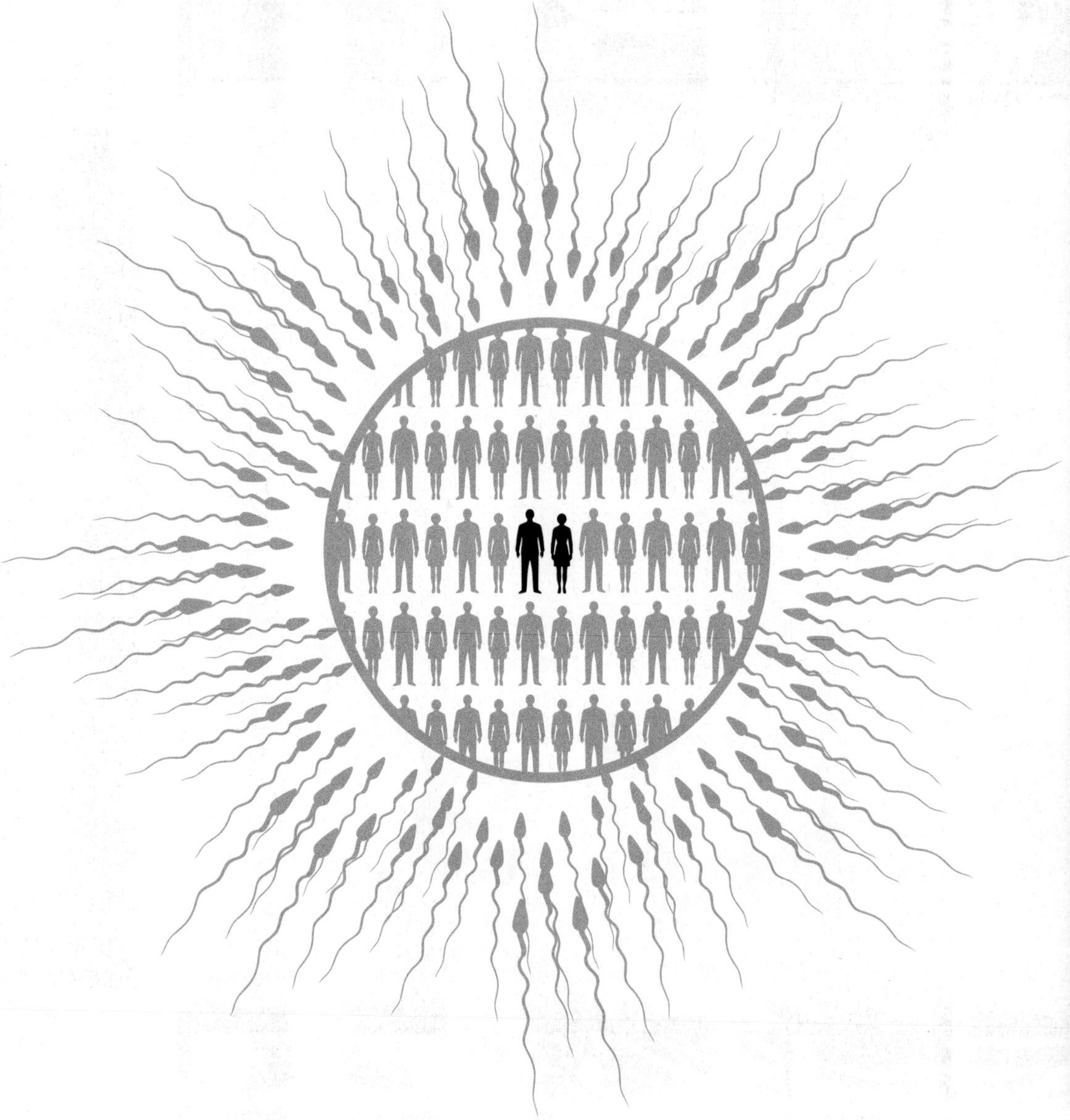

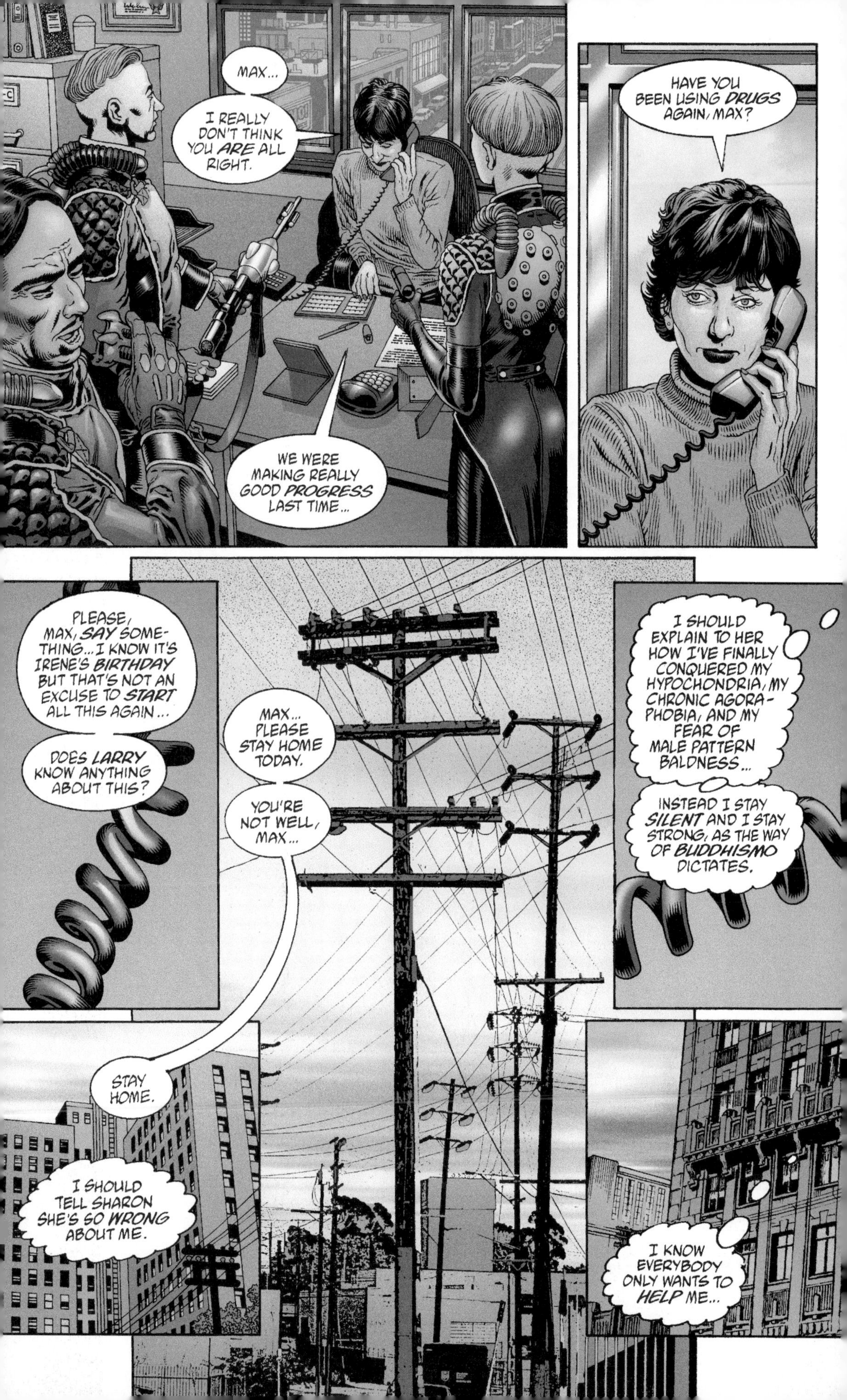
MAX...
I REALLY DON'T THINK YOU ARE ALL RIGHT.
WE WERE MAKING REALLY GOOD PROGRESS LAST TIME...
HAVE YOU BEEN USING DRUGS AGAIN, MAX?
PLEASE, MAX, SAY SOME-THING... I KNOW IT'S IRENE'S BIRTHDAY BUT THAT'S NOT AN EXCUSE TO START ALL THIS AGAIN...
DOES LARRY KNOW ANYTHING ABOUT THIS?
MAX... PLEASE STAY HOME TODAY.
YOU'RE NOT WELL, MAX...
I SHOULD EXPLAIN TO HER HOW I'VE FINALLY CONQUERED MY HYPOCHONDRIA, MY CHRONIC AGORA-PHOBIA, AND MY FEAR OF MALE PATTERN BALDNESS...
INSTEAD I STAY SILENT AND I STAY STRONG, AS THE WAY OF BUDDHISMO DICTATES.
STAY HOME.
I SHOULD TELL SHARON SHE'S SO WRONG ABOUT ME.
I KNOW EVERYBODY ONLY WANTS TO HELP ME...

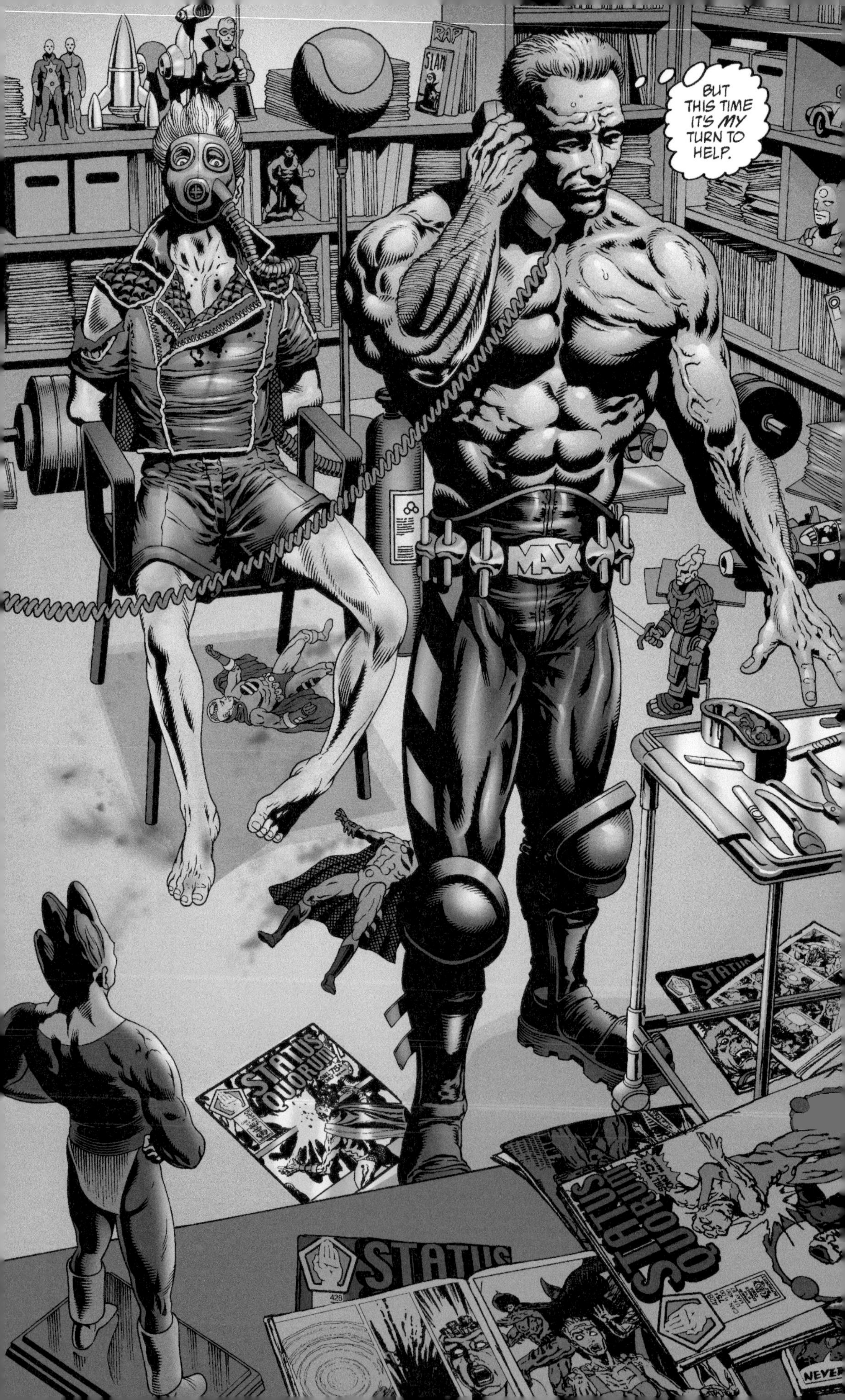
BUT THIS TIME IT'S *MY* TURN TO HELP.
RAP
SLAM
MAX
STATUS QUORUM
STATUS

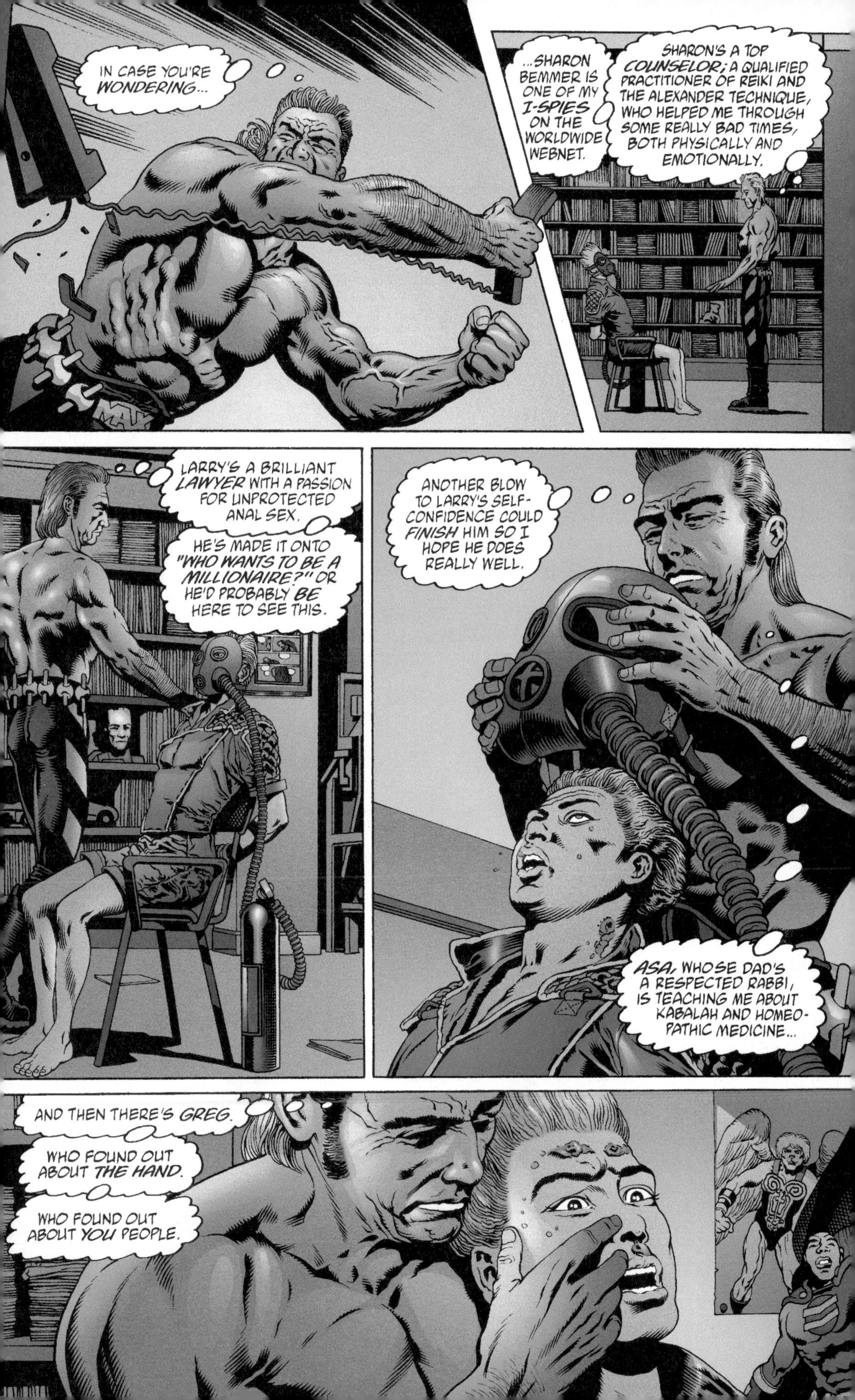
IN CASE YOU'RE WONDERING...
...SHARON BEMMER IS ONE OF MY I-SPIES ON THE WORLDWIDE WEBNET.
SHARON'S A TOP COUNSELOR; A QUALIFIED PRACTITIONER OF REIKI AND THE ALEXANDER TECHNIQUE, WHO HELPED ME THROUGH SOME REALLY BAD TIMES, BOTH PHYSICALLY AND EMOTIONALLY.
LARRY'S A BRILLIANT LAWYER WITH A PASSION FOR UNPROTECTED ANAL SEX.
HE'S MADE IT ONTO "WHO WANTS TO BE A MILLIONAIRE?" OR HE'D PROBABLY BE HERE TO SEE THIS.
ANOTHER BLOW TO LARRY'S SELF-CONFIDENCE COULD FINISH HIM SO I HOPE HE DOES REALLY WELL.
ASA, WHOSE DAD'S A RESPECTED RABBI, IS TEACHING ME ABOUT KABALAH AND HOMEO-PATHIC MEDICINE...
AND THEN THERE'S GREG.
WHO FOUND OUT ABOUT THE HAND.
WHO FOUND OUT ABOUT YOU PEOPLE.

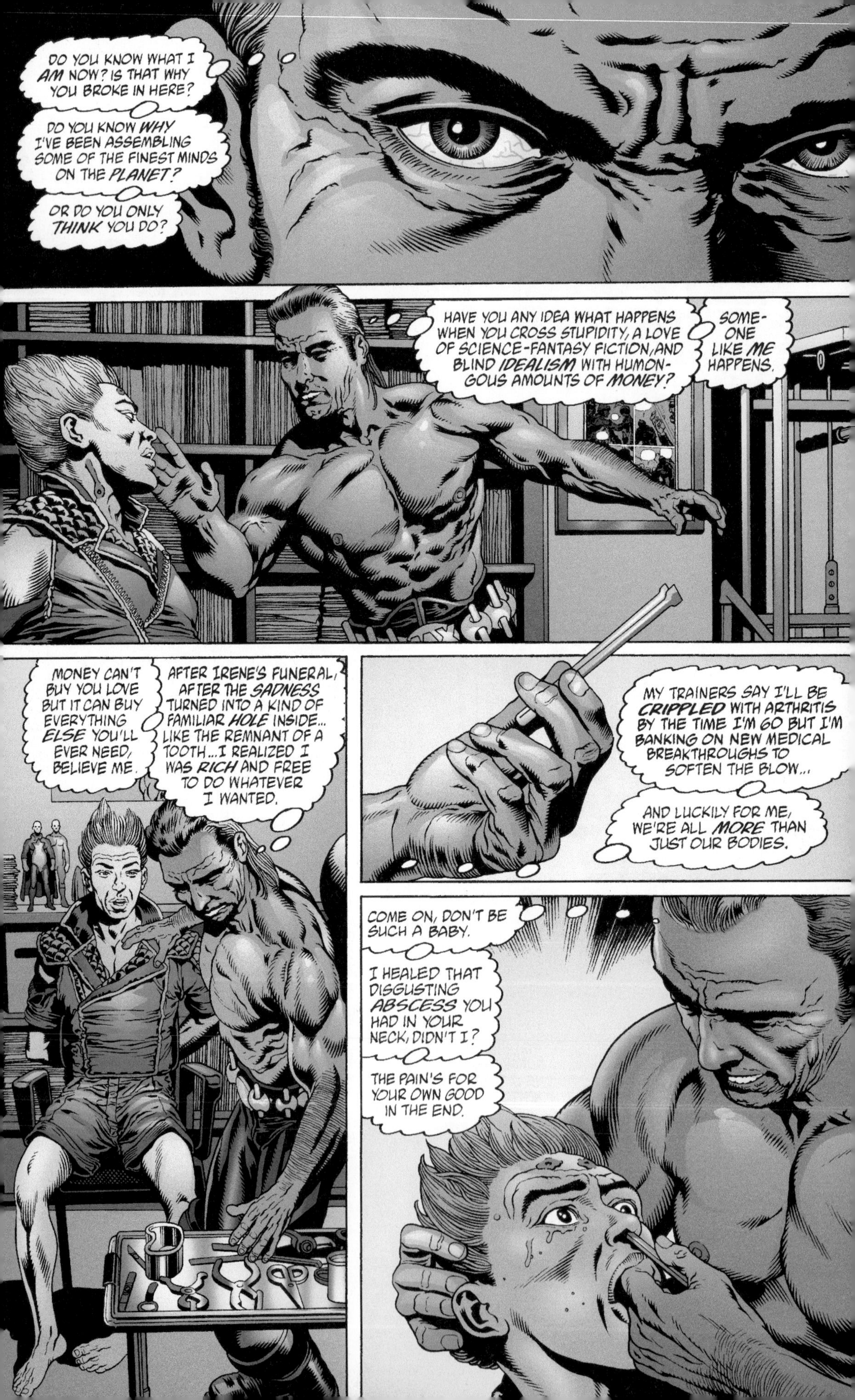
DO YOU KNOW WHAT I AM NOW? IS THAT WHY YOU BROKE IN HERE?
DO YOU KNOW WHY I'VE BEEN ASSEMBLING SOME OF THE FINEST MINDS ON THE PLANET?
OR DO YOU ONLY THINK YOU DO?
HAVE YOU ANY IDEA WHAT HAPPENS WHEN YOU CROSS STUPIDITY, A LOVE OF SCIENCE-FANTASY FICTION, AND BLIND IDEALISM WITH HUMON-GOUS AMOUNTS OF MONEY?
SOME-ONE LIKE ME HAPPENS.
MONEY CAN'T BUY YOU LOVE BUT IT CAN BUY EVERYTHING ELSE YOU'LL EVER NEED, BELIEVE ME.
AFTER IRENE'S FUNERAL, AFTER THE SADNESS TURNED INTO A KIND OF FAMILIAR HOLE INSIDE... LIKE THE REMNANT OF A TOOTH...I REALIZED I WAS RICH AND FREE TO DO WHATEVER I WANTED.
MY TRAINERS SAY I'LL BE CRIPPLED WITH ARTHRITIS BY THE TIME I'M 60 BUT I'M BANKING ON NEW MEDICAL BREAKTHROUGHS TO SOFTEN THE BLOW...
AND LUCKILY FOR ME, WE'RE ALL MORE THAN JUST OUR BODIES.
COME ON, DON'T BE SUCH A BABY.
I HEALED THAT DISGUSTING ABSCESS YOU HAD IN YOUR NECK, DIDN'T I?
THE PAIN'S FOR YOUR OWN GOOD IN THE END.

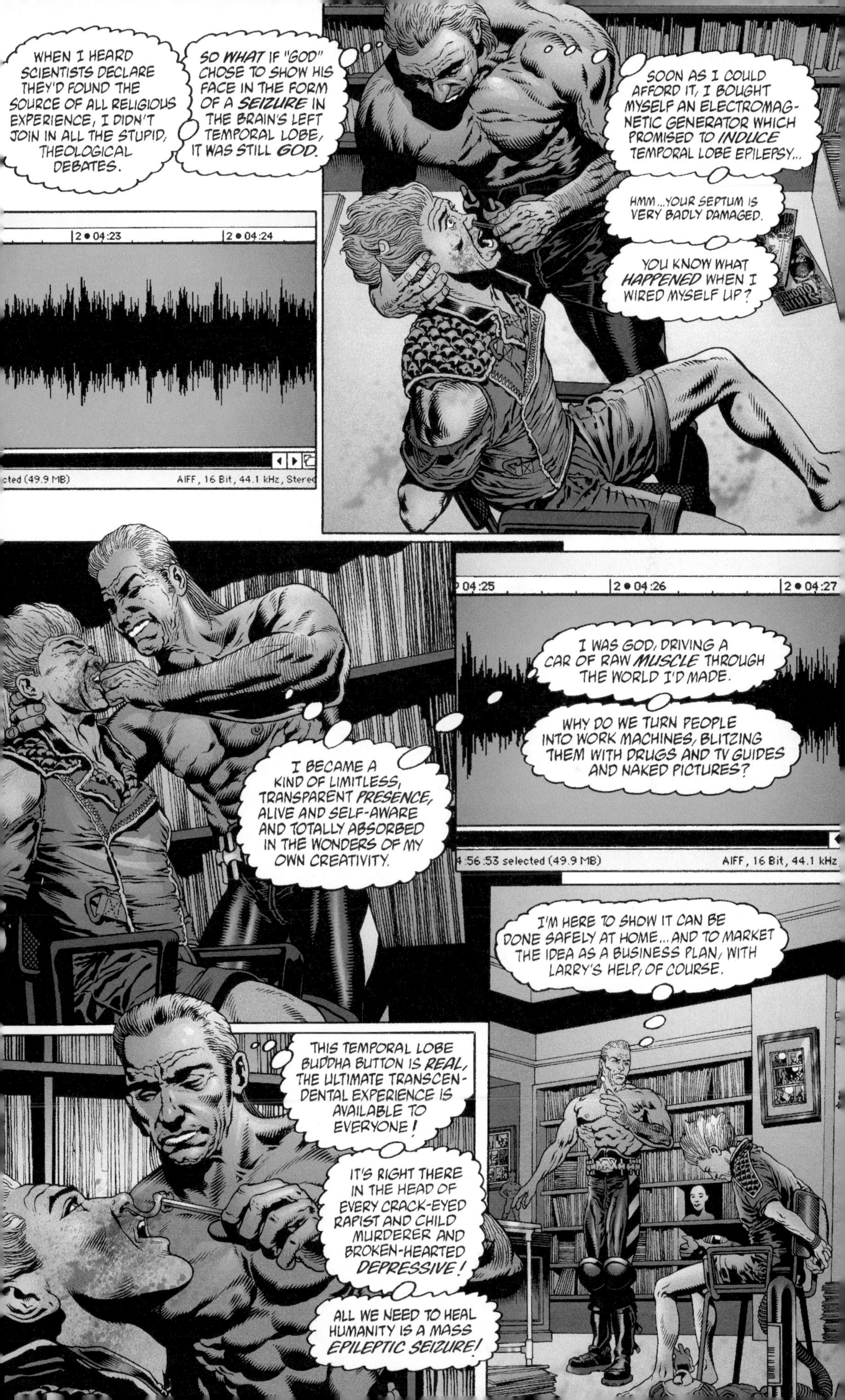
WHEN I HEARD SCIENTISTS DECLARE THEY'D FOUND THE SOURCE OF ALL RELIGIOUS EXPERIENCE, I DIDN'T JOIN IN ALL THE STUPID, THEOLOGICAL DEBATES.
SO WHAT IF "GOD" CHOSE TO SHOW HIS FACE IN THE FORM OF A SEIZURE IN THE BRAIN'S LEFT TEMPORAL LOBE, IT WAS STILL GOD.
2 • 04:23
2 • 04:24
cted (49.9 MB)
AIFF, 16 Bit, 44.1 kHz, Stereo
SOON AS I COULD AFFORD IT, I BOUGHT MYSELF AN ELECTROMAGNETIC GENERATOR WHICH PROMISED TO INDUCE TEMPORAL LOBE EPILEPSY...
HMM...YOUR SEPTUM IS VERY BADLY DAMAGED.
YOU KNOW WHAT HAPPENED WHEN I WIRED MYSELF UP?
04:25
2 • 04:26
2 • 04:27
I WAS GOD, DRIVING A CAR OF RAW MUSCLE THROUGH THE WORLD I'D MADE.
WHY DO WE TURN PEOPLE INTO WORK MACHINES, BLITZING THEM WITH DRUGS AND TV GUIDES AND NAKED PICTURES?
I BECAME A KIND OF LIMITLESS, TRANSPARENT PRESENCE, ALIVE AND SELF-AWARE AND TOTALLY ABSORBED IN THE WONDERS OF MY OWN CREATIVITY.
4:56:53 selected (49.9 MB)
AIFF, 16 Bit, 44.1 kHz
I'M HERE TO SHOW IT CAN BE DONE SAFELY AT HOME...AND TO MARKET THE IDEA AS A BUSINESS PLAN, WITH LARRY'S HELP, OF COURSE.
THIS TEMPORAL LOBE BUDDHA BUTTON IS REAL, THE ULTIMATE TRANSCENDENTAL EXPERIENCE IS AVAILABLE TO EVERYONE!
IT'S RIGHT THERE IN THE HEAD OF EVERY CRACK-EYED RAPIST AND CHILD MURDERER AND BROKEN-HEARTED DEPRESSIVE!
ALL WE NEED TO HEAL HUMANITY IS A MASS EPILEPTIC SEIZURE!

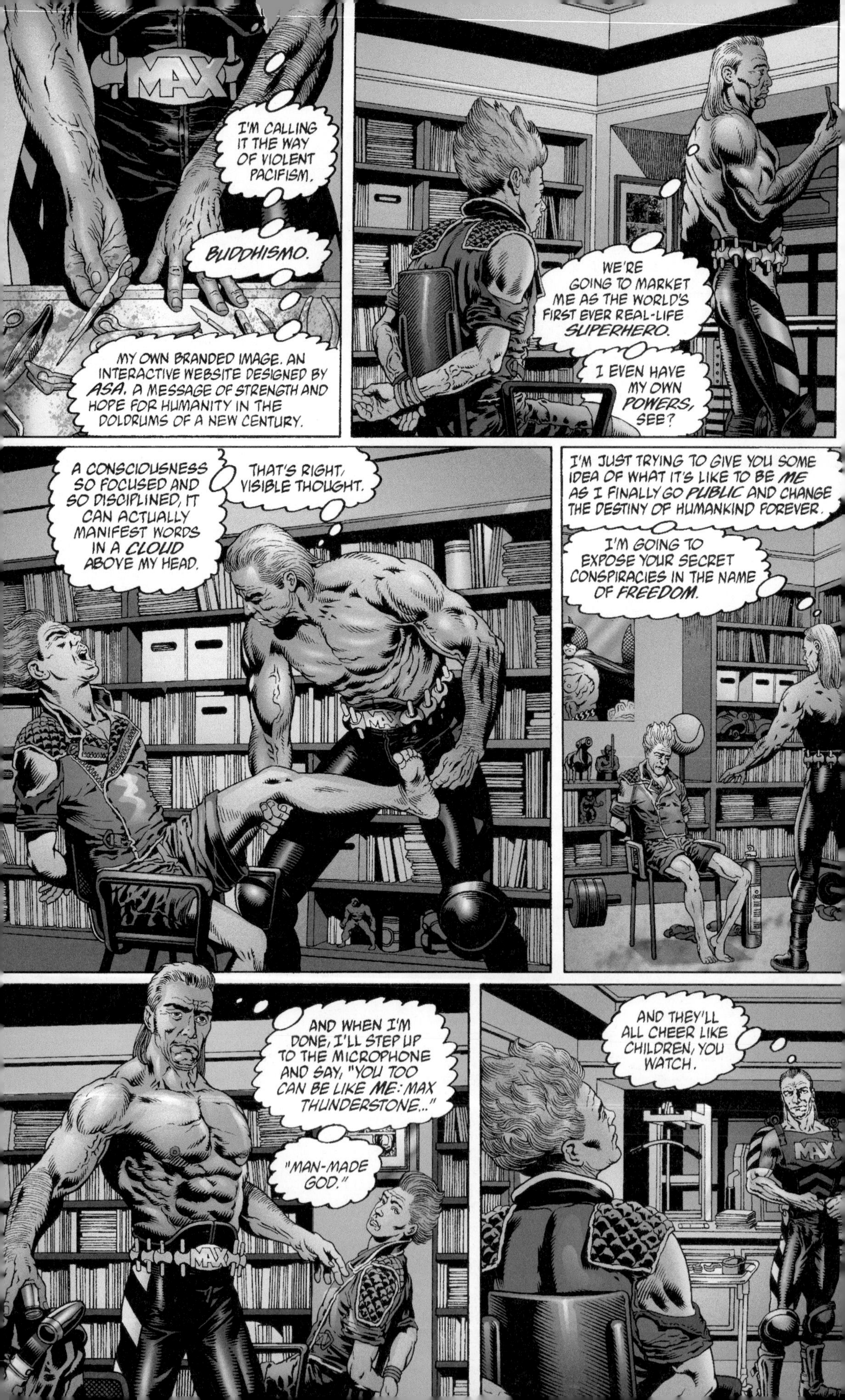
I'M CALLING IT THE WAY OF VIOLENT PACIFISM.
BUDDHISMO.
MY OWN BRANDED IMAGE. AN INTERACTIVE WEBSITE DESIGNED BY ASA. A MESSAGE OF STRENGTH AND HOPE FOR HUMANITY IN THE DOLDRUMS OF A NEW CENTURY.
WE'RE GOING TO MARKET ME AS THE WORLD'S FIRST EVER REAL-LIFE SUPERHERO.
I EVEN HAVE MY OWN POWERS, SEE?
A CONSCIOUSNESS SO FOCUSED AND SO DISCIPLINED, IT CAN ACTUALLY MANIFEST WORDS IN A CLOUD ABOVE MY HEAD.
THAT'S RIGHT, VISIBLE THOUGHT.
I'M JUST TRYING TO GIVE YOU SOME IDEA OF WHAT IT'S LIKE TO BE ME AS I FINALLY GO PUBLIC AND CHANGE THE DESTINY OF HUMANKIND FOREVER.
I'M GOING TO EXPOSE YOUR SECRET CONSPIRACIES IN THE NAME OF FREEDOM.
AND WHEN I'M DONE, I'LL STEP UP TO THE MICROPHONE AND SAY, "YOU TOO CAN BE LIKE ME: MAX THUNDERSTONE..."
"MAN-MADE GOD."
AND THEY'LL ALL CHEER LIKE CHILDREN, YOU WATCH.

MY MOTHER'S NAME WAS *IRENE SHATT*; SHE WOULD HAVE BEEN 83 YEARS OLD TODAY, SO THIS IS QUITE AN IMPORTANT DATE FOR ME.

WE ONLY *ARGUED* THAT LAST TIME BECAUSE SHE WANTED *TWO* LOTTERY TICKETS AND I'D BOUGHT *ONE* FOR HER AND NOT FOR MYSELF, WHICH MEANT I'D *HALVED* OUR CHANCES OF WINNING...

IT'S SO *STUPID*, ISN'T IT? WHEN YOU THINK ABOUT IT,

ALL THE STUPID REASONS PEOPLE FIND TO HATE ONE ANOTHER ON THE ROCKET RIDE TO THE *GRAVE*.

I WAS *STILL* ANGRY AT HER WHEN I CAME *HOME* FROM MY JOB AT THE STORE.

I COULDN'T WAIT TO TELL HER I'D HEARD GOD WAS ONLY A NEUROLOGICAL *SPASM*...AND THEN I FOUND HER JUST... *SITTING* THERE, LOOKING SO SMALL AND SO *DONE*, WITH THE *TV* ON.

SHH. RELAX...

I WAS IN SHOCK FOR ABOUT FOUR... OR MAYBE IT WAS *FIVE*... MINUTES BEFORE I NOTICED THE TICKET, FROZEN IN HER HAND,

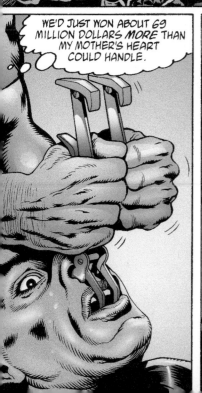

WE'D JUST WON ABOUT 69 MILLION DOLLARS *MORE* THAN MY MOTHER'S HEART COULD HANDLE.

YOU CAN IMAGINE MY CONFLICTING EMOTIONS THAT DAY.

IN FACT...

YOU CAN PROBABLY EVEN *SEE* THEM.

HTT!

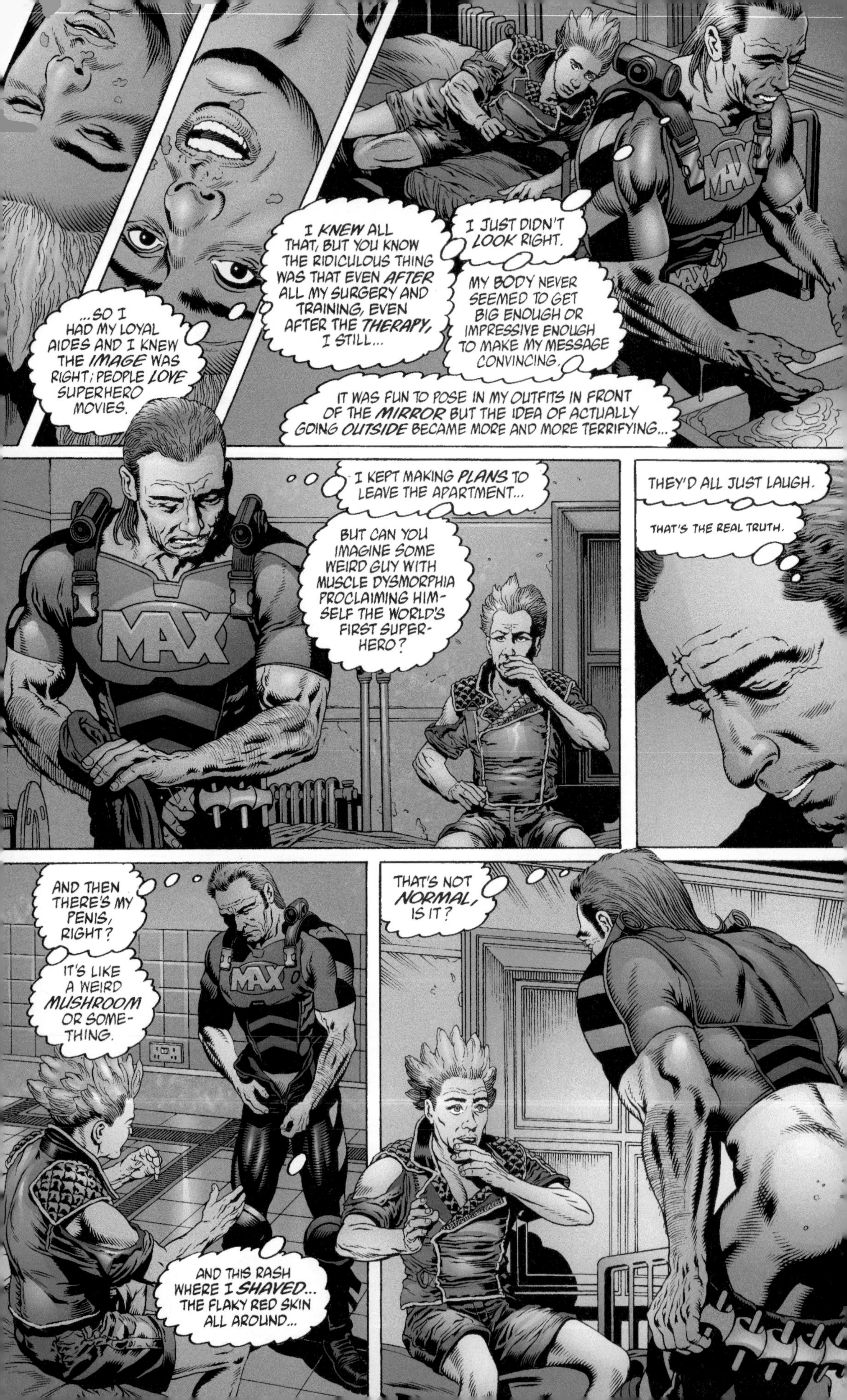
...SO I HAD MY LOYAL AIDES AND I KNEW THE IMAGE WAS RIGHT; PEOPLE LOVE SUPERHERO MOVIES.
I KNEW ALL THAT, BUT YOU KNOW THE RIDICULOUS THING WAS THAT EVEN AFTER ALL MY SURGERY AND TRAINING, EVEN AFTER THE THERAPY, I STILL...
I JUST DIDN'T LOOK RIGHT.
MY BODY NEVER SEEMED TO GET BIG ENOUGH OR IMPRESSIVE ENOUGH TO MAKE MY MESSAGE CONVINCING.
IT WAS FUN TO POSE IN MY OUTFITS IN FRONT OF THE MIRROR BUT THE IDEA OF ACTUALLY GOING OUTSIDE BECAME MORE AND MORE TERRIFYING...
I KEPT MAKING PLANS TO LEAVE THE APARTMENT...
BUT CAN YOU IMAGINE SOME WEIRD GUY WITH MUSCLE DYSMORPHIA PROCLAIMING HIMSELF THE WORLD'S FIRST SUPERHERO?
THEY'D ALL JUST LAUGH.
THAT'S THE REAL TRUTH.
AND THEN THERE'S MY PENIS, RIGHT?
IT'S LIKE A WEIRD MUSHROOM OR SOMETHING.
AND THIS RASH WHERE I SHAVED... THE FLAKY RED SKIN ALL AROUND...
THAT'S NOT NORMAL, IS IT?
MAX

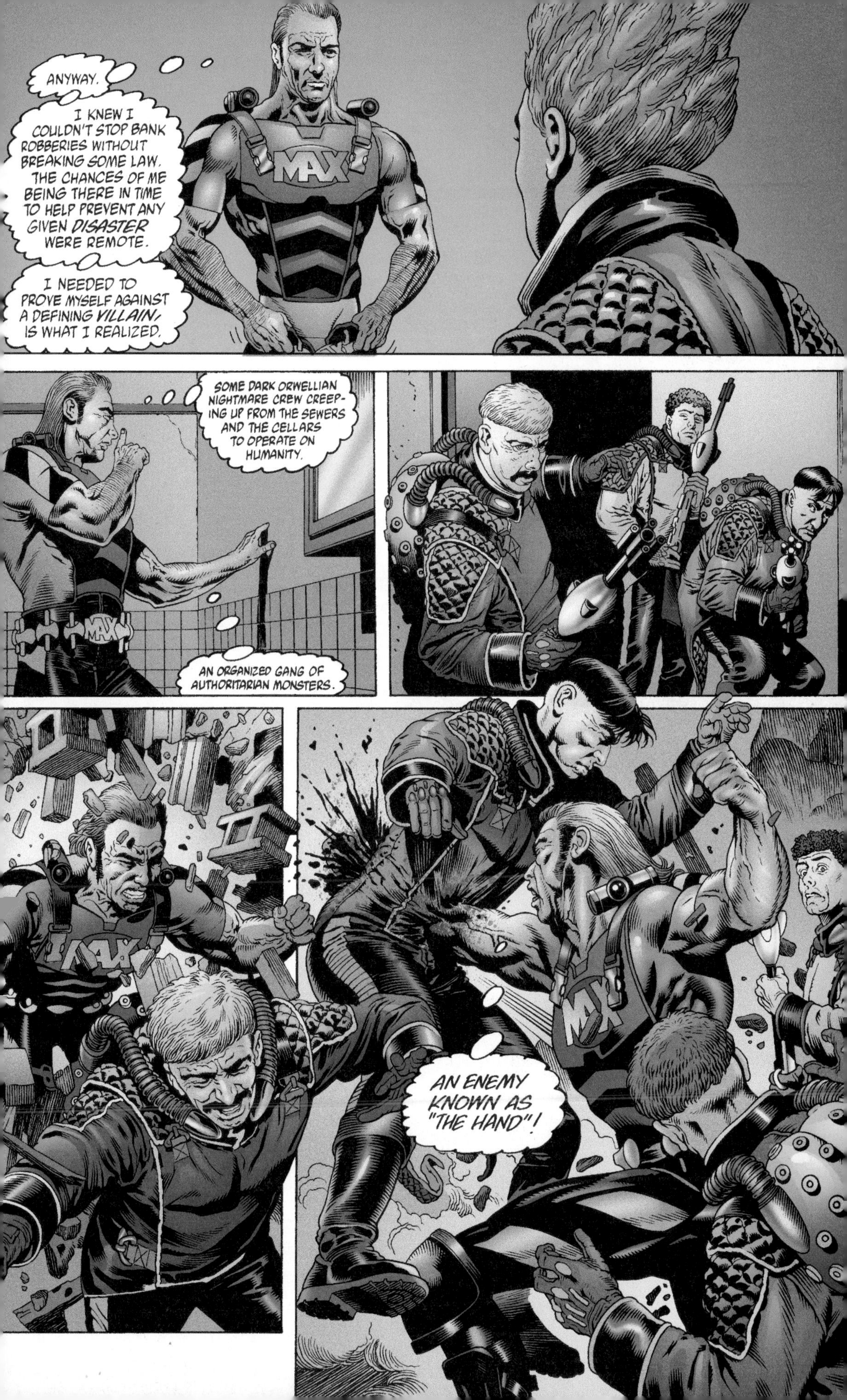
ANYWAY.
I KNEW I COULDN'T STOP BANK ROBBERIES WITHOUT BREAKING SOME LAW. THE CHANCES OF ME BEING THERE IN TIME TO HELP PREVENT ANY GIVEN DISASTER WERE REMOTE.
I NEEDED TO PROVE MYSELF AGAINST A DEFINING VILLAIN, IS WHAT I REALIZED.
MAX
SOME DARK ORWELLIAN NIGHTMARE CREW CREEPING UP FROM THE SEWERS AND THE CELLARS TO OPERATE ON HUMANITY.
AN ORGANIZED GANG OF AUTHORITARIAN MONSTERS.
AN ENEMY KNOWN AS "THE HAND"!

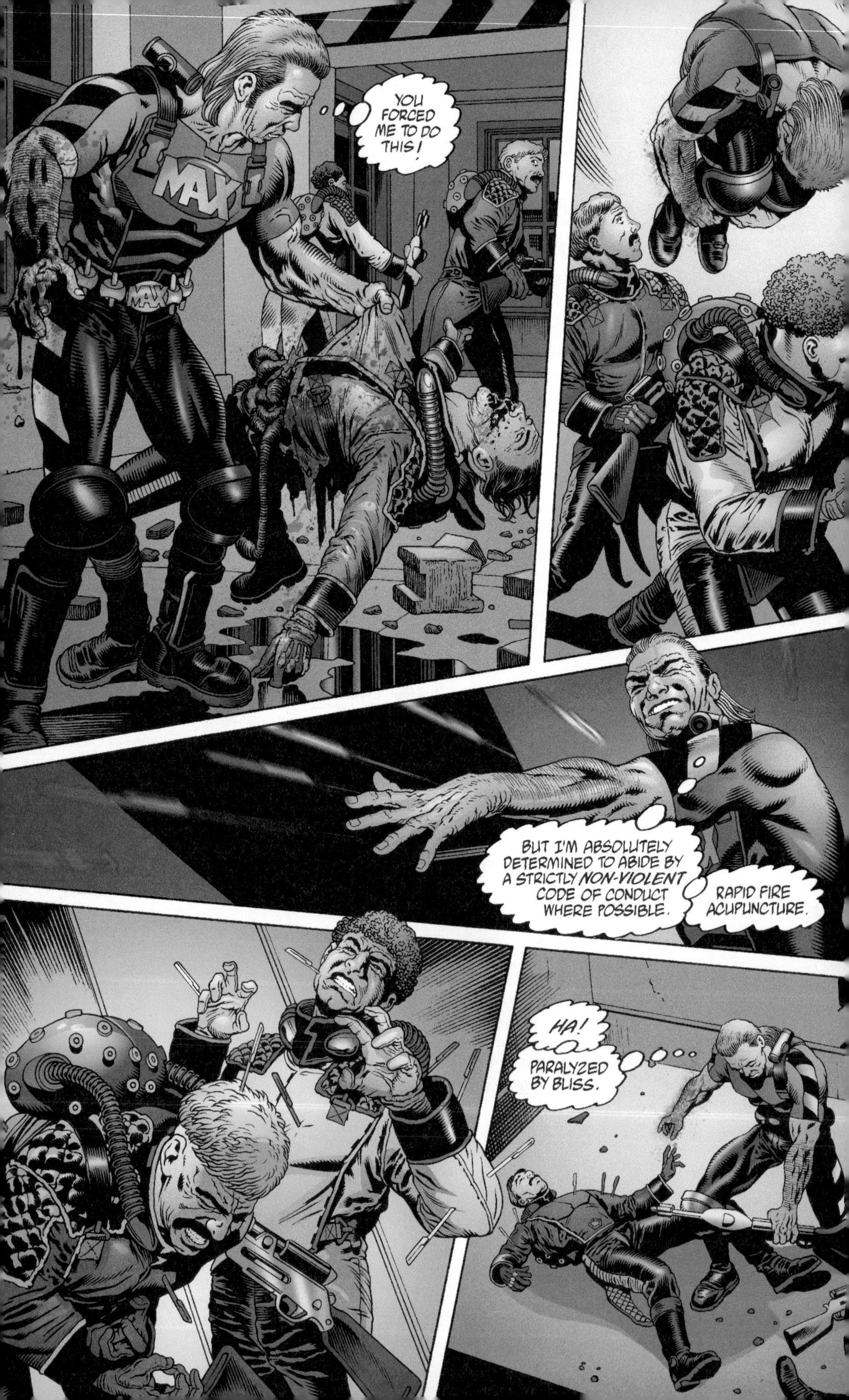
YOU FORCED ME TO DO THIS!
BUT I'M ABSOLUTELY DETERMINED TO ABIDE BY A STRICTLY NON-VIOLENT CODE OF CONDUCT WHERE POSSIBLE.
RAPID FIRE ACUPUNCTURE.
HA!
PARALYZED BY BLISS.

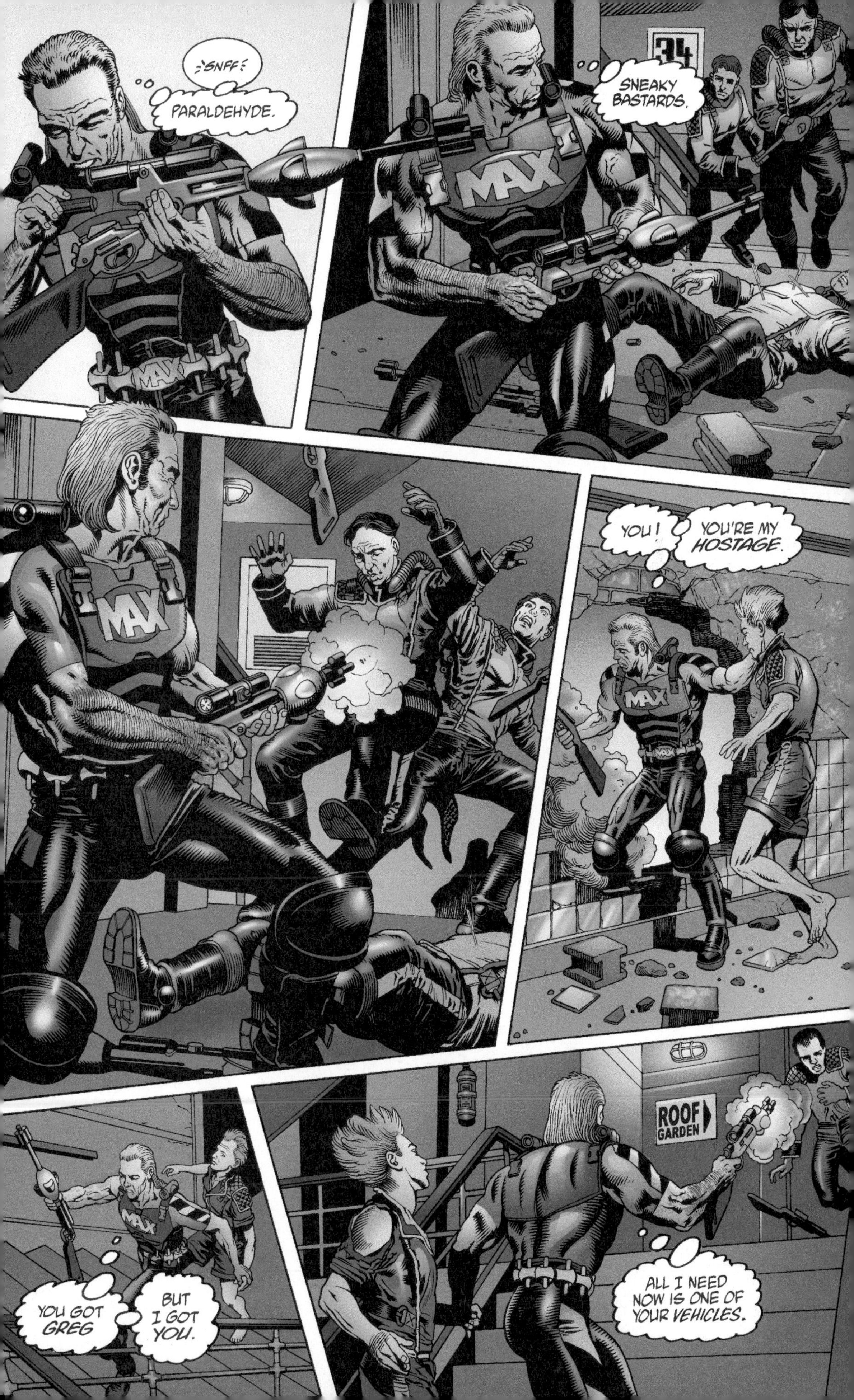
:SNFF:
PARALDEHYDE.
SNEAKY BASTARDS.
34
MAX
MAX
YOU!
YOU'RE MY HOSTAGE.
MAX
ROOF GARDEN
YOU GOT GREG
BUT I GOT YOU.
ALL I NEED NOW IS ONE OF YOUR VEHICLES.

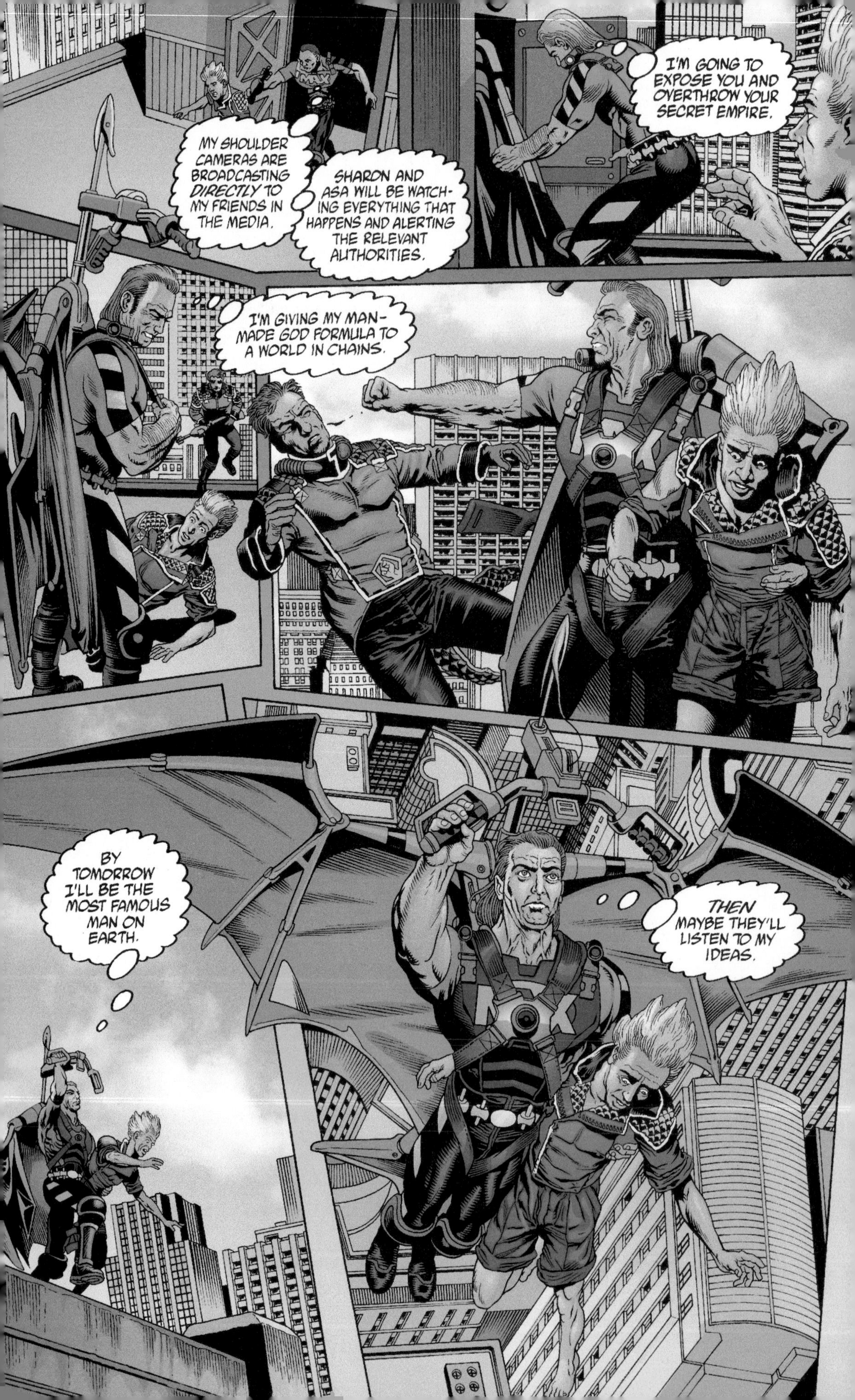
MY SHOULDER CAMERAS ARE BROADCASTING *DIRECTLY* TO MY FRIENDS IN THE MEDIA.
SHARON AND ASA WILL BE WATCHING EVERYTHING THAT HAPPENS AND ALERTING THE RELEVANT AUTHORITIES.
I'M GOING TO EXPOSE YOU AND OVERTHROW YOUR SECRET EMPIRE.
I'M GIVING MY MAN-MADE GOD FORMULA TO A WORLD IN CHAINS.
BY TOMORROW I'LL BE THE MOST FAMOUS MAN ON EARTH.
THEN MAYBE THEY'LL LISTEN TO MY IDEAS.

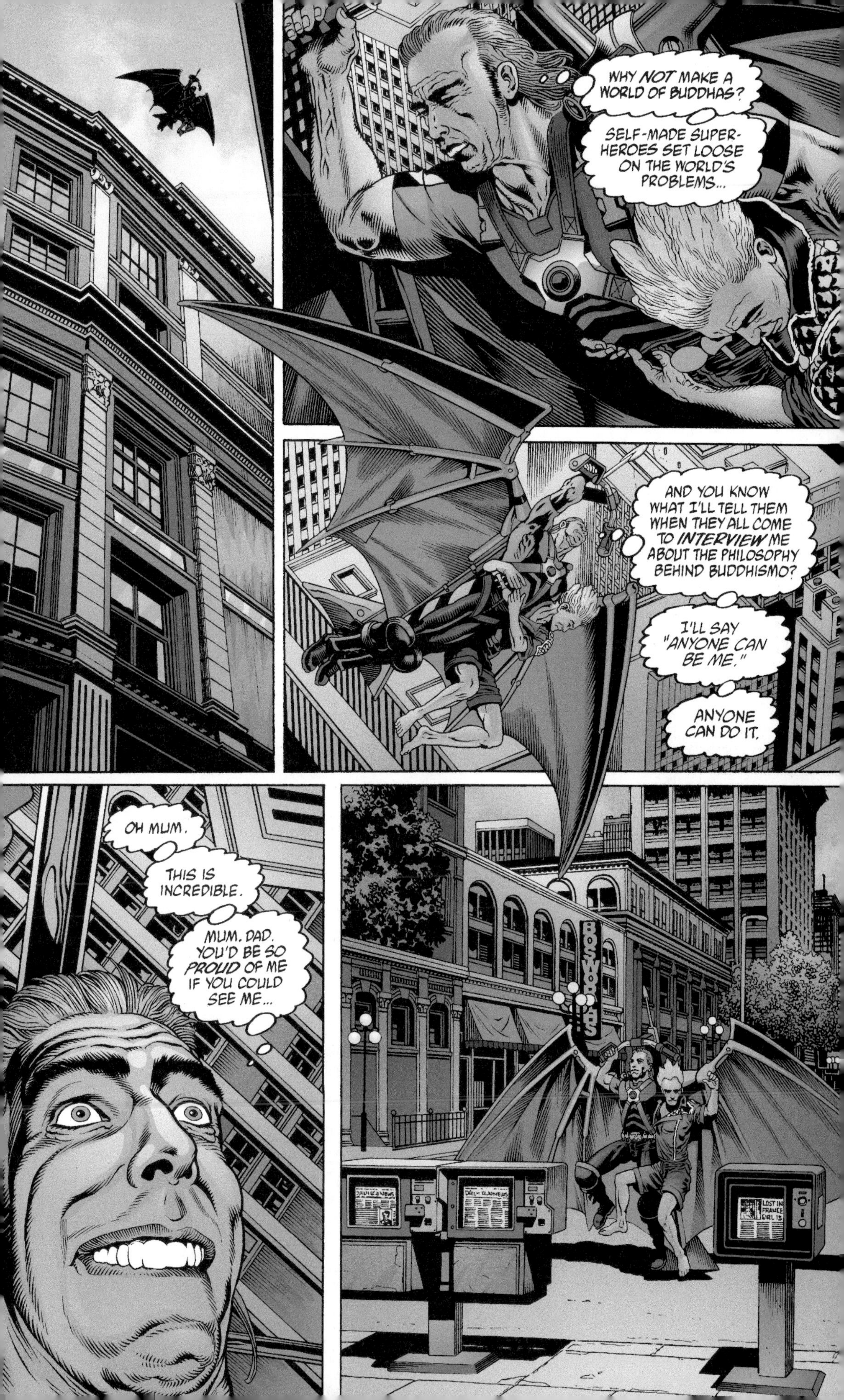
WHY NOT MAKE A WORLD OF BUDDHAS?
SELF-MADE SUPER-HEROES SET LOOSE ON THE WORLD'S PROBLEMS...
AND YOU KNOW WHAT I'LL TELL THEM WHEN THEY ALL COME TO INTERVIEW ME ABOUT THE PHILOSOPHY BEHIND BUDDHISMO?
I'LL SAY "ANYONE CAN BE ME."
ANYONE CAN DO IT.
OH MUM.
THIS IS INCREDIBLE.
MUM. DAD. YOU'D BE SO PROUD OF ME IF YOU COULD SEE ME...
BOSWORTHS

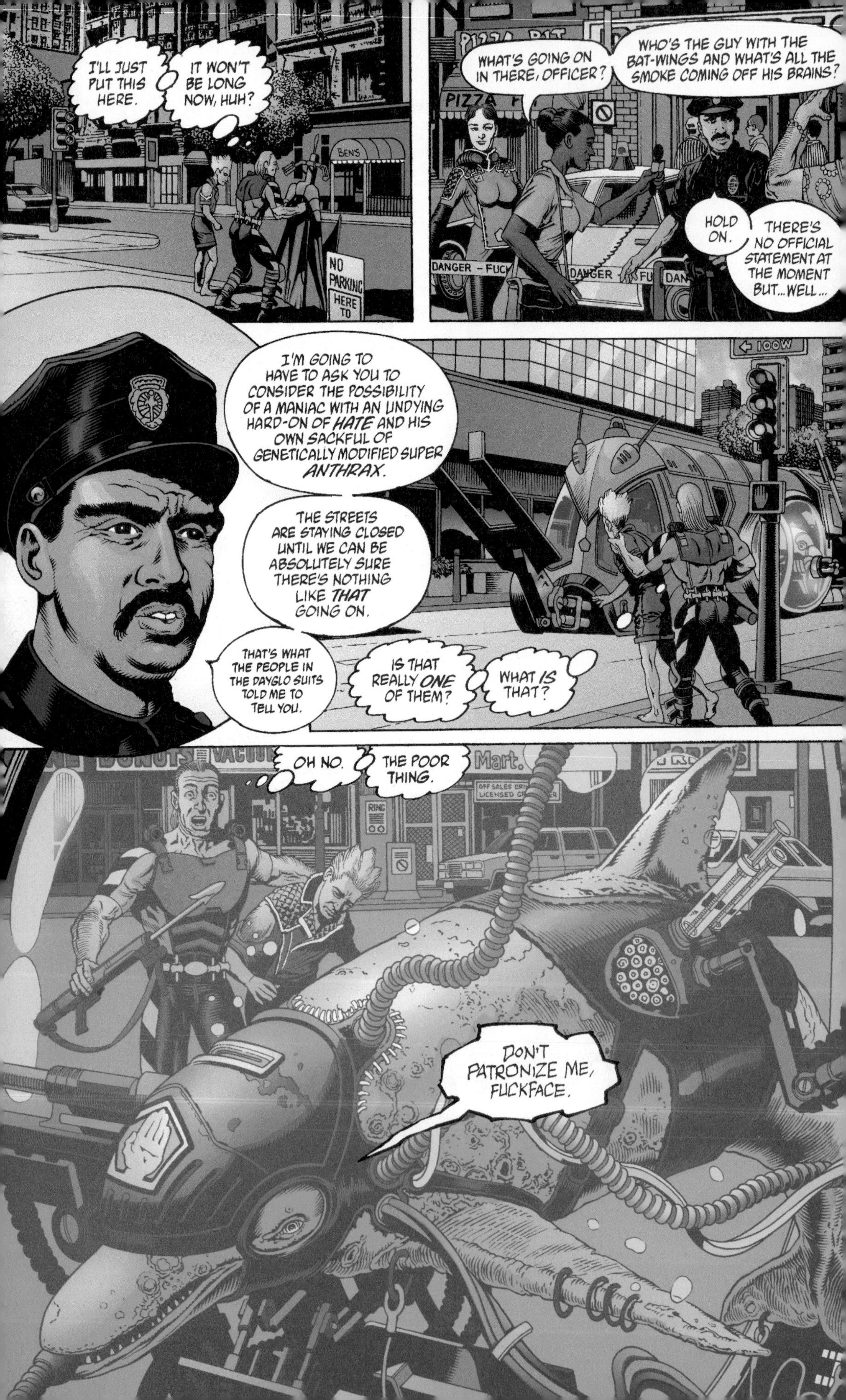
I'LL JUST PUT THIS HERE.
IT WON'T BE LONG NOW, HUH?
BEN'S
NO PARKING HERE TO
PIZZA PIT
PIZZA
WHAT'S GOING ON IN THERE, OFFICER?
WHO'S THE GUY WITH THE BAT-WINGS AND WHAT'S ALL THE SMOKE COMING OFF HIS BRAINS?
HOLD ON.
THERE'S NO OFFICIAL STATEMENT AT THE MOMENT BUT...WELL...
DANGER – FUC
DANGER – FU
DAN
I'M GOING TO HAVE TO ASK YOU TO CONSIDER THE POSSIBILITY OF A MANIAC WITH AN UNDYING HARD-ON OF HATE AND HIS OWN SACKFUL OF GENETICALLY MODIFIED SUPER ANTHRAX.
THE STREETS ARE STAYING CLOSED UNTIL WE CAN BE ABSOLUTELY SURE THERE'S NOTHING LIKE THAT GOING ON.
THAT'S WHAT THE PEOPLE IN THE DAYGLO SUITS TOLD ME TO TELL YOU.
IS THAT REALLY ONE OF THEM?
WHAT IS THAT?
100W
OH NO.
THE POOR THING.
DONUTS
VACUU
Mart.
OFF SALES DRI LICENSED G
RING
DON'T PATRONIZE ME, FUCKFACE.

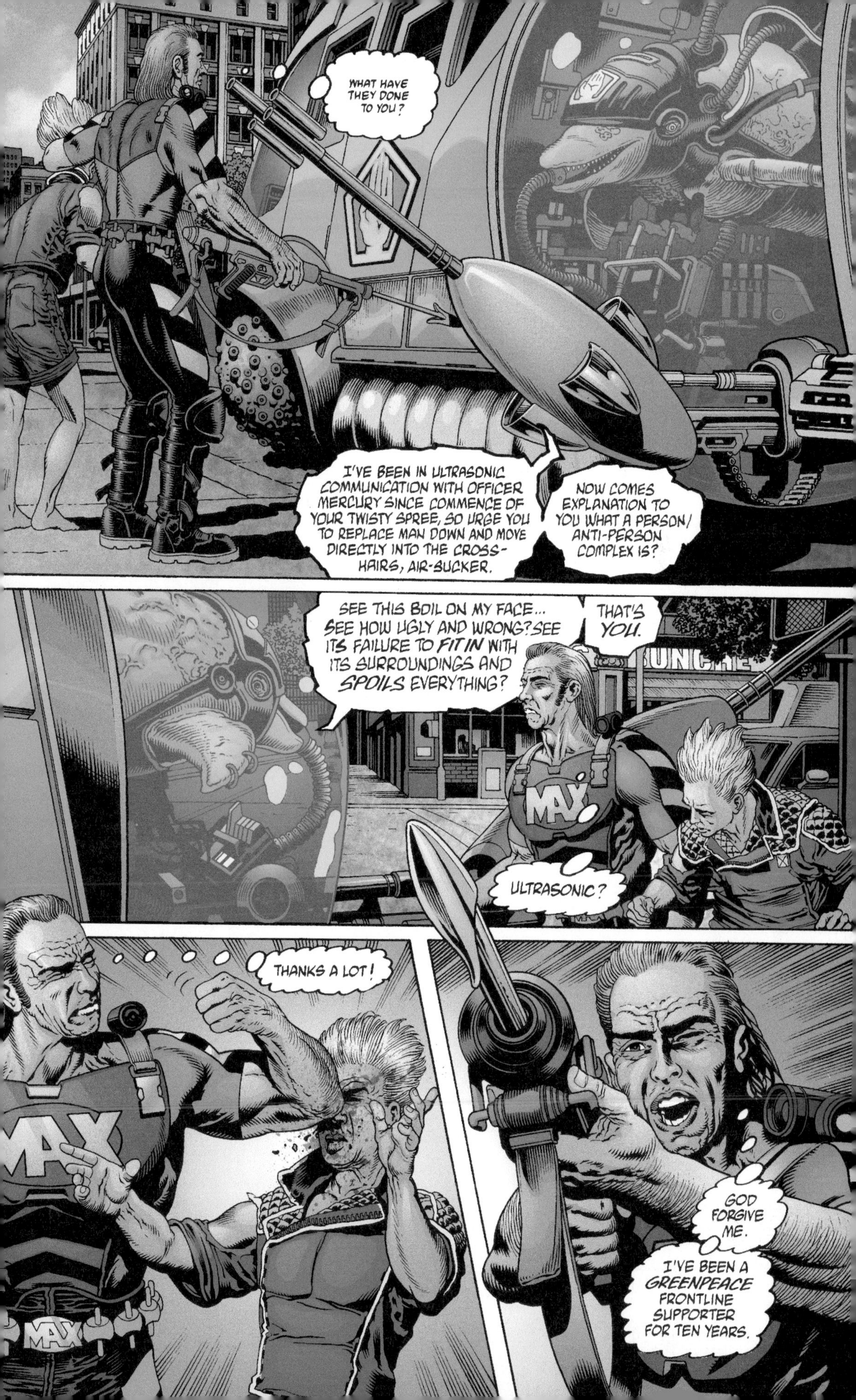
WHAT HAVE THEY DONE TO YOU?
I'VE BEEN IN ULTRASONIC COMMUNICATION WITH OFFICER MERCURY SINCE COMMENCE OF YOUR TWISTY SPREE, SO URGE YOU TO REPLACE MAN DOWN AND MOVE DIRECTLY INTO THE CROSS-HAIRS, AIR-SUCKER.
NOW COMES EXPLANATION TO YOU WHAT A PERSON/ ANTI-PERSON COMPLEX IS?
SEE THIS BOIL ON MY FACE... SEE HOW UGLY AND WRONG? SEE ITS FAILURE TO FIT IN WITH ITS SURROUNDINGS AND SPOILS EVERYTHING?
THAT'S YOU.
ULTRASONIC?
MAX
THANKS A LOT!
MAX
MAX
GOD FORGIVE ME.
I'VE BEEN A GREENPEACE FRONTLINE SUPPORTER FOR TEN YEARS.

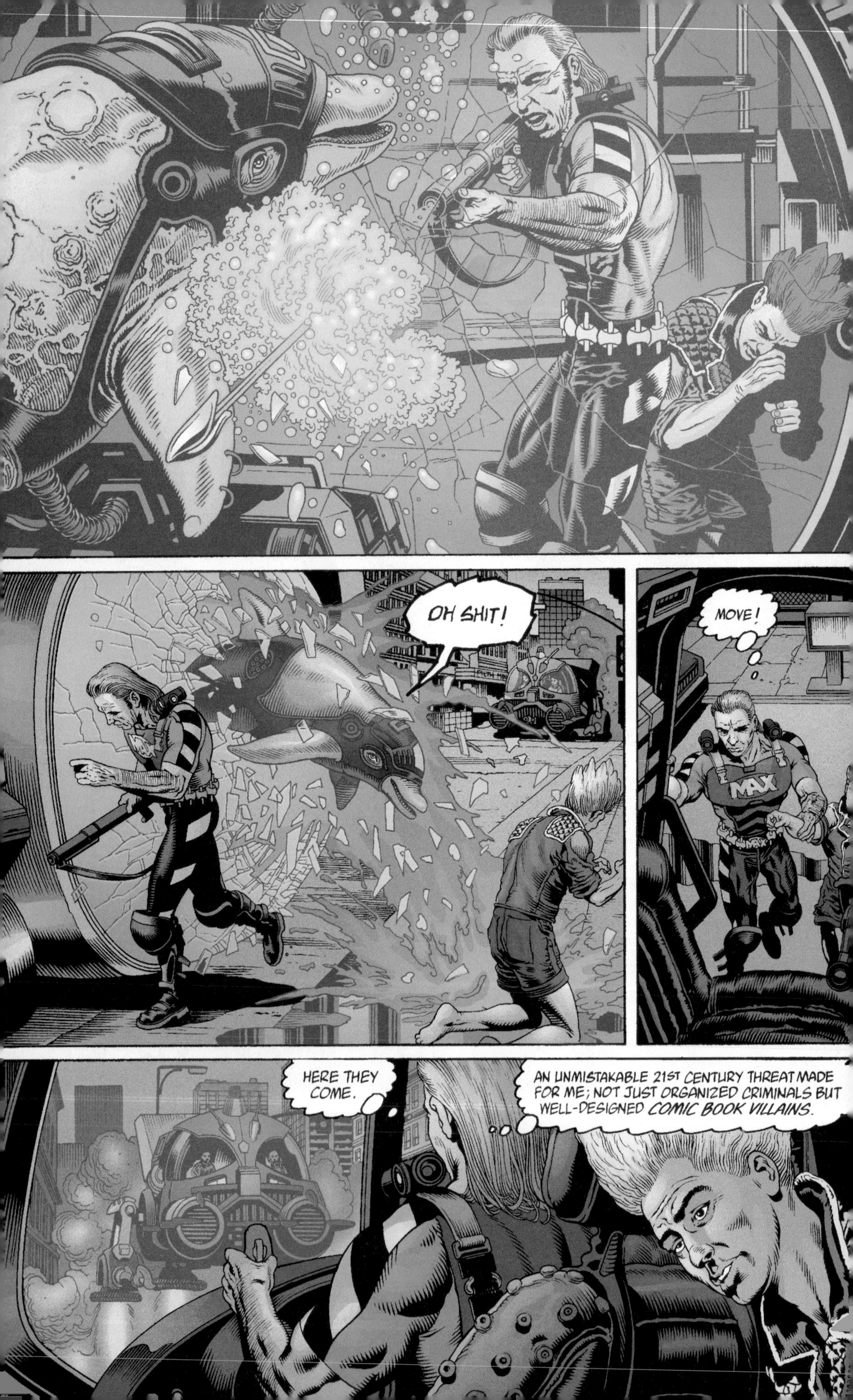
OH SHIT!
MOVE!
HERE THEY COME.
AN UNMISTAKABLE 21ST CENTURY THREAT MADE FOR ME; NOT JUST ORGANIZED CRIMINALS BUT WELL-DESIGNED COMIC BOOK VILLAINS.

IT'S ALL HAPPENING SO *FAST*...NOW...NOW I'M *OUTSIDE*.

I'M OUTSIDE AND EVERYONE CAN *SEE* ME.

POWER BOOST

ENGAGE FORKLIFT

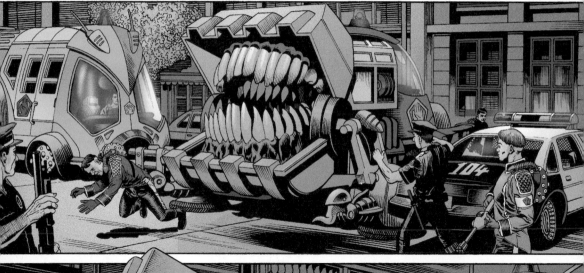

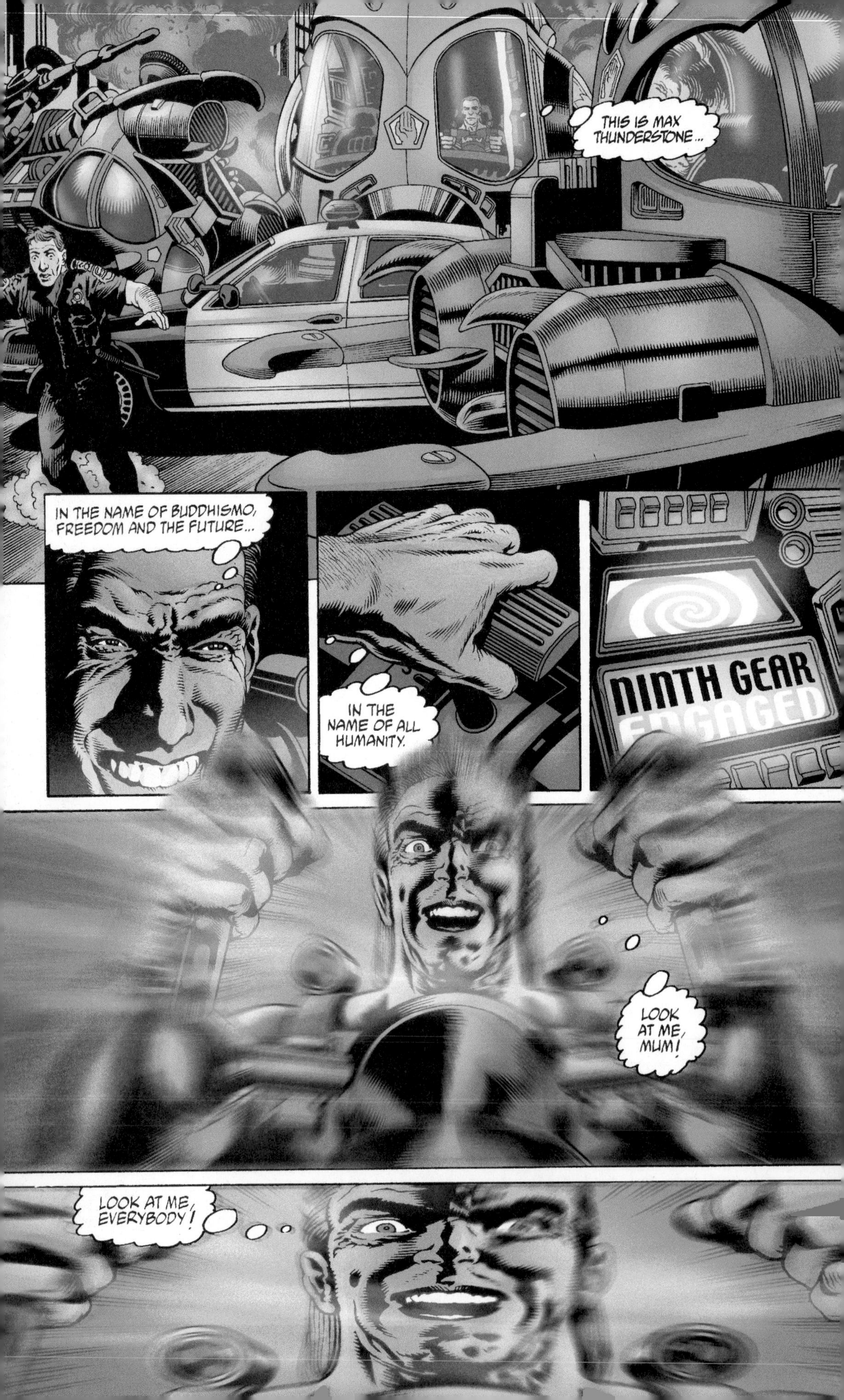
THIS IS MAX THUNDERSTONE...
IN THE NAME OF BUDDHISMO, FREEDOM AND THE FUTURE...
IN THE NAME OF ALL HUMANITY.
NINTH GEAR
ENGAGED
LOOK AT ME, MUM!
LOOK AT ME, EVERYBODY!

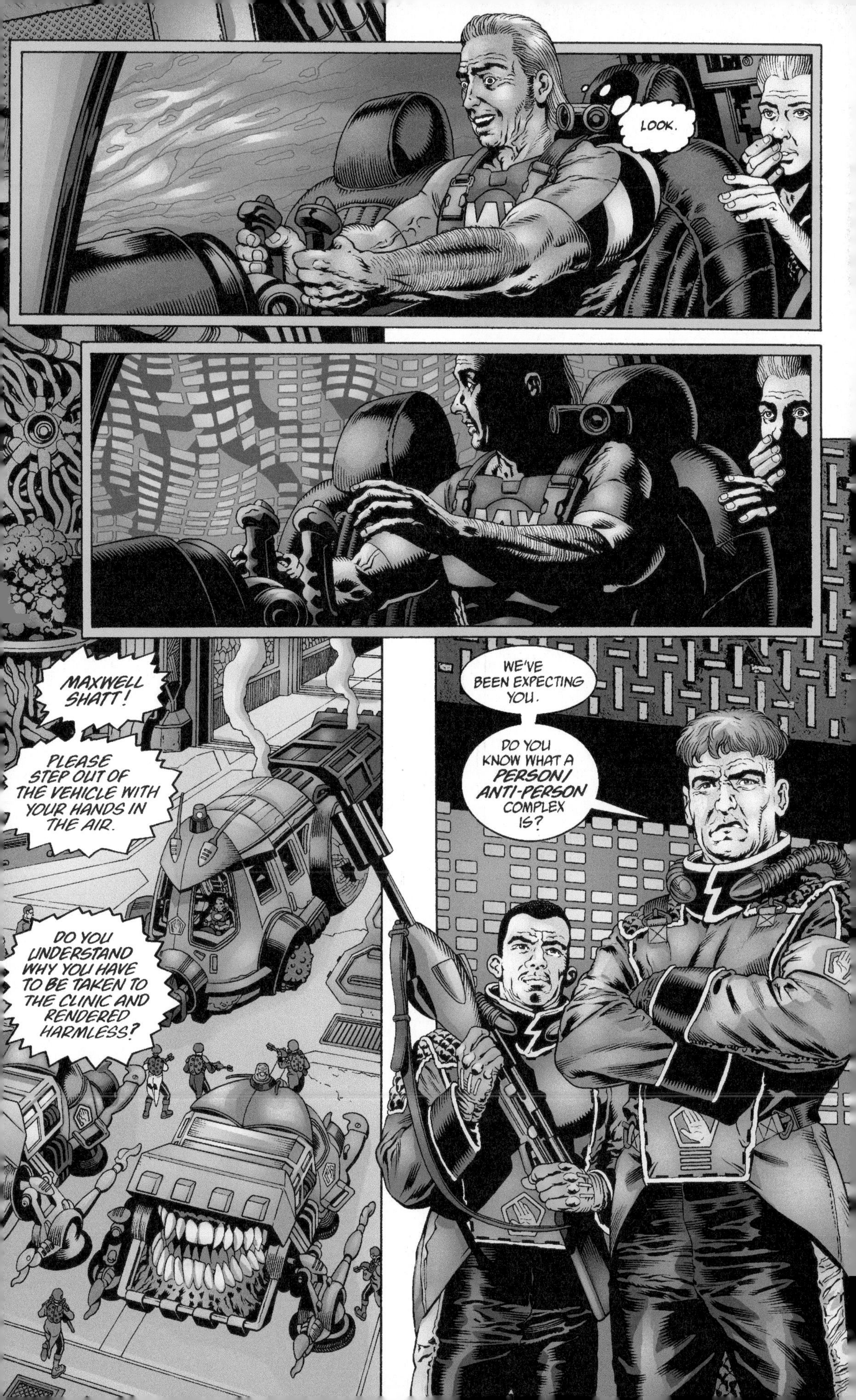
LOOK.
MAXWELL SHATT!
PLEASE STEP OUT OF THE VEHICLE WITH YOUR HANDS IN THE AIR.
DO YOU UNDERSTAND WHY YOU HAVE TO BE TAKEN TO THE CLINIC AND RENDERED HARMLESS?
WE'VE BEEN EXPECTING YOU.
DO YOU KNOW WHAT A PERSON/ ANTI-PERSON COMPLEX IS?

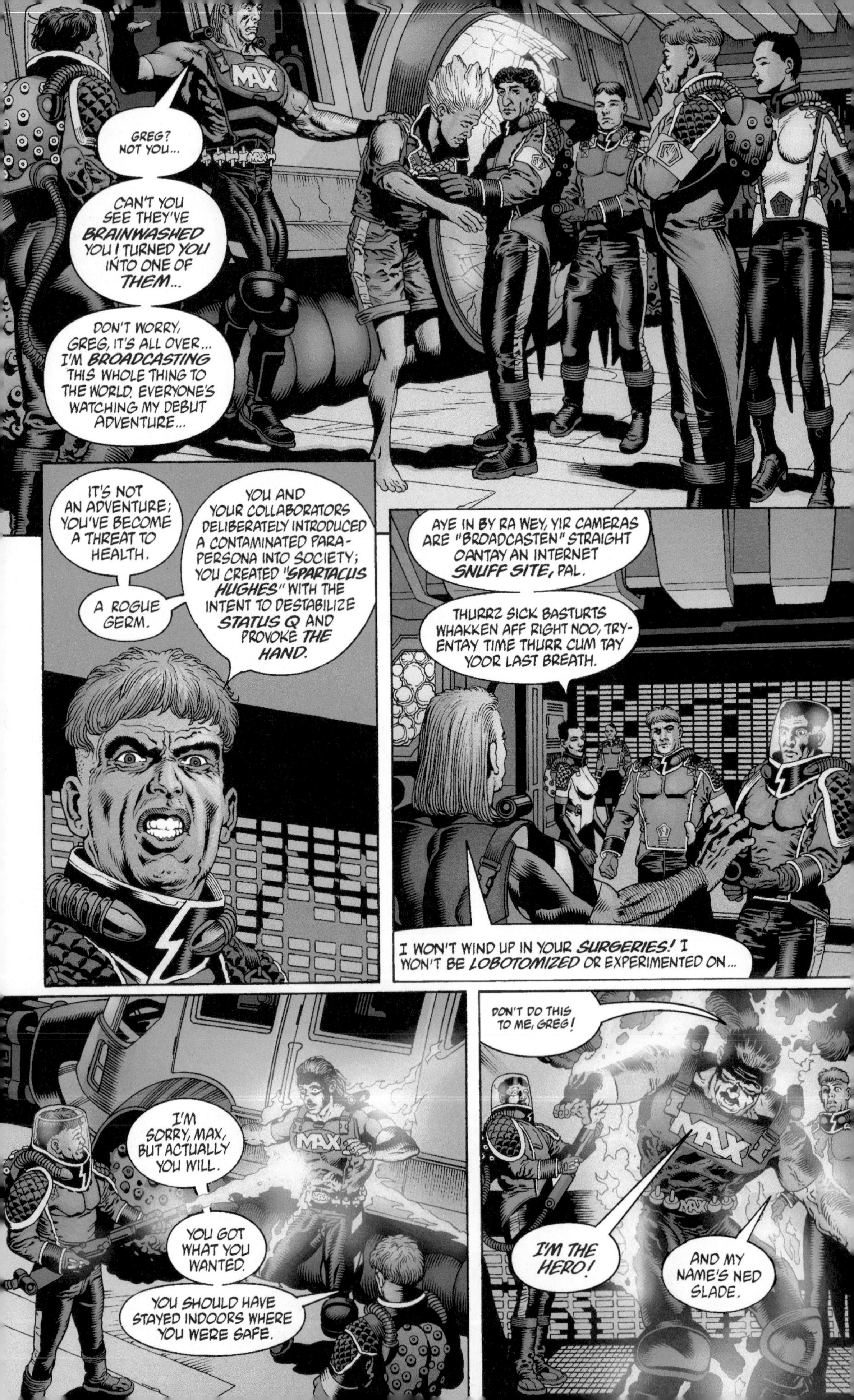
GREG? NOT YOU...
CAN'T YOU SEE THEY'VE BRAINWASHED YOU! TURNED YOU INTO ONE OF THEM...
DON'T WORRY, GREG, IT'S ALL OVER... I'M BROADCASTING THIS WHOLE THING TO THE WORLD. EVERYONE'S WATCHING MY DEBUT ADVENTURE...
IT'S NOT AN ADVENTURE; YOU'VE BECOME A THREAT TO HEALTH.
A ROGUE GERM.
YOU AND YOUR COLLABORATORS DELIBERATELY INTRODUCED A CONTAMINATED PARA-PERSONA INTO SOCIETY; YOU CREATED "SPARTACUS HUGHES" WITH THE INTENT TO DESTABILIZE STATUS Q AND PROVOKE THE HAND.
AYE IN BY RA WEY, YIR CAMERAS ARE "BROADCASTEN" STRAIGHT OANTAY AN INTERNET SNUFF SITE, PAL.
THURRZ SICK BASTURTS WHAKKEN AFF RIGHT NOO, TRY-ENTAY TIME THURR CUM TAY YOOR LAST BREATH.
I WON'T WIND UP IN YOUR SURGERIES! I WON'T BE LOBOTOMIZED OR EXPERIMENTED ON...
I'M SORRY, MAX, BUT ACTUALLY YOU WILL.
YOU GOT WHAT YOU WANTED.
YOU SHOULD HAVE STAYED INDOORS WHERE YOU WERE SAFE.
DON'T DO THIS TO ME, GREG!
I'M THE HERO!
AND MY NAME'S NED SLADE.

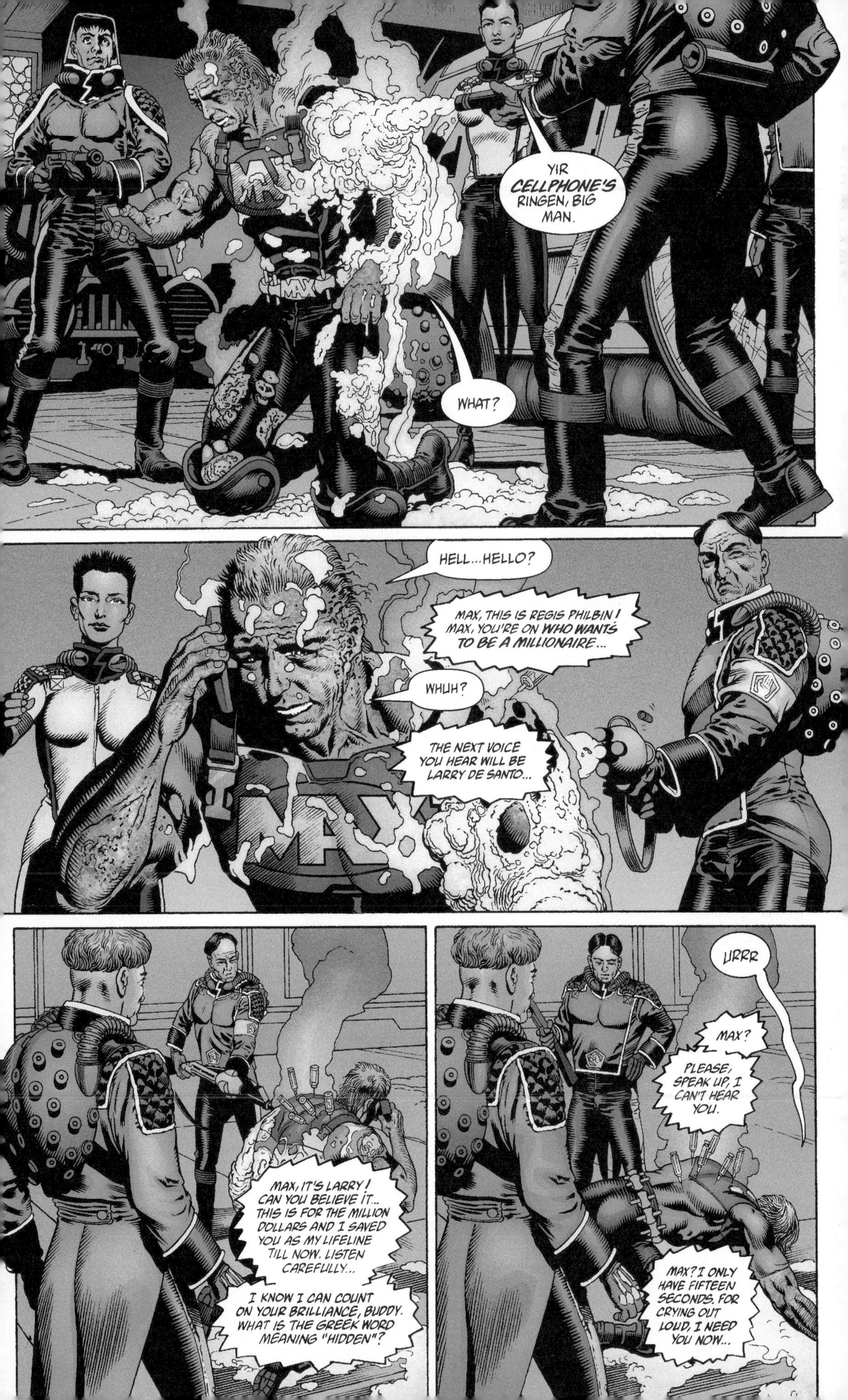

YIR CELLPHONE'S RINGEN, BIG MAN.
WHAT?
HELL...HELLO?
MAX, THIS IS REGIS PHILBIN! MAX, YOU'RE ON WHO WANTS TO BE A MILLIONAIRE...
WHUH?
THE NEXT VOICE YOU HEAR WILL BE LARRY DE SANTO...
MAX, IT'S LARRY! CAN YOU BELIEVE IT... THIS IS FOR THE MILLION DOLLARS AND I SAVED YOU AS MY LIFELINE TILL NOW. LISTEN CAREFULLY...
I KNOW I CAN COUNT ON YOUR BRILLIANCE, BUDDY. WHAT IS THE GREEK WORD MEANING "HIDDEN"?
URRR
MAX?
PLEASE, SPEAK UP, I CAN'T HEAR YOU.
MAX? I ONLY HAVE FIFTEEN SECONDS. FOR CRYING OUT LOUD, I NEED YOU NOW...

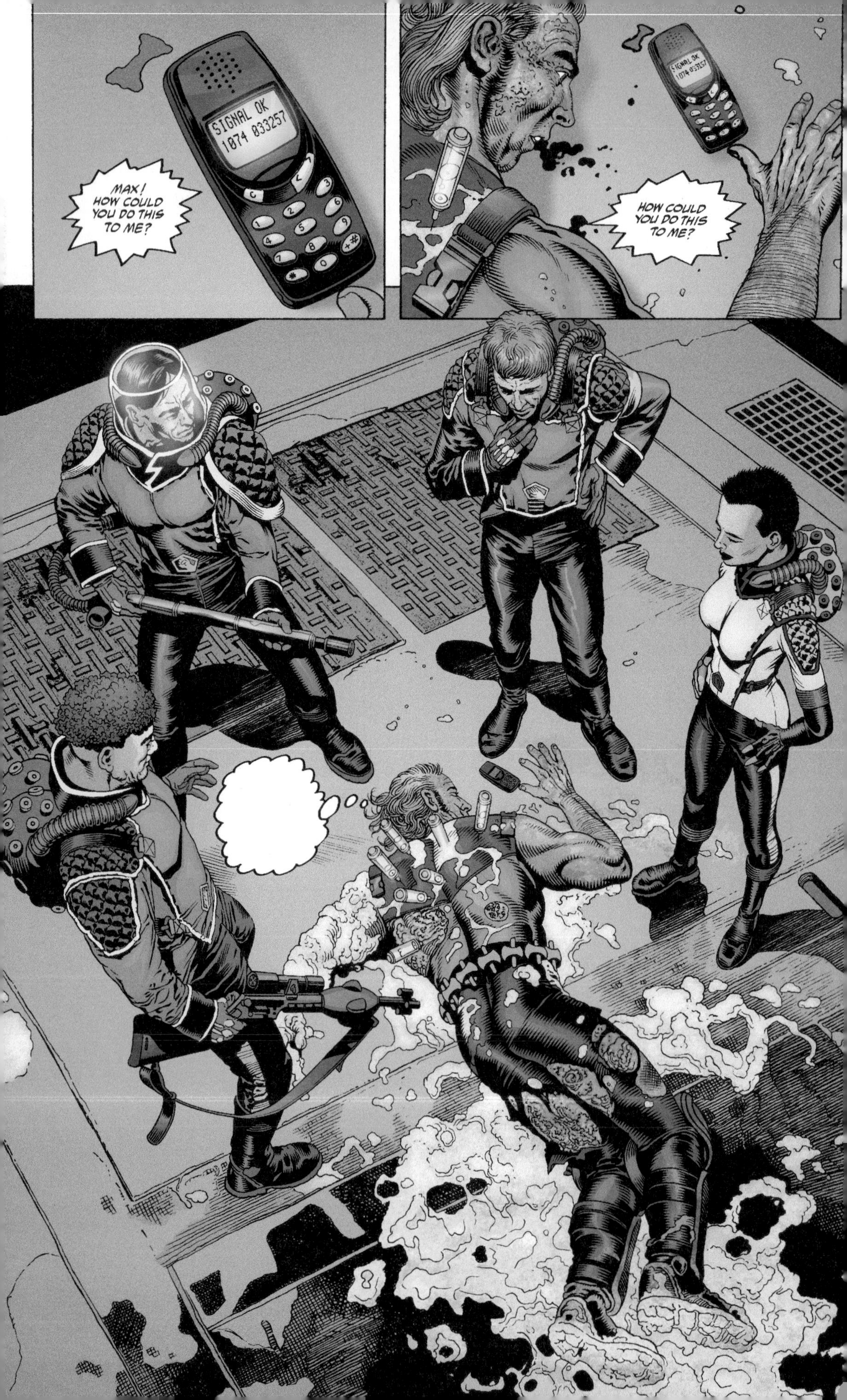
SIGNAL OK
1074 033257
MAX! HOW COULD YOU DO THIS TO ME?
SIGNAL OK
1074 033257
HOW COULD YOU DO THIS TO ME?

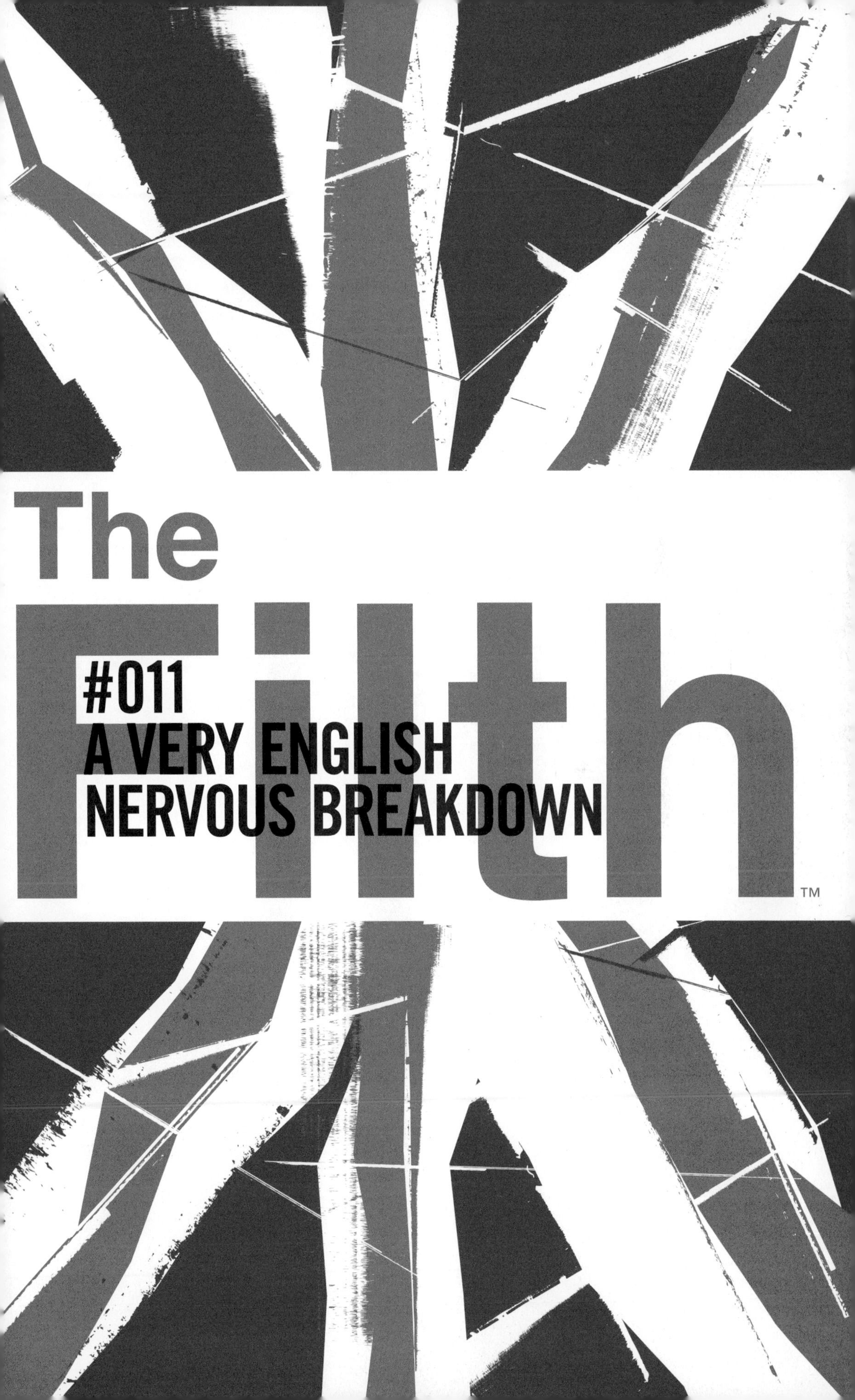
The Filth™
#011
A VERY ENGLISH
NERVOUS BREAKDOWN

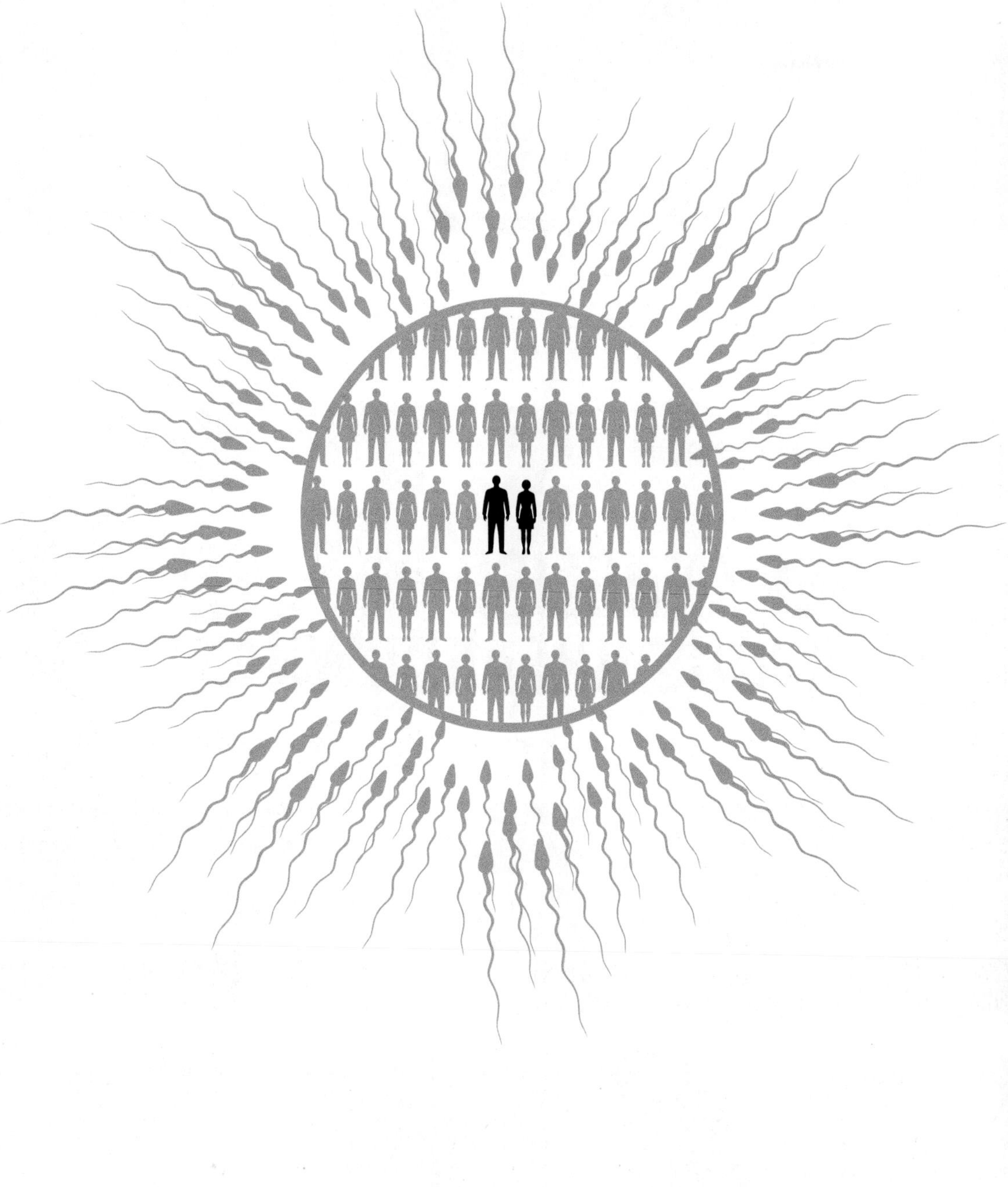

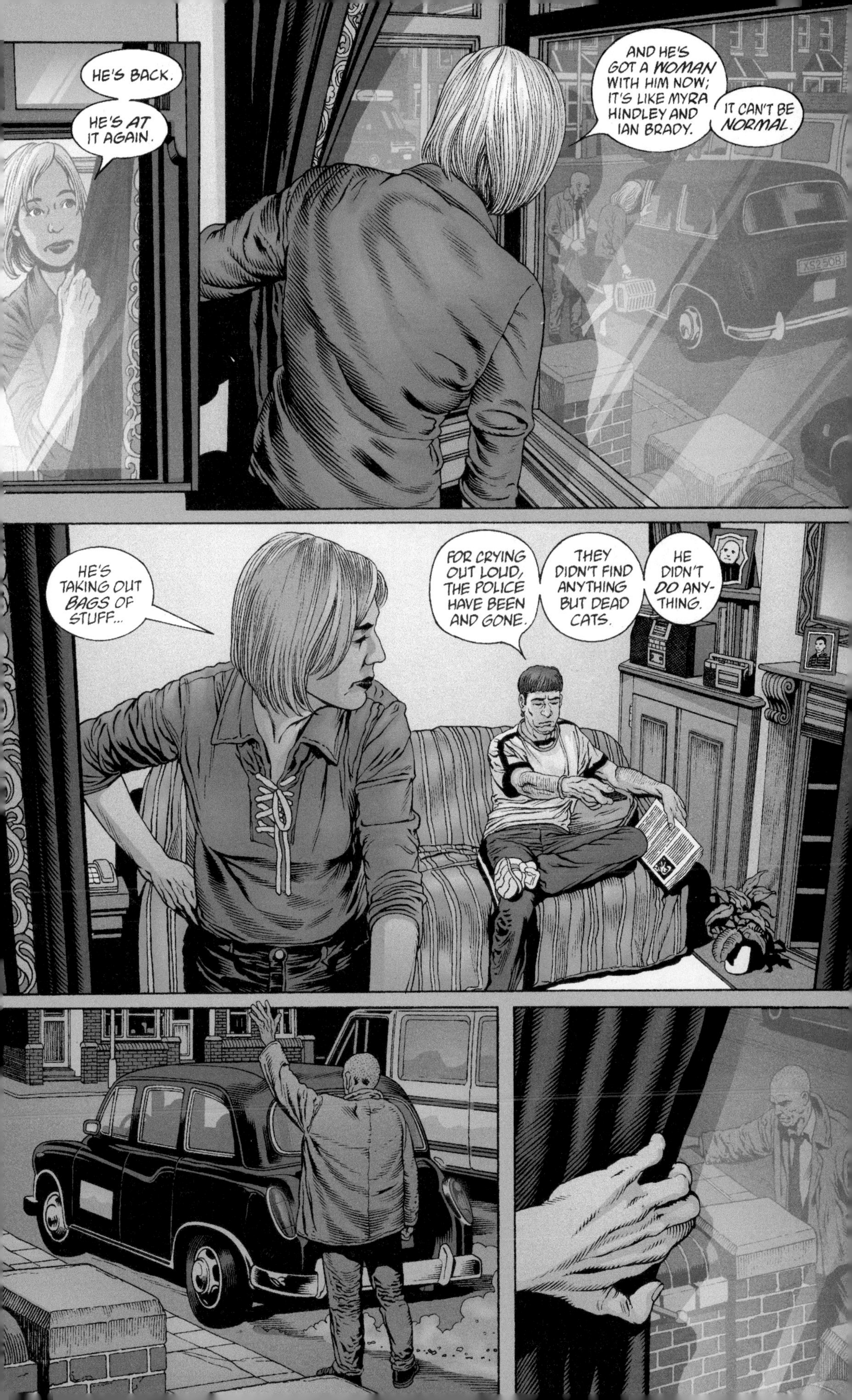
HE'S BACK.
HE'S AT IT AGAIN.
AND HE'S GOT A WOMAN WITH HIM NOW; IT'S LIKE MYRA HINDLEY AND IAN BRADY.
IT CAN'T BE NORMAL.
HE'S TAKING OUT BAGS OF STUFF...
FOR CRYING OUT LOUD, THE POLICE HAVE BEEN AND GONE.
THEY DIDN'T FIND ANYTHING BUT DEAD CATS.
HE DIDN'T DO ANYTHING.

THIS WAS MY *PLACE.*

I COULD UNWIND HERE AND BE KIND.

THIS HOUSE WAS WHERE I COULD COME TO GET AWAY FROM THE *HORROR.* WHERE I COULD FORGET THE JOB...

THAT'S WHAT YOU ALL *TOLD* ME.

GREG'S JUST A SAFE HOUSE, YOU SAID. HE'S NOT *REAL,* HE'S JUST A COVER STORY...

MY LOVELY CAT'S GONE. THE POLICE DUG UP MY BACK GARDEN. I'VE LOST MY JOB. THE NEIGHBORS THINK I'M A PEDOPHILE...

I'VE GOT NOTHING TO *LOSE* NOW, DO I?

SO I'M JUST GOING TO STAY HERE.

AND WAIT FOR THEM TO COME AND *GET* ME AGAIN.

MAYBE I *AM* JUST A LOONY WITH A STOLEN FACE.

MAYBE YOU'RE ALL RIGHT AND GREG IS JUST AN ARTIFICIAL PERSONALITY THEY INJECT INTO YOUR HEAD AND THERE YOU ARE.

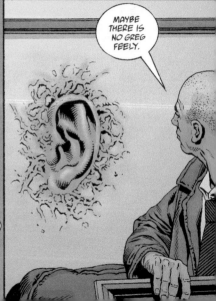

MAYBE THERE IS NO GREG FEELY.

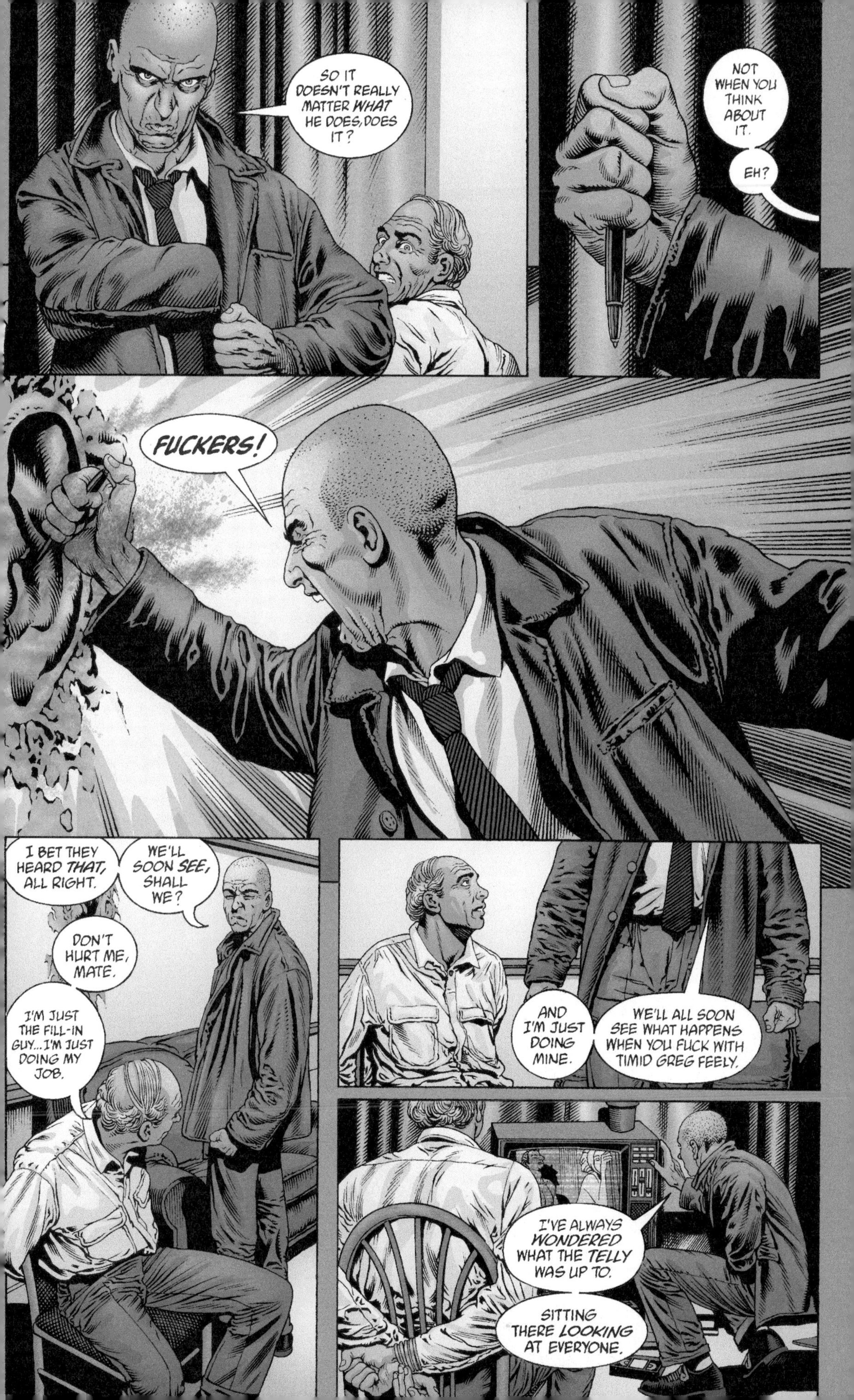
SO IT DOESN'T REALLY MATTER WHAT HE DOES, DOES IT?
NOT WHEN YOU THINK ABOUT IT.
EH?
FUCKERS!
I BET THEY HEARD THAT, ALL RIGHT.
WE'LL SOON SEE, SHALL WE?
DON'T HURT ME, MATE.
I'M JUST THE FILL-IN GUY...I'M JUST DOING MY JOB.
AND I'M JUST DOING MINE.
WE'LL ALL SOON SEE WHAT HAPPENS WHEN YOU FUCK WITH TIMID GREG FEELY.
I'VE ALWAYS WONDERED WHAT THE TELLY WAS UP TO.
SITTING THERE LOOKING AT EVERYONE.

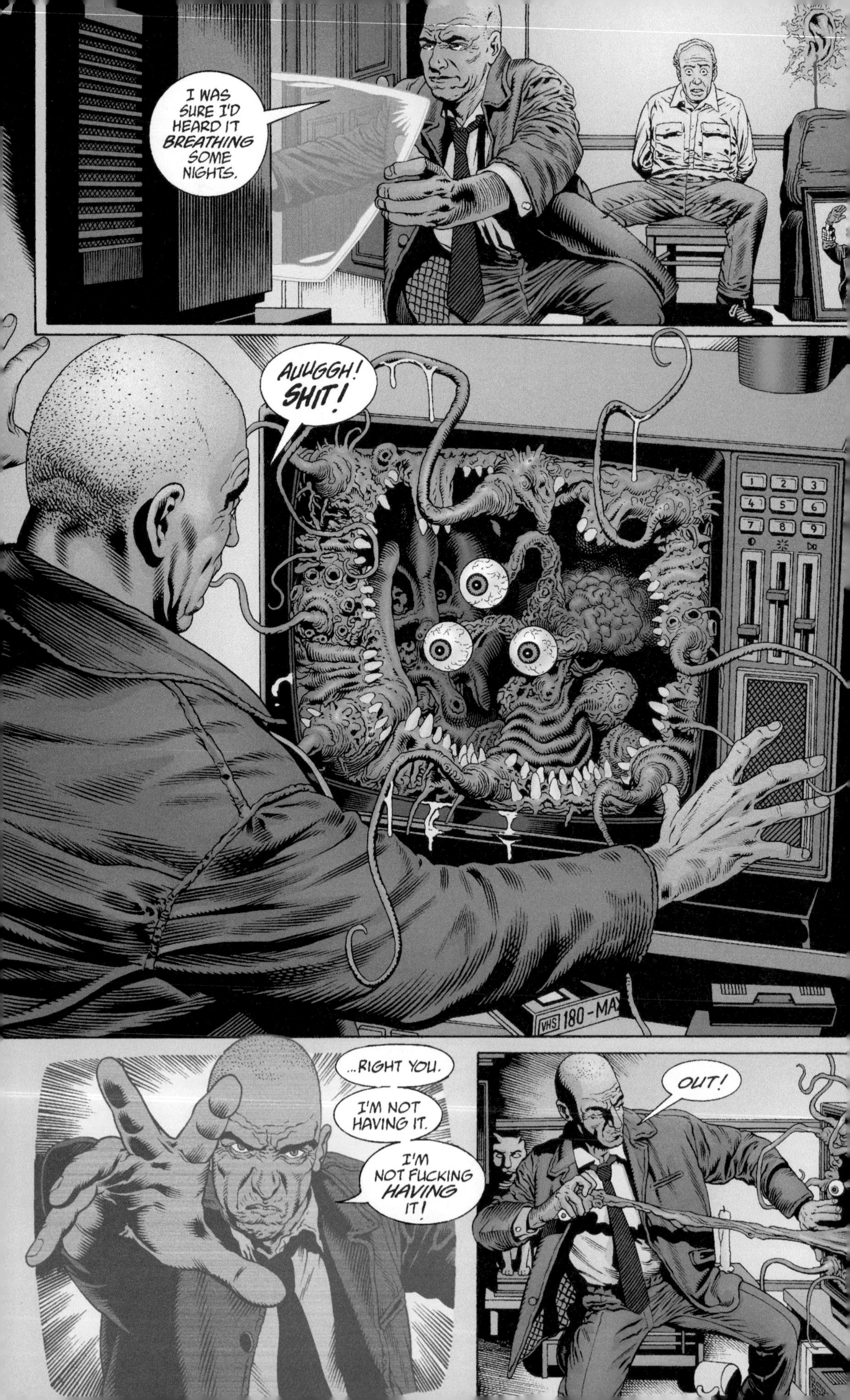

I WAS SURE I'D HEARD IT BREATHING SOME NIGHTS.
AUUGGH! SHIT!
VHS 180-MAX
...RIGHT YOU.
I'M NOT HAVING IT.
I'M NOT FUCKING HAVING IT!
OUT!

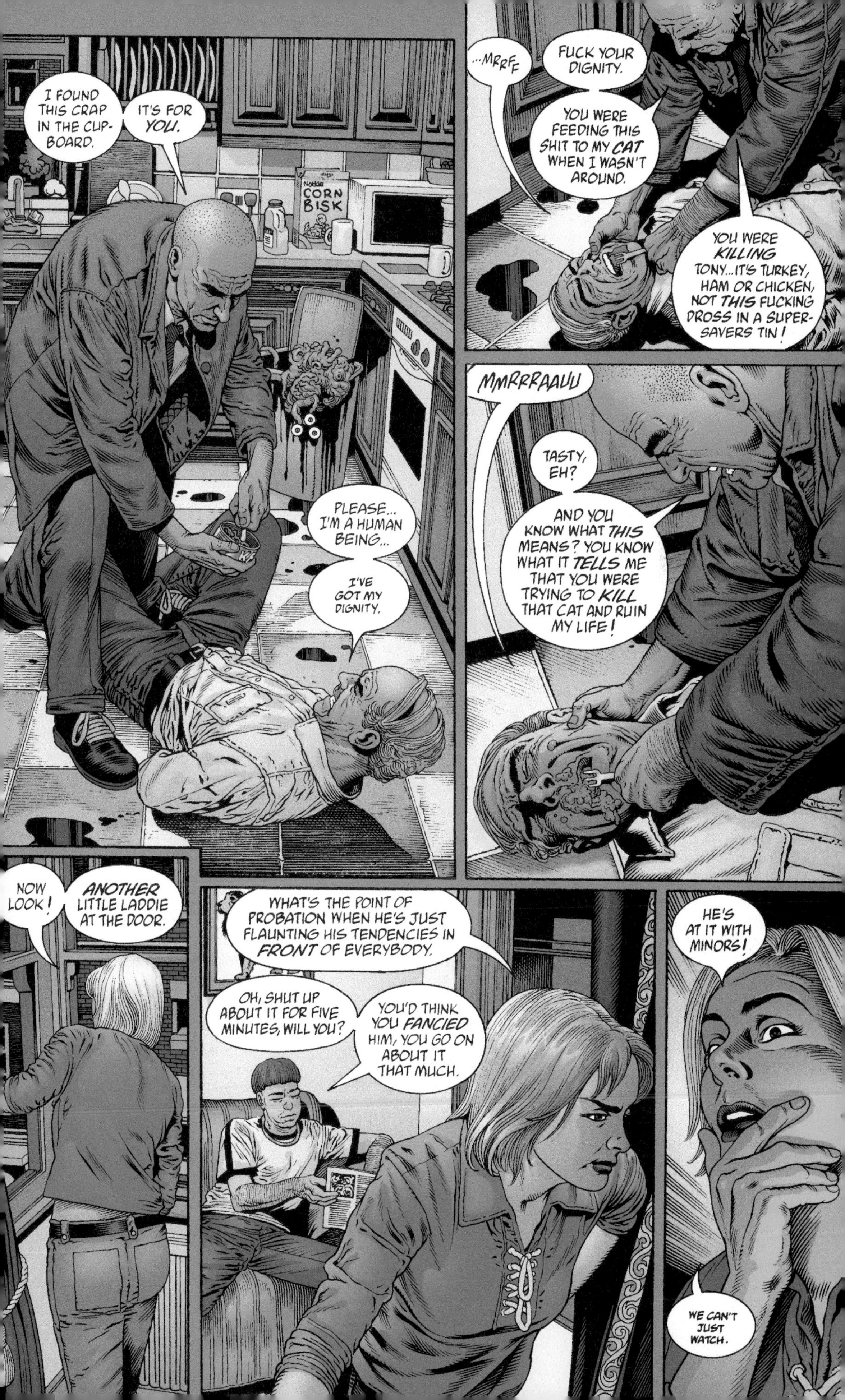
I FOUND THIS CRAP IN THE CUPBOARD.
IT'S FOR YOU.
CORN BISK
PLEASE... I'M A HUMAN BEING...
I'VE GOT MY DIGNITY.
...MRRFF
FUCK YOUR DIGNITY.
YOU WERE FEEDING THIS SHIT TO MY CAT WHEN I WASN'T AROUND.
YOU WERE KILLING TONY...IT'S TURKEY, HAM OR CHICKEN, NOT THIS FUCKING DROSS IN A SUPER-SAVERS TIN!
MMRRRAAUU
TASTY, EH?
AND YOU KNOW WHAT THIS MEANS? YOU KNOW WHAT IT TELLS ME THAT YOU WERE TRYING TO KILL THAT CAT AND RUIN MY LIFE!
NOW LOOK!
ANOTHER LITTLE LADDIE AT THE DOOR.
WHAT'S THE POINT OF PROBATION WHEN HE'S JUST FLAUNTING HIS TENDENCIES IN FRONT OF EVERYBODY.
OH, SHUT UP ABOUT IT FOR FIVE MINUTES, WILL YOU?
YOU'D THINK YOU FANCIED HIM, YOU GO ON ABOUT IT THAT MUCH.
HE'S AT IT WITH MINORS!
WE CAN'T JUST WATCH.

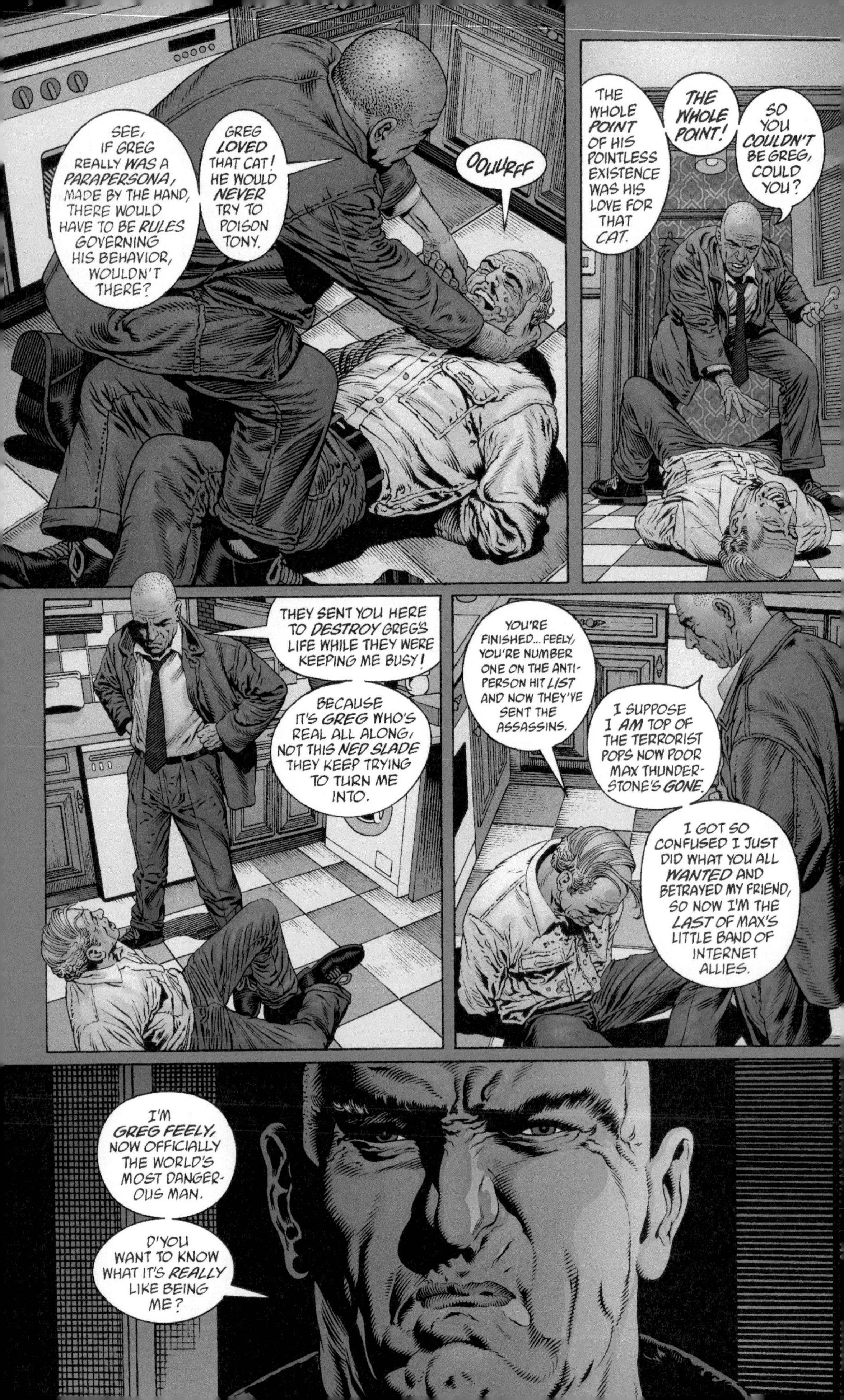
SEE, IF GREG REALLY *WAS* A *PARAPERSONA*, MADE BY THE HAND, THERE WOULD HAVE TO BE *RULES* GOVERNING HIS BEHAVIOR, WOULDN'T THERE?
GREG *LOVED* THAT CAT! HE WOULD *NEVER* TRY TO POISON TONY.
OOUURFF
THE WHOLE *POINT* OF HIS POINTLESS EXISTENCE WAS HIS LOVE FOR THAT *CAT*.
THE WHOLE POINT!
SO YOU *COULDN'T* BE GREG, COULD YOU?
THEY SENT YOU HERE TO *DESTROY* GREG'S LIFE WHILE THEY WERE KEEPING ME BUSY!
BECAUSE IT'S *GREG* WHO'S REAL ALL ALONG, NOT THIS *NED SLADE* THEY KEEP TRYING TO TURN ME INTO.
YOU'RE FINISHED... FEELY, YOU'RE NUMBER ONE ON THE ANTI-PERSON HIT *LIST* AND NOW THEY'VE SENT THE ASSASSINS.
I SUPPOSE I *AM* TOP OF THE TERRORIST POPS NOW POOR MAX THUNDER-STONE'S *GONE*.
I GOT SO CONFUSED I JUST DID WHAT YOU ALL *WANTED* AND BETRAYED MY FRIEND, SO NOW I'M THE *LAST* OF MAX'S LITTLE BAND OF INTERNET ALLIES.
I'M *GREG FEELY*, NOW OFFICIALLY THE WORLD'S MOST DANGER-OUS MAN.
D'YOU WANT TO KNOW WHAT IT'S *REALLY* LIKE BEING ME?

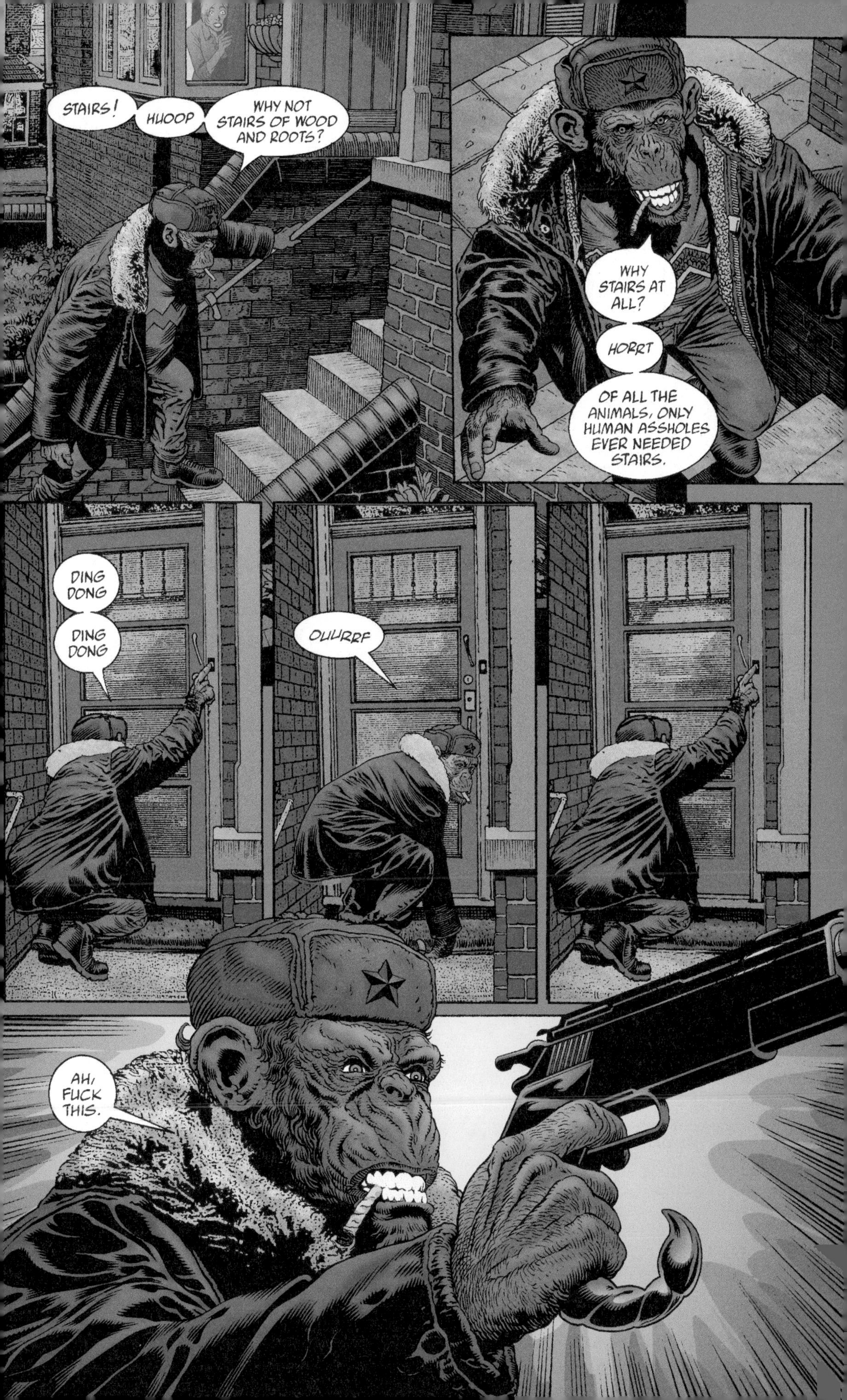
STAIRS!
HUOOP
WHY NOT STAIRS OF WOOD AND ROOTS?
WHY STAIRS AT ALL?
HORRT
OF ALL THE ANIMALS, ONLY HUMAN ASSHOLES EVER NEEDED STAIRS.
DING DONG
DING DONG
OUURRF
AH, FUCK THIS.

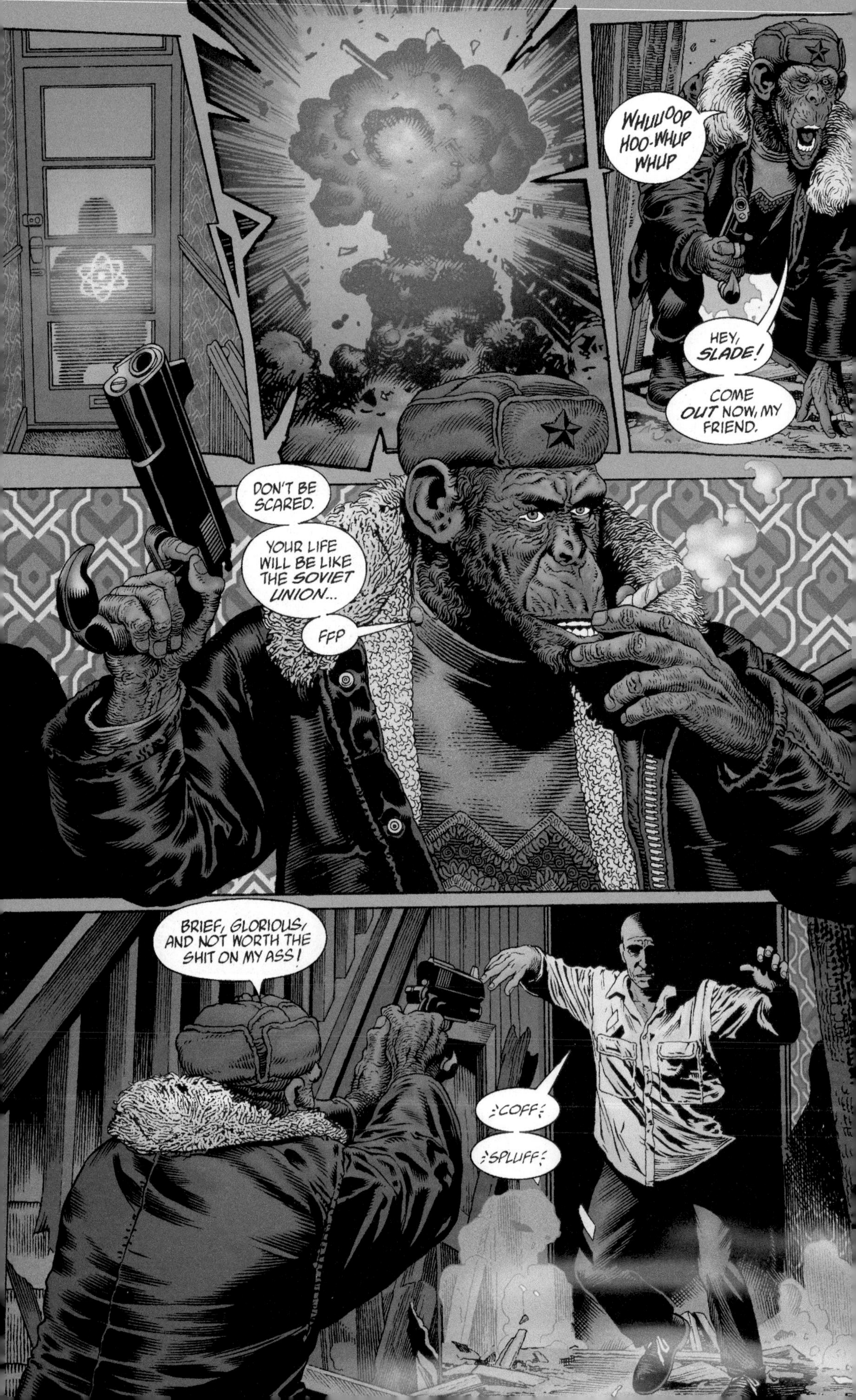
WHUUOOP HOO-WHUP WHUP
HEY, SLADE!
COME OUT NOW, MY FRIEND.
DON'T BE SCARED.
YOUR LIFE WILL BE LIKE THE SOVIET UNION...
FFP
BRIEF, GLORIOUS, AND NOT WORTH THE SHIT ON MY ASS!
COFF
SPLUFF

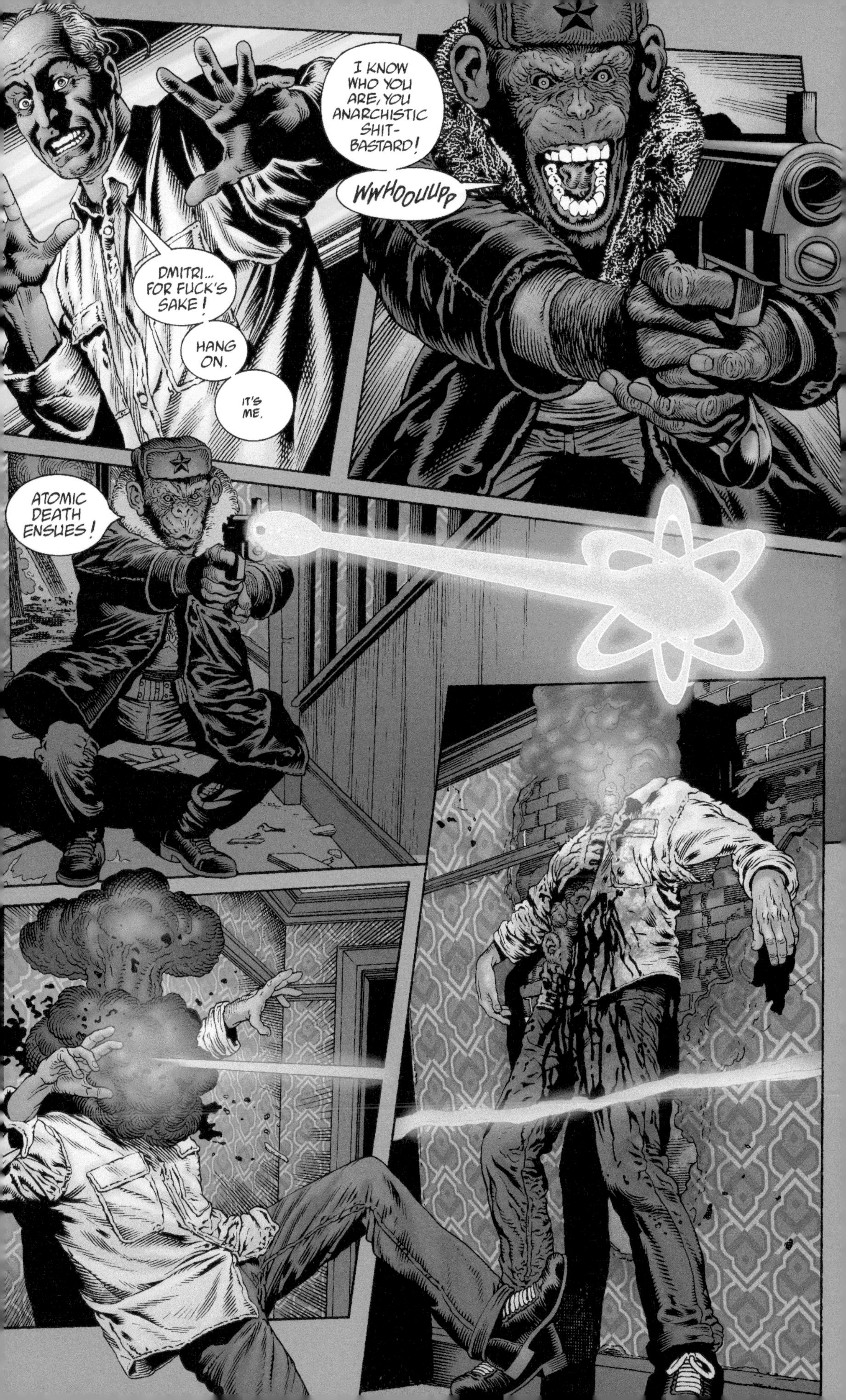
I KNOW WHO YOU ARE, YOU ANARCHISTIC SHIT-BASTARD!
WWHOOUUPP
DMITRI... FOR FUCK'S SAKE!
HANG ON.
IT'S ME.
ATOMIC DEATH ENSUES!

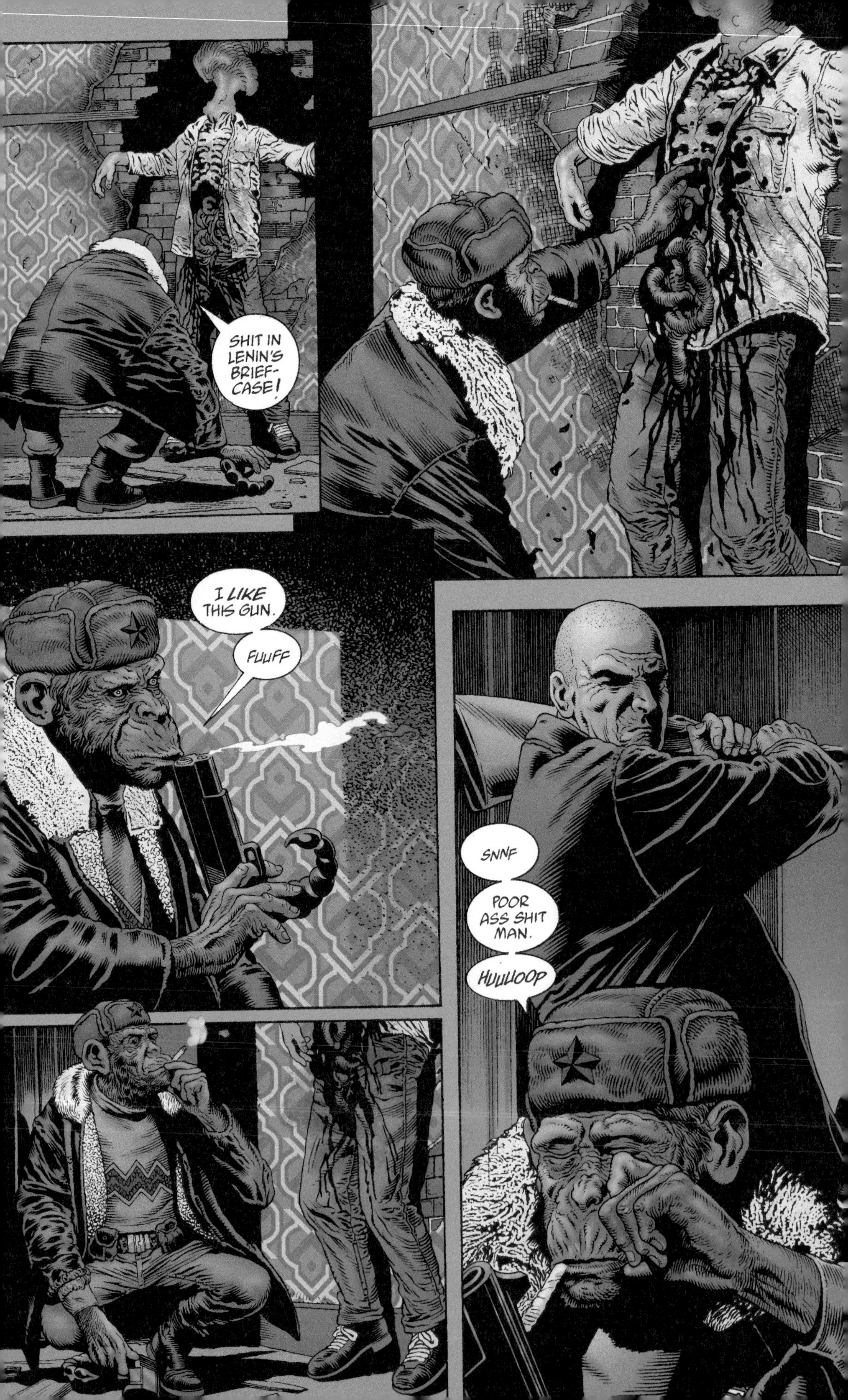
SHIT IN LENIN'S BRIEF-CASE!
I LIKE THIS GUN.
FUUFF
SNNF
POOR ASS SHIT MAN.
HUUUOOP

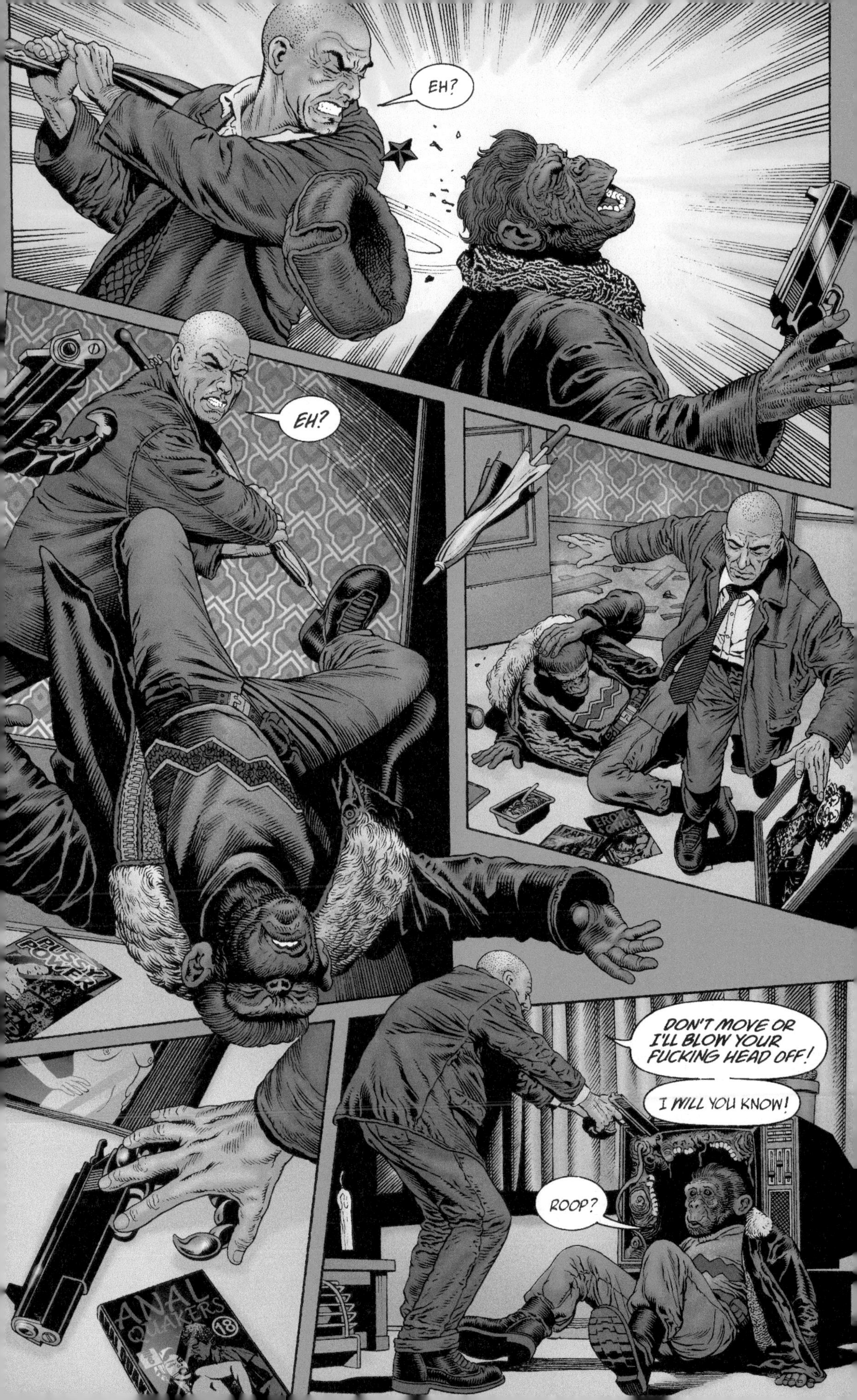
EH?
EH?
DON'T MOVE OR I'LL BLOW YOUR FUCKING HEAD OFF!
I WILL YOU KNOW!
ROOP?

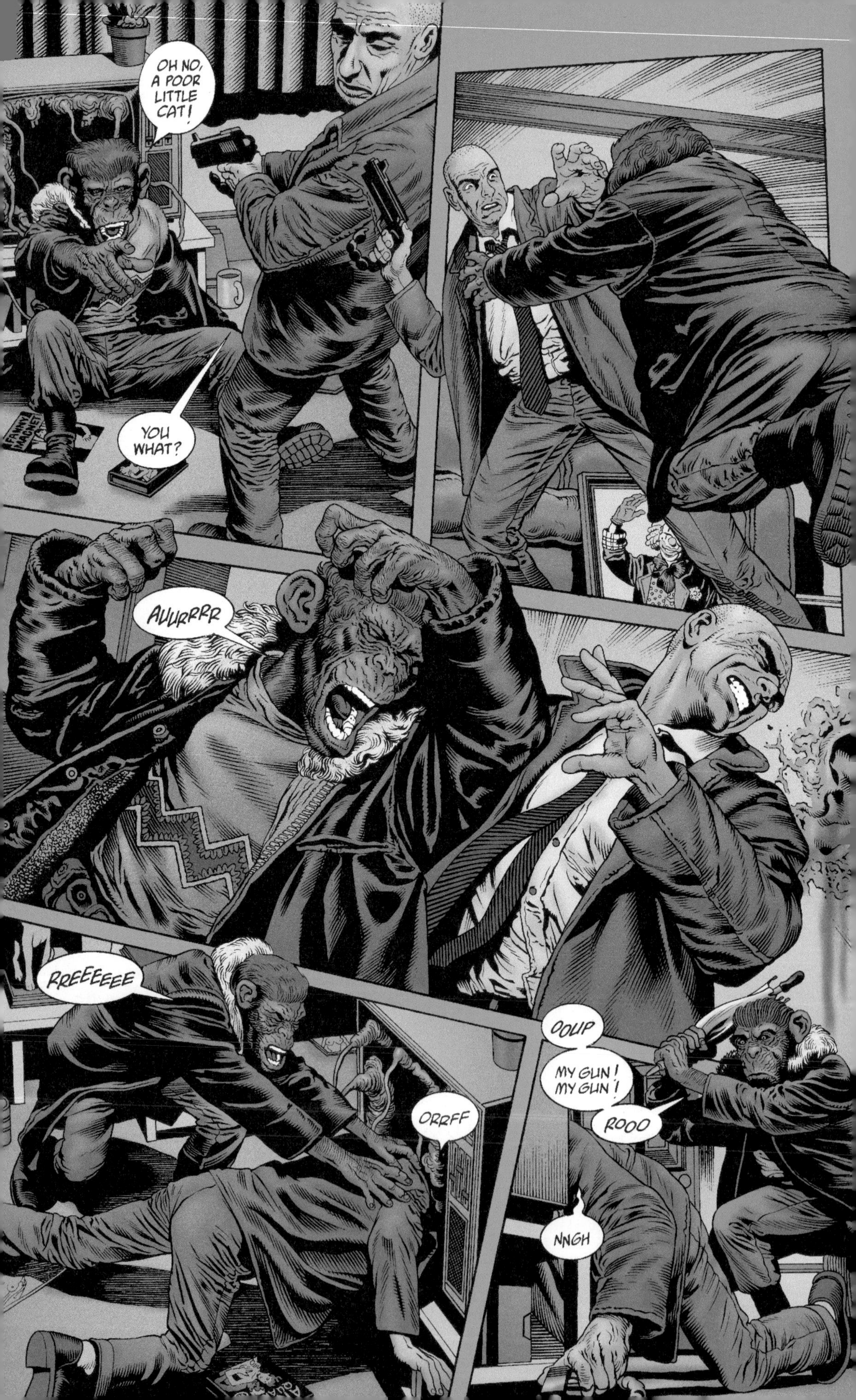
OH NO, A POOR LITTLE CAT!
YOU WHAT?
AUURRRR
RREEEEEEE
ORRFF
OOUP
MY GUN! MY GUN!
ROOO
NNGH

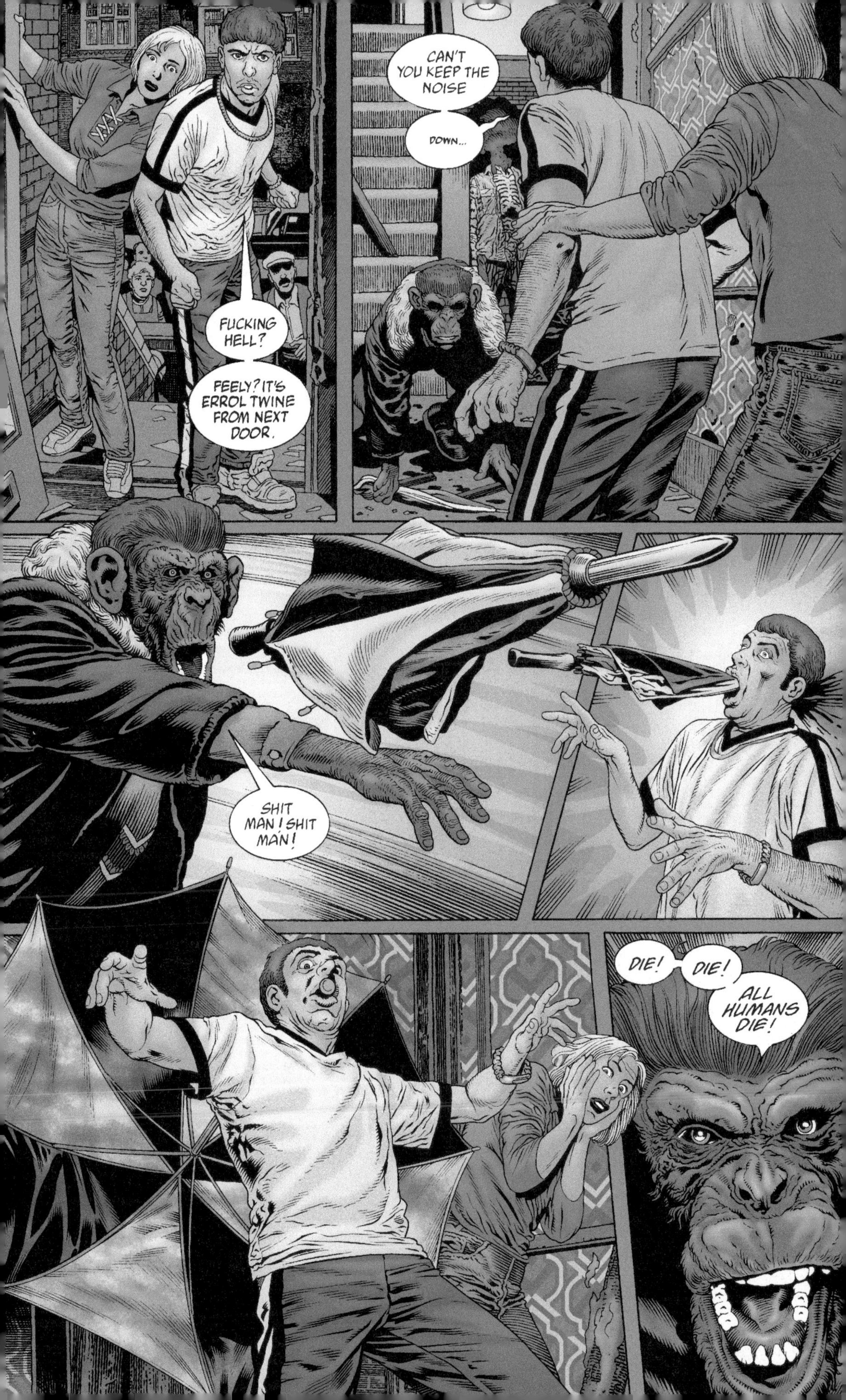
FUCKING HELL?
FEELY? IT'S ERROL TWINE FROM NEXT DOOR.
CAN'T YOU KEEP THE NOISE
DOWN...
SHIT MAN! SHIT MAN!
DIE!
DIE!
ALL HUMANS DIE!

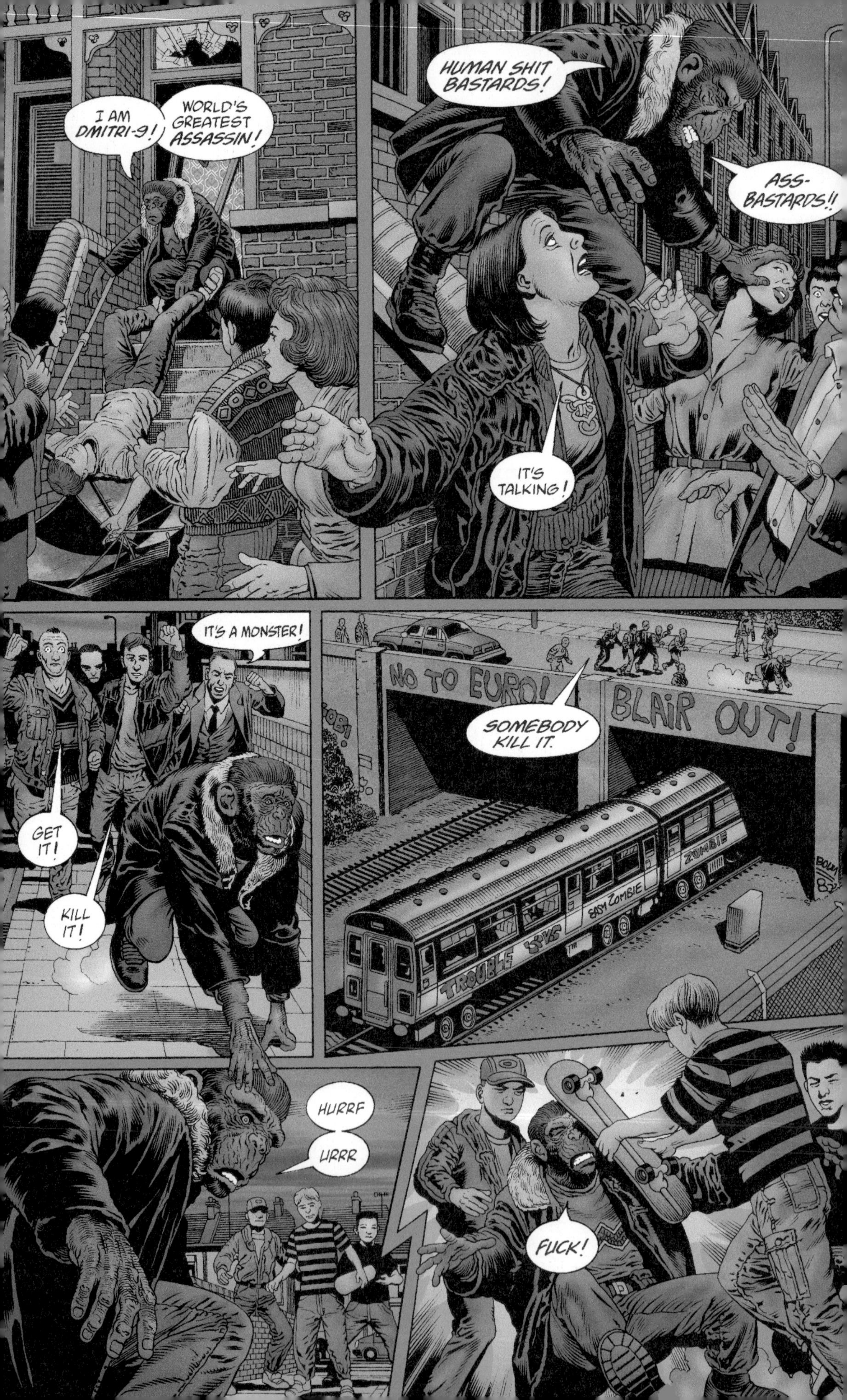
I AM DMITRI-9!
WORLD'S GREATEST ASSASSIN!
HUMAN SHIT BASTARDS!
ASS-BASTARDS!!
IT'S TALKING!
IT'S A MONSTER!
GET IT!
KILL IT!
NO TO EURO!
BLAIR OUT!
SOMEBODY KILL IT.
ZOMBIE
HURRF
URRR
FUCK!

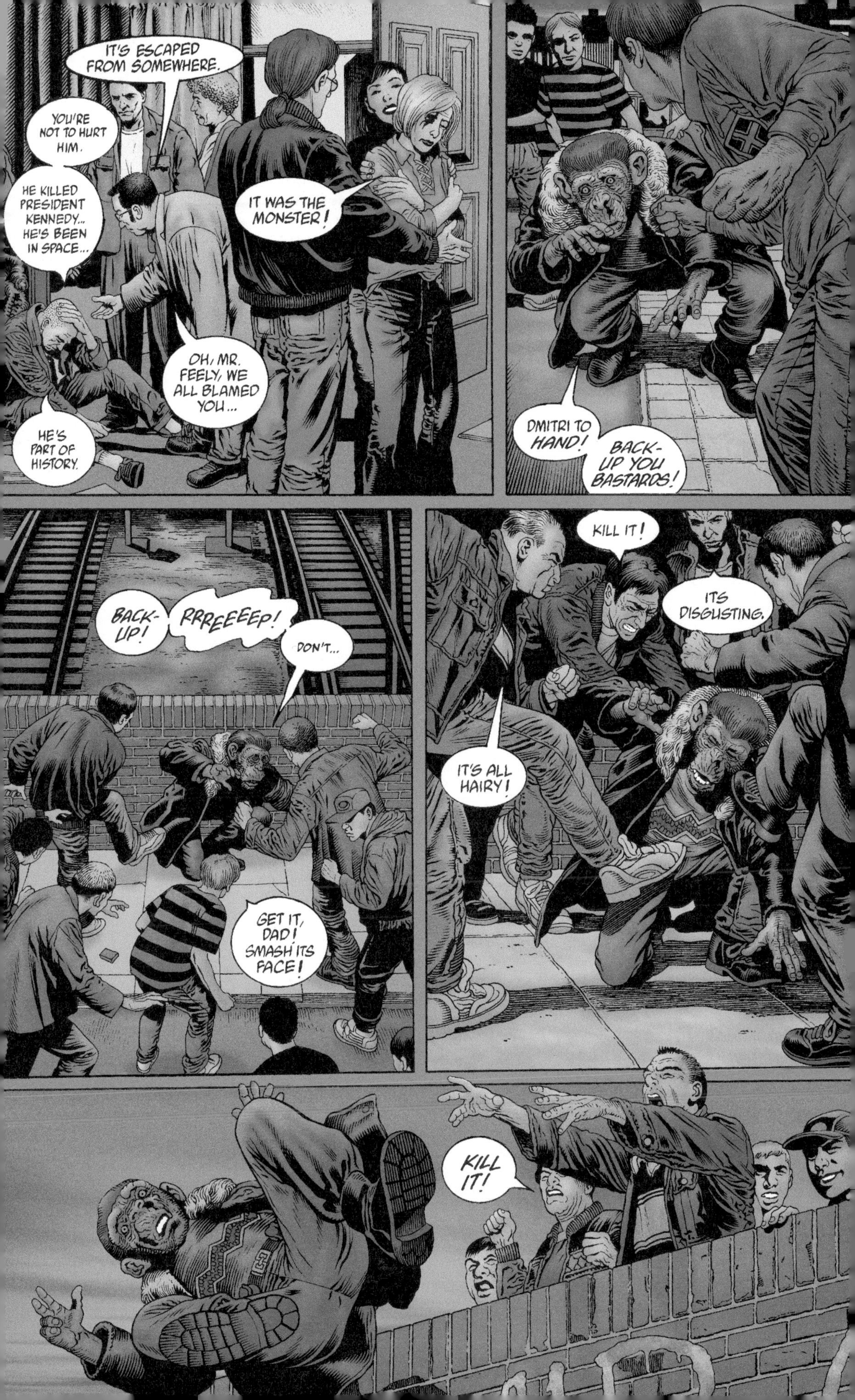
IT'S ESCAPED FROM SOMEWHERE.
YOU'RE NOT TO HURT HIM.
HE KILLED PRESIDENT KENNEDY... HE'S BEEN IN SPACE...
IT WAS THE MONSTER!
OH, MR. FEELY, WE ALL BLAMED YOU...
HE'S PART OF HISTORY.
DMITRI TO HAND!
BACK-UP YOU BASTARDS!
BACK-UP!
RRREEEEp!
DON'T...
GET IT, DAD! SMASH ITS FACE!
KILL IT!
ITS DISGUSTING.
IT'S ALL HAIRY!
KILL IT!

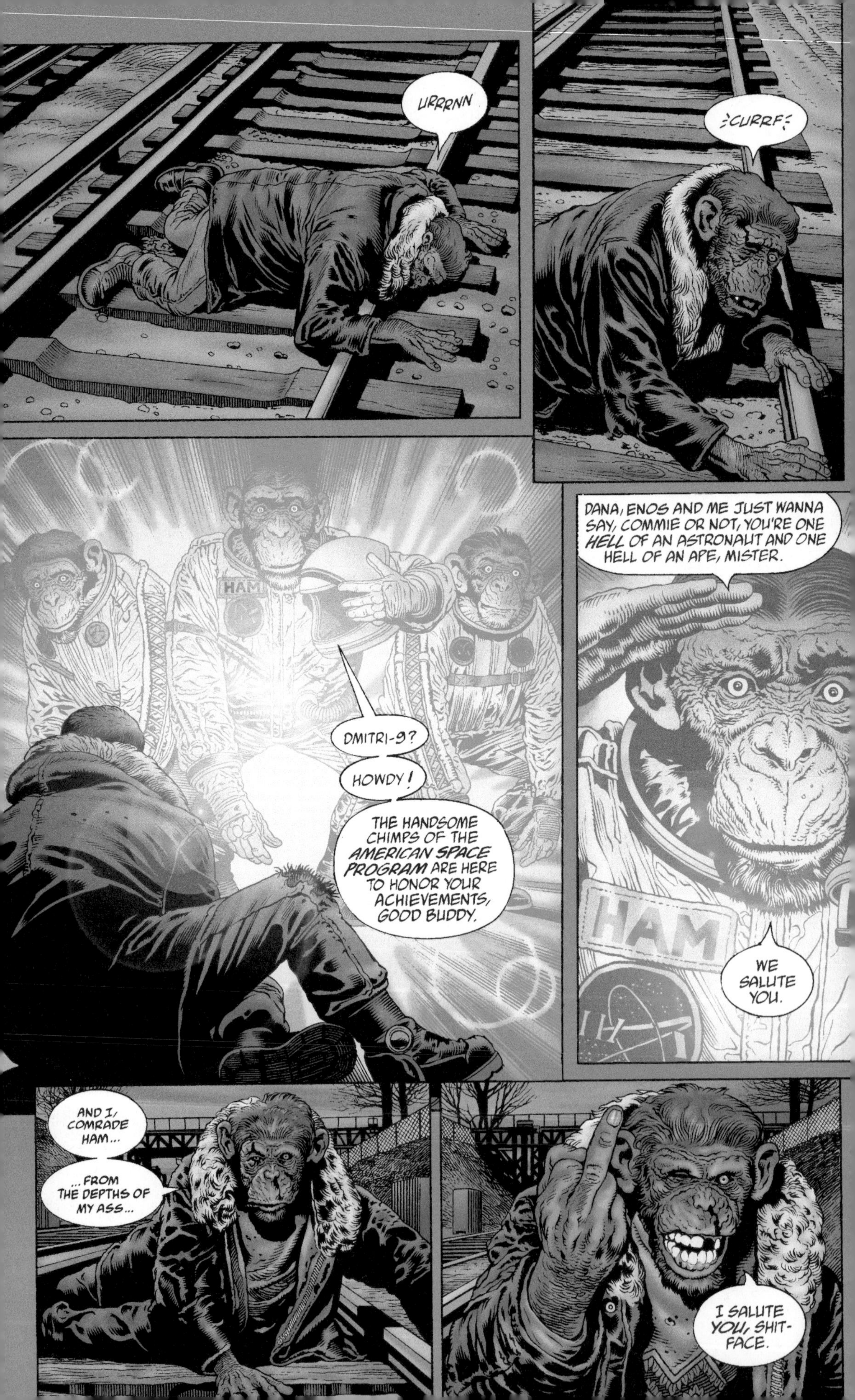
URRRNN
CURRF
DMITRI-9?
HOWDY!
THE HANDSOME CHIMPS OF THE AMERICAN SPACE PROGRAM ARE HERE TO HONOR YOUR ACHIEVEMENTS, GOOD BUDDY.
DANA, ENOS AND ME JUST WANNA SAY, COMMIE OR NOT, YOU'RE ONE HELL OF AN ASTRONAUT AND ONE HELL OF AN APE, MISTER.
WE SALUTE YOU.
AND I, COMRADE HAM...
...FROM THE DEPTHS OF MY ASS...
I SALUTE YOU, SHIT-FACE.
HAM

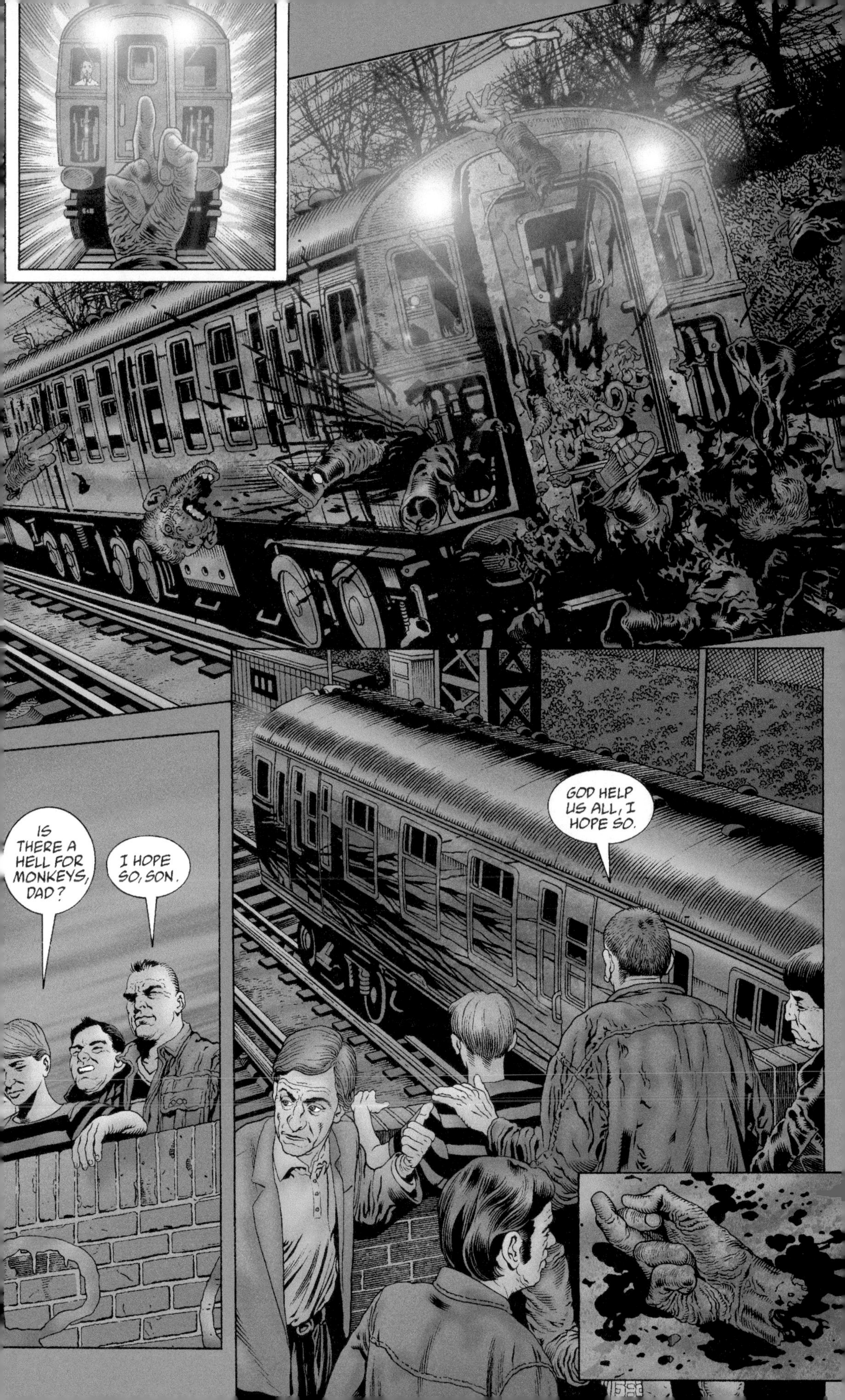
IS THERE A HELL FOR MONKEYS, DAD?
I HOPE SO, SON.
GOD HELP US ALL, I HOPE SO.

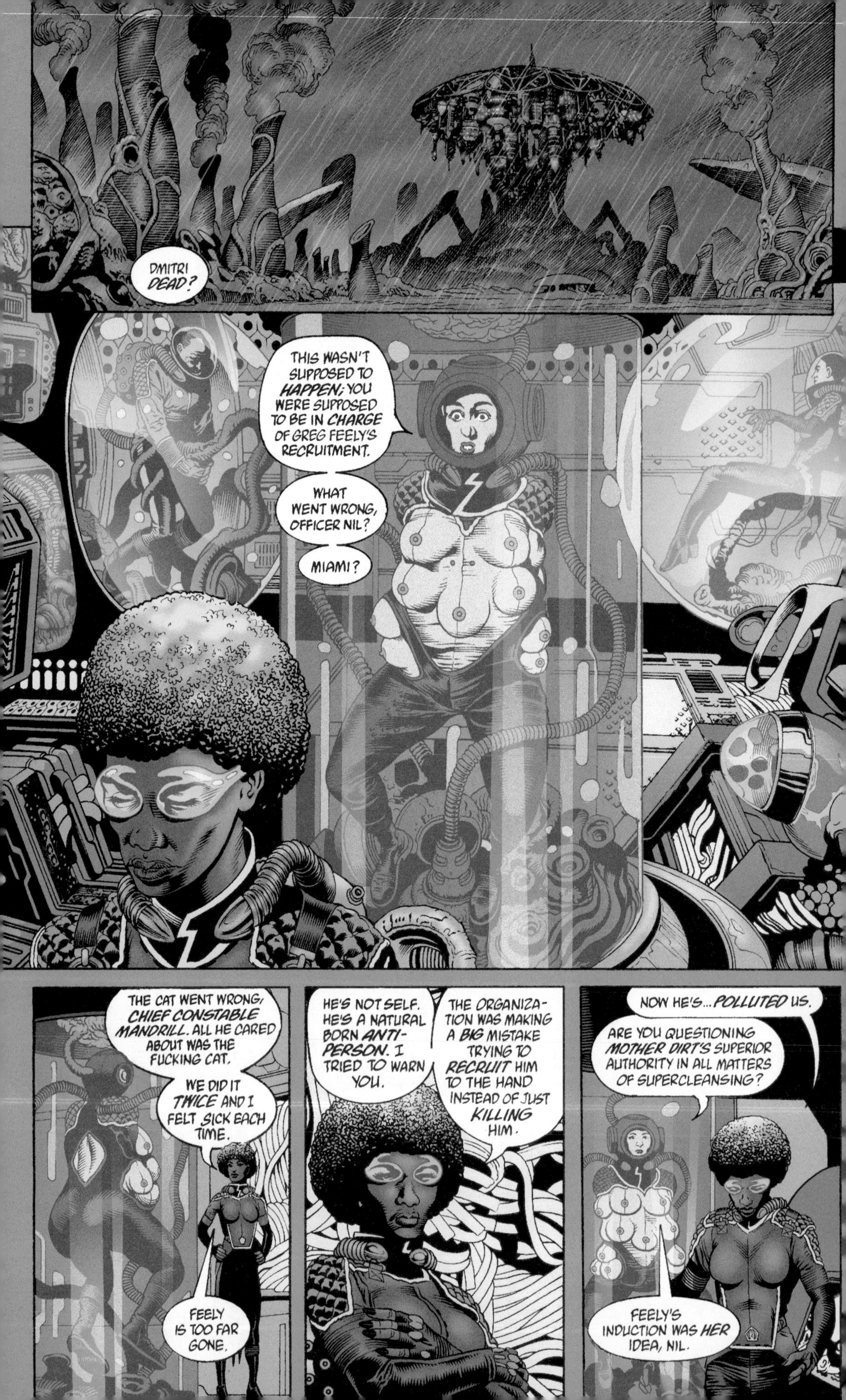

DMITRI DEAD?
THIS WASN'T SUPPOSED TO HAPPEN; YOU WERE SUPPOSED TO BE IN CHARGE OF GREG FEELY'S RECRUITMENT.
WHAT WENT WRONG, OFFICER NIL?
MIAMI?
THE CAT WENT WRONG, CHIEF CONSTABLE MANDRILL. ALL HE CARED ABOUT WAS THE FUCKING CAT.
WE DID IT TWICE AND I FELT SICK EACH TIME.
FEELY IS TOO FAR GONE.
HE'S NOT SELF. HE'S A NATURAL BORN ANTI-PERSON. I TRIED TO WARN YOU.
THE ORGANIZATION WAS MAKING A BIG MISTAKE TRYING TO RECRUIT HIM TO THE HAND INSTEAD OF JUST KILLING HIM.
NOW HE'S... POLLUTED US.
ARE YOU QUESTIONING MOTHER DIRT'S SUPERIOR AUTHORITY IN ALL MATTERS OF SUPERCLEANSING?
FEELY'S INDUCTION WAS HER IDEA, NIL.

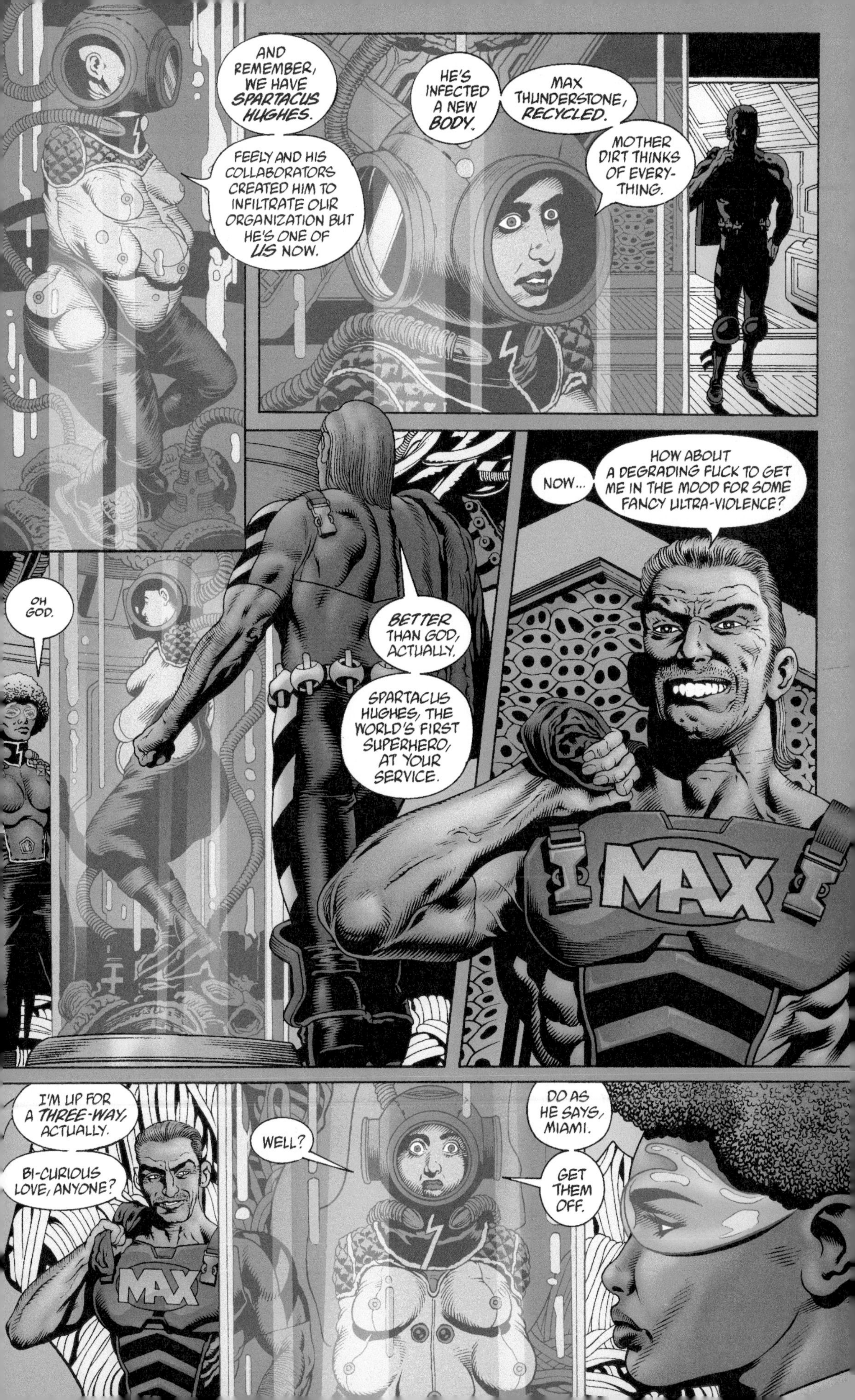
AND REMEMBER, WE HAVE *SPARTACUS HUGHES*.
FEELY AND HIS COLLABORATORS CREATED HIM TO INFILTRATE OUR ORGANIZATION BUT HE'S ONE OF *US* NOW.
HE'S INFECTED A NEW *BODY*.
MAX THUNDERSTONE, *RECYCLED*.
MOTHER DIRT THINKS OF EVERY-THING.
NOW...
HOW ABOUT A DEGRADING FUCK TO GET ME IN THE MOOD FOR SOME FANCY ULTRA-VIOLENCE?
OH GOD.
BETTER THAN GOD, ACTUALLY.
SPARTACUS HUGHES, THE WORLD'S FIRST SUPERHERO, AT YOUR SERVICE.
MAX
I'M UP FOR A *THREE-WAY*, ACTUALLY.
BI-CURIOUS LOVE, ANYONE?
MAX
WELL?
DO AS HE SAYS, MIAMI.
GET THEM OFF.

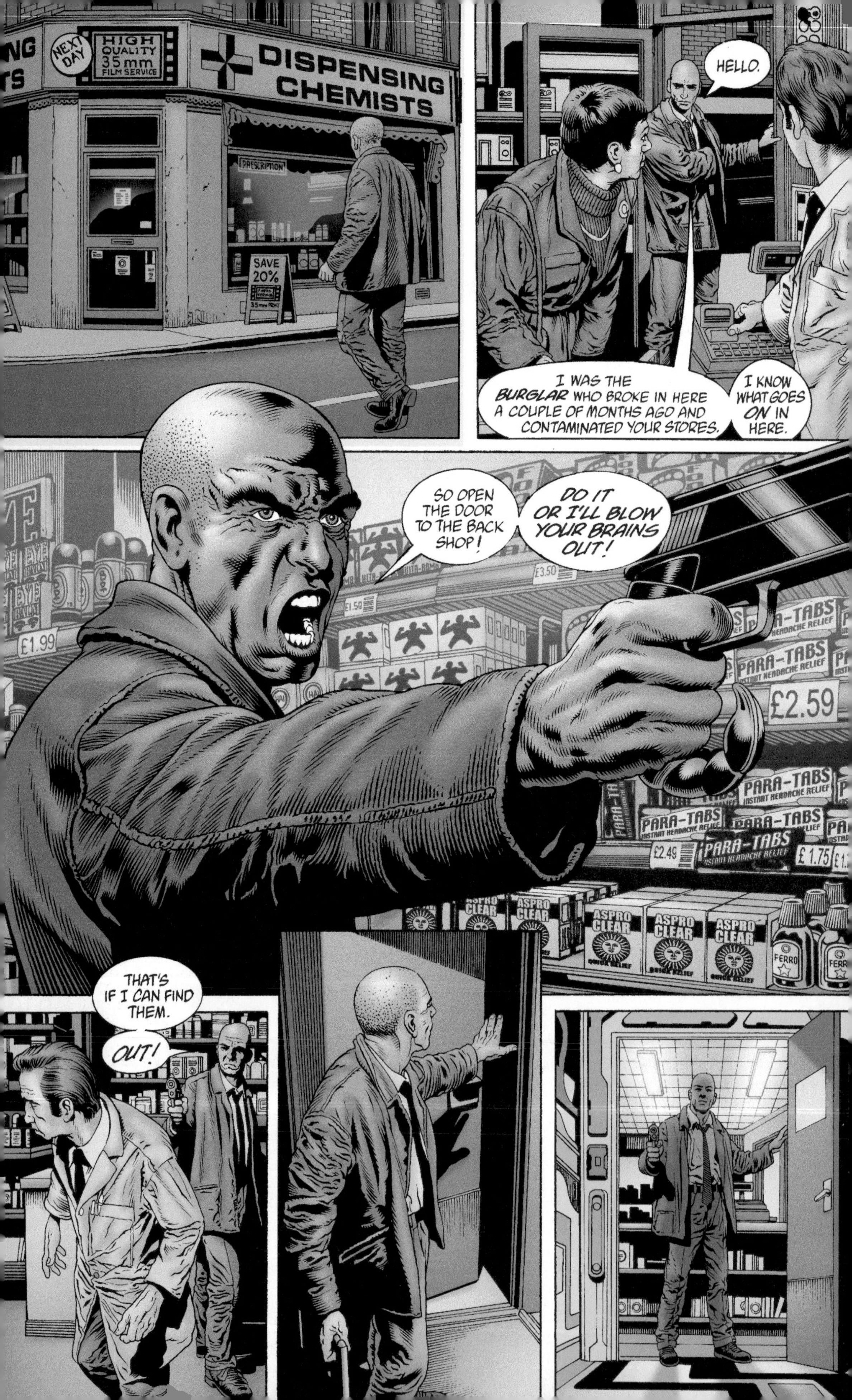
NEXT DAY
HIGH QUALITY 35mm FILM SERVICE
DISPENSING CHEMISTS
PRESCRIPTION
SAVE 20%
HELLO.
I WAS THE BURGLAR WHO BROKE IN HERE A COUPLE OF MONTHS AGO AND CONTAMINATED YOUR STORES.
I KNOW WHAT GOES ON IN HERE.
SO OPEN THE DOOR TO THE BACK SHOP!
DO IT OR I'LL BLOW YOUR BRAINS OUT!
£1.99
£3.50
£1.50
PARA-TABS INSTANT HEADACHE RELIEF
£2.59
£2.49
£1.75
ASPRO CLEAR QUICK RELIEF
FERRO
THAT'S IF I CAN FIND THEM.
OUT!

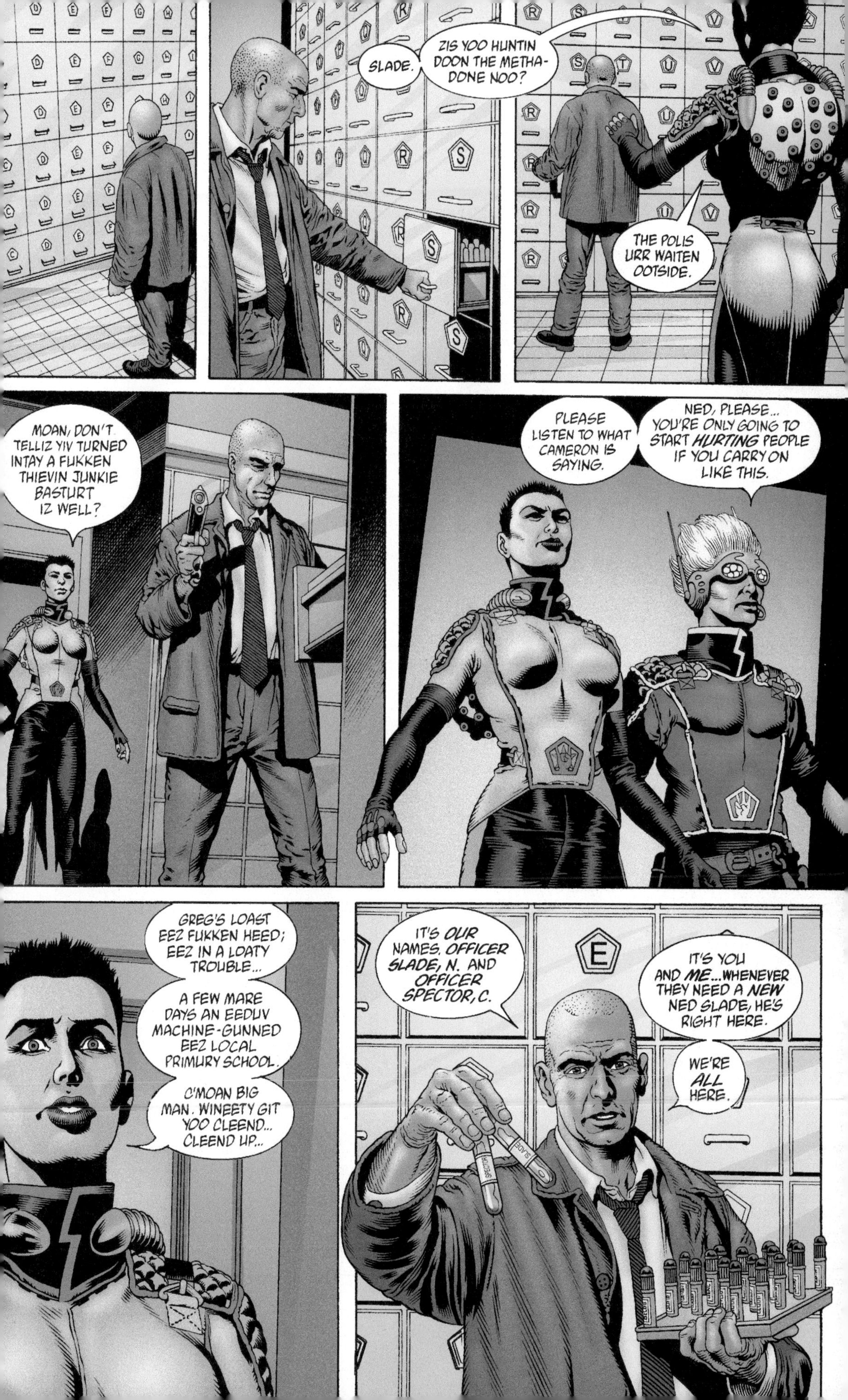
SLADE.
ZIS YOO HUNTIN DOON THE METHA-DONE NOO?
THE POLIS URR WAITEN OOTSIDE.
MOAN, DON'T TELLIZ YIV TURNED INTAY A FUKKEN THIEVIN JUNKIE BASTURT IZ WELL?
PLEASE LISTEN TO WHAT CAMERON IS SAYING.
NED, PLEASE... YOU'RE ONLY GOING TO START HURTING PEOPLE IF YOU CARRY ON LIKE THIS.
GREG'S LOAST EEZ FUKKEN HEED; EEZ IN A LOATY TROUBLE...
A FEW MARE DAYS AN EEDUV MACHINE-GUNNED EEZ LOCAL PRIMURY SCHOOL.
C'MOAN BIG MAN. WINEETY GIT YOO CLEEND... CLEEND UP...
IT'S OUR NAMES. OFFICER SLADE, N. AND OFFICER SPECTOR, C.
IT'S YOU AND ME... WHENEVER THEY NEED A NEW NED SLADE, HE'S RIGHT HERE.
WE'RE ALL HERE.

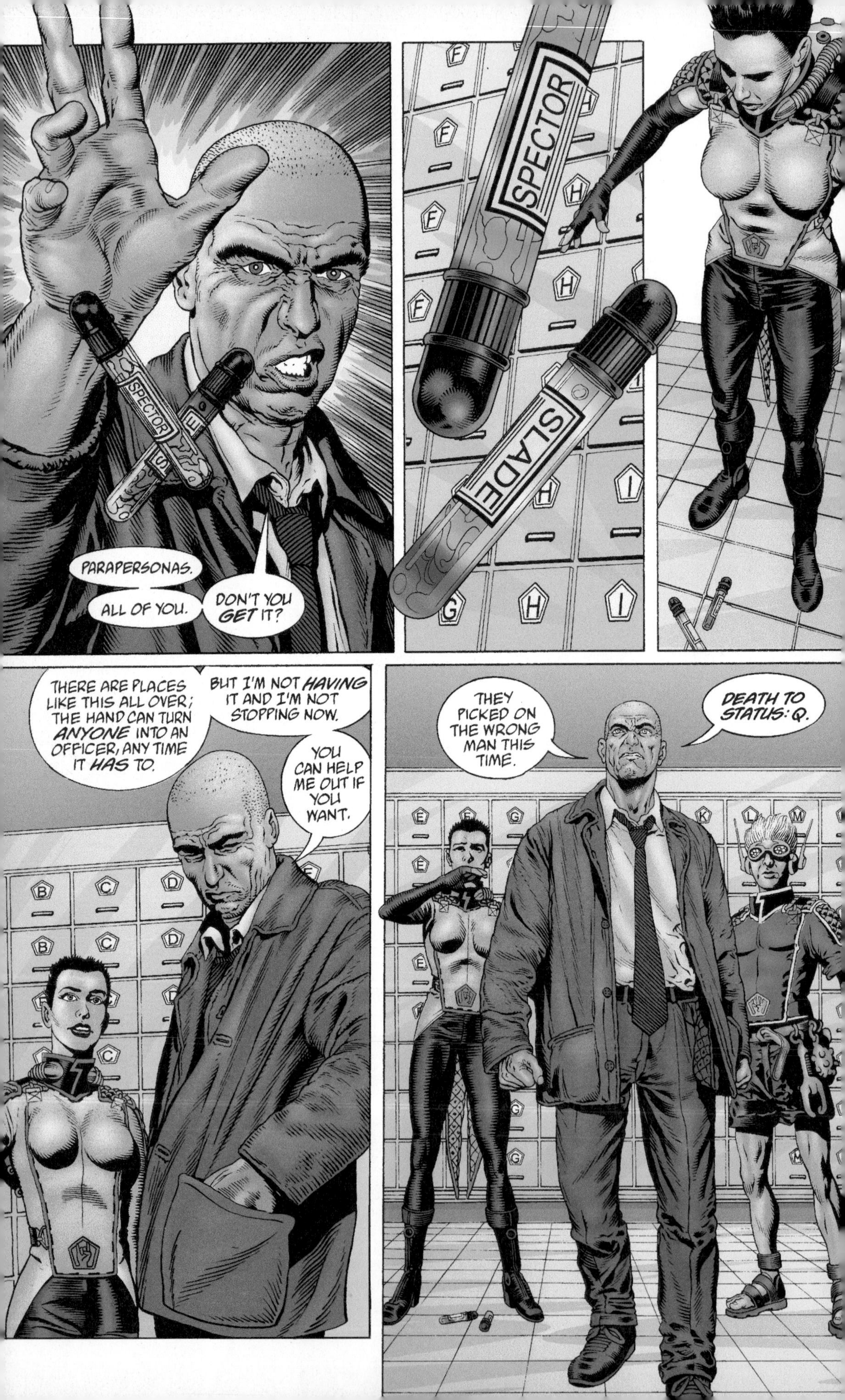

SPECTOR
SPECTOR
SLADE
PARAPERSONAS.
ALL OF YOU.
DON'T YOU GET IT?
THERE ARE PLACES LIKE THIS ALL OVER; THE HAND CAN TURN ANYONE INTO AN OFFICER, ANY TIME IT HAS TO.
BUT I'M NOT HAVING IT AND I'M NOT STOPPING NOW.
YOU CAN HELP ME OUT IF YOU WANT.
THEY PICKED ON THE WRONG MAN THIS TIME.
DEATH TO STATUS: Q.

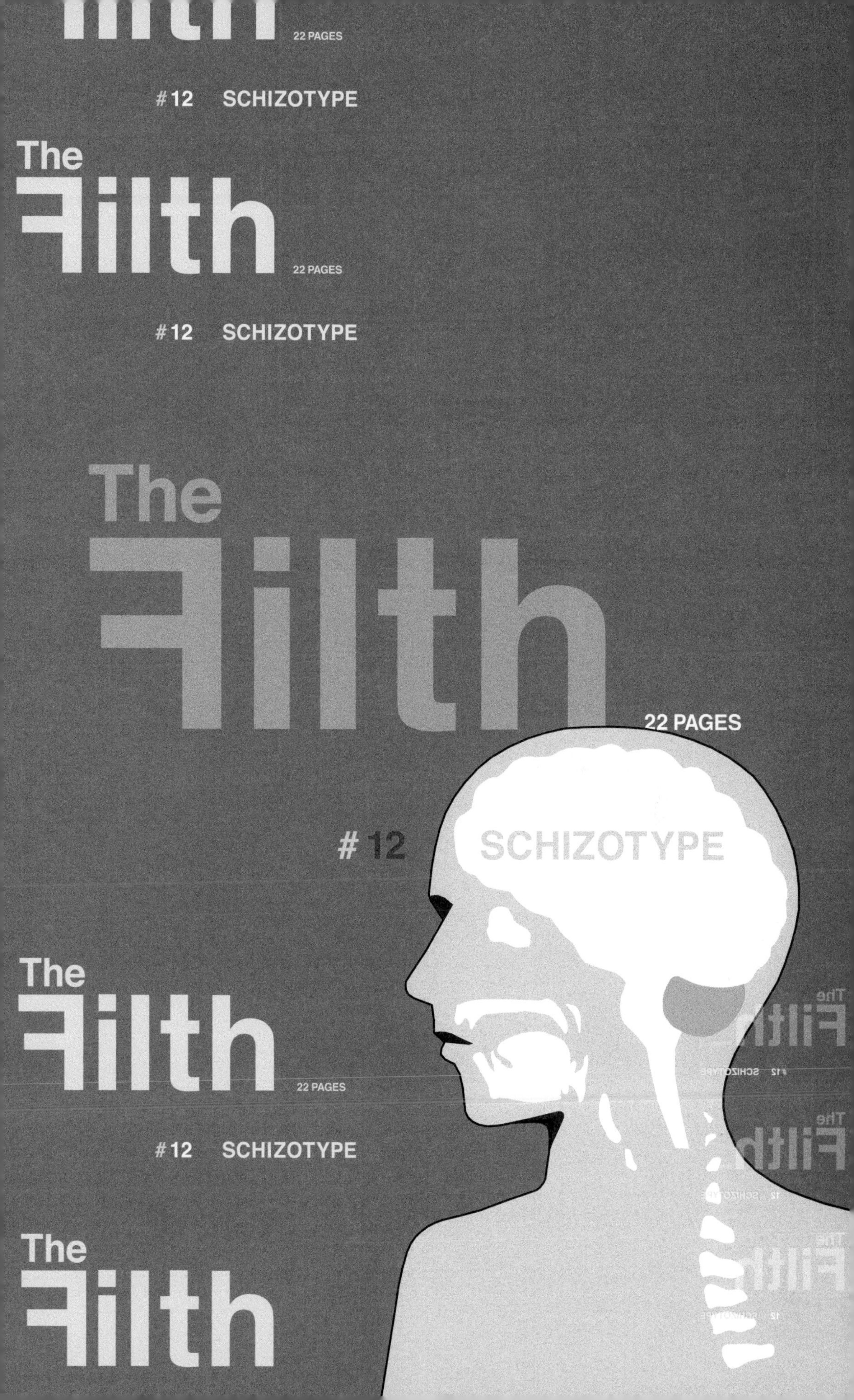

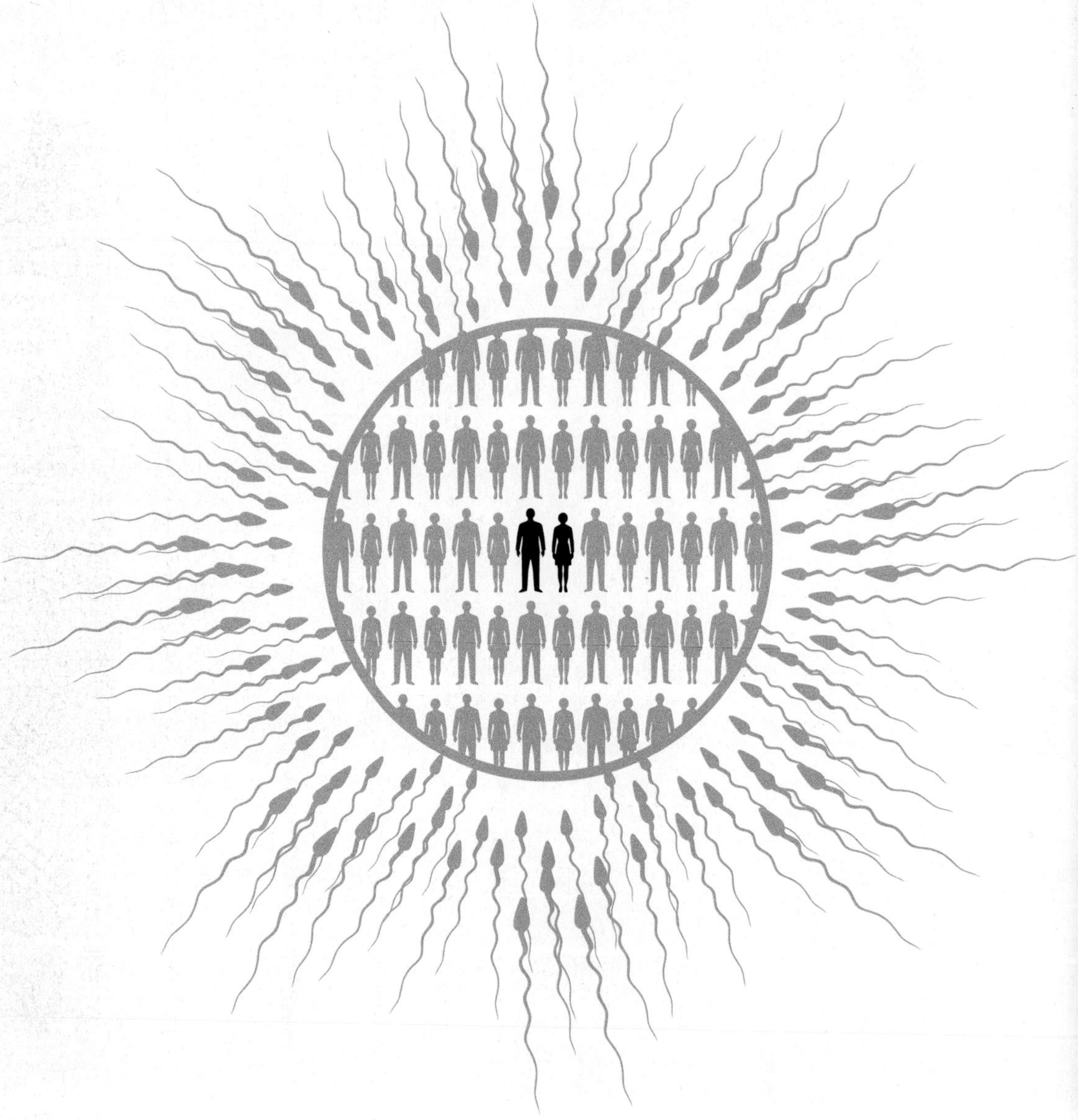

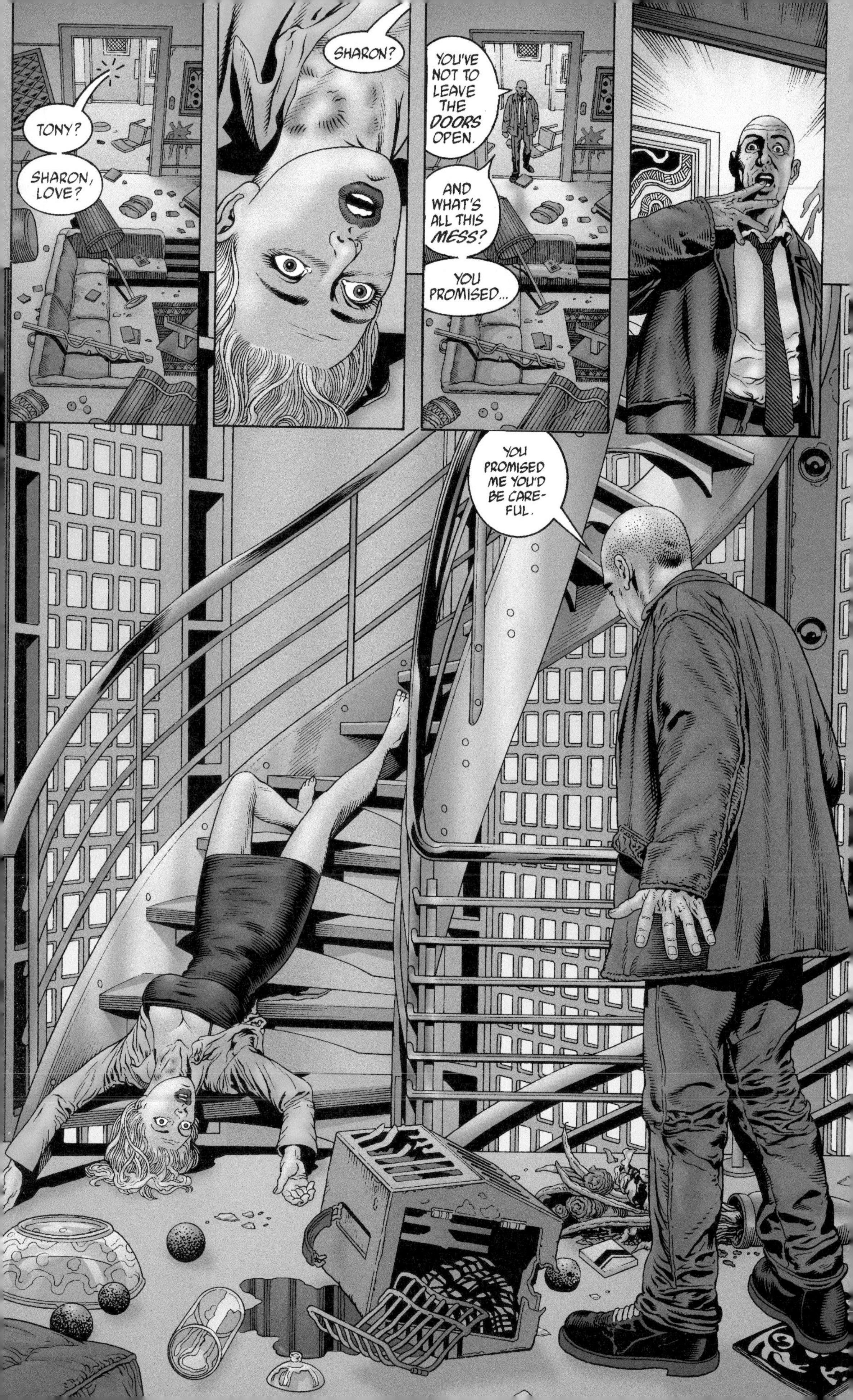
TONY?
SHARON, LOVE?
SHARON?
YOU'VE NOT TO LEAVE THE DOORS OPEN.
AND WHAT'S ALL THIS MESS?
YOU PROMISED...
YOU PROMISED ME YOU'D BE CARE-FUL.

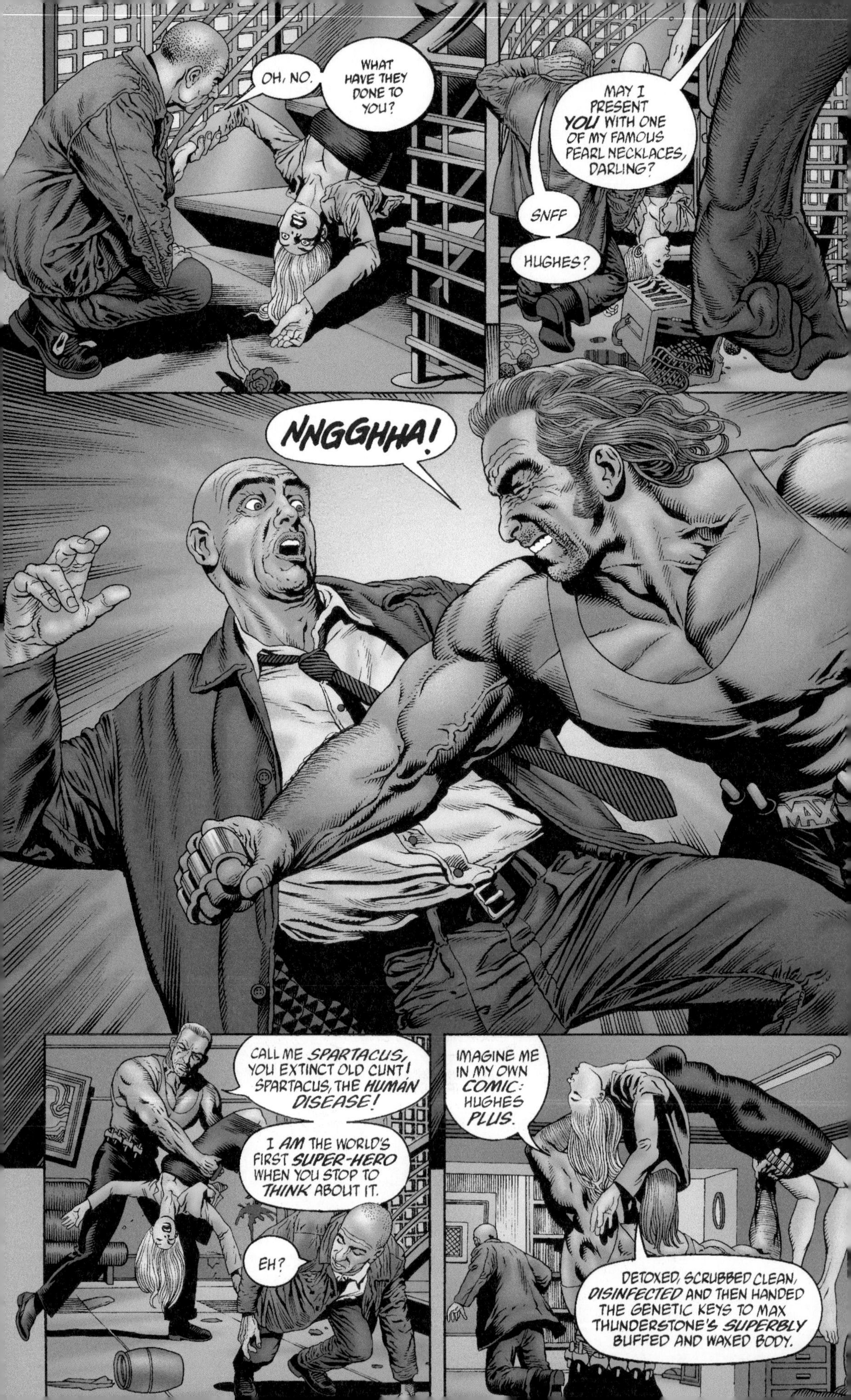
OH, NO.
WHAT HAVE THEY DONE TO YOU?
MAY I PRESENT YOU WITH ONE OF MY FAMOUS PEARL NECKLACES, DARLING?
SNFF
HUGHES?
NNGGHHA!
CALL ME SPARTACUS, YOU EXTINCT OLD CUNT! SPARTACUS, THE HUMAN DISEASE!
I AM THE WORLD'S FIRST SUPER-HERO WHEN YOU STOP TO THINK ABOUT IT.
EH?
IMAGINE ME IN MY OWN COMIC: HUGHES PLUS.
DETOXED, SCRUBBED CLEAN, DISINFECTED AND THEN HANDED THE GENETIC KEYS TO MAX THUNDERSTONE'S SUPERBLY BUFFED AND WAXED BODY.

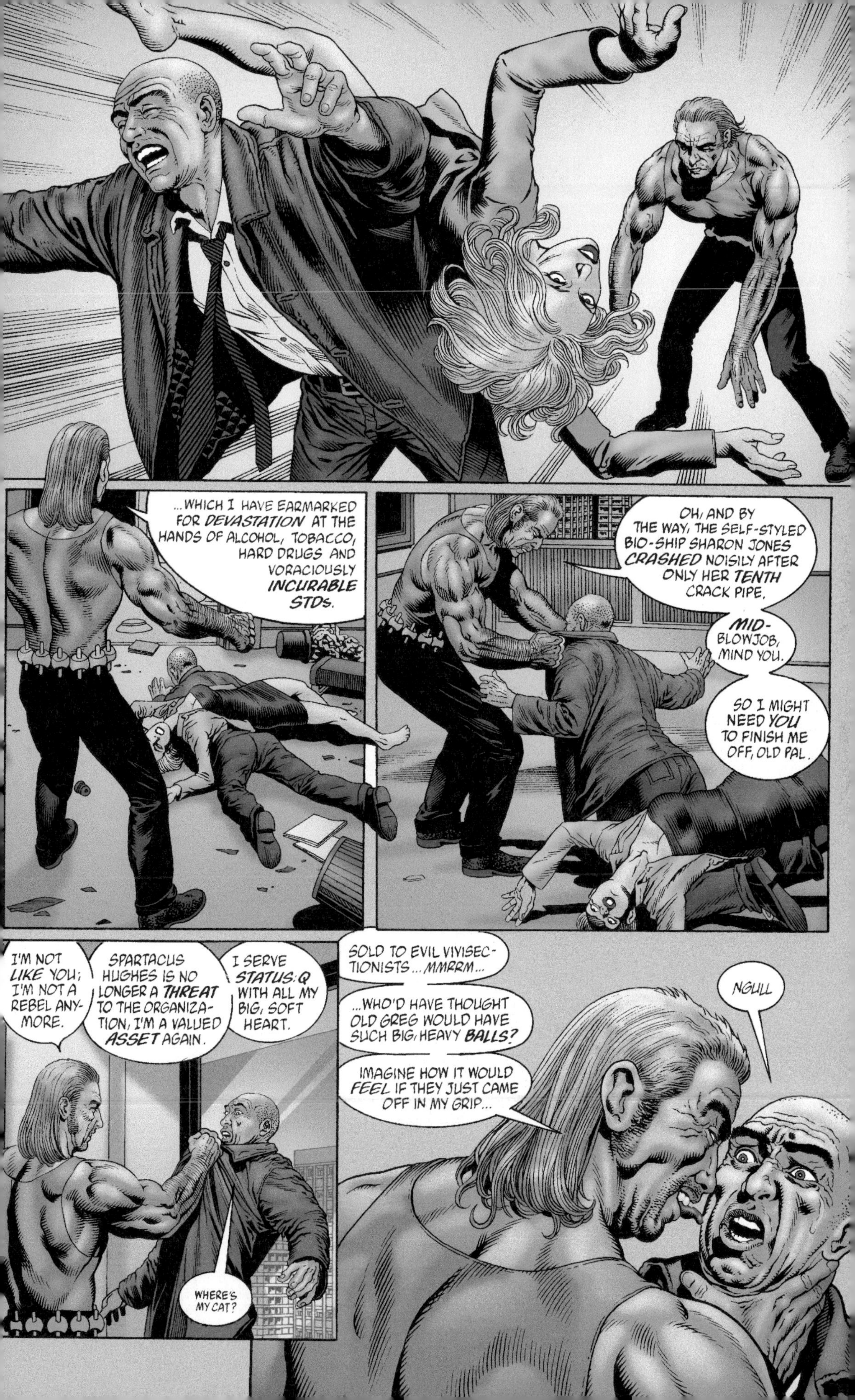
...WHICH I HAVE EARMARKED FOR DEVASTATION AT THE HANDS OF ALCOHOL, TOBACCO, HARD DRUGS AND VORACIOUSLY INCURABLE STDs.
OH, AND BY THE WAY, THE SELF-STYLED BIO-SHIP SHARON JONES CRASHED NOISILY AFTER ONLY HER TENTH CRACK PIPE.
MID-BLOWJOB, MIND YOU.
SO I MIGHT NEED YOU TO FINISH ME OFF, OLD PAL.
I'M NOT LIKE YOU; I'M NOT A REBEL ANY-MORE.
SPARTACUS HUGHES IS NO LONGER A THREAT TO THE ORGANIZA-TION, I'M A VALUED ASSET AGAIN.
I SERVE STATUS:Q WITH ALL MY BIG, SOFT HEART.
WHERE'S MY CAT?
SOLD TO EVIL VIVISEC-TIONISTS... MMRRM...
...WHO'D HAVE THOUGHT OLD GREG WOULD HAVE SUCH BIG, HEAVY BALLS?
IMAGINE HOW IT WOULD FEEL IF THEY JUST CAME OFF IN MY GRIP...
NGULL

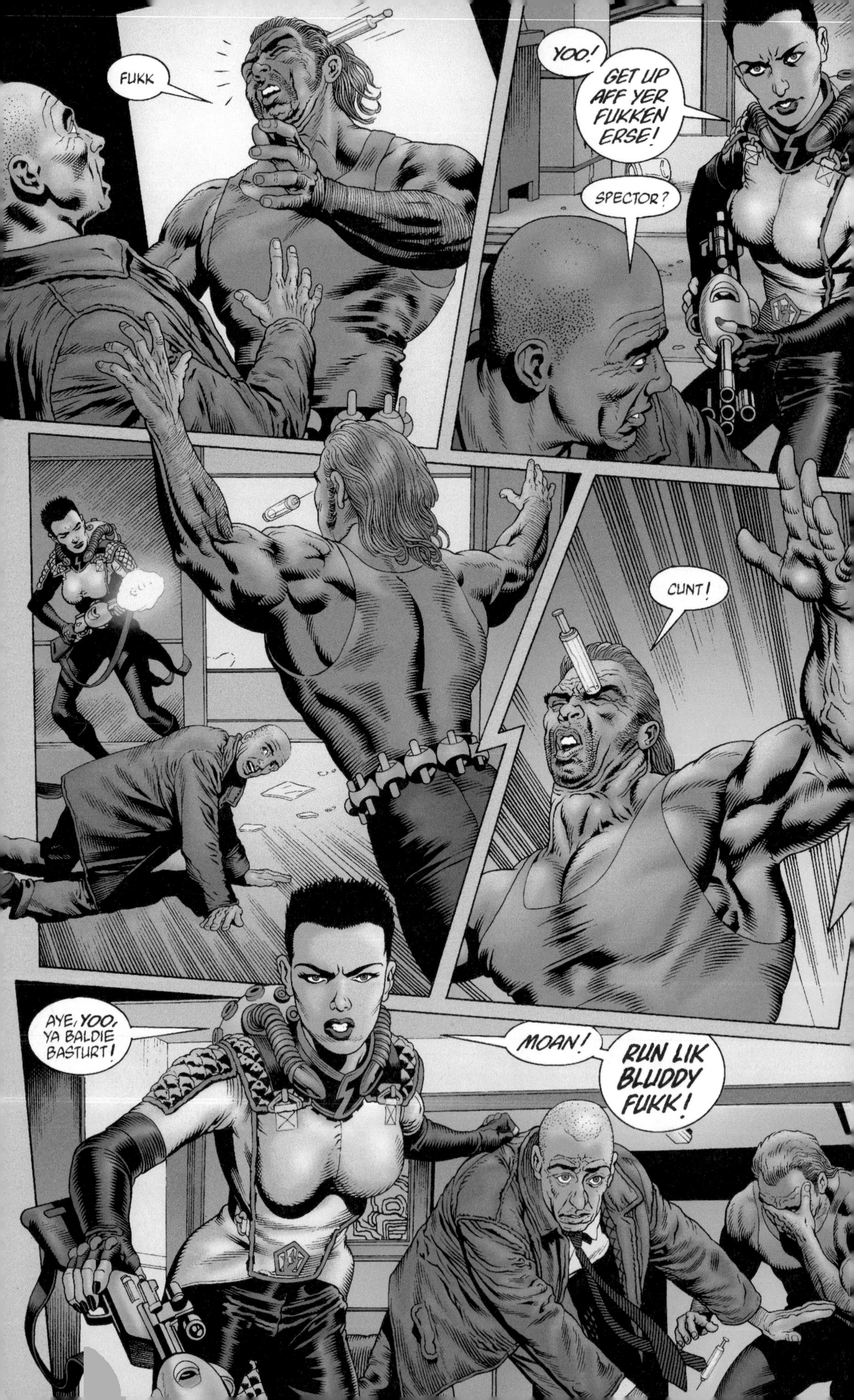
FUKK
YOO!
GET UP AFF YER FUKKEN ERSE!
SPECTOR?
CUNT!
AYE, YOO, YA BALDIE BASTURT!
MOAN!
RUN LIK BLUDDY FUKK!

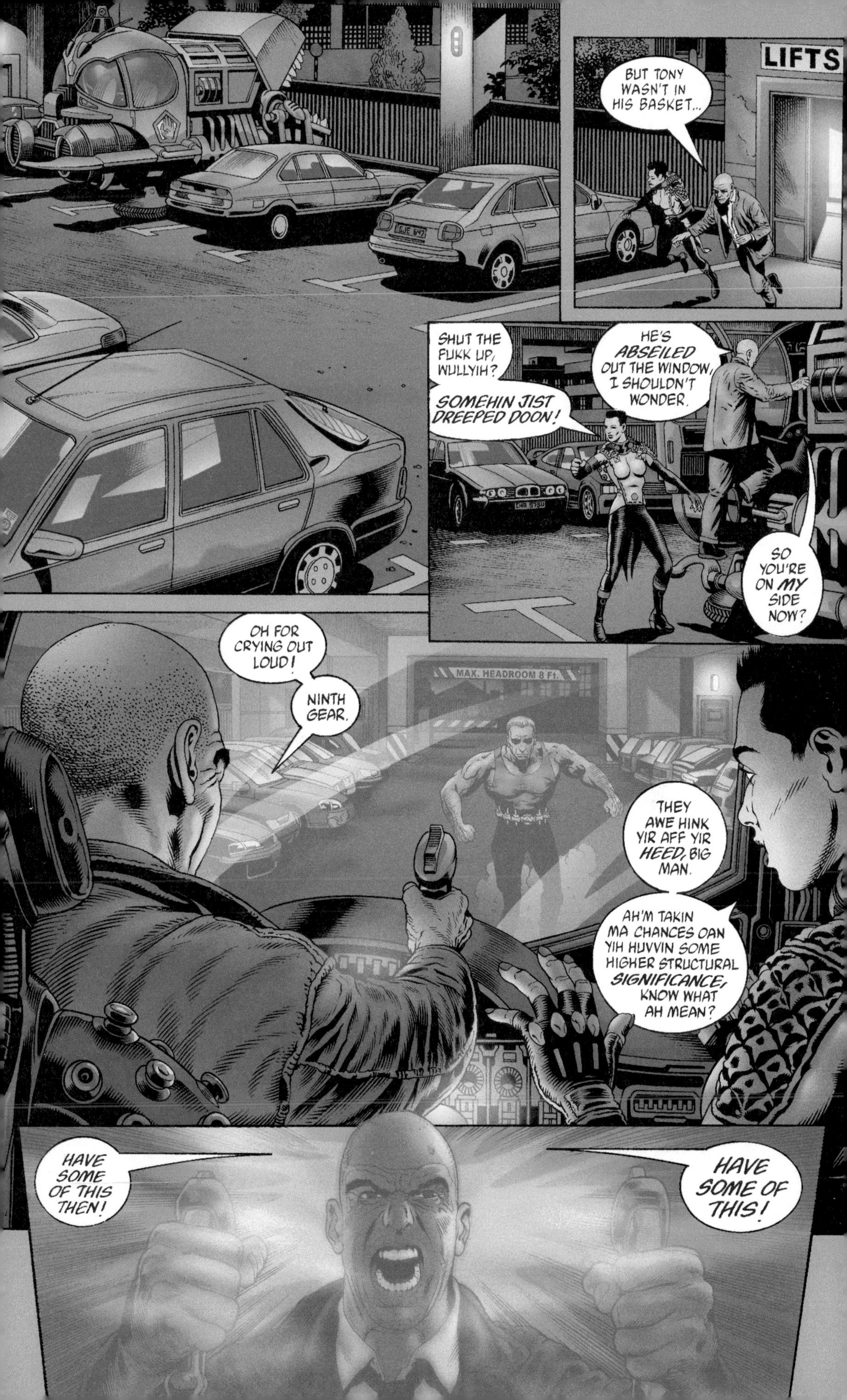
LIFTS
BUT TONY WASN'T IN HIS BASKET...
SHUT THE FUKK UP, WULLYIH?
SOMEHIN JIST DREEPED DOON!
HE'S ABSEILED OUT THE WINDOW, I SHOULDN'T WONDER.
SO YOU'RE ON MY SIDE NOW?
MAX. HEADROOM 8 Ft.
OH FOR CRYING OUT LOUD!
NINTH GEAR.
THEY AWE HINK YIR AFF YIR HEED, BIG MAN.
AH'M TAKIN MA CHANCES OAN YIH HUVVIN SOME HIGHER STRUCTURAL SIGNIFICANCE, KNOW WHAT AH MEAN?
HAVE SOME OF THIS THEN!
HAVE SOME OF THIS!

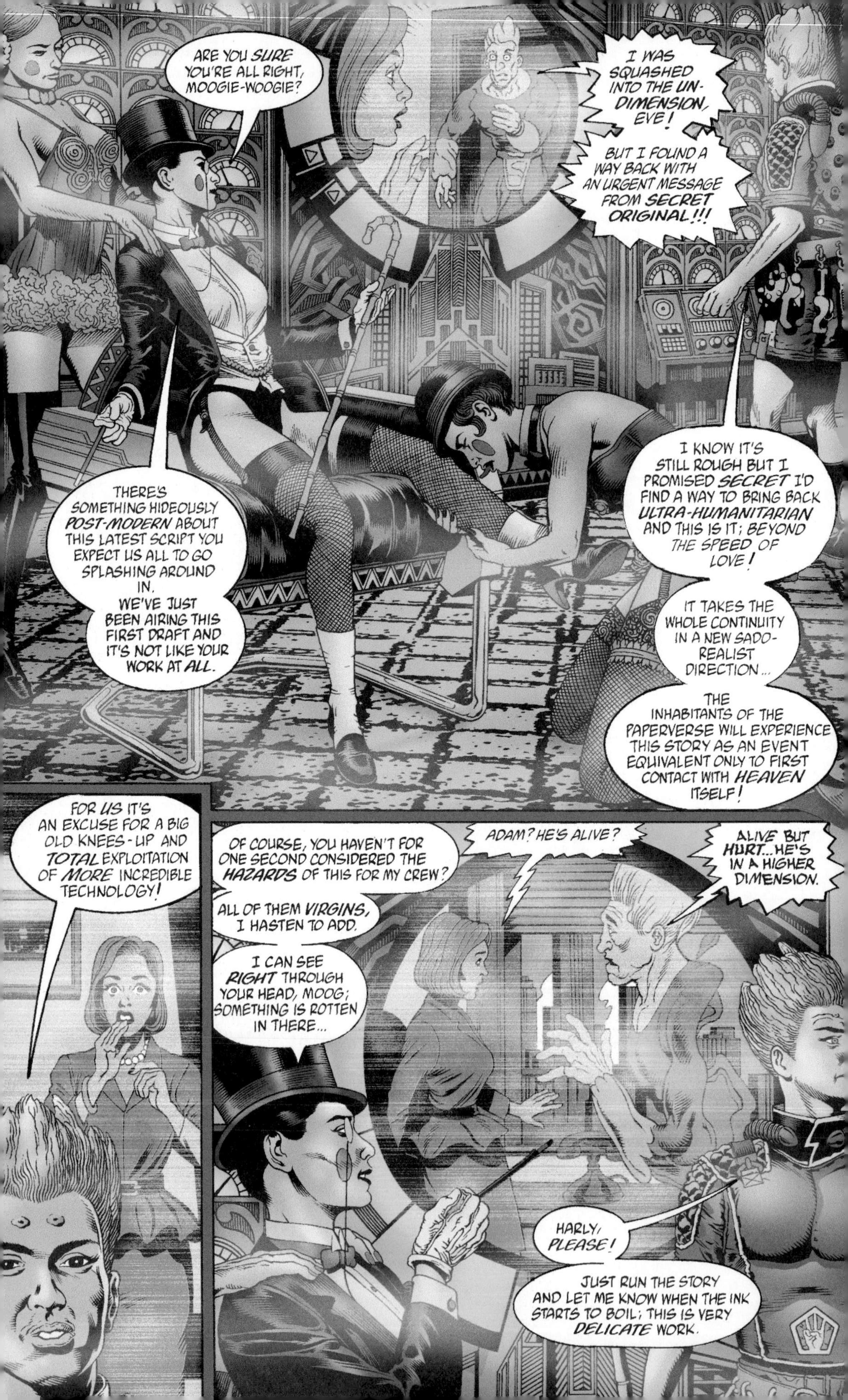
ARE YOU SURE YOU'RE ALL RIGHT, MOOGIE-WOOGIE?
I WAS SQUASHED INTO THE UN-DIMENSION, EVE!
BUT I FOUND A WAY BACK WITH AN URGENT MESSAGE FROM SECRET ORIGINAL!!!
THERE'S SOMETHING HIDEOUSLY POST-MODERN ABOUT THIS LATEST SCRIPT YOU EXPECT US ALL TO GO SPLASHING AROUND IN.
WE'VE JUST BEEN AIRING THIS FIRST DRAFT AND IT'S NOT LIKE YOUR WORK AT ALL.
I KNOW IT'S STILL ROUGH BUT I PROMISED SECRET I'D FIND A WAY TO BRING BACK ULTRA-HUMANITARIAN AND THIS IS IT; BEYOND THE SPEED OF LOVE!
IT TAKES THE WHOLE CONTINUITY IN A NEW SADO-REALIST DIRECTION...
THE INHABITANTS OF THE PAPERVERSE WILL EXPERIENCE THIS STORY AS AN EVENT EQUIVALENT ONLY TO FIRST CONTACT WITH HEAVEN ITSELF!
FOR US IT'S AN EXCUSE FOR A BIG OLD KNEES-UP AND TOTAL EXPLOITATION OF MORE INCREDIBLE TECHNOLOGY!
OF COURSE, YOU HAVEN'T FOR ONE SECOND CONSIDERED THE HAZARDS OF THIS FOR MY CREW?
ALL OF THEM VIRGINS, I HASTEN TO ADD.
I CAN SEE RIGHT THROUGH YOUR HEAD, MOOG; SOMETHING IS ROTTEN IN THERE...
ADAM? HE'S ALIVE?
ALIVE BUT HURT...HE'S IN A HIGHER DIMENSION.
HARLY, PLEASE!
JUST RUN THE STORY AND LET ME KNOW WHEN THE INK STARTS TO BOIL; THIS IS VERY DELICATE WORK.

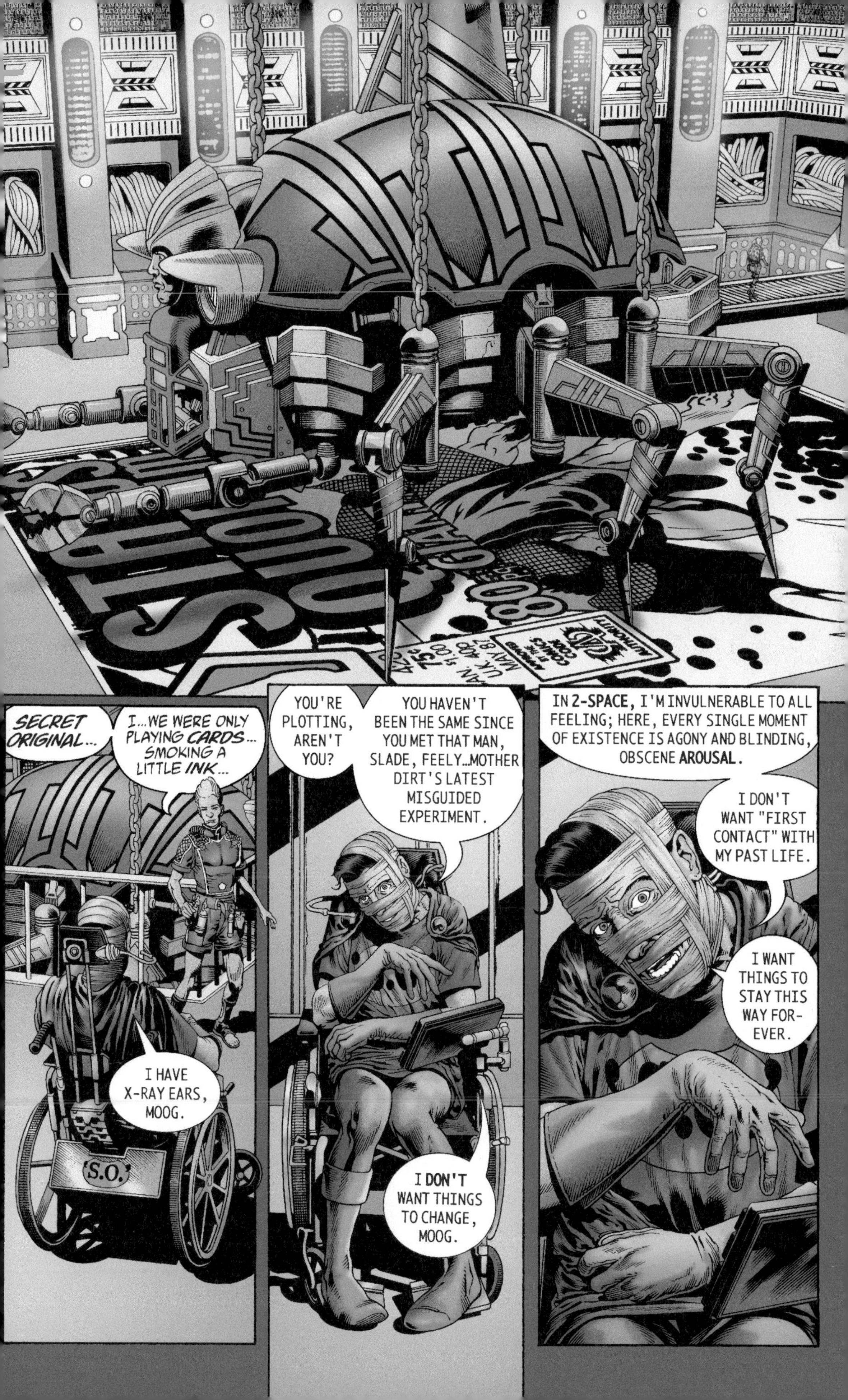
SECRET ORIGINAL...
I...WE WERE ONLY PLAYING CARDS... SMOKING A LITTLE INK...
I HAVE X-RAY EARS, MOOG.
YOU'RE PLOTTING, AREN'T YOU?
YOU HAVEN'T BEEN THE SAME SINCE YOU MET THAT MAN, SLADE, FEELY...MOTHER DIRT'S LATEST MISGUIDED EXPERIMENT.
I DON'T WANT THINGS TO CHANGE, MOOG.
IN 2-SPACE, I'M INVULNERABLE TO ALL FEELING; HERE, EVERY SINGLE MOMENT OF EXISTENCE IS AGONY AND BLINDING, OBSCENE AROUSAL.
I DON'T WANT "FIRST CONTACT" WITH MY PAST LIFE.
I WANT THINGS TO STAY THIS WAY FOR-EVER.

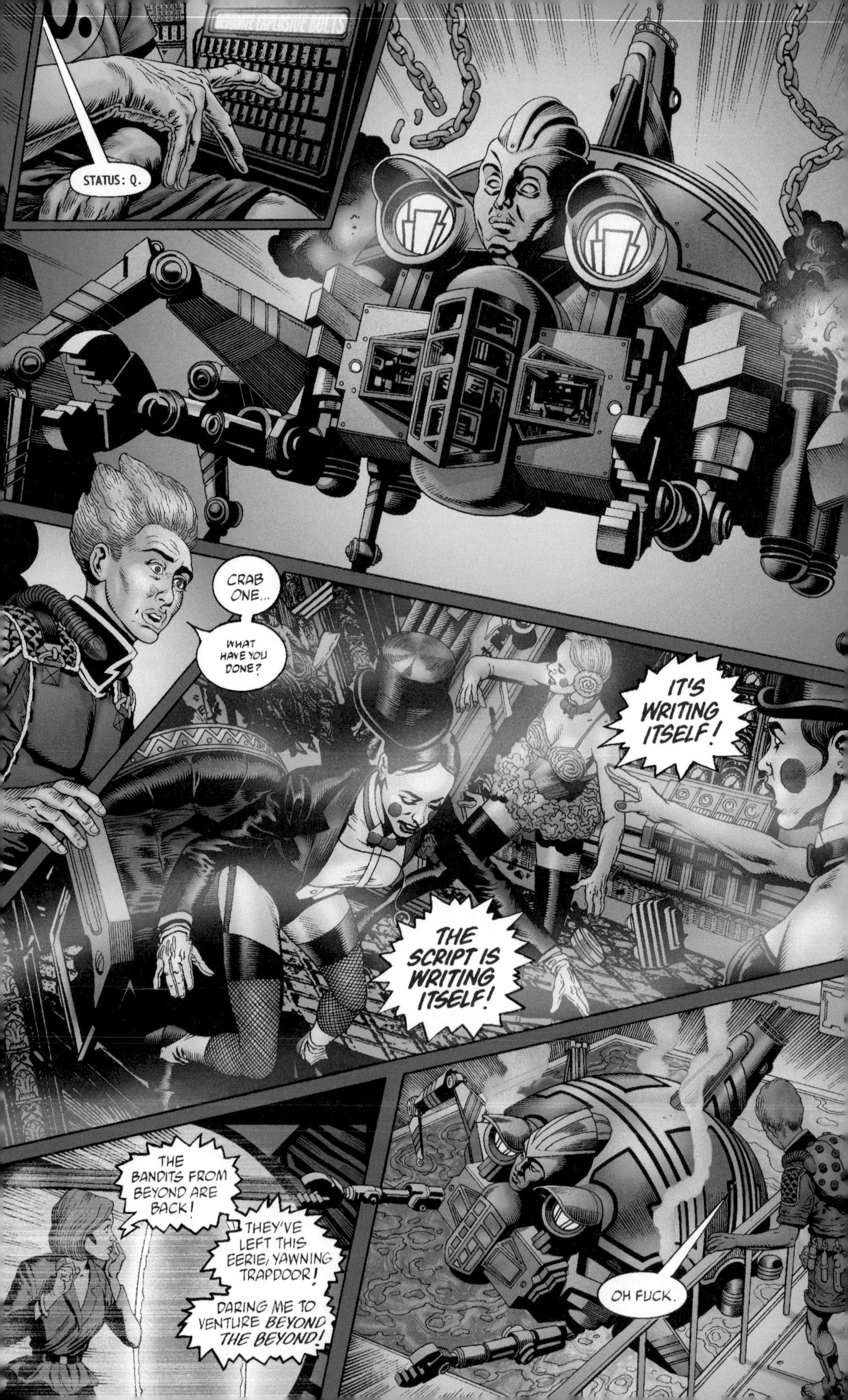
EXPLOSIVE BOLTS
STATUS: Q.
CRAB ONE...
WHAT HAVE YOU DONE?
IT'S WRITING ITSELF!
THE SCRIPT IS WRITING ITSELF!
THE BANDITS FROM BEYOND ARE BACK!
THEY'VE LEFT THIS EERIE, YAWNING TRAPDOOR!
DARING ME TO VENTURE BEYOND THE BEYOND!
OH FUCK.

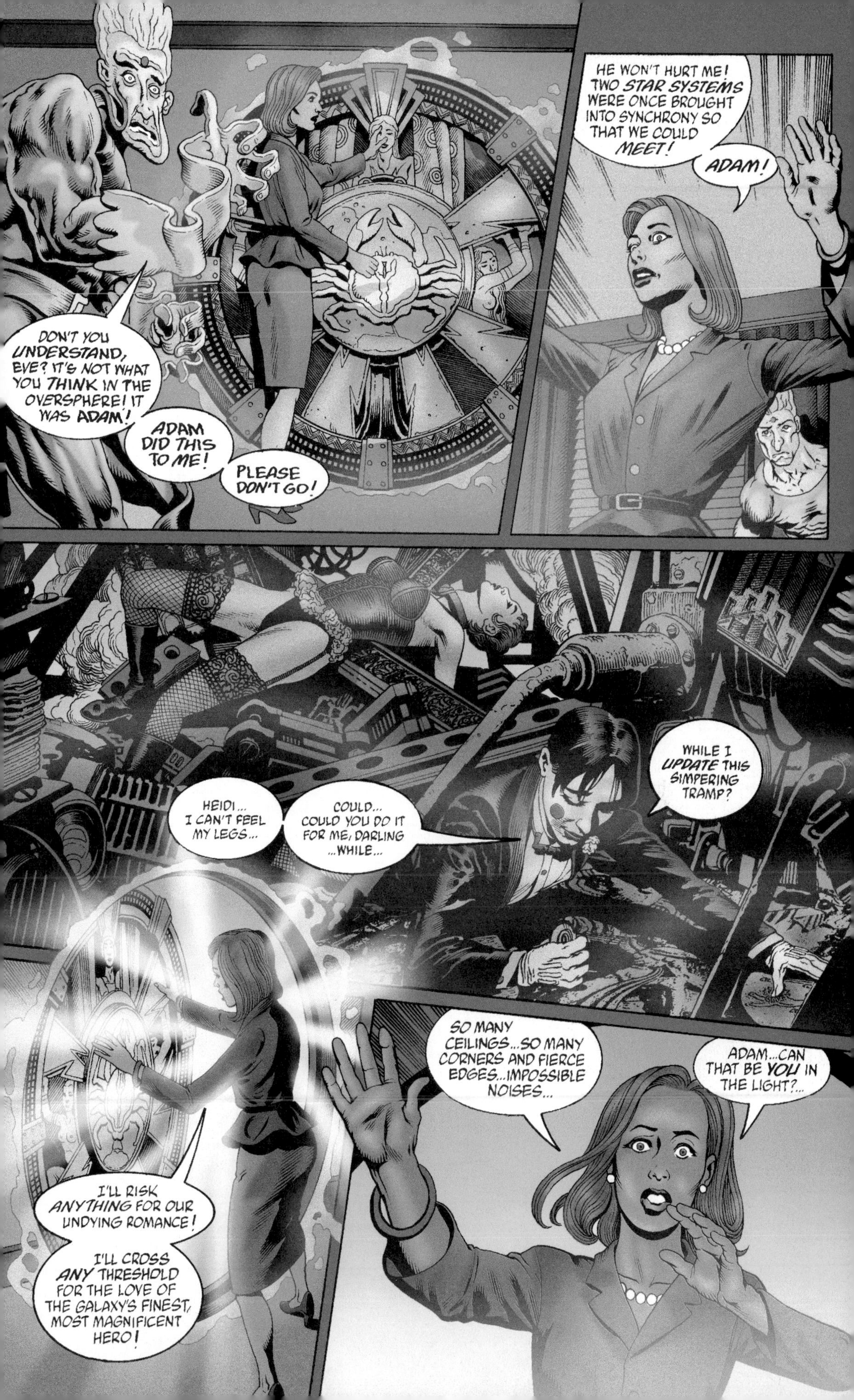
DON'T YOU UNDERSTAND, EVE? IT'S NOT WHAT YOU THINK IN THE OVERSPHERE! IT WAS ADAM!
ADAM DID THIS TO ME!
PLEASE DON'T GO!
HE WON'T HURT ME! TWO STAR SYSTEMS WERE ONCE BROUGHT INTO SYNCHRONY SO THAT WE COULD MEET!
ADAM!
HEIDI... I CAN'T FEEL MY LEGS...
COULD... COULD YOU DO IT FOR ME, DARLING ...WHILE...
WHILE I UPDATE THIS SIMPERING TRAMP?
I'LL RISK ANYTHING FOR OUR UNDYING ROMANCE!
I'LL CROSS ANY THRESHOLD FOR THE LOVE OF THE GALAXY'S FINEST, MOST MAGNIFICENT HERO!
SO MANY CEILINGS...SO MANY CORNERS AND FIERCE EDGES...IMPOSSIBLE NOISES...
ADAM...CAN THAT BE YOU IN THE LIGHT?...

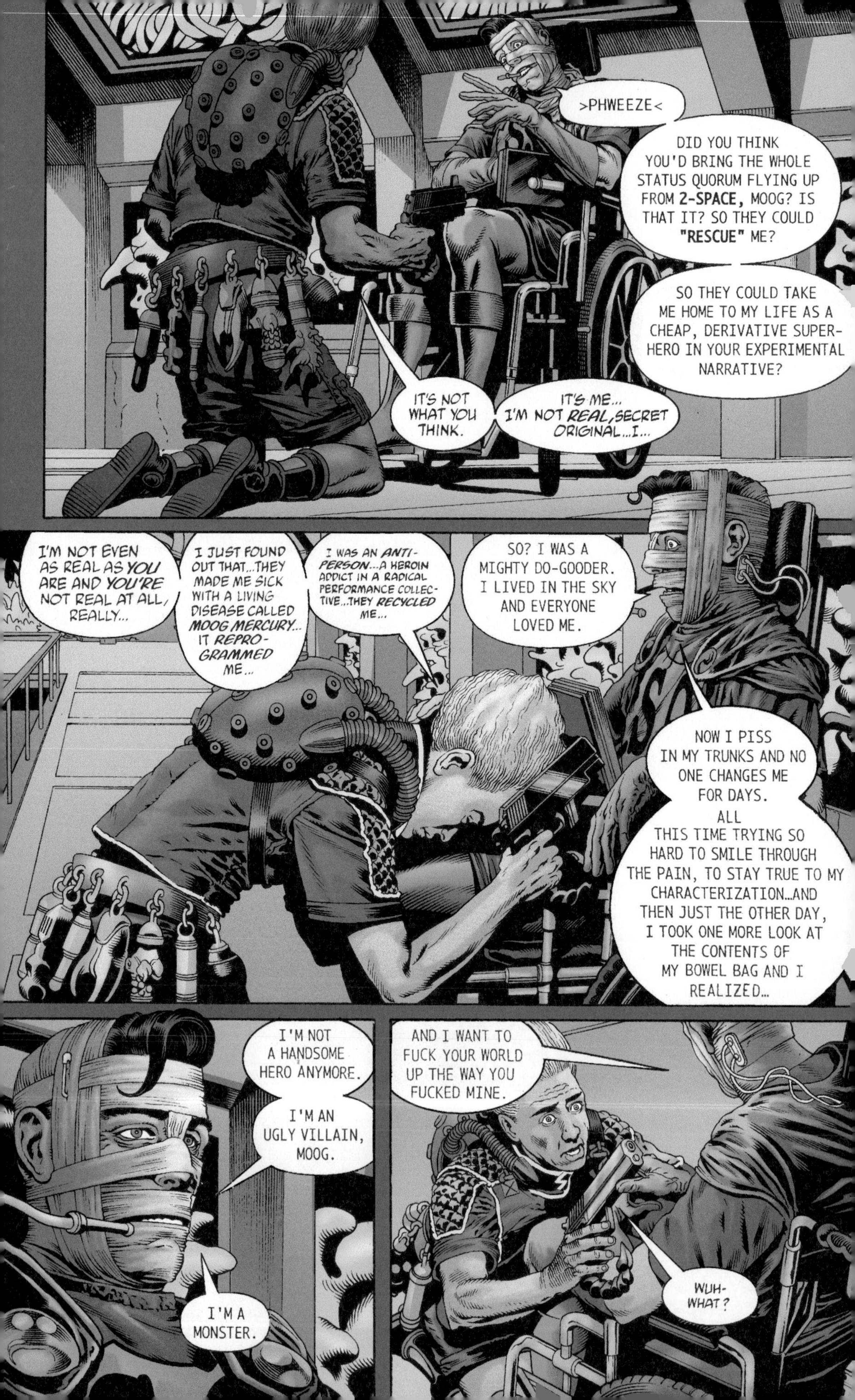
>PHWEEZE<
DID YOU THINK YOU'D BRING THE WHOLE STATUS QUORUM FLYING UP FROM 2-SPACE, MOOG? IS THAT IT? SO THEY COULD "RESCUE" ME?
SO THEY COULD TAKE ME HOME TO MY LIFE AS A CHEAP, DERIVATIVE SUPER-HERO IN YOUR EXPERIMENTAL NARRATIVE?
IT'S NOT WHAT YOU THINK.
IT'S ME... I'M NOT REAL, SECRET ORIGINAL...I...
I'M NOT EVEN AS REAL AS YOU ARE AND YOU'RE NOT REAL AT ALL, REALLY...
I JUST FOUND OUT THAT...THEY MADE ME SICK WITH A LIVING DISEASE CALLED MOOG MERCURY... IT REPRO-GRAMMED ME...
I WAS AN ANTI-PERSON...A HEROIN ADDICT IN A RADICAL PERFORMANCE COLLEC-TIVE...THEY RECYCLED ME...
SO? I WAS A MIGHTY DO-GOODER. I LIVED IN THE SKY AND EVERYONE LOVED ME.
NOW I PISS IN MY TRUNKS AND NO ONE CHANGES ME FOR DAYS.
ALL THIS TIME TRYING SO HARD TO SMILE THROUGH THE PAIN, TO STAY TRUE TO MY CHARACTERIZATION...AND THEN JUST THE OTHER DAY, I TOOK ONE MORE LOOK AT THE CONTENTS OF MY BOWEL BAG AND I REALIZED...
I'M NOT A HANDSOME HERO ANYMORE.
I'M AN UGLY VILLAIN, MOOG.
I'M A MONSTER.
AND I WANT TO FUCK YOUR WORLD UP THE WAY YOU FUCKED MINE.
WUH-WHAT?

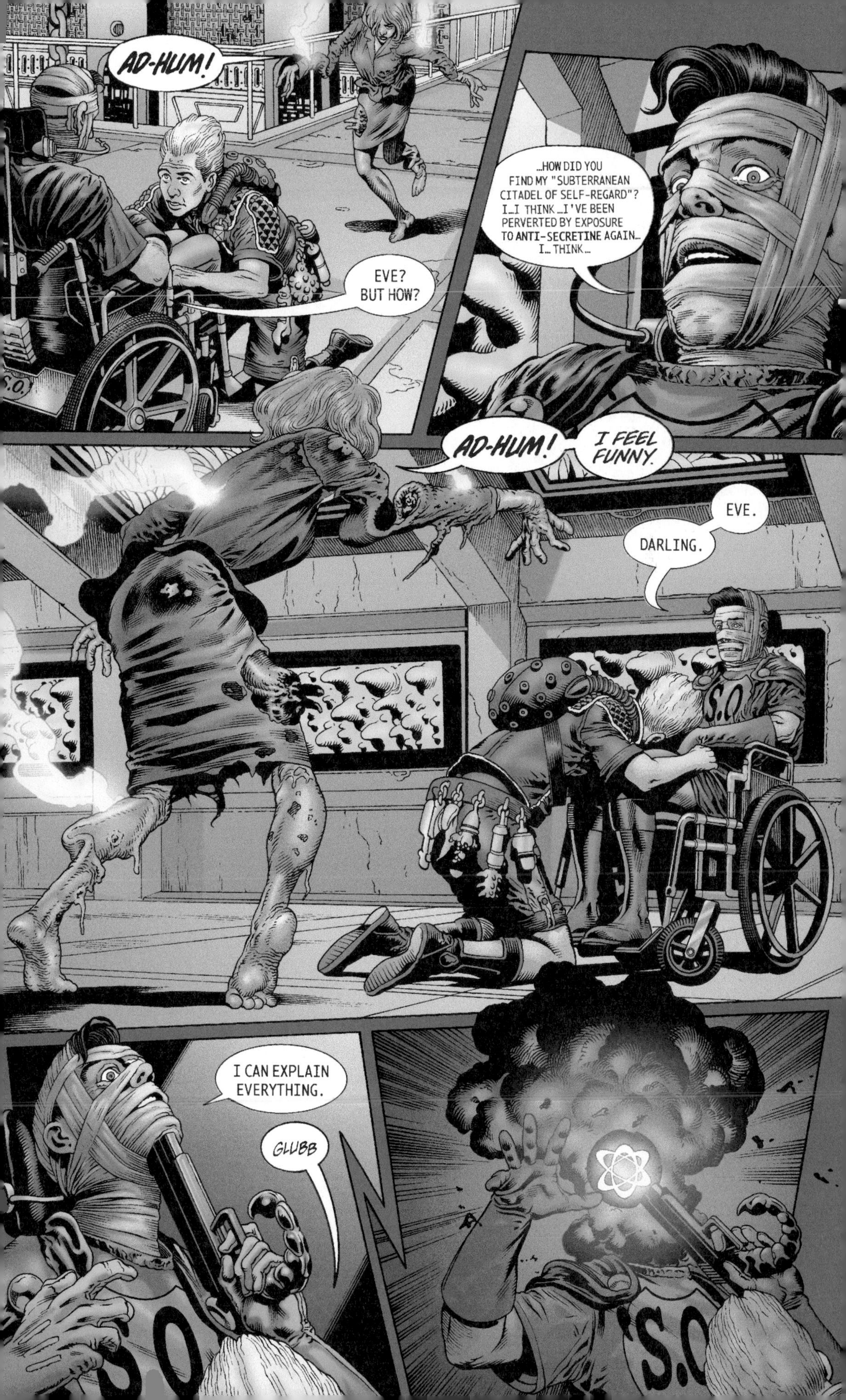

AD-HUM!
EVE? BUT HOW?
...HOW DID YOU FIND MY "SUBTERRANEAN CITADEL OF SELF-REGARD"? I...I THINK...I'VE BEEN PERVERTED BY EXPOSURE TO ANTI-SECRETINE AGAIN... I... THINK...
AD-HUM!
I FEEL FUNNY.
EVE.
DARLING.
I CAN EXPLAIN EVERYTHING.
GLUBB
S.O
S.O

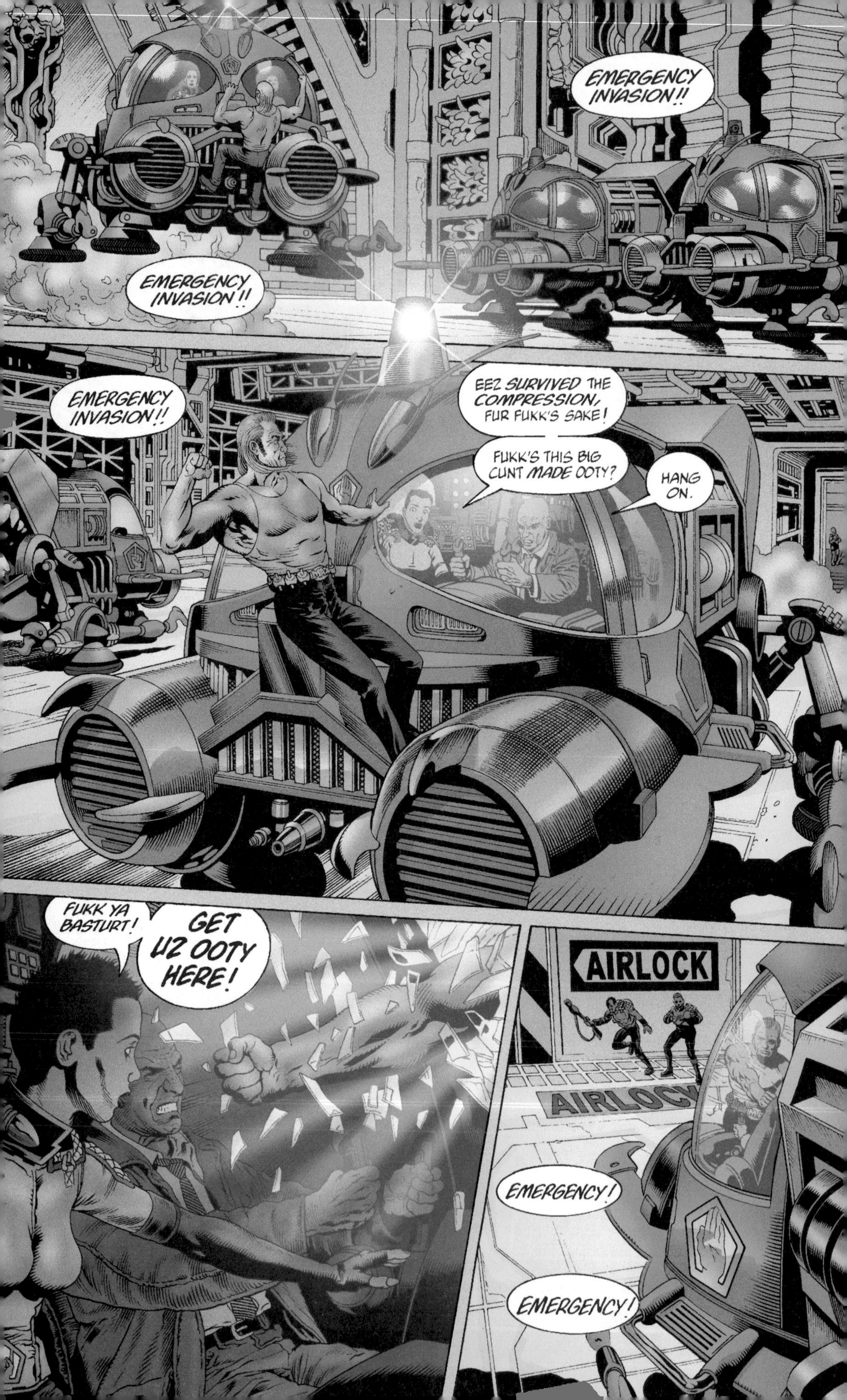
EMERGENCY INVASION!!
EMERGENCY INVASION!!
EMERGENCY INVASION!!
EEZ SURVIVED THE COMPRESSION, FUR FUKK'S SAKE!
FUKK'S THIS BIG CUNT MADE OOTY?
HANG ON.
FUKK YA BASTURT!
GET UZ OOTY HERE!
AIRLOCK
AIRLOCK
EMERGENCY!
EMERGENCY!

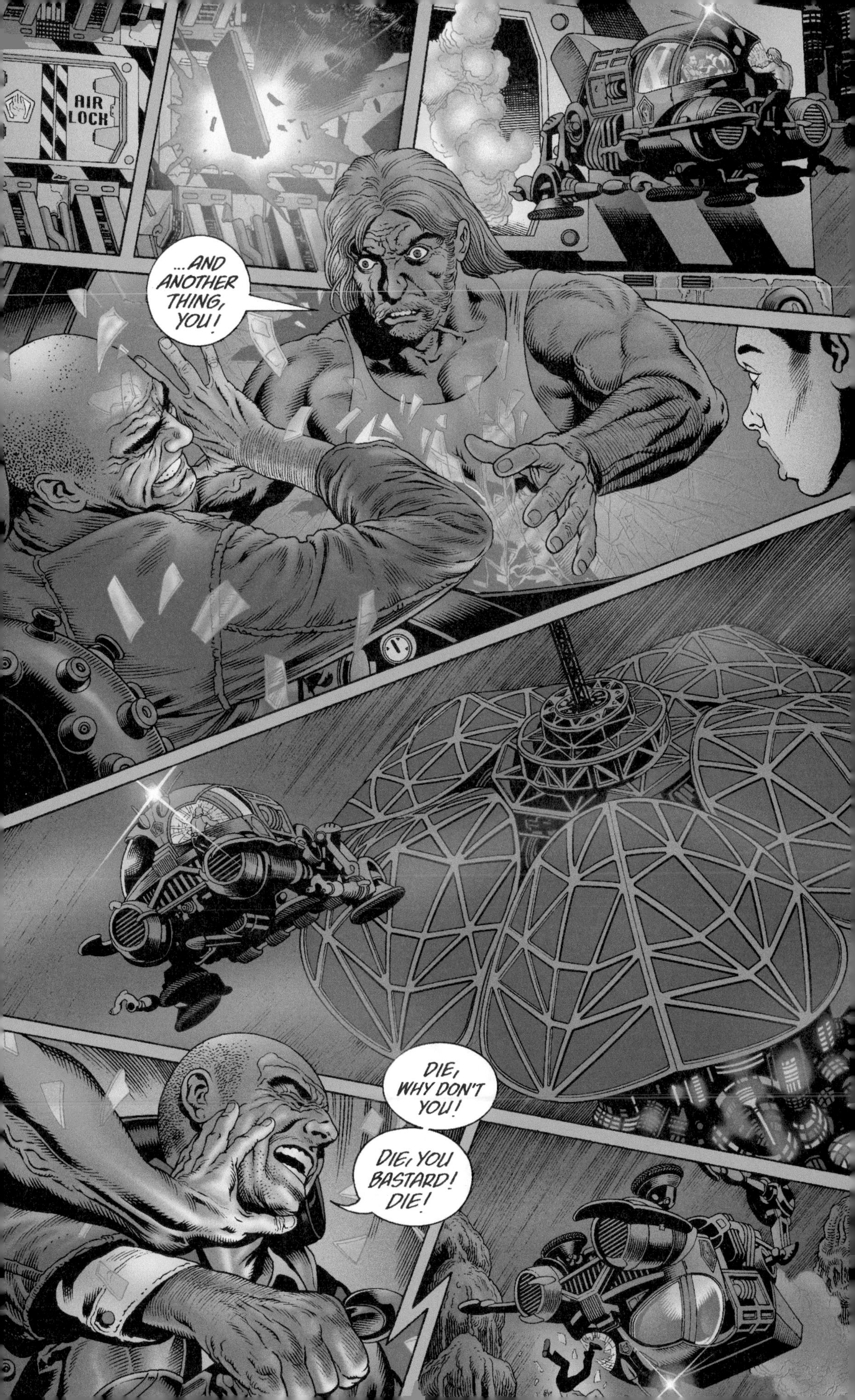
AIR LOCK
...AND ANOTHER THING, YOU!
DIE, WHY DON'T YOU!
DIE, YOU BASTARD! DIE!

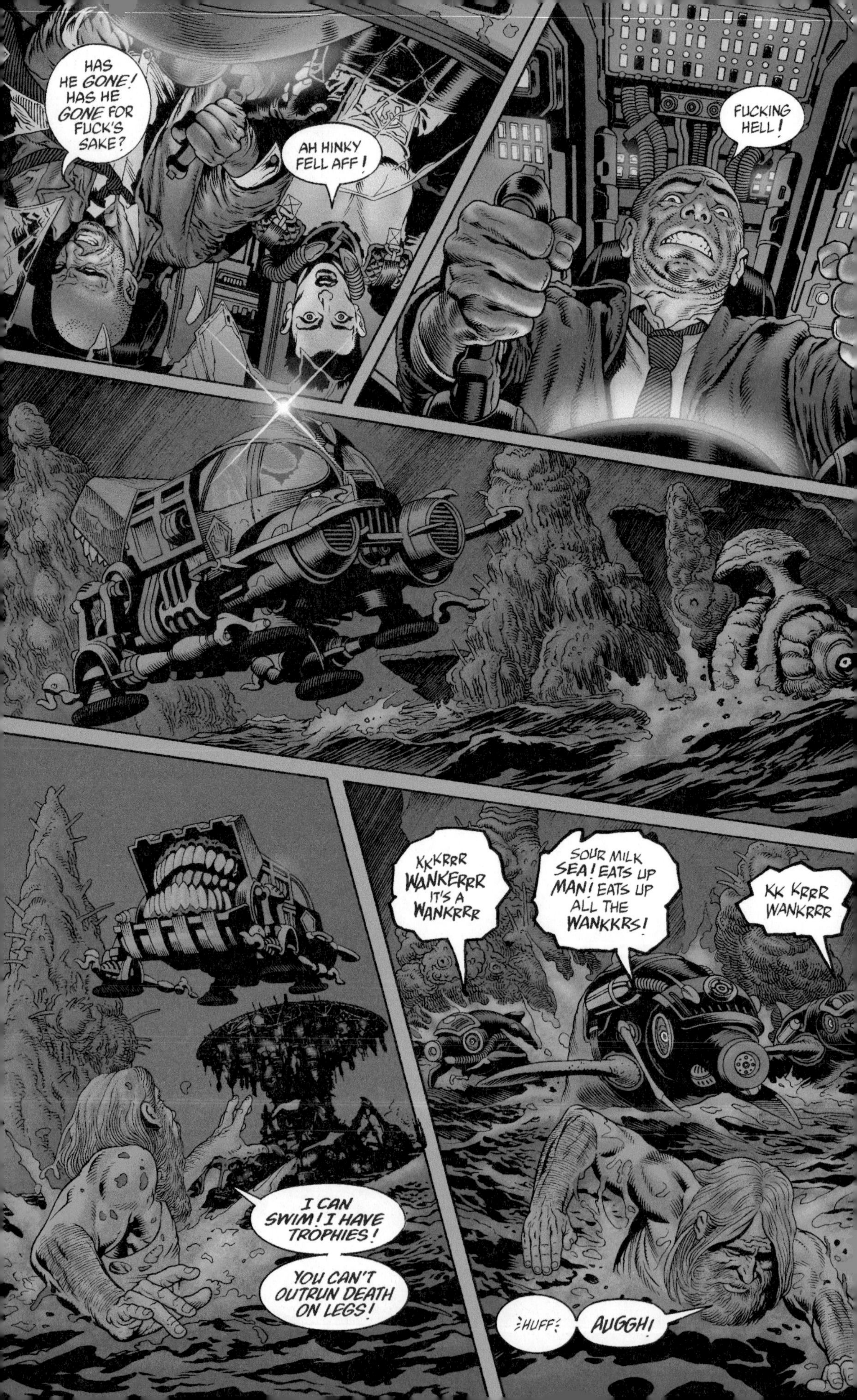
HAS HE GONE! HAS HE GONE FOR FUCK'S SAKE?
AH HINKY FELL AFF!
FUCKING HELL!
I CAN SWIM! I HAVE TROPHIES!
YOU CAN'T OUTRUN DEATH ON LEGS!
KKKRRR WANKERRR IT'S A WANKRRR
SOUR MILK SEA! EATS UP MAN! EATS UP ALL THE WANKKRS!
KK KRRR WANKRRR
HUFF
AUGGH!

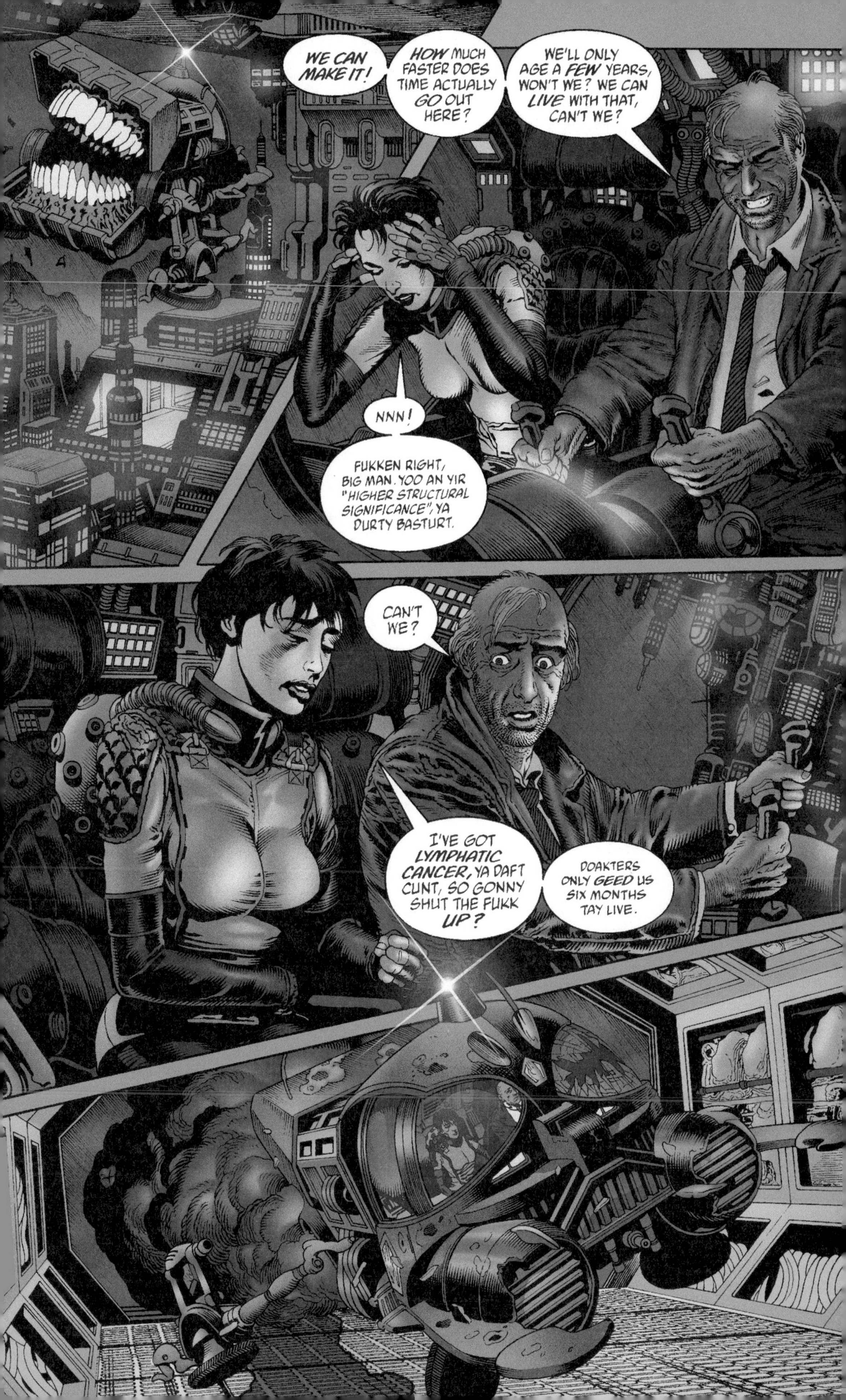
WE CAN MAKE IT!
HOW MUCH FASTER DOES TIME ACTUALLY GO OUT HERE?
WE'LL ONLY AGE A FEW YEARS, WON'T WE? WE CAN LIVE WITH THAT, CAN'T WE?
NNN!
FUKKEN RIGHT, BIG MAN. YOO AN YIR "HIGHER STRUCTURAL SIGNIFICANCE", YA DURTY BASTURT.
CAN'T WE?
I'VE GOT LYMPHATIC CANCER, YA DAFT CUNT, SO GONNY SHUT THE FUKK UP?
DOAKTERS ONLY GEED US SIX MONTHS TAY LIVE.

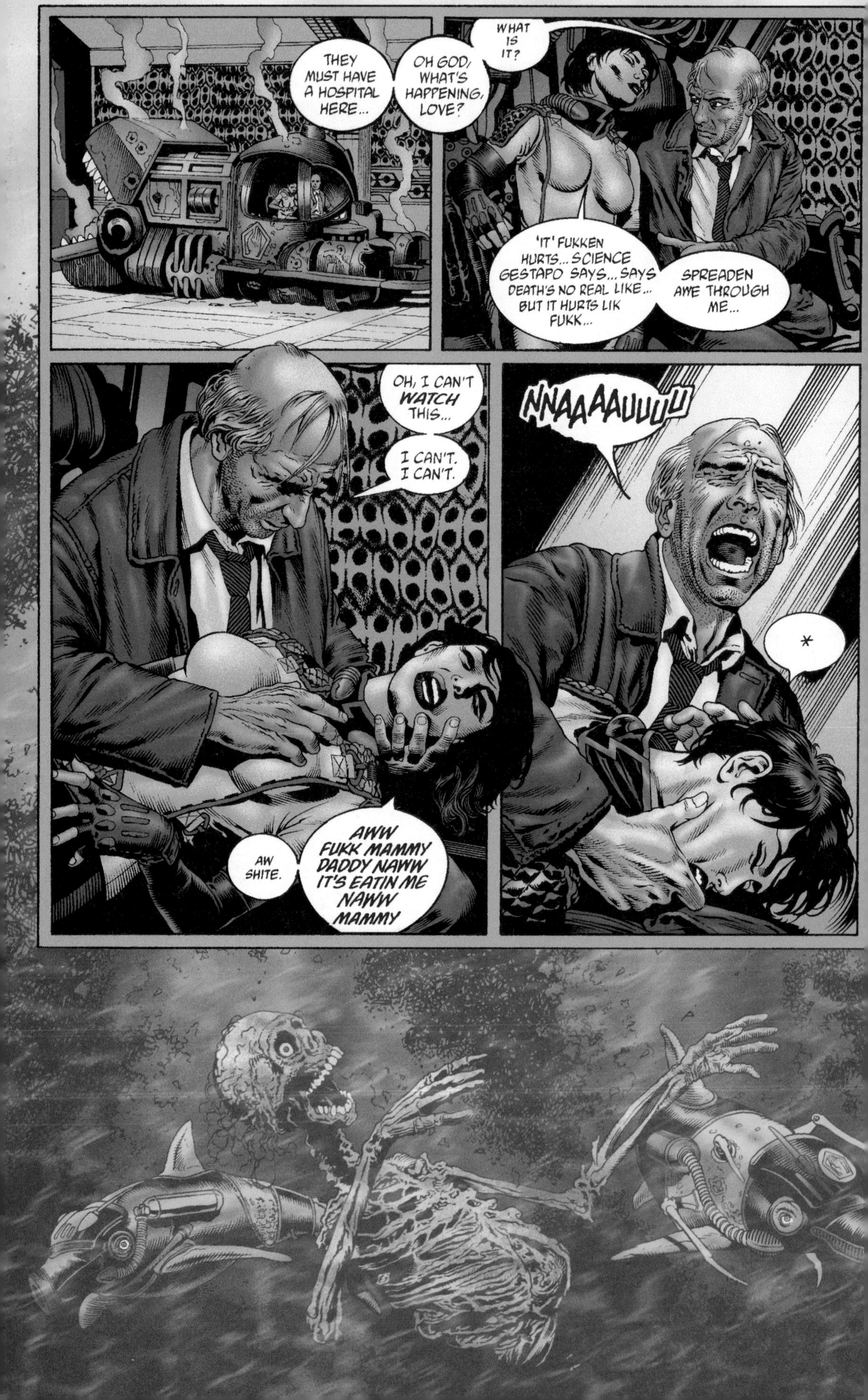
THEY MUST HAVE A HOSPITAL HERE...
OH GOD, WHAT'S HAPPENING, LOVE?
WHAT IS IT?
'IT' FUKKEN HURTS... SCIENCE GESTAPO SAYS... SAYS DEATH'S NO REAL LIKE... BUT IT HURTS LIK FUKK...
SPREADEN AWE THROUGH ME...
OH, I CAN'T WATCH THIS...
I CAN'T. I CAN'T.
AW SHITE.
AWW FUKK MAMMY DADDY NAWW IT'S EATIN ME NAWW MAMMY
NNAAAAAUUUU
*

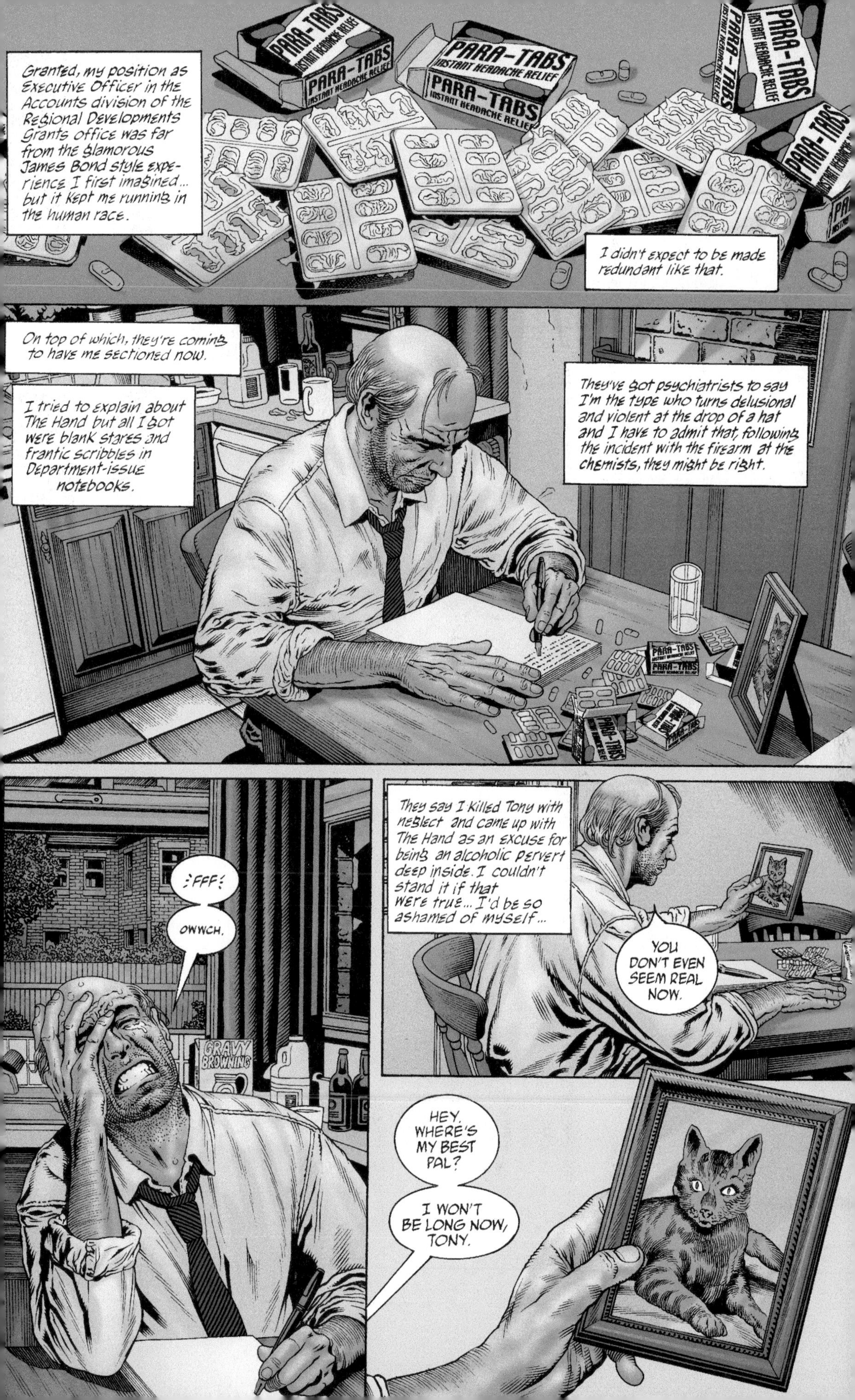

Granted, my position as Executive Officer in the Accounts division of the Regional Developments Grants office was far from the glamorous James Bond style experience I first imagined... but it kept me running in the human race.
PARA-TABS INSTANT HEADACHE RELIEF
I didn't expect to be made redundant like that.
On top of which, they're coming to have me sectioned now.
I tried to explain about The Hand but all I got were blank stares and frantic scribbles in Department-issue notebooks.
They've got psychiatrists to say I'm the type who turns delusional and violent at the drop of a hat and I have to admit that, following the incident with the firearm at the chemists, they might be right.
:FFF:
OWWCH.
GRAVY BROWNING
They say I killed Tony with neglect and came up with The Hand as an excuse for being an alcoholic pervert deep inside. I couldn't stand it if that were true... I'd be so ashamed of myself...
YOU DON'T EVEN SEEM REAL NOW.
HEY. WHERE'S MY BEST PAL?
I WON'T BE LONG NOW, TONY.

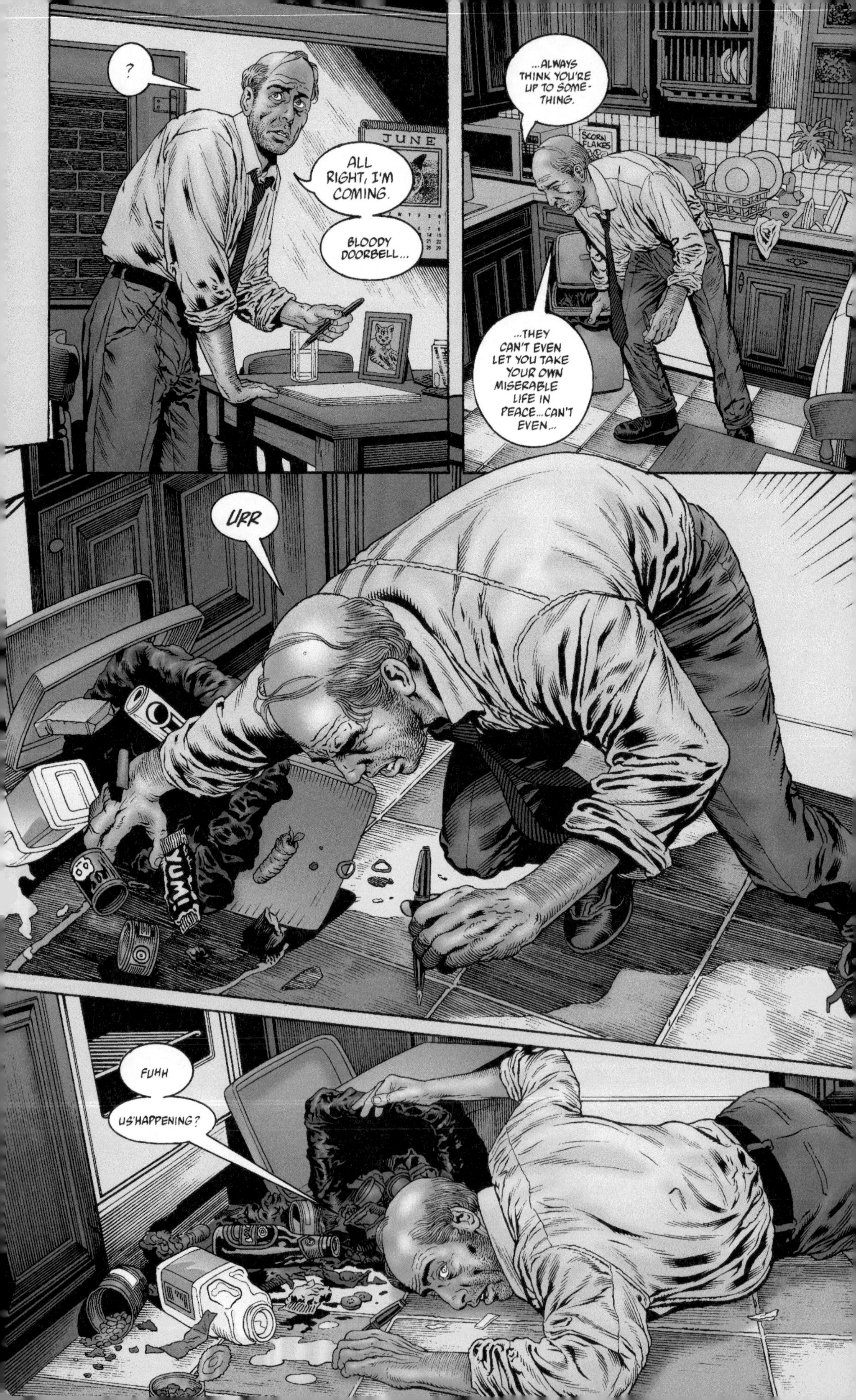
?
ALL RIGHT, I'M COMING.
BLOODY DOORBELL...
JUNE
...ALWAYS THINK YOU'RE UP TO SOMETHING.
SCORN FLAKES
...THEY CAN'T EVEN LET YOU TAKE YOUR OWN MISERABLE LIFE IN PEACE...CAN'T EVEN...
URR
YUM!
FUHH
US'HAPPENING?

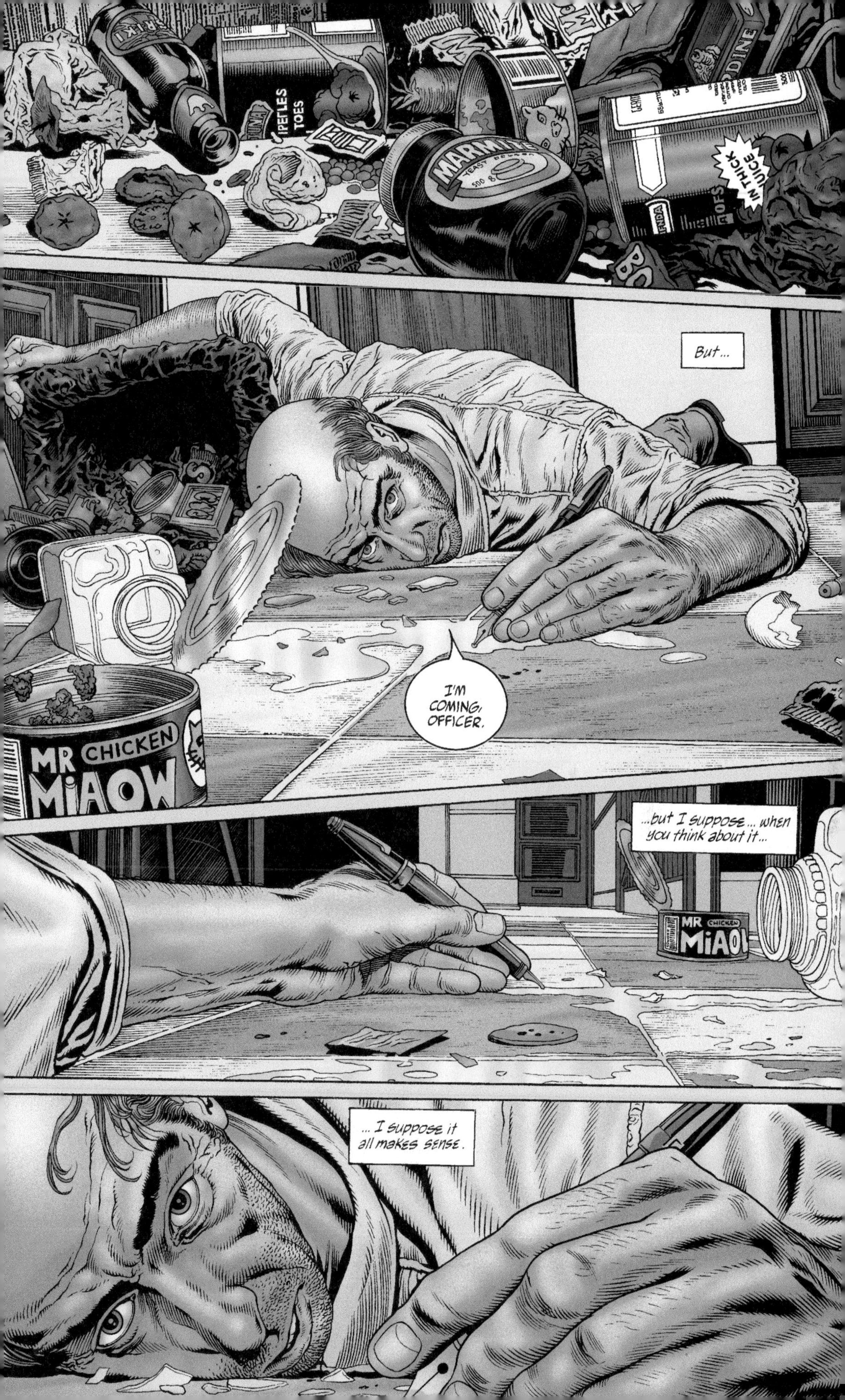
MARMITE
IN THICK JUICE
But...
I'M COMING, OFFICER.
MR CHICKEN MIAOW
...but I suppose... when you think about it...
MR CHICKEN MIAOW
... I suppose it all makes sense.

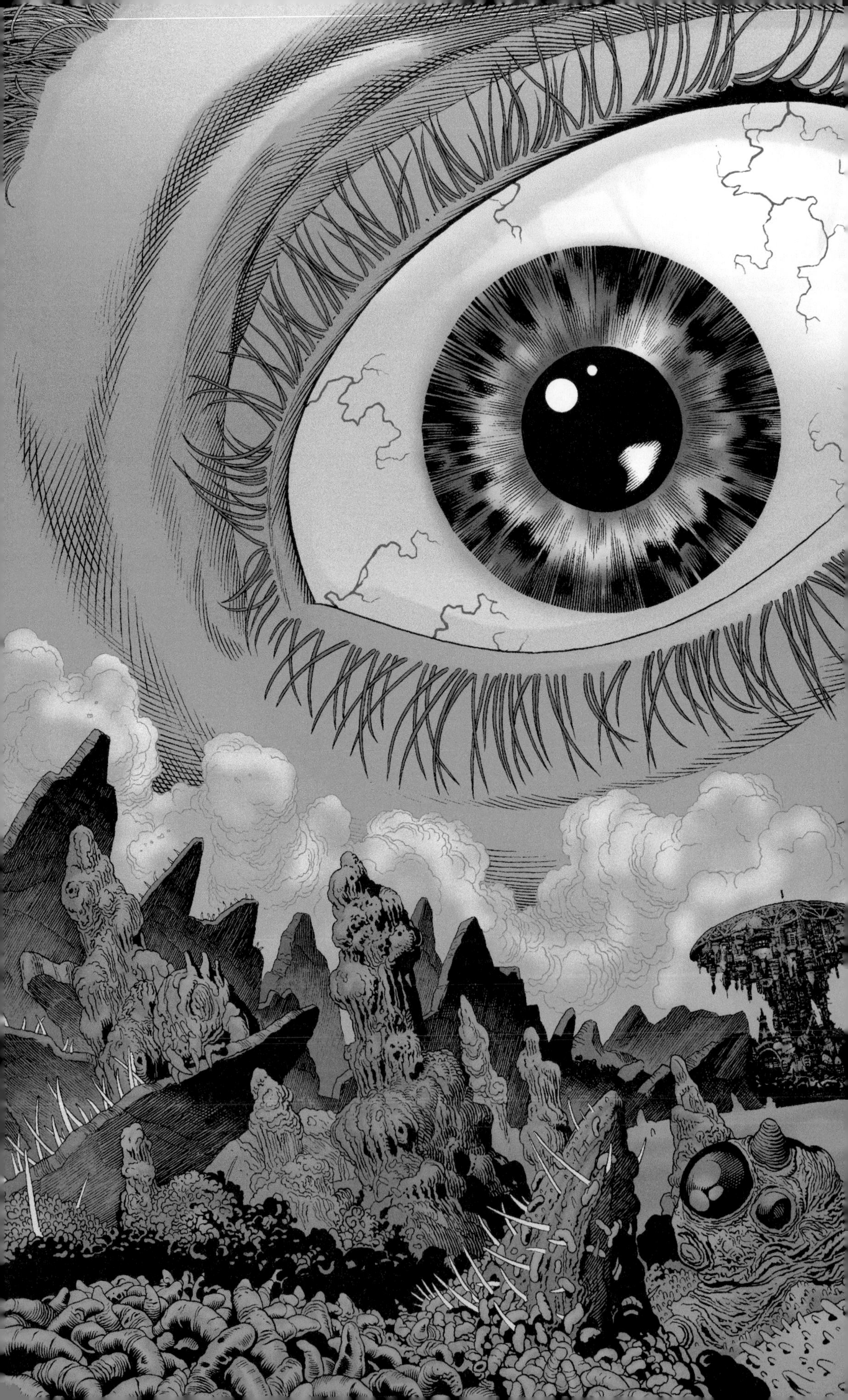

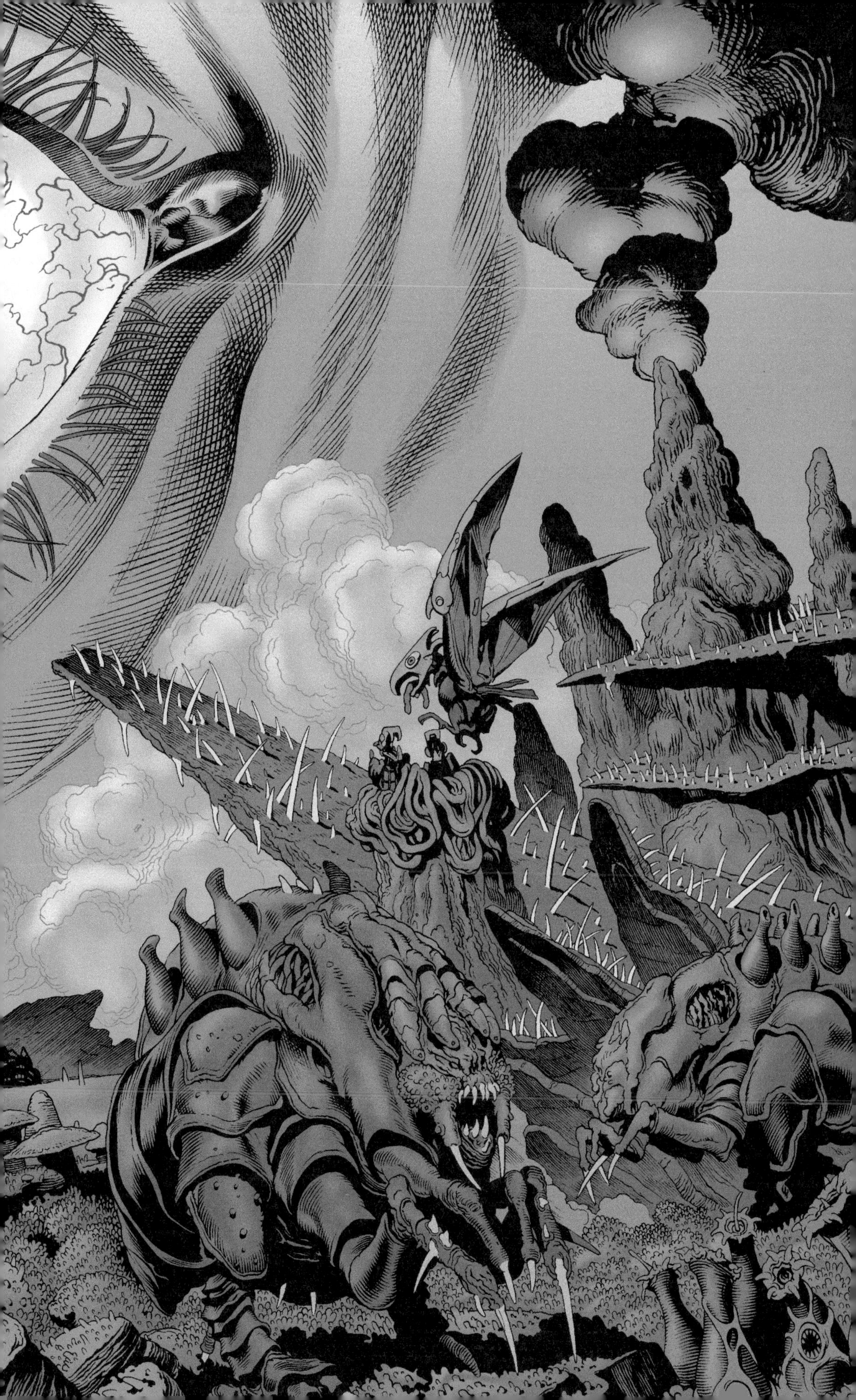

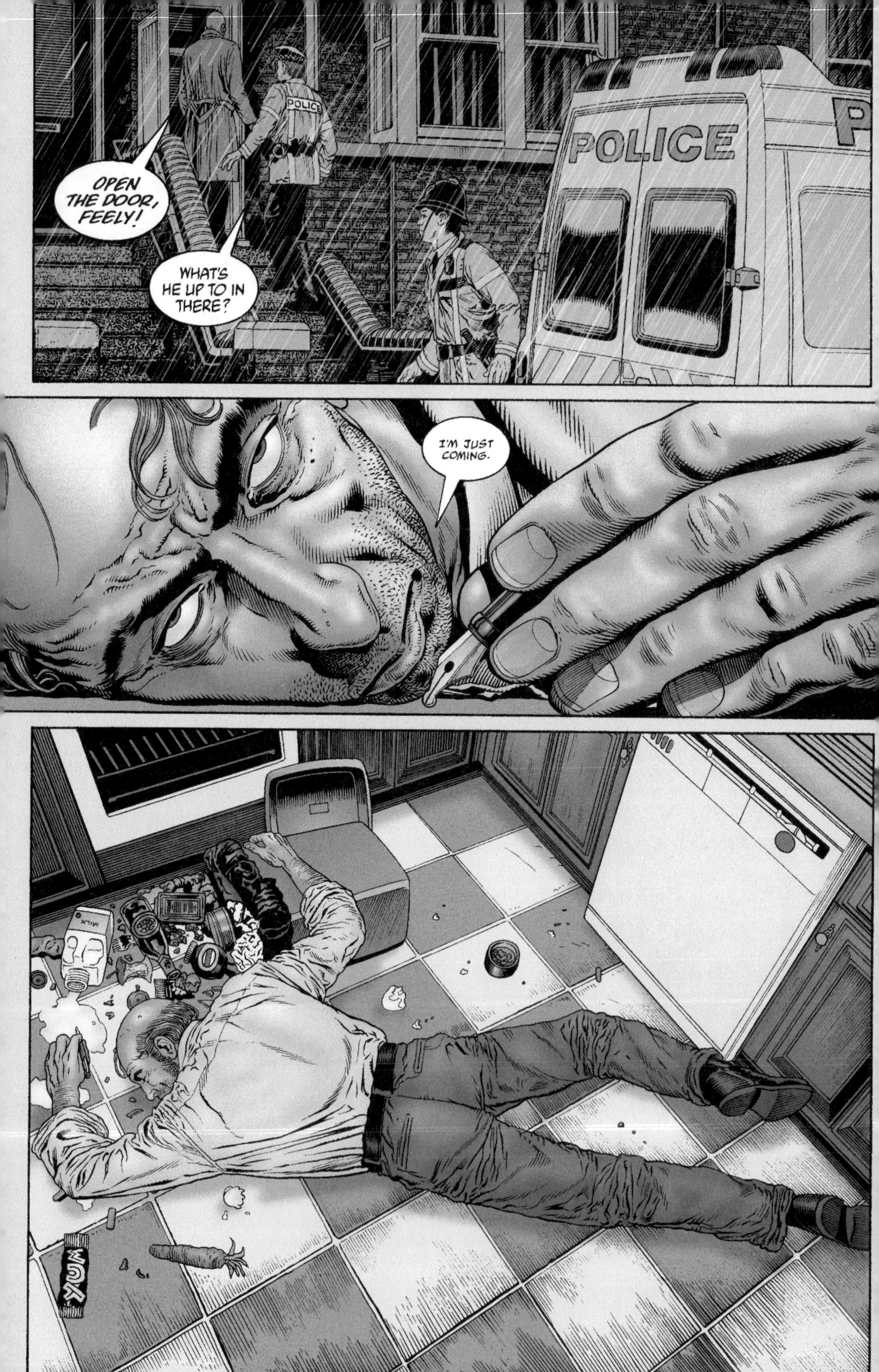
POLICE
POLICE
OPEN THE DOOR, FEELY!
WHAT'S HE UP TO IN THERE?
I'M JUST COMING.

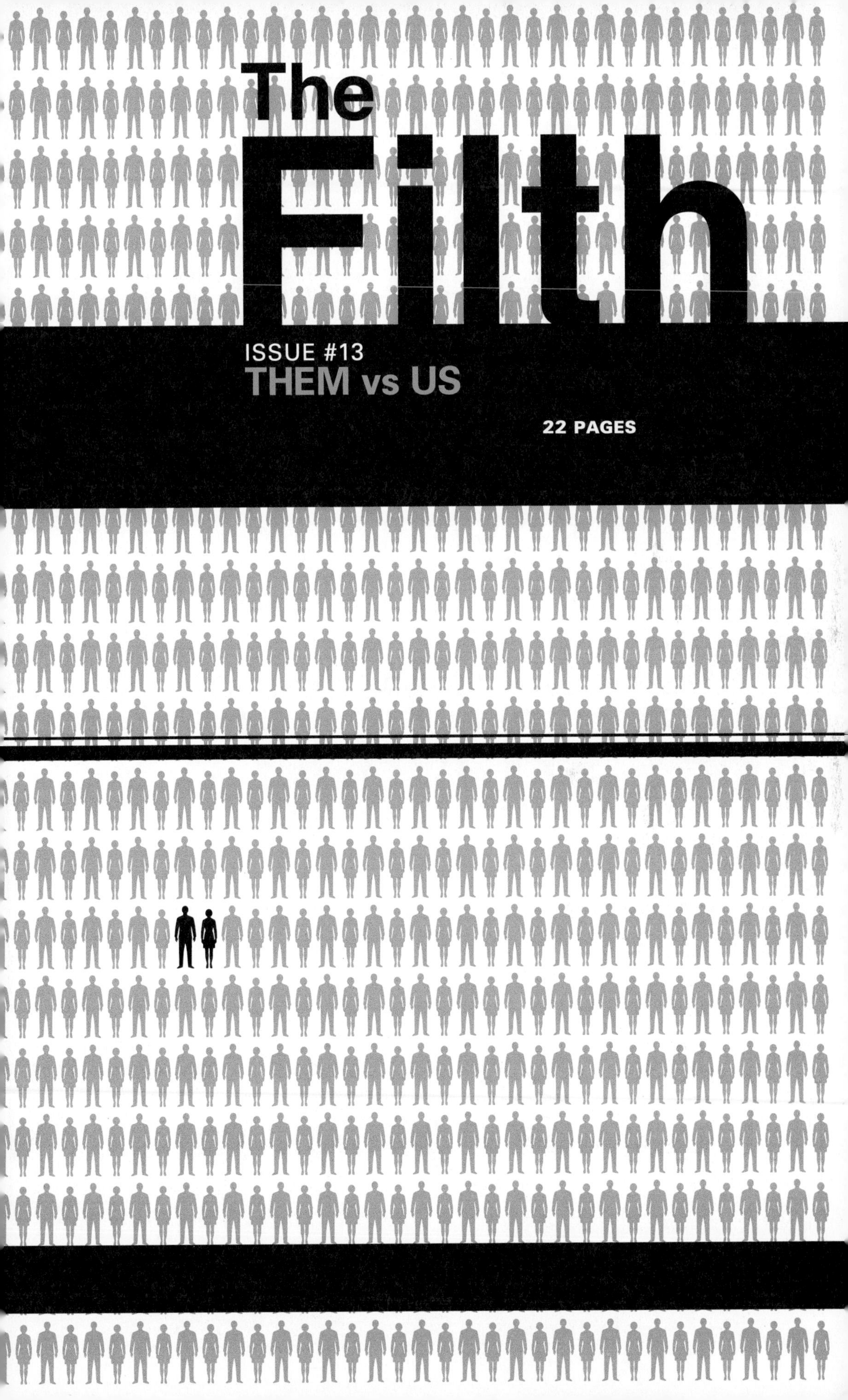
The Filth
ISSUE #13
THEM vs US
22 PAGES

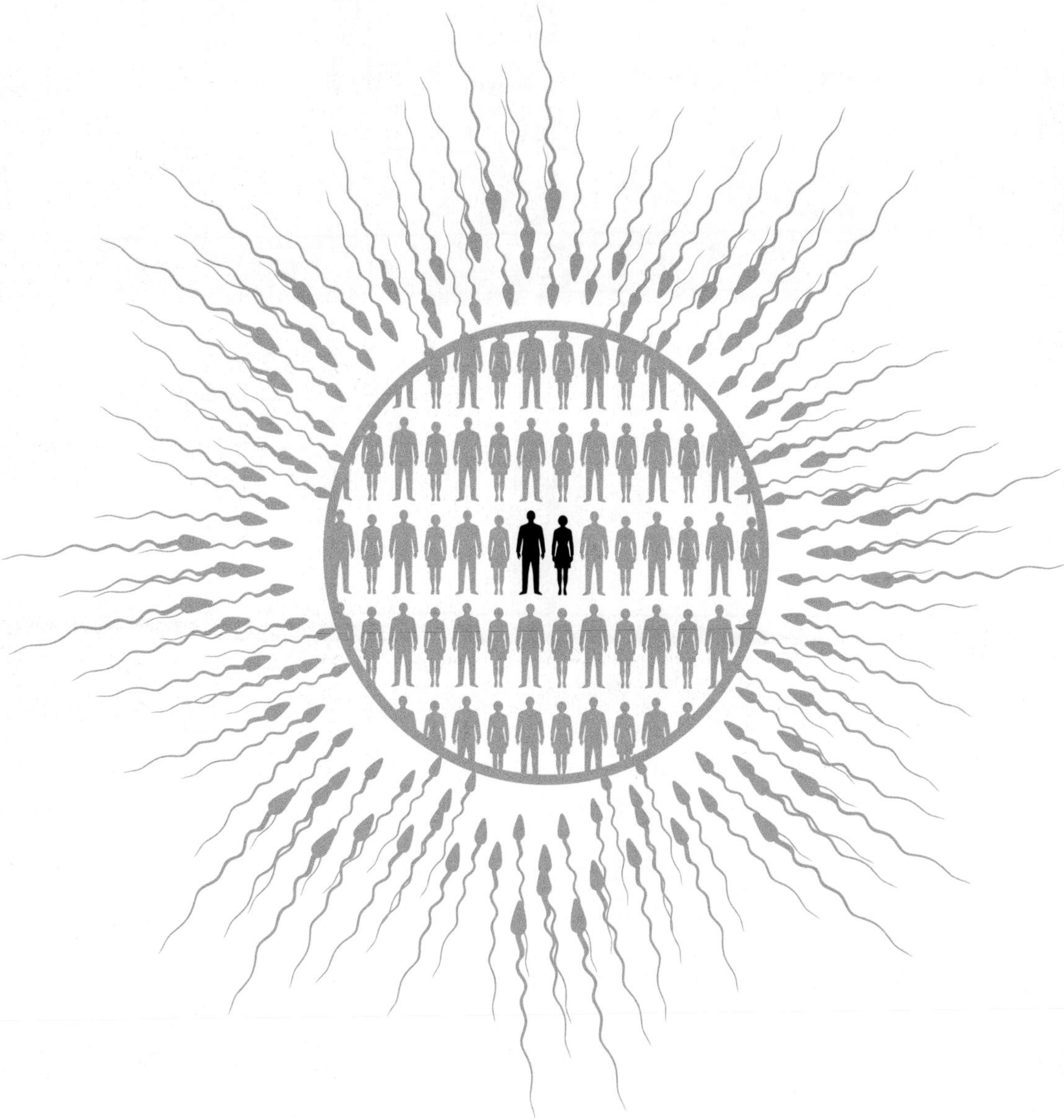

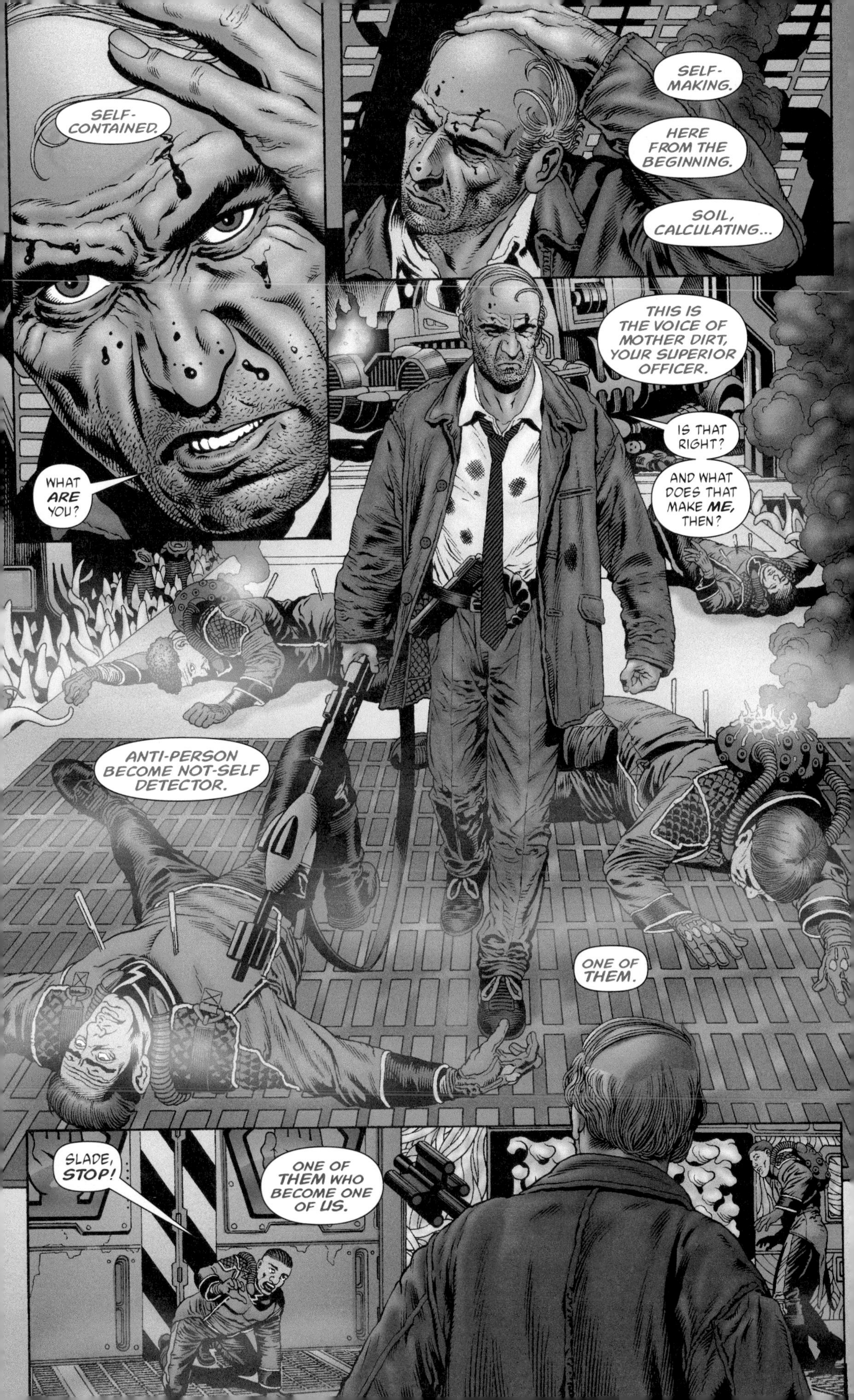
SELF-CONTAINED.
SELF-MAKING.
HERE FROM THE BEGINNING.
SOIL, CALCULATING...
WHAT ARE YOU?
THIS IS THE VOICE OF MOTHER DIRT, YOUR SUPERIOR OFFICER.
IS THAT RIGHT?
AND WHAT DOES THAT MAKE ME, THEN?
ANTI-PERSON BECOME NOT-SELF DETECTOR.
ONE OF THEM.
SLADE, STOP!
ONE OF THEM WHO BECOME ONE OF US.

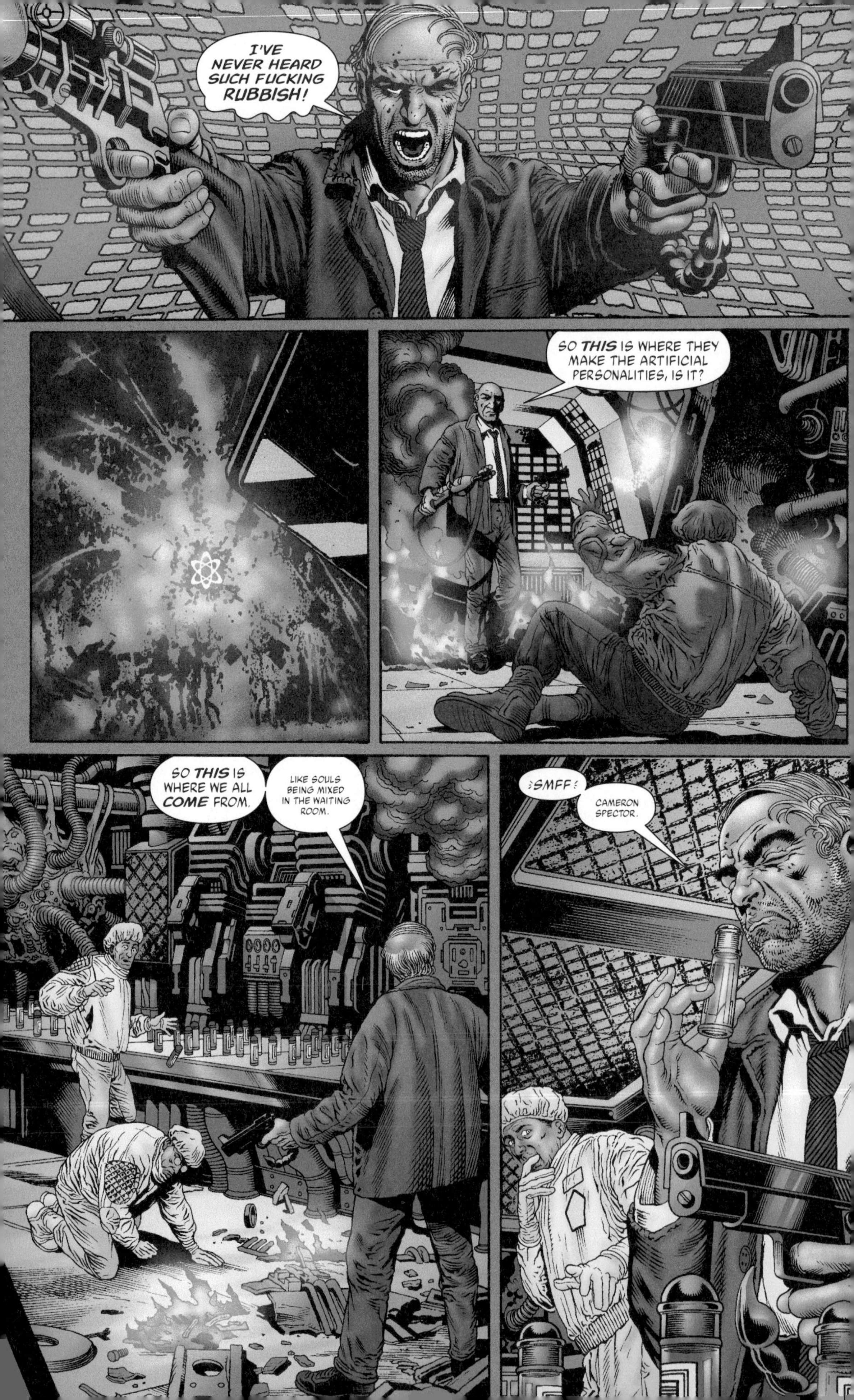
I'VE NEVER HEARD SUCH FUCKING RUBBISH!
SO THIS IS WHERE THEY MAKE THE ARTIFICIAL PERSONALITIES, IS IT?
SO THIS IS WHERE WE ALL COME FROM.
LIKE SOULS BEING MIXED IN THE WAITING ROOM.
SMFF
CAMERON SPECTOR.

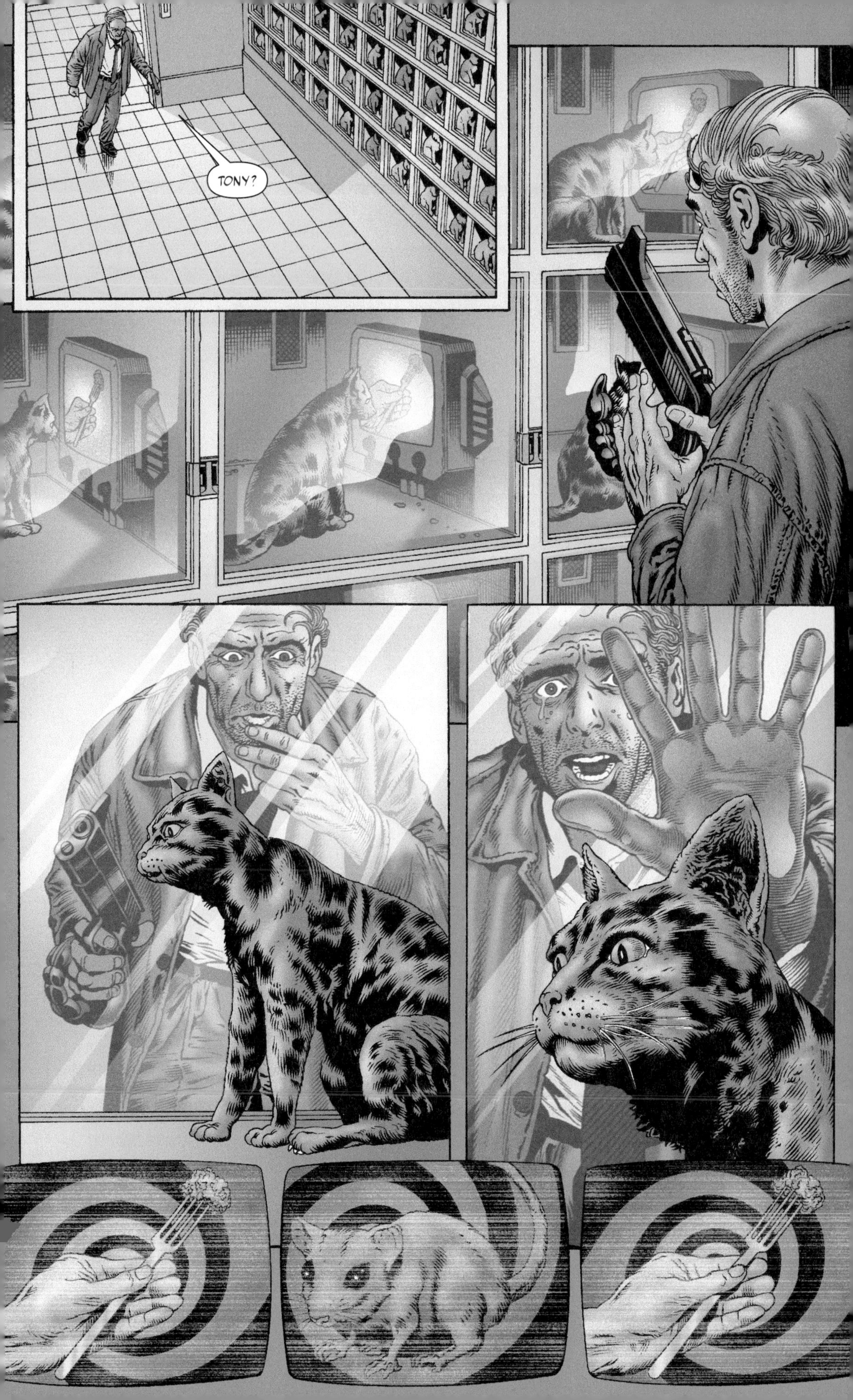
TONY?

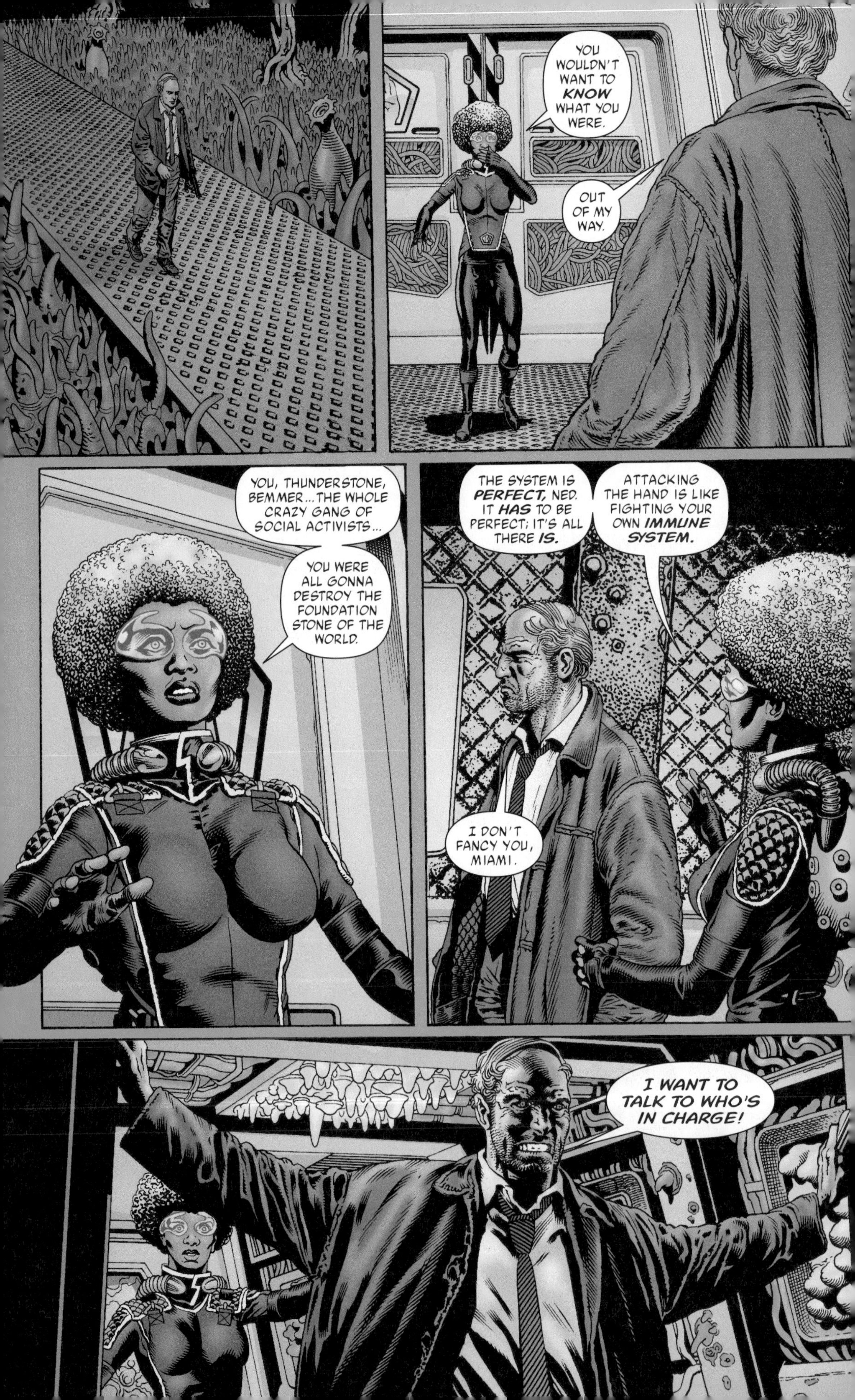
YOU WOULDN'T WANT TO KNOW WHAT YOU WERE.
OUT OF MY WAY.
YOU, THUNDERSTONE, BEMMER... THE WHOLE CRAZY GANG OF SOCIAL ACTIVISTS...
YOU WERE ALL GONNA DESTROY THE FOUNDATION STONE OF THE WORLD.
THE SYSTEM IS PERFECT, NED. IT HAS TO BE PERFECT; IT'S ALL THERE IS.
ATTACKING THE HAND IS LIKE FIGHTING YOUR OWN IMMUNE SYSTEM.
I DON'T FANCY YOU, MIAMI.
I WANT TO TALK TO WHO'S IN CHARGE!

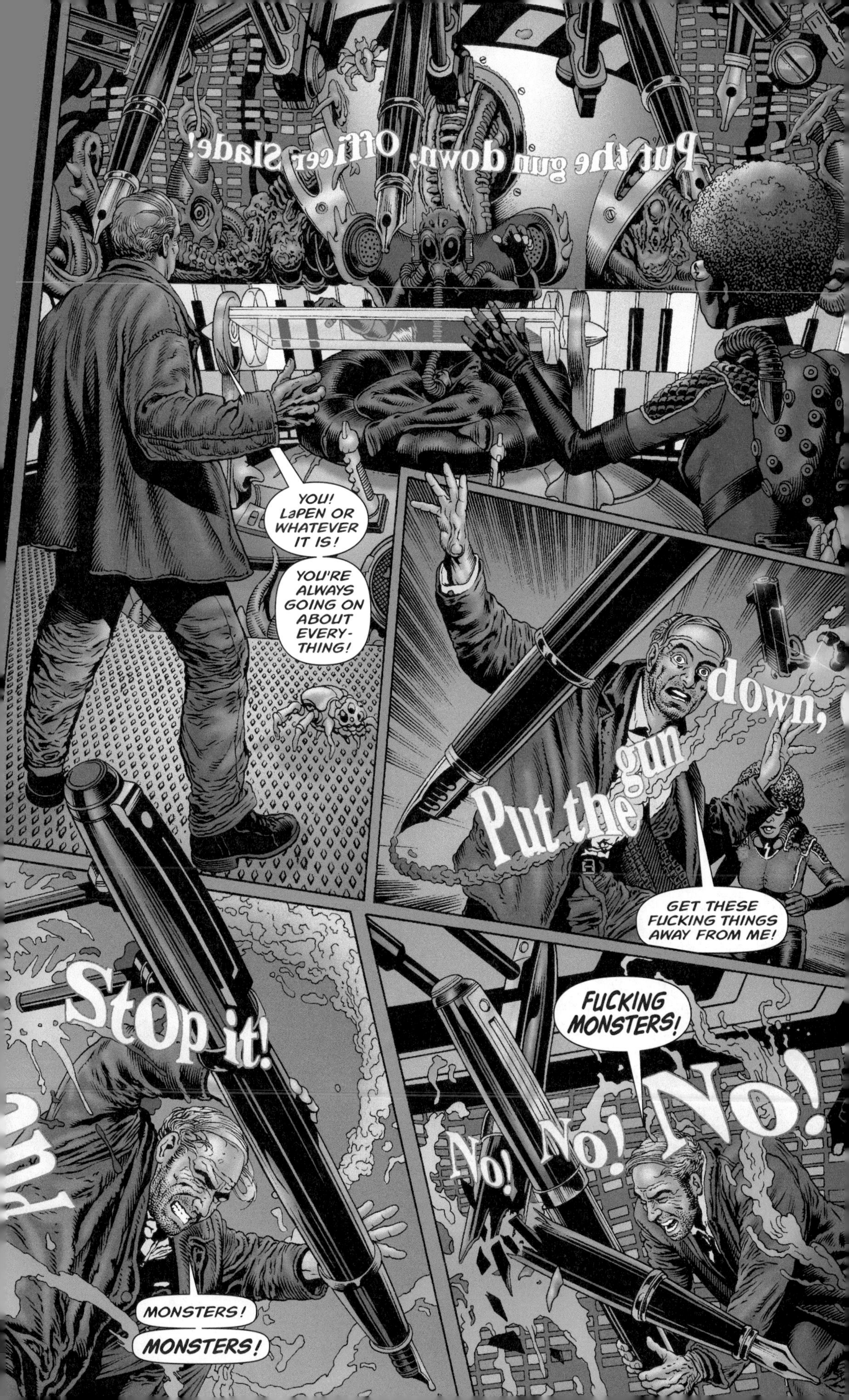
Put the gun down, Officer Slade!
YOU! LaPEN OR WHATEVER IT IS!
YOU'RE ALWAYS GOING ON ABOUT EVERY-THING!
Put the gun down,
GET THESE FUCKING THINGS AWAY FROM ME!
Stop it!
MONSTERS!
MONSTERS!
FUCKING MONSTERS!
No! No! No!

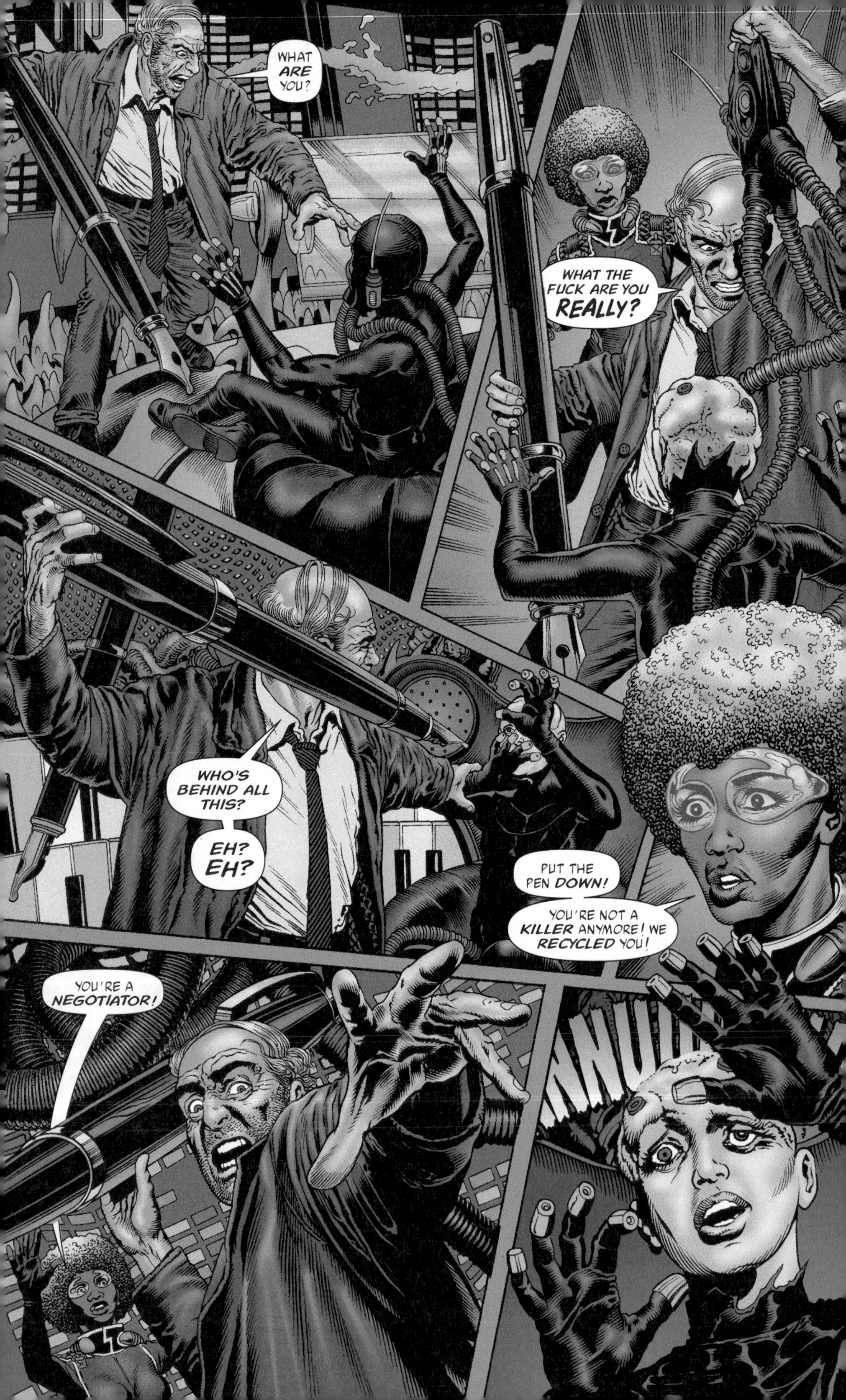
WHAT ARE YOU?
WHAT THE FUCK ARE YOU REALLY?
WHO'S BEHIND ALL THIS?
EH? EH?
PUT THE PEN DOWN!
YOU'RE NOT A KILLER ANYMORE! WE RECYCLED YOU!
YOU'RE A NEGOTIATOR!

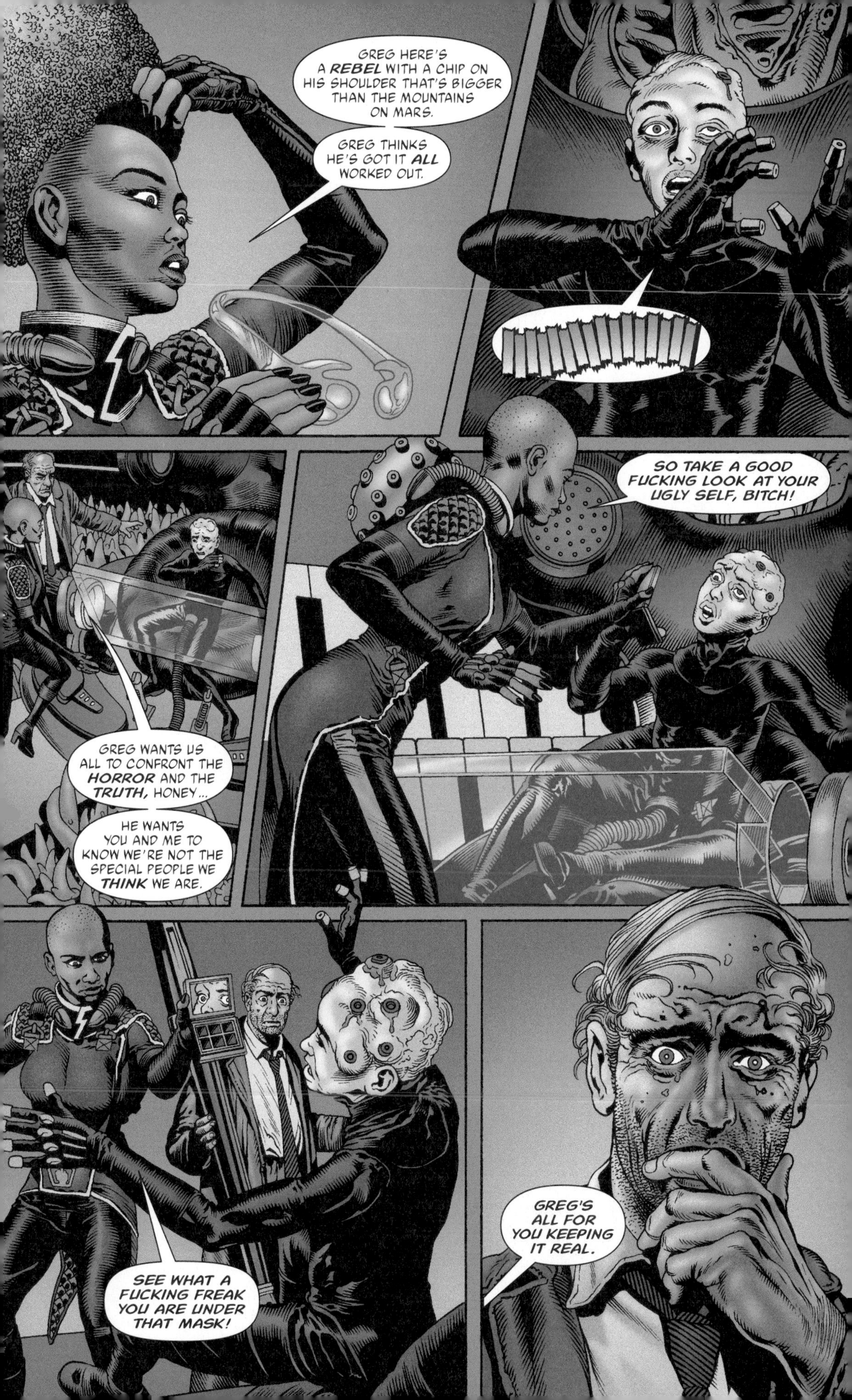
GREG HERE'S A **REBEL** WITH A CHIP ON HIS SHOULDER THAT'S BIGGER THAN THE MOUNTAINS ON MARS.
GREG THINKS HE'S GOT IT **ALL** WORKED OUT.
GREG WANTS US ALL TO CONFRONT THE **HORROR** AND THE **TRUTH,** HONEY...
HE WANTS YOU AND ME TO KNOW WE'RE NOT THE SPECIAL PEOPLE WE **THINK** WE ARE.
SO TAKE A GOOD FUCKING LOOK AT YOUR UGLY SELF, BITCH!
SEE WHAT A FUCKING FREAK YOU ARE UNDER THAT MASK!
GREG'S ALL FOR YOU KEEPING IT REAL.

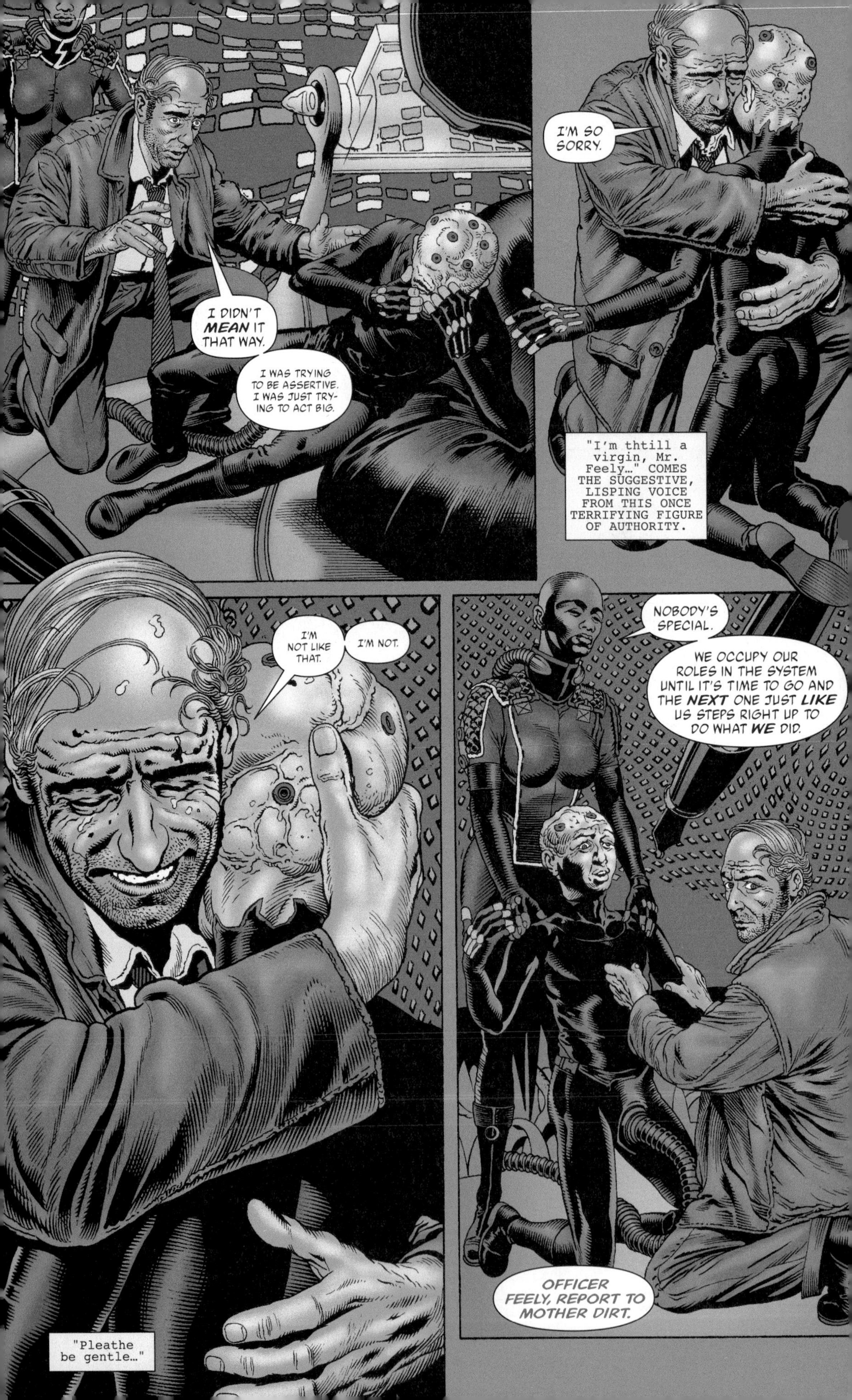
I DIDN'T MEAN IT THAT WAY.
I WAS TRYING TO BE ASSERTIVE. I WAS JUST TRY-ING TO ACT BIG.
I'M SO SORRY.
"I'm thtill a virgin, Mr. Feely..." COMES THE SUGGESTIVE, LISPING VOICE FROM THIS ONCE TERRIFYING FIGURE OF AUTHORITY.
I'M NOT LIKE THAT.
I'M NOT.
"Pleathe be gentle..."
NOBODY'S SPECIAL.
WE OCCUPY OUR ROLES IN THE SYSTEM UNTIL IT'S TIME TO GO AND THE NEXT ONE JUST LIKE US STEPS RIGHT UP TO DO WHAT WE DID.
OFFICER FEELY, REPORT TO MOTHER DIRT.

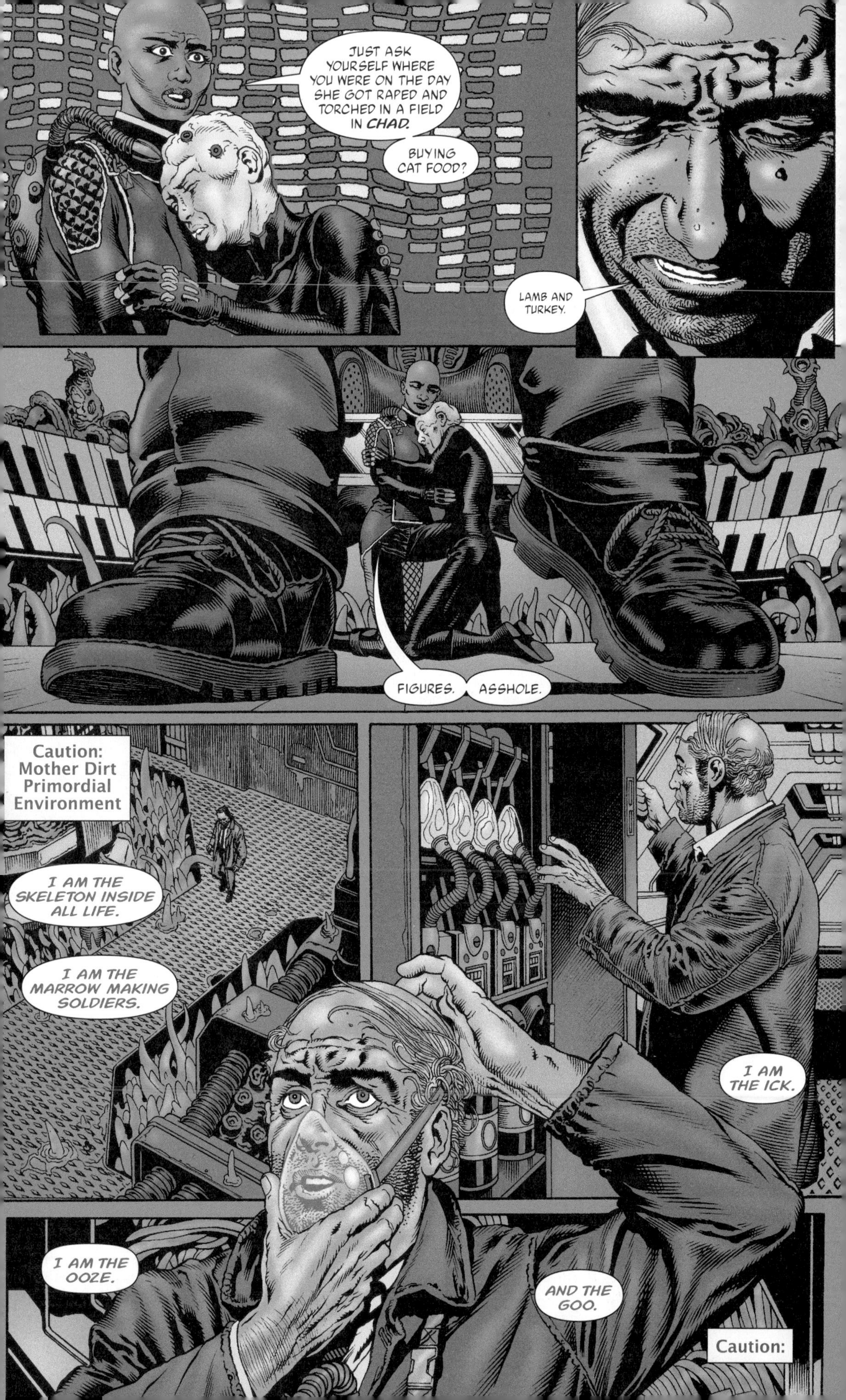
JUST ASK YOURSELF WHERE YOU WERE ON THE DAY SHE GOT RAPED AND TORCHED IN A FIELD IN CHAD.
BUYING CAT FOOD?
LAMB AND TURKEY.
FIGURES.
ASSHOLE.
Caution: Mother Dirt Primordial Environment
I AM THE SKELETON INSIDE ALL LIFE.
I AM THE MARROW MAKING SOLDIERS.
I AM THE ICK.
I AM THE OOZE.
AND THE GOO.
Caution:

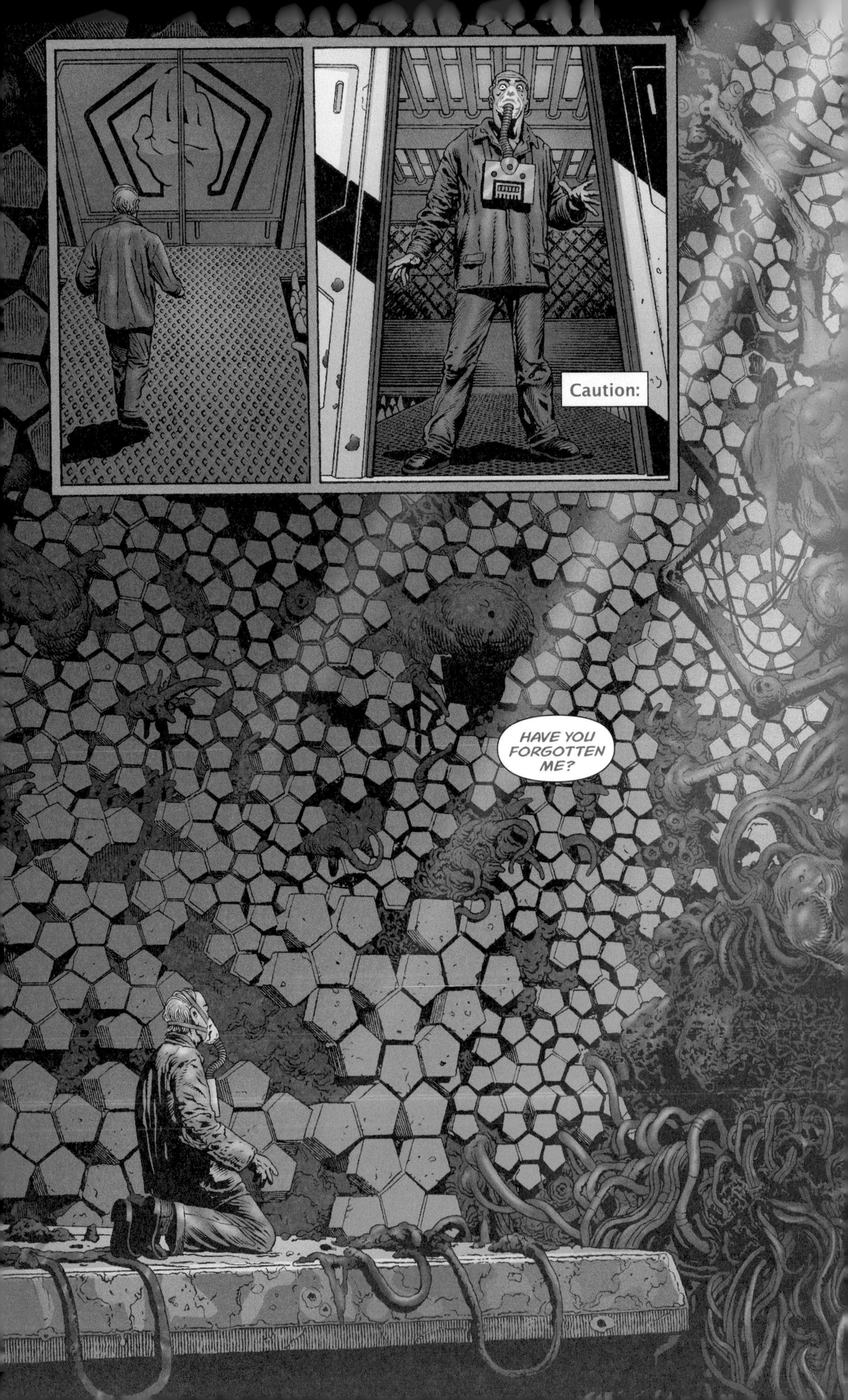

Caution:
HAVE YOU FORGOTTEN ME?

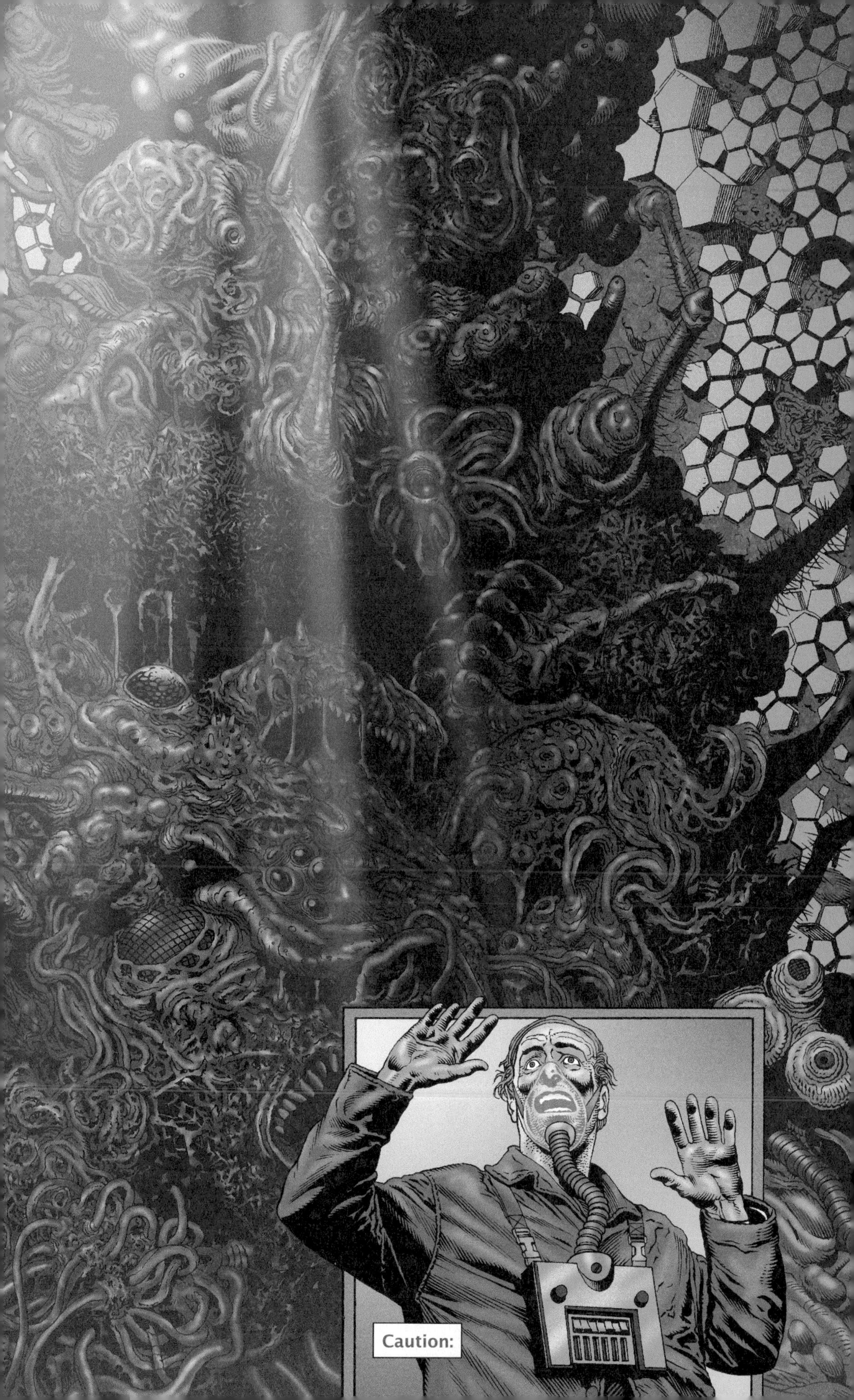
Caution:

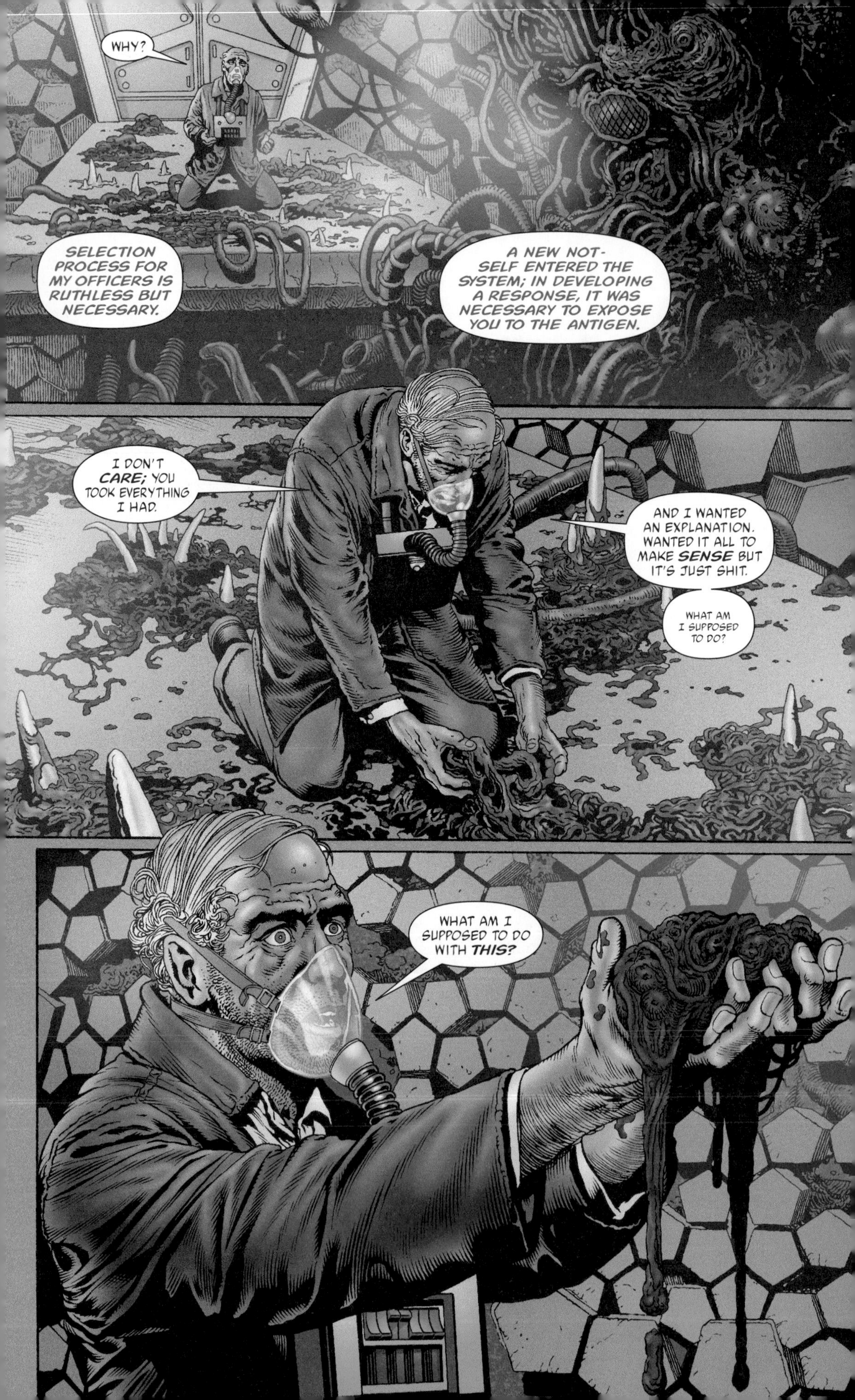

WHY?
SELECTION PROCESS FOR MY OFFICERS IS RUTHLESS BUT NECESSARY.
A NEW NOT-SELF ENTERED THE SYSTEM; IN DEVELOPING A RESPONSE, IT WAS NECESSARY TO EXPOSE YOU TO THE ANTIGEN.
I DON'T CARE; YOU TOOK EVERYTHING I HAD.
AND I WANTED AN EXPLANATION. WANTED IT ALL TO MAKE SENSE BUT IT'S JUST SHIT.
WHAT AM I SUPPOSED TO DO?
WHAT AM I SUPPOSED TO DO WITH THIS?

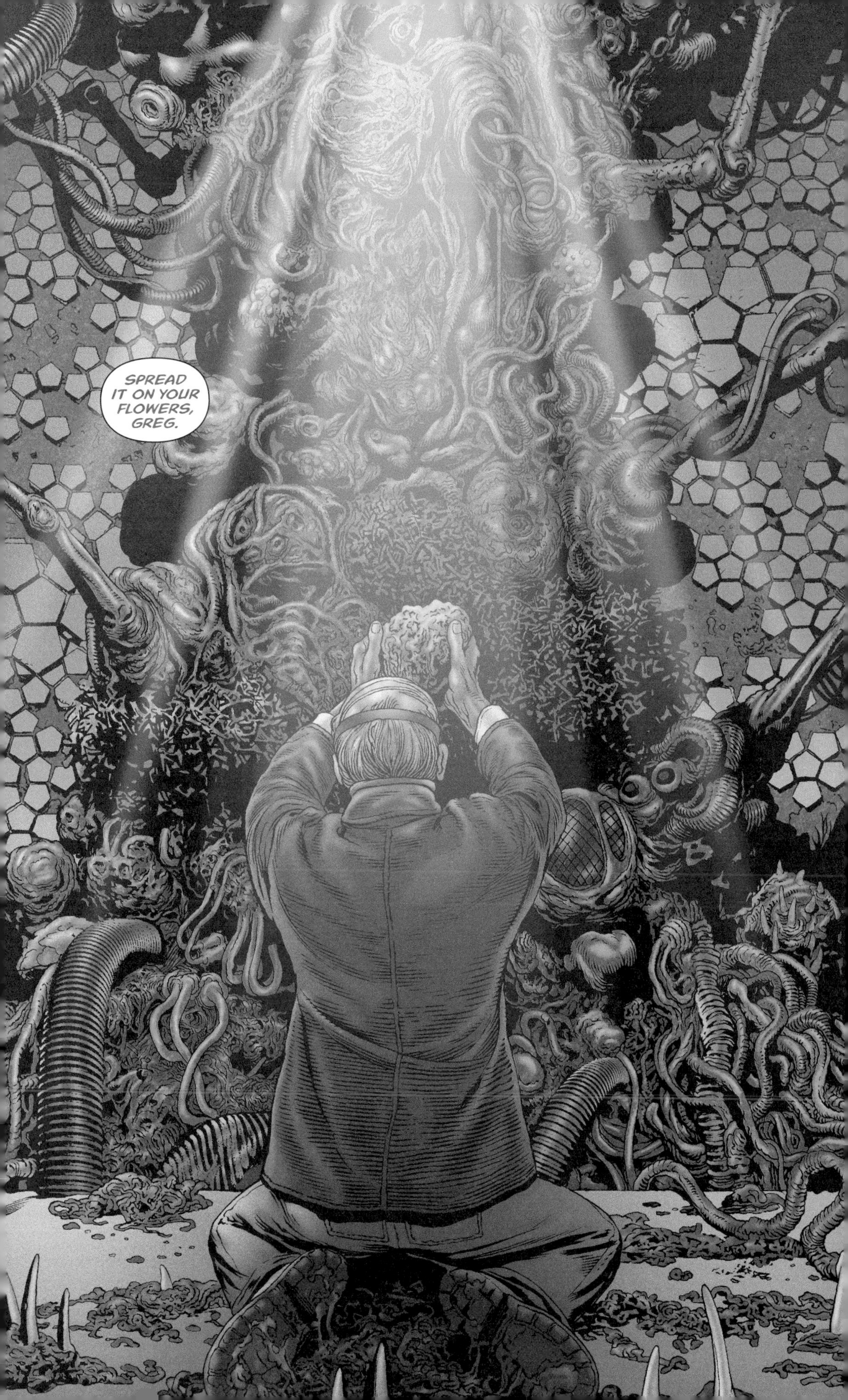
SPREAD IT ON YOUR FLOWERS, GREG.

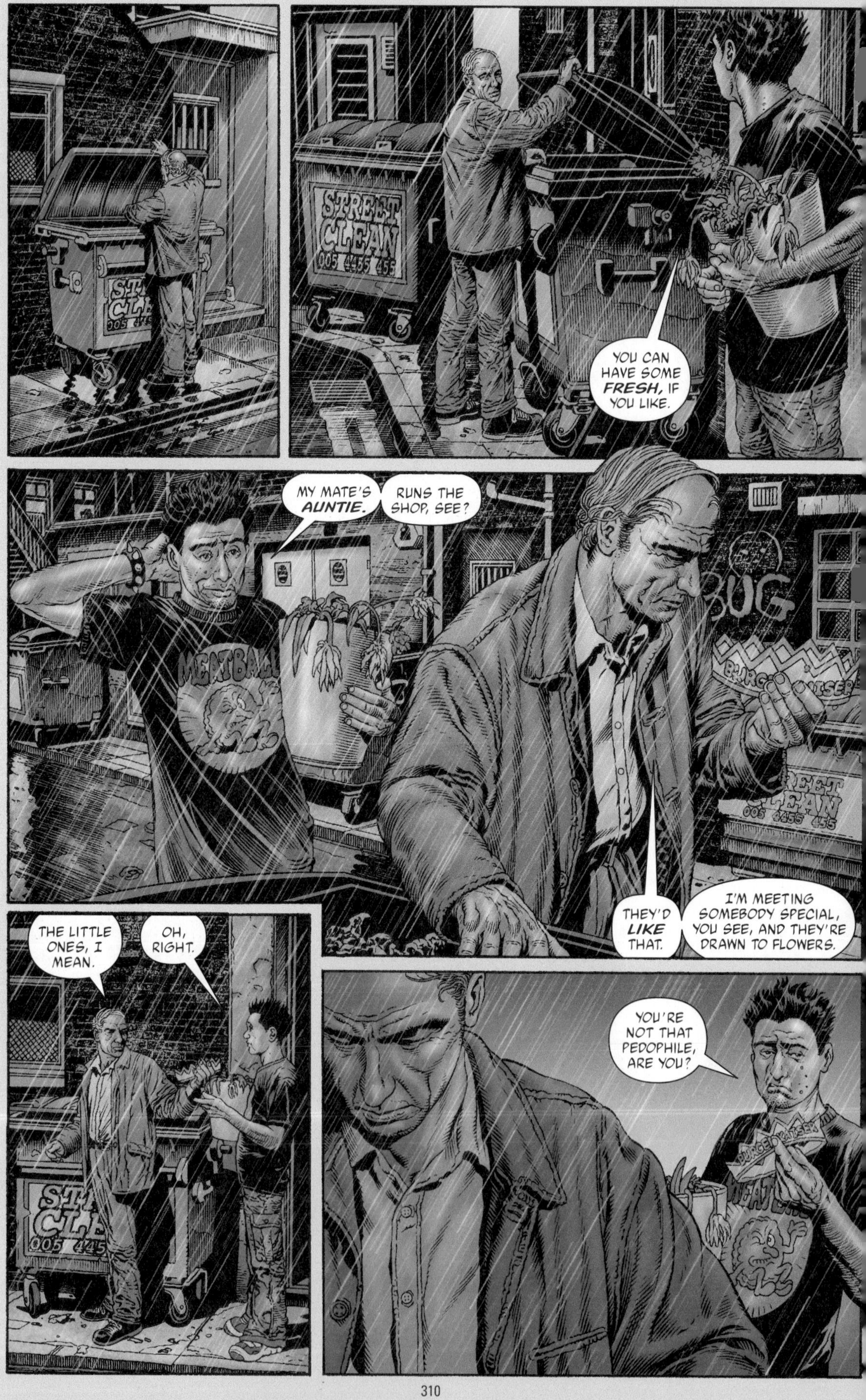
STREET CLEAN 005 4455 455
YOU CAN HAVE SOME *FRESH,* IF YOU LIKE.
MY MATE'S *AUNTIE.*
RUNS THE SHOP, SEE?
BUG
THEY'D *LIKE* THAT.
I'M MEETING SOMEBODY SPECIAL, YOU SEE, AND THEY'RE DRAWN TO FLOWERS.
THE LITTLE ONES, I MEAN.
OH, RIGHT.
YOU'RE NOT THAT PEDOPHILE, ARE YOU?

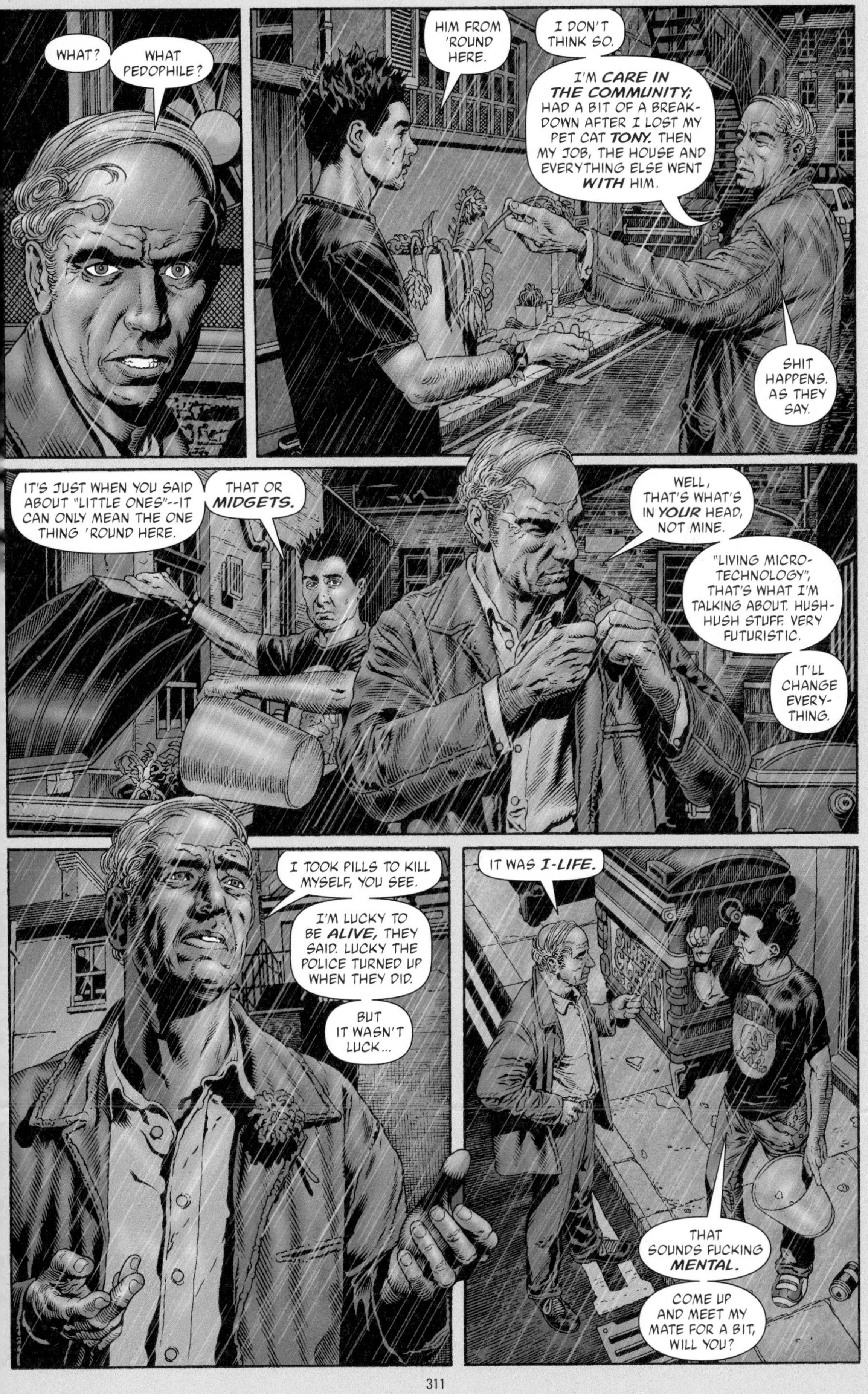
WHAT?
WHAT PEDOPHILE?
HIM FROM 'ROUND HERE.
I DON'T THINK SO.
I'M CARE IN THE COMMUNITY; HAD A BIT OF A BREAK-DOWN AFTER I LOST MY PET CAT TONY. THEN MY JOB, THE HOUSE AND EVERYTHING ELSE WENT WITH HIM.
SHIT HAPPENS. AS THEY SAY.
IT'S JUST WHEN YOU SAID ABOUT "LITTLE ONES"--IT CAN ONLY MEAN THE ONE THING 'ROUND HERE.
THAT OR MIDGETS.
WELL, THAT'S WHAT'S IN YOUR HEAD, NOT MINE.
"LIVING MICRO-TECHNOLOGY", THAT'S WHAT I'M TALKING ABOUT. HUSH-HUSH STUFF. VERY FUTURISTIC.
IT'LL CHANGE EVERY-THING.
I TOOK PILLS TO KILL MYSELF, YOU SEE.
I'M LUCKY TO BE ALIVE, THEY SAID. LUCKY THE POLICE TURNED UP WHEN THEY DID.
BUT IT WASN'T LUCK...
IT WAS I-LIFE.
THAT SOUNDS FUCKING MENTAL.
COME UP AND MEET MY MATE FOR A BIT, WILL YOU?

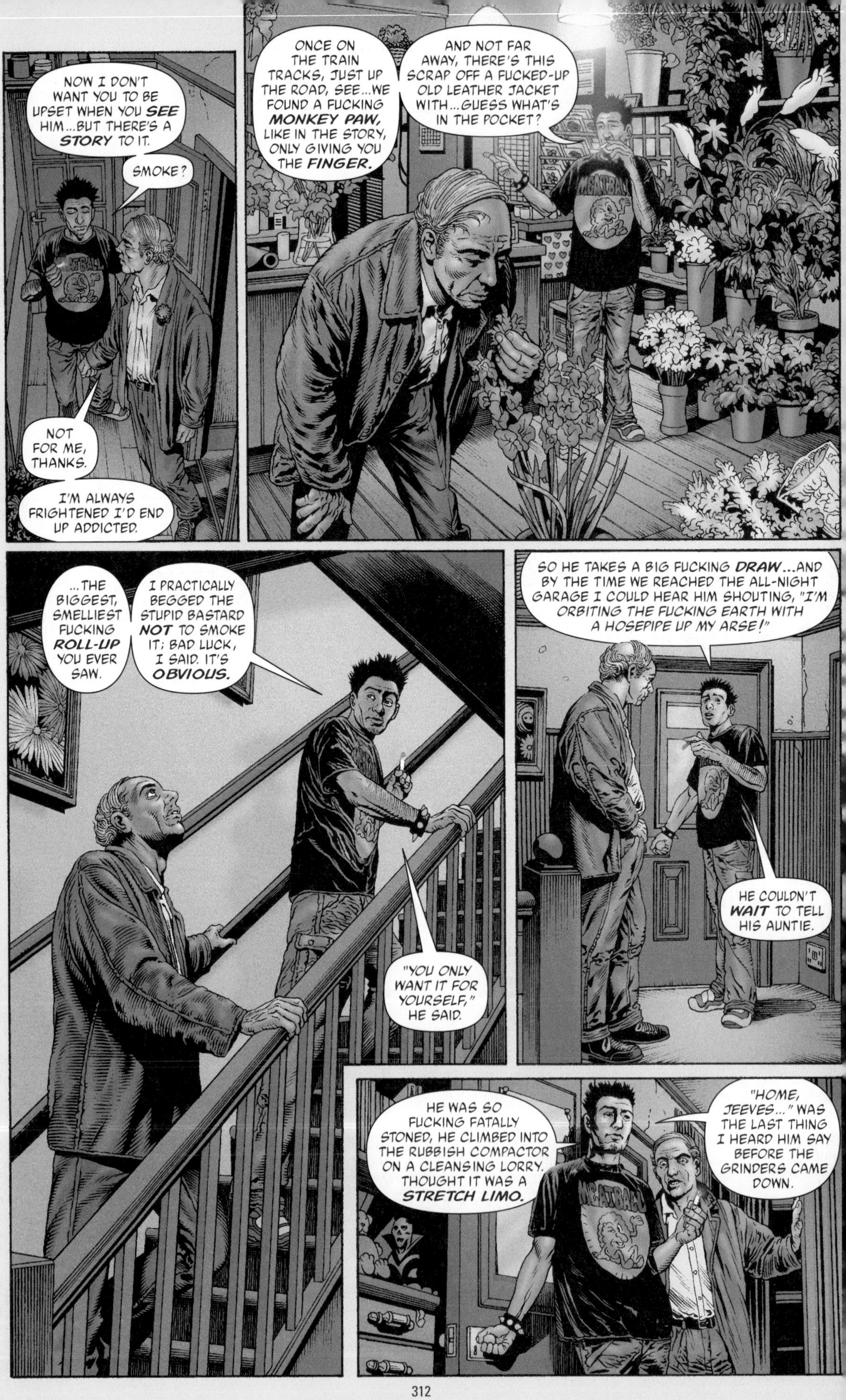
NOW I DON'T WANT YOU TO BE UPSET WHEN YOU SEE HIM...BUT THERE'S A STORY TO IT.
SMOKE?
NOT FOR ME, THANKS.
I'M ALWAYS FRIGHTENED I'D END UP ADDICTED.
ONCE ON THE TRAIN TRACKS, JUST UP THE ROAD, SEE...WE FOUND A FUCKING MONKEY PAW, LIKE IN THE STORY, ONLY GIVING YOU THE FINGER.
AND NOT FAR AWAY, THERE'S THIS SCRAP OFF A FUCKED-UP OLD LEATHER JACKET WITH...GUESS WHAT'S IN THE POCKET?
...THE BIGGEST, SMELLIEST FUCKING ROLL-UP YOU EVER SAW.
I PRACTICALLY BEGGED THE STUPID BASTARD NOT TO SMOKE IT; BAD LUCK, I SAID. IT'S OBVIOUS.
"YOU ONLY WANT IT FOR YOURSELF," HE SAID.
SO HE TAKES A BIG FUCKING DRAW...AND BY THE TIME WE REACHED THE ALL-NIGHT GARAGE I COULD HEAR HIM SHOUTING, "I'M ORBITING THE FUCKING EARTH WITH A HOSEPIPE UP MY ARSE!"
HE COULDN'T WAIT TO TELL HIS AUNTIE.
HE WAS SO FUCKING FATALLY STONED, HE CLIMBED INTO THE RUBBISH COMPACTOR ON A CLEANSING LORRY. THOUGHT IT WAS A STRETCH LIMO.
"HOME, JEEVES..." WAS THE LAST THING I HEARD HIM SAY BEFORE THE GRINDERS CAME DOWN.

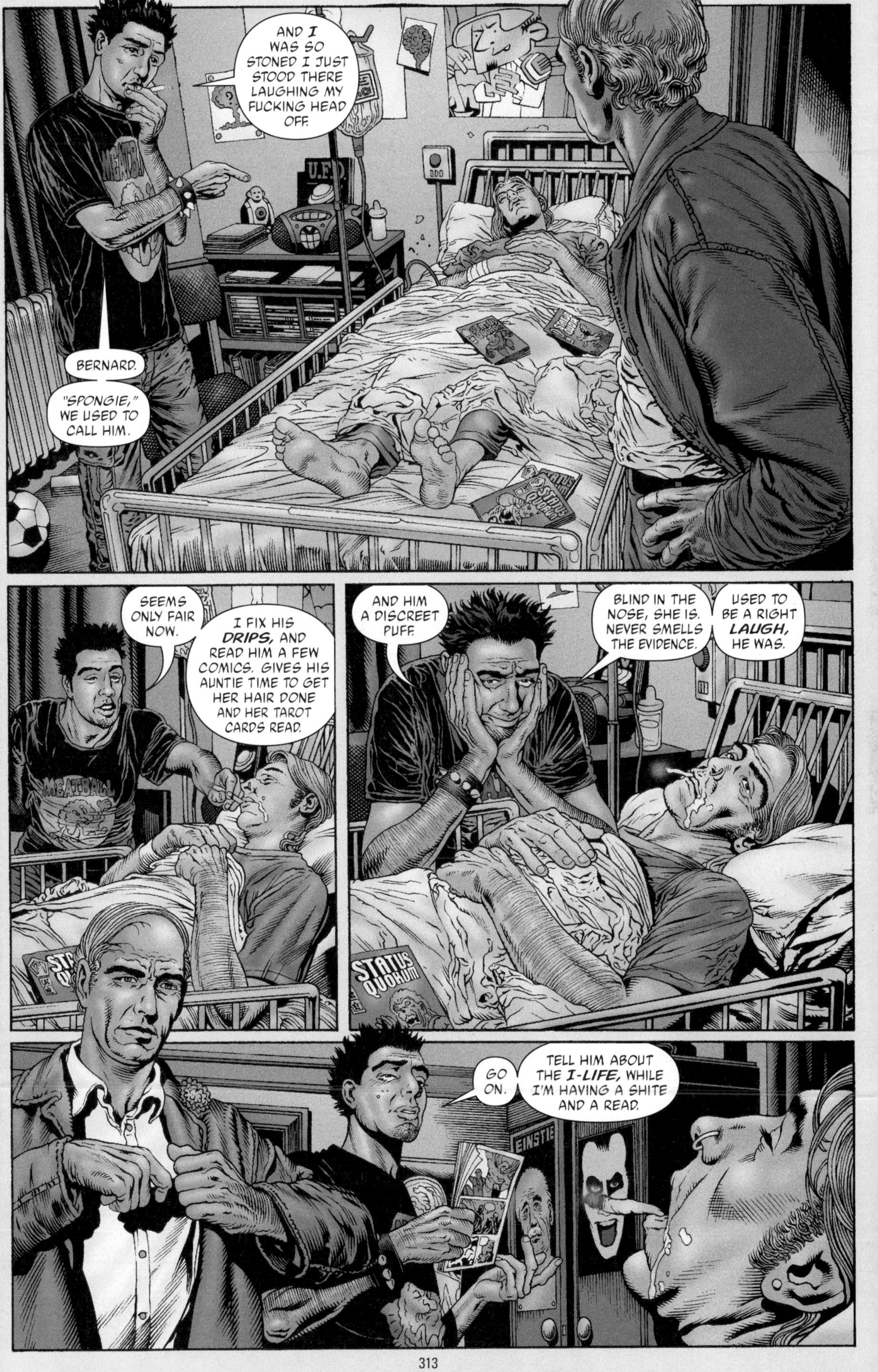
AND *I* WAS SO STONED I JUST STOOD THERE LAUGHING MY FUCKING HEAD OFF.
BERNARD.
"SPONGIE," WE USED TO CALL HIM.
U.F.O.
STATUS QUORUM
SEEMS ONLY FAIR NOW.
I FIX HIS *DRIPS,* AND READ HIM A FEW COMICS. GIVES HIS AUNTIE TIME TO GET HER HAIR DONE AND HER TAROT CARDS READ.
AND HIM A DISCREET PUFF.
BLIND IN THE NOSE, SHE IS. NEVER SMELLS THE EVIDENCE.
USED TO BE A RIGHT *LAUGH,* HE WAS.
STATUS QUORUM
GO ON.
TELL HIM ABOUT THE *I-LIFE,* WHILE I'M HAVING A SHITE AND A READ.

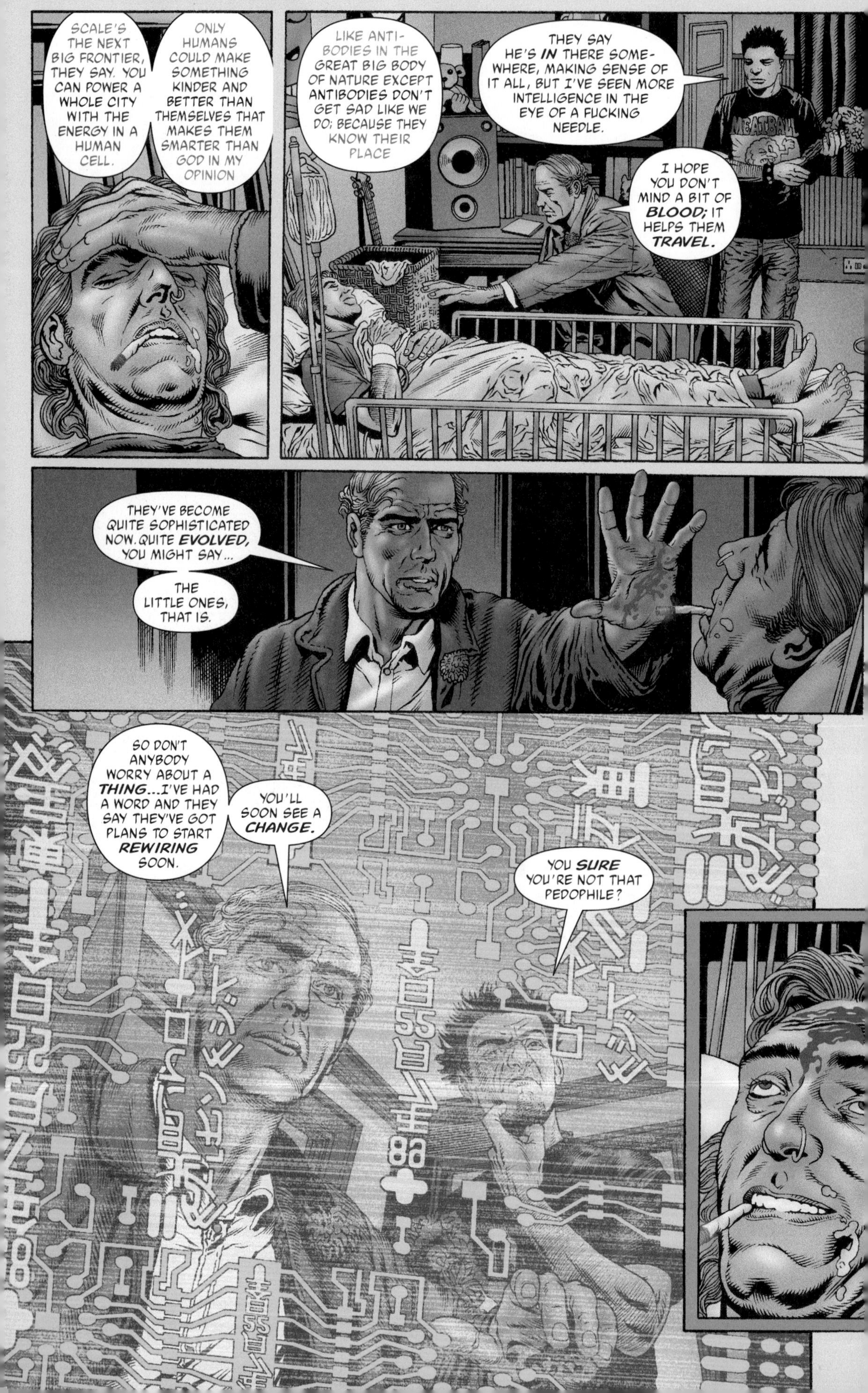
SCALE'S THE NEXT BIG FRONTIER, THEY SAY. YOU CAN POWER A WHOLE CITY WITH THE ENERGY IN A HUMAN CELL.
ONLY HUMANS COULD MAKE SOMETHING KINDER AND BETTER THAN THEMSELVES THAT MAKES THEM SMARTER THAN GOD IN MY OPINION
LIKE ANTI-BODIES IN THE GREAT BIG BODY OF NATURE EXCEPT ANTIBODIES DON'T GET SAD LIKE WE DO; BECAUSE THEY KNOW THEIR PLACE
THEY SAY HE'S IN THERE SOME-WHERE, MAKING SENSE OF IT ALL, BUT I'VE SEEN MORE INTELLIGENCE IN THE EYE OF A FUCKING NEEDLE.
I HOPE YOU DON'T MIND A BIT OF BLOOD; IT HELPS THEM TRAVEL.
THEY'VE BECOME QUITE SOPHISTICATED NOW. QUITE EVOLVED, YOU MIGHT SAY...
THE LITTLE ONES, THAT IS.
SO DON'T ANYBODY WORRY ABOUT A THING...I'VE HAD A WORD AND THEY SAY THEY'VE GOT PLANS TO START REWIRING SOON.
YOU'LL SOON SEE A CHANGE.
YOU SURE YOU'RE NOT THAT PEDOPHILE?

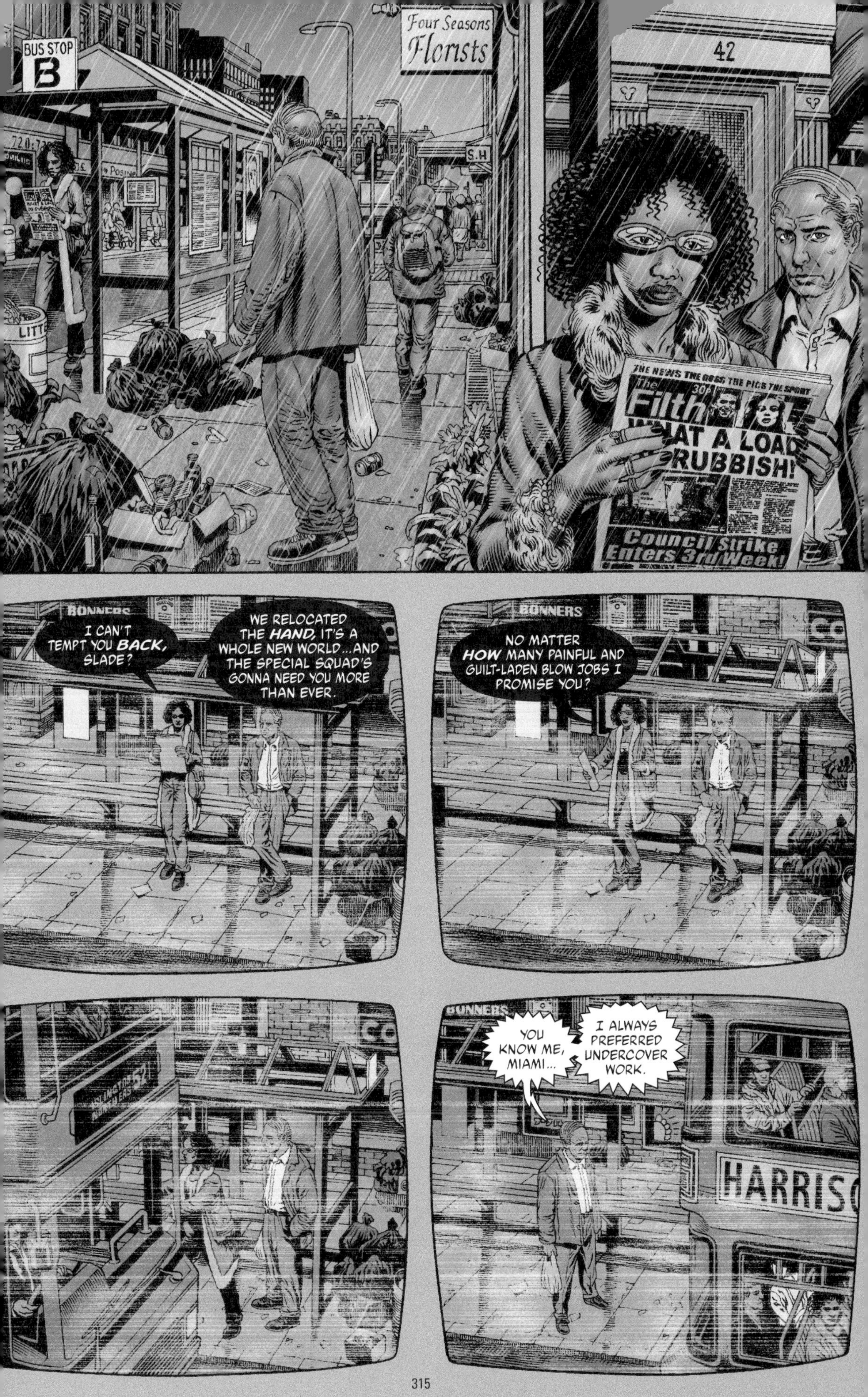
BUS STOP
B
Four Seasons
Florists
42
S.H
THE NEWS THE GOSS THE PICS THE SPORT
The Filth
WHAT A LOAD
RUBBISH!
Council Strike
Enters 3rd Week!
BONNERS
I CAN'T TEMPT YOU BACK, SLADE?
WE RELOCATED THE HAND, IT'S A WHOLE NEW WORLD...AND THE SPECIAL SQUAD'S GONNA NEED YOU MORE THAN EVER.
BONNERS
NO MATTER HOW MANY PAINFUL AND GUILT-LADEN BLOW JOBS I PROMISE YOU?
BONNERS
YOU KNOW ME, MIAMI...
I ALWAYS PREFERRED UNDERCOVER WORK.
HARRISO

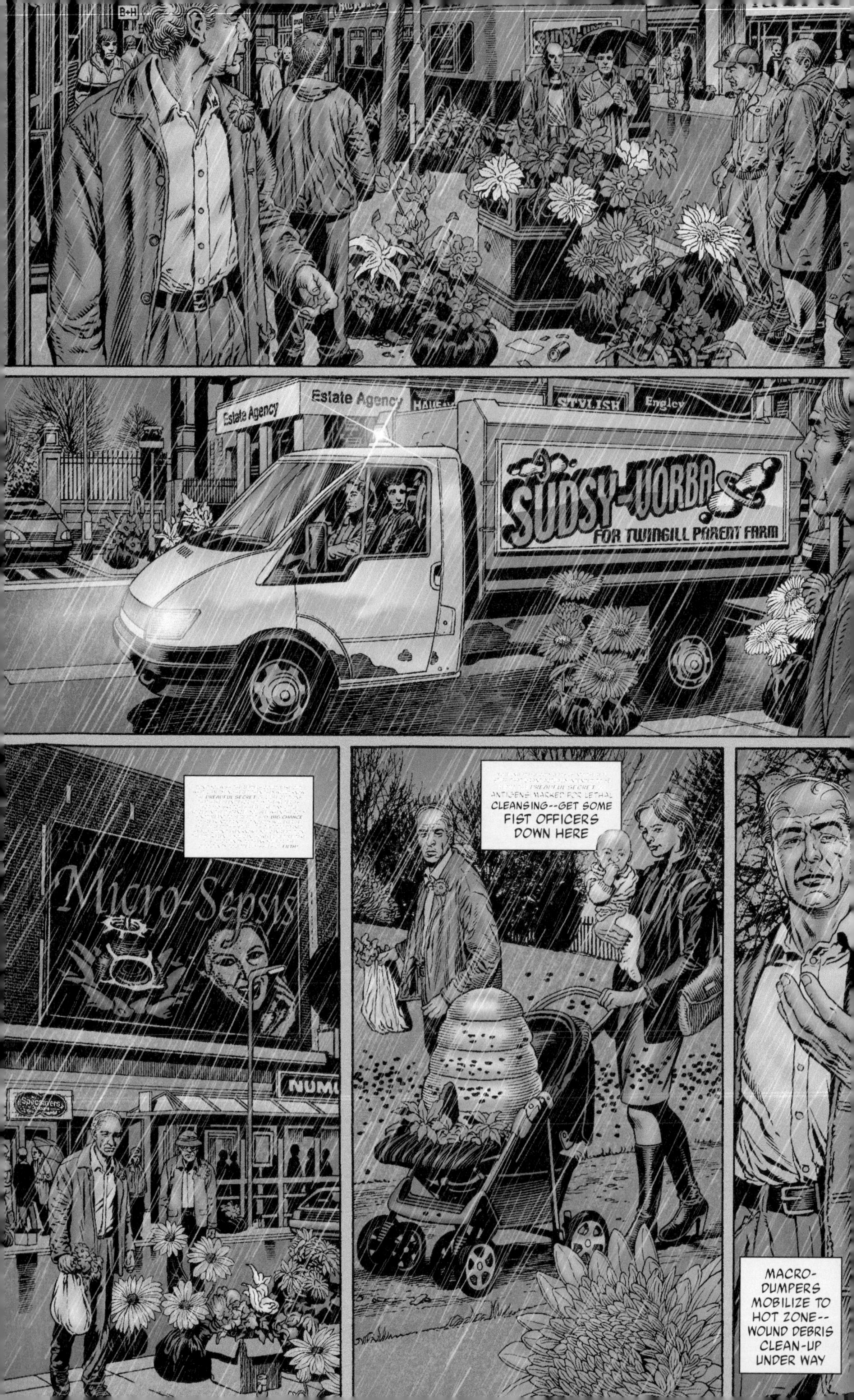
Estate Agency
Estate Agency
STYLISH
SUDSY-VORBA
FOR TWINGILL PARENT FARM
Micro-Sepsis
DREADFUL SECRET
BIG CHANCE
FILTH!
DREADFUL SECRET
ANTIGENS MARKED FOR LETHAL
CLEANSING--GET SOME
FIST OFFICERS
DOWN HERE
MACRO-
DUMPERS
MOBILIZE TO
HOT ZONE--
WOUND DEBRIS
CLEAN-UP
UNDER WAY

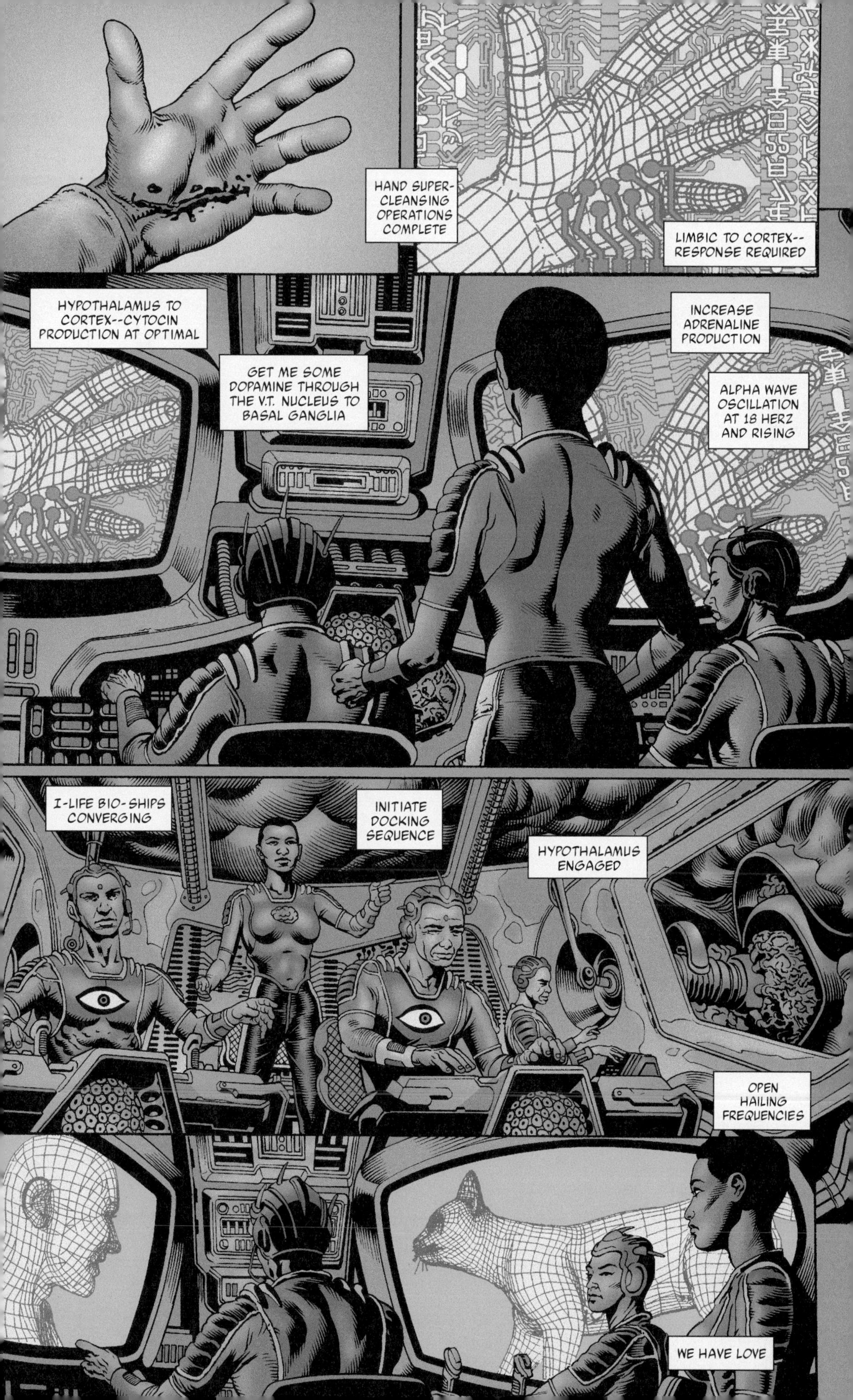
HAND SUPER-CLEANSING OPERATIONS COMPLETE
LIMBIC TO CORTEX--RESPONSE REQUIRED
HYPOTHALAMUS TO CORTEX--CYTOCIN PRODUCTION AT OPTIMAL
GET ME SOME DOPAMINE THROUGH THE V.T. NUCLEUS TO BASAL GANGLIA
INCREASE ADRENALINE PRODUCTION
ALPHA WAVE OSCILLATION AT 18 HERZ AND RISING
I-LIFE BIO-SHIPS CONVERGING
INITIATE DOCKING SEQUENCE
HYPOTHALAMUS ENGAGED
OPEN HAILING FREQUENCIES
WE HAVE LOVE

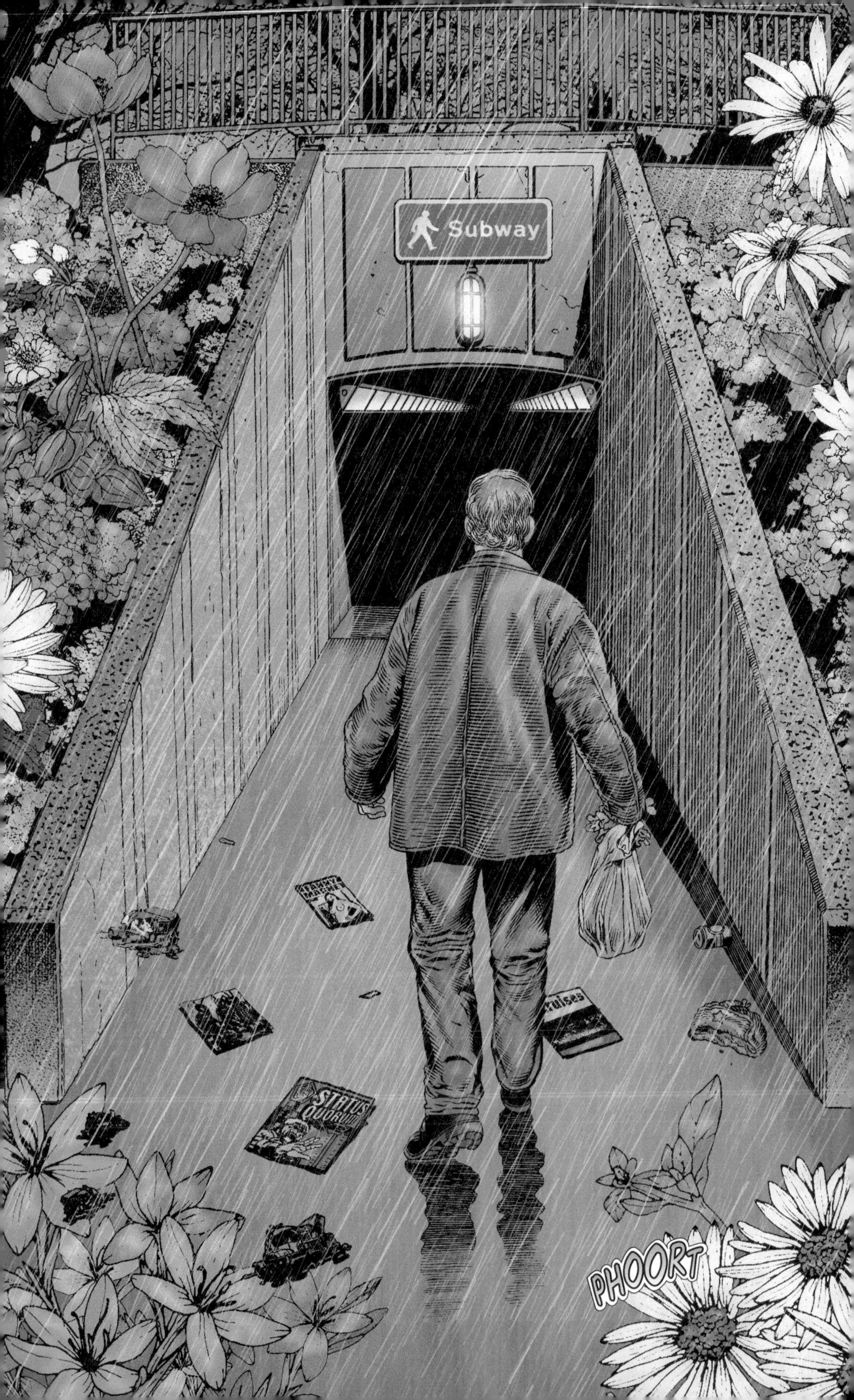
Subway
STATUS QUORUM
PHOORT

THE OOZE AND THE GOO

Wading into THE FILTH with Grant Morrison and Chris Weston

disease/kobolds/underworld/reproduction/subterranean geology/
pressure/antibiotics/immune system/sperm sailing and the
cloacina etc./
                                    room - this one's been
                                    turned off...

what are you doing, love?
I'm making the ultimate porno/

YOU BECOME
STUNNED
UNTOUCHABLE.

• Klinzhlu in Amsterdam
He's in police station telli shung.
gets cock out
Wow say cops.
'They're selig semen in...'

bellamy/TV21/kubrd/
plutonian/purple/ultraviolet/
petrol blue/

crackcomics.com: a division of grantmorrison.com

Early notes by Morrison and augmented dolphin designs by Weston.

This early teaser text for the series first appeared on Morrison's now-dormant website www.crackcomicks.com.

WHAT IS THE FILTH?

"Visit the centre of the earth

There you will find the global fire

Rectify it of all dirt

Drive it out with love and ire..."

sang Benedictus Figula

"The filth is Gerry Anderson for paranoid schizophrenics; a fluorescent Day-Glo trip through an abyss of internet porn, 'ironic' humor and disease pathology," roars writer Morrison, dispatching three massive warriors of the Uruk-Hai with a single razor-edged arc of his legendary Elven blade, Durinduryll, the Sword That Never Shuts Up. *"It's bigger, wilder, uglier and more heart-rending than the best summer blockbuster movie and if, like me, you love the awful smells of failure, shame, male pattern baldness and seedy compromise, then you're sure to revel in the squirming twists and turns of this exotic international spy-fi thriller, where games of identity, madness and planetary hygiene combine with perverted sex, kitchen sink realism and ultra-technology to blind the mind's eye and infect the soul forever. Sights to scupper the sanity! Philosophies to burst the frontal lobes! People with combovers having sex! 'Certified UnCool Brutalist Pop-Fic EVERY MONTH for a twelvemonth and a day!'"*

Yeah, right! And that's only the half of it. Grant Morrison's first creator-owned series since the groundbreaking cult hit THE INVISIBLES is a harrowing 13-issue rake through the middens of 21st century life, love, death and low self-esteem.

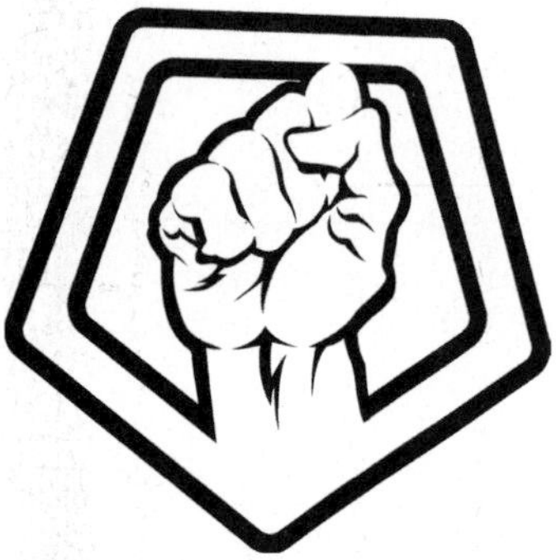
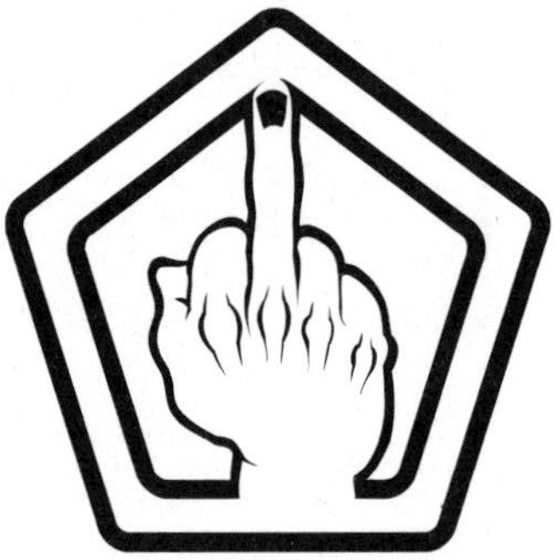
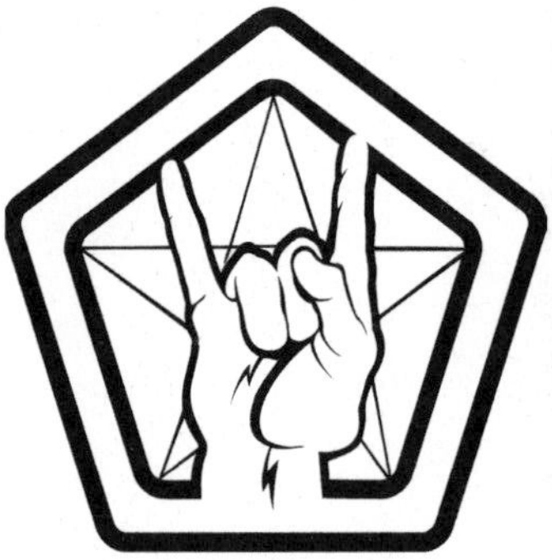

THE HAND STRIKES
THE HAND CARESSES
THE HAND INVOKES
THE HAND SIGNALS
THE HAND GIVES AND TAKES

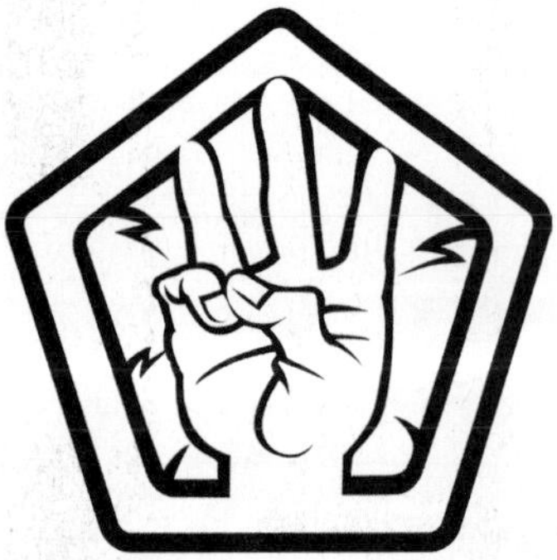
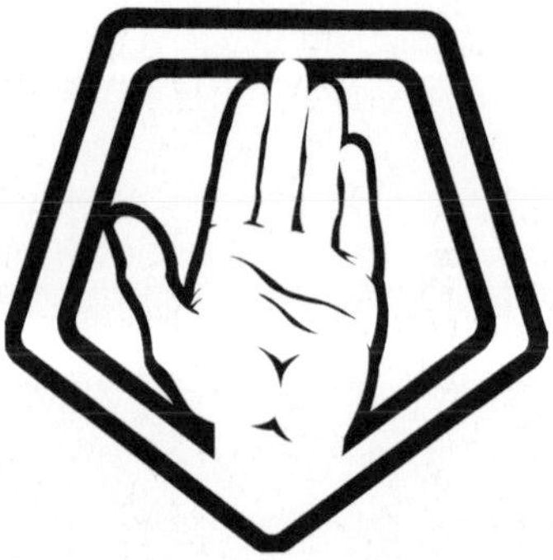
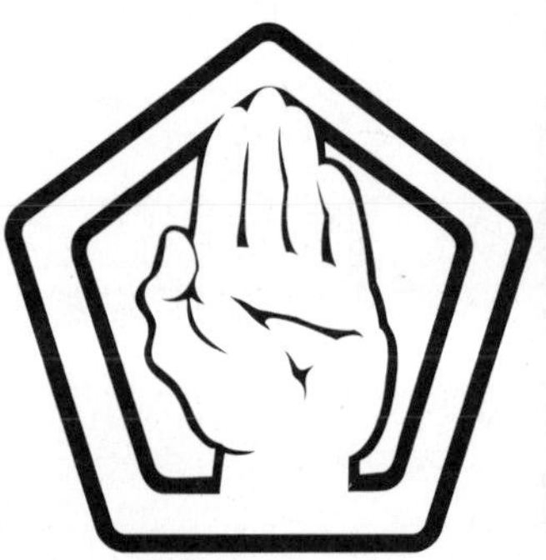

WE ARE THE HAND THAT WIPES THE ARSE OF THE WORLD

PREPARE FOR INOCULATION.
STAY CLOSE TO THE SICK BAG.
THIS IS THE FILTH.

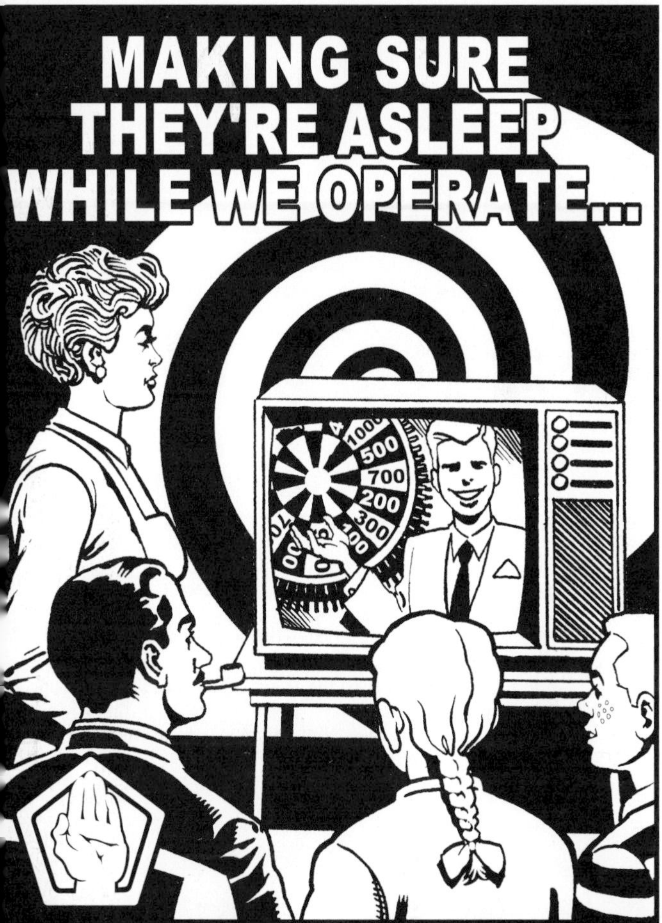
MAKING SURE
THEY'RE ASLEEP
WHILE WE OPERATE...
1000
500
700
200
300
100

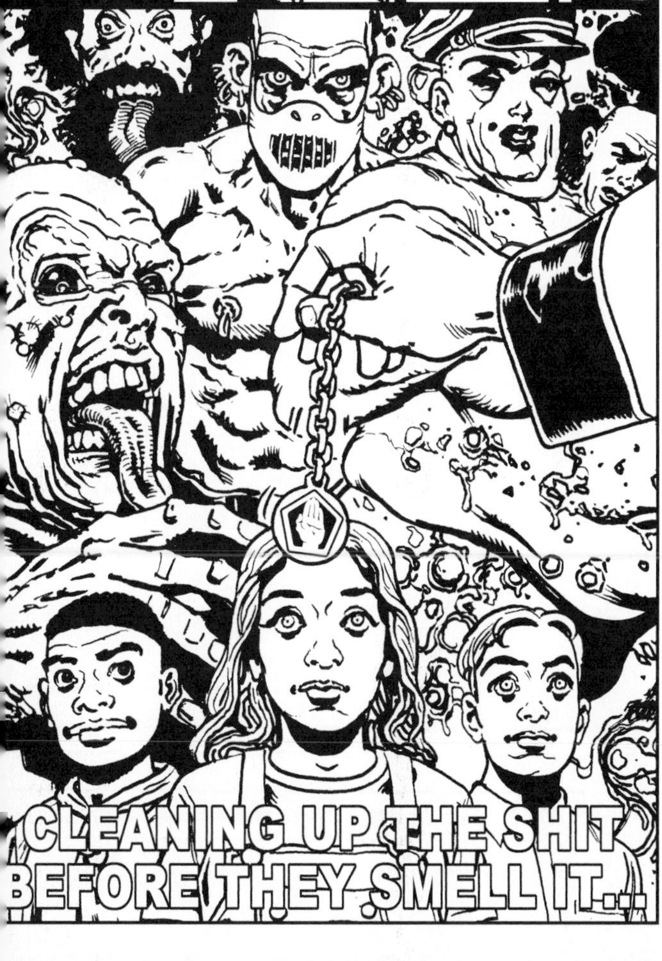
CLEANING UP THE SHIT
BEFORE THEY SMELL IT...

Hand propaganda posters.

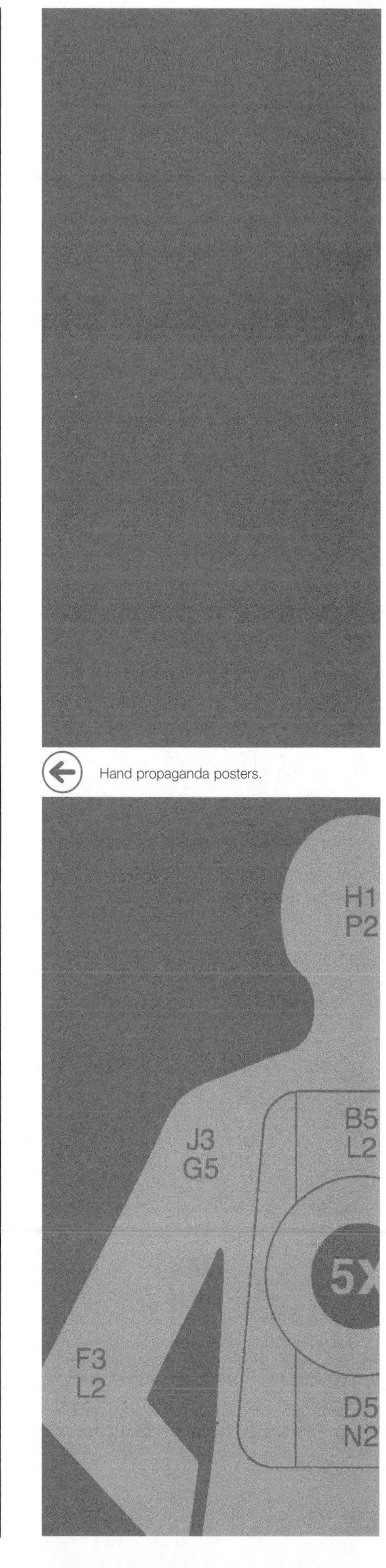
H1
P2
J3
G5
B5
L2
5X
F3
L2
D5
N2

THE PAPERVERSE

A creation of Hand Inkytech, the Paperverse is a so-called "concept-farm." Memetically-engineered for maximum imaginative crop yield, the Paperverse is an ongoing 2-dimensional narrative universe based on traditional American comic book fiction — these type of "super-hero" stories were found to be least resistant to real science considerations and therefore more fertile ground for development of imaginary technologies. Impossible machinery can be implanted within these permanently rolling "continuities," nourished into possibility and finally harvested into 3-D existence to enhance the ongoing operations of the hand.

Outlandish technologies and weapons are "written in" to the "story," tested by the "characters" in living scenarios maintained and farmed by experts. A large percentage of retrieved concepts are too frail to survive the return from the pressures of 2-D, of course, and disintegrate upon decompression into three dimensions, but this problem is now being attended to as the narrative development of "invulnerable" weapons and technology accelerates and yields spectacular durable results. Some fascinating and bizarre artifacts have already been recovered from the crushing fathoms of the Paperverse but this aspect of hand work has always been regarded as slightly frivolous and controversial by the higher echelons of the organization and remains so to this very day.

Secret Original concept sketches by Morrison.

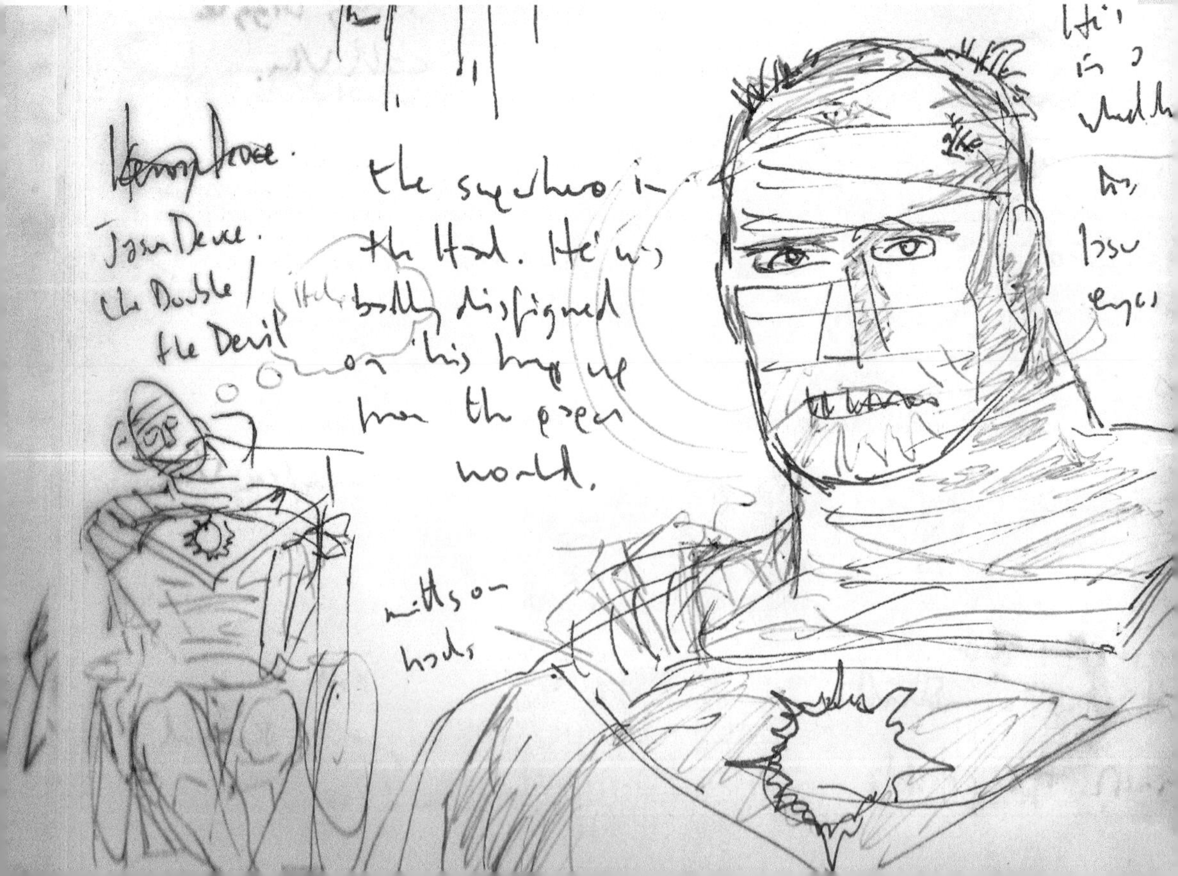
Jason Deuce.
the Double /
the Devil
the superhero in
the Hand. He was
badly disfigured
on his way up
from the paper
world.

THE STATUS QUORUM

The Status Quorum are fictional protectors of the Paperverse. Their journeys to other planets, dimensions and planes of existence are specifically designed for minimal scientific friction and maximum concept-crop yield.

The team at the beginning of THE FILTH #3 comprises:

ALPHA SAPIENS: Is Bill Tomney, a educationally-subnormal cleaner whose simple brain allows him to play host to the time-travelling micro-city of the Morlockoi. This minute, utopian society of tomorrow travels back in time to take over Bill's head. By enhancing his abilities and using the now-super-intelligent Alpha Sapiens as a messenger, the little visitors from the future go about the business of making human society better and more effective. Alpha Sapiens' primary mission is to arrange current events so that the world of today will eventually shrink and become the perfect, loving world of the majestic, miniaturized Morlockoi!!!

ULTRA-HUMANITARIAN: This Buddhist super-hero is an avatar of the Bodhisattva Avalokitesvara and has vowed to use his "siddhis" or super-powers to rid the earth of the so-called Four Sorrows of Existence — hunger, sickness, old age and death. So far, only hunger has partially succumbed to the might of Ultra-Humanitarian but his fight continues undaunted. His stare can shame a mountain range, his anger can turn the sun to water! Thank God he's on our side!

DARK STRANGER: This sinister lord of night and flies based his whole modus operandi on the life cycle of the swarming insects he found feasting on the corpses of his parents after returning from summer camp one year to find them dead — their bodies fought over by five separate serial killers, five undying maniacs Dark Stranger has vowed to destroy!

ZUR-VANN: One of mankind's oldest gods, Zur-Vann has returned from a 6,000-year-long mercy mission into space, only to find his mighty race long destroyed. Sole survivor of a tribe of ancient man-gods who once tamed the primal Earth, Zur-Vann now fights against the forces of chaos which threaten everyday life in Omnitropolis!

WOMANITE: Womanite is a new element: a soft mineral substance, created in his lab by Professor Mervin Coyle. A lonely bespectacled loser, Coyle sought to create his own sexy, synthetic companion but instead produced this ultra-militant feminist heroine. Womanite has only one weakness and that is Anti-Womanite — a living substance created to destroy her by the insane Professor Coyle, her enduring enemy. If Anti-Womanite ever touches Womanite the world will explode and possibly the universe as well.

MACHINE GIRL: Tess Bradlock was once a promising young gymnast until the horrific car crash, which left her father in a wheelchair and lovely Tess burned beyond all recognition and crippled from the ankles up. The distraught Doctor Bradlock invented and built the wind-up "machine girl" suit which allows Tess to move freely and "help people." Only dad can fix the suit which runs for five hours before needing "tinkering." Machine Girl's ponytail is made of living fiber optic filaments which respond to Tess' control and can be used either as a deadly weapon or as a handy computer interface!

The seventh member of the Status Quorum — and its first chairman — is SECRET ORIGINAL — now trapped in the three-dimensional world as the first living being to travel from fiction to reality. Crushed and folded into a wheelchair by the immense stresses of his passage from the 2-D world of the Paperverse, Secret Original is no longer an active member of the Status Quorum!

Designs for the Status Quorum by Weston.

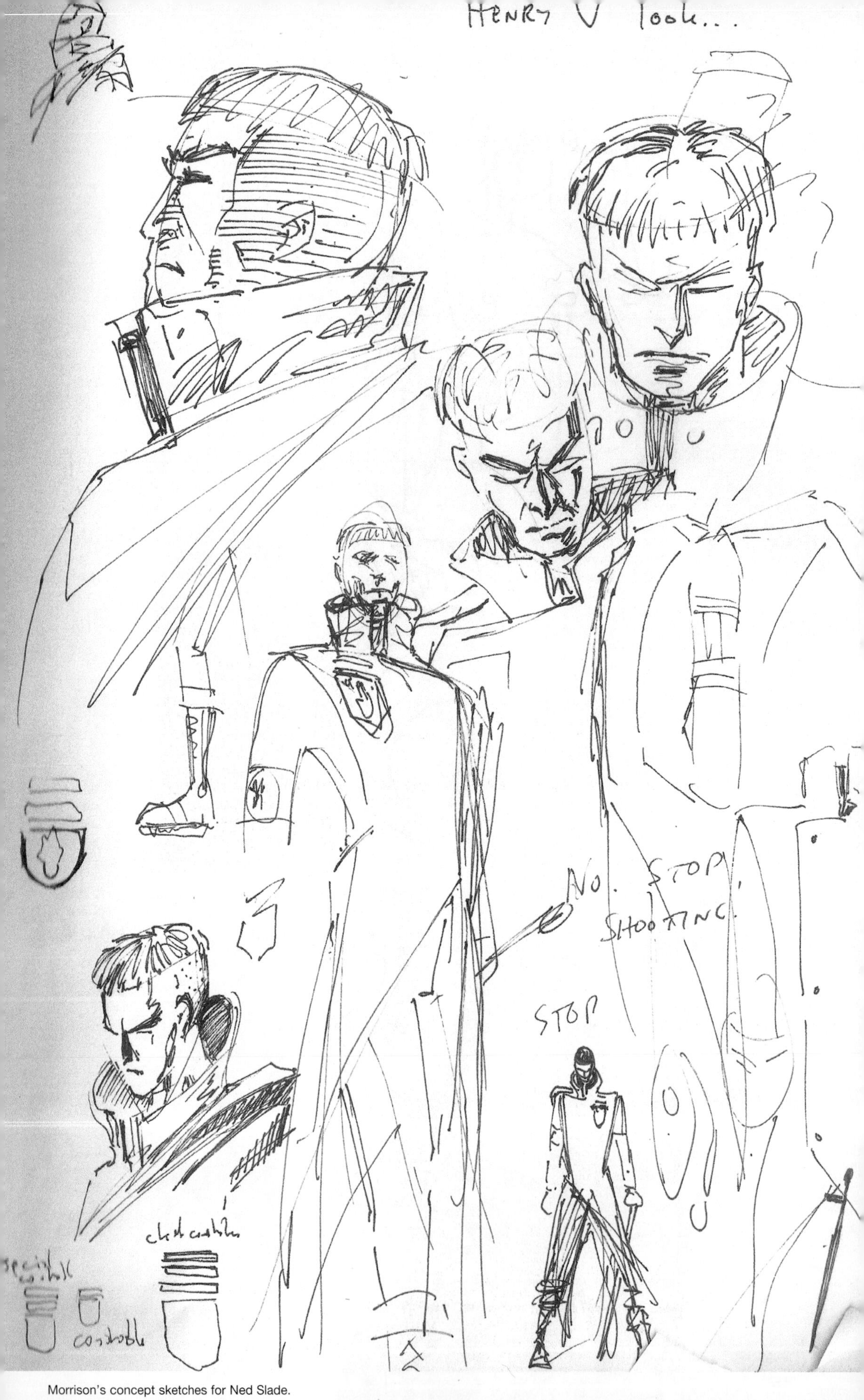
HENRY V look...
NO. STOP, SHOOTING.
STOP

Morrison's concept sketches for Ned Slade.

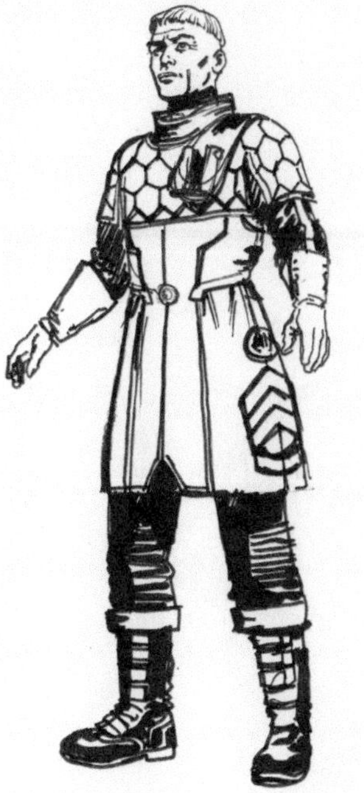

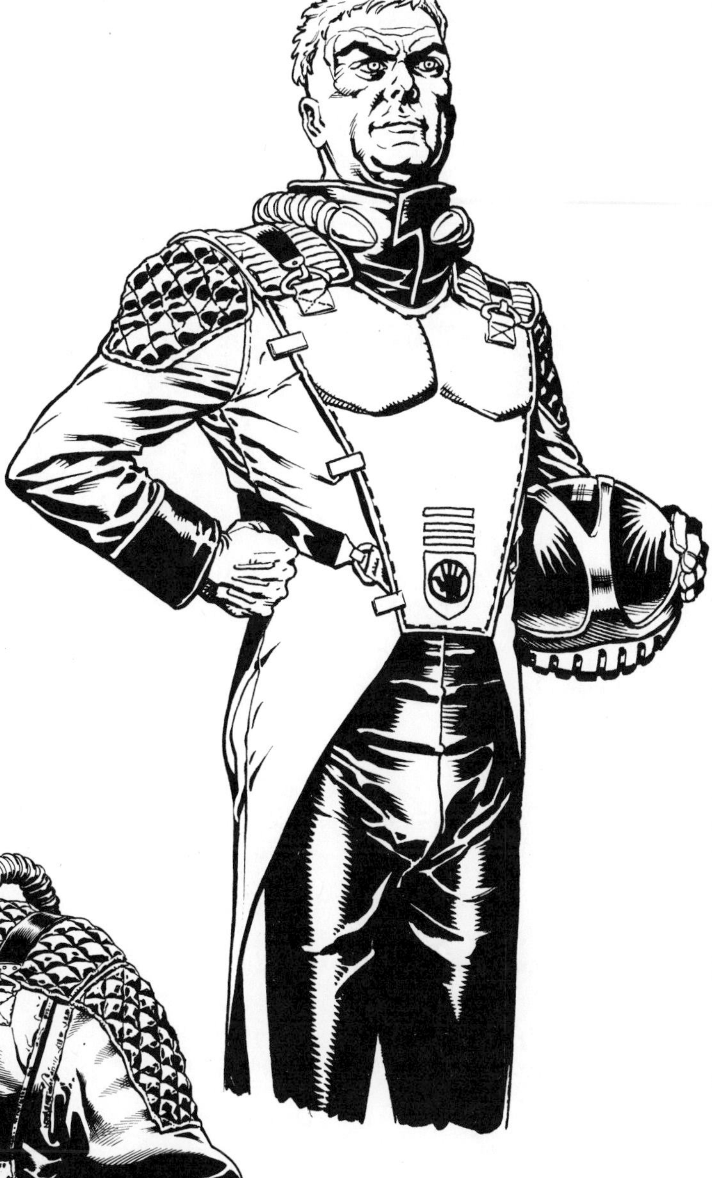

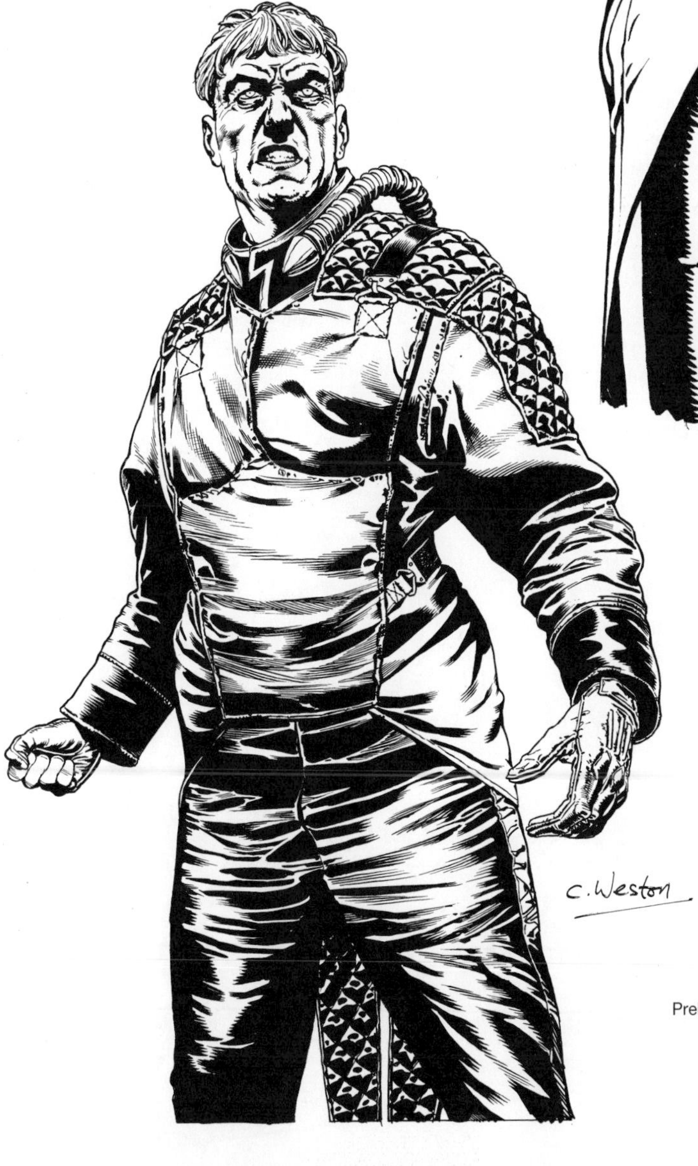
C. Weston

Preliminary and final character designs by Weston.

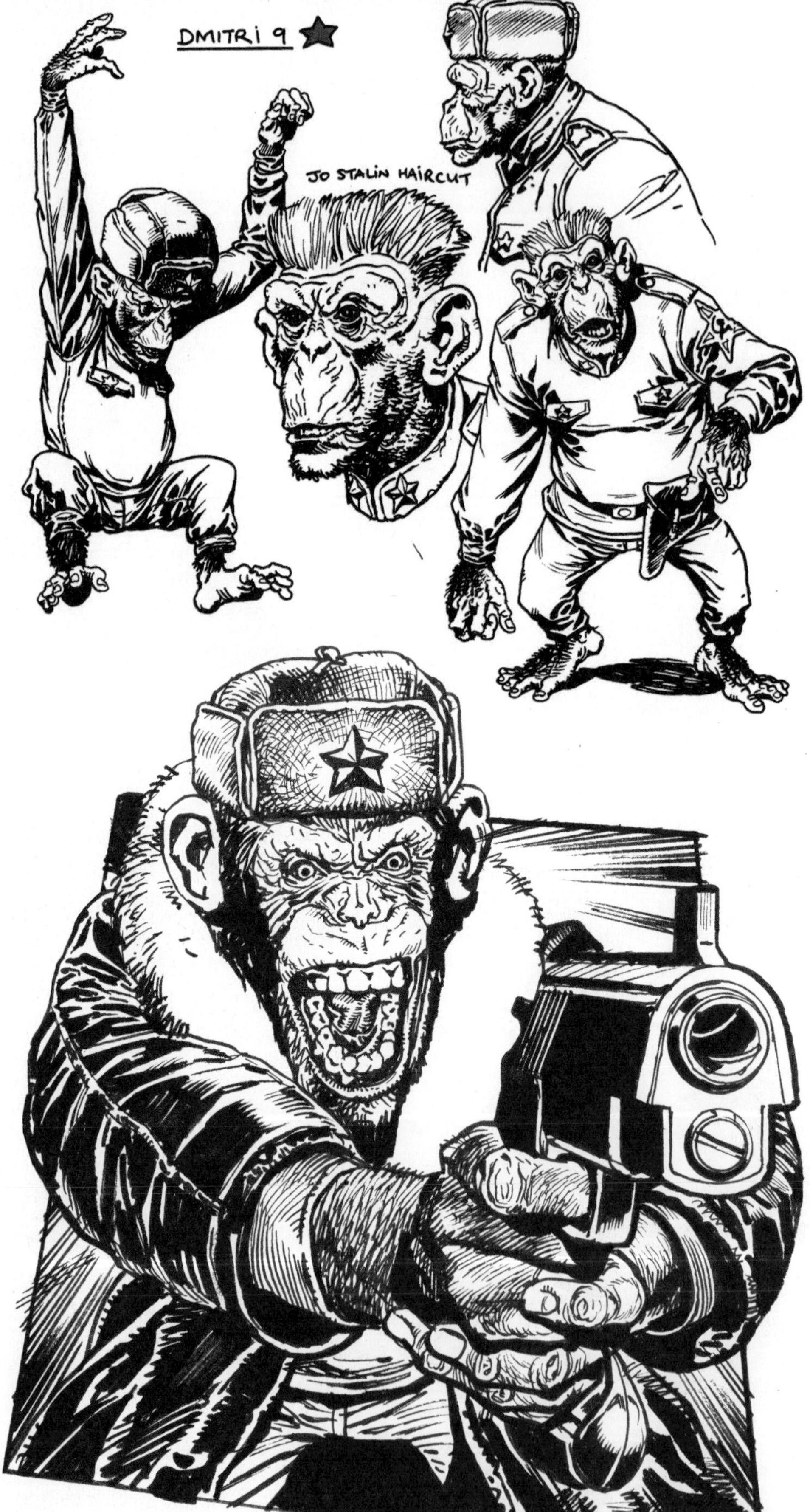
DMITRI 9
JO STALIN HAIRCUT

Sketches and character designs by Weston for Dmitri-9.

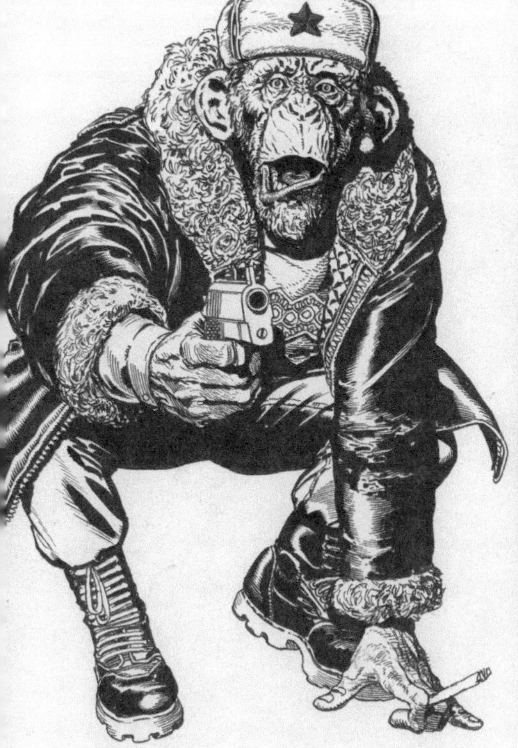

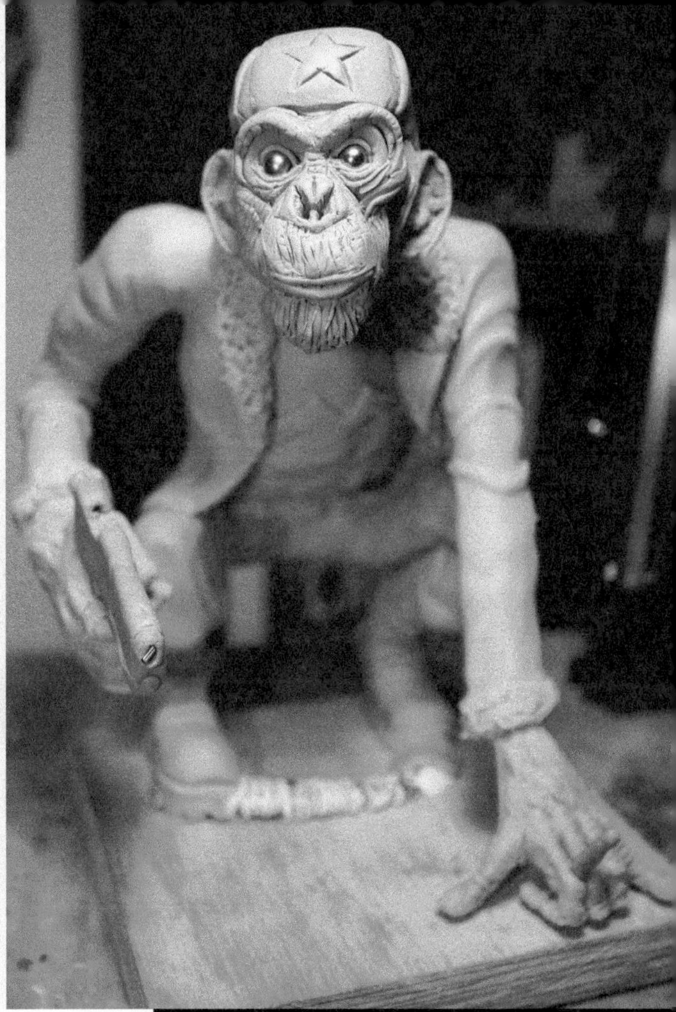

A Dmitri-9 maquette sculpted by FILTH fan Eric Tengren.

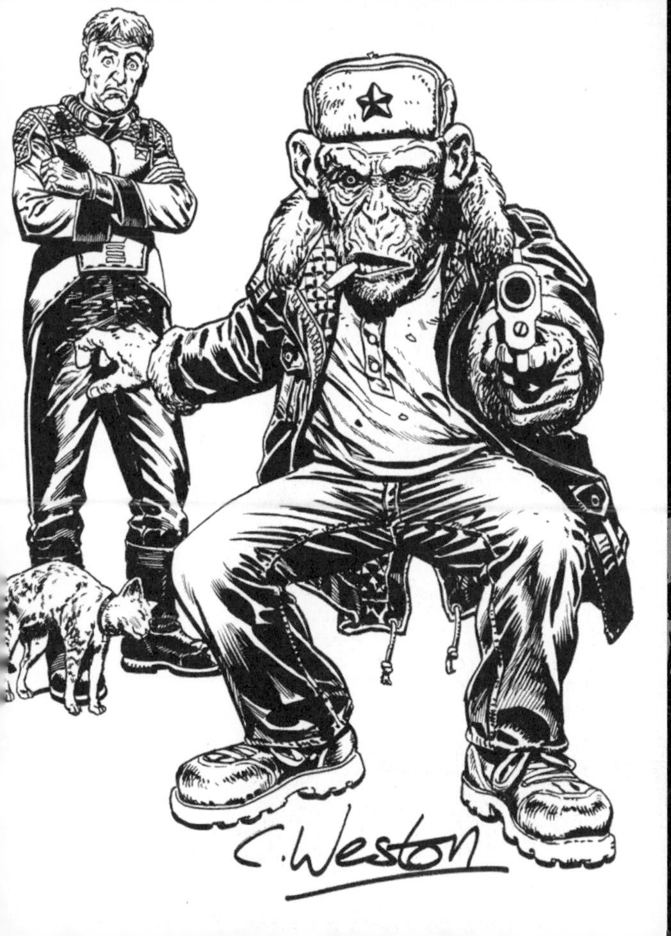
C.Weston

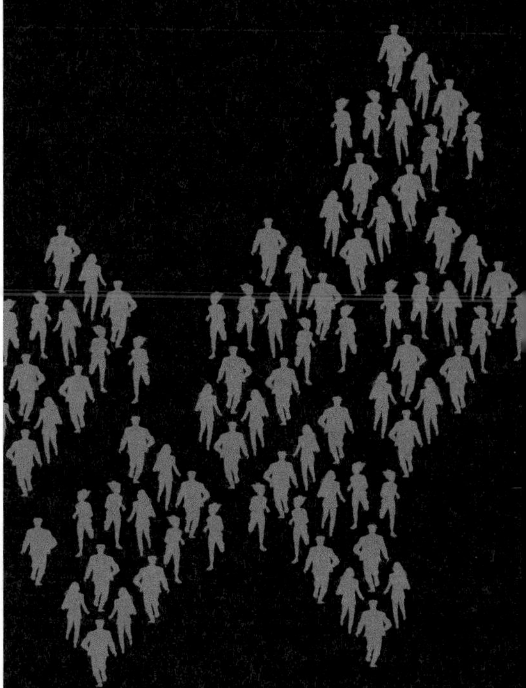

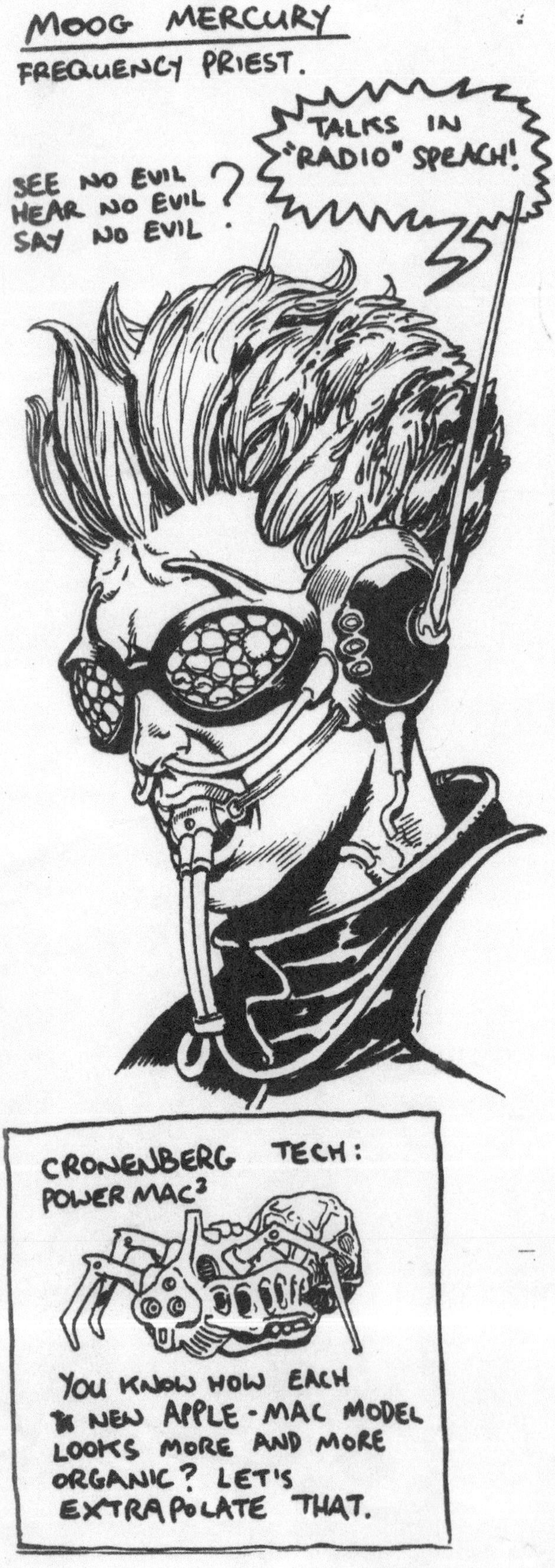
MOOG MERCURY
FREQUENCY PRIEST.
TALKS IN "RADIO" SPEACH!
SEE NO EVIL
HEAR NO EVIL ?
SAY NO EVIL.
CRONENBERG TECH:
POWER MAC^3
YOU KNOW HOW EACH NEW APPLE-MAC MODEL LOOKS MORE AND MORE ORGANIC? LET'S EXTRAPOLATE THAT.

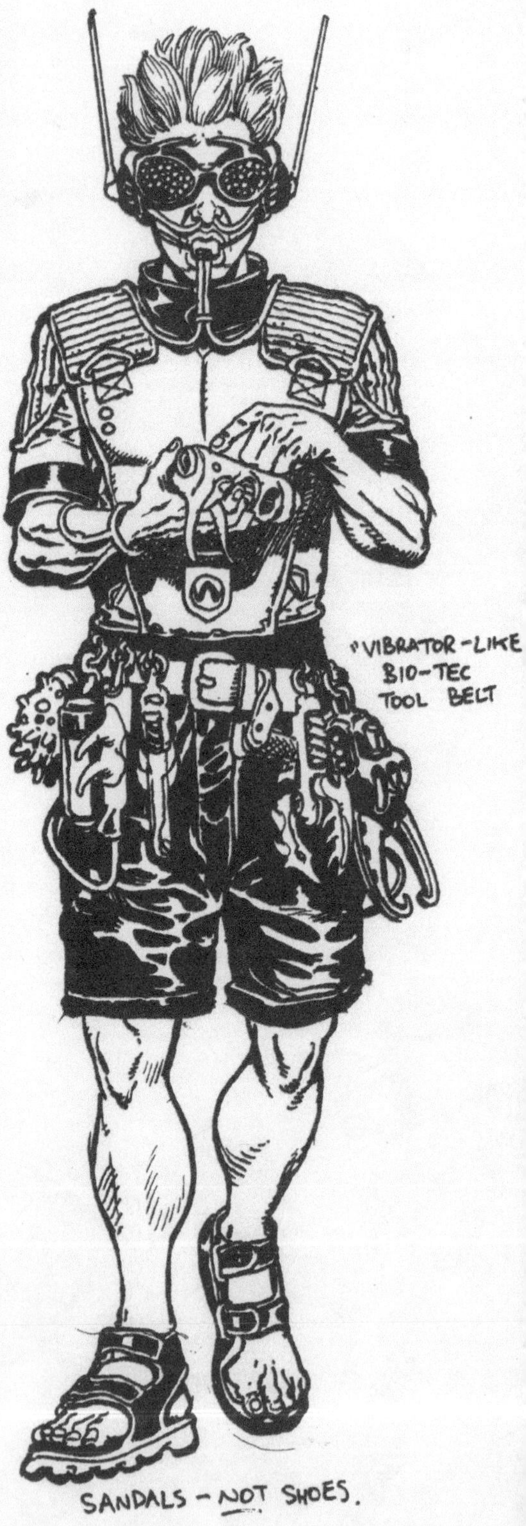
"VIBRATOR-LIKE
BIO-TEC
TOOL BELT
SANDALS - NOT SHOES.

Weston designs for Miami Nil and Moog Mercury.

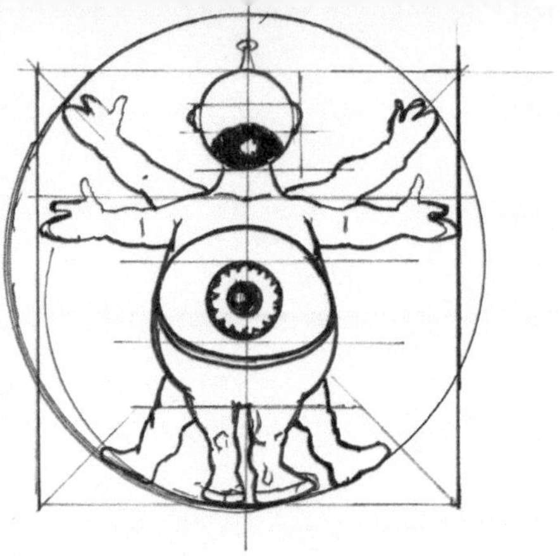

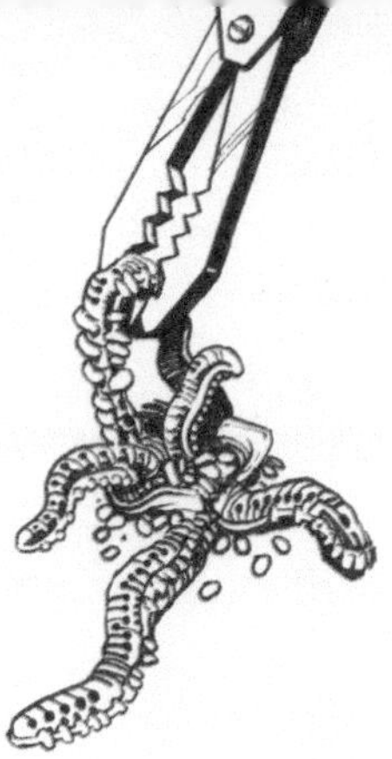

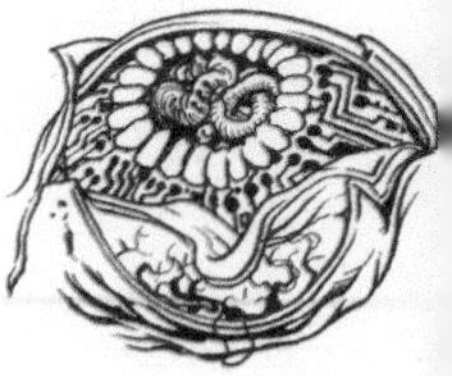

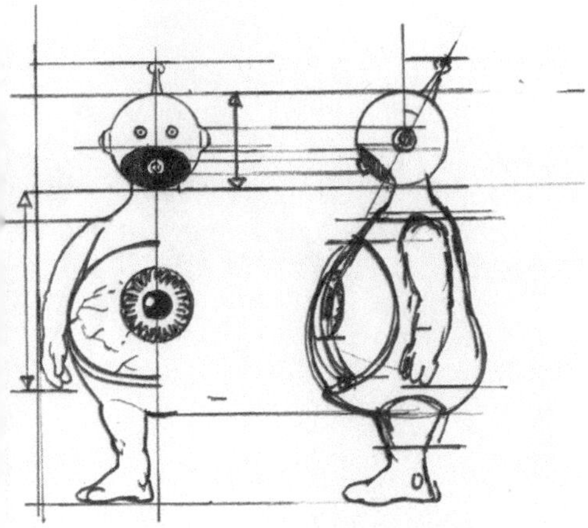

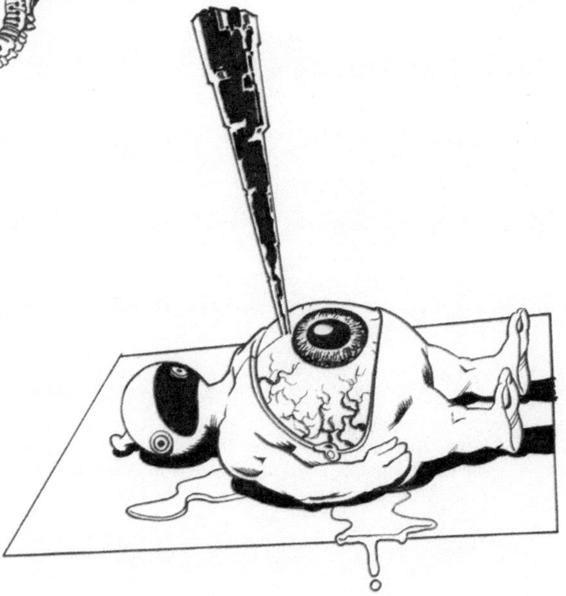

Ant children and iLife sketches by Weston.

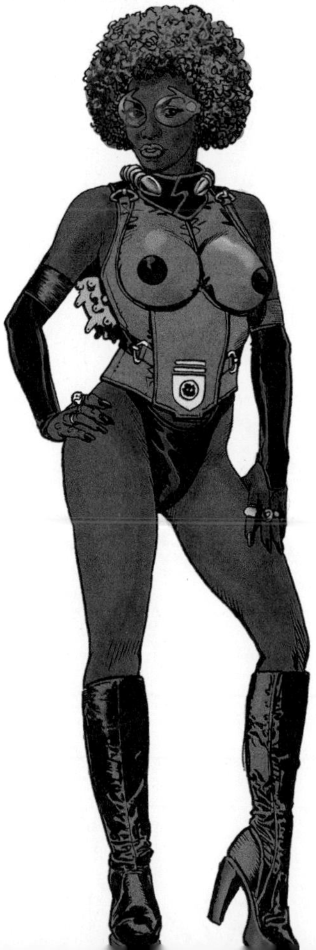

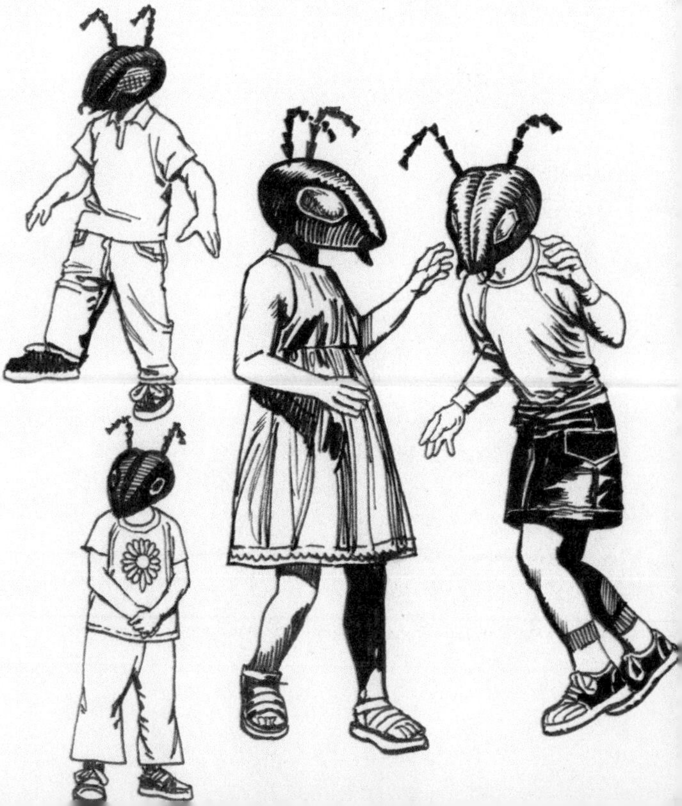

THE CRAB

Designed for supercompression into the Paperverse, Crab One is the only one of the Hand wonder machines able to convert its structure from three dimensions to two and protect its crew from the distorting pressures of this incredible trip.

Crab One is captained by fraulein Harlotte Church, the only Hand agent to have attained distinction in all five divisions of the organisation.

Her crew is comprised of five lucky "virgins," each hand-picked from insane asylums and brothels around the world. When the band begins to play, when it's time to dive into the grinding, infinitely flattened jet-blue depths of the Paperverse, the girls take up their stations and sing their songs of loss and love and cynical scorn.

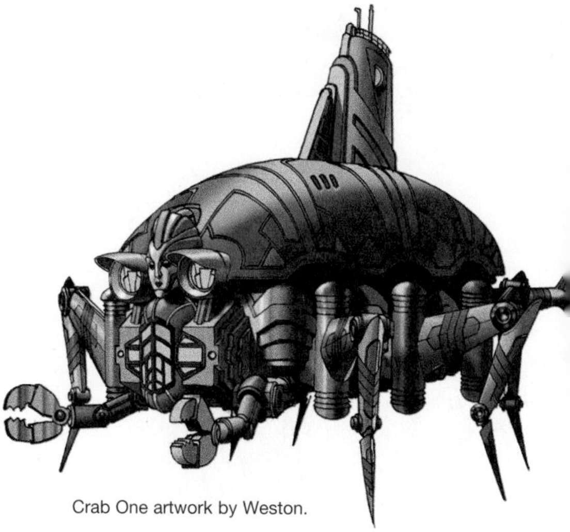

Crab One artwork by Weston.

Preliminary text description and Crab One crew designs by Morrison.

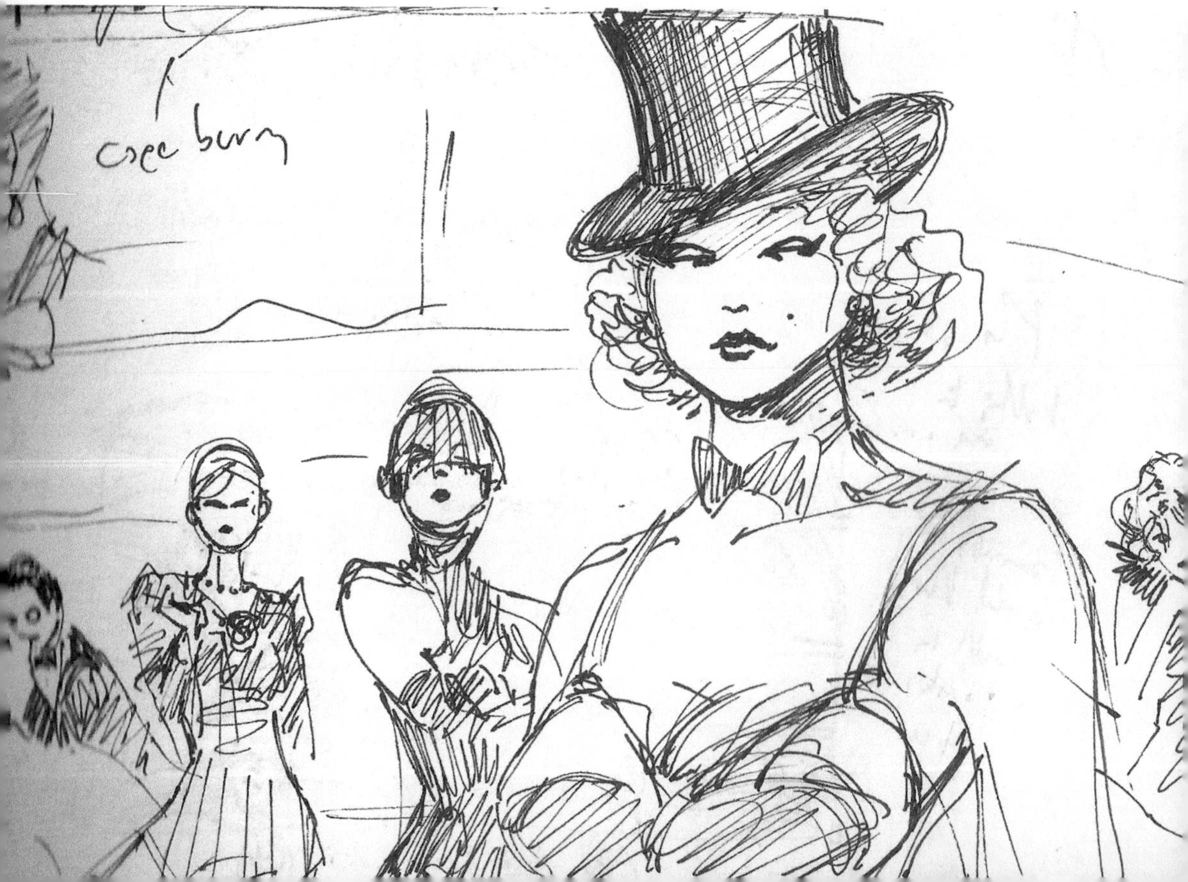

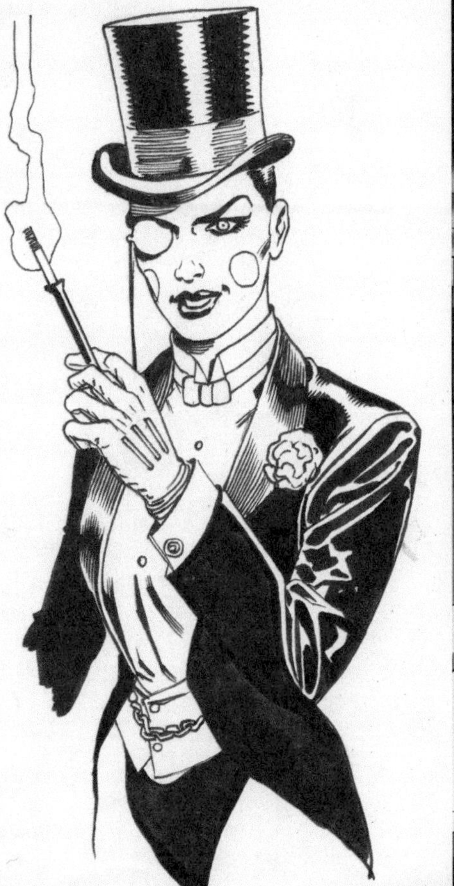

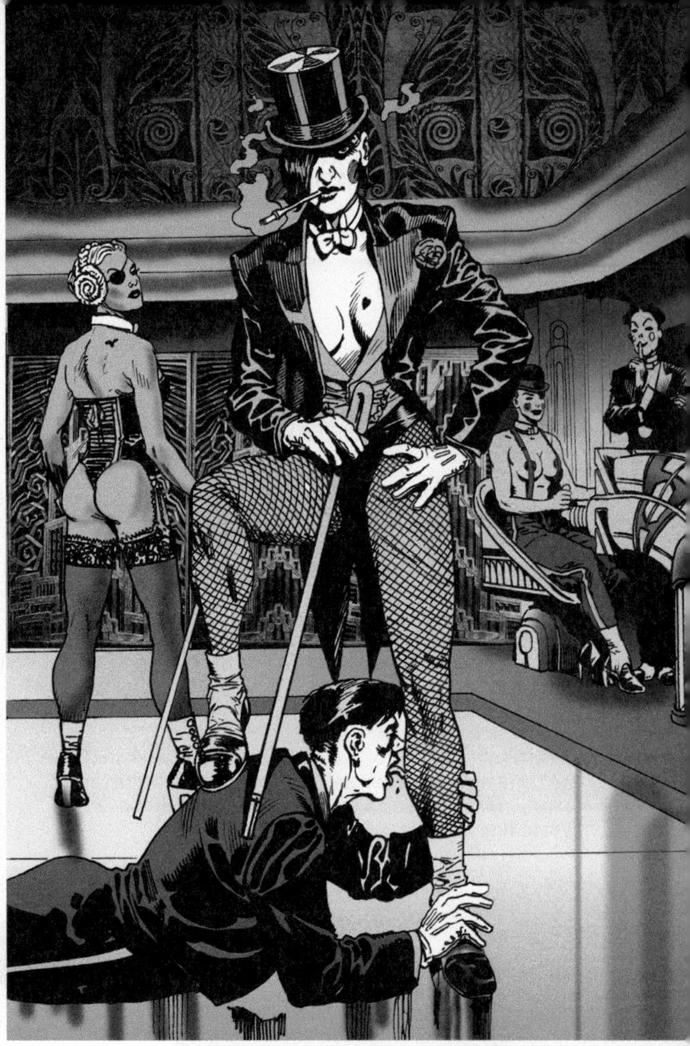

Captain Harlotte of the Crab One by Weston.

Crab One artwork by Weston.

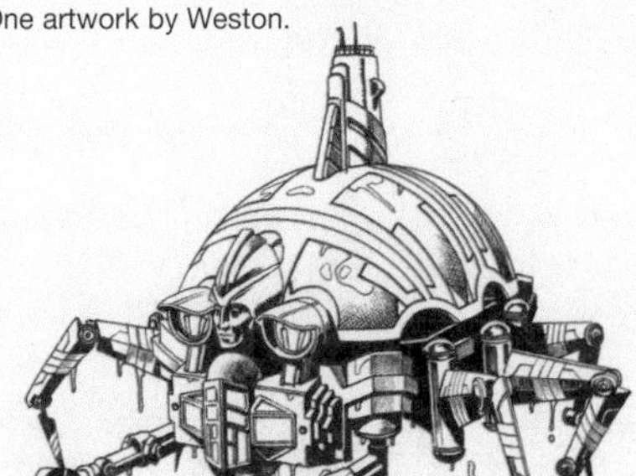

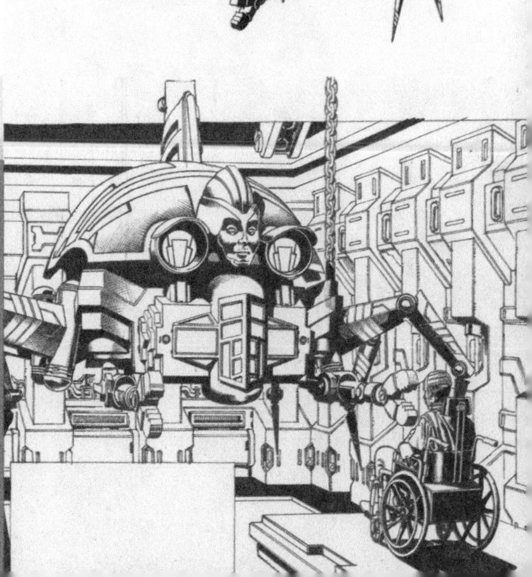

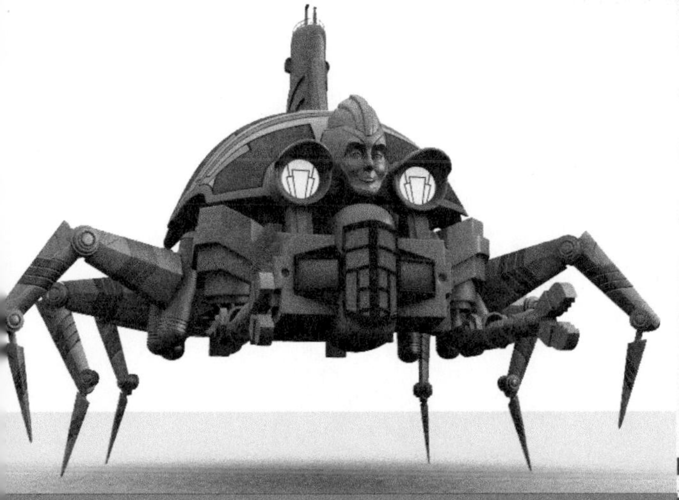

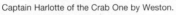

A computer model of Crab One rendered by Gary Erskine.

THE DUMPTRUCK

The Hand Standard Series Dumptruck is a custom-built Cleansing vehicle brought to life by Hand Inkytech.

Each officer of the Hand is assigned a 2-seater personal Dumptruck.

The wheels of the Dumptruck are convertible into thrusters in aerial and submarine modes. Windows are fully evil-proofed and polaroid filtered. Engines run on refined 5-star ink and the Dumptruck can eat and digest five times its own weight in raw garbage in a 12-hour period.

The Dumptruck can accelerate to Ninth Gear — at these speeds space compacts and time begins to flow like a fast-moving beer, providing access to The Crack.

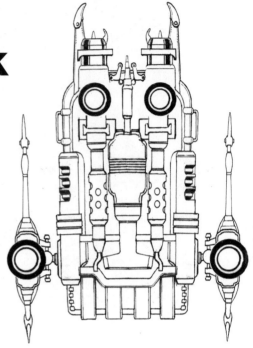

Weston's preliminary sketches and final designs for the Dumptruck.

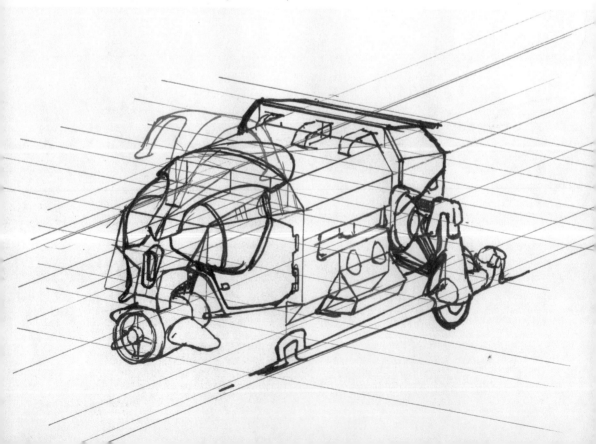

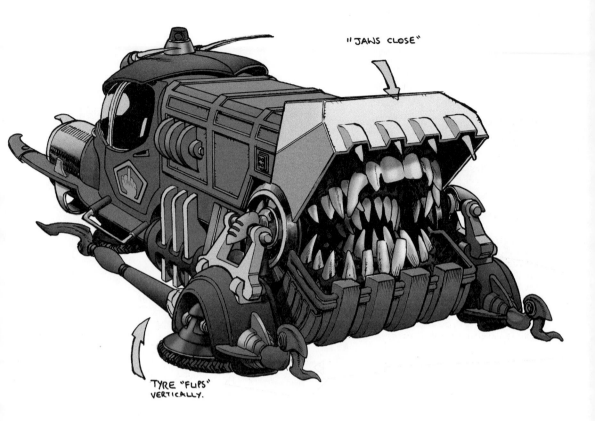

"JAWS CLOSE"

TYRE "FLIPS" VERTICALLY.

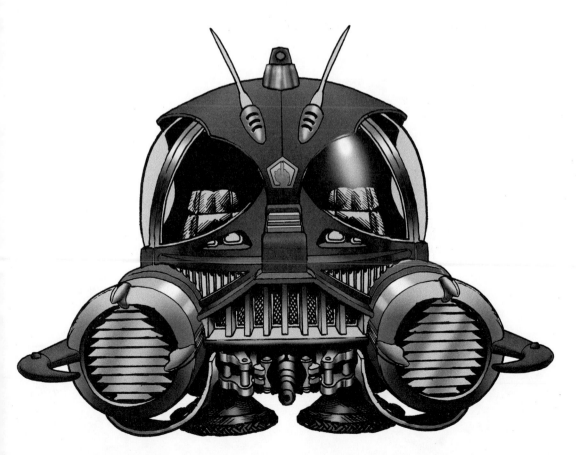

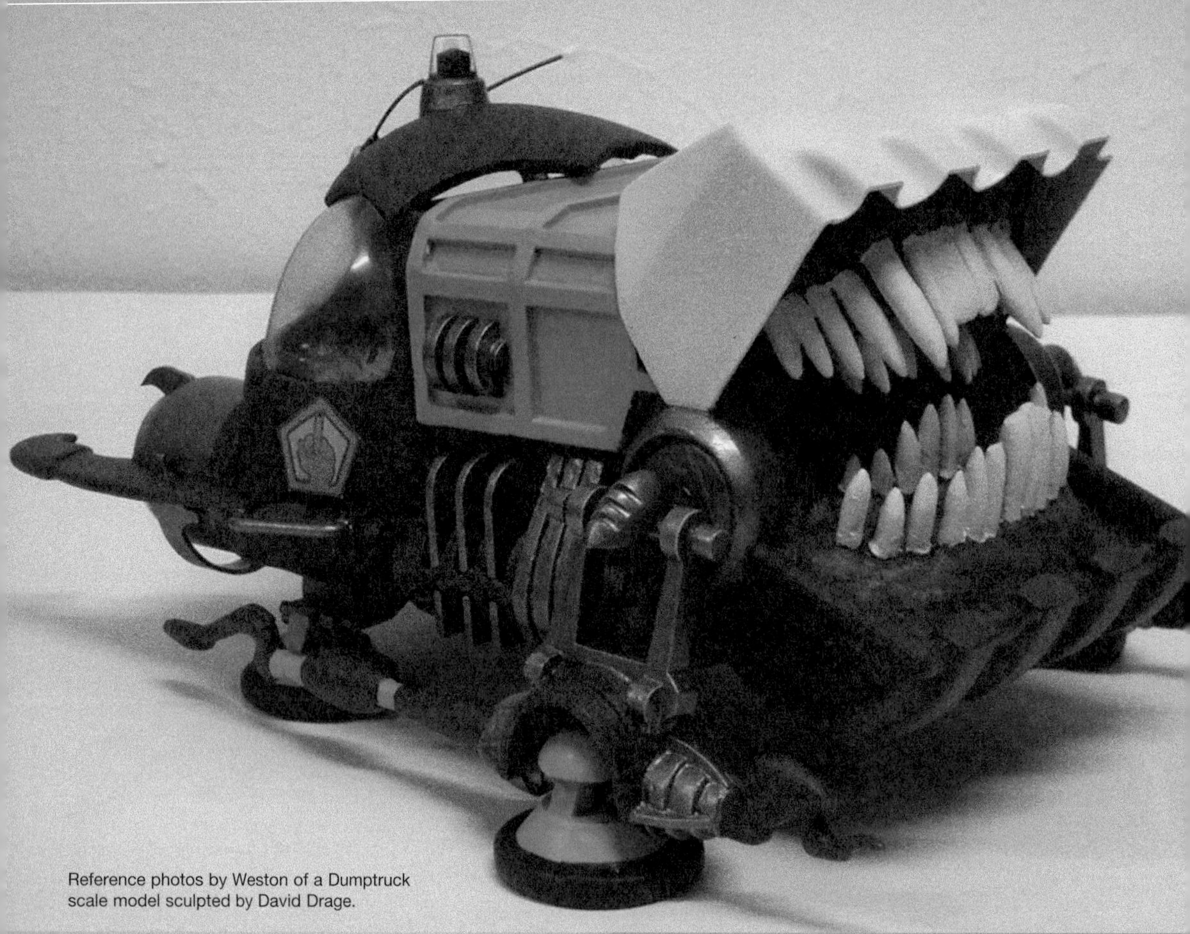

Reference photos by Weston of a Dumptruck scale model sculpted by David Drage.

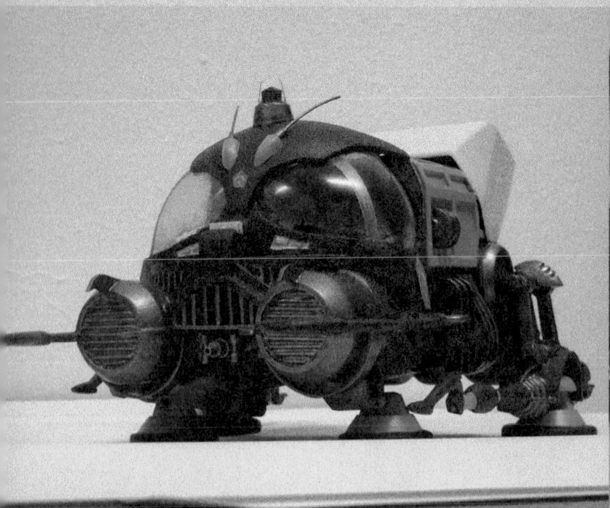

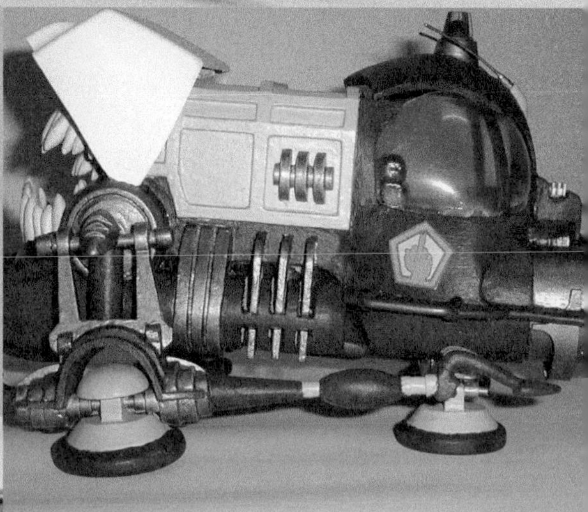

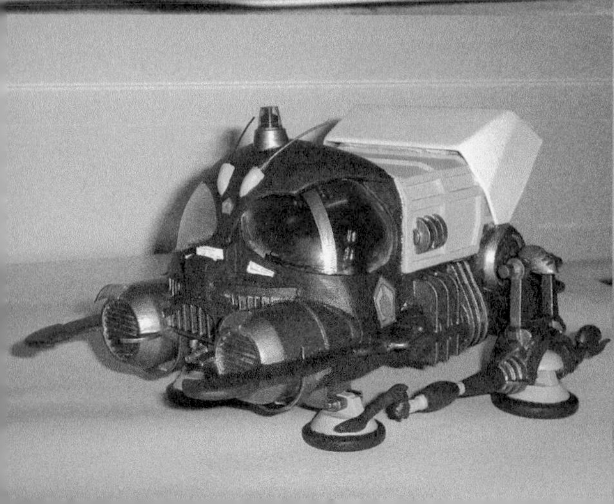

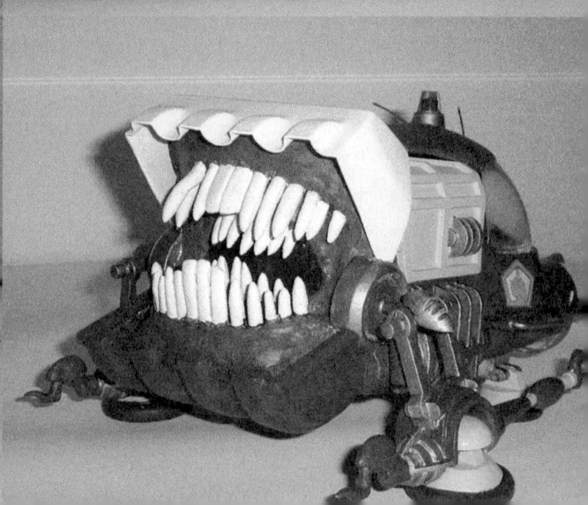

THE FILTH UNCENSORED!

Grant Morrison's complete script for the infamous "Pornomancer" chapter from THE FILTH #5, accompanied by unexpurgated artwork by Chris Weston.

Company: DC COMICS/Vertigo

Series: **the filth #5**

Title: **pornomancer** (22 pages)

Writer: Grant Morrison

Artist: Chris Weston

PAGE 1

Frame 1   Full page splash to open on. Go straight for the gut again, Chris — here's our protagonist, porn star Anders Klimakks in action. He's dressed as the devil, with little horns and a forked clipped fake beard on his chin. He turns to look back over his shoulder at us with a grin (he always talks to camera, 'Alfie' style). Anders is in the midst of humping an actress dressed as an Amish girl with a ball gag in her mouth and her hands tied to the bedhead.

ANDERS: HEY!
ANDERS: COME ON IN!
ANDERS: DON'T BE SHY.

PAGE 2

Frame 1   Dozens of tiny close-up digital panels flickering across the entire page — fast cut shots of the sex film in superheated video-screen resolution. This mosaic of porn tiles is overlaid with a couple of horizontal frames.

BALLOON: UH
BALLOON: BITCH
BALLOON: AH
BALLOON: COCK
BALLOON: BABY
BALLOON: OHH
BALLOON: DEATH
BALLOON: HARDER
BALLOON: TRAMP

Frame 2   First of the horizontals shows a close up of a girl's hand with a cigarette between her fingers. Painted red nails.

ANDERS: WHO WOULD GIVE A FLOATING FUCK TO SEE THESE CRAZY MOVIES WHERE PEOPLE WITH STRICT RELIGIOUS PRINCIPLES GET TURNED INTO SHIT-WORSHIPPING PERVERTS BY THE DEVIL?

Frame 3   Pull back. The Amish girl, naked to the waist except for her untied, disarrayed bonnet. She takes a drag of her cigarette, bored. Anders in head and shoulders shot, foreground, is having his make-up touched up by a production girl. In background, a couple of guys are moving the lights and cameras. Anders shoots us his sidelong glance and wicked grin. He's always likeable and open.

ANDERS: ONLY THE STAUNCH FUNDAMENTALISTS OF THE WORLD.
ANDERS;   AND THAT IS LUCKY FOR ME.
ANDERS: TODAY IS 'ANAL QUAKERS', SEQUELS TWO AND THREE.

Frame 4   Closer on Anders. Red face. Horns. Grin to camera.

ANDERS: 5 HOURS FOR ME IN MAKE UP TO BECOME THE PRINCE OF DARKNESS AND FUCK SOME GIRL.
ANDERS: I FEEL LIKE I AM THE ELEPHANT MAN OF SEX.

PAGE 3

Frame 1   More tiny digital flickers.

BALLOON: UH
BALLOON: AH
BALLOON: HARDER
BALLOON: COCK
BALLOON: TRAMP
BALLOON: OHH
BALLOON: DEATH
BALLOON: BITCH
BALLOON: BABY

Frame 2   Horizontal insert. Close up on Anders fingers lighting a joint with a cigarette lighter.

ANDERS: THEN THERE IS REAL LIFE, WHERE BASICALLY I'M THE COMPLETE OPPOSITE OF THE JUDAEO-CHRISTIAN SATAN FIGURE; ANDERS KLIMAKKS IS A HAPPY KIND OF GUY WITH A WIDE RANGE OF INTERESTS.
ANDERS: BUT EACH PORNO ACTOR MUST HAVE HIS OWN SPECIALTY IF HE WANTS TO BE THE BIG STAR.

Frame 3 Anders holds the joint between his teeth and talks as he puffs some smoke. He makes an erect fist.

ANDERS: MAYBE IF THIS <u>ONE</u> GUY HAS THE KING OF COCKS, THEN THE <u>OTHER</u> GUY WHO IS NOT SO BIG MUST BE ABLE TO STAY HARD LIKE A POLICEMAN'S TRUNCHEON, YEAH?
ANDERS: THEN THERE IS THE <u>NEXT</u> GUY, WHO CAN MAKE THE GENETIC OINTMENT FLY ACROSS THE ROOM LIKE A SHELL FROM A HOWITZER.

Frame 4 As Frame 3 on the previous page. The girl tilts her head back against the wall and pouts a couple of smoke rings into the air. Her knees drawn up to her chest. Anders leans back, slumped and happy and blurred in his seat. He languidly points a video remote control at us.

ANDERS: EVERY STAR HAS THIS ONE SPECIAL THING NO OTHER HAS GOT.
ANDERS: BUT, I AM PROUD TO SAY, THERE IS ONLY THE ONE GUY IN THE ADULT BUSINESS WHO FIRES THE <u>BLACK</u> JUICE.

Frame 5 The digital flickers freeze and stop. As black ink jets across the camera and the face of the girl.

ANDERS: AND THAT GUY IS <u>ANDERS KLIMAKKS</u>.

PAGE 4

Frame 1 Cut to a police interview room in LA. Cop turning to look past us as he fills a plastic cup from the water dispenser. This is Detective Nick Welliwell. He's just used a remote to freeze the image on a small TV screen.

WELLIWELL: THEY FOUND YOU STROLLING BUCK <u>NAKED</u> DOWN THE MEDIAN STRIP ON HIGHWAY 101, ANDERS.

Frame 2 Close on water from the spigot filling the cup.

Frame 3 Welliwell walks towards us, carrying the cup. We see only his midsection.

WELLIWELL: YOU WERE CARRYING OVER <u>FIFTY</u> HARDCORE MAGAZINES, VIDEOS AND DVDs IN A TOMMY BAG.

Frame 4 Puts cup down beside some sex DVDs and videos on a table — all starring Anders Klimakks. 'BEELZEBUGGER 2: THE SECOND COMING OF EVIL', 'DAD'S NAVY', 'ANAL QUAKERS', 'VIDEO CLIMAX 3', 'BUDDHIST BUTT BABES', 'SPUNK JIHAD'.

WELLIWELL: AND YOU HAVE NO <u>MEMORY</u> HOW YOU GOT TO BE THERE?

Frame 5 Anders Klimakks. The sports bag on the table. He's carefully putting hardcore material back inside with one hand and picking up his water with the other. DVDs, videos, some magazines.

ANDERS: I TOLD YOU MY BRAIN HAS THIS MEDICAL FUCK-UP, MAN.
ANDERS: THESE ARE ALL THE MEMORIES I HAVE.

Frame 6 Anders Klimakks drinks some water. The porno is scattered on the table.

ANDERS: WHAT'S IN THIS <u>BAG</u> IS ANDERS KLIMAKKS.

PAGE 5

Frame 1 Cut to the roof of the police station. Welliwell stands at the edge looking over the city. He's having a smoke from a crack pipe. His partner John Whim joins him on the rooftop.

WHIM: SO AN AMNESIAC PORNO ACTOR FLASHES HIS DICK AT THE FAST LANE.
WHIM: IF I HAD <u>HIS</u> DICK, I'D BE TAKING OUT ADS IN THE <u>LA TIMES</u>.
WHIM: WHERE'S OUR CASE?
WELLIWELL: HE SHOOTS JET BLACK PEARLS, JOHN.
WELLIWELL: FOR CHRIST'S SAKE, THAT KIND OF THING ATTRACTS ATTENTION.

Frame 2 Welliwell is lifting a glass crack pipe to his lips, looking out thoughtfully. Whim appears behind him, a little concerned by his colleague's drug use but not wanting to say much.

WHIM: SO WE'RE HOLDING THIS GUY FOR FEDERAL?
WELLIWELL: *HUINN!*
WELLIWELL: THIS IS <u>WAY</u> BEYOND FEDERAL.
WELLIWELL: I EVER TELL YOU MY OLD MAN WAS A COP IN NEW YORK CITY?

Frame 3 Tight close. Detective closes his eyes and blows a cloud of smoke. He passes the pipe to the other guy who looks a little dubious and refuses.

WHIM: EVERY FUCKING DAY OF MY <u>LIFE</u>, NICK.
WHIM: YOU GOTTA LAY OFF THE CRACK PIPE.
WELLIWELL: WHO MADE <u>YOU</u> MY MOTHER?
WELLIWELL: GO ON. TRY SOME. YOU'LL FEEL GREAT.
WELLIWELL: I USED TO HEAR MY OLD MAN AND HIS CREEPY BUDDIES SOMETIMES, TELLING GHOST STORIES OR TALKING ABOUT ALL THE UNNATURAL SHIT THEY'D SEEN ON THE JOB.

Frame 4 Overhead shot. The detectives look over the parapet. Down in the car park, a Filth patrol vehicle pulls into the disabled space.

WELLIWELL: THERE WAS THIS ONE STORY ABOUT A CLEAN-UP CREW WHO COME UP FROM TUNNELS UNDER THE OLD PRECINCT HOUSE.
WELLIWELL: A SPECIAL SQUAD OF <u>UNTOUCHABLES</u> THEY MAKE DEAL WITH THE SHIT THE REGULAR GUYS WOULDN'T TOUCH.

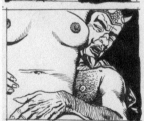

Frame 5 Aerial shot of Los Angeles.

WELLIWELL: 'THE FILTH'... THAT'S WHAT THE OLD MAN AND HIS BUDDIES CALLED THEM.
WELLIWELL: CREEPY, HUH?
WELLIWELL: FUCKING CREEPY BUDDIES.

PAGE 6

Frame 1 Filth dumptruck in the car park.

Frame 2 People turn to look past us, reacting to the arrival of the Filth officer off-panel, whose POV we share.

Frame 3   Hand officer Jenesis Jones enters the station with absolute self-confident sexiness in her weird Hand uniform and Joan of Arc wig. All around her are little pull out panels showing close ups of her lips or her hand as it moves through space. Her boots on the floor. Her bum seen from behind. Build up a composite mosaic of her movement into the police station so that we're seeing it all at once. Jenesis Jones of the Filth has arrived. She's an officer of the Finger.

Frame 4   Desk cop.

Frame 5   Move in for a head and shoulder shot as Jones lifts her ID.

JONES: OFFICER JONES: HAND SUPERCLEANSING.
JONES: PRIORITY AUTHORISATION.
JONES: ANDERS KLIMAKKS, PLEASE.

PAGE 7

Frame 1   Zoom in on the ID. We can read the name JONES, JENESIS.

Frame 2   Jones is showing her ID to Anders Klimakks in the interview room.

ANDERS: THERE IS NOTHING MORE I CAN SAY.
ANDERS: HOW ABOUT THE STORY OF YOU;
YOU'RE A VERY SEXY LADY, THAT'S FROM WHERE
I'M SITTING.

Frame 3   She reaches into her coat. Very business like.

JONES: WELL... I KNOW YOU CAME OUT OF
NOWHERE FIVE YEARS AGO.
JONES: I KNOW YOU HAVE A NOVELTY PENIS
WHICH DEFIES MEDICAL ANALYSIS.
JONES: OTHERWISE, DON'T TRY TO FUCK WITH
ME, ANDERS; I HAVE PMS.

Frame 4   She lays her purse on the table.

JONES: SPERM SPECIMEN.
JONES: PLEASE.

Frame 5   Looking down over Anders Klimakks' shoulders as he stands up and gets his cock out.

ANDERS: SURE.

Frame 6   Officer Jones' eyes widen as she stares at what we can't see.

ANDERS: THIS IS WHAT I DO FOR A LIVING.
JONES: JESUS!

PAGE 8/9

Frame 1   Anders Klimakks' memories come to life. Tall vertical panel showing our hero in longshot, leaning against the brightly lit window of an Amsterdam sex shop. Neon and flesh and shiny covers. People pass like ghosts.

ANDERS: PORNO IS MY LIFE. IN THE WORLD OF
ANDERS KLIMAKKS, IF THE GUY IS HARD AND THE
GIRL COMES, THE PEOPLE WILL PAY.
ANDERS: HERE IS AMSTERDAM WHERE I MADE MY
FIRST MOVIE.
ANDERS: 'MY LEFT-HAND COCK'.

Frame 2   These panels are a sequence of flowing images — panels which create a Z-shaped eye motion as we zoom and twist leading the reader across the page. First we see Jones looking at Anders as he comes across someone's head in a movie. We see only his top half.

JONES: FORGET FIVE YEARS AGO.
JONES: WHAT ARE YOU DOING IN LOS ANGELES,
ANDERS?
ANDERS: I LIKE TO TRAVEL. I LIKE TO FUCK. I LIKE
TO MAKE BIG BUCKS.
ANDERS: HARDCORE IS A GOOD BUSINESS FOR
ME.

Frame 3   Far off longshot of a transatlantic passenger jet — KLM. Its trajectory on the page is such that it could easily have spurted from Anders' unseen cock in the previous image. The plane heads up to the top right of the page.

Frame 4   The plane comes towards us, slowly turning in the sky.

Frame 5   The plane comes closer, turning to pass us, heading towards the bottom right of the page.

ANDERS: I KNOW I FLEW FROM SCHIPHOL TO LA
BECAUSE I HAVE THE TICKET STUBS.

Frame 6   Zoom into the window of the plane where Anders is looking out and down.

ANDERS: ALSO I HAVE THE E-MAIL THAT BROUGHT
ME HERE SO I KNOW I WAS HIRED TO WORK ON
THIS ONE MOVIE.

PAGE 9

Frame 1   Anders POV through the little plane window. Below, the flat circuit board sprawl of LA passes.

Frame 2   The plane is a tiny object seen in the sky above an observatory dome.

Frame 3   The dome is part of a stylish conversion in the Hollywood Hills. Now we see a long shot of Anders walking towards the front door.

ANDERS: WHAT WOULD YOU DO IF THE ORSON
WELLES OF HARDCORE ASKED YOU TO PUT YOUR
DICK IN HIS LATEST PRODUCTION?

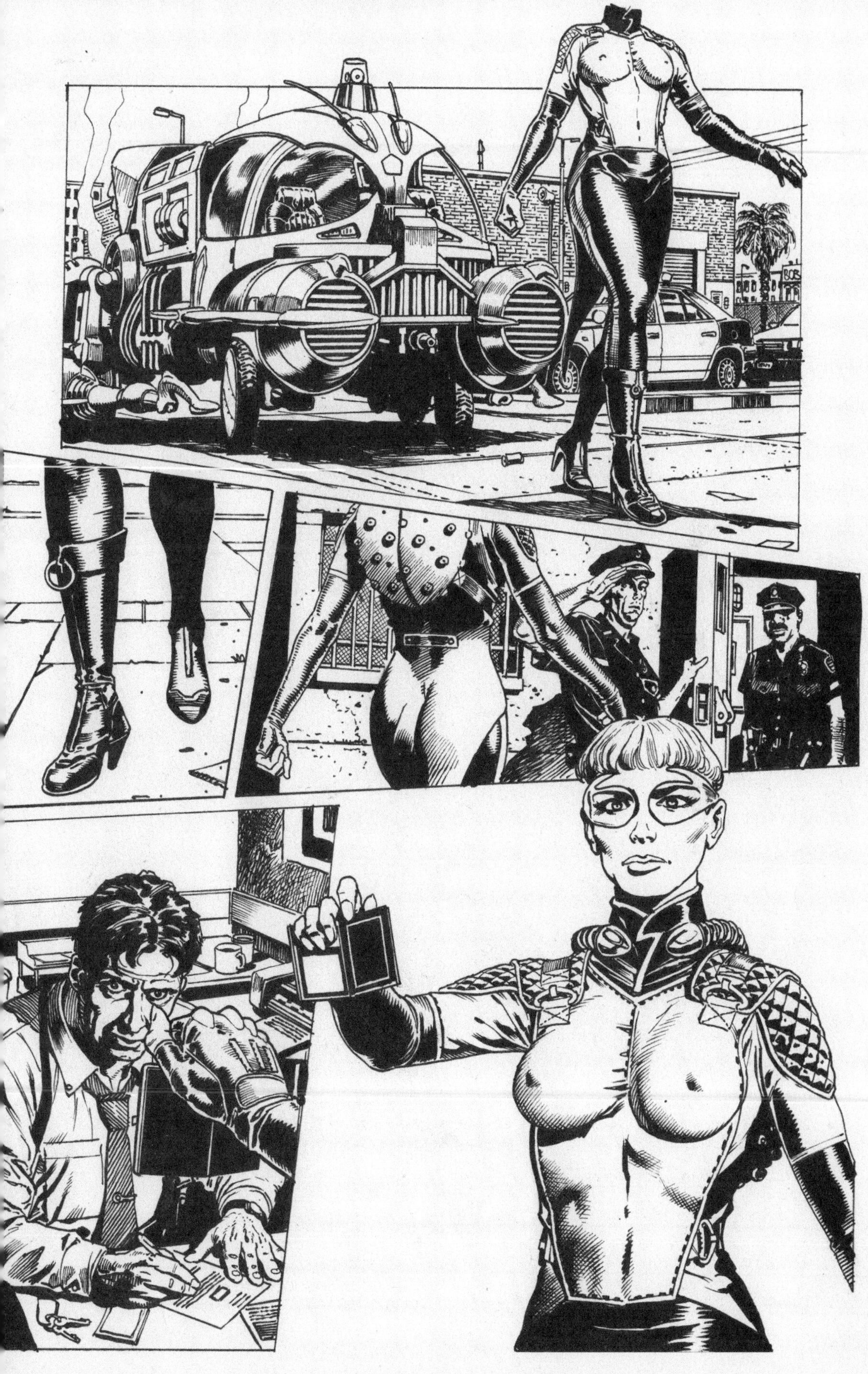

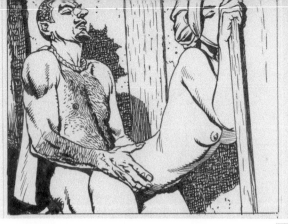

Frame 4   Anders, seen in the fish-eye style of a door camera. He looks up.

ANDERS: OKAY, SO THIS GUY HAS A SCUMBAG REPUTATION WITH ALL THE GIRLS BUT FOR ME THIS WOULD BE BIG-TIME.

Frame 5   Head and shoulders of Anders. He turns to smile that charming, roguish smile once more and jerks his thumb as the front door opens. A silhouette appears — a man in a cowboy hat. We can see the camera mounted high on the doorframe for continuity with the previous panel.

ANDERS: HIS NAME IS <u>TEX PORNEAU</u>.

Frame 6   Tall vertical panel, the mirror of Frame 1. Close up on the heavily shadowed, mysterious face of the terrifying, outrageous spirit of unstoppable rapacious sexuality — TEX PORNEAU. His eyes glitter like cold blue ice in the shadows under the brim of his Stetson. He holds up a Panasonic DV.

PORNEAU: THE LATIN MOTTO ABOVE THE DOOR IS ALSO MY MEDITATIONAL MANTRA.
PORNEAU: IT READS *'FUCK... OR BE FUCKED'*.

JONES: TEX PORNEAU BOUGHT YOU A FLIGHT TICKET AND INVITED YOU TO APPEAR IN HIS LATEST PRODUCTION.
JONES: SOMETHING TASTY ENTITLED *'THE RAPE OF BEVERLEY HILLS'*, RIGHT?

Frame 4   The Jacuzzi seen from above. Porneau is showing the huge hot tub to Anders. A weirdly colored bubbling liquid is being pumped into the basin.

PORNEAU: PEOPLE SAY SIZE DOESN'T MATTER, ANDERS.
PORNEAU: YOU AND I KNOW DIFFERENT.
PORNEAU: SIZE IS <u>EVERYTHING</u>.

Frame 5   Anders smiles in close-up.

ANDERS: THAT WAS THE <u>NAME</u> OF THIS MOVIE; I DON'T KNOW WHICH GIRL WAS BEVERLEY HILLS.
ANDERS: I CAN'T REMEMBER...

Frame 6   The Jacuzzi is filled with writhing naked girls and Anders Klimakks. The strangely-hued water boils and froths as the orgy gets underway.

ANDERS: IT'S TRULY FUCK OR BE FUCKED, MAN.

PAGE 10

Frame 1   Jones takes off her coat, keeping her eye on us.

JONES: I'VE HEARD OF HIM.
JONES: IT'S NOT TEX PORNEAU WE'RE INTERESTED IN, ANDERS, IT'S <u>YOU</u>.
JONES: THIS SPECIALTY OF YOURS...

Frame 2   Anders is walking into Tex Porneau's mansion — Porneau himself walks about constantly naked and with a permanent hard-on which is hidden behind pixilations, the way they do on TV. He's a well-muscled man in his 50s, Germanic.

TEX: THEY TELL ME YOU HAVE THE BLACK JIZZ OF THE DEVIL IN YOUR BALLS, MISTER.
TEX: CARE TO <u>PROVE</u> IT?

Frame 3   Jones hangs her coat, glancing back at us. There's a slow-burning gradually building and thickening of the sexual tension.

PAGE 11

Frame 1   We're looking at Anders in the flashing colored light. He's being pulled down in to a seething mass of flesh, arms wide. He looks ecstatic, drugged to the eyeballs.

ANDERS: THIS WATER IS LIKE TOO MUCH <u>JELLY</u>.
ANDERS: THIS IS NOT BUBBLES.
ANDERS: ARE THERE FISH HERE?

Frame 2   From behind Anders. His arms are wide. He's silhouetted by the light of the rising sun. The entire circular chamber inside the dome is blazing with intense light. People thrash and the water explodes and bubbles, gouting like lava. Things turn cubist.

Frame 3   Screaming terror, huge 'fish' forms thrash in the bubbling weirdly colored Jacuzzi froth. People sucked under into the maelstrom of slithering bodies, thrashing coiling tails. The light is intense. Wild

screaming cubist chaos. Anders looks up at us, into the light, arms wide in supplication.

ANDERS: WHY IS EVERYONE SCREAMING?

Frame 4   Tex films the splattering horror. Lit from below. Frightened girls crouch by his chair, gazing in terror. In foreground, froth rises, clutching hands and screaming mouths as heads bob past in front of us, trying to escape from the Jacuzzi. Normal POV now, simple stark super-real image without the cubist distortions. Fierce light.

Frame 5   Cut to Anders in longshot, staggering naked along the highway. Sun overhead. Noon light. Cars flash by streaking into strobes and lines. Jones walks beside him.

ANDERS: LUCKY I MANAGED TO GET MYSELF AND MY BAG OF MEMORIES OUT OF THERE.

PAGE 12

Frame 1   Officer Jones leans across the table, engrossed, besotted. She leans her head on her arms which are crossed on the desk. Faint wisps of visible infra-red radiation rise from her as she heats up.

JONES: MY... ah... MY JOB IS TO IDENTIFY AND TARGET THINGS THAT DON'T BELONG IN THE WORLD.
JONES: I WANT TO KNOW WHY TEX PORNEAU NEEDS YOUR SEMEN.

Frame 2   Anders and Jones face one another across the table. Anders is beating off under there but we don't see anything, we just know what's going on. More infra-red.

ANDERS: FOR ME IT SEEMS LIKE... LIKE EVERYBODY WANTS MY SEMEN, MISS.
ANDERS: I SHOULD NOW MENTION THAT I'M JUST ABOUT READY TO EJACULATE.

Frame 3   Same POV. Jones climbs up onto the table, heading towards Anders Klimakks as if magnetised by lust. She's picking up the purse. He's looking down, hand pumping under the table. His body is perfectly sculpted. He's struck this dramatic pose before.

JONES: HERE.
JONES: I'LL CATCH IT IN THIS.

Frame 4   Same POV. Jones crawls across the table. Fumes of radiant infra-red heat as the scene dissolves into heat distribution patterns.

JONES: YOU DO KNOW I FIND YOU VERY ATTRACTIVE, MR. KLIMAKKS.

Frame 5   Zoom in for a close-up. His left hand pulls her head forward. Their lips part to kiss. All is red and hot. In between the two faces is TV static.

ANDERS: ANDERS.

PAGE 13

Frame 1   The static fills a long thin horizontal panel across the top of the page.

Frame 2   Jones lies on her back, head tilted towards us, upside down. She lifts her arm to speak into her wrist radio. Her clothes have been pulled open, trousers around her ankles.

JONES: SHIT.
JONES: FUCK.

Frame 3   Move around to the side as she lifts her wrist radio to her lips.

JONES: JONES TO CENTRAL!
JONES: I'VE COMPLETELY BLOWN THIS ASSIGNMENT.
JONES: ANDERS KLIMAKKS OVERWHELMED ME WITH SOME KIND OF MAXI-PHEROMONE AND GOT AWAY.

Frame 4   Her free hand moves down to scoop between her legs.

JONES: I NEED TO CONFIRM PERSON/ANTI-PERSON COMPLEX ALERT. STATUS: V.

Frame 5   Close. She lifts her hand into shot and we see what looks like ink hanging in strings from her fingers.

JONES: REQUEST IMMEDIATE LETHAL CLEANSING BACK-UP.

PAGE 14

Frame 1   Establishing shot of Tex Porneau's observatory home. Skyline of the LA basin and the Hollywood hills. Beautiful orange sky of late afternoon. Dusty sunstruck haze of LA. The light blazing in the mirrored walls of downtown skyscrapers way off in the basin.

Frame 2   The cops at the ornate door of the observatory. It's the same place we saw earlier (page 9). They look at one another a little nervously. Detective Nick Welliwell takes another gulp of crack. Cameras everywhere.

WELLIWELL: BUSY ADDRESS.
WELLIWELL: THERE'S EVEN A <u>FED-EX</u> TRUCK, FOR CHRIST'S SAKES.
WHIM: DON'T YOU THINK YOU'RE STARTING TO ABUSE THAT STUFF?

Frame 3   Welliwell rings doorbell.

WELLIWELL: FUCK YOU.
WELLIWELL: IT'S RECREATIONAL. IT'S UNDER CONTROL.

Frame 4   From behind. The door opens and we're behind the naked Tex Porneau himself. The detectives look down at his unseen dick with shock. Blows smoke and drops the crack pipe.

WELLIWELL: TEX PORNEAU?
WELLIWELL: DETECTIVES WHIM AND WELLIWELL. <u>LAPD</u>. WE'RE HERE TO TALK TO YOU ABOUT ANDERS...
WELLIWELL: SHIT.

Frame 5   Powerful head and shoulders shot capturing the full Tex Porneau mystique. Huge cigar in his fingers. Eyes shadowed by his hat brim, glittering in the gloom. Germanic, stocky, monstrous. Behind him, figures creep forward from the depths of the house. Tex should have a few huge sleek Dobermans around too. Stealth fighter dogs.

TEX;   NO TIME FOR TALK, HONEY.
TEX: YOU CAME TO MY DOOR. THAT MEANS *'FUCK OR BE FUCKED'*.

PAGE 15

Frame 1   The detectives look a little perplexed but try to stay tough and in charge of this situation. Reality is slowly falling away however. People come up behind the cops, stealthy perverts and hollow-eyed porno stars carrying hoods, harnesses, restraints, clothing, wigs, whatever. These are the Extras — the endless parade of weirdoes trapped in Tex's never-ending sex film.

WELLIWELL: YEAH. SURE THING, SCUMBAG.
WELLIWELL: WE'RE HERE TO ASK A FEW VERY SERIOUS AND...

Frame 2   The cops are suddenly overwhelmed. A rubber doll like face is being rolled down over Welliwell's forehead. He's going into real panic. The grinning, drugged and dressed-up Extras restrain his arms and legs, pinning him.

WELLIWELL: <u>AUU CHRIST! JESUS CHRIST, <u>NO</u>!</u>
WELLIWELL: <u>WHAT <u>IS</u> THAT THING!</u>
WELLIWELL: <u>WHAT'S THAT COMING DOWN THE HALL, JOHN!!</u>

Frame 3   The pervs pull a mask over Whim's head. His arms flail.

WELLIWELL: *GNNUMMF*
WHIM: NO... JESUS, NO YOU CAN'T DO THIS *TRRWMMF*

Frame 4   Max is behind Detective Whim, mounting him with a cold thin smile. We can only see Whim's boggling eyes through the holes in his insectile bondage mask. His zipped mouth gives away nothing of the intense feelings Whim is experiencing.

WHIM: <u>NAUUUU</u>
TEX: JUST <u>RELAX</u>. YOU'RE VERY BEAUTIFUL WHEN YOU LET GO. VERY SEXY, BABY.

Frame 5   Tex leering.

TEX: THAT'S GOOD, YEAH. YOU CAN TAKE IT.
WHIM: <u>MMWHHAAUU</u> (From off)

PAGE 16

Frame 1   Rolling from foreground, a monstrous dungball of garbage — cans and bin bags and newspapers and old curries — that's rolled around the house by slaves in gimp gear. They crawl across the ball, moving it the way dung beetles herd their shit globe across the desert, rolling it here and there. This huge ball stopped for a moment. The struggling fetishized detectives are being pulled towards the horrible giant ball. Welliwell is shrieking. Whim is broken, limp.

WELLIWELL: MMMUUIIIII
TEX: GOOD GIRLS.
TEX: NOW GO, JOIN IN, AND DON'T <u>BOTHER</u> ME.
TEX: I'M CREATING PORNOGRAPHIC HISTORY.

Frame 2   The scarab-people help Whim up onto the ball of garbage where he can only cling there like one of them. Tex looks down and point off panel, showing the struggling Welliwell something awful which is coming in from off panel.

TEX: A NEW WORLD DEMANDS A NEW KIND OF <u>HARDCORE</u>. YOU'LL ALL LEARN THAT SOON ENOUGH.
TEX: I WANT YOU ALL TO MEET ONE OF THE STARS OF MY <u>ULTIMATE</u> MOVIE.

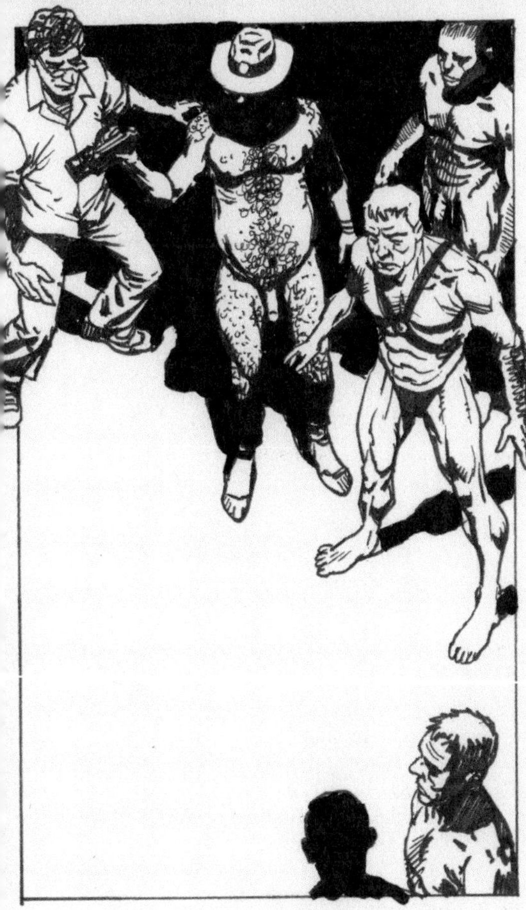
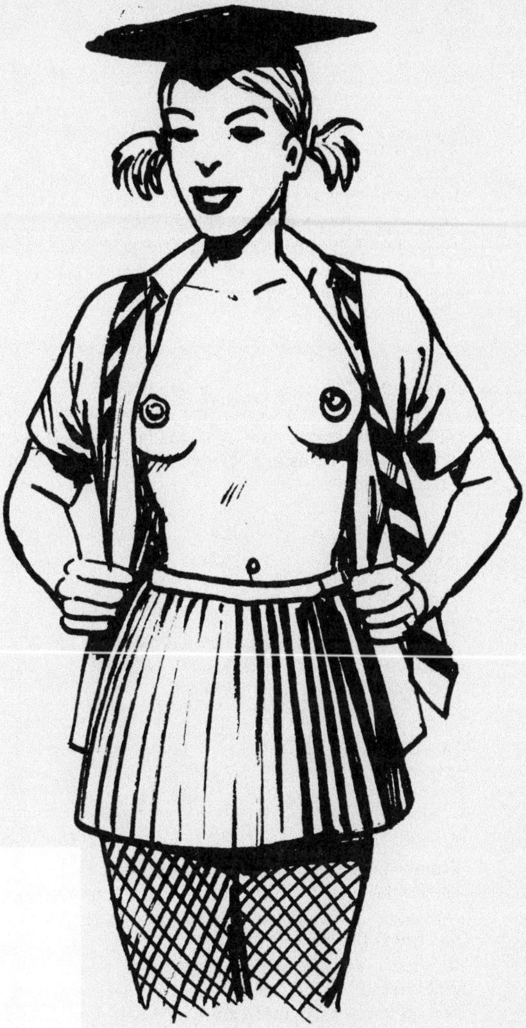
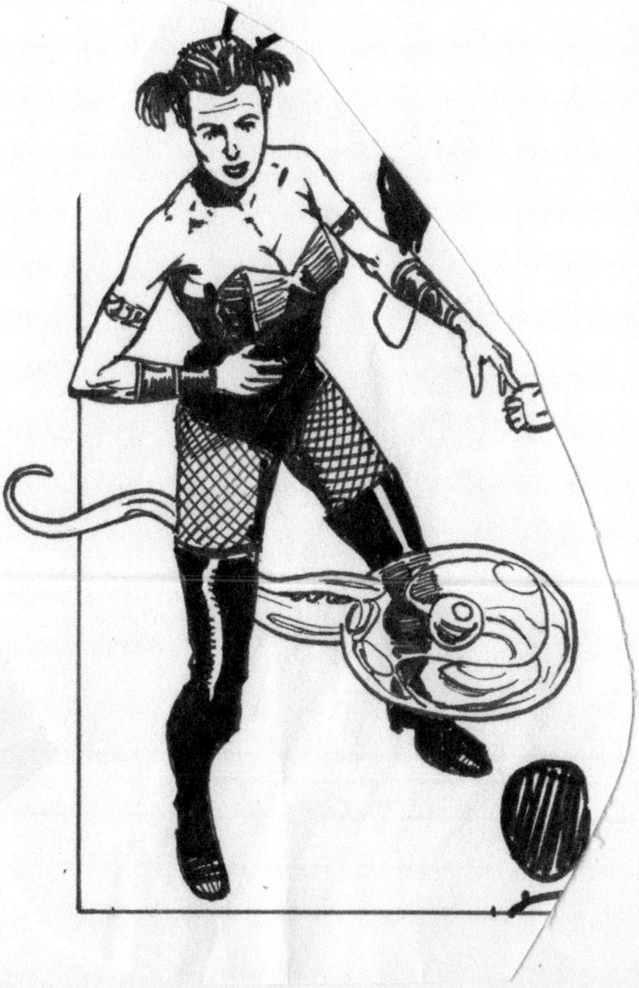
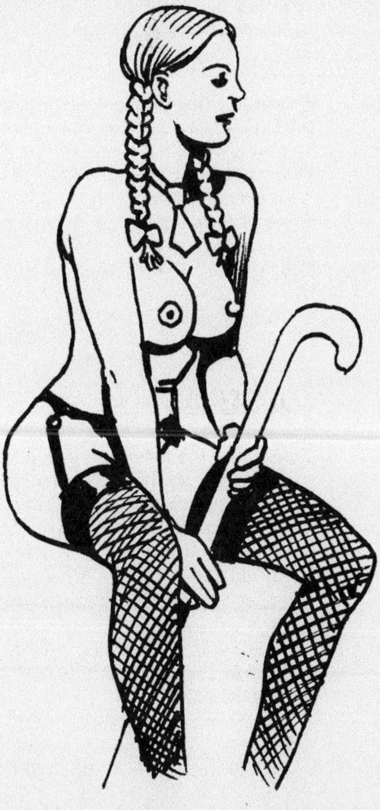

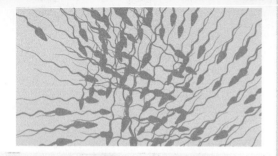

Frame 3   Around the corner.

TEX: <u>NOT ME! BY GOD, NOT TEX!</u>
TEX: <u>I'M GONNA FUCK THE ABYSS RAW!</u>
TEX: <u>I'M GONNA MAKE IT HOLLER LIKE LOLITA!</u>

Frame 4   Tex turns round and grabs a poor guy in a FedEx outfit. Tex has his DV camera in one hand, always ready.

FEDEX: LISTEN, MISTER... THIS IS SOME PLACE YOU GOT HERE BUT I... I THINK THERE'S BEEN A <u>MISTAKE</u>.

PAGE 18

Frame 1   We follow Tex towards a viewing window up a spiral stair. He's dragging the Fed-Ex guy behind him and his creeping capering posse of Extras follow. Crying women in corners.

FEDEX: PLEASE, WHAT ARE YOU DOING?... IN THE NAME OF CHRIST, I'M JUST THE DELIVERY GUY.
FEDEX: <small>YOU CAN'T FUCKING DO THIS...</small>
TEX: DON'T GIVE ME THIS UNPROFESSIONAL BULLSHIT, HONEY.
TEX: I GET A THOUSAND GIRLS THROUGH HERE WHO MANAGE TO DO WHAT THEY'RE TOLD <u>WITHOUT</u> BLEATING LIKE LOSERS.

Frame 2   Fed-Ex tries to protest but he's having a weird feathered crest strapped under his chin by Tex's relentless entourage of Extras.

FEDEX: PLEASE... I HAVE TWO YOUNG BOYS!

Frame 3   Cardboard beak arrangement on elastic is pulled over the Fed-Ex guy's face. Tex takes up position behind him, hand on his shoulder, cooing menacingly in the hapless man's ear.

FEDEX: <small>I ONLY CAME TO MAKE A DELIVERY</small>
TEX: YOU'LL GET YOUR DELIVERY, PRINCESS.
TEX: TEX PORNEAU STYLE.

Frame 4   Tex is filming over the guys shoulder as he penetrates him from behind. We're close up, so we don't see anything other than the reactions. Bug eyed Fed-Ex guy, grinning icy Tex as he films his masterpiece.

FEDEX: **WAAUUH GODDD!**
TEX: YOU <u>LIKE</u> THAT, HUH? JUST A SHY LITTLE ENGLISH <u>SCHOOLGIRL</u>, AREN'T YOU?
TEX: YOU WANT TO SEE DADDY FUCK <u>LOS ANGELES</u> HUH?
TEX: <u>DADDY CHAOS?</u>
TEX: **DADDY DEATH?**

(Tex's yells get bigger, more orgasmic)

Frame 5   Tall vertical. The observatory. The centre of the dome is pulled back and the observatory shoots light in to the air.

TEX: **<u>DADDY MADNESS!</u>**

(Letters get huge in a ridiculous crescendo)

Frame 3   A huge, magnified sperm glides like a shark between the girls' legs towards Tex. It propels itself through the air with a long tail.

TEX: DON'T WORRY.
TEX: THIS ONE'S <u>DORMANT</u>. NEUTERED.

Frame 4   Tex Porneau crouches down to pet the eerie giant spermatozoon. A mad light in his eye.

TEX: UNLIKE ITS MANY, MANY GREEDY BROTHERS.

PAGE 17

Frame 1   Big background shot of the mansion interior cut into tall verticals to register the movement as the ball rolls away grotesquely with Detectives Whim and Welliwell now indistinguishable form the crawling, faceless scarab people. Four insect figures now scramble purposefully across the ball, piloting it off down the corridor into the interior of the mansion.

TEX: THE EXISTENTIALISTS <u>FALTERED</u> ON THE BRINK OF THE GAPING <u>VOID</u>.

Frame 2   The creeping crawling people roll the garbage ball away.

TEX;   'NAUSEA'... THAT'S WHAT THOSE LIMP-DICK INTELLECTUALS FELT.
TEX: THEY WERE <u>AFRAID</u> OF THE BIG BLACK PIT. SCARED OF LOSING THEIR WEENY-WEENY DICKLETS IN THE ASSHOLE OF BEING!

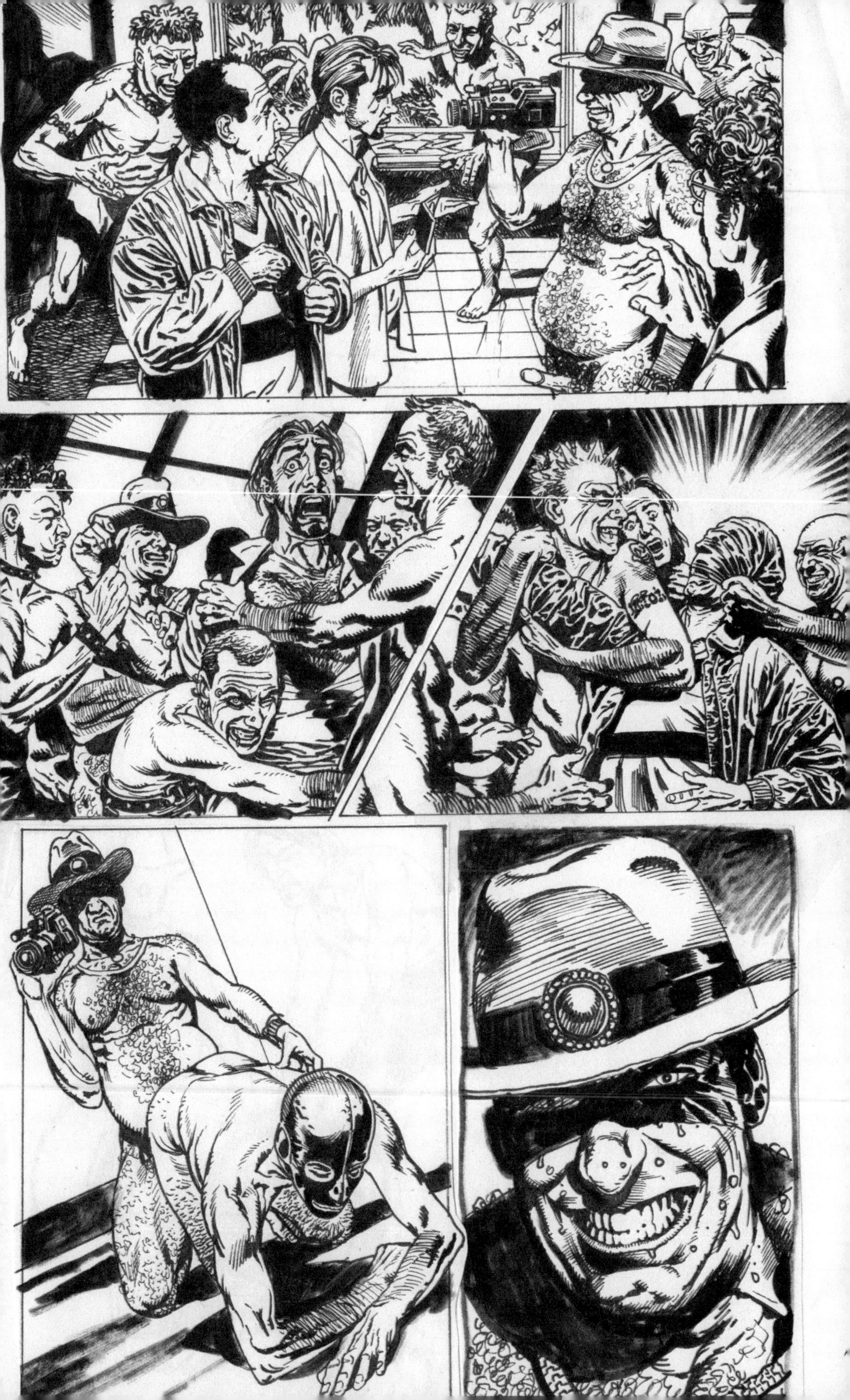

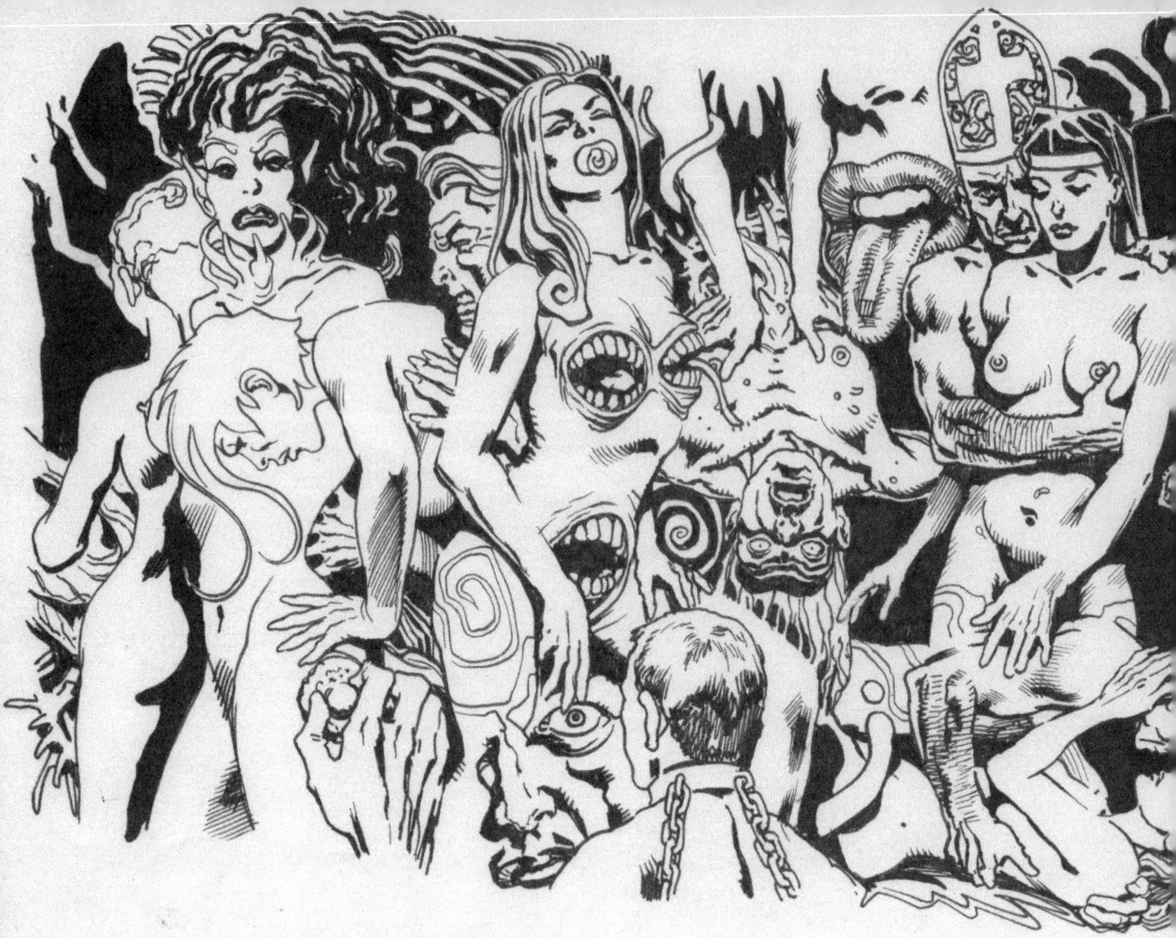

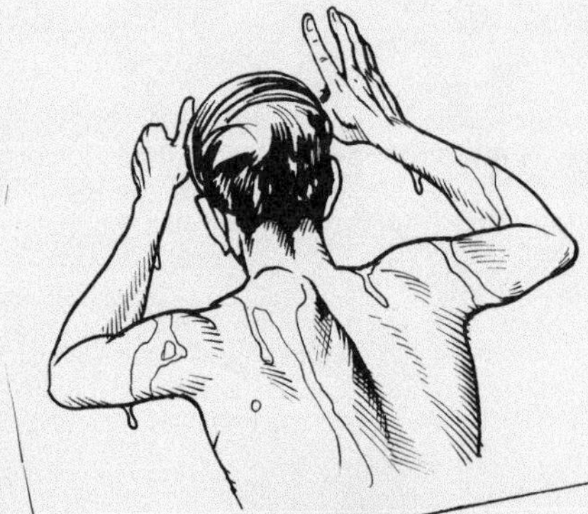

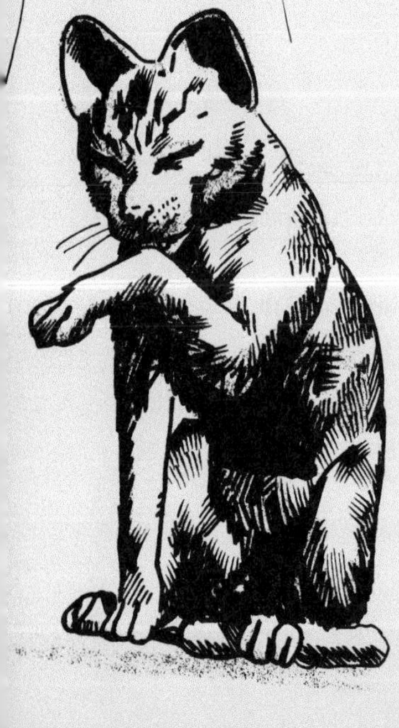

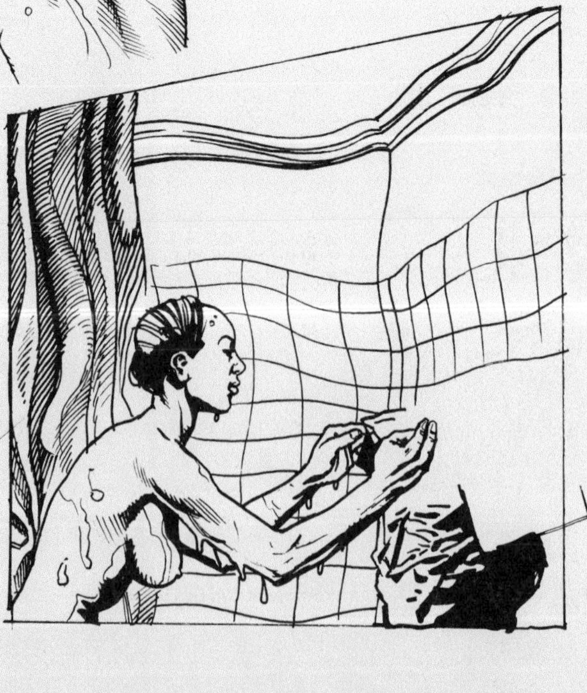

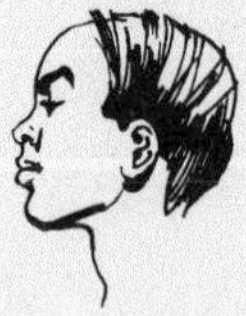

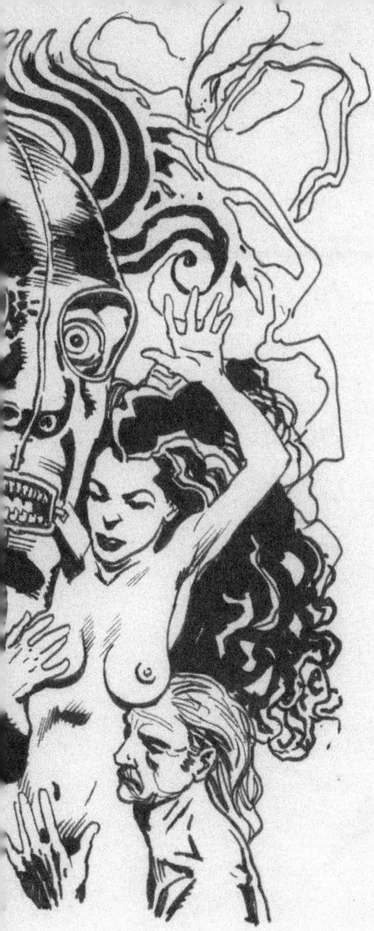

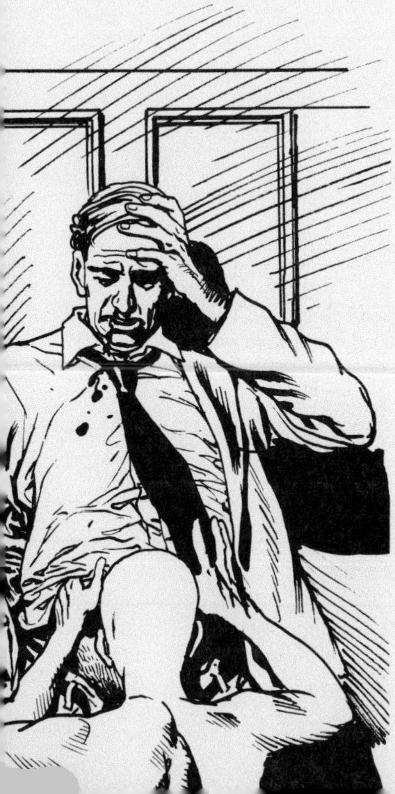

PAGE 19

Frame 1 Giant sperm leap from the bubbling boiling Jacuzzi hurtling skyward towards the open dome.

Frame 2 Tex throws the shocked, traumatized FedEx guy aside. Marches forward with his erect penis hidden behind pixel fuzz.

TEX: THESE NEW KIDS... WITH THEIR SLEAZECORE HEROIN VOMIT PORN... THESE DROOPY PUNKS THINK THEY CAN STEAL THE HARDCORE CROWN FROM TEX PORNEAU.
TEX: FORGET IT.

Frame 3 Tex's cowboy boots in foreground ground level as he walks out of shot. In background the pervs descend upon the Fed-Ex guy and drag his flailing body away.

TEX: TRIPLE IMAX 3-D SUPER-EXTREME HARDCORE.
TEX: THE ULTIMATE EQUATION...

Frame 4 Overhead shot as Tex walks out onto the circular deck around the dome. There are cameras on tripods, pointing at Beverley Hills.

TEX: SEX = DEATH = BUCKS!
TEX: I AM THE FUTURE!

Frame 5 Tex Porneau mans the cameras profile from waist up, angling the camera down as he fucks a girl up the ass. His arm around her waist, she's bent over the balcony rail, eyes wide with alarm and shock as he calmly glides in.

TEX: ARE YOU READY FOR THE MONEY SHOT, MISS HILLS?
TEX: SCENE ONE!
TEX: TAKE 1!

PAGE 20

Frame 1 Horizontal shot. Filth patrol vehicle racing towards us with streaming speedlines of streets around.

DMITIRI: I THOUGHT YOU SAY YOU REMEMBERED HOW TO DRIVE, SHIT-FOR-HEAD?

Frame 2 Close in on the driver and passenger. The driver is Dmitri 9. The chimpanzee assassin. The passenger Ned Slade. Slade looks at some pornos, Dmitri is intense, smoking a big joint.

DMITIR; HOOUUP
DMITIR: HAVE A NICE DAY! HAVE A NICE DAY!
DMITRI: LET THEM SPEND ONE DAY IN A FREEZING COLD SPACESUIT FULL OF SHIT!
SLADE: CHIMP-LANGUAGE FOR '*WE'RE DEPLOYING DUMPTRUCKS TO SECURE THE CLEAN-UP ZONE'*.
SLADE: GOT THAT?
SLADE: THIS IS SLADE: I'M TRYING MY BEST TO FIT IN.

Frame 3 Three vertical panels. Longshot of Jones running across the street. Evening shades now on the clean streets of Beverly Hills' rich shopping pavilions.

RADIO: ANDERS KLIMAKKZZ///ACTIVITY IN ZONE MAY HEAT UP AROUND////STATUS: W ALERT
RADIO: ///ORDERS FROM///
JONES: WHAT ?
JONES: I CAN'T HEAR.

Frame 4 She comes closer. Yells into her wrist radio.

JONES: THERE'S THIS... <u>CRACKLING</u> NOISE FROM EVERYWHERE. THE HILLS... THIS SMELL...
JONES: IT'S LIKE FIRECRACKERS AND AMMONIA OR...

Frame 5 Closer. She reacts as she sees Anders off panel.

JONES: I <u>GOT</u> HIM!
JONES: HE'S ON <u>RODEO DRIVE!</u>

PAGE 21

Frame 1 Horizontal. Anders turns, he's with a gorgeous looking, impeccably dressed woman. We're looking over Jones' shoulders as she aims her hypo gun at Anders.

JONES: <u>ANDERS KLIMAKKS!</u>
ANDERS: HAVE WE MET?
ANDERS: DO YOU WANT ME TO SIGN YOUR PANTIES?

Frame 2 Move in on Anders. The face of genuine innocence, he shows off his new suit proudly. The glamorous woman hangs on his arm and offers a challenging look.

ANDERS: THIS BEAUTIFUL HORNY LADY WAS BUYING ME A TERRIFIC <u>SUIT</u>, YOU SEE...
WOMAN;   PLEASE... YOU <u>CANNOT</u> KILL THIS MAN.
WOMAN: DO YOU REALISE HE HAS A TEN INCH PENIS?

Frame 3 Looking up, past Jones' head as she lifts it, sensing something from above. We can see up past the storefronts to the sky where a weird swarm can be seen, turning like swallows in flight and angling sharply downwards.

JONES: OH, YES I DO.
JONES: STAND AWAY!
JONES: ANDERS KLIMAKKS: YOU HAVE BEEN IDENTIFIED AS A POTENTIALLY LETHAL ANTI-PERSON!

Frame 4 Anders looks up. A faint frown of recognition.

ANDERS: AH.
ANDERS: MAYBE <u>THIS</u> IS WHY MY SPUNK HAS BEEN GROWN TO GIANT SIZE AND USED AS A WEAPON.

Frame 5 Overhead shot. Jones looks up can't believe what she's seeing. We have vague hints of shapes diving down towards her. Shadows on the ground.

JONES: NO
JONES: FUCKING
JONES: WAY.
JONES: **HAND ASSIST!**

PAGE 22

Frame 1 Then BANG shock end splash as the sperm of Anders Klimakks explode through Jones and the woman with her shopping bags. In background, the fastest of the monster cells are bursting through the womb of any woman they can find. It's the giant size sperm invasion of Beverly Hills.

the filth created by Morrison and Weston
grant morrison writer
chris weston penciller
gary erskine inker
hifi color & seps
clem robins lettering
carlos segura cover artist
steve bunche associate editing
karen berger editor
more filth at crackcomicks.com & vertigocomics.com

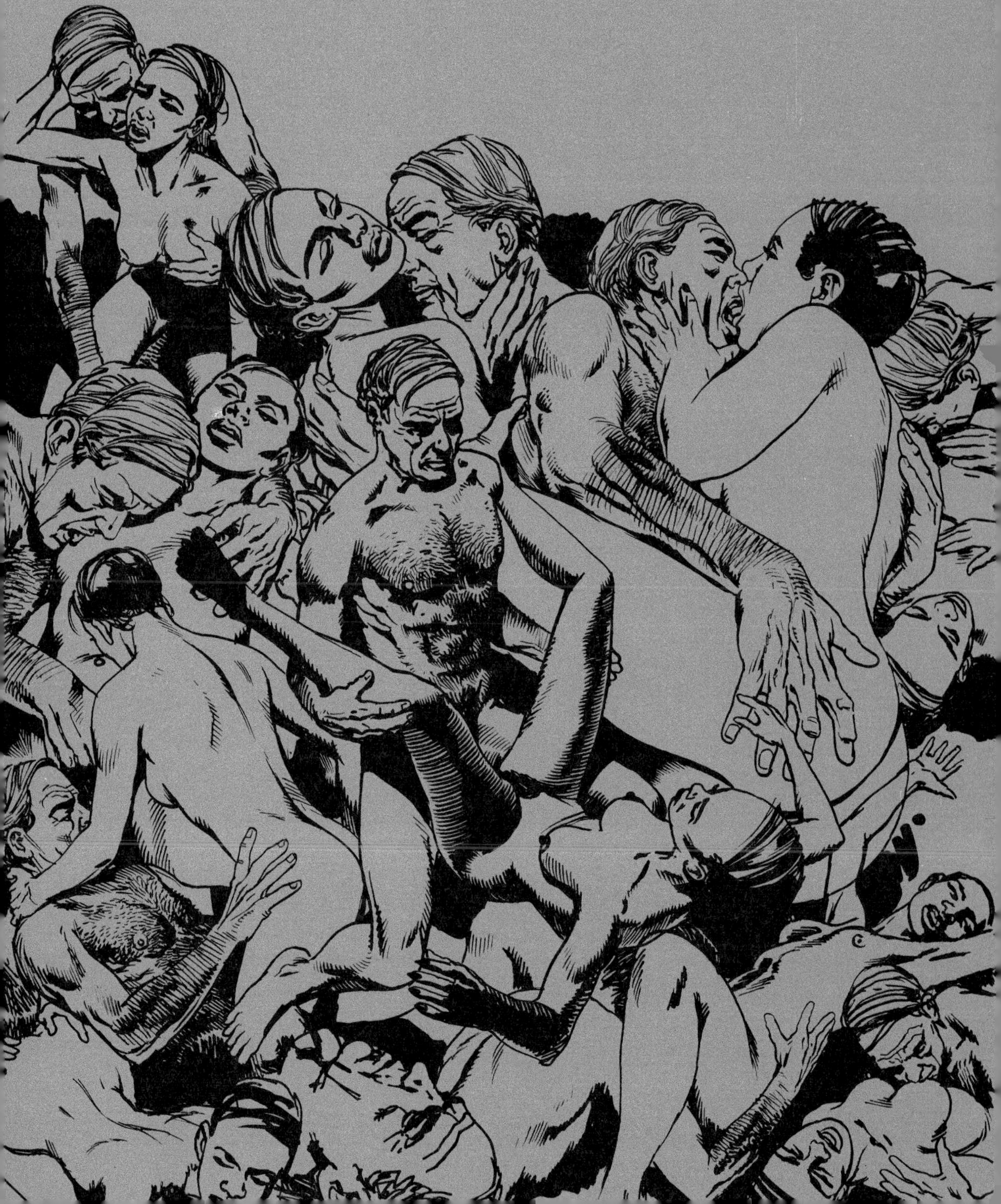

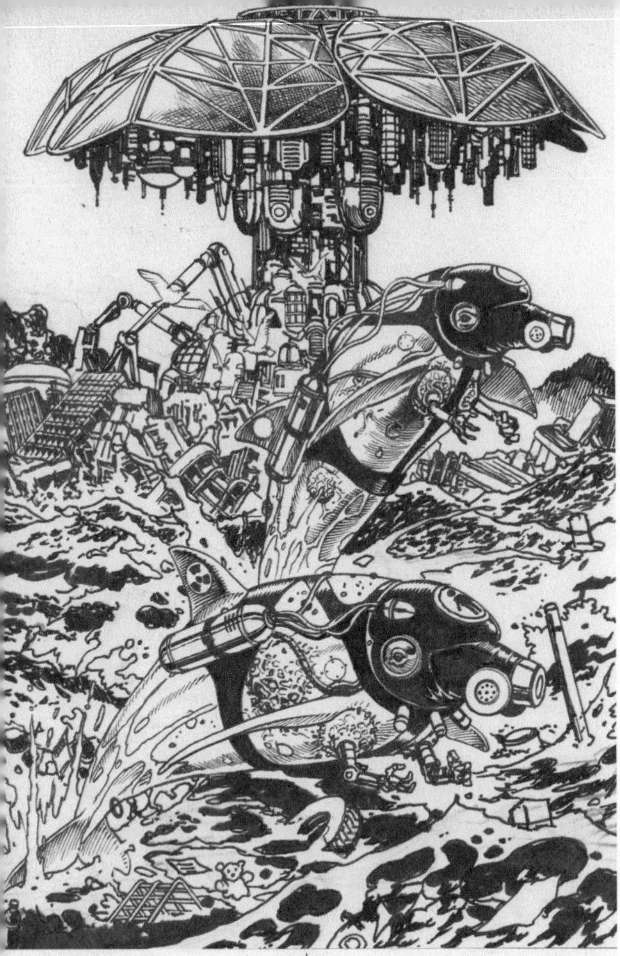

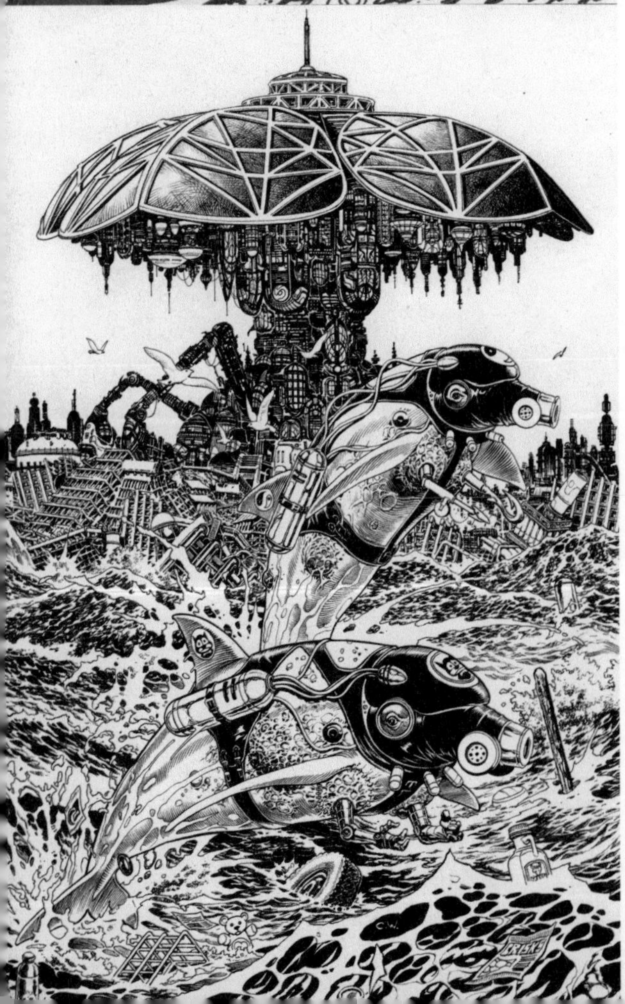

Promotional art for the series drawn by Weston, colored by Matt Hollingsworth, and featured in Diamond's *Previews* catalog.

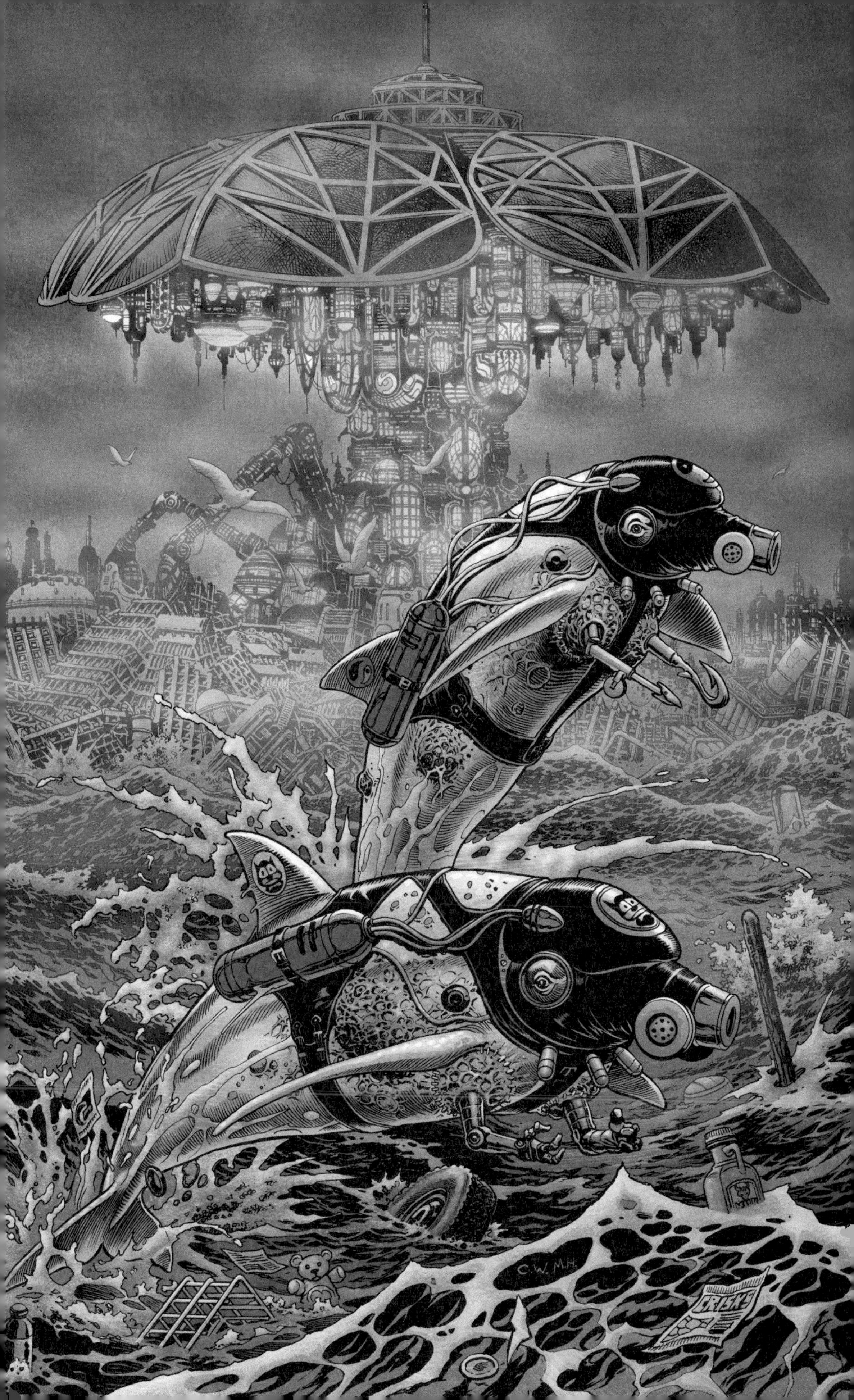
C.W.M.H.

BIOGRAPHIES

Grant Morrison has been working with DC Comics for more than 20 years, beginning with his legendary runs on the revolutionary titles ANIMAL MAN and DOOM PATROL. Since then he has written numerous bestsellers — including JLA, BATMAN and *New X-Men* — as well as the critically acclaimed creator-owned series THE INVISIBLES, SEAGUY, THE FILTH, WE3 and JOE THE BARBARIAN. Morrison has also expanded the borders of the DC Universe in the award-winning pages of SEVEN SOLDIERS, ALL-STAR SUPERMAN, FINAL CRISIS, BATMAN, INC. and ACTION COMICS.

In his secret identity, Morrison is a "counterculture" spokesperson, a musician, an award-winning playwright and a chaos magician. He is also the author of the *New York Times* bestseller *Supergods*, a groundbreaking psycho-historic mapping of the superhero as a cultural organism. He divides his time between his homes in Los Angeles and Scotland.

Chris Weston is a British illustrator who has enjoyed a long career working for the comic-strip industries on both sides of the Atlantic. After getting his start drawing Judge Dredd for the weekly UK magazine *2000 AD*, Weston has gone on to contribute art to BATMAN, SUPERMAN, *The Fantastic Four*, SWAMP THING, and THE INVISIBLES for DC and Marvel. However, he is probably best known for his work on two creator-owned series: THE FILTH (with writer Grant Morrison) and *Ministry of Space* (with writer Warren Ellis). His more recent comics work includes the J. Michael Straczynski-written and Eisner Award-nominated Marvel series *The Twelve*, for which he also wrote a prequel story entitled *The Twelve: Spearhead* that won an AICN Comics Award for Best One-Shot. Since then he has branched out into the world of film concept art and storyboards, working with director Albert Hughes on movie projects like *The Book of Eli* and a live-action adaptation of Katsuhiro Otomo's *Akira*. Most recently, Weston has enjoyed a popular and growing sideline in producing limited-edition silkscreen prints based on popular films.

Gary Erskine began his comics career drawing for Marvel UK and the British anthology magazines *2000 AD* and *Crisis*. In 1993 he left Marvel UK to create the Tundra graphic novels *The Lords of Misrule* with writers Dan Abnett and John Tomlinson and *Pale Horse* (later published by Dark Horse as *Hypersonic*) with writers Steve White and Dan Abnett. A third, unfinished Tundra project — *City of Silence* with writer Warren Ellis — was reborn in 2000 as an acclaimed Image miniseries.

In 2002 Erskine was approached by artist Chris Weston to ink Grant Morrison's groundbreaking Vertigo maxiseries THE FILTH, and his Vertigo work continued in the titles ARMY@LOVE with writer/artist Rick Veitch and GREATEST HITS with writer David Tischman and artist Glenn Fabry. Over the years he has also collaborated with Mark Millar, Garth Ennis, James Robinson, Kurt Busiek, Alex De Campi, and Brian Wood on a wide variety of features, including *Captain America*, *Judge Dredd*, *The Avengers*, *The Massive*, *Star Wars*, *Doctor Who*, *The Terminator*, and *Transformers*.

In addition to his comics work, Erskine teaches design workshops, provides story-boards and concept art to the video game, film, and television industries, and mentors film students at the Royal Conservatoire of Scotland. He is currently working on motion comics for Madefire as well as crafting the independent comics titles *Roller Grrrls*, *Incendiary.US*, and *Zachariah Gunn: Dakota*. He lives in Glasgow, Scotland, with his wife, Mhairi, and their cats, Meg and Mog, and he dislikes writing in the third person.